AMERICAN
Reform and Reformers

A Biographical Dictionary

Edited by Randall M. Miller
and Paul A. Cimbala

G
P

Greenwood Press
Westport, Connecticut • London

618716

Library of Congress Cataloging-in-Publication Data

American reform and reformers : a biographical dictionary / edited by
  Randall M. Miller and Paul A. Cimbala.
    p.   cm.
  Includes bibliographical references and index.
  ISBN 0–313–28839–9 (alk. paper)
  1. Social reformers—United States—Biography—Dictionaries.
I. Miller, Randall M.   II. Cimbala, Paul A. (Paul Alan).
HQ1412.A46   1996
303.48'4'0922—dc20
  [B]   95–16048

British Library Cataloguing in Publication Data is available.

Library of Congress Catalog Card Number: 95–16048
ISBN: 0–313–28839–9

First published in 1996

Greenwood Press, 88 Post Road West, Westport, CT 06881
An imprint of Greenwood Publishing Group, Inc.

Printed in the United States of America

∞

The paper used in this book complies with the
Permanent Paper Standard issued by the National
Information Standards Organization (Z39.48–1984).

10 9 8 7 6 5 4 3 2 1

Copyright Acknowledgments

The authors and publisher gratefully acknowledge permission to use the following:
Excerpts from Washington Gladden, Sermon, 5 October 1897, and Sermon, ''Strengths
and Weaknesses of Organized Labor,'' 28 April 1901, both from Washington Gladden
Papers (Ohio Historical Society). Copyrights to the Ohio Historical Society's
Washington Gladden Collection (MIC 4) have not been dedicated to the public.
Excerpts from Betty Friedan, *It Changed My Life*, reprinted by permission of Curtis
Brown, Ltd. Copyright 1963, 1964, 1966, 1970, 1971, 1972, 1973, 1974, 1975, 1976,
1985, 1991, by Betty Friedan.

Contents

Acknowledgments

Compiling and editing this book on American reform in some ways mirrored the experience of reform itself. It was a cooperative enterprise that profited from a mix of perspectives and talents. Although not all the contributors agree on definitions of reform or the relative significance of particular reforms and reformers, they do share a sense of common purpose and conviction regarding the need for this dictionary and the importance of reform in American history and culture generally.

Foremost in making this book possible was Cynthia Harris, executive editor, reference books, at Greenwood Press. She nurtured the idea for such a book, encouraged and instructed the editors throughout its development, and guided it through the production process. This is her book as much as ours.

Others deserving thanks include David Allmendinger, Paula Benkart, Marion Roydhouse, and Stephen Whitfield, whose readings of the introductory section improved its content and style, and whose suggestions regarding the scope of the overall work enlarged the editors' vision. Barbara Costa at Fordham University and Stephanie McKeller-Auer at Saint Joseph's University performed countless administrative chores with their usual efficiency. Marc Pascente of Fordham University checked time-line dates. Nancy McCarthy, director of the Office of Research at Fordham University, provided essential funds for photocopying and postage. Daniel Curran, dean of the College of Arts and Sciences at Saint Joseph's University, supported the project with faculty development funds. The library staffs at Saint Joseph's University, Fordham University, the University of Pennsylvania, Haverford College, Swarthmore College, Bryn Mawr College, Temple University, the Free Library of Philadelphia, and the Library of Congress were uniformly helpful.

We dedicate this book to those teachers who introduced us to the reform tradition of Western civilization and insisted that reform is a noble calling—especially Paul G. Fried, William Barlow, David Clark, James C. Duram, David Powell, and Warren VanderHill at Hope College (for Randall Miller) and David H. Burton, Francis X. Gerrity, and Randall M. Miller at Saint Joseph's University (for Paul Cimbala).

Introduction

RANDALL M. MILLER

This biographical dictionary presents substantial life-and-times treatments of major American reformers and the reforms they most directly affected. Each chapter combines biography with historical analysis of a particular reform to establish the context and character of the movement each biographical subject represented. The chronology at the end of the volume runs from the late eighteenth century to the present. The definition of ''American'' reform dictates such an approach, for since the creation of the republic, American reformers have believed in America as a special society capable of being reshaped to achieve a more perfect world. The exfoliation of reforms over the past two centuries attests to the persistent power of this belief in American life. Indeed, as several chapters suggest, a reform spirit continues to inform American private belief and public behavior.

The idea of America as a regenerative force preceded, and in some ways precipitated, the creation of an independent United States, but it emanated most powerfully from the American Revolution. The Revolution fostered both an obligation and an opportunity to reshape government, society, and even the human condition. Freed from the past, Americans could make their own future. Such liberty also made Americans self-conscious and critical of their republican experiment. Without a sense of purpose and without self-criticism, Americans believed, no nation could prosper and no people could properly govern themselves. American reformers from the late eighteenth century until today have used revolutionary rhetoric and invoked the Revolution's legacy to justify their calls for renewal, though admittedly others have drawn on similar language and inheritance to contest the means and ends of various reforms. Although no consensus about the exact course of American reform emerged from the Revolution or after, an abiding sense of special purpose, of reform, has run through American history. That is the rationale for these essays, which collectively mark the contours and individually probe the content of American reform identity and activity.

Since the days of the Puritans, Americans have sought to reconcile individual responsibility and community demands. However much they have celebrated getting ahead and have elevated self-made men to political and social pedestals, while seeming to ignore the means by which such men acquired their wealth and power, Americans also have charged all people with moral responsibilities to their communities. The Judeo-Christian core of American morality, especially the heavily Calvinist cast of early American religion and rules of public behavior, combined with the Revolutionary sense of mission to invest Americans with a sense of moral obligation. If America was the ''new Israel,'' a redeemer nation—as countless sermons and speeches have echoed since the dawn of the republic—it must, reformers insisted, build a just society, lest God visit His wrath on it as He did on the Israel of old. Indeed, during the nineteenth century God's judgment seemed imminent to the heavily Protestant intellectual and religious establishment witnessing the commercial and industrial transformation of America. Many reformers also have believed that Americans needed to act while their institutions and society were still in a plastic state capable of being reformed. Before the mold had set, reform must occur.

The belief in the mutability of American society gained strength from the liberal tradition that harks back to the days of Jefferson and Jackson. Americans generally have believed in progress, as the prospects of improving their condition and creating a new society require that they do. Such beliefs have pointed Americans' civic and moral duties away from self-indulgence and toward a sense of collective responsibility for others. Reformers unvaryingly reminded Americans of those obligations.

Prosperity added to the moral obligation of the few to share their wealth in ways that would improve the lot of the many. In his ''gospel of wealth'' Andrew Carnegie summed up an attitude underlying much American belief when he argued that prosperity must bring about public good. Although Carnegie and many other Americans left the final responsibility for uplift with the individual rather than the society, as historian Daniel Boorstin observed in *Democracy and Its Discontents* (New York, 1974), the American struggle for equality and justice ''has been, in large part, the struggle of some Americans for the rights of *other* Americans,'' and the ''some'' often were ''haves'' reaching out to ''have nots.'' The activism of propertied whites in the antislavery and civil rights crusades, and the concern of such patricians as the two Roosevelt presidents for the downtrodden, are but two examples of such outreach.

The sense of common purpose, from its various sources, has encouraged and shaped American reform for over two centuries. It has helped make possible the translation of sentiment into interest, the mobilizing of popular support to right moral and civic wrongs. It also has made American reform less radical than it might have been if the sources of reform and the reformers themselves had come from desperation and alienation.

American reform has been almost wholly homegrown. While borrowing and adapting ideas and responding to philosophical impulses from abroad, American reformers have relied on native ideas, interests, and identities to make their case for particular reforms. Jane Addams, for example, visited Toynbee Hall in London and sat at the feet of Tolstoy in Russia, but the settlement house movement she did so much to define in the United States was adapted to American circumstances and needs, and rooted in American institutions and language. Opponents of reform—from, for example, proslavery apologists charging abolitionists with being agents of a British conspiracy during the 1840s and 1850s, to business leaders charging labor organizers with being agents of Old World socialism and anarchism during the 1880s and 1890s, to segregationists charging civil rights activists with being tools of Soviet communism during the 1950s—have depicted reformers as outsiders. By using the language of their native American culture and by being principally natives of that culture, however, American reformers have been able to counter claims that the changes they have proposed are ''un-American.'' The reformers' emphasis on persuasion rather than violence, and their interest in recruiting popular support, repeatedly have pulled their cause close to the center of American consciousness and conscience. Because of their own faith in American democratic values and institutions, American reformers have operated openly rather than in secret societies. In the United States, which French observer Alexis de Tocqueville rightly characterized as a nation of joiners, reform succeeded by appealing to Americans' voluntarism, by enlisting people who wanted to combine to effect change.

This dictionary's interest rests on reform rather than on radicalism—on the reshaping and redirecting of society rather than on its uprooting. In emphasizing reform over radicalism—indeed, in distinguishing between the two—the dictionary borrows from Raymond Williams's *Keywords: A Vocabulary of Culture and Society* (New York, 1976) in recognizing that such terms as ''reform'' and ''radical'' are fluid and sometimes interchangeable, and that their meanings are rooted in particular historical contexts. However much American reformers might not deserve the label ''radical,'' many of them were regarded (and in several instances regarded themselves) as radicals in their own day and proposed substantial changes in social structure and the redistribution of power. In fact, the lines separating reform from radicalism have remained blurred and porous, so that clear distinctions between reformer and radical often have proven problematic. One generation's radical outcast might be embraced as another generation's reformer hero or heroine. The abolitionists, for example, were so transformed in Northerners' collective estimation from the 1830s through the 1860s.

From Thomas Paine's day onward, radical ideas have inspired reform efforts, and reforms have become radical. Antislavery, for example, moved from the cautious, gradual abolition strategies of the Quakers and the Revolutionary era generation to the immediatism and moral certainty of the evangelicals and Garrisonian abolitionists. Internal tensions regarding direction and purpose within a ''reform'' movement might make it simultaneously more conservative and more radical. Such was the case in antislavery when the failures of gradualism and moral suasion gave way to calls by some for accommodations with and entrance into the political world, and to calls by others for self-purification and further removal from the corrupting influences of society and politics.

Still, reform and radicalism were (and are) not wholly synonymous. They have sought and have achieved different outcomes. One of the striking common characteristics of American reform over time has been its combination of idealism and realism, with pragmatism often tempering visionary renderings of what American society ought to be. Reformers expected to change society by argument and action. Understanding American society and beliefs, adapting to political realities, and appealing to public conscience and self-interest forced reformers to consider the practical aspects of how to enlist popular support for their ideas and programs. The reformers included in this dictionary have encouraged, sustained, and led organized efforts at reform. They were not just writers or advocates; in most cases they were also builders and coalition seekers. Where true radicals were alienated from the larger American culture, which they considered beyond redemption, reformers commonly sought alliances with powerful elements and the general public in a culture they hoped to redeem.

The reformers selected for inclusion in this collection principally have operated outside of government, although many of them have sought to influence public policy and even to gain control of local, state, or the federal government and several of them have held governmental office. American reformers traditionally expected the words and actions of their public appeals to have political consequences. Defining government's place in reform proved more difficult. During the nineteenth century many reformers, from temperance to health advocates, emphasized individual self-control as the way to improve self and society. In the view of Ralph Waldo Emerson, among others, social amelioration began with self-regeneration. But during the twentieth century many reformers, from prohibitionists to environmentalists, have looked to government to regulate private as well as public behavior. The emphasis in reform shifted increasingly, if incompletely, from internal to external control, and from voluntarism to public agency. As government became more important in all aspects of social life and policy, more reformers focused attention on its structure, politics, and personnel. Some, especially the Populists and Progressives, and modern civil rights activists, made civic reform central to their overall programs for social and economic change.

Despite the importance of government in reform thinking, this dictionary's emphasis is on social rather than civic reform. An undercurrent of distrust of government courses through American history, and even those reformers most insistent on using public policy have remained ambivalent about entrusting too much authority to government. Indeed, some modern reformers have charged that from the New Deal through the Great Society, government has blunted the thrust of reform, muting and even transmuting it in ways that reinforce rather than reorient American institutions. They have warned that conceding responsibility for reform to government rather than assuming it themselves has left Americans morally flaccid. From the 1960s on, one of the most powerful forces in American reform has been the effort to return moral and civic responsibility to the individual, making each person feel responsible for keeping the environment clean, choosing life or death in abortion, coming out for civil rights, whatever. In any case, reformers, not government, have initiated change; government has responded to and managed social changes proposed and demanded by those outside government. The essays in this dictionary reflect the struggle between private and public controls that has marked American reform throughout its history.

In addition to providing individual essays on representative reformers from major movements, this dictionary as a whole provides insight into the evolving nature of American reform. One of the more significant developments in American life has been the growing specialization of people's skills, interests, and occupations. The complexity of modern life and the demands for efficiency often have discouraged a holistic approach to solving social problems. Social reform, too, has become specialized. In the late eighteenth century through the mid-nineteenth century, one would find an interlocking directorate of American reformers; the same individuals were engaged in a host of social reform efforts, ranging from penal reform to antislavery to temperance, under the overarching assumption that all evils were interconnected and thus required coordinated action to cleanse America. By the twentieth century, reformers tended to focus on a single issue, sometimes to the exclusion of all others. To be sure, Jane Addams and Martin Luther King, Jr., among others, moved outward from single concerns to a more embracing vision of change, and antiwar activists and feminists of the 1960s and 1970s framed their protests in global terms; nevertheless, specialization is one mark of modern American reform that distinguished it from its late eighteenth- and early nineteenth-century forebears.

American reform has not been linear. A reform time line reveals that reforms crashed upon America in waves, each with, in the words of Ronald Walters in *American Reformers 1815–1860* (New York, 1978), "a decade or more of intense activity followed by periods of relative apathy about social problems." Intense reform activity erupted during the 1830s and 1840s, the late nineteenth and early twentieth centuries, the 1930s, and the 1960s but abated soon after each surge, generally when a war siphoned off and redirected energy to the nation's service. Each wave left residues of reform interest and ideas about strategy in the American consciousness that subsequent reformers picked up, and many reform movements long outlived their founders because of the institutions they built. Still, each reform surge has had its own character and focus. Each new reform generation wrote its own agenda, built its own institutions, fashioned its own instruments. The religious assumptions and drives of antebellum reform receded by the twentieth century as science advanced in public respect; reliance on self-control yielded to demands for governmental regulation; and so on.

Although this dictionary places American reform at the center of American history, it makes no claim to being a comprehensive history of American reform. Rather, its purpose is to provide in-depth examinations of major American reform movements through essays on representative reformers and, thereby, to chart the process of American reform action and draw a collective portrait. This dictionary thus functions both as a reference work and as an extended essay on the character and impact of reform in America. As Ralph Waldo Emerson observed, in America, where the people are in a constant state of inventing and remaking themselves, all Americans are reformers at certain times in their lives. Reform constitutes the marrow of American identity. Examining American reform thus promises to reveal insights into American's true and ideal selves.

In compiling the essays, the editors chose not to impose any uniform theory of social or protest movements or of personality types on the contributors. The contributors approached their subjects as historians rather than as social theorists. We believe that no single theory can explain the variety and complexity of reform movements, but for editorial purposes we have adopted Anthony Blasi's definition of a social movement to identify which movements might be included in our volume. Blasi argues in *Early Christianity as a Social Movement* (New York, 1989) that social movements are made up of more than an organization alone, encompassing as well popular participation and the beliefs and actions that promote social change. We also recognized that each reform movement had its own specific causes within the larger historical context of American culture and the culture of reform, so no single explanatory device will fit all the reforms together. The variety, even the contradictory nature, of American reform marks its character as much as do its common roots in religious and civic culture.

No particular personality type emerged from the biographies. Although several reformers came from reformer families and many held strong religious convictions, no single factor determined why they became reformers. The environmental context and family background that pushed one person toward reform might have pulled another person away from it. The contributors repeatedly point to the idiosyncratic aspects of circumstance, personality, and historical context that led a person to reform. Regarding context, it is significant that as early as the 1830s, it was possible to make a career of reform. Increased literacy rates, technological advances that reduced the cost of printing, and transportation improvements that created a national market for ideas as well as goods allowed one to make a living writing books or editing a newspaper or journal. Reform became a profession, however low-paying and precarious. For women especially, a career in reform promised a way to exercise public power by influencing public opinion and by building institutions. Yet what personality factors inclined people to devote their lives to a cause remain unclear. Consequently, we have left any collective portrait of "the American reformer" for readers to draw. We also have eschewed applying labels such as "conservative" or "liberal" to individuals, for such terms lack consistency in an ambiguous world where reformers can believe simultaneously in the innate depravity of humankind and the idea of progress, the corrupt nature of government and the need for public controls, or the tyranny of the majority and the desirability of democratic appeals.

The vast and unwieldy nature of the subject has discouraged scholars from trying to package the whole of American reform in one book. Not since William Dwight Bliss's *Encyclopedia of Social Reform* (New York, 1897) has anyone attempted an inventory of reform generally. Bliss's reach was wide, as evinced by his book's subtitle—*Including Political Economy, Political Science, Sociology, and Statistics, Covering Anarchism, Charities, Civil Service, Currency, Land and Legislation Reform, Penology, Socialism, Social Purity, Trades Unions, Woman Suffrage, etc.*—and then global in his revised edition of the encyclopedia—*The New Encyclopedia of Social Reform, Including All Social-Reform Movements and Activities, and the Economic, Industrial, and Sociological Facts and Statistics of All Countries and All Social Subjects* (New York, 1908). However useful they may be in identifying the myriad social reform movements across the Western world and in reminding readers of the transatlantic connections to American reform, Bliss's works, with their generous definitions of reform, often miss the peculiar dynamic and character of American reform development.

To date, only Thomas H. Greer, in *American Social Reform Movements: Their Patterns Since 1865* (New York, 1949), and Robert H. Walker, in *Reform in America: The Continuing Frontier* (Lexington, Ky., 1985), have ventured general histories of American reform. Only Arthur M. Schlesinger, in *The American as Reformer* (Cambridge, Mass., 1950), has offered a rounded view of the American reform personality from the Revolution through the twentieth century, arguing that reform has been inherent in the American character that derived from a Puritan conscience and an Enlightenment philosophy. For a good profile of American reform, one must rely on the materials collected in Robert H. Walker, ed., *The Reform Spirit in America: A Documentation of the Patterns of Reform in the American Republic* (New York, 1976).

There are excellent biographical dictionaries and reference works on American radicalism, the American Left, the civil rights movement, American peace movements, a variety of particular reforms, and the relationship between religion and reform, especially for the nineteenth century (see especially Robert H. Abzug, *Cosmos Crumbling: American Reform and the Religious Imagination* [New York, 1994]). There also are several hundred sketches of American reformers included in Alden Whitman, ed., *American Reformers: An H. W. Wilson Biographical Dictionary* (New York, 1985). But no single volume has combined full-bodied biography and history to observe the variety and particularity of American reformers and reform over two centuries, and no volume has included many post–World War II reform interests and personalities. Meeting those needs for a longitudinal, comparative perspective and attention to recent developments is the purpose of this dictionary.

Each chapter has been written by an authority on the particular reform or reformer under review. Each chapter includes an up-to-date bibliography of the principal works on the reform and reformer, with endnotes citing sources for quotations or very specific information in the text. A time line on American reform shows the connection between reforms and the changing reform interests over time, and arranges the subjects in this dictionary in chronological order. A detailed subject index provides easy access to subjects treated throughout the book.

Jane Addams
and the Settlement House Movement

LOUISE W. KNIGHT

Jane Addams's contemporaries hailed her as "the leader and prophet of the settlement movement in America" and the movement's "grandmother," and declared Hull House "the Mother House."[1] Such acknowledgments suggest the breadth of her influence but fail to convey its shallow depth. Although her views on settlement purpose and method were respected by those active in the movement, she was more often honored than imitated. This development, often the fate of prophets, was perhaps inevitable in a movement that valued settlement autonomy over conformity to any national definition or standard.

How does one sum up the settlement house movement? Although settlement workers launched or supported hundreds of local, state, and national reforms during the movement's peak years of 1893–1922, no single reform or set of reforms was distinctly identified with the settlement. Indeed, during these years the movement, or elements within it, campaigned for the entire Progressive reform agenda. That agenda included access for all Americans to excellent public education, protective labor laws for women and children, woman's suffrage, municipal reform, recreational facilities, affordable housing for low-income people, and city planning.

Yet the settlement movement was something more than the sum of the Progressive agenda. Although the movement was certainly a source of social reform ideas and social reformers, it was intended by its most visionary leaders as something more—as a reform in itself. The settlement was meant to be a new process by which public policy would be developed and social conditions improved.

An urban minister of the Anglican Church, Samuel A. Barnett, and his wife and fellow worker Henrietta Barnett, founded the world's first settlement, Toynbee Hall, in London in 1884. Believing that university men of the middle and upper classes had a civic obligation to educate themselves about the lives of the working poor in the industrial neighborhoods of London, the couple invited young Oxford graduates to join them in taking up collective residence in the East End. As "residents" of the settlement house, the young men would spend their free time (outside their city jobs) becoming involved in the life of the neighborhood. Clubs, classes, local political organizing, and social reform might follow in response to neighbor interest, but the most important development would be the friendships formed between neighbors and residents, and the mutual education that would result.

The settlement, as Canon Barnett conceived it, was a class-conscious institution—one that acknowledged the existence of class differences. But in conceiving of the settlement, Barnett also challenged the class structure by rejecting the prevailing upper-class prejudices that the working poor did not "deserve" or could not benefit from the "advantages" (education, culture, and the arts) available to the upper classes, and that the working poor were not capable of or interested in being active citizens in a democracy. The residents were meant, of course, to help their neighbors, a fact that made the settlement part of the upper-class tradition of noblesse oblige, but they were also expected to be helped by them, to learn from them. Thus the settlement was potentially conservative and radical, condescending and democratic, all at the same time.

In which of these two directions a settlement went often depended more on the personal style and values of its head resident than on anything else. Barnett, a gentle, spiritual man, treated everyone—neighbors and residents alike—with quiet respect, and his example was an influence on Toynbee Hall residents. But as settlements spread in England and the United States, the conventional expectations and class prejudices of some settlement leaders often served to reinforce the attitudes of class and race superiority that residents brought with them to the neighborhoods. Settlement leaders did not always live up to the high ideals they embraced. This human shortcoming underlines the importance of noting the difference between their words and their deeds, between theory and practice.

One American settlement leader, Jane Addams, stayed closer in practice to the Toynbee Hall model than most of her colleagues. Like Barnett, she believed that the residents had as much to learn from their neighbors as their neighbors had to learn from them. For her, unlike for some head residents, this was not an abstract idea but an insight that grew out of her own experience.

Jane Addams—social reformer, peace activist, author, and lecturer—was born 6 September 1860 in Cedarville, Illinois, a small village fourteen miles south of the Illinois–Wisconsin border. She was the fifth surviving child of John Huy Addams and Sarah Weber Addams. Her mother died when Jane was two and a half, so her early sense of herself was most influenced by her father, a wealthy landowner, miller, banker, investor, and state legislator. His moral rectitude and civic-mindedness made a great impression on his daughter. She also found inspiration in the family and village recollections of her mother as a kind and generous neighbor to the poor of Cedarville.

Determined from childhood to accomplish something in life, Addams became fascinated in high school by social reform. Ralph Waldo Emerson and Charles Dickens were her favorite authors. Her stepmother—her father remarried when Jane was eight—was a woman of culture and social ambition who further broadened Addams's horizons through her love of literature and the arts.

Addams's drive to achieve was strong. Although she was determined to earn a Bachelor of Arts degree at the new Smith College in Massachusetts, her father insisted on sending her to the local Rockford Seminary. The school did not offer the B.A., but she took all the courses she could that would qualify her to receive one. By graduation, her plan was to become a doctor and live and work among the poor.

Still in pursuit of a B.A., Addams planned to attend Smith College before seeking her medical degree. Her parents, feeling she was too ill and weak to go east the following fall, forbade it. Frustrated, Addams lived at home that summer, unsure of her future. Then her father died unexpectedly in August. These two disappointments were followed by a third. That October, while the family was living in Philadelphia, she enrolled with her sister for two semesters of medical studies. Addams did not complete the degree, however, because of back problems that originated in a childhood illness. Major surgery and slow recovery followed.

The years immediately following college were, in some ways, the most difficult of Addams's life. Full of dreams about changing the world, she felt constrained by society's expectations—ones her father had shared and that her stepmother continued to express forcefully—that a single, unmarried daughter of prosperous means (Addams had received a large inheritance upon her father's death) should devote herself to family and travel, and should seek to marry as soon as possible. Addams's letters to her friend Ellen Gates Starr provide a record of her misery during this time.

At first, to compensate, Addams sought meaning for her life in the study of "culture," particularly through books. She read not only her favorite authors from college—Thomas Carlyle, Ralph Waldo Emerson, George Eliot, and Matthew Arnold—but also new ones, such as Leo Tolstoy, Auguste Comte, Herbert Spenser, John Stuart Mill, and Karl Marx. In their various ways, these authors explored the question that came to dominate Addams's life during these years: what was her responsibility as a human being to those who suffered? Slowly, her determination to work with the poor returned, strengthened by her sense that, in their suffering and their joy, they held a key to life's meaning that had escaped her.

By 1886 or 1887 Addams had decided, as she later noted in her autobiography, to rent a house in a poor district of a city where, along with other young women who would join her, she would try to act on the ideas she had absorbed from her extensive education while also trying to "learn of life from life itself."[2] Her ideas about how to reform society, enriched by her wide reading, spurred her to act, but so did her need to feel alive again and her desire to end her isolation from the rest of humanity. Founding Hull House was both an effort to

make an objective difference and a personal necessity. She formulated her motives and goals for the settlement house out of her own experience.

Addams does not say when she first learned of Toynbee Hall, but by the
spring of 1888 she had decided to visit it. In Madrid at the time, traveling with
friends, she confessed her dream to Ellen Gates Starr. They agreed they would
start a settlement in Chicago, where Ellen had been teaching school and had
many friends. Encouraged by her friend's enthusiasm, Addams departed for
London. She was deeply impressed by what she found at Toynbee Hall in the
poverty-stricken East End, but most of all by its compassionate head resident,
Canon Barnett, who would remain a lifetime friend. By 19 September 1889,
Addams and Starr had rented a formerly elegant, now neglected, old house on
Chicago's West Side; had lined up several women to join them as residents and
volunteers; and had opened the doors to the community of mostly German, Irish,
and Italian immigrants who lived in the surrounding tenements. Although Starr
was cofounder of Hull House, they agreed Addams would be head resident,
probably because her wealth was underwriting the costs of launching the settlement and, having no need to support herself, she had the free time to run it that
Ellen, having to earn her living, did not.

Many have assigned the honorific ''America's first settlement house'' to
Neighborhood Guild, which was founded in 1886, three years before Hull
House, on the Lower East Side of New York City, and a case can be made for
the claim. The Guild rationale, as set forth by its founder, Stanley Coit, sought
to give neighbors a voice in governance by organizing entire neighborhoods into
self-governing guilds, but it did not emphasize what the residents would learn
or the idea of ''mutual benefit.'' Furthermore, the idea of organizing neighborhoods into guilds was adopted in modified form by only a few settlements, and
Coit himself, who continued to found guilds in England and America, drew a
distinction between his guilds and settlements.

The first two American settlements that adopted the Toynbee Hall model were
Hull House in Chicago and the College Settlement in New York City, founded
by a group of alumnae (including nongraduates) of Smith, Wellesley, and several
other New England women's colleges. The College Settlement opened its doors
only two weeks after Hull House, on 1 October. Each settlement had made its
initial plans unaware of the other's intent. Thus it was that independent efforts
by college alumnae in the Northeast and Midwest launched the American settlement house movement in the fall of 1889.

The settlement idea spread rapidly. In October 1890, an African-American
woman and Hampton Institute graduate, Janie Porter Barrett, opened the Locust
Street Social Settlement in her home in Hampton, Virginia; the following year
three more settlements opened in New York and Chicago. By 1900, fifteen years
after Toynbee Hall began, in America alone there were between 50 and 103
settlements, depending on how ''settlement'' was defined (those with religious
affiliations were often excluded). But whichever definition one used, the official
figures were always low because the leaders in the field, whose personal net-

works produced the lists, were all white and from cities in the Northeast and Midwest. Jewish settlements in New York and Chicago were usually known, but Southern, rural, and black settlements were mostly omitted from early counts. By 1922 there were, by one "official" count, 500 settlements in the United States; the number may have marked the movement's peak.

From the beginning, women were drawn in disproportionate numbers to settlements. There were always significantly more women than men residents nationwide, and until the 1950s the majority of head residents were women. Women had always done work for the poor and been active in churches, two traditions that fed into settlements, but the settlement was uniquely appealing to women in that it offered an alternative to marriage—that is, a place to live, a group of people to live with, and a structure that presumed single women would live independent working lives. For the first generation of college-educated women, those graduating in the 1880s and 1890s, these characteristics made the settlement particularly attractive.

With these facts in mind, some historians have argued that the settlement provided a valuable kind of women's community, where they could develop their own strengths as actors in the public realm without interference from men. Many early settlements were sex-segregated and had the potential to be this kind of community (Denison House, the College Settlement in New York City, and Henry Street, for example, accepted only female residents for many years), but some of the settlements whose female residents and head residents were the most active in the "public realm," like Hull House and the University of Chicago Settlement, accepted men residents early. Hull House broke the barrier first, admitting men in late 1891; they soon numbered (and would remain for many years) a third of all Hull House residents. What was significant about Hull House was not the absence of men but their nondominant presence. Masculinity carried no extra authority there. The women of Hull House who emerged as local, state, and national leaders of various Progressive reforms, including Jane Addams, gained valuable experience at Hull House working with and leading men residents.

As the idea's prompt adoption in the United States suggests, the settlement house, although perceived as an innovation, drew on familiar elements in the Anglo-American—and African-American and Jewish—religious charitable traditions. Like a Christian city mission, the settlement came into a poor neighborhood out of concern for the conditions there. But whereas a mission's purpose was conversion, the settlement's was mutual education and cooperation.

Although religious faith often motivated settlement workers, early theorizers about the settlement philosophy, beginning with Canon Barnett, stressed that the settlement did not proselytize. Nevertheless, churches founded religious settlement houses to proselytize to the immigrant and African-American populations in the cities; in fact, among settlements—loosely defined—religious settlements were soon numerous. Between 1897 and 1906, 157 new settlements were established in the United States, 70 of them founded by churches. In 1910, out of 413 settlements that participated in one survey, 167 were religious settlements.

Viewing the movement from this perspective, it was essentially Christian, not only in motive but also in purpose. During the 1890s and after, the rapid spread of religious settlements was fueled by the activism of Protestant ministers inspired by the Social Gospel, the self-help efforts of black urban churches, and the urban mission work of the Catholic Church. Despite their numbers, however, the church-based settlements never captured the leadership of the movement. The National Federation of Settlements, founded in 1911 by the early pioneers—all of whom, including Addams, shared Barnett's view on prosyletizing—long resisted accepting as a member any settlement that served as a mission.

Settlements established by African Americans to serve their communities often were founded by churches, and some, like the Institutional Church and Social Settlement of Chicago, were churches and settlements at the same time. Others, like the Abraham Lincoln Centre, also in Chicago, were founded by blacks and whites together, to serve racially integrated communities.

Settlements shared an interest in forming personal relations with the poor with another new kind of organization imported from England, the Charity Organization Society (COS). By the 1890s, when American settlements first became numerous in major cities, COS efforts were well established in the United States. COS proponents typically viewed the poor as responsible for their poverty, crediting able-bodied men with moral decrepitude if they remained poor. COS workers saw themselves as ''reformers.'' Their reform goals were to make the delivery of charity more scientific and to reform the individual poor person. These goals became those of the modern social work profession—a fact that is hardly surprising, given that profession's origins in the COS movement. By contrast, settlement leaders—or at least the most progressive ones—tended to see poverty as mainly caused by environmental conditions like low pay, poorly ventilated and unsafe housing, unsanitary streets, and unclean water.

Another difference, much discussed, lay in whom the two movements served. COS was concerned with efficiently providing the ''worthy'' poor with food, clothing, and shelter. Settlements mainly dealt with the working poor and avoided giving charity, except to neighbors in crisis. The distinction was important, although it was usually lost on visitors, newspaper reporters, and, later, some historians.

Although national COS and settlement leaders argued about theory, cooperation was extensive at the local level. Despite the fact that the COS and settlement philosophies and goals differed, many COS offices were housed in settlements, and some COS groups even founded settlements. COS volunteers, like those with ties to prosyletizing churches, tended to have a conservative influence on settlements.

In keeping with the Toynbee Hall model, American universities were actively involved in settlements from the start. Those founded by professors or alumni were usually called ''university'' (for men) or ''college'' (for women) settlements. These groups often saw settlements as "laboratories" where college or seminary students could "study poverty." Several early male settlement leaders, such as Robert Woods and Charles Stover, with close ties to universities or seminaries, enthusiastically promoted the "settlement as laboratory" idea and the term "university settlement."

Jane Addams disagreed. As early as 1892, before a gathering of settlement leaders at a social ethics conference, she argued in favor of the idea of the "social settlement" and stressed the importance of knowing the neighbors as people, not as objects of study.[3] In 1899, in her lengthiest, most carefully crafted essay on settlements, "A Function of the Social Settlement" (strategically published in an academic journal), Addams took up the question again. The settlement, she argued, "stands for application, not for research; for universal interest, as opposed to specialization."[4]

Addams's reasons for rejecting the "settlement as laboratory" model went to the heart of her understanding of what a settlement was. In this essay she defined it as "an effort to apply knowledge to life, to express life itself in terms of life." Unlike the philanthropist, who seeks "to do good," or the sociologist, who "thirst[s] for data and analysis," the resident's "more . . . human desire" was for the workingman and workingwoman to have the opportunity to develop the "moral and intellectual qualities upon which depend the free aspects and values of living."[5] The settlement resident's purpose was life-transforming, both for herself or himself and for the neighbors. A desire for factual knowledge was too narrow and impersonal a motive for such work, Addams felt. Although Hull House residents did some studies of the neighborhood, and although Addams never argued against such work—indeed, she thought "investigations" valuable—she continued to point out the dangers of the "settlement as laboratory" model.

Addams's thoughtful speeches at the 1892 conference, published the following fall in the prestigious *The Forum* magazine, marked her emergence as a national leader of the fledgling American settlement movement. A year later she helped bring settlements to national and international prominence by organizing the first national and world conference on settlements, the Congress on Social Settlements, as part of the series of congresses held under the auspices of the Chicago World's Fair (the Columbian Exposition). Addams and Graham Taylor organized the first regional federation of settlements in Chicago in 1894, and she was one of the eleven founders of the National Federation of Settlements in 1911, of which she was promptly elected the first president.

The types of activities they undertook were another way to define settlements, yet even among the early settlements, patterns were difficult to discern. Kindergartens, children's clubs, and classes were the most widespread; but, as if to prove the point that no particular activity was defining, Denison House had neither a kindergarten nor children's clubs in its early years. Henry Street Settlement, initially called the Nurses' Settlement, had only one club and no kindergarten at first. Some—like South End House, Henry Street, Hull House,

Chicago Commons, and University of Chicago Settlement—were particularly active in local politics and municipal reform; others were determinedly apolitical. Some settlements, most notably Hull House, had rich cultural offerings: drama clubs, literature classes, lectures, music classes, concerts. Others offered little beyond crafts. Some emphasized vocational education; others, literacy; still others, citizenship. Some worked closely with labor unions (Denison House, Hull House, South End House, University Settlement); others, fearing to alarm their communities, distanced themselves from the labor movement. (It should be noted that none of these activities was the sole purview of settlements. Missions, churches, temples, and other local organizations also undertook them.) In fact, a majority of settlements was always focused, some exclusively, on meeting the needs of the neighborhood through service. The average settlement house, as Ruth Crocker has persuasively argued, was no ''spearhead'' for reform, except at the neighborhood level.[6]

What made a settlement reform-minded (in the broader sense) was, of course, the outlook of its residents, which was influenced, at least in part, by the outlook of the head resident, particularly by his or her expectations of the residents. Consensus in the movement regarding the residents' role was absent from the beginning, although initially there was some agreement that the presence of residents was the most distinctive characteristic of settlements. In 1896 a survey of American settlements by the National Conference of Charities and Corrections found that the field considered the residents' presence essential to the settlement's ''identity.''[7]

Most of the early head residents were familiar with Barnett's belief that settlements were not to impose their solutions to neighborhood problems but to learn what the neighbors wanted changed. In one of her 1892 speeches, Addams echoed and elaborated on the point: ''[The] residents must be emptied of all conceit of opinion and all self-assertion.''[8] This belief, in turn, shaped Barnett's and Addams's method of leading their settlements. At Hull House, as at Toynbee Hall, the residents governed themselves through a committee of all residents that met weekly to set fees for room and board, vote on new residents after a trial period, decide what projects the House would undertake as a whole, and determine the House expectations of residents regarding shared tasks, such as answering the front door and tending the playground. Although Addams chaired the committee on most occasions, her power was limited by the parliamentary rules that governed the meetings, and her proposals were sometimes rejected.

Addams, like Barnett, gave Hull House residents the freedom to choose how to spend their time. She encouraged them to pursue their own interests. ''Miss Addams,'' a volunteer recalled, ''had a rare way of . . . letting [people] work out their own plans.''[9] The freedom she gave residents was a policy that flowed directly out of her belief that a key purpose of the settlement was to teach the resident about life outside his or her own social class. Canon Barnett had first sounded the theme, but Addams was alone among the American settlement leaders in making a strong case for pursuing that goal. For her, the twin goals of social reform and self-reformation were inextricably intertwined. It was an old Protestant theme carried forward by Barnett and Addams into the settlement movement.

During the period before World War I, most settlements had no governing committee to which all residents belonged, although several (including Chicago Commons) had executive committees whose membership was elected by the residents.[10] Greenwich House in New York City did have a full residents' committee and in other ways was modeled closely on Hull House. Its founder, Mary Simkhovitch, was, along with Graham Taylor, one of the settlement founders (she was second generation) who caught the Toynbee Hall/Hull House spirit.

Residents at settlement houses were typically restricted in other ways as well. Like most head residents, Robert Woods viewed the volunteer residents as "his" staff, to be deployed as he saw fit after consulting them regarding their views. When residents at South End House departed, restless under his command, he decided the only solution was to change from residents to paid staff.

This attitude and the trend toward paid staff were repeated at most settlements during the 1890s. At the University Settlement in New York, for example, volunteer residents were expected to "cooperate" with the head worker and to "offer suggestions" for new policies.[11] At another settlement, volunteer residents were expected to "contribute" four hours a day. Probably as a result of the extensive demands placed on volunteer residents at most settlements, frequent turnover was also a problem. In response, as the twentieth century progressed, nearly all settlement houses converted to paid staff. By contrast, at Hull House, turnover was low and residents remained volunteers until after Addams's death in May 1935.

The degree of a resident's freedom to design his or her own settlement experience was hardly a minor detail. It affected the amount of creativity a resident could exercise and her or his freedom to undertake controversial work or make controversial public statements. In tight regimes, residents with new, or simply their own, ideas were seen as troublemakers. At Denison House, for a time, residents were forbidden to develop new projects on their own. Residents at such settlements were far less likely to originate fresh reform ideas. Although historians have rightly praised settlement workers for being, in Allen Davis's words, "progressive with a vengeance," the movement as a whole was more conservative than the views of its most prominent leaders would suggest.[12] In that, the settlement movement was similar to most reform movements.

But the fact that the ideal resident—an open-minded learner exploring her or his own interests—was not perfectly or even widely realized should not obscure the ideal's power to transform a particular resident from a defender of the status quo to a campaigner for social and economic change. The experience of settlement residence was, when properly designed, the reason the settlement movement became, for a time, a reform-nurturing movement. When residents really learned from their neighbors, they arrived at a new understanding of the causes of social problems. The energy and ideas for state and national reforms came

mostly from the leadership and the residents of the pioneer settlements. Jane
Addams, Robert Woods, Charles Stover, Graham Taylor, Mary McDowell, and
Lillian Wald had founded settlement houses by 1895. To their ranks were added
residents of their settlements who became nationally known reformers in their
own right: Julia Lathrop, Florence Kelley, Alice Hamilton, and Robert Hunter
(all from Hull House); Albert Kennedy (South End House); and Raymond Rob-
ins (Chicago Commons). Many of these individuals, plus others who came later
(Eleanor Roosevelt, Harold Ickes, Louise deKoven Bowen, Sophonisba Breckinridge, Edith and Grace Abbott), wrote movingly of the impact of their settlement experiences on their understanding of the obstacles facing the unemployed
and the working poor.

The settlements were also the source of loyal networks for political mobilization that were part of what made these reformers so effective in their efforts.
Addams worked closely with the individuals just named on one or more reforms
at the state and national levels. Ideas first conceived at settlement dining room
tables were sometimes transformed into national policy, after much letter writing
and consulting, data gathering, speechmaking and testifying, and private sessions
with elected officials. These reformers worked in tandem when they could, and
agreed to disagree when they had to. The lines of cooperation remained strong
in part because the settlement leaders did not demand consensus on every issue.
Alliances emerged and fell apart amiably as the issues changed.

Community organizing, always an engine for reform, was also part of the
original settlement vision and practiced by some houses. Experience had shown,
Addams wrote in 1904, that the settlement's neighbors ''have in themselves
reservoirs of moral power and civic ability . . . [and] that one can count upon
tremendous aids from within the neighborhoods.''[13] The residents' task was to
arouse their neighbors to collective action and to ''interpret the public opinion
of their neighborhood'' to those who lived outside it.[14]

Examples of what Addams meant stud the history of Hull House: its clubs
for children and adults, which were self-governing organizations with consti-
tutions and voting members; its cooperative coal society (headed by a neighbor
with a neighborhood membership) was designed to keep fuel costs down by
eliminating the middle man. Other community organizing included the campaigns to defeat the corrupt local alderman, the effort of the Hull House Wom-
en's Club to lobby city hall to improve garbage and sanitation services, and the
settlement's support for the right of unions to organize and strike. As Addams
said many times, she wished to work with others, not for others.[15] This was part
of what she meant by ''social democracy,'' a concept about which she wrote a
great deal.

Very few settlements, however, embraced community organizing and democratic self-governance as part of their agenda. Instead, elements of the Hull
House approach were borrowed piecemeal. Lillian Wald at Henry Street eventually established self-governing clubs. Robert Woods at South End House tried
to encourage neighbors to lobby for better garbage services. Denison House

welcomed union organizers to hold meetings there. It was not until the 1950s, however, that the approach became central to the methods of some settlements.

Racism, combined with classism, kept many settlement leaders from doing more to encourage community activism earlier. They feared an empowered community and thought the educated class better equipped than illiterate immigrants or African Americans to handle power. Despite their years of living in ethnically diverse communities, many residents and head residents felt themselves to be racially superior, particularly to southern European immigrants and African Americans, whose numbers were on the increase in major American cities between 1900 and 1920. Settlements located in areas where black people began to settle in increasing numbers often refused to serve them and even relocated to white neighborhoods, sometimes handing over the old settlement building to the African-American community to run—which, in the case of Christamore House in Indianapolis, it did with great success. Some white settlements, like Henry Street, founded separate branches in black neighborhoods.

Addams's deep convictions about democracy and the essential equality of human beings helped her to avoid practicing much of the racism prevalent in white society. She was, it appears, the first white head resident to invite a black resident to join a settlement serving a white community. Harriet Rice, a graduate of Wellesley College and a medical doctor by profession, was a resident of Hull House, with one or two breaks, from 1892 to at least 1904. Addams supported a prominent Chicago woman's effort to become the first black member of the Chicago Women's Club, supported African-American Chicagoans who sought to start a settlement house in a predominantly black neighborhood, and fought (but failed) to have the black delegates from the southern states seated at the 1912 Bull Moose convention.

Addams's methods as head resident, her emphasis on "learning from life," and her respect for a community's knowledge and for the principles of democracy contributed to her distaste for what she called "professionalism"—a distaste she extended to the profession of social work, which began to be an influence in settlement houses and elsewhere after the turn of the century. Addams felt that those who sought to "do good" professionally were dangerous in their self-righteousness, in their disdain for the wisdom of the common people, and in their minute concern with method.[16] Although social workers, like everyone else, were welcome at Hull House, and although Addams had close friends involved in shaping the profession, she never considered herself a "social worker" (even though she was often introduced as one) or spoke on the need for training in the field of settlement work.

Addams's nephew chose to include only two accomplishments on the stone that marked her grave in the cemetery at Cedarville (she died 25 May 1935). It reads, "Jane Addams of Hull House and the Women's International League for Peace and Freedom." Her involvement in the peace movement began in 1898, triggered in part by the outbreak of the Spanish–American War, but was inspired, at a deeper level, by ideas on nonviolence she first absorbed from the

Christian writings of Leo Tolstoy, which she read in the 1880s and 1890s. A visit to Tolstoy in Russia in 1896 moved her deeply, even as it raised questions in her mind about whether he was committed to nonviolence in all its forms. Eventually Addams opposed World War I at great personal cost. She founded the Women's International League for Peace and Freedom in 1919 and served as its president until 1929.

Despite the differences she had with social workers, and despite her expanding and controversial role in the international peace movement, Addams remained a prominent settlement leader until her death. She continued to be much sought-after as a speaker on the subject of settlements. Her famous and popular classic, *Twenty Years at Hull-House, with Autobiographical Notes*, published in 1910, made her name a household word and synonymous with the movement, but her most definitive writings on settlements remain her two 1892 speeches and her 1899 journal article.

Addams would not have labeled herself as a reformer either (''writer and lecturer'' was how she chose to describe herself), but she wrote and thought a good deal about the subject of reform. Her views on the sources of the reform impulse were consistent with her desire to nurture residents' individuality. ''The variation of the established type,'' she once wrote, ''is at the root of all change.''[17] Thus did she apply Darwin's theory of the evolution of species to explain social change. Although historians tend to call ''reformers'' those activists who promote a public policy reform agenda, Addams understood her greatest reform to be the creation of conditions at Hull House in which each resident could develop his or her individuality as a full human being, could become ''a variation from established type'' and therefore a source of social change. The record of the accomplishments of Hull House residents, unique among the residents of American settlements, testifies to her success.

In holding such views, Addams stood in opposition to strong trends within the settlement movement and wider society. By the 1910s, residents increasingly were trained social workers, although untrained paid and volunteer residents could be found at settlements in reduced numbers for many years. In time, resident programs disappeared altogether, replaced by paid, trained staff who went home every night.

The final trend, confirming the nonreform, conservative leanings of most settlements, was the increasing involvement of the business community, directly and indirectly, in settlement financing. Although businessmen had always supported settlements and served on their boards, the emergence after World War I of the federated charity fund-raising organizations—Community Chests—consolidated their influence. By the 1930s, if not before, many settlements were receiving the majority of their funding from these sources. Fearing such influences, Addams persuaded Hull House's board of directors to avoid such funding. The policy was changed only after her death.

Government funding, another trend that began in the 1930s, further inhibited settlements from seeking reforms. By the 1940s most settlements were community-based social service agencies, more often extensions of the government than critics of society—if they ever had been, which of course most had not.

Jane Addams and her colleagues in the settlement movement did not see eye to eye on many policy issues regarding settlement houses, but because of the decentralized nature of the movement (it was twenty-two years old before it felt the need for a national organization) and Addams's belief in individual freedom, these disagreements remained mostly uncontested. Despite Addams's enormous personal appeal as a much-loved public figure, her influence on the directions taken by the settlement movement was not great. Her greatest reform was Hull House. As its cofounder and head resident, she gave herself and others the opportunity to help to change America.

NOTES

1. Mary Sayles, "Settlement Workers and Their Work," *Outlook* 78 (1904): 311; Jane Addams to Alice Addams Haldeman, 23 February 1893, Jane Addams Papers, Jane Addams Peace Collection (Swarthmore College); Paul Kellogg, "Twice Twenty Years at Hull-House," *The Survey* 64 (1930): 266.

2. Jane Addams, *Twenty Years at Hull-House* (New York, 1910), 85.

3. This speech was later published as "The Objective Value of a Social Settlement," first in the *Forum* magazine (under a different title) and then in Henry C. Adams, ed., *Philanthropy and Social Progress* (New York, 1893).

4. Jane Addams, "A Function of the Social Settlement," *Annals of the American Academy of Political and Social Science* 13 (1899): 336.

5. Ibid., 50.

6. Ruth Hutchinson Crocker, *Social Work and Social Order: The Settlement Movement in Two Industrial Cities, 1889–1930* (Champaign-Urbana, Ill., 1992), 211, 222–225.

7. Harry P. Kraus, *The Settlement House Movement in New York City, 1886–1914* (New York, 1980), 31.

8. Jane Addams, "The Subjective Necessity for Social Settlements," in Adams, ed., *Philanthropy and Social Progress*, 24.

9. Louise deKoven Bowen, *Growing Up with a City* (New York, 1926), 88.

10. Louise C. Wade, *Graham Taylor: Pioneer for Social Justice, 1851–1938* (Chicago, 1964), 150.

11. Daniel Murphy, "Some Functions of a Settlement Resident," *Annual Report of University Settlement Society, 1912* (New York, 1912), 33.

12. Allen F. Davis, *Spearheads for Reform: The Social Settlements and the Progressive Movement, 1890–1914* (New York, 1967), x.

13. Jane Addams, "Neighborhood Improvement," in *Proceedings of the 31st National Conference of Charities and Corrections* (New York, 1904), 457.

14. Jane Addams, "Remarks," National Conference of Charities and Corrections, *Proceedings of the 23rd National Conference* (Boston, 1897), 136.

15. James Weber Linn, *Jane Addams: A Biography* (New York, 1936), 387.

16. Jane Addams, "A Modern Lear," repr. in Christopher Lasch, ed., *The Social Thought of Jane Addams* (New York, 1965), 118; Jane Addams, "Presidential Address,"

in International Congress of Women at the Hague, April 28th-May 1st, 1915, *Report* (Chicago, 1915), 22.

17. Jane Addams, *The Spirit of Youth and the City Streets* (New York, 1909), 8.

BIBLIOGRAPHY

Addams, Jane. "Hull House, Chicago: An Effort toward Social Democracy." *The Forum* 14 (1892): 226–241.

―――. "A New Impulse to an Old Gospel." *The Forum* 14 (1892): 345–358. [The *Forum* articles were reprinted with new titles, "The Objective Value of a Social Settlement," and "The Subjective Necessity for Social Settlements," in Henry C. Adams, ed. *Philanthropy and Social Progress.* New York, 1893.]

―――. "A Function of the Social Settlement." *Annals of the American Academy of Political and Social Science* 13 (1899): 323–345.

―――. *Twenty Years at Hull-House.* New York, 1910.

Barbuto, Domenica Maria. " 'The Matrix of Understanding': The Life and Work of Mary Kinsbury Simkovitch." Ph.D. diss., State University of New York at Stony Brook, 1992.

Bryan, Mary Lynn McCree, ed. *The Jane Addams Papers Microfilm.* Ann Arbor, Mich., 1985.

Carson, Mina. *Settlement Folk: Social Thought and the American Settlement Movement, 1885–1930.* Chicago, 1990.

Crocker, Ruth Hutchinson. *Social Work and Social Order: The Settlement Movement in Two Industrial Cities, 1889–1930.* Champaign-Urbana, Ill., 1992.

Davis, Allen F. *Spearheads for Reform: The Social Settlements and the Progressive Movement, 1890–1914.* New York, 1967.

―――. *American Heroine: The Life and Legend of Jane Addams.* New York, 1973.

Doe, Seung Ja. "Christian Perspective on Poverty: An Ideological Foundation for Social Work, 1880–1920." Ph.D. diss., Washington University, 1990.

Knight, Louise W. "Jane Addams and Hull House: Historical Lessons on Nonprofit Leadership." *Nonprofit Management and Leadership* 2 (1992): 125–141.

Kraus, Harry P. *The Settlement House Movement in New York City, 1886–1914.* New York, 1980.

Lasch-Quinn, Elisabeth. *Black Neighbors: Race and the Limits of Reform in the American Settlement House Movement, 1890–1945.* Chapel Hill, N.C., 1993.

Staples, George Henry. "Stanley Coit and the Neighborhood Guild: Ethical Idealism and Social Reform in New York City." Ph.D. diss., City University of New York, 1991.

―――. "Hull House and the Settlement Movement: A Centennial Reassessment." *Journal of Urban History* 17 (1991): 410–420.

Trolander, Judith Ann. *Settlement Houses and the Great Depression.* Detroit, 1975.

Wade, Louise C. "The Heritage from Chicago's Early Settlement Houses." *Journal of the Illinois State Historical Society* 60 (1967): 411–441.

Woods, Robert A., and Albert J. Kennedy, eds. *The Handbook of Settlements.* New York, 1911.

Jessie Daniel Ames and the White Women's Anti-Lynching Campaign

ROBERT F. MARTIN

In 1930 Coleman Livingston "Coley" Blease, campaigning in the Democratic primary for reelection to the U.S. Senate from South Carolina, declared to the voters of the Palmetto State, "Whenever the Constitution comes between me and the virtue of the white women of South Carolina, then I say 'to hell with the Constitution!' "[1] Blease was arguably as vacuous as he was flamboyant, but like many other Dixie demagogues in search of votes, he knew, almost instinctively, how to tap his region's deepest fears and most profound prejudices for the sake of political gain. His defiant justification of vigilante violence in retribution for the alleged rape of white women by black men was a simple but succinct expression of the volatile nexus of the South's complex and interrelated mythologies of race and gender. Yet even as Blease uttered his notorious words, a cadre of liberal white Southerners was already emerging to challenge lynching and the deadly and degrading patterns of belief that underlay the crime. Prominent among this band of dissenters was Jessie Daniel Ames, founder of the Association of Southern Women for the Prevention of Lynching (ASWPL). Throughout the 1930s the ASWPL mounted a narrowly focused but increasingly effective campaign against the most violent manifestation of Southern racism.

Although initially more a function of frontier social instability than of racial tension, by the late nineteenth and early twentieth centuries lynching had become an increasingly Southern and racist phenomenon. By 1909 the number of lynchings in the nation was approximately half what it had been in 1890. During this same period, the number of white victims declined from approximately 32.2 percent to about 11.4 percent, and the proportion of such crimes occurring in the South rose from roughly 82 to 92 percent of the total. Lynching, like other manifestations of de jure and de facto racism, was at least in part a legacy of attitudes informed by slavery and the turbulence of the Reconstruction era, and a corollary of the suppression of populism and the rise of Progressivism. Disfranchisement and segregation were often touted by Southern Progressives as reforms that would foster more stable race relations and remove the vexing issue of race from regional politics, thus enabling white Southerners to debate more freely the myriad social and economic problems confronting the South. And, if not touted, lynching was at least tolerated by many presumably enlightened Southerners as an unfortunate but sometimes necessary dimension of Southern race relations.

Racism and related violence surged in the immediate aftermath of World War I; however, Progressivism and the U.S. involvement in World War I had already begun to awaken some Southerners to the complexity and injustices inherent in their region's race relations. Although disheartened by the postwar situation, these fledgling liberals looked to the future with determination and optimism. During the 1920s young men and women of both races became involved in the nascent interracial work of such groups as the intercollegiate Young Women's and Young Men's Christian Associations, the women's missionary work of the Methodist Episcopal Church South, the Fellowship of Reconciliation, and, most notably, the Commission on Interracial Cooperation (CIC).

The CIC was a response to the violence and social turmoil that swept the nation immediately after the Great War. Longing for order and stability, those involved in the CIC sought peace through accommodation and reconciliation rather than repression. Funded largely by Northern philanthropy, this loose-knit association of black and white Southerners led by Will Alexander worked at the state and community levels to secure rudimentary justice, defuse tension, thwart violence, and promote contacts across racial lines. It soon became the most extensive force for interracial cooperation in the South during the interwar years.

The CIC initially was dominated by men. Many among the male leadership feared that women would be either too radical or too conservative, or they felt that issues such as lynching, linked in the popular mind with sexuality and race, were inappropriate for female consideration. Many Southern women activists were, however, increasingly interested in, and sometimes more enlightened on, questions of race than were some of their male counterparts. In time, both black and white women began to swell the ranks of the CIC and to demand a more prominent place in its activities. As a result, the Interracial Commission created a department of woman's work, and by 1924 eleven statewide women's groups were functioning across the South. The women attempted to facilitate interracial communication and to make health, educational, and recreational facilities more readily available to African Americans. It was through such work that Jessie Daniel Ames first became deeply involved in the fledgling interracial movement in the South.

Born on 2 November 1883, to James M. and Laura Leonard Daniel, in Palestine, Texas, Jessie Daniel spent her childhood and adolescence in the small towns of Overton and Georgetown in eastern Texas. The psychological roots of her activism, however, sprang less from her social environment than from her familial matrix. Daniel's childhood was marred by feelings of inadequacy and insecurity, stemming largely from the fact that she felt overshadowed by her older sister, Lulu, whose charm and intelligence made her their father's favorite.

Shortly after Jessie Daniel's graduation from Southwestern College in Georgetown, in 1902, her father moved the family to Laredo, Texas, where she met Roger Post Ames, a military surgeon thirteen years her senior; they were married in 1905. According to historian Jacquelyn Dowd Hall, the marriage was plagued by sexual incompatibility and by family tensions resulting from the Ames family's hostility toward Jessie. Although the marriage was characterized by prolonged separation and emotional strain, the Ameses had three children before Roger Ames's death in 1914. Hall suggests that Jessie Ames's unhappy and unfulfilling marriage compounded feelings of inadequacy and insecurity that resulted initially from an unsatisfying relationship with her father, who considered her less able and less feminine than her older sister. Consequently, Ames was never secure in her sexuality, and throughout her life had difficulty establishing and maintaining intimate relationships. As a defense mechanism, she developed a rather bold, aggressive, and somewhat domineering persona, which perhaps alleviated her insecurity but compounded her loneliness. Ames found in public life some of the satisfaction and fulfillment denied her in private relationships. Her insecurity bred in her a competitiveness and drive for success that served her well in the public sphere. It may also have intensified her sense of commitment to the powerless and victimized in society.

Following her father's death in 1911, Jessie joined her mother in the operation of the family-owned telephone company in Georgetown, Texas. Both women developed considerable business skill and earned the respect of the community. Her career in business enabled Ames to develop a measure of self-confidence and economic independence, both of which were assets when she became involved in public affairs. First as a local organizer for the Texas Equal Suffrage Association and then as its state treasurer, she began to emerge as an effective and formidable leader of the women of the Lone Star State.

When the Texas Equal Suffrage Association became the Texas League of Women Voters following the ratification of the Nineteenth Amendment, Ames was an active leader, agitating for educational, penal, and legal reforms that would benefit women, children, and the disadvantaged in her state. As she worked on behalf of a variety of progressive measures, Ames grew increasingly aware of the seamlessness of the social fabric and began to understand that injustice against one group was injurious to society as a whole. By the early 1920s, Ames's recognition of racial injustice, her awareness of the contradictions in a white-only reform movement, and her revulsion at the activities of the Ku Klux Klan precipitated her increased involvement in interracial work. An experienced public speaker, she worked first as a volunteer for the CIC, speaking out against racism, injustice, and the deleterious effects of both upon the South. Her volunteer work was so effective that she soon became a part-time field worker in Texas, and within less than a year was the first female executive director of a state interracial committee as well as field representative for the entire Southwest. Ames was experienced in both business and political activism, and thus brought to the cause of interracial work skills that were relatively rare among the women of her era. She was articulate, organized, efficient, and pragmatic in her approach to problems.

As southwestern field representative of the CIC, Ames's most extensive endeavor was an educational and legislative campaign against lynching. Although she called for anti-lynching laws, her primary objective was education. She doubted that statutes could end lynching unless white public opinion condemned it. Throughout the 1920s she investigated lynchings, called for more accurate and objective press coverage of mob violence, and sought to rally public opinion against the Klan.

Although often opposed by powerful political and social elements in Texas, Ames enjoyed her interracial work, regarding these turbulent years as some of the most satisfying of her public career. Combative by nature, she relished a fight, and rarely did she have more formidable foes than those in Texas in the 1920s. Under Ames's leadership the Texas CIC became one of the most successful state operations. It was therefore not surprising that in 1928, when the position of director of woman's work became vacant, a nominating committee representing the women of the CIC recommended Ames for the job. Although Will Alexander worried that her somewhat unconventional demeanor might alienate many Southerners, he acquiesced in the recommendation. Ames accepted, and assumed her responsibilities in the summer of 1929. Although her independence and assertive personality made her controversial, especially with some of the CIC's male leaders, who felt that she "had a touch of the suffragette about her" and "was against men," Ames brought energy, ability, commitment, and efficiency to the job.[2] She did not, however, find her labors for the CIC wholly satisfying. She objected to the segregated nature of the women's work and felt that her role within the CIC limited her ability to have a significant impact upon the problems of her region. The resurgence of lynching in the early 1930s afforded her an opportunity for the kind of service she envisioned.

In spite of the popularity of the Klan, during the 1920s lynching was not only opposed by Southern liberals but also became increasingly unacceptable among many image- and dollar-conscious businessmen in the South's urban centers. There was a statistical decline in lynchings during the decade, but the practice remained viable in rural areas where the South's traditional cultural patterns remained intact. The economic distress and social instability of the Great Depression led to a resurgence of the practice in the early 1930s.

Will Alexander of the CIC responded to the renewed violence by organizing the Southern Commission for the Study of Lynching, which undertook to better understand both the socioeconomic and the legal dimensions of the crime. Women were largely excluded from its investigatory endeavors, and many were unhappy with this exclusion. Ames took advantage of this dissatisfaction to launch a new endeavor that rested solely on the white women of the South. She was never enthusiastic about the CIC's investigatory approach to lynching, believing prevention efforts at the local level were more efficacious and important than an understanding of the problem as a whole. Consequently, she persuaded Alexander to call a regional conference of women at which they could design their own agenda for dealing with racial violence. Out of a gathering in Atlanta, Georgia, in November 1930 and another in Dallas, Texas, a few days later emerged the Association of Southern Women for the Prevention of Lynching. The handful of charter members were women who were officers in their respective Protestant denominations, and the majority had been involved in church race relations programs as well as in the CIC women's work.

Despite Ames's protestations to the contrary, as it expanded, those participating in the ASWPL's campaign constituted something of an elite group among Southern women. The leadership clearly was not drawn from the broad spectrum of Southern white womanhood. Although the ASWPL aimed its anti-lynching program at the rural South, almost three-quarters of its leadership lived in the larger towns and cities of the region. Also, the average age of the leadership was forty-eight—many had been born before the turn of the century, and interpreted both social problems and their solutions in terms of a Victorian, evangelical frame of reference shaped in the nineteenth-century rural South. In time, the ASWPL's leadership expanded to include a larger number of women who resided in the countryside or small towns, but it retained its urban quality.

The leadership was atypical in other ways. A substantial number worked, at least for a time, outside the home. Most who had careers were engaged in clerical or professional occupations. Their educational level also was exceptional. Many had at least some college or university experience, and a few had graduate training. They were, however, typical in that most were married and had children. Their husbands were generally from the region's professional, business, or ministerial ranks. In other words, these couples were respected members of the community. Of those leaders whose religious affiliation is known, the majority came from the Methodist Episcopal Church South. Presbyterians, too, were disproportionately represented. Southern Baptists, the largest Protestant denomination in the South, accounted for only 11 percent of the leadership.

Although it is more difficult to determine the socioeconomic status of the rank and file of the ASWPL, they appear to have been less likely to have worked outside the home and to have had education beyond high school. Like their leaders, however, they were likely to be married with families, and they and their husbands in most cases were members of rural and small town economic and social elites.

Regardless of their social station, the women of the ASWPL thought of themselves as Southern ladies. Although they challenged some of the more restrictive features of their region's gender roles, they did not reject in its entirety the conception of ''Southern lady'' and in fact sought to use their image as ladies as an instrument in their war against lynching. They were not rebels challenging the fundamental racial and gender assumptions of their civilization, merely Southern ladies seeking to ameliorate some of the worst manifestations of their section's racism and the more demoralizing and degrading features of its notions about femininity. So conscious were they of their regional identity that they excluded women who were not from the South or who had not lived there sufficiently long to be legitimately identified with it.

The ASWPL also barred from membership many who had a legitimate claim to the designation ''Southerner.'' It was not the first organized expression of Southern women's opposition to lynching. From Ida B. Wells in the late nineteenth and early twentieth centuries to the NAACP's Anti-lynching Crusaders in the 1920s, African-American women had struggled to stem the tide of extralegal violence against black men and had leveled criticism at the sexual and racial myths that underlay lynchings.

Although working in a common cause, Ames and the founders of the ASWPL chose to exclude their black sisters from the new organization. Black women who had solicited the support of white women in their anti-lynching endeavors often resented their exclusion. Ames and her associates, however, felt that it was essential for the ASWPL to be a white movement if it was to raise an effective voice against lynching and the racial and gender assumptions used to justify it.

Lynching was customarily justified as retribution for the rape of a white woman by a black man. This reflected cultural assumptions about the degradation of African-American men and the vulnerability of white women. In fact, alleged sexual assault precipitated lynching in less than a quarter of the documented cases between 1882 and 1946. Although little noted by the white South, the rape of black women by white men was a more common occurrence.

Ames was well aware of the contradiction between myth and reality with regard to lynching, and she sought to make this contradiction known as one means of undermining the crime. She and her associates, however, were not simply trying to end mob violence in Dixie. They were also challenging the myth of female inferiority, vulnerability, and dependence upon male protectors for their virtue and security. As the women of the ASWPL began questioning their region's assumptions about both race and gender, they found themselves confronting not only women who believed the myths, such as those who in 1932 founded The Women's National Association for the Preservation of the White Race, but also myriad men who professed to be the protectors of Southern womanhood. Their opponents sometimes condemned ASWPL women as misguided or reviled them as degraded betrayers of their race and region. The opposition was so virulent because for white men the issue was not merely protection but also, in a sense, possession. Black men were not to possess white women, who were the property of white men. To do so was to step across the bounds of caste, to challenge the superiority of whites. The ASWPL was, then, questioning not only racial but also caste and gender stereotypes and roles that were a sacred part of Southern culture.

ASWPL supporters believed that the white women of the South, in whose name the crime of lynching was often committed, were in a unique position to attack the practice and the assumptions that underlay it. To allow black women to join their campaign would diminish its effectiveness. Thus, to the chagrin of many black and some white opponents of lynching, the ASWPL remained lily white.

Throughout its existence the ASWPL operated on a shoestring. With a budget only a fraction as large as that of the CIC, Ames, the ASWPL's only salaried employee, managed to work effectively throughout the 1930s and early 1940s. The key to her success was her reliance upon volunteers and a preexisting network of religious and secular women's organizations to provide cohesiveness for the ASWPL.

The structure of the ASWPL was quite simple. A regional central committee met annually in Atlanta to issue resolutions, set policy, and provide moral support for the membership. Executive committees and small central councils in each state coordinated the ASWPL's investigatory, educational, and political activities at the state level and served as a link between the regional leadership and local membership. The association was actually rather loose-knit and had a relatively small membership, but it reached many people through its connections with the network of women's organizations across the South. Eventually, the ASWPL had councils in all eleven former Confederate states as well as in Oklahoma and Kentucky, with more than 40,000 active members at the local level engaging in activities ranging from education, to political action, to efforts to prevent imminent lynchings. Those states with the greatest extralegal violence against blacks, such as Mississippi, had the most active ASWPL organizations. Likewise, those areas where violence was minimal, such as Virginia and the southern Appalachians, received little or no attention.

Although only a small minority of Southern women were actively involved in the ASWPL, it secured a sufficiently broad base of support to enable it to make a credible claim to be speaking for the white women of the South. According to Jacquelyn Hall, by the early 1940s, 109 women's associations with a combined membership in excess of 4 million supported the ASWPL's work. These included the women's organizations of the major Protestant denominations, the national and regional federations of church women, the YWCA, and business and professional women's clubs. The mainstay of its support was the women's organizations of the major Protestant churches in the South, which both endorsed the ASWPL and included anti-lynching literature in their educational materials. The most important of these denominational groups was the Methodist Women's Missionary Council. No Catholic women were prominent in the ASWPL. Jewish women, although not in major leadership roles, gave both the ASWPL and the interracial movement in general strong support.

By working through existing religious and secular organizations, the ASWPL was able to reach into many of the rural and small town areas of the South while maintaining the all-important aura of an indigenous organization. The charge of outside agitation was fatal to any reform effort in Dixie, and its structure and manner of operation enabled the ASWPL legitimately to rebut such accusations and contend that it represented the women of the South.

The ASWPL was often criticized not only by conservative white Southerners, who opposed its philosophy and scorned its objectives, but also by some of the more radical younger activists in groups such as the Fellowship of Reconciliation, the Committee on Economic and Racial Justice, and the NAACP. The young radicals frequently criticized the CIC and the ASWPL for their caution and conservatism. It is true that the ASWPL was cautious and conservative, but they were a calculated caution and conservatism born of the conviction that to proceed too quickly or to adopt too radical a position might antagonize many individuals within the network of religious and secular women's groups upon whose cooperation it depended, and at the same time alienate the larger Southern audience whom the ASWPL hoped to convert. Much of the ASWPL's work, especially in the early years, was educational. Although it initially regarded lynching as a matter of social pathology, in time the ASWPL concluded that it was a product of the prejudice of society as a whole, and thus an act for which the white South in its entirety was responsible. The message of the ASWPL was threefold in its attacks on lynching. It contended that the practice dishonored Southern women, diminished respect for and undermined the effectiveness of law enforcement, and tarnished the reputation of the United States in the eyes of much of the rest of the world.

The ASWPL proceeded carefully when it came to the question of rape, which was a very real fear among many white women in the South. Members constantly reiterated that the actual incidence of rape of white women by black men was relatively low, but they could not deny that it sometimes occurred. They took the position that whenever sexual violence against white women by black men did occur, it should be addressed within the context of the law. With regard to the even more delicate matter of consensual relations between white women and black men, the ASWPL initially chose not to address the issue, but by the end of the 1930s it was quietly trying to deal with this question. Generally, the ASWPL condemned such relations, considering them a violation of decency and of the color line. Behind the scenes members sought to minimize such sexual contacts, recognizing their potentially volatile consequences for individuals and communities.

The ASWPL circulated thousands of pamphlets to church and secular women's organizations in an effort to disseminate the socioeconomic and cultural truth about lynching. Much of this material was designed to dispel the myth that lynching was customarily retribution for black men's rape of white women, and to suggest the destructive effects of mob violence. Generally, the literature was low key and informative, designed to appeal to reason rather than to the emotions. Perhaps more important than the literature circulated were the speeches that Ames and the other ASWPL women delivered. By the late 1930s, hundreds of Southern women were speaking publicly against lynching. When addressing audiences, they might sometimes be graphic and forthright in their appeal to the emotions, but rarely did they resort to the sensational.

Increasingly, the ASWPL, like the NAACP, CIC, and other groups, became actively involved in the investigation of lynchings. By 1941 it had undertaken forty-six such case studies. White women gathered information from the local white population and were sometimes surprisingly successful in gleaning facts from uneasy and suspicious black residents in the vicinity of a lynching, in order to construct a more accurate picture of the circumstances surrounding a particular act of violence. Once information had been collected, the ASWPL was able, through speeches or word of mouth, to disseminate the truth about lynchings, thus further helping to undermine the stereotypical picture of the crime.

During the 1930s Ames became more innovative in her attacks on lynching. Inspired by the popularity of folk drama, she sponsored a contest in search of plays that would sensitively and effectively portray the terrors of racial violence. The two winning entries were *Country Sunday* by Walter Spearman and *Lawd, Does you Undahstan?* by Ann Seymour. Usually presented in churches and colleges, these plays were sometimes controversial but often successful in bringing home to limited numbers of white Southerners the horrors of racial violence. To reach the wider audience of regional popular opinion, Ames relied largely upon the press. She stressed contradictions between condemnatory editorials and inflammatory reporting. She attacked the press for its portrayal of women as helpless and vulnerable, and its inherent assumptions about the bestiality and depravity of alleged black perpetrators of sexual crimes. Gradually, she gained the support of major newspapers, and by the late 1930s she professed to see a marked change in the policies of the press, in general, regarding lynching.

Beyond the level of moral suasion and education, the ASWPL attacked lynching more directly. Local law enforcement officers were frequently half-hearted in their opposition to lynch law. This failure was in part a product of fear, and in part a result of the fact that sheriffs and other law officers knew that powerful political elements sometimes condoned or even participated in the mobs (and opposing them would be an act of political suicide). The women of the ASWPL circulated anti-lynching petitions at the local level and presented them to authorities, in an effort to demonstrate that opposition to lynch mobs was a politically viable alternative to submission. They also tried to persuade law enforcement officials to sign pledges expressing their opposition to lynching. By 1941, 1,355 officers had complied, and the ASWPL could report that in a single year, police officers in forty cases had successfully opposed lynch mobs.

Conversely, the ASWPL increasingly exposed by name officers who failed to uphold the law. Sometimes the women themselves became directly involved in trying to thwart lynchings. Whenever local or regional ASWPL activists became aware of impending trouble, they pressured law enforcement officials and civic leaders to do their duty. At the same time, assuming that communities would be less likely to engage in vigilante violence if threatened with exposure, they kept in touch with the Associated Press and other sympathetic news media to assure that trouble would not go unpublicized. The women also worked quietly to persuade their husbands and sons that lynching was hardly the chivalric act portrayed in Southern mythology, and that to engage in such activity was to go against the wishes of those they professed to protect. Although such incidents were relatively rare, women, sometimes even those who were victims or whose families were victims of interracial sexual violence, occasionally confronted mobs in an effort to prevent lynching and uphold the legal process.

The impact of the ASWPL is difficult to assess. Various cultural, social, and economic factors were converging in the South by the late 1930s and early 1940s to reduce the incidence of lynching. There is, however, evidence suggesting that the ASWPL significantly reduced vigilante violence in those areas where it was active. At least one sociological survey found that during the twelve-year history of the ASWPL, the rate of decline in lynching was generally greater in counties in which it was active than in those in which it was not. The average county during the organization's history had 35 percent as many lynchings as it had had in the previous decade. Counties where the ASWPL was most active had only 26 percent as many. Furthermore, in the latter counties there was generally a dramatic decrease in the number of lynch victims surrendered to mobs by law officers.

Jessie Daniel Ames believed that the patient, persistent, persuasive course of the ASWPL was the key to the ultimate eradication of lynching in the South. She had little faith in federal anti-lynching statutes and refused to endorse the NAACP's efforts in the 1930s to secure passage of the Costigan-Wagner federal anti-lynching bill. Although such a refusal was contrary to the position taken by much of the liberal community in the South and the nation, Ames believed that publicly endorsing the bill would do little more than drive lynching underground and undermine the educational and local interventionist approach the ASWPL had built up over the years. She may also have feared that federal legislation would threaten her own hard-won role as a significant player on the stage of Southern social action. In any case, the sharp decline in reported lynchings by the early 1940s seemed to confirm for her the efficacy of the ASWPL's strategy.

By 1942 the apparent decrease in lynchings persuaded Ames that although interracial violence was not forever banished from the South, the socially sanctioned, institutionalized lawlessness that had plagued the region for decades was at an end. Furthermore, the practice of justifying lynching in the name of white Southern womanhood was, she believed, no longer viable. Consequently, in 1942, convinced that its goals were largely accomplished, she quietly dissolved the ASWPL.

After the Southern Regional Council superseded the Commission on Interracial Cooperation in the mid-1940s, Ames retired to Tryon, North Carolina. For a number of years she remained active in the cause of social justice, mobilizing and registering potential black voters and serving for a time as superintendent of Christian social relations for the Western North Carolina

Conference of the Methodist Church. In 1968 waning energy and crippling arthritis forced her to move to a nursing home in Texas, where she remained until her death on 21 February 1972.

Like a number of other liberal endeavors of its era, the contributions of the ASWPL were for a time overshadowed by the more ambitious, aggressive, and dramatic civil rights crusade of the 1950s and 1960s. Ultimately, however, as historians have sought to recover the work of earlier generations of socially conscious Southerners, they have recognized that although it was conservative, ''paternalistic,'' and cautious by the standards of subsequent generations of activists, the work of Jessie Daniel Ames and her associates in the ASWPL was a significant part of the ferment of cultural and social change beginning to seethe beneath the surface of Southern life prior to World War II.

NOTES

1. George B. Tindall, *The Emergence of the New South, 1913–1945* (Baton Rouge, La., 1967), 171.

2. Wilma Dykeman and James Stokely, *Seeds of Southern Change: The Life of Will Alexander* (New York, 1962), 116.

BIBLIOGRAPHY

Ames, Jessie Daniel. *Southern Women and Lynching*. Rev. and repr. Atlanta, 1936.

———. *Toward Lynchless America*. Washington, D.C., [1939?].

———. *The Changing Character of Lynching*. Atlanta, 1942.

Ayers, Edward L. *The Promise of the New South: Life After Reconstruction*. New York, 1992.

Dudley, Julius Wayne. ''A History of the Association of Southern Women for the Prevention of Lynching, 1930–1942.'' Ph.D. diss., University of Cincinnati, 1979.

Dykeman, Wilma, and James Stokely. *Seeds of Southern Change: The Life of Will Alexander*. New York, 1962.

Hall, Jacquelyn Dowd. *Revolt Against Chivalry: Jessie Daniel Ames and the Women's Campaign Against Lynching*. New York, 1979.

———. '' 'A Truly Subversive Affair': Women Against Lynching in the Twentieth-Century South.'' In Carol Ruth Berkin and Mary Beth Norton, eds. *Women of America: A History*. Boston, 1979.

Raper, Arthur. *The Tragedy of Lynching*. 2nd ed. New York, 1970.

Tindall, George Brown. *The Emergence of the New South, 1913–1945*. Baton Rouge, La., 1967.

Woodward, C. Vann. *Origins of the New South, 1877–1913*. Baton Rouge, La., 1971.

Roger Baldwin and the American Civil Liberties Union

SAMUEL WALKER

Roger Baldwin founded the American Civil Liberties Union (ACLU) and served as its director from 1920 to 1950. Through the ACLU he helped to shape the special character of modern American legal culture, in which many social and political conflicts are resolved through litigation concerning individual rights. Indicative of the ACLU's and Baldwin's success in bringing civil liberties cases before the public is the fact that the ACLU has been involved in about 80 percent of the landmark civil liberties cases decided by the Supreme Court since the 1920s. Baldwin shaped the direction of the ACLU, especially its championing of freedom of speech in a period when it was considered a radical and dangerous idea, and he was almost single-handedly responsible for the organization's survival in its early years.

A member of a family that could trace its roots back to the earliest colonial settlements in America, Baldwin was born in Wellesley, Massachusetts, on 21 January 1884, to Frank and Lucy Nash Baldwin. Although his father was a politically conservative businessman, Baldwin learned a patrician ethos of community service from other members of the family. His uncle William H. Baldwin, a railroad executive, was active in many social reform causes and was a founder of the National Urban League. As a child, Baldwin grew accustomed to the presence of prominent individuals as guests in the house, with dinner table discussions focusing on important social and political issues.

Upon graduating from Harvard in 1904, Baldwin was uncertain about a career. He was torn between entering the business world and public service. Members of his family, notably Uncle William, had managed to combine both. He finally consulted with his father's attorney, the future Supreme Court Justice Louis Brandeis, who recommended a professional commitment to public service. Baldwin earned a master's degree from Harvard in 1905 and then moved to St.

Louis, where he was a social worker and part-time instructor at Washington University. In 1908 he became the chief probation officer for the local juvenile court.

During his twelve years in St. Louis, Baldwin established the work habits that characterized the rest of his life. With boundless energy, he threw himself into the world of social reform and soon became a prominent figure in the community. He had no private life in the conventional sense, devoting virtually all of his waking hours to meetings or social events related to his work. His social background and personal charm won friends and support from many wealthy and otherwise conservative people. In 1910 Baldwin had been appointed secretary of the St. Louis Civic League, a Progressive reform organization supported by the business and professional elite. His activities involved reforming city government, improving child welfare, and promoting racial justice.

Baldwin gained a national reputation as a civic reformer, publishing several articles about his activities in *The Survey*, an important Progressive reform journal. He became an expert on the juvenile court, and in 1908 he helped to organize the National Probation Association. Baldwin was coauthor of *Juvenile Courts and Probation* (1916), which became the standard reference book on the operation of a juvenile court. It embodied the philosophy of *parens patriae*, which holds that the court should treat the delinquent as a parent would. Under this philosophy, juvenile courts dispensed with most of the formal procedures required in adult criminal courts. Ironically, fifty-one years later the U.S. Supreme Court declared this approach unconstitutional in an ACLU-sponsored suit (*In re Gault* [1967]). Baldwin, still alive at the time, quietly objected to the decision.

Initially, Baldwin was a politically moderate Progressive reformer, believing that the social and economic institutions of American society were basically sound. Like many other Progressives, he believed that political reform would give people greater control over government and lead to greater social justice. Gradually, however, he became more concerned about the plight of the poor, and his thinking began to move in a radical direction. Baldwin was particularly shaken by a 1916 St. Louis referendum that legalized racial segregation in residential housing. This event challenged his assumption that majority rule would necessarily improve social justice. Given his later involvement in the ACLU, it is noteworthy that Baldwin did not consider the possibility of challenging the St. Louis segregation ordinance through litigation.

The outbreak of World War I in 1914 accelerated Baldwin's growing pessimism about the prospects for incremental social reform. He became increasingly disillusioned with the social work profession because it seemed to focus on case work, providing help to individual victims of poverty, rather than on social reform that would address the underlying causes of poverty. In March 1917, as the U.S. entry into World War I appeared imminent, Baldwin made a bold career move that would shape the rest of his life. Quitting his job in St. Louis, he moved to New York City to join the staff of the American Union Against

Militarism (AUAM), which had led the opposition to U.S. entry into the war. After the United States declared war on Germany in April, he and the AUAM secretary, Crystal Eastman, established the Civil Liberties Bureau within the AUAM to provide information and assistance to conscientious objectors to military service. The leaders of the AUAM, the noted reformers Lillian Wald and Paul U. Kellogg, strongly objected to this activity, however. Within a few months the organization split, with Eastman and Baldwin forming the National Civil Liberties Bureau (NCLB). Eastman soon withdrew because of poor health, and Baldwin assumed the reins at the NCLB, which evolved into the ACLU.

Baldwin's work with the NCLB focused on assistance to conscientious objectors and defending free speech for opponents of the war. At the outset he believed he could achieve these goals by negotiating quietly behind the scenes with government officials. He and many of them came from the same Ivy League background, and he knew some of them personally. The administration's suppression of civil liberties, however, turned Baldwin into a radical. The government banned the Civil Liberties Bureau's publications from the mail in the summer of 1917, and the Justice Department and the War Department began spying on the organization. By early 1918 many government officials regarded the NCLB as a dangerous radical organization that might be guilty of violating the Espionage Act. Baldwin's principal contacts in the government finally severed all official connection with him. This was a personal trauma, shattering his belief that the administration was staffed by people who shared his principles. In late August 1918, the Justice Department raided the NCLB offices, seized its records, and for a time seriously considered indicting Baldwin and other NCLB leaders.

At the same time, Baldwin faced a personal crisis with respect to military service. In the late summer of 1918, he received notice to appear for induction into the military. Holding true to his principles as a conscientious objector, he informed his draft board that he would refuse to cooperate in any way. He was arrested, tried, convicted, and sent to prison in November 1918. Addressing the judge at the time of his sentencing, Baldwin delivered a forthright statement of his objection to compulsory military service. His speech was immediately regarded as an important statement of moral and political principles. It was reprinted in *The Nation* and some other journals, and was privately distributed by the NCLB. The speech and his willingness to go to jail for his principles established Baldwin's national reputation in liberal reform circles.

Baldwin served nine months in jail. In characteristic fashion, he adopted an energetic program of activity, reading extensively, tending the jail's garden, and organizing a self-help group among the inmates. He also kept his wide circle of friends informed about his activities with regular letters. The prison experience completed his development into a political radical. Baldwin decided to devote the rest of his life to efforts on behalf of the working class. Upon his release from jail in the summer of 1919, he traveled around the country for several months, taking jobs as a common laborer. In late 1919 he returned to

New York City and, at the urging of his friends, agreed to reorganize the NCLB into a new organization devoted to the defense of civil liberties. This became the American Civil Liberties Union, which was officially founded in January 1920.

Baldwin was the driving force behind the ACLU between its founding and his retirement in 1950. The organization probably would not have survived the hostile political climate of the 1920s without him. The qualities he had exhibited in St. Louis—his enormous energy, his extensive network of contacts, and his personal charisma—served the ACLU very well by inspiring other people to support the cause of civil liberties. In particular, Baldwin recruited many brilliant lawyers into the ACLU, which became a vehicle for their contributions to the development of American constitutional law. As a fund raiser, he secured contributions from wealthy individuals, many of whom trusted him because of his elite social background and his evident commitment to high principles.

During these early years the ACLU's program was greatly shaped by Baldwin's personal views on civil liberties. His priorities included free speech for political radicals and labor union organizers, amnesty for persons imprisoned during World War I, and racial equality. Largely because of his influence, the ACLU initially was relatively uninterested in several issues that later became a major part of its program. He was prudish about public discussions of sexuality, and the ACLU devoted little effort to combating censorship of sexually oriented literary works. Nor was he much interested in separation of church and state or the violations of due process by law enforcement agents during Prohibition.

On the central issue of freedom of speech for unpopular political ideas, Baldwin opposed all restrictions based on the content of the ideas being expressed, a position that eventually shaped the course of American law. The ACLU consistently defended the First Amendment rights of unpopular groups such as the Communists, the Ku Klux Klan, and the American Nazis. Because of its defense of the rights of Communists, the ACLU was repeatedly attacked as a dangerous and ''un-American'' organization. Its defense of the rights of the Klan and anti-Semites evoked strong criticism from many liberals and left-wingers.

In terms of strategy, Baldwin was at first extremely skeptical about the prospects for protecting civil liberties through litigation. This is somewhat surprising, given the ACLU's subsequent successes in this area. Through the 1920s and the early 1930s, however, his assessment was not unrealistic. The courts were almost completely hostile to civil liberties in those years. Baldwin believed that rights could be achieved through ''direct action,'' demonstrations and political action by the masses of workers.

Direct action was a popular ACLU tactic in the 1920s. Baldwin and others often demonstrated on behalf of freedom of speech. On several occasions ACLU leaders were arrested for trying to read the Declaration of Independence or the Constitution. In a time when the courts had not yet upheld the First Amendment rights of unpopular groups, the ACLU's objective was to dramatize the idea that free speech was an ''old-fashioned American liberty.'' In 1924 Baldwin was arrested in Paterson, New Jersey, and convicted of unlawful assembly. Three years later the New Jersey Supreme Court overturned his conviction on the grounds that it violated the First Amendment. This was one of the very few court decisions affirming freedom of speech or assembly during the 1920s.

As the director of the ACLU, Baldwin's practices often contradicted his principles. Although he believed in democracy, he was an extremely autocratic administrator, unwilling or unable to delegate responsibility. On a number of occasions he manipulated the operations of the ACLU board of directors to secure policy decisions he wanted. He found it difficult to separate his personal devotion to the cause of civil liberties from the realities of daily living, and expected equal commitment from his employees. He developed a reputation as a terrible employer who paid horrendously low wages. Baldwin himself took an extremely low salary, believing that it was an honor and a duty to serve the cause of civil liberties.

Baldwin married Madeline Doty, an active Progressive reformer, in 1919, shortly after his release from prison. The wedding was performed by Baldwin's friend and colleague Norman Thomas. In their wedding vows, Baldwin and Doty rejected the traditional view of marriage and committed themselves to an egalitarian relationship, including the sharing of housework. Their relationship became strained, however, and Doty moved to Geneva, Switzerland, in 1925 to work with the Women's International League for Peace and Freedom. They divorced in 1935, and the following year Baldwin married Evelyn Preston, who had inherited wealth from her family's interests in the Standard Oil Company. Her inheritance compensated for Baldwin's very low ACLU salary and helped to support a lifestyle that included a New York City town house and vacation properties in New Jersey and Martha's Vineyard.

Every year Baldwin took a trip across the country to speak on behalf of civil liberties and to recruit local ACLU leaders. From 1920 until well into the late 1940s, he was widely regarded as the personal embodiment of civil liberties principles. He actively cultivated this image, and a number of liberal journalists eagerly assisted, in large part because he was a genuinely charismatic figure who occupied a unique place in American society at the time. A 1925 article on him was titled "The Legend of Roger Baldwin," and one published in 1930 characterized him as the "Galahad of Freedom."

Although he published more than 100 articles and several books, Baldwin was not an intellectual. Restless and energetic, he thrived on public speaking and working with the many committees and organizations devoted to reform causes. Philosophically, he always described himself as an anarchist, but he never took the time to set forth an extended statement of his views. His published work consists primarily of short pieces on topical issues.

Although the ACLU was the principal focus of Baldwin's life, he also was involved in numerous other issues and organizations. The ACLU was only one of four organizations he helped to found in 1920. The most important of these was the American Fund for Public Service, popularly known as the Garland

Fund. Charles Garland had inherited about $1 million but had philosophical objections to inherited wealth. Baldwin persuaded him to create a private foundation that would support social reform efforts. Through the 1920s the Garland Fund supported several left-liberal publications, some experimental educational efforts, and a number of political defense funds, many of which were associated with the ACLU. For all practical purposes, Baldwin directed the Garland Fund by controlling the selection of its board of directors, many of whom were also involved in the ACLU. During the prosperity of the 1920s the assets of the Fund continued to grow, but the Great Depression wiped out the value of its assets. It became defunct in the 1930s.

The range of Baldwin's reform activities outside of the ACLU was extraordinary. Following the family tradition, he supported racial justice, holding positions within the National Urban League and maintaining close ties with the NAACP. He was an opponent of the death penalty, working with the American League to Abolish Capital Punishment. Along with many other liberals and leftists, he became deeply committed to the antifascist side in the Spanish Civil War. He worked with the North American Committee to Aid Spanish Democracy, the Spanish Refugee Relief Campaign, and other antifascist organizations. He also was associated with numerous left-wing and prolabor groups, including the Labor Defense Council, the American Committee for the Protection of the Foreign Born, the Tom Mooney Defense Committee, and the U.S. Congress Against War.

Baldwin was deeply interested in international human rights issues, maintaining an extensive correspondence with activists around the world and taking several trips abroad. In the 1920s he helped to found the International Committee for Political Prisoners and was a leader of the League Against Imperialism. He edited a collection titled *Letters from Russian Prisons* (1925), an early exposé of political repression in the Soviet Union. His interest in international affairs created occasional conflict with the board of directors of the ACLU, which insisted on focusing on civil liberties within the United States. On this and some other issues, Baldwin's personal views were not always the same as the policies of the ACLU.

One of the greatest controversies surrounding Baldwin's career involves his relationship with communism and the Communist party. Over the years, his attitude toward communism as a political philosophy and his relations with American Communists changed substantially. These changes provide an important index of his own evolving assessment of the prospects for human freedom in America and abroad.

In 1927 Baldwin took an extended leave of absence from the ACLU and traveled through Europe, where he became more aware of the arrogance of European colonialism and the emerging dangers of totalitarianism. He was initially denied entry into England, primarily because of his publicly expressed interest in independence for India. On the basis of his observations in the Soviet Union, Baldwin published *Liberty Under the Soviets* (1927), a detailed account of the status of religious minorities, pacifists, women, and other groups in that country. He also noted briefly the growing repression under Joseph Stalin.

Although wary of Soviet-style communism abroad, in the 1920s Baldwin maintained a supportive but wary attitude toward American Communists. He and the ACLU vigorously defended their First Amendment rights. As a pacifist, however, he objected to the Communists' advocacy of violence. He also objected to their secrecy and their attempts to suppress the free speech rights of critics of the Soviet Union. In 1931 Baldwin was expelled from the League Against Imperialism by Communist members who disagreed with his position on the struggle for Indian independence.

In the early 1930s Baldwin's political outlook swung sharply to the left as a result of the Great Depression and the rise of fascism in Europe. On two occasions in 1934 he made public statements that seemed to indicate his personal support for communism. Fifty years later, these statements were still being cited by conservative critics of the ACLU as evidence of the organization's Communist leanings. Beginning in 1935, Baldwin became a prominent leader in the Popular Front, a coalition of the Communist party and other liberal and left-wing organizations.

Baldwin was a particularly important participant in the Popular Front because of his extraordinary network of contacts, his reputation as a fighter for social justice, and his skill at creating organizations. In many instances, his name alone or a letter from him was a crucial factor in establishing a new committee or organization. Baldwin held an official position with the American League for Peace and Democracy (formerly the American League Against War and Fascism), the most important Popular Front organization.

By 1937 Baldwin was becoming disillusioned with both communism and the Popular Front as a result of two political developments: Stalinist repression in the Soviet Union and the rise of the New Deal in the United States. The Moscow Trials and other evidence of repression under Stalin convinced him that the Soviet Union was not the progressive force he had imagined it to be. Many of his experiences with the American Communist party added to his growing disillusionment. Baldwin gradually severed his ties with Popular Front organizations, quitting the American League for Peace and Democracy in 1939.

By then he had become a staunch anticommunist. In early 1940 he helped to promulgate an official policy barring Communists from leadership positions in the ACLU. Under the policy, he helped to expel Elizabeth Gurley Flynn, a Communist, from the ACLU board of directors. Her expulsion became the most controversial event in the history of the ACLU because the organization had imposed a political test for its leaders, in violation of its own long-standing principles. Through the rest of his life, Baldwin was dogged by the criticism that he had betrayed both his civil liberties principles and Flynn, a longtime personal friend and original member of the ACLU.

The New Deal also had a profound impact on Baldwin's views on the prospects for human freedom. Although initially very critical of the Roosevelt administration, mainly on the grounds that it was hostile to the rights of labor, Baldwin soon discovered that many of Roosevelt's appointees were sympathetic to civil liberties. Coupled with his growing disillusionment with communism and other radical movements, this restored Baldwin's faith in American constitutional democracy. He quickly became a skilled Washington insider, establishing close relations with government officials, lobbying for civil liberties issues, and advising the administration on government appointments.

Baldwin's move to the political center also manifested itself in a change in the ACLU's litigation program. The Supreme Court, in a historic shift in judicial philosophy beginning in 1937, started to rule in favor of civil liberties in a large number of cases. As a result of Roosevelt appointments to the Court, there was a solid group of justices sympathetic to civil liberties by 1940. The change in the Court's orientation convinced Baldwin that litigation could be an effective strategy for protecting civil liberties. Consequently, the ACLU stepped up its legal program and began bringing many cases before the Supreme Court.

The change in Baldwin's political orientation in the late 1930s included a new perspective on the problems of labor. When he founded the ACLU, the rights of working people had been one of his, and the ACLU's, principal causes. After the enactment of the Wagner Act (1935) and the emergence of labor as a major political and economic force, Baldwin became more concerned about internal labor union democracy. His growing criticisms of labor union bureaucracies caused many of his allies in the labor movement to accuse him of becoming antilabor.

The status of civil liberties during World War II was very different than it had been during World War I. Instead of a massive repression of dissent, the government remained remarkably tolerant. Only a small number of persons suffered prosecution because of their views. Because Baldwin and other ACLU leaders enjoyed access to top government officials, they were able to lobby successfully on civil liberties issues. The tolerant atmosphere was an important index of the ACLU's gains over the previous twenty years. Civil liberties principles, including freedom of speech, were widely accepted by administration officials, the Supreme Court, and much of the opinion-making elite.

At the same time, however, some serious violations of civil liberties occurred during the war. The worst was the evacuation and internment of about 120,000 Japanese Americans on the West Coast. To Baldwin's dismay, the ACLU was bitterly split over whether to fight the government's action. A conservative faction did not want the ACLU to oppose it. The same group also objected to ACLU opposition to the government's prosecution of a group of alleged American fascists. Baldwin found himself in the extremely difficult position of having to carry out ACLU policies to which he strongly objected.

The ACLU also was deeply split during the Cold War in the late 1940s and 1950s. It strongly opposed loyalty oaths and the Smith Act prosecution of top Communist party leaders, but it was uncertain about how to respond to some anticommunist measures. A conservative faction on the ACLU board of directors did not want to challenge many of those measures. A number of prominent ACLU leaders endorsed both the purposes and the tactics of the House Un-American Activities Committee. Because of his own unpleasant experience with the Communist party, Baldwin was ambivalent about some Cold War issues.

The most controversial aspect of the ACLU's role in the Cold War involved the Federal Bureau of Investigation (FBI). Baldwin and the ACLU did not criticize the Bureau's actions, many of which were later found to be illegal. Baldwin's relationship with FBI Director J. Edgar Hoover began in 1924. The ACLU had been highly critical of the role of the Bureau of Investigation (as it was then called) in spying on political organizations. In 1924 Baldwin met with Hoover, who had just been appointed director of the Bureau, and was extremely impressed with his assurances that illegal spying had ended. Baldwin promised to assure his many liberal friends that the Bureau was no longer a threat to liberty.

From 1924 on, Baldwin maintained an uncritical view of the FBI. In the early 1940s Hoover persuaded him not to publish an article critical of the Bureau's civil rights enforcement efforts. Baldwin and the ACLU also failed to pursue reports of renewed FBI spying. In 1940 the FBI began spying systematically on the ACLU and designated Baldwin for detention in the event of a national emergency. This spying escalated to massive proportions during the Cold War. The release of the FBI's files on the ACLU in the mid-1970s also revealed that some ACLU leaders, notably Morris L. Ernst, had maintained questionable relations with the Bureau.

Despite its ambivalence about many Cold War issues, the ACLU embarked on an expanded program of defending civil liberties in the post–World War II era. It adopted a strong position on separation of church and state, opposing religious practices in the public schools, and stepped up its campaign against censorship, fighting restrictions on novels, poetry, and films. The ACLU also worked closely with the National Association for the Advancement of Colored People (NAACP) and was a prominent member of the national civil rights coalition. The expanded ACLU program of activity both reflected and helped to shape changing public attitudes on these issues. Many liberals and moderates, for example, saw no contradiction between ending government censorship in the arts while restricting the rights of Communists. A number of ACLU leaders saw these goals as preserving and extending the democratic process. Baldwin was deeply ambivalent about many Cold War measures. He was deeply alarmed by the anticommunist assault on freedom of expression but was very distrustful of the Communist party, in large part because he felt that it was directed by the Soviet Union and not an indigenous form of radicalism. As the Supreme Court became more sympathetic to civil liberties, particularly under Chief Justice Earl Warren, the ACLU won many cases expanding the scope of individual rights.

Baldwin's career as director of the ACLU came to an end in 1950. Influential members of the ACLU board of directors concluded that because of a changing political and legal environment, the organization needed a director with greater skills as an administrator than Baldwin possessed. He had always been little interested in the mundane tasks of administration, such as maintaining membership files, and was unable to delegate responsibility. His main contributions had always been as a publicist, speaking and writing on behalf of civil liberties. The board of directors forced Baldwin to resign, appointing him chair of the National Committee, which advised the ACLU on policy questions, and designating him director of international work. In that role he pursued his long-standing interest in international human rights issues.

Although deeply hurt by his forced resignation, and despite the fact that he was sixty-six years old, Baldwin plunged into his new role with much the same energy that he had brought to the ACLU thirty years earlier. He traveled around the world and wrote many articles on international problems, such as human rights in the Middle East. He remained in close contact with the ACLU during the last thirty-one years of his life and was occasionally consulted on questions of policy. In January 1981 President Jimmy Carter awarded Baldwin the Medal of Freedom, the country's highest civilian honor. Baldwin died on 26 August, 1981, at the age of ninety-seven.

In the thirty-one years between Baldwin's retirement as director and his death, the ACLU grew enormously. By 1981 it had more than 200,000 members, staffed affiliate offices in all but four states, a Washington office with more than ten full-time lobbyists, and special projects devoted to such issues as prisoners' rights and reproductive rights. The ACLU handled an estimated 7,000 legal cases each year and appeared before the U.S. Supreme Court more often than any other organization except the federal government. The ACLU's program had expanded considerably since Baldwin's time, embracing a range of new civil liberties issues such as prisoners' rights, reproductive rights, children's rights, and lesbian and gay rights.

The ACLU's basic position on freedom of speech, which held that the First Amendment protected the expression of ideas, no matter how unpopular, had not changed since Baldwin founded the organization in 1920. By the time of his death, the ACLU could legitimately claim to have exerted a major influence on American law and policy. There was an imposing body of constitutional law protecting individual rights in the areas of free speech, separation of church and state, free exercise of religion, due process of law, equal protection, and privacy. Most important, over the span of Baldwin's career, civil liberties had moved from the periphery to the center of American concepts of basic rights.

BIBLIOGRAPHY

Baldwin, Roger. "The Faith of a Heretic." *The Nation* 107 (9 November 1918): 54.
———. "Working Outside." *The World Tomorrow* 7 (July 1924): 202–203.
———. "Where Are the Pre-War Radicals?" *The Survey* 55 (1 February 1926): 560.
———. *Liberty Under the Soviets.* New York, 1927.
———. "Free Speech for Nazis?" *The World Tomorrow* 16 (November 1933): 613.

———. ''Negro Rights and the Class Struggle.'' *Opportunity* 12 (September 1934): 264–269.

———. ''Japanese-Americans in Wartime.'' *American Mercury* 59 (December 1944): 655–670.

———. ''Hope for a World Bill of Rights.'' *The New Republic* 119 (19 July 1948): 9.

———. ''Reds and Rights.'' *The Progressive* 4 (June 1948): 5–6.

———. ''Communist Conspirators and the Bill of Rights.'' *The Progressive* 5 (April 1949): 14.

Baldwin, Roger, and Bernard Flexner. *Juvenile Courts and Probation*. New York, 1916.

Duffus, Robert L. ''The Legend of Roger Baldwin.'' *American Mercury* 5 (August 1925): 408–414.

Lamson, Peggy. *Roger Baldwin: Founder of the American Civil Liberties Union, A Portrait*. Boston, 1976.

MacDonald, Dwight. ''The Defense of Everybody.'' *New Yorker* 29 (11 July 1953): 31ff.; (18 July 1953): 29ff.

Murphy, Paul L. *World War I and the Origin of Civil Liberties in the United States*. New York, 1979.

Walker, Samuel. *In Defense of American Liberties: A History of the ACLU*. New York, 1990.

———. *The American Civil Liberties Union: An Annotated Bibliography*. New York, 1992.

Westin, Alan F., and Roger Baldwin. ''Recollections of a Life in Civil Liberties.'' *Civil Liberties Review* 2 (Spring 1975): 39–72; (Fall 1975): 10–40.

Catharine Beecher and Domestic Relations

KATHLEEN C. BERKELEY

Four years before her death in 1878, Catharine Esther Beecher, who once had ranked among the "most famous women in America," decided to take stock of her life's accomplishments and present them, for the last time, to her public.[1] Her achievements had been legendary: founder of several institutes of higher education for women, including the once prestigious Hartford Female Seminary; the driving force behind the American Woman's Educational Association; and the author of close to thirty publications on such pressing social issues as educational reform, religion and ethics, slavery and abolition, the condition of women's health, dress, diet, calisthenics, the principles of domestic science, and the rights and duties of American women. With her place in the limelight increasingly usurped by the fame of her sister Harriet Beecher Stowe; the growing notoriety surrounding her brother Henry Ward Beecher; and the budding career as a woman's rights advocate of her half sister Isabella Beecher Hooker, she issued her carefully crafted autobiography as a reminder of her "integrity of purpose and her professional commitment to the cause of women."[2]

Fearful, perhaps, that Isabella's brand of feminism was gaining ground, Beecher wrote her memoir also as a call to arms. Several years before, in public lectures and in print, she had castigated the woman's movement for "uniting all the antagonisms that are warring on the family state" and had characterized the movement as a dangerous mix of spiritualism, free love, free divorce, family limitation, and agitation for the ballot.[3] By 1874 her concern for the rising tide of feminism seemed no less urgent. By dedicating *Educational Reminiscences and Suggestions* to those "who as Housekeepers, Mothers, and Schoolteachers, are to decide the Safety and Prosperity of our country," Beecher exhorted her constituency of middle-class white women to continue advocating the philosophy that had guided her half-century career as an educational reformer and advocate of domestic female autonomy.[4]

Catharine Beecher's reform impulse, like that of so many women and men of her generation, originated in the economic, social, and cultural transformations that characterized the first half of the nineteenth century. The decline of self-sufficient family farms in portions of the Northeast, coupled with the opening of the West, drained a significant portion of land-hungry, marriageable-age men from the older, settled region. At the same time, many of these older agrarian communities were undergoing an urban metamorphosis as a result of nascent industrial development. These economic and demographic changes influenced cultural developments, especially in the areas of religion, family, and gender relations. Concomitant with the flowering of evangelical Protestantism, which attributed human agency to personal salvation and linked an individual's salvation to that of society, was the emergence of a gender ideology that ascribed mutually exclusive interests and responsibilities to men and women. If men claimed the public world of business and politics for themselves, which they did, then the private world of the family became the purview of women.

Through thought and deed, Beecher, who never married or managed her own household, contributed to the formation of this new ideology of domesticity. Her version of the ideology, however, contained a subversive twist. Central to the public–private dichotomy was a corresponding set of assumptions about men's and women's characters: men were inherently aggressive, competitive, and individualistic; women were naturally passive, nurturing, and pious. Although Beecher, like so many nineteenth-century reformers, believed in the redemptive power of American women, she disagreed vehemently with those who argued that female moral agency was innate. Even as she extolled the virtues of female benevolence and self-sacrifice, she stressed that these were not inborn personality traits but acquired characteristics that needed to be taught to young women at an early age. For Beecher, the key to society's salvation lay in educating and training women for their responsibilities.

When Beecher began her work in education in the 1820s, first as a teacher in New London, Connecticut, and then as the founder of the Hartford Female Seminary, public support for educating women beyond the acquisition of ornamental skills was tepid at best, and teaching was still a man's occupation. In the decade and a half following the Civil War, as Beecher's career was drawing to a close, private female seminaries and colleges flourished, several originally all-male private and public colleges became coeducational, state-supported teacher training colleges were in vogue, and teaching was fast becoming a woman's profession. Beecher does not deserve sole credit for these changes, but her literary and institutional contributions definitely shaped the direction American education took in the nineteenth century.

Prior to Beecher's entrance into the area of educational reform, educating women was deemed controversial because it gave them ''an identity outside the family.''[5] Beecher's genius in promoting an education for women equal to that which their male counterparts received lay in her recognition that the American public feared a classical education might render women unfit for their domestic duties. Beecher effectively defused this argument by linking advances in women's education to their primary social responsibilities as wives and mothers, which she identified as women's true profession. Her views first appeared in 1827 in the *American Journal of Education*:

When we consider the amazing responsibilities resting upon the mother of a family, and the fact, that her own characteristics, feelings and sentiments will inevitably be impressed upon the plastic mind of her offspring, it would seem as if this alone would render the subject of female education an object of the highest interest.[6]

Beecher's convictions appear evolutionary rather than revolutionary. She and her contemporaries in educational reform—Emma Willard, Mary Lyon, and Zilpah Grant—built their arguments favoring a classical education for women on the foundation laid by Revolutionary era educational reformers like Benjamin Rush and Judith Sargent Murray. Rush explicitly advocated advances in women's education by attaching significant political weight to the social responsibilities of mothering. According to the tenets of ''Republican Motherhood,'' the new nation's success depended on knowledgeable women because they bore the primary responsibility for supervising their children's early education. This maternal duty was especially weighty in the case of sons, who needed careful training before claiming their rightful place as citizens.

Beecher's generation of educational reformers, with her in the lead, made more explicit the connection between a woman's influence on her family and her influence on society:

But it is not in domestic relations alone that the female character operates. There is no refined, well educated woman, but can exert an immediate influence upon a father, husband, or brother, and thus upon the general interests of society.[7]

However indirect a woman's influence might appear, Beecher presented a convincing argument that society gained when women received an education comparable with that of men.

Beecher believed that women coming of age in antebellum America needed an education superior to that which their mothers had received because this generation confronted a world far different from that of their predecessors. She emphasized this point by linking her philosophy of education and womanhood to the demands of a modernizing society. Mastering the environment depended on acquiring knowledge, especially of science and technology, and learning ''time management'' skills rather than relying on instinct and traditional modes of thought and action. Beecher underscored this point in her advice manual, *A Treatise on Domestic Economy*, which was a best-seller from its publication in

1841 until the mid-1850s and was adopted as a textbook by the Massachusetts state board of education in 1842:

There is no one thing more necessary to a housekeeper in performing her varied duties than a *habit of system and order. . . .* A wise economy is nowhere more conspicuous, than in a systematic *apportionment of time* to different pursuits.[8]

No longer could young women learn the arts of household management from their mothers' personal, informal instruction. Modern times demanded a more rigorous and systematic formal education. Women needed instruction, Beecher wrote, "in the formation of habits of investigation, of correct reasoning, of persevering attention, of regular system, of accurate analysis and of vigorous mental action."[9]

Beecher not only advocated an education for women that went well beyond the limitations of ornamental instruction, but she also provided a powerful rationale for training women for the profession of teaching. Since the stated purpose of female education was the production of better wives and mothers, it seemed obvious that the task of preparing young women for their domestic duties properly belonged to women. Here, too, Beecher's philosophy built on educational concepts embedded in the ideology of "Republican Motherhood." She adroitly assisted in the shift from public acceptance of educating mothers so that they could instruct their children at home to educating women "to teach the children of others."[10] She did so by reconceptualizing and expanding the mothering role to include a teaching function. That this teaching duty eventually led women out of their households and into schools and academies confirmed Beecher's belief that the boundaries separating the private, domestic sphere from the public, social sphere were flexible rather than fixed. A nagging question remained, however: How could women instruct the next generation unless they themselves were knowledgeable? Beecher's answer was succinct and to the point: women needed to be schooled in how to teach.

Beecher was hardly the product of the systematic and rigorous training she advocated for women; nor in her youth had she anticipated that she would carve out a professional career for herself and for the generations of women educators who followed in her footsteps. In fact, until her twenty-second year, Beecher expected that her life would follow a different, much more traditional course.

Born in East Hampton, New York, on 6 September 1800, to Lyman Beecher and Roxanna Foote Beecher, Catharine was the oldest of eight surviving children from her father's first marriage. Schooled at home by her mother and her Aunt Mary (Roxanna's sister became part of the Beecher household when Catharine was born) until the age of ten, she was a reluctant student of the domestic arts. According to Beecher's preeminent biographer, Kathryn Kish Sklar, the young pupil chafed under her mother's strict instruction.[11] Aunt Mary's coaxing achieved better results from Catharine, who remembered that "She [Aunt Mary] secured my enthusiastic devotion by the high appreciation she seemed to have of my childish services.''[12]

When the Beechers moved from the village of East Hampton to the bustling town of Litchfield, Connecticut, in 1809, Catharine left her mother's ''parlor'' school for Sarah Pierce's academy. Begun in 1791, Pierce's school drew its pupils from leading families in the region. Although Pierce offered her female students a ''full academic curriculum,'' it was not a demanding one; the emphasis was on instruction in the ''social graces.''[13] Beecher flourished in this environment. Mastering the academic component of the curriculum was easy for her, and she earned top honors in the school's first competition in 1814. She enjoyed her years at Pierce's academy because the school provided her with an outlet for her sociability; ''concocting plans for amusement'' was far more important to her than studying.[14]

Beecher's carefree childhood came to an abrupt end in 1816 when tuberculosis claimed her mother's life; Aunt Mary had succumbed to the same disease three years earlier. At her mother's death, Beecher left school to take charge of her father's household. Even after Lyman Beecher remarried the following year, she remained at home, assisting her new stepmother, Harriet Porter. To Catharine fell the task of caring for her siblings, especially after the arrival in 1818 of Frederick, the first of four children born to Harriet and Lyman Beecher.

In 1819 Beecher escaped the confines of the Litchfield household by embarking on an extended visit to relatives living in Massachusetts and Rhode Island. Six months later, when she returned home, she focused her energies on polishing her ornamental skills—painting, poetry writing, and piano playing—and her domestic arts—needlework—in preparation for a temporary teaching position at a girls' school in New London. She also met Alexander Metcalf Fisher, a brilliant professor of mathematics and natural philosophy at Yale. After a bumpy courtship (to which her father contributed), the couple became engaged in January 1822. They planned to marry the following year, after Fisher returned from a year of study abroad.

Beecher's carefully orchestrated life, revolving around her impending marriage and the eventual assumption of maternal duties, came to an abrupt and tragic end in April 1822, when Alexander Fisher died in a shipwreck off the coast of Ireland. Grief-stricken, she received no solace from her father. The close, loving, supportive relationship of her early childhood had become strained even before her father's meddling in the courtship.

Simultaneous to but independent of Beecher's acquaintance with Fisher, her father had begun pressuring her to start the process of religious introspection that would culminate in her conversion and mark her entry into adulthood. However, she found it difficult to adhere to her father's Calvinist teachings, which stressed the sovereignty of an angry God, the doctrine of human depravity, the need for repentance, and total submission to God. Beecher was beginning the process of parting company with her father over the concept of human depravity and original sin in favor of a theology that stressed free will, the uncorrupted nature of the individual, and ''the conviction that God was just and merciful.''[15] Adding to the growing tension between father and daughter was the fact that Fisher, although a religious man, had not had a conversion experience before death claimed him. Beecher found it difficult to reconcile her father's teachings with the thought that Fisher's unconverted soul was doomed.

It was only a matter of months before Beecher left her father's house, seeking refuge first with her Boston relatives and then with Fisher's parents. Her conflict with her father continued, albeit through correspondence. In January 1823 she wrote:

When I think of Mr. Fisher and remember his blameless . . . life, his . . . efforts to do his duty both to God and man, I believe that a merciful Savior has not left him to perish at last . . . and that in the Day of Judgement we shall find that . . . God is influenced in bestowing his grace by the efforts of men . . . and that there was more reason to hope for one whose whole life had been an example of excellence, than for one who had spent all his days in guilt and sin.[16]

The strain between father and daughter eventually abated. Although Catharine returned to the Beecher fold, she continued to assert her independence from her father by remaining unconverted. In 1823, still unconverted, she joined his church; three years later she led a revival at her school. Nonetheless, as her voluminous writings on theology, ethics, and moral instruction indicate, Beecher had rejected the religious orthodoxy of her father. Shortly before his death in 1863, she made a complete break with Lyman Beecher's faith by joining the church to which her mother had belonged in her youth, the Episcopal Church.

Her stay at the Fishers' home provided Beecher with the opportunity to reflect on her future. Poring over Alexander Fisher's books, she discovered the pleasures of intellectual stimulation; self-discovery also revealed the deficiencies in her formal education at Pierce's academy. A chance remark by a family friend concerning the lack of a good school for girls in Hartford, the necessity of earning a living if she wanted to remain independent of her father, and the bittersweet windfall of $2,000 from Fisher's will constituted all the impetus she needed. Moving to Hartford, she rented a room above a harness shop and founded Hartford Female Seminary.

Beecher took a gamble when she opened her school in 1823. Although she wrote to her father that ''there seems to be no very extensive sphere of usefulness for a single woman but that which can be found in the limits of a school room,'' she was mistaken.[17] In the 1820s, when she opened the doors of Hartford Female Seminary, the majority of young women who worked outside the home were domestic servants, milliners, seamstresses, and factory operatives. If women found employment in schools during the 1820s, they were more than likely hired for summer terms, when boys were absent. Until late in the century, male-dominated school boards in communities across the country clung to the notion that women could neither supervise boys nor serve as appropriate role models for them, even while they were hiring women as cheap replacements for men. The feminization of the teaching profession, which began in Massachusetts during the mid-to-late 1830s, was complete by the 1880s. Beecher was indeed ahead of her times.

Of the five institutions Beecher was instrumental in founding, Hartford Female Seminary was the most successful. By the time she left Hartford in 1832 to follow her father to Cincinnati, where he became president of Lane Theological Seminary and where she founded, a year later, the short-lived Western Female Institute, Hartford Female Seminary had acquired a widespread reputation for academic excellence. The school's eventual decline was due, in part, to the rise of the public high school movement. Beecher's resumption of the principalship near the end of her life did little to revive the faltering institution. Of the three remaining institutions that were founded under the aegis of Beecher's organization, the American Woman's Educational Association, only Milwaukee Female Seminary (later Milwaukee Female College) endured.

Hartford Female Seminary stands out because the school was truly a family affair. Beecher's first venture at running a school, like many of her future endeavors, depended on the support of her siblings and, in later instances, in-laws. She and several of her siblings created a second home in Hartford, living together, studying together, and sometimes working together. Her brother Edward was her mentor (and Latin tutor) until he left the city in 1824 to pursue theological studies. Her sister Mary shared teaching responsibilities at the school until her marriage to Thomas Perkins in 1827. Harriet, who later became a teacher at the school, began there as a pupil, as did a younger brother. Catharine relied heavily on Harriet after Mary's retirement into domesticity. In fact, Harriet assumed responsibility for running the school in 1829 when Catharine, suffering from "nervous prostration," retreated to Boston, where her father resided.

Beecher's depression in the fall of 1829 had its root cause in a recent setback she had suffered while striving to implement facets of her educational philosophy. Although Hartford Female Seminary began as a modest one-room school above a harness shop, it became something much larger and more significant than its name implied. The school served as Beecher's educational laboratory, where over the course of nine years she experimented with and refined many of her ideas about the future direction of women's education. Twice during her tenure she attempted to alter its function and structure. Her professed goals were threefold: to transform the instruction offered at Hartford Female Seminary in order to make it equivalent to that available at any endowed institution of higher education available to men; to professionalize teaching for middle-class white women like herself, who, for a variety of reasons, remained single; and, in keeping with her evolving theological stance, to create an environment conducive to molding the moral character of her students and faculty. Her first attempt to implement her educational goals met with modest success; her second venture did not.

Three years of teaching had allowed Beecher ample time to observe and experience the "defects and difficulties in the mode of teaching and conducting [female] schools" points she addressed in the 1827 article she published in the *American Journal of Education*.[18] Simply put, women's schools were not equal to men's schools. The breadth of the curriculum offered to women and men was similar, but the depth of knowledge was not. Beecher blamed the difference on the structural and organizational limitations imposed on women's education. The limited physical space of women's schools—often one or two rooms stuffed with teachers, tutors, and pupils all reciting at once—was detrimental to learning. Moreover, the division of labor of the faculties at men's and women's schools differed significantly. Beecher preferred the "college plan," an organizational innovation recently adopted at some of the leading men's schools. Under this plan, administrators, faculty, and boards of trustees had separate but complementary duties. At women's schools the principals were responsible for the administrative, financial, and maintenance functions of their institutions, and they taught. Unlike their male counterparts, principals and teachers at women's schools were expected to offer instruction in a variety of subjects rather than specialize in a specific discipline. Although this instructional mode might have sufficed a decade earlier, Beecher wrote, "the amount of knowledge required to complete the education" of young women in the 1820s rendered this system obsolete.[19]

Beecher was determined to transform her "private school into an endowed seminary."[20] With an endowment, the school's immediate future was secured and she could turn her attention to expanding the school's physical facilities and introducing (in however modified a form) the "college plan." Much to Beecher's surprise, her plans received a cool reception from Hartford's leading male citizens, who were "surprised and almost dismayed" by her request for an endowment.[21] Undeterred by their rebuff, she turned to their wives and found success. Fund-raising among women provided Beecher with the capital she needed to expand the school and taught her a valuable lesson about the importance of cultivating a female network. When Hartford Female Seminary opened its doors in the fall of 1827, Beecher, in her capacity as principal, supervised eight teachers in a beautiful new building that "contained ten recitation rooms, a lecture room, and a study hall that could accommodate 150 pupils."[22]

The reluctance of the city's most influential and powerful men to support Beecher's educational endeavors left a lasting impression. In her memoir she recalled, perhaps with a trace of bitterness, that while the city fathers refused to endow her school for girls, there were several endowed colleges for men within a thirty-mile radius of Hartford. Men, she could only assume, were not committed to putting women's and men's education on an equal footing. From her creation, in the mid-1840s, of the Central Committee for Promoting National Education to her founding of the American Woman's Education Association in 1852, Beecher cultivated the support of middle- and upper-class white women for her goal of establishing endowed institutions of higher education for women.

The aim of these institutions was to train women for their "true professions": teaching, health care, and domestic economy.[23]

Between 1829, when Beecher wrote *Suggestions Respecting Improvements in Education*, and 1831, when she published *The Elements of Mental and Moral Philosophy*, the theological underpinnings of her educational philosophy became more pronounced. Her intellectual journey, which began in 1828, when she took charge of a course in moral philosophy previously taught by a member of her staff, also had a practical bent. Within a year she had determined to take her school in a new direction by proposing the addition of a department of moral instruction and the transformation of Hartford Female Seminary into a boarding school. Both objectives were revolutionary. The former implied that the school and the female teacher, not the church and a male minister, would be responsible for instilling morality in young women; the latter removed daughters from the confines of private homes to a dormitory where they lived with other young women and were supervised by a spinster teacher.

Integral to Beecher's philosophy was her positive view of human agency and reason, and her belief that habit, or training, was essential to the formation of an individual's character. Moreover, because of the influence of personal habits (good or bad) on the human will, she stressed the need for early intervention in a child's moral training, lest the mind become "disordered." "A well managed child could not turn out badly," wrote an observer of Beecher's school.[24]

Cultivating good habits, which Beecher defined as obedience, self-denial, self-sacrifice, and self-government, depended not only on moral instruction in the classroom but also on management of the environment beyond the classroom. "The hours spent outside the classroom," she wrote, "are the hours of access to the heart, hours in which character is developed, and in which opportunities for exerting beneficial influence are continually occurring."[25] The construction of a residence hall at the school met both Beecher's requirements for a managed environment for her teaching staff and students and her personal need for independence from her family by providing her with an inexpensive, secure, and comfortable home.

For Beecher, the proper formation of a child's mind was essential not only to the salvation of an individual's soul but also to that of the nation's spirit. Such high stakes required that those who engaged in this business be trained, rewarded, and honored. In *Suggestions Respecting Improvements in Education*, she broadened the scope of motherhood to include teaching and ministerial duties and called for its professionalization: "What is *the profession of a Woman*? Is it not to form immortal minds, and to watch, to nurse, and to rear the bodily system?"[26] Beecher's philosophy also struck a careful balance between empowering women like herself, for whom marriage was not an option, and upholding the gender conventions of her society:

The writer cannot but believe that all female institutions . . . ought to be conducted exclusively by females, *so soon as suitable teachers of their own sex can be prepared.* . . .

Until this day no other profession could with propriety admit the female aspirant, nor till this day has the profession of a teacher been the road to honour, influence, and emolument. But the feelings of an enlightened society are fast changing. . . . The time is not far distant when it will become an honourable profession . . . [to which] woman is gladly welcomed. . . . *She*, also, can discern before her the road to honourable independance [*sic*] . . . where she need not outstep the proscribed boundaries of feminine modesty, nor diminish one of those retiring graces that must ever constitute her most attractive charms.[27]

Beecher's educational philosophy may have been visionary, but she wisely tempered it with a bow to gender conventions. After all, how could Americans quibble with a profession that gave women economic independence and the esteem of a grateful society while ensuring the protection of their feminine charms?

Beecher's success with her second reform effort hinged on three objectives: hiring a leading woman educator to head the proposed department of moral instruction, raising a tidy sum for construction of a residence hall, and overcoming any prejudices parents might harbor about boarding their daughters in residence halls located on school grounds rather than placing them with individual families living near the school. Unfortunately, her plans went awry. Beecher was unsuccessful in her attempt to lure Zilpah Grant, a woman with impeccable religious and educational credentials, from her post at Mary Lyon's school; she was stymied in her effort to raise the school's endowment (her goal was $20,000); and she was unprepared for the community's lack of support for the dormitory concept. Upon receipt of Grant's rejection of what she considered a generous offer, Beecher went into a depression that lasted through December 1829.

Although Beecher returned to her school in 1830, she longed for something else. When the trustees of Lane Theological Seminary in Cincinnati offered her father the presidency, and he suggested that she join the family pilgrimage to the Queen City of the West, she seized the opportunity. Economic promise had enticed both New Englanders and immigrants to move west. Fearful that "Catholics and infidels" would dominate (and debase) the region, father and daughter viewed the West as the battleground for the nation's soul. Although their means differed (Lyman training young men for the ministry and Catharine training young women for the teaching profession), their ends were the same.

Unfortunately for the Beechers, Cincinnati was unlike either Hartford or Boston. Their initial reception by Cincinnati society was warm, but relations between the "better sort" and the Beechers soon cooled. The Beechers' air of superiority did not sit well with Cincinnatians. In particular, Catharine's imperious manner alienated influential members of society whose financial support she so desperately needed for her educational cause. Cincinnatians also were extremely skittish about the escalating controversy over slavery. Many of the leading merchant families, who made their money in the Southern trade, were not inclined to support abolition. Moreover, during the previous few years, whites from all levels of society had grown increasingly uncomfortable with the city's free black community because of its reputation for harboring fugitive slaves; working-class whites resented competing for jobs with free blacks. The Beechers unwittingly found themselves embroiled in a community conflict over slavery in 1834 when Lane Theological Seminary students, led by Theodore Dwight Weld, began a series of debates on immediate abolition versus gradualism and colonization, and put their abolitionist views into practice in the black community. Although the Beechers had not raised the issue, and in fact were supporters of the more moderate stance, they were tarred with the brush of radicalism.

A year before the controversy at Lane, Beecher opened the doors of her second school, Western Female Institute. Less interested in either teaching or the day-to-day management of the school, which she turned over to her sister Harriet and Mary Dutton (a friend from the Hartford school), she preferred to promote her cause of training teachers to "save the West from darkness and damnation."[28] She also joined forces with leading education reformers of the day—William Russell, William C. Woodbridge, George B. Emerson, and Horace Mann—in their drive to eradicate the pernicious use of competition (emulation) and ranking in American schools. Yet even as Beecher gained national prominence in the field of educational reform, Beecher's popularity sank. Her school suffered the loss of patronage by Cincinnati's social and economic elite. With students and funding in short supply, she sought assistance for her cause outside the local community. Just as she had done in her Hartford Seminary days, Beecher looked to middle- and upper-class white women for that support.

In 1836 Beecher planned a promotional tour through the East that kept her out of Cincinnati for six months. This action suited her because it allowed her to ignore the intertwining of professional and personal problems associated with the imminent collapse of her school and new arrangements within the Beecher household. Catharine's stepmother, Harriet Porter Beecher, had died the previous year, and her father had wasted little time in finding a third wife, Lydia Beals Jackson. Although the grown Beecher children and the new Mrs. Beecher never developed a comfortable relationship, Lyman's third marriage was especially stressful for Catharine, who increasingly felt unwelcome in her father and stepmother's household.

Beecher's Eastern tour netted a collection of potential benefactors and teachers. But a combination of circumstances limited her success: the loss of her institutional base when Western Female Institute finally closed in 1837, the lingering ill effects of the antiabolition and antiblack mob violence that had wracked Cincinnati the previous summer, and a perceived challenge to Beecher's prominence as an advocate for American women's unique social identity and responsibilities. While traveling in the East, Beecher discovered that a woman who had once considered enrolling in the Hartford school was poised to tap Beecher's sources for a cause that she and her family found troublesome. The person was Angelina Grimké, and the cause was the creation of "Abolition Societies among ladies of the non-slave-holding states."[29]

It was within this context that Beecher decided to counter Grimké's ideas by firing the first salvo of what became a public debate over the social responsibilities of American women. In 1837 Beecher published *An Essay on Slavery and Abolition, with Reference to the Duty of American Females*, which began by distinguishing between the "moral and conscientious character" of abolitionists and their misguided support for measures that were neither "peaceful [n]or Christian . . . but calculated to generate . . . recrimination and angry passions."[30] In particular, Beecher found fault with the movement's emphasis on immediate emancipation, which she viewed as "unduly provocative," and the decided lack of concern by abolitionists for the consequences of their actions. She abhorred social strife and remained steadfast in her belief that American society was best served by a gradual approach to ending slavery. She believed that this solution, which was less disruptive to social harmony, would achieve the greater goal of establishing a "peaceable Kingdom" in America. Grimké apparently thought otherwise. In *Letters to Catherine E. Beecher, in Reply to an Essay on Slavery and Abolitionism* (1838), she accused Beecher of "bartering principle for an unholy peace."[31]

Central to Beecher's and Grimké's debate over means versus ends within the abolition movement was a second, and very much related, issue: "the just bounds of female influence, and the times, places, and manner in which it can be appropriately exerted."[32] Beecher favored an orderly, hierarchical society ordained by God: child to parent, pupil to teacher, servant to master, wife to husband, citizen to magistrate, and man to God. Although female subordination did not imply female inferiority, she believed that men and women differed in temperament, and that these differences called forth separate spheres of duty and social responsibility. Women legitimated their social power by appealing to Christian principles of kindness, generosity, peace, and benevolence, and they exerted their influence within the domestic and social circle.

Beecher's vision of American womanhood was not hidebound, nor did it advocate female submissiveness. The source of female power was not innate and God-given; instead, female authority was based on principles (albeit Christian ones) that were learned through moral instruction. By treating the "domestic and social circle" as a single sphere, Beecher provided a convincing rationale for women to expand their influence beyond their households and into society. Moreover, by infusing mothering with a teaching function that extended beyond the family circle, she created a useful and honorable position for single women as "mothers" of society's children. As the historian Kathryn Sklar has noted, the subtlety of Beecher's philosophy of womanhood derived from its ability to glorify domesticity even as it reconceptualized and politicized it.[33] There were, however, limits to female power. Women exerted their influence on society indirectly through their social roles as wives, mothers, and teachers. Thus, the home and the classroom were their stage. Beecher abhorred a more direct representation of female influence, especially in the realm of politics. Political power was something men exercised. Beecher believed that it was foolhardy for women to engage in this pursuit because it undermined the gender hierarchy that was central to the maintenance of the social order.

Drawn into a controversy she had not necessarily intended, Grimké replied to Beecher in a series of letters published in the abolitionist press during the latter months of 1837. The bulk of her response addressed various points of disagreement between the two reformers pertaining to the abolition movement and the character of its participants: the strategy of immediacy, colonization, the Christian impulse of abolitionists (or lack thereof), the consequences of abolition on society, and prejudice. In three concluding letters Grimké sketched out her theory of womanhood, which stood in stark contrast to Beecher's. Rejecting Beecher's belief in an ordained social hierarchy in favor of the principle of equality, Grimké labeled the former ''an assertion without proof'' and used Christian doctrine—''in Christ Jesus there is neither male nor female''—in support of the latter.[34] Even as she clothed herself in her religious faith, however, Grimké rejected the notion that ''rights'' were a gift from God; without respect to differences based on color, sex, or status, she insisted that humans had rights ''because they are moral beings'' endowed with the ''same moral nature.''[35]

Grimké's repudiation of differences between men and women ''based on the mere circumstance of sex'' paved the way for her rejection of the doctrine of separatism, which she held as injurious to both sexes:

By this doctrine, man has been converted into the warrior, and clothed with sternness . . . ; whilst woman has been taught to lean . . . to sit as a doll . . . to be admired for her personal charms . . . caressed and humored as a spoiled child, or converted into a mere drudge [for] the convenience of her lord and master.[36]

No artificial boundary separated men's and women's social responsibilities or their exercise of power: ''whatever is morally right for a man to do, it is morally right for a woman to do.''[36] Logic dictated that the opposite dictum also held. Questioning Beecher's view that it was the peculiar duty of women to educate society's children, Grimké concluded that it was the duty of men to cooperate with women in this ''high and holy venture.''[37] No matter the consequences, Grimké did not shy away from expressing her convictions, even if they challenged Beecher's lifework.

The implications of Grimké's views were not lost upon Beecher. Grimké had raised important questions about the limitations of women's social power and had offered an alternative vision of womanhood in which power was exercised directly, through the political process. While Beecher shrank from the idea that women should engage in politics, Grimké called for women to claim political participation as their birthright:

Now, I believe it is woman's right to have a voice in all the laws and regulations by which she is to be *governed*, whether in Church or State; and that the present arrangements of society on these points, are *a violation of human rights, a rank usurpation of power.* . . . I contend that woman has just as much right to sit in solemn counsel in Conventions, Conferences . . . and General Assemblies, as man—just as much right to it . . . in the Presidential chair of the United States.[38]

As Beecher's and Grimké's ideological clash suggests, the influence and exercise of female power in American society, so integral to feminism, was contested terrain in the antebellum era. In 1837 it was not a foregone conclusion that Beecher's vision of womanhood would falter while Grimké's conceptualization would prevail. Over the next two decades, American women pressed forward with their competing claims for the source and direction of their influence and responsibilities.

After her clash with Grimké, a depressed Beecher retreated to her father's household. Over the next few years she turned inward. Writing and occasional visits to her favorite water cure establishment became her therapy. By the mid-1840s, buoyed by the financial success of her domestic advice manual, which brought independence from her family, Beecher returned to an active public agenda. She envisioned women's education as the great social leveler, uniting the interests and resources of the upper classes with the faith and industry of the working and middle classes. Pressing forward with her plans for uniting American women of all ranks beneath the democratic banner of a female-led education movement, she turned to former pupils for help, cultivated support from women's church groups, and managed to secure the endorsement of America's leading male educational reformers, Horace Mann and Henry Barnard.

In 1844 Beecher founded the Central Committee for Promoting National Education after persuading her brother-in-law Calvin Stowe to serve as its titular head. Putting a reluctant Stowe at the helm was in keeping with Beecher's belief that men lent prestige to her cause, although she expected to run the Committee. Stowe eventually found his replacement, William Slade, the former governor of Vermont. As the organization's general agent, Slade's responsibilities were limited to making local arrangements and supporting Beecher's endeavors—promotional fund-raising tours in the East and teacher training. Unfortunately for Catharine, Slade was not as malleable as Stowe. In 1848 they parted company, with Slade renaming Beecher's organization the National Board of Popular Education. Working her connections in the East, in 1852 Beecher founded her last organization devoted to the cause of women's education, the American Woman's Education Association. In addition to the support of her now famous younger sister, Harriet Beecher Stowe, Catharine persuaded a number of influential female literary figures, among them Sarah Josepha Hale, Lydia Sigourney, and Catharine Sedgwick, to serve on the organization's board of managers. Over the next four years the American Woman's Education Association sponsored three institutions organized according to the ''college plan'' Beecher had advocated some thirty years earlier.

While Beecher's movement flourished, the ideas that Grimké advocated sputtered along, impeded by the lack of an autonomous institutional base. The "woman's question" tore apart the abolition movement even as Grimké retired from public life after her marriage to the Beechers' old nemesis, Theodore Weld. Nonetheless, a handful of women and men, most of whom were associated with William Lloyd Garrison's radical wing of the abolition movement, nurtured the concept of woman's rights. In 1848 Elizabeth Cady Stanton's meeting at Seneca Falls, New York, produced the famous feminist document "A Declaration of Sentiments," but women registered few concrete gains in promoting their political equality before the Civil War. Not until 1869, when woman's rights advocates founded two suffrage associations, did an autonomous movement exist; success, however, was fifty years in the future.

Early in 1856 Beecher made two decisions that, however unintentional, signaled an end to her career as an educator. She severed her relationship with Milwaukee Female College, and a few months later ended her association with the American Woman's Education Association. Having devoted several years to the Milwaukee venture, she had looked to the school for a permanent home. When the trustees refused to subsidize the building of a private residence for Beecher, she disengaged herself.

Milwaukee Female College endured and became the most successful of the institutions founded by Beecher's organization, although its future was hardly assured when Beecher left. Meanwhile, the other two institutions eventually foundered for lack of resources. After 1856 Beecher never formalized her relationship with the American Woman's Education Association, which limped along until it disbanded in 1862, but she continued to promote its cause long after its demise. The association never realized her goal of securing a sizable endowment for each institution it founded, and scholars have attributed a number of causes to its and Beecher's lack of success.

Beecher's intractability probably led her to reject the advice of those who cautioned her to consolidate the association's resources and urged her to consider denominational support for the colleges. Then, too, as Beecher often lamented, support for private women's colleges was neither as deep nor as widespread as support for private men's colleges. The Civil War also disrupted and redirected the path of American reform. In education the movement to include a teacher training curriculum in the public high schools expanded during the postwar years, and states responded to the Morrill Act of 1862 by promoting vocational education for women through the establishment of state-supported normal schools.

Although Beecher's influence on reform waned after the Civil War, her contributions were noteworthy. Her most important ideas about professionalizing teaching and claiming it as a respectable option for women became part of mainstream thought by midcentury. Her articles criticizing emulation appeared in the leading education journals of her day, and her writings on domestic economy laid the foundations for the field of home economics that emerged after her death. Of equal importance were Beecher's contributions to the emerging debate over the origins and scope of woman's influence on society. Although her ideas about womanhood became more contested in the post–Civil War era, especially when cast in the light of the debates over the Fourteenth and Fifteenth Amendments to the Constitution, Beecher did not relinquish her position without a fight. Retirement from public life was not something she relished. She wrote endlessly, traveled, and lectured whenever possible. As support for woman's suffrage gained ground, she redoubled her critique of the movement. In December 1870 Beecher debated woman's rights activist Mary Livermore at Boston's Music Hall, and expanded and published her address, *Woman's Suffrage and Woman's Profession*, in 1871.[39]

Never having a home to call her own, Beecher moved about in her last years, from relative to relative. In 1877 she made her last move, retiring to the Elmira, New York, home of her brother Thomas. The generosity of her brother and sister-in-law, the availability of a nearby water cure establishment, and the presence of Elmira College, where she could lecture to young women, made her last year tolerable. Two days after suffering a debilitating stroke, Catharine Esther Beecher died in her sleep on 12 May 1878.

NOTES

1. Jeanne Boydston, Mary Kelly, and Anne Margolis, *The Limits of Sisterhood: The Beecher Sisters on Women's Rights and Woman's Sphere* (Chapel Hill, N.C., 1988), 13.

2. Kathryn Kish Sklar, *Catharine Beecher, a Study in American Domesticity* (New York, 1976), 270.

3. Catharine Beecher, *Woman's Suffrage and Woman's Profession* (Hartford, Conn.: 1871), dedication page.

4. Catharine Beecher, *Educational Reminiscences and Suggestions* (New York, 1874), dedication page.

5. Barbara Miller Solomon, *In the Company of Educated Women: A History of Women in Higher Education in America* (New Haven, 1985), xviii.

6. Catharine Beecher, ''Female Education,'' *American Journal of Education* 2 (1827): 219–222, 264–269. The quote is on 221.

7. Ibid., 221.

8. Catharine Beecher, *A Treatise on Domestic Economy* (New York, 1841), 222.

9. Kathryn Kish Sklar, ''Catharine Beecher,'' in G. J. Barker-Benfield and Catharine Clinton, eds., *Portraits of American Women: From Settlement to the Present* (New York, 1991), 178.

10. Joan M. Jensen, ''Not Only Ours but Others: The Quaker Teaching Daughters of the Mid-Atlantic, 1790–1850,'' *History of Education Quarterly* 24 (1984): 3.

11. Sklar, *Catharine Beecher*, 7.

12. Ibid., 7–8.

13. Milton Rugoff, *The Beechers: An American Family in the Nineteenth Century* (New York, 1981), 43.

14. Sklar, *Catharine Beecher*, 18.

15. Boydston, Kelly, and Margolis, *The Limits of Sisterhood*, 34.

16. Ibid., 34–35.

17. Ibid., 35.

18. Beecher, ''Female Education,'' 219.

19. Ibid.; Joan N. Burstyn, ''Catharine Beecher and the Education of American Women,'' *New England Quarterly* 47 (1974): 398–399.

20. Sklar, *Catherine Beecher*, 72.

21. Ibid., 74.

22. Rugoff, *The Beechers*, 56.

23. *Third Annual Report of the American Woman's Education Association and of the General Agent, May 1855* (New York, 1855), 8.

24. The statement is attributed to Angelina Grimké when she toured Hartford Female Seminary in 1831.

25. Beecher, *Educational Reminiscences*, 68.

26. Boydston, Kelly, and Margolis, *The Limits of Sisterhood*, 43.

27. Ibid., 45.

28. Rugoff, *The Beechers*, 174.

29. Catharine Beecher, *An Essay on Slavery and Abolition with Reference to the Duty of American Females* (Philadelphia, 1837), 5.

30. Ibid., 14–17.

31. Esther L. Bruland, ''Great Debates: Ethical Reasoning and Social Change in Antebellum America: The Exchange Between Angelina Grimké and Catharine Beecher'' (Ph.D. diss., Drew University, 1990), 175. Whether by accident or design, in her reply to Beecher, Grimké misspelled Catharine's name. Beecher also made a mistake, addressing Grimké as Miss A. D. Grimké (her middle initial was E.).

32. Beecher, *An Essay on Slavery*, 98.

33. Sklar, *Catharine Beecher*, 134–136.

34. Angelina E. Grimké, *Letters to Catharine E. Beecher, in Reply to An Essay on Slavery and Abolition, Addressed to A. E. Grimke* (Boston, 1838), 103, 108.

35. Ibid., 114–115.

36. Ibid., 115–116.

37. Ibid., 122.

38. Ibid., 119.

39. Catharine Beecher, *Woman's Suffrage and Woman's Profession* (Hartford, Conn., 1871). Perhaps too close for comfort for Catharine was the conversion to the suffrage cause of her youngest sister, Isabella Beecher Hooker. Twenty-two years younger than Catharine, Isabella represented a new generation of women. Although she grew up under the shadow of her famous sister, and attended the Hartford and Cincinnati schools, Isabella eventually rejected her sister's theory of social power for women in favor of female political power. Hooker's thoughts crystallized during the period in which Catharine Beecher's public career was drawing to a close. See Isabella Beecher Hooker, *Shall Women Vote? A Matrimonial Dialogue* (n.p., 1860) and *A Mother's Letter to a Daughter on Woman Suffrage* (Hartford, Conn., 1870).

BIBLIOGRAPHY

Boydston, Jeanne, Mary Kelly, and Anne Margolis. *The Limits of Sisterhood: The Beecher Sisters on Women's Rights and Woman's Sphere*. Chapel Hill, N.C., 1988.

Bruland, Esther Louise. "Great Debates: Ethical Reasoning and Social Change in An- tebellum America: The Exchange Between Angelina Grimké and Catharine Bee- cher." Ph.D. diss., Drew University, 1990.

Burstyn, Joan N. "Catharine Beecher and the Education of American Women." *New England Quarterly* 47 (1974): 386–403.

Chambers, Carol L. "Heavenly Influences: Catharine Beecher and the Moral Sphere of Nineteenth Century Women." M.A. thesis, Indiana University, 1984.

Green, Nancy. "Female Education and School Competition, 1820–1850." *History of Education Quarterly* 18 (1978): 129–142.

Lindley, Susan H. "Woman's Profession in the Life and Thought of Catharine Beecher: A Study of Religion and Reform." Ph.D. diss., Duke University, 1974.

Rugoff, Milton. *The Beechers: An American Family in the Nineteenth Century.* New York, 1981.

Sklar, Kathryn Kish. *Catharine Beecher, a Study in American Domesticity.* New Haven, 1973; New York, 1976.

Solomon, Barbara M. *In the Company of Educated Women: A History of Women in Higher Education in America.* New Haven, 1985.

Charles Loring Brace
and Children's Uplift

ERIC C. SCHNEIDER

The name of Charles Loring Brace is most closely associated with the "placing out" movement, which sought to remake urban America by taking poor children from the streets and placing them in rural Protestant foster families. There is some justification for the link between Brace and placement, since his New York Children's Aid Society transported over 85,000 New York City children to country homes between 1853 and 1894. The agency's efforts inspired similar efforts in virtually every major American city, and Brace emerged as the leading spokesman for nineteenth-century child-saving. Placement, which stemmed from a belief in the moral plasticity of children and had its roots in evangelical efforts to convert the poor, is in many ways representative of American reform. It was optimistic, promising a simple solution to the problem of poverty; it relied on the efforts of volunteers; and it offered an arena for individual action. But placement was only a part of Brace's agenda for uplifting urban children, and it declined in significance as his programs evolved and evangelical fervor cooled.

Historians, focusing on placement, have described Brace as a romantic reformer, as a hard-boiled individualist who mistrusted even the ordinary restraints of family, and as an anti-institutionalist. However, in 1894 the New York Children's Aid Society administered twenty-one industrial schools, thirteen night schools, six lodging houses, three reading rooms, a summer home offering short vacation stays for urban children, the Seaside Sanitarium for mothers and children, and a farm school for adolescent boys. Together these institutions served over 30,000 individuals in 1894, whereas the Society placed only 1,940 children during that same year. Clearly, there was more to Brace than a romantic hope of breaking up the dangerous class by turning its children into yeomen farmers. Any evaluation of Charles Loring Brace must examine the evolution of the New

York Children's Aid Society, assess its role in creating urban institutions, and question the curious interpretation of Brace's career.

There were four parts to nineteenth-century child-saving. The first, the asylum movement, began in the 1820s and hoped to reform delinquent and neglected children through an institutional regimen based on discipline and order. The second, placing-out, developed in the 1850s in reaction to the failures of large-scale ''congregate'' institutions and to the growing population of the immigrant poor. Led by Charles Loring Brace, critics of the asylum argued that the family was ''God's reformatory'' and that placement offered the best chance for changing a street urchin's life and reforming urban society. Farm schools, also dating from the mid-nineteenth century, provided a third form of child-saving, one that was not as radical as placing urban children directly into families and that seemed like a more humane form of institutionalization than the congregate asylum. Finally, Brace and other reformers created a network of urban institutions, such as industrial and night schools, that tried to uplift the poor in their own neighborhoods and sought to use the child as an agent of reform in his or her own family. Although the New York Children's Aid Society formed urban institutions in the 1850s, this approach to child-saving became more significant during the 1870s and 1880s. While each of these approaches to child-saving was distinct, they were not mutually exclusive. Rather, each served a specific population, and together they formed the foundation on which the Progressive generation built the modern child welfare system.

Charles Loring Brace was born in Litchfield, Connecticut, on 19 June 1826, to John Brace and Lucy Porter Brace, the second of their four children. Lucy Porter, descended from a prominent Maine family, had married John Brace in 1820. John Brace had been educated by his two aunts, who founded Litchfield Academy as a school for girls and who supported his education at Williams College. After graduating from Williams, he toyed with being a minister before becoming head teacher of his aunts' school. In 1833, the Hartford Female Seminary hired Brace as principal, and he remained there until becoming editor of the *Hartford Courant* in 1849.

Charles Brace's youth in Hartford was shaped by his family's teaching and by the sermons of Horace Bushnell. Following family tradition, he studied at home, with his father supervising his education after his mother's death in 1840. John Brace tutored his son in the classics and English literature until Charles passed his examinations and entered Yale College in 1842. On Sundays, Brace attended Horace Bushnell's North Congregational Church. Bushnell's sermons, including one entitled ''Unconscious Influence,'' which Brace claimed ''influenced his whole life,'' are key to understanding Brace's later child-saving work.[1] Bushnell rejected traditional Calvinist doctrine with its emphasis on a decisive conversion experience as the only route to salvation. He argued that formal education and precepts were less important in child-rearing than the daily workings of family life that a child imitated unconsciously. Bushnell pursued these themes in his influential *Views of Christian Nurture*, first published in serial

form in 1846. He stressed the malleable nature of the child rather than its inherent good or evil, arguing that the childhood years were crucial for moral
education and that the family was the linchpin of the child's moral development.
Brace later drew upon Bushnell's environmentalism in stressing both the peril
posed by unchurched and homeless urban children, and the opportunity to remold them in rural Christian families.

Brace took several years to find his path. He graduated from Yale in 1846,
at age twenty, and, like many young New England college graduates, he briefly
taught school. Brace had considered going into the ministry while he was in
college, perhaps to imitate his mentor Horace Bushnell, and he enrolled at Yale
Divinity School in 1847. The following year Brace transferred to Union Theological Seminary in New York, a bastion of religiously liberal Presbyterians and
Congregationalists, but the move failed to convince him that the ministry was
the right career choice. Brace began visiting the poor at the Blackwell's Island
almshouse, which stirred his soul but furthered his doubt about organized religion. Writing to his father, he remarked that religion did not seem to touch daily
life: "There's so much of the dogma . . . and so little which makes men better
men."[2] At this time, Brace also suffered a personal blow: the death of his
younger sister, Emma, to whom he was particularly close. In search of a calling
and looking to bury his grief, he decided to travel in Europe with two of his
childhood friends, John and Frederick Olmsted.

The young vagabonds trekked through England, Scotland, northern Ireland
(where Brace met his future wife, Letitia Neill), and Germany in the summer
and fall of 1850. Brace was particularly interested in German culture and "home
life," and in the operations of the family-style reformatory Rauhe Haus. (Rauhe
Haus, or rough house, cared for Hamburg's criminal and vagrant youth in cottages holding twelve children, each under the supervision of an older "brother."
The program emphasized agricultural labor in a "family" setting.) When the
Olmsteds returned to New York, Brace continued his travels. He ventured into
the Austro-Hungarian Empire, where he was imprisoned for approximately a
month on suspicion of being an agent for Hungarian nationalists. Brace, like
many Americans of his generation, was sympathetic to the democratic, nationalist movements seeking to overthrow ossified European monarchies. He was
not, however, a revolutionary agent, and the protest of the American embassy
in Vienna eventually secured his release. Brace returned to New York in 1851,
imbued with a renewed faith in democratic individualism and suspicion of governmental and institutional restraints on individual liberty.

Upon his return, Brace began to work as a city missionary, visiting the poor
for Lewis Pease's Five Points Mission, rather than as a conventional minister.
"I don't care a straw for a city pastor's place," he wrote his father. "I want to
raise up the outcast and homeless, to go down among those who have no friend
or helper."[3] City missionaries hoped to secure the American republic by converting the unchurched and Catholic poor to evangelical Protestantism. The Five
Points Mission, supported by the Methodists and located in a former brewery

in one of New York's worst slums, held prayer meetings and dispatched visitors into the homes of the poor to pray, leave religious tracts, and dispense advice. After a few months, Brace became disillusioned. Like many home visitors before him, he concluded that missionary work with the adult poor was nearly hopeless. Moreover, with immigrants arriving from Germany and Ireland at the rate of nearly 1,000 per weekday, he saw the number of the poor swelling beyond the capacity of the city missionaries to convert them. City streets swarmed with child beggars, "baggage smashers" (who stole baggage under the pretense of carrying it), and street peddlers from whom he believed the next generation of criminals and prostitutes would be recruited. Brace concluded that reaching these children offered the only possibility of preventing social disaster.

George W. Matsell, the city's police chief, had already brought the reform community's attention to the existence of child vagrants with a report to the mayor in 1849. He estimated the number of wayward and homeless children at 10,000 and warned that without schooling or training in a trade, they would be fit only for a life of crime. In response to the alarming report, several clergymen began to offer Sunday services for children, and Brace joined their efforts, organizing special Boys' Meetings.

The boys proved to be a difficult audience to capture and hold. Well-meaning preachers were confronted with cries of "Gas! Gas!" when the boys detected pious platitudes, and the more ineffectual had their meetings interrupted by disputes over pews and rock-throwing incidents, or heard their sermons being imitated in newsboys' accents. Questions designed to elicit spiritual considerations received practical replies instead. If a minister asked when they were happiest, the boys answered earnestly, " 'When we'd plenty of hard cash, sir,' " or if asked who would take them if they lost their parents, the reply came, " 'The Purlice, sir, the Purlice.' "[4] Even when speakers were wiser or more effective, the ministers concluded that they exerted only a brief influence over their flock. In order to make a more lasting impact, the group decided in 1853 to form a new organization, the Children's Aid Society, devoted exclusively to children, and to offer its directorship to the twenty-seven-year-old Charles Loring Brace.

Brace undertook his new role cautiously. He gave himself two years to see if work with children was indeed his calling, and at the same time he settled his personal affairs. In June 1854, he returned to Ireland and married Letitia Neill; they journeyed back to New York in the fall. Neill had taught in a Belfast "ragged school," and she soon began teaching and visiting the poor through the Children's Aid Society. Brace was hesitant about committing himself fully to the Society, still thinking that he might become a minister, and apparently it was Neill who convinced him that his future lay in child-saving.

For Brace and others in his generation, reform supplied a substitute career for the ministry. At a time when Protestantism was becoming feminized and the manly efficacy of ministers was questioned, reform allowed a man the opportunity to engage the world actively while doing God's work. Brace had been fleeing the arid regions of dogma since he left the seminary, and he put into practice a secularized Protestantism that aimed at creating a new community out of the urban wilderness.

The first circular issued by the Children's Aid Society in 1853 announced virtually its entire plan for uplifting society by saving poor children. The Society hoped to expand its Boys' Meetings to every district in the city, to form industrial schools in order to begin teaching vagrant children trades and to bring middle-class volunteers into contact with the poor, to open lodging houses so that street children could have inexpensive and safe places to stay overnight, and to place children with farmers, manufacturers, and families in the countryside. Placing-out was only a part of the Society's work, and it flowed quite naturally from the rest of the program. While the urban institutions aided children who lived at home or who were unwilling to leave the city, placing-out was supposed to supply families to those children who had none.

At the time that Brace inaugurated his programs, the major existing institutions for reforming wayward and delinquent children were the congregate asylums and reformatories founded in the second quarter of the nineteenth century. The New York House of Refuge (1825), the Boston House of Reformation (1826), and the Philadelphia House of Refuge (1827) were the first; by midcentury nearly every major American city had established a similar institution. Although the asylum movement was not nearly as uniform as it has been portrayed, generally it aimed to segregate youthful offenders from adult prisoners and to instill self-discipline through work and a carefully regimented schedule. The asylums were constructed at the same time as workhouses and houses of correction, and were part of a movement to categorize and discipline the poor. By their third decade, the congregate reformatories were widely perceived as failures. In the name of reform, street children marched in lockstep around buildings, worked and ate in silence, had their labor contracted out to entrepreneurs for making brass nails or caning chairs, and for infractions of the rules endured corporal punishments that included whippings, gagging, and hanging by the thumbs. Brutality met with spirited resistance: inmates ran away, sang or shouted obscenities during sermons and remained quiet in choir, set fires, attacked guards, and ruined their work. Judges became reluctant to sentence children guilty only of vagrancy or minor thefts to such institutions, and therefore let them go with warnings the children knew carried little weight. It was this group, the status offenders and the petty criminals on the verge of more serious offenses, that Brace hoped to divert from the reformatory and the prison.

Brace objected to congregate asylums in principle. He argued they were relics of "monastic days" and that their most successful graduates learned subservience and deceit while losing their "manly vigor." Such boys had virtues with "an almshouse flavor," while their vices did not "present the frank character of a thorough street boy."[5] These boys had lost their independence and initiative, and therefore had not been readied for citizenship in a democratic society. Brace already feared that American cities were becoming Europeanized with vast districts housing only the degraded and pauperized who threatened to pass their degeneracy on to the next generation. Instead of breaking up this dangerous class, the congregate asylum brought it together and allowed its vices to fester.

Brace proposed creating new environments for urban children by placing them with rural families, either immediately or after a short period of training in a family-style institution. He believed that children were naturally interested in planting and harvesting crops and taking care of farm animals. He argued that work in sunshine and the soil was "medicinal" to the diseased minds of the children of urban vice and poverty.[6] Reform stemmed from a combination of the pastoral and the nurture found in a good family.

Brace's position was part of an emerging critique of the asylum that had its roots in antebellum reform culture. The language of child-saving suggests its affinity with the evangelical movements of the antebellum era. Like temperance and antislavery reformers, child-savers looked to individual conversions as the basis for societal reform. Reflecting their liberal Protestantism, however, they saw this conversion occurring gradually, under the maternal and familial influence embodied in Christian nurture.

Brace and the other proponents of placing-out and family-style institutions were domestic reformers. They called the asylum mechanical and artificial, and argued that although its discipline procured order, it failed to touch inmates' hearts and therefore failed to reform them. They proposed that poor children be remade in the image of the families they joined. Children ideally were incorporated into the family circle: "adopted" in effect if not in law. The precise shape that domestic reform took depended on the child. Older male children received more of a pastoral emphasis, whereas girls and younger boys were subject more to maternal influences. The more delinquent child might be trained in a family-style institution, while the merely wayward or neglected could be placed immediately into a family.

Brace modified domestic reform in one important way. He was a classical liberal who believed in the rule of the marketplace, and this shaped all aspects of his child-saving, from placement to lodging houses to industrial schools. To Brace, the newsboy, in particular, symbolized the possibility of individual entrepreneurship. The newsboy was hindered by his illiteracy, his ignorance of God, and his exposure to the disorder and freedom of city streets, but he possessed spirit and independence that no one could teach and that institutions such as the asylum destroyed. Brace designed placement and the other policies of the Children's Aid Society in such a way as to place the fewest constraints on a boy's development. Domestic reform and Christian nurture were mixed with a heavy dose of individualism.

Debates between the asylum managers and their critics occurred at the conventions of institution managers in 1857 and 1859, and continued at the National Conference on Charities and Corrections meetings until nearly the end of the century. Congregate institutions continued to be built, but placing-out and family-style reformatories developed as major alternatives. Citizens in Boston, Baltimore, Philadelphia, Washington, Cleveland, Chicago, and San Francisco, among other cities, formed societies to place-out children, and both public and private farm schools were built throughout the Northeast and the Middle West.

Family-style or farm schools were the part of domestic reform not usually associated with Brace. The Children's Aid Society did not open a farm school until 1894, but Brace always recognized the farm school as a necessary complement to placement in order to train delinquent children before placing them. He frequently cited the Rauhe Haus example to his American audiences, and he called the farm/family school "as near the natural condition" as could be found in an institution.[7] In the farm school model, children lived in cottages under the supervision of house "parents." Ideally, they formed bonds of affection with these parents and internalized their values. Instead of the corporal punishment found in congregate asylums, the family-style school relied on "family discipline." Children lost privileges, such as dessert or recess, or were deprived of affection for their misbehavior. After a short stay—usually from several months to over a year—children either returned to their parents or were placed out.

The actual operation of the farm/family school varied, depending on whether it was a public or private institution and whether its inmates were male or female. Private schools had the easiest time of it because they could admit the children who seemed most likely to succeed with mild, parental discipline, and always had the option of committing a particularly troublesome child to a state reformatory. Public farm schools usually worked with a more troubled group of youngsters because they could not determine who was committed. However, they still had the option of having a difficult youth transferred into the adult penal system. Farm schools for boys stressed raising crops and doing chores; those for girls focused on cooking, sewing, and doing laundry. In both cases, children were readied to rejoin a family after their release.

The Children's Aid Society acquired fame from immediate placement—the second part of the domestic reform model. It was one of the first agencies to place children directly into families, and it attempted placement on an unheard-of scale. Brace did not intend to set up a bureaucratic system for placing children; he believed that former street children, particularly older boys, were independent agents, used to caring for themselves and requiring little oversight by the Society.

Because street boys were so independent, Brace refused to indenture them to a farmer or tradesman for a certain number of years. Arrangements were kept quite loose for the benefit, Brace maintained, of both parties. Boys who were unhappy with their placements could leave without obtaining anyone's permission, and a farmer dissatisfied with a boy could dismiss him as he could any farmhand. Apparently some boys took advantage of the labor shortage in the countryside and moved from farm to farm, pursuing better deals for themselves. Brace noted with approval that some farmers promised land or farm animals to boys as inducements to stay. He believed that the marketplace regulated placement.

It was less clear to others that the marketplace model worked. Critics argued that the Society placed children haphazardly and did not follow up to see how they were doing. Spokesmen in Western states, usually asylum managers, complained that the agency transported delinquents who went on to commit other crimes. (Eventually a number of Midwestern states required that societies transporting children post bonds for their good behavior and restricted the admission of ''mentally deficient'' or diseased children.) The marketplace did not seem to protect younger children from exploitation, nor could it protect society from older boys bent on criminal careers.

The methods used by the Society and other placement agencies, at least in the early years, left room for criticism. Agents scoured the city dumps, piers, and flophouses for likely candidates for placement, and apparently they asked few questions of potential recruits or of potential families. The first group to go west (to Michigan) with the Children's Aid Society illustrates its methods. The party left New York in September 1854 and took a steamer up the Hudson to Albany. Along the way, two of the group of forty-six were taken by fellow passengers. In Albany, the party acquired an additional youngster who volunteered to go west. The boys approached the agent, saying, '' 'Here's a boy what wants to go to Michigan, sir; can't you take him with us?' '' No one knew the boy, who said he was orphaned, but he looked honest and the agent concluded that ''if left to float here a few months longer, his end is certain.'' He told the boy he could come '' 'if you will have your face washed and hair combed within a half an hour.' ''[8]

Over the years the pattern became more routinized. Usually an agent led parties of five to thirty children and took the train for upstate New York or the Middle West. (Ninety-one percent of all placements went to New York, New Jersey, Illinois, Iowa, Missouri, Indiana, Ohio, Michigan, and Kansas.) Upon arriving at their destination, the children were dispersed to families for lodging, then gathered the next day in a large space, such as the local church or town hall. The curious and the childless, drawn to the spectacle by circulars distributed in the area, applied for children and went off with their choices. The party then moved on to the next town, until all children were spoken for. After the first several years, local committees were formed to review the applications for children, and the town fathers decided on the suitability of applicants. But for the first decade or so, controls were fairly lax, and life-changing decisions were made in the time it took a child to wash up.

The child's status in the new family was ambiguous, which contributed to instability. Despite the emphasis on placing orphans, nearly 70 percent of the children had at least one surviving parent; frequently the Children's Aid Society did not bother with the legal nicety of obtaining custody over its charges. Not surprisingly, its policy forbade contact between the child and its biological family, but this was difficult to enforce. Since the children were not indentured or adopted, neither the agency nor the family of placement could do very much about those children who were old enough and sufficiently independent to write or even visit their biological families. And parents were sometimes successful in negotiating the terms of a child's stay and in retrieving the child afterward— about one in ten returned home, and another two in ten went to other family or to friends.

The Society had difficulty in accounting for all of its children. Children and the families into which they were placed were encouraged to correspond with the Society, but this did not always occur and a number of children simply disappeared. For example, the Society placed 960 children in Kansas between 1867 and 1893, but despite visits and correspondence, almost 10 percent of them could not be traced. In response to critics of child placement, the Society, like other agencies, began to adopt new methods.

By the 1870s the Society became more careful in selecting, processing, and following children. After a lawsuit filed against the Brooklyn Children's Aid Society in 1872 by parents seeking to recover their son, the New York Society made sure to determine a child's legal status before placement. It began to rely more on other agencies for referrals rather than taking children directly from the streets, and thereby avoided potential legal problems. Both farm schools and immediate placement agencies started exhibiting more care and instituting more formal procedures during the 1870s and 1880s. They hired agents to visit and report on placed children, required more careful checks on families taking children, and monitored changes in placements. Gradually, placement was evolving into foster care.

The changing market for children contributed to this process. American families, including farm families, were growing smaller and more intimate by the end of the nineteenth century. As a result, they began to exclude strangers, such as boarders, young workers, and domestics, from the household. Where once older children were at a premium in placement, now the demand shifted to younger children who could become part of the family. Circulars advertising the availability of children make this quite clear. They stopped describing sturdy youngsters who could work as laborers or domestics, and began to emphasize the need for good homes for younger children. By the early twentieth century, placement delivered young children, most commonly girls under the age of three, into middle-class homes for adoption. Since younger children could not fend for themselves, virtually all child-saving agencies became more bureaucratized and developed a core of professionals who administered their programs.

Domestic reform had several limitations that were not apparent at the time and were untouched by professionalization. Although domestic reform was a fundamentally more humane way of treating wayward and delinquent children than incarcerating them in asylums, it still held that the locus of reform was in the individual. Instead of attacking the social conditions that were producing more and more poor children, the domestic reform agenda called for removing children from the city one by one and grafting Protestant, rural, and familial virtues onto their characters. Domestic reform may have been the best method for saving vagrant children that Victorian America could devise, but it hardly addressed the enormity of the problem or its cause. Moreover, the expression of domestic reform was hindered by factors of gender, race, religion, and class.

Gender shaped the entire reform program. Males comprised 61 percent of the children placed between 1853 and 1893, which reflected Brace's attitudes toward the effect of vice and the possibility of reform. Brace romanticized the newsboys and male street traders he encountered. Although he feared for their futures, he admired their plucky independence, their generosity with one another, their ingenuity, and their ability to survive on the streets. He wrote that the street boy "has a rather good time of it, and enjoys many of the delicious pleasures of a child's roving life." Their swearing, tobacco chewing, and petty thievery were "not so bad as they look." By contrast, girls had "more of the feminine dependence on affection," missed family life, and found living on the streets much harder than boys did. Most important, girls in the street trades were subject to sexual advances, and if they succumbed, their fall was deeper and the "crime" seemed "to sap and rot the whole nature." Moreover, the chances for reform were slim. If a girl somehow managed to escape the streets, she found that she missed the stimuli of the wild life she had led, her bad name dogged her, and "all the wicked have an instinct of her former evil courses; the world and herself are against reform."[9] The emphasis on boys' reform followed naturally from Brace's opinions on the effects of street life.

Brace's opinions about girls' reformability stemmed from experience as well as from his commonplace ideas about the nature of womanhood. The Society attempted to assist older girls by opening an inexpensive lodging house in response to the increasing number of homeless during the Civil War. Brace feared his lodging house might become a "Reformatory for Magdalenes" and set an age limit of eighteen for entrance. But "sweet young maidens . . . who gave the most touching stories of early bereavement and present loneliness, whose voices arose in moving hymns of penitence, and whose bright eyes filled with tears" at the Sunday sermon turned out to be skillful liars working the streets during the day and returning to the lodging house at night to corrupt the other inmates. Limiting the age and guessing at the virtue of an applicant was the best the lodging house's matron could do.[10]

One might argue that girls learning "vice" from one another was no different from boys becoming more adept at pickpocketing during a stay in a reform school. However, contemporaries did not see it that way. Most believed, as did Brace, that vice "soiled" a girl permanently and that reform was difficult if not impossible. Although some women reformers challenged this notion, the problem of moral contagion was a recurring one, and it was faced (but not solved) by every agency interested in reforming adolescent girls.

Race also proved to be a difficult issue for nineteenth-century child-savers. Many institutions excluded African Americans or, as in the case of the Children's Aid Society, opened what was in effect a segregated institution. Although the Society did not exclude African Americans from its industrial schools or lodging houses, these youngsters encountered hostility from the other youths.

African-American youngsters found that white families were reluctant to take them, and therefore the length of time they remained institutionalized was longer than for whites.

Religious antagonism was yet another problem. For example, after the opening of one industrial school that offered instruction in carpentry, provided free lunches, and gave lessons in rudimentary educational skills, the boys "smashed our windows; they entered the premises at night and carried off everything they could find; they howled before the door, and yelled 'Protestant School!' "[11] More serious were the charges that the Society and similar agencies deliberately transported Catholic children to the West in order to make Protestants of them. Many of the street children placed in country homes were at least nominally Catholic and, not surprisingly, priests anathematized the Children's Aid Society from their pulpits. Brace dismissed Catholics' objections as the desperate efforts of the priesthood seeking to retain control over the immigrant masses. He inveighed against "priestcraft" and "Romanism," which he, like many Protestant Americans, believed were the superstitious relics of an Old World order. This hostility continued until the end of the century, when Catholic child-saving agencies were finally accepted as peers by the Protestant ones and worked out agreements to refer clients.

Finally, domestic reform was embedded in relations of class. To the Children's Aid Society supporters, who included some of New York City's most prominent and wealthy families, the Society was presented as a bulwark against the dangerous class. Brace warned that society had left the poor to their "misery and temptation." "Now these children arise and wrest back with bloody and criminal hands, what the world were [*sic*] too careless or too selfish to give."[12] The only way to deal with the problem of crime and disorder was to educate, employ, and change the character of the children of the poor. Placement seemed like the ideal way to break up the dangerous class, because it transported the most likely recruits into the countryside, where they could learn the values they needed to take advantage of an open society. Domestic reform joined self-interest with benevolence, promising to save both the wealthy and the waifs.

Clients saw domestic reform somewhat differently. Families used the agency to train their children or to board them until a bout of sickness or unemployment passed. Placement provided some youngsters with a chance to escape difficult family situations, to gain an education, and to live modest and hard-working lives. The lucky few, who were plucked from poverty and adopted by their families, provided highly touted examples of social mobility at work. But the howling before the door, the rocks thrown through the windows, the avowals of conversion traded for a bag of coal, the number of runaways from placement—however bewildering to the child-savers—suggest that at least some of the poor doubted the ideology of benevolence.

The poor also helped to shape the course of reform. Child-savers, including Brace, gradually deemphasized placement and the domestic reform model, and paid more attention to urban institutions. One reason for the shift was the lack of interest on the part of urban children in being sent to the country. Perhaps in difficult economic times they were willing to try their luck at jobs on farms, but more were interested in employment opportunities in the city's growing manufacturing sector. Brace established industrial schools and lodging houses and added more social services in order to prepare street children for the industrial workforce. By 1881 fewer than one in seven of the children served by the Society went into placement, with the remainder attending one of the urban programs. At the same time, Brace retained his hope for bringing the classes into contact.

The Newsboys' Lodging House, one of the first urban institutions established by the Children's Aid Society, illustrates Brace's marketplace model for charity. Brace treated the newsboys as "independent little dealers" and kept the lodging house on a strict fee-for-service basis. However, he decided to give them "much more for their money than they could get anywhere else."[13] A bed and a bath cost 6 cents, and dinner an additional 4 cents; boys were asked to contribute the fees for those who could not afford to pay. Brace hoped to encourage boys to attend religious services, to learn to read and write, and even to recruit others for placement. He also respected the boys' ability to detect the "gaseous." The manager firmly evicted troublemakers. The Society's first night school evolved out of the lessons for newsboys.

Industrial schools provided a different set of lessons for boys. Brace expected the industrial schools to teach marketable skills to urban youth and to be self-supporting, but both of these hopes were dashed. The industrial schools began as workshops, but Brace quickly found out that they could not compete with the factory system that produced goods more cheaply. Moreover, the boys showed up irregularly, destroying any kind of production schedule, and displayed little enthusiasm for working steadily. Not only were the workshops uneconomical, but they provided boys with skills that machines were making obsolete. The failure of the workshops led Brace to reconceptualize them as industrial "schools" that taught habits of work, punctuality, and discipline rather than specific skills.

The movement for industrial schools and manual training, dating from the 1870s, had a narrower vision than did domestic reform. Domestic reform had held out the hope that poor children would remake themselves in the image of the families with whom they were placed. Reformers like Brace recalled their own youth in communities that were not as sharply divided into distinct classes, and they could realistically hope that a sense of community could be regenerated through missionary work and activities like placement. By the last quarter of the nineteenth century, such hopes were growing dimmer. Brace still expressed the belief that voluntary societies could bring the classes together, but his programs reflected a different reality. An exploration of the form of manual training called the object system provides a perfect example.

Brace believed that the object system was a natural way of educating youngsters. It emphasized learning by the senses—that is, having students observe concrete objects rather than memorizing abstract principles. The object system seemed to offer the possibility of individualizing lessons and making the child an active participant in education. Unfortunately, it turned out somewhat differently. As taught in most industrial schools, the object system proved to be as dull and mechanical as anything that preceded it. Manual training, frequently exacting woodworking exercises (and military drill, which was a popular form of recreational activity), was believed to be particularly appropriate for the limited mentality of working-class boys. Repetitive physical activity was thought to ingrain habits of moral rectitude. Boys learned precision, attention to detail, obedience—skills not learned in the street trades—and were fitted for factory labor.

Reformers also developed programs for girls, but they continued to reflect a traditional concern for the domestic sphere rather than attention to the industrial labor market. For example, Brace did not claim that the sewing lessons provided to girls in the industrial schools served any practical purpose. He admitted that competition for jobs in the garment trades led to very depressed wages and rather dim job prospects. However, he did not believe that this was important. Through the lessons learned at the industrial school, he wrote, girls "had no difficulty in securing places as upper servants, or they soon married into a better class."[14] Girls learned food preparation, cleaning, sewing, and laundering as well as punctuality and dependability. The young women who were counted as successes either supported themselves as domestics or married a farmer or "mechanic," in which case they could apply their training to their families. In both instances, they had been returned safely to the domestic sphere.

Young children, particularly girls, were thought to be effective in transmitting the cultural lessons learned from child-savers to their families. The Children's Aid Society had opened six industrial schools for vagrant girls by 1855. Brace persuaded a number of prominent society women to help instruct the girls in sewing, knitting, and crocheting, and to help prepare them for admission to the public schools; but it was the interaction between the girls and their patrons that Brace believed was most important. He wanted the girls to model themselves on the upper-class women rather than on the prostitutes and dance-hall girls they encountered in the streets. Brace declared that schools that had begun in "riot and disorder" became "attentive, affectionate family-schools." The girls were cleaner and better-behaved, and brought the influences of the industrial schools home to their families by singing "sweet songs of purity and religion . . . in their squalid homes."[15]

Reformers looked to the child as a means of entry into the working-class family. They hoped to refashion the leisure time of working-class children, substituting supervised activities for street games and enticing children to attend boys' clubs, participate in sewing circles, host reading clubs, or join saving-stamp societies (buying stamps for pennies in order to encourage thrift). The children were to become guides to the parents and little engines of reform within the home.

Programs for boys and girls depended on a fraying spirit of voluntarism. A number of observers commented on the middle-class abandonment of the city in the late nineteenth century as the expansion of trolley lines permitted mass suburbanization. Even in the city, exclusive residential districts allowed an increased level of class and ethnic segregation than already existed. The retreat from the city was also a retreat from working-class crime and disorder, and Brace noted that fewer individuals were volunteering to uplift the poor. At the same time, the demand for more careful placement and supervision of children fueled the professionalization of social welfare.

Ironically, Brace supported the same professionalization that threatened his vision of urban reform. He recognized that serving the poor could not be "mere holiday work," and he gladly paid the teachers and agents of the Children's Aid Society who bore primary responsibility for administering the industrial and night schools.[16] As the requirements of placing and visiting children multiplied, so did the professionals. These individuals organized meetings to exchange ideas, developed university courses to train their successors, and gave child-saving the full-time attention that volunteers could not. They presided over the birth of child welfare that was shorn of its religious parentage and of the hope that charity could unite the classes.

Brace attempted to transform his city with a program of daring simplicity. Over time, it necessarily became more complex, more realistic, and more limited. By the time of his death on 11 August 1890, Charles Loring Brace had presided over the transformation of child-saving into child welfare. Placement had become foster care, industrial schools trained youth for the industrial workforce, and the missionaries and volunteers yielded to social workers and bureaucrats. It is not at all clear that Brace was aware of how dramatically he had changed child-saving and of how that change had altered his hope for a community regenerated by Christian nurture. The Children's Aid Society, like other private child-saving agencies, engaged in a dialogue with benefactors and clients, and changed its program in order to meet their changing demands. As a result, the pastoral vision of newsboys turned into yeomen farmers became an urban vision of a social service agency fitting youngsters for an industrial society.

Yet Brace's name is still associated with orphan trains and child placement, and he is called an anti-institutionalist. His vision of a community remade through Christian love is appealing even as we recognize its impracticality. The history of child-saving shows that social problems are too complex to be confronted piecemeal, through the salvation of individuals. Brace's vision belongs to the tradition of cultural reform that tackles the problem of poverty by trying to change the individual's values rather than confronting the structures of inequality that produce poverty. It remains alluring because it is so quintessentially a part of the American reform tradition.

NOTES

1. Quoted in Emma Brace, *The Life of Charles Loring Brace, Chiefly Told in His Own Letters* (New York, 1894), 8.
2. Ibid., 76.
3. Ibid., 154.
4. Charles Loring Brace, *The Dangerous Classes of New York and Twenty Years' Work Among Them*, (3rd ed., New York, 1880; repr. Montclair, N.J., 1967), 80–81.
5. Ibid., 76, 236.
6. Ibid., 400–401.
7. Ibid., 402.
8. Ibid., 248.
9. Ibid., 114–117.
10. Ibid., 305–306.
11. Ibid., 177.
12. New York Children's Aid Society (CAS), *Annual Report* no. 4 (1857), 5–6.
13. Brace, *Dangerous Classes*, 100.
14. Ibid., 96.
15. CAS, *Annual Report* no. 2 (1855), 10.
16. Brace, *Dangerous Classes*, 137.

BIBLIOGRAPHY

Annual Reports of the New York Children's Aid Society, Nos. 1–10, Feb. 1854–Feb. 1863. Repr. New York, 1971.

Bellingham, Bruce. '' 'Little Wanderers': A Socio-Historical Study of the Nineteenth-Century Origins of Child Fostering and Adoption Reform, Based on Early Records of the New York Children's Aid Society.'' Ph.D. diss., University of Pennsylvania, 1984.

Bender, Thomas. *Toward an Urban Vision: Ideas and Institutions in Nineteenth-Century America.* Baltimore, 1982.

Boyer, Paul. *Urban Masses and Moral Order in America, 1820–1920.* Cambridge, 1978.

Brace, Charles Loring. *The Dangerous Classes of New York and Twenty Years' Work Among Them*, 3rd ed. New York, 1880; repr. Montclair, N.J., 1967.

Brace, Emma. *The Life of Charles Loring Brace, Chiefly Told in His Own Letters.* New York, 1894.

Hawes, Joseph M. *Children in Urban Society: Juvenile Delinquency in Nineteenth-Century America.* New York, 1971.

Holt, Marilyn Irvin. *The Orphan Trains: Placing Out in America.* Lincoln, Nebr., 1992.

Langsam, Miriam Z. *Children West: A History of the Placing-out System of the New York Children's Aid Society, 1853–1890.* Madison, Wis., 1964.

Rothman, David J. *Discovery of the Asylum: Social Order and Disorder in the New Republic.* Boston, 1971.

Schneider, Eric C. *In the Web of Class: Delinquents and Reformers in Boston, 1810s–1930s.* New York, 1992.

Wohl, R. Richard. ''The 'Country Boy' Myth and Its Place in American Urban Culture:

The Nineteenth Century Contribution.'' In Donald Fleming and Bernard Bailyn, eds. *Perspectives in American History*, Vol. 3, Cambridge, Mass., 1969: 77–156.
Zelizer, Viviana A. *Pricing the Priceless Child: The Changing Social Value of Children.* New York, 1985.

Earl Browder
and American Communism

JAMES G. RYAN

During the 1930s the American public still stereotyped Marxists as stocky, swarthy figures advocating revolution in thick Slavic accents. Suddenly there appeared a slender new American Communist party general secretary: blue-eyed, sandy-haired, ruddy-complected Earl Browder. Still possessing boyish good looks in his forties, Browder repudiated violent change. In his Great Plains twang—more Kansan than that of Governor Alf Landon, one conservative commentator conceded—Browder told listeners that communism was "Twentieth Century Americanism."

Few Americans born after World War II associate the Communist party with reform. During the Great Depression, however, Communists seemed to appear wherever people protested economic or racial injustice. In early 1930, just months after the stock market crash, the Communist Party of the U.S.A. (CPUSA) led mass demonstrations against wage cuts and layoffs. Marxists agitated among the unemployed, demanding jobs or full pay, and fought every relief cut. They organized unskilled workers more than five years before the Congress of Industrial Organizations (CIO) appeared. Three decades before the modern civil rights movement, the CPUSA proclaimed itself the "Negro party," nominating African-American James W. Ford as its vice presidential candidate in 1932 and 1936. The Communists led rent strikes and antieviction campaigns in Northern cities. They also focused the world's attention on Southern injustice. They rallied behind Angelo Herndon, an African-American organizer sentenced to eighteen years' imprisonment under a Georgia antebellum insurrection law and also behind nine young black men sentenced to death for allegedly raping two white women on a moving freight train near Scottsboro, Alabama. Communists also protested deportations of Mexican-American laborers.

Browder, the greatest public-relations expert in party history and the best speaker before Angela Davis, led the CPUSA to its most dramatic successes in American life from 1934 to 1945. He carried the startling message that his party wanted to cooperate with all progressives to Madison Square Garden, university campuses, and African-American churches across the land. In so doing, Browder helped the Communists to surpass the Socialists and become the largest political party to the left of Franklin D. Roosevelt's New Deal. Indeed, CPUSA influence stretched far beyond its 100,000 members to reach fellow-traveling intellectuals, figures in Hollywood, and other opinion makers. Communists controlled many of the CIO's labor unions and played a prominent role in state-level political reform organizations: End Poverty in California, Minnesota's Farmer-Labor party, and Washington's Commonwealth Federation. Browder brought his followers to the borders of legitimacy in American politics. By contrast, after Moscow forced his removal in 1945, the party rushed headlong into oblivion.

Browder was born on 20 May 1891 into a family that was both nationalistic and reform-oriented. He later boasted that his earliest traceable ancestors, three Welsh brothers, had arrived in Dinwiddie County, Virginia, not long after the Mayflower reached New England. Browders had fought in every major conflict before World War I. Earl's place of birth, Wichita, Kansas, was almost precisely in the nation's geographical center.

Acute poverty stimulated his parents' interest in reform. Earl's father, William, youngest of eighteen siblings, took Martha Hankins Browder, his sixteen-year-old bride, to Kansas from their native Illinois during the 1870s. Living in a dugout, they attempted to homestead at the very time foreign competition had pushed American wheat and corn prices to record lows. To add to the Browders' economic hardships, drought ruined their crops and disease claimed two of their children. By the time Earl was born in 1891, his parents had lost their property and were renting a small house in Wichita. There William taught elementary school, suffered a nervous breakdown, and became an invalid, forcing Earl to drop out of third grade to help support the family at age nine. An energetic youth, he worked as an errand boy and a telegraph messenger, then rose from office boy, to clerk, to accountant for a wholesale drug company. William tutored him at night, imparting an elementary school education. Martha added her potent anticlericalism and love of literature. Earl never fully overcame his intellectual deprivation, however, and spent his adulthood taking on self-improvement projects.

Location played a important role in attracting Browder to American reform. During the 1890s his native Kansas was the epicenter of the People's party, which became the largest third party in American history. As Browder came to political awareness, populism, though in retreat, influenced his thinking profoundly. Indeed, while most Kansans returned to their traditional Republican loyalties, the Browder family clung to populism even as its numbers dwindled. Soon William was calling himself a Socialist and young Earl was peddling copies of *Appeal to Reason*, the nation's premier radical newspaper. He joined the Socialist party (SP) at age sixteen.

Five years later, in 1912, Browder, now married, moved to Kansas City, Kansas. Although the twentieth century's second decade proved to be socialism's high-water mark in America, Browder, a restless radical, could not find the ideal home for his energies. He spent time in nearly all the era's political and labor movements. He left the SP in 1913 after its membership removed with a recall election the charismatic "Big Bill" Haywood. Browder did not join Haywood's Industrial Workers of the World. Instead, he tried to radicalize the American Federation of Labor (AFL) from within by entering the Workers' Educational League, the Kansas City branch of William Z. Foster's Syndicalist League of North America. That same year Browder joined the local chapter of the Bookkeepers, Stenographers, and Accountants Union. The members elected him president in 1914, and he also became a delegate to the Kansas City (Missouri) Central Labor Countil. He enjoyed organizing and retained his union position after he began managing a farmers' cooperative outside the city in 1916. Browder also found time to serve on the national council of the Grangers' Cooperative League of North America; occasionally, he contributed articles to its journal.

Although Browder roamed from organization to organization between 1912 and 1916, these were not wasted years. They constituted a decisive, formative period in his career, during which Browder developed a keen understanding of American radical politics. His actions nurtured nativist tendencies that never deserted him—even after he had spent more than a decade in the Soviet-dominated CPUSA.

In 1917 Browder finally found a cause that enchanted him and consumed his spare time: nonviolent resistance to American entry into World War I. His beliefs and actions cost him dearly. Refusal to register with the Selective Service brought a term in the Platte County jail from December 1917 to November 1918. Proselytizing against the military brought imprisonment in Leavenworth Penitentiary from July 1919 until November 1920.

The two incarcerations affected Browder in quite different ways. The Platte County jailer welcomed Browder, his brother R. Waldo, and his future brother-in-law Thomas R. Sullivan because their presence brought federal support money. The convicts were treated almost as guests and were accorded every amenity the law allowed. Browder passed idle hours reading, discussing politics, and writing a book on accounting. He emerged essentially unchanged, returned to Kansas City, rejoined the SP, and tried to win converts to its left wing.

By contrast, Leavenworth altered Browder's personality in two fundamental ways. First, the icy environment, incredible overcrowding, merciless regimentation, and rigidly enforced rule of silence killed the romantic in Browder. In its place emerged a steely toughness that would enable him to spend a quarter-century championing a highly unpopular cause hostile to his nation's fundamental faith in capitalism. The second change concerned ideology. While in Leavenworth, the angry Browder made an emotional commitment to the Bolshevik Revolution because of its militance and success. He emerged from prison a zealot, deserted his wife and son, moved to New York, and joined the Communist party. Although his action was cruel, his timing could hardly have been better.

Not long before, international communism had undergone its first historic "change of line." Previously, followers had expected Soviet-style uprisings and had eschewed association with reformers, especially in labor. By 1920, however, except in Russia, the "World Revolution" had stalled. That spring, V. I. Lenin wrote a pamphlet, *Left Wing Communism: An Infantile Disorder*, that sanctioned cooperation with other progressive elements. When American party members finally received a translation a year later, they found that a gulf of ill will separated them from most of organized labor. One high party official, James P. Cannon, had worked with Browder in Kansas City. He realized that Browder had more experience in the AFL than most other CP members. By coincidence, at that same time, early 1921, three representatives from Moscow were touring the nation, recruiting an American delegation to the First Congress of the Red International of Labor Unions (known by its Russian abbreviation, Profintern). Cannon introduced Browder to the visitors. They liked his Midwestern and AFL background, and chose him to lead the U.S. contingent to the gathering that July. Although Browder had obtained a lucrative head bookkeeper's position with a wholesale company in New York City, he resigned and began rounding up delegates who could claim union support.

Once in Moscow, Browder, without any conscious effort, charmed his Soviet hosts. Profintern head Solomon A. Lozovsky became a close friend who later aided Browder's career. Organizing the delegation did not make Browder America's top Communist, but it did locate him in the second stratum of leaders.

Browder's first Moscow visit had another result. William Z. Foster, who went along as an observer, decided to join the party. One of the nation's best-known left-wing unionists, Foster was an important convert. He brought along his Chicago-based Trade Union Educational League (TUEL), which quickly became the Profintern's American section. Once the Soviets provided financial backing, its power soon rivaled the Communist party's political leadership in New York. Foster entered the movement on his own terms. Browder became his assistant, editing the TUEL's paper, the *Labor Herald*, and doing much of the legwork during negotiations between the Chicago and New York factions. Browder's efforts, energy, and efficiency brought him recognition but not respect. He became known as Foster's "man Friday" and was often derided as "Foster's boy." By the mid-1920s he seemed destined to remain a high-level apparatchik for life.

The year 1926 brought an unexpected turning point in Browder's career. Summoned to assist Foster in a CPUSA factional dispute being settled in Moscow, Browder broke with his mentor and linked his future to the rising Joseph Stalin. For the rest of his career, Browder tried to champion Stalinism and the American reform tradition simultaneously. Foster, angered at Browder's insubordination, left him in the Soviet Union as America's Profintern delegate.

Soviet leaders quickly found better uses for Browder's time and talents. At Solomon Lozovsky's behest, they asked him to join an international labor delegation to China, then being ravaged by civil war. Bravely, Browder swallowed his fears. Taking the assignment, he helped to establish the Pan-Pacific Trade Union Secretariat, centered first at Hankow and later at Shanghai. Helping to teach Chinese workers the concept of unionization, Browder remained in East Asia for most of 1927 and 1928, heading the organization and editing its journal. In China he proved his courage and dedication to the Communist International (Comintern). He had become a noted American Communist overseas while he was still little known at home.

Like much of the CPUSA's overall history, the crisis that brought Browder to the verge of leadership concerned Russian, not American, events. In December 1927, Stalin and Nikolai Bukharin engineered Leon Trotsky's expulsion from the Soviet Communist party. The following year Stalin consolidated all power in the Soviet Union by ousting his former ally Nikolai Bukharin. Foreign Communists made similar purges. The American party removed Trotskyist James Cannon in 1928 and, more significantly, Bukharin's friend, CPUSA General Secretary Jay Lovestone, the following year. Numerous followers of both were ostracized, depleting the party's highest ranks.

Browder returned from East Asia in January 1929 and subsequently displayed his independence from Foster yet again. Soon Profintern head Lozovsky began telling CPUSA figures that Browder would make the best general secretary. Resident Comintern representative Boris Mikhailov offered to promote Browder's candidacy. Surprised and not yet ready to lead amid the intraparty chaos, Browder demurred. In October, however, the CPUSA abolished the general secretary's post and created a three-person secretariat to run the organization, as Communist parties often did during times of crisis. Max Bedacht, as acting secretary, led the troika, which included *Daily Worker* editor Robert Minor and Browder as head of agitation and propaganda (Agitprop). Browder quickly realized that he possessed the ability to lead the CPUSA, and he delivered the main report at the party plenum in the spring of 1930.

That June, under great Comintern pressure, the CPUSA reorganized yet again. Bedacht, a poor leader, assumed Browder's duties. A reconstituted and longer-lasting secretariat appeared, consisting of William W. Weinstone (organizational secretary), William Z. Foster (trade union secretary), and Browder (administrative secretary). Although Browder's title gave him nominal leadership, Weinstone and Foster remained contenders for power. Behind the facade of public unity the three men battled privately for two years. Browder's pluck and a good measure of luck helped him win out. Decisive factors included his own ambition, Weinstone's aversion to hard work and his lengthy visits to Moscow and Western Europe, and Foster's 1932 heart attack and prolonged convalescence. At its April 1934 convention, the CPUSA re-created the general secretary's post and awarded it to Browder.

Browder accurately anticipated the Comintern's monumental change of orientation in 1935. As Adolf Hilter's shadow over Europe lengthened, the world Communist movement abandoned revolutionary rhetoric and adopted an unprecedented strategy: the Popular Front. Marxists in every land began seeking to unite progressive forces against the Nazi menace and to find links to indigenous radical traditions. Tirelessly, for nearly five years, Communists urged Western democracies to join the Soviet Union in adopting collective security measures.

Browder never possessed the charisma of Socialist leaders Eugene Debs and Norman Thomas. Yet, in championing both Stalinism and patriotism, he inspired domestic Communists as no party head had done before or has done since. Claiming links to American revolutionaries and abolitionists, he rapidly became a public figure. His voice was heard on national radio in 1936, and his photograph appeared on *Time* magazine's cover in 1938. Over Foster's objections, Browder convinced Moscow that Communist party support for President Franklin D. Roosevelt, first tacit and then open (the Democratic Front), was the specific form the Popular Front should take in the United States.

Great Britain's and France's appeasement of Germany at Munich caused the Soviet Union to despair of realizing its collective security goals. Accordingly, in August 1939, it signed a separate nonaggression treaty with Hitler. Nine days after the accord's completion, Hitler ignited World War II by invading Poland, which Great Britain and France had pledged to defend. The Nazi–Soviet pact dumbfounded Browder and other American Communists. The Comintern gave no advance warning of its first major line change since 1935. Learning of the treaty through the media was a rude shock; in July the Marxist leader had told a Charlottesville, Virginia, audience that there was "as much chance of Russo-German agreement as of Earl Browder being elected President of the Chamber of Commerce."[1] The pact presented Browder with a painful choice between American Communist needs and those of the Soviet Union. By shortwave radio, Comintern chief Georgi Dimitrov ordered Browder to follow Moscow, but the CPUSA head risked foreign censure and angered domestic militants Foster and Alexander Bittelman by procrastinating for weeks.

From September through late October 1939, Browder led his followers down a unique and somewhat schizophrenic path. It set the American Communist apart from other Western Communist parties. By late September the British, French, and German Communist parties, originally war supporters, had all abandoned their anti-fascist crusades. Once apprised of Soviet foreign policy's new course, they demanded peace with the Nazis and denounced Allied governments for continuing the conflict. Browder, however, feared a direct rupture with President Roosevelt's position would be a political disaster. However, he could not bring himself to defy Moscow openly; he even hid the existence of the Dimitrov messages from other CPUSA leaders.[2]

At the height of the American Communist crisis, federal authorities unexpectedly intervened, indicting Browder on a decade-old minor passport violation. Never before had the national government jailed a CPUSA head. Many bewildered Communists believed Roosevelt now wanted to outlaw the party, and that Browder's arrest constituted the first step toward that goal. American Communists immediately began attacking the president in the wildest terms, and continued to do so for the next twenty months.

By temporizing and refusing to take a principled, independent stand on the Nazi–Soviet pact, Browder lost a critical portion of his party's following. For many intellectuals and other American radicals, the German–Soviet agreement and the CPUSA's response proved to be the end of an American leftist dream.

Browder spent fourteen months during 1941 and 1942 in the Atlanta Penitentiary on a passport fraud technicality. The incarceration proved a subtle yet crucial turning point in his career and life, leaving psychological scars that never healed fully. Two decades earlier a sojourn at Leavenworth, though painful, had shaped the youthful, romantic Browder into a tough revolutionary, possessing the self-discipline necessary to support a highly unpopular cause. The months in Atlanta, however, wounded him severely. Browder carried to the maximum-security facility all the fears and insecurities one might expect to find in a prisoner approaching age fifty. Once there, he faced a situation he had not encountered at Leavenworth. No longer an anonymous Midwestern radical, Browder fascinated federal investigators. In addition to giving him the customary prison physical examination, they now probed his psyche.

To Browder's generation, in a land with few community-based mental health centers, psychiatric and psychological examinations were unfamiliar and very threatening. Browder lived in a society where only the very rich and the very sick saw a psychiatrist. He of course was neither, and found the experience terrifying. Browder especially feared involuntary commitment to a mental institution. Although it could be for a term of unspecified, possibly lifelong, duration, commitment was considered a reasonable and routine way to treat the "abnormal" in 1941. That involuntary commitment was rarely used to punish political dissent in the United States did not lessen Browder's fright. He knew his unpopular views could be equated with pathology, a phenomenon that later became tragically common in Stalinist Russia.

The most significant event during Browder's incarceration was Hitler's invasion of the Soviet Union on 22 June 1941. Suddenly, Stalinists everywhere became staunch advocates of collective security. Without blushing, the CPUSA began espousing the very preparedness efforts it had opposed since the autumn of 1939. Thenceforth, the party stood among the most martial groups in the nation and ardently courted those who had been sympathizers in the 1930s. It seemed willing to sacrifice anything to secure American entry into the conflict.

Japan's attack on Pearl Harbor in December 1941, which brought the United States into the war and made the Anglo–Soviet–American alliance possible, proved a boon to CPUSA for the Marxists. Now one could fight for communism and Americanism simultaneously. Fifteen thousand CPUSA members rushed into the armed forces. Many others joined the merchant marine or entered war-

related industries. Government persecution ended, though the party never regained all the acceptance it enjoyed in 1938.

The change of line brought anxiety to Browder. He worried about both his
party leadership and his health. Suddenly, at his emotional nadir, President Roosevelt commuted his sentence in order to further "national unity." Liberated,
Browder soon displayed marked changes. Although he had always enjoyed the
limelight, he now felt an unquenchable thirst for status. This, in turn, impaired
his judgment. Much as *Pravda* praised Stalin daily, the CPUSA press had long
heaped adulation upon Browder. He had always enjoyed, but had never taken
seriously, his cult of personality during the 1930s. After 1942 he showed every
sign of believing party propaganda lauding his brilliance, wisdom, and origi-
nality of thought.

Browder received unprecedented acceptance during 1942 and 1943. Three
times he visited Undersecretary of State Sumner Welles in Washington, to discuss foreign policy. The two corresponded on numerous occasions. Browder's
State Department colloquies did more to enhance his already abundant self-
esteem than any other events since 1934. Browder felt vindicated by history.
Freed by the president himself, he believed he had become a recognized figure
in national politics. A significant measure of credulity crept in also, and a severe
error of judgment quickly followed.

Browder felt a controversial adviser of his stature might want to communicate
with the administration more discreetly. Shortly thereafter, mutual friends introduced him to Josephine Truslow Adams, an inveterate CPUSA sympathizer
whom the Communists valued for her famous family name and "impeccable
DAR Credentials."[3] She used a genuine, though tenuous, tie to Eleanor Roosevelt to dupe Browder into believing she enjoyed access to the president. Thinking he now had a pipeline to the White House, Browder sought appropriate
acclaim within international Communist circles. Moreover, the CPUSA's wartime isolation from Moscow and the Comintern's 1943 liquidation allowed him
the illusion that he commanded a truly autonomous Marxist organization.

In November 1943 Roosevelt and Winston Churchill held their first meeting
with Stalin at Teheran, Iran, where they set the date for invading Western Europe
and displayed harmony exceeding the most optimistic expectations. The three
leaders issued a deliberately vague declaration, pledging to work together during
the war and the forthcoming peace. Browder, who felt an overwhelming desire
to see the East–West alliance maintained, took the communiqué's statements
literally. He deduced correctly that the Allied leaders' accord indicated complete
agreement on subsequent wartime strategy, but he inferred erroneously that the
new consonance "could never have been hammered out in the absence" of an
"overall agreement on the world that is to emerge from the war." He insisted
that the declaration signified "a fundamental and long-term policy held *in common* [Browder's emphasis] by the three great powers signing it." At last the
capitalist democracies had accepted the Soviet Union "as a permanent member

of the family of nations.'' For Browder, postwar unity had become ''the only hope'' for continuing ''civilization in our time,'' and had to extend indefinitely.[4]

Browder decided his role resembled those of Communist partisan leaders in occupied Europe's underground Popular Fronts. He concluded it was his duty as an independent Communist boss to apply the forthcoming East–West détente to domestic politics. Although Browder possessed neither philosophical aptitude nor economics training, he resolved to blaze his own path as a pioneering Marxist theoretician. He launched what he considered his greatest contribution to his party's ideology: the Teheran Thesis.

Unity required prosperity, so Browder set forth a bold economic program. He noted that mobilization had doubled the size of America's economy, citing the 1943 national income figure of $188 billion. Military orders comprised nearly $90 billion of this, however, and the nation had to find substitute peacetime markets never imagined before. Browder proposed class collaboration to achieve a two-part program: expanding foreign sales geometrically and doubling the domestic adult wage earner's purchasing power. First, he envisioned a $40 billion scheme that would create ''great semi-governmental development corporations'' sending $6 billion in Anglo–American investments yearly to Latin America, Africa, and Europe, $20 billion to Asia, and $2 billion to the Soviet Union. At no time did he seem aware of Third World objections to economic imperialism, and he did not anticipate the postwar national liberation movements in European colonies. Second, the United States could invest in human capital through an array of social programs aimed at the vast majority who spent their entire income on life's necessities.[5]

Browder never foresaw the possibility of an extended Cold War or the prosperity it would bring to the United States. Like many Americans of his generation, he feared World War II's boom would presage a return to depression conditions. But beyond doubt, his Teheran projections represented wishful thinking. Political leaders, East and West, ignored them.

If the Teheran Thesis surprised Communists, Browder's next move shocked them profoundly. At a January 1944 National Committee meeting, he told his followers to stop banging their heads against the two-party system's ''stone wall.'' Because the Communists sought a long-term alliance with other reform forces, they would reorganize as a nonpartisan left-wing pressure group. Browder, who had not cleared the proposal with Moscow, transformed the CPUSA into the Communist Political Association (CPA), boasting that now the movement was ''standing on its own feet for the first time.''[6] Although Browder's action caught everyone by surprise, only William Z. Foster and Samuel A. Darcy objected. Browder spent 1944 idolized by his followers. They believed his bold, creative Marxism would lead them to full political legitimacy as a minor but integral part of the reformist New Deal coalition.

Browder's ambition finally exceeded his abilities. Seeking a mainstream national figure's stature in both foreign and domestic affairs, Browder began to display an ugly hubris. Believing he had earned personal greatness, he was determined to achieve it. Eleven months after the the the CPUSA became the CPA, disaster struck suddenly. Once Hitler's defeat removed the common enemy, the Soviet–American alliance crumbled rapidly. Just as the Cold War was beginning, the French Communist party's theoretical journal published a scathing attack on Browder's revisions of Marxism. Purportedly written by Jacques Duclos, the French CP's second highest figure, it praised Browder's perennial rival William Z. Foster and echoed criticisms Foster had made within the highest American Communist circles. Browder had sent the texts of intraparty debates to Moscow for aid in suppressing Foster's dissent. Publication virtually guaranteed that the Soviets had launched the attack.

Browder's followers quickly stampeded, but he defiantly refused to humble himself and admit heresies. Foster, smelling total victory, fanned the controversy and blocked face-saving compromises. In July the American Communists, perceiving Stalin's hand behind the message, deposed Browder and reconstituted the CPUSA. Expelled from the CPUSA in February 1946, Browder never gained reinstatement and left public life in 1950 as a political outcast. After the death of his wife in 1955, he lived alone, dying in Princeton on 27 June 1973.

Under Foster's leadership the party issued weekly blasts against ''Browderism'' and remained a political force until the 1948 election. Then it squandered its CIO following by trying to build a large antiwar party around former Vice President Henry Wallace. Overwhelming defeat brought isolation and invited attack. The Truman administration used the Smith Act to imprison virtually the entire CPUSA leadership for alleged advocacy of violent revolution. During the McCarthy period the party conducted its own intramural witch-hunt. Most leaders not in prison went underground, emerging only in the mid-1950s. Soviet Premier Nikita Khrushchev's 1956 revelation of Stalin's crimes and the Soviet Union's suppression of the Hungarian rebellion caused thousands to abandon the movement. A truncated CPUSA limped into the 1960s but was eclipsed by a broader, antihierarchical New Left. The Soviet Union's collapse opened archives revealing that the CPUSA enjoyed generous financial support until the end. A ghost of the CPUSA survived in the 1990s but its strength remained unknown because the party's national office refused to release membership figures.

Writers and commentators have related Browderism to Italy's, France's, and Spain's liberal ''Eurocommunist'' parties of the 1970s, which sought a democratic route to power. Actually, Browderism was a mutant form of Stalinism less akin to Eurocommunism than was once believed. Browder, more than any other individual, personified the CPUSA's most fundamental contradiction: the interplay of genuine American radicalism and subservience to the Soviet Union. Browder made major innovations in the party's tactics, but he always sought protection from left-wing rival Foster by going to Moscow for support. Browder's leadership, at times almost schizophrenic, tried to harmonize Stalinism with Great Plains populism. Browder's tragedy, and that of the CPUSA, was that attempting the impossible wrecked his career and helped destroy the party's influence, leaving a vacuum on America's political left that remained unfilled half a century later.

NOTES

1. *Daily Worker*, 6 July 1939.
2. Theodore Draper interview with Browder, 12 October 1955, p. 246 Theodore Draper Papers (Robert W. Woodruff Research Library, Emory University).
3. Joseph P. Lash, *Eleanor and Franklin* (New York, 1971), 905.
4. Earl Browder, *Teheran: Our Path in War and Peace* (New York, 1944), 30; and "Teheran: History's Greatest Turning Point" (speech delivered at Bridgeport, Conn., 12 December 1943), in Earl Browder Papers (Special Collections, Syracuse University).
5. Browder, *Teheran: Our Path*, 78, 81.
6. Earl Browder, *Teheran and America, Perspectives and Tasks* (New York, 1944), 43.

BIBLIOGRAPHY

Aronowitz, Stanley. *False Promises: The Shaping of American Working-Class Consciousness*. New York, 1973.

Baxendall, Rosalyn Fraad. *Words on Fire: The Biography and Writings of Elizabeth Gurley Flynn*. Newark, N.J., 1985.

Dennett, Eugene V. *Agitprop: The Life of an American Working-Class Radical*. Albany, N.Y., 1990.

Draper, Theodore. *American Communism and Soviet Russia: The Formative Period*. New York, 1960.

Healey, Dorothy, and Maurice Isserman. *Dorothy Healey Remembers: A Life in the American Communist Party*. New York, 1990.

Howe, Irving, and Lewis Coser. *The American Communist Party: A Critical History*. Boston, 1957.

Isserman, Maurice. *Which Side Were You On? The American Communist Party During World War II*. Middletown, Conn., 1982.

Jaffe, Philip J. *The Rise and Fall of American Communism*. New York, 1975.

Johanningsmeier, Edward P. *Forging American Communism: The Life of William Z. Foster*. Princeton, 1994.

Keeran, Roger. *The Communist Party and the Auto Workers Unions*. Bloomington, Ind., 1980.

Kelley, Robin D. G. *Hammer and Hoe: Alabama Communists During the Great Depression*. Chapel Hill, N.C., 1990.

Klehr, Harvey. *The Heyday of American Communism: The Depression Decade*. New York, 1984.

Kraditor, Aileen. *"Jimmy Higgins": The Mental World of the American Rank-and-File Communist, 1930–1958*. Westport, Conn., 1988.

Naison, Mark. *Communists in Harlem During the Great Depression*. Urbana, Ill., 1983.

Nelson, Steve, James R. Barrett, and Rob Ruck. *Steve Nelson, American Radical*. Pittsburgh, 1981.

Ottanelli, Fraser. *The Communist Party of the United States: From the Depression to World War II.* New Brunswick, N.J., 1991.

Ryan, James G. *Earl Browder: The Failure of American Communism.* Tuscaloosa, Ala., 1996.

Scales, Junius, and Richard Nickson. *Cause at Heart: A Former Communist Remembers.* Athens, Ga., 1987.

Shipman, Charles. *It Had to Be Revolution: Memoirs of an American Radical.* Ithaca, N.Y., 1993.

Starobin, Joseph R. *American Communism in Crisis, 1943–1957.* Berkeley, Calif., 1972.

Weinstein, James. *Ambiguous Legacy: The Left in American Politics.* New York, 1975.

Yoneda, Karl G. *Gambatte: Sixty Years' Struggle of a Kibei Worker.* Los Angeles, 1985.

César Chávez
and Migrant Workers

RICHARD GRISWOLD DEL CASTILLO

César Chávez rose from humble beginnings as a migrant farm worker to become the founder of a farm worker union that drew world attention to the plight of America's most oppressed group of workers. He established the Farm Workers Association (FWA) in California in 1962. After several years of organizing and five years of bitter strife, in 1970 he gained union recognition and labor contracts from grape growers in the San Joaquin Valley. Chávez became the best-known Mexican-American labor or reform leader of his generation, gathering support from organized labor, Protestant and Catholic churches, progressive intellectuals and students, and international labor organizations. His union went on to improve wages and working conditions for all farm workers by setting industry standards. Chávez's struggle to force agribusiness to recognize the basic rights of farm workers continued throughout his life. Even after his death in 1993, he remains an inspiring example of a leader who aroused America's conscience regarding the poor.

César Estrada Chávez was born on 31 March 1927 in Yuma, Arizona, the child of Mexican-born parents, Librado and Juana Estrada, who had settled on a small farm. He grew up, with his four brothers and sisters nourished by the values of his family and the rural Mexican community. From his mother he learned the importance of nonviolence and self-sacrifice, and from his grandmother the values of the Catholic faith. As a youth, he experienced racial discrimination in school, and he absorbed from the Mexican community the folklore of their struggle against oppression in Mexico during the Revolution. In 1939, because of the depression, the Chávez family lost their farm and joined the migrant stream flowing west into California.

For the next ten years, the Chávez family worked as migrants, moving from farm to farm, following the crops up and down California and taking odd jobs to supplement their income when there was no farm work. During this period César encountered the conditions that he would dedicate the rest of his life to changing: wretched migrant camps, corrupt labor contractors, meager wages for backbreaking work, and bitter racism.

In 1942 César's father was injured in a car accident and unable to work for a month. César decided to quit school (he had completed the eighth grade) and work full-time in the fields with his brothers and sisters to help support the family. Chávez's migrant period introduced him to labor organizing. While moving from crop to crop, his father had joined several unions—the Tobacco Workers, the Cannery Workers, the National Farm Labor Union (NFLU), the Packing House Workers, and the Agricultural Workers Organizing Committee (AWOC). The family participated in many strikes during the late 1930s and 1940s and became very active in union activities, although they never served in a leadership capacity.

Chávez joined the Navy in 1944, and like thousands of other Mexican Americans in the service, he discovered a wider world. He went to San Diego for training and learned that Mexicans were not the only ones discriminated against because of their nationality or language. Sent to the South Pacific, he served as a coxswain's apprentice on Saipan and Guam, assisting in ferrying ship pilots in and out of the harbor.

When Chávez was discharged from the Navy in 1946, he returned to the family home in Delano California, and resumed work in the fields. On 22 October 1948, he married Helen Fabela, whom he had first met when his family had passed through Delano following the crops. She had been born in Brawley, California, in 1928, to Mexican campesino parents. Her family also had been migrant workers during the 1930s and 1940s. Helen was an important partner to her husband as he began to fulfill his dream of doing something to improve the lot of the farm workers. The Chávezes eventually settled in San Jose, where César worked for a lumber company, and began raising a family of eight children.

César Chávez's introduction to community organizing began in 1952 when he met Father Donald McDonnell, a Catholic priest who was trying to build a parish in the San Jose barrio of Sal Si Puedes. From McDonnell, Chávez learned the church's social doctrines on labor organizing and social justice; he also read the *Life of Gandhi*, a book that made a deep impression on him. Mahatma Gandhi's values struck a responsive chord: the complete sacrifice of oneself for others, the severe self-discipline, and the self-abnegation to achieve a higher good. These values Mexican farm workers could understand, not only in religious terms but also in their daily experience. Especially important to Chávez's moral development was Gandhi's teaching on nonviolence, which echoed his mother's admonitions and teachings. The philosophy of nonviolence later became the hallmark of Chávez's leadership of the farm worker movement.

Another organizer who was at work in the Sal Si Puedes barrio in San Jose also changed young Chávez's life. In 1952 Fred Ross had been sent as an organizer for Saul Alinsky's Community Service Organization (CSO). Chávez was genuinely impressed by Ross's sincerity and his message. He talked about local concerns as well as the CSO's advocacy of Mexican rights in police brutality cases. The night they met, Fred Ross wrote in his diary: "I think I've found the guy I'm looking for." Chávez recalled, "My suspicions were erased. As time went on, Fred became sort of my hero. I saw him organize, and I wanted to learn."[1]

Soon Chávez was working full-time for the CSO. In it he learned an important lesson that became the foundation of his organizing style: helping people and expecting their help in return was a way to build a strong organization. Chávez worked in many of the small towns of the San Joaquin Valley and eventually rose to executive director of the CSO in California. While working for this organization, he recruited Dolores Huerta, Antonio Orendain, and Gil Padilla, some of his first lieutenants in founding the UFW. In Los Angeles, Chávez met and worked with the early founders of the Mexican American Political Association (MAPA), Eduardo Quevedo and Bert Corona. They had formed an association in 1959 to advance the Chicano community's political interests in the state. In the early 1960s the CSO, MAPA, and the Viva Kennedy Clubs became important training grounds for young Mexican Americans who were self-consciously beginning to call themselves Chicanos, a slang term that for decades had been used by natives to denigrate newly arrived Mexican immigrants.

At its 1962 annual convention, Chávez proposed that the CSO support a union movement for farm workers. The board refused to back his project, arguing that the CSO was a civil rights, not a labor, organization. Chávez then resigned in order to devote himself to building an independent farm workers' union. Soon after his resignation, AWOC, an AFL-CIO farm union organization, offered him a job as a paid organizer; he turned it down because he wanted to be able to work with "no strings attached." In 1962 the Chávez family moved to Delano, a small town in the San Joaquin Valley, where César began recruiting efforts. On 30 September, Chávez's Farm Workers Association (FWA) held its first convention, with 150 delegates in attendance. It was at this meeting that the organization adopted its distinctive union flag, a black eagle on a red field. For the next three years, Chávez slowly built up the membership of the FWA. Using his CSO training, he emphasized the service aspect of his organization. He traveled extensively, talking to the workers to see what they thought about a union and the services it should provide. He went out into the fields, camps, and colonias, distributing questionnaires that people could fill out and mail in, and talking to thousands of workers.

Prior to Chávez's full-time commitment to farm labor organizing, there had been a long history of struggle in the fields. One of the earliest agricultural unions, organized by Mexicans in California, was the Imperial Valley Workers' Union (La Unión de Trabajadores del Valle Imperial). In 1928, with more than 2,700 members, the union went on strike, attempting to increase the piece rate for cantaloupe picking, reform the labor contractor system, and get accident insurance for workers. The growers tried to end the strike by getting court orders against picketing, organizing armed vigilante groups, urging the police to make mass arrests, and red-baiting the union leadership with hysterical media accounts. Within a year, the growers defeated the union. In the process, they established a pattern for handling future farm labor strikes that lasted well into the 1970s.

Despite this early setback, California became a focus for labor organizing activity in the 1930s. In 1933, for instance, 5,000 Mexican berry pickers in El Monte organized a union, the Confederación de Uniones de Campesinos y Obreros Mexicanos (CUCOM), which went on strike to raise hourly pay for pickers. Strikers were joined by a more militant, Communist-led labor union that included some Mexican organizers, the Cannery and Agricultural Workers' Industrial Union (C&AWIU), with 7,000 workers. Because the growers were Japanese farmers who feared a nativist backlash, the Mexican union won its wage demands.

The C&AWIU moved on to organize cotton workers in the San Joaquin Valley. The result was a prolonged and violent strike in 1933. In that strike 12,000 cotton pickers, 75 percent of whom were Mexicans, confronted the powerful San Joaquin Valley Agricultural Labor Bureau, representing the cotton growers. Events followed a familiar pattern: evictions, court orders, arrests, and violence. The growers hired goons and strikebreakers, who surrounded union meetings at the towns of Pixley and Arvin and killed three farm workers. During the strike, hospitals refused to admit wounded and sick strikers and their families. People starved because there were no relief or charity funds available; nine infants died of malnutrition. When the violence and suffering could no longer be ignored, state and federal officials intervened to negotiate a compromise settlement. The strike ended.

Throughout the 1930s, hundreds of agricultural strikes occurred. Many were spontaneous walkouts in protest over the numerous injustices. During the postwar years the American Federation of Labor (AFL) organized the National Farm Labor Union (NFLU). Led by Hank Hasiwar and Ernesto Galarza, the union launched a number of strikes throughout California. Along with several thousand Mexican workers, the Chávez family participated in a cotton strike the union organized in 1948. A few months earlier, the union had begun a strike against the DiGiorgio Corporation, a family-run corporation that was one of the largest fruit growers in the United States. The struggle against the DiGiorgios lasted two and a half years, until it was broken by the use of a government injunction under the Taft-Hartley Act, the recruitment of braceros as strikebreakers, and red-baiting by the California Senate Committee on Un-American Activities.

This was the history of farm labor organizing that Chávez sought to reverse during the 1960s. His Farm Workers Association grew, nourished by personal sacrifice and dogged commitment. The Chávez family frequently went without food and clothing to pay union expenses. He felt that the union would be stronger if, in its early years, it relied only on its membership for financial support. Chávez was the only farm worker union official in the nation whose salary came 100 percent from the farm workers themselves. By August 1965 his faith in the union was beginning to earn rewards. The union numbered 1,000 dues-paying members and had more than 50 locals.

From the beginning Chávez had thought of "La Causa" as a movement that would be motivated in part by appeals to race and nationality. When he had worked for the Community Service Organization, he had confronted the issue of Mexican chauvinism and had been uncompromising in fighting for the inclusion of blacks from the organization. Although the staff and hundreds of volunteer workers were predominantly Anglo, the core leadership of the NFWA was Mexican American. The union's soul remained with the Mexican-American workers.

After a series of small strikes that concessions for agricultural workers in McFarland and Porterville, the UFW had its baptism by fire. The union had been asked to join the Filipino grape workers who were on strike for higher wages. After an emotional meeting, on 15 September 1965, Mexican Independence Day, the UFW members voted to join them. They needed little convincing; the members seemed spontaneously to join a struggle that they had long considered their own. It was also at the outset of this struggle that the organization changed its name, reflecting its ambition, and became the National Farm Workers Association (NFWA).

The Delano grape strike was the largest in the history of California. The region covered a 400-square-mile area and involved thousands of workers. The job of organizing picket lines to patrol the fields fell to inexperienced farm workers and urban volunteers who worked side by side. The sheer dimensions of the ranches and farms made it impossible constantly to maintain pickets at all the entrances. Inevitably, scab workers (called *esquiroles*) found their way into the fields, and the union had to find a way of convincing them to join the strike. The picket line then became a noisy place. The picketers cajoled, argued, pleaded, orated, and shamed the scabs in Spanish, Tagalog, and English, trying to get them to join the strike. Picketers walked the dusty borders of the fields holding hand-painted signs—"Huelga," "Delano Grape Striker," "Victoria!," accompanied by the NFWA black eagle.

Whatever its practical effect, Chávez saw the picket line as offering an educational and recruiting experience, and as the place where one could feel the confrontation between the worker and the grower. It became a way of building a strong membership. He would later say; "The picket line is where a man makes his commitment, and it is irrevocable; the longer he's on the picket line, the stronger the commitment. . . . The picket line is a beautiful thing, because it does something to a human being."[2]

From the beginning of the strike, Chávez had emphasized the importance of nonviolence as a strategy. In doing so, he met the Mexican cultural belief in machismo head-on, exhorting the volunteers and picketers:

If someone commits violence against us, it is much better—if we can—not to react against the violence but to react in such a way as to get closer to our goal. People don't like to see a non-violent movement subjected to violence, and there's a lot of support across the country for nonviolence. That's the key point we have going for us. We can turn the world if we can do it non-violently.[3]

Chávez's main activity during the early months of the strike was giving speeches at various college campuses across the state to galvanize support for the striking farm workers. The national news media helped to generate sympathy for the strike. Television news crews visited Delano and filmed the drama of the confrontations at the picket line. The NBC special ''The Harvest of Shame,'' depicting the tragic conditions of migrant labor in the United States, had begun to make people more aware of the farm workers' plight. Reporters from the big-city newspapers and national magazines traveled to Delano to interview Chávez, other union officials, and the growers. Chávez spoke about how the farm work-ers were fighting for their civil rights and economic justice, a message that neatly fit the growing national concern with civil rights. Publicity became increasingly important when the union decided to launch a boycott to put pressure on the growers to recognize the union and sign contracts. They targeted the most iden-tifiable grape products from the largest Delano growers. When Walter Reuther visited Delano in December 1965, the grape strike and boycott had become a national news item.

Other dramatic events added momentum to the strike and boycott. Three months after Reuther's visit, on 16 March 1966, Chávez organized a march from Delano to Sacramento to dramatize the strike and win the support of the governor, Edmund ''Pat'' Brown. Chávez marched with the procession as it left Delano. They carried the American and Mexican flags, the NFWA and AWOC banners, and a flag with the image of the Virgin of Guadalupe, the patron saint of Mexico. The march helped recruit more members and spread the spirit of the strike. As they passed through each small farming town, hundreds of workers greeted them. Others joined the march to carry the flags to the next town.

Just prior to the end of the pilgrimage, the first grower, Schenley, announced that it was willing to sign a contract with the NFWA. On 7 April the agreement was made public. In a triumphant mood, the pilgrimage ended a few days later on the steps of the state capitol. The union and its supporters had won their first victory and demonstrated the power of their cause. This marked the first time in American history that a grassroots farm labor union had gained recognition by a corporation. (In Hawaii, some years earlier, the Longshoremen's Union had won a contract for pineapple workers.)

The other large growers remained unsigned. The most important was the DiGiorgio Fruit Corporation, which controlled thousands of acres of pear, plum, apricot, and citrus trees, and marketed its products under the S&W Foods and TreeSweet labels. Robert DiGiorgio, the patriarch of the family, sat on the board of directors of the Bank of America, and the family had access to capital and government. The family, which had broken strikes and unions since the 1930s, had come to symbolize the concentrated power of the growers—so much so that in his novel *The Grapes of Wrath*, John Steinbeck had used the DiGiorgios as a model for the grower named "Gregorio."

Chávez was convinced the boycott could break the corporation's grip on the industry. He rallied hundreds of volunteers who remembered the previous struggles against the DiGiorgios to enlist in the boycott drive. Within a short time, the company agreed to enter into negotiations regarding an election, but Chávez broke them off when company guards attacked a picketer at Sierra Vista. When negotiations finally resumed, Chávez discovered that DiGiorgio had invited the Teamsters Union to recruit among vineyard workers. Thus, beginning in mid-1966, the two unions began an on-and-off jurisdictional fight that lasted more than ten years and resulted in violence, injury, and deaths.

About this time, in order to consolidate its power, the AWOC and the NFWA formally merged to form one united union within the AFL-CIO. Although some debate about the wisdom of this move occurred, not a single farm worker voted against it. Under the final merger agreement, a new organization, the United Farm Workers Organizing Committee (eventually to become the United Farm Workers of America, AFL-CIO), was formed with Chávez as its director. The UFW became a full member of the AFL-CIO and, as a result, received millions of dollars of emergency aid during the early years of struggle. This was the first time that a predominantly Mexican union had been incorporated within mainstream organized labor. Over the years the relationship proved to be mutually supportive, and the UFW never seemed to be hampered in its independence of action.

During the next four years the UFWOC grew in strength, nourished by the support of millions of sympathetic Americans who sacrificed for the farm workers. Hundreds of student volunteers lived on poverty wages in the big cities to organize an international boycott of table grapes. Scores of priests, nuns, ministers, and church members donated time, money, facilities, and labor to the farm workers' cause. Organized labor pumped millions of dollars into the UFWOC strike fund. Millions of Americans gave up eating table grapes. All this was inspired by the example of Chávez, a soft-spoken, humble leader who quietly worked to revolutionize grower–worker relations.

In 1967 the union moved from its cramped offices on Albany Street in Delano to new buildings on land it had purchased with the help of private donations and contributions from AFL-CIO affiliates. The new headquarters, known as "The Forty Acres," was located near the city dump on forty acres of alkali land. Volunteers had built a complex of buildings, including a service and administrative center, a medical clinic, and a cooperative gas station. It became the center of the farm workers union movement in California until the union moved its headquarters to Keane, a small town just outside of Bakersfield, in 1970.

On 1 April 1967, the newspapers announced the signing of a union contract between DiGiorgio Fruit Corporation and the UFWOC. It included wage increases for workers, set up a special fund for health and welfare benefits, provided for unemployment compensation, and specified that hiring would be done through the union labor hall. UFWOC strikes continued against other Delano growers, and by October seven more wineries had signed contracts with the union.

During a strike against the Guimarra Corporation, Chávez began a fast to protest the mounting talk of violence. In characteristic fashion, he told no one. He did not know how long it was going to last. On the fourth day, he decided to hold a meeting of the strikers to announce his intentions: ''I told them I thought they were discouraged, because they were talking about short cuts, about violence. They were getting so mad with the growers, they couldn't be effective anymore.''[4]

After the meeting with the membership, Chávez walked to The Forty Acres. He set up his monastic cell in the storage room of the service station with a small cot and a few religious articles. Soon hundreds of farm worker families began appearing, to show their support for Chávez and to join the daily mass that he attended. A huge tent city housing thousands of farm workers sprang up surrounding the gas station. There was a tremendous outpouring of emotion during the masses. Every day hundreds stood in line to meet and talk to Chávez.

The national media helped to make the 1968 fast a major event. As the fast went into its twentieth day, letters of support came from congressmen and senators, union and religious leaders. During the fast, Chávez would not let a doctor examine him because he felt that ''Without the element of risk, I would be hypocritical. The whole essence of penance . . . .would be taken away.''[5] When Chávez finally decided to end his fast, on the twenty-fifth day, he asked Senator Robert Kennedy to be present. On 11 March 1968 a mass was celebrated at a county park with more than 4,000 farm workers in attendance, along with reporters from the major papers and television networks. The mass was said on the back of a flatbed truck. Chávez was too weak to stand or speak, so Jim Drake read a message he had written earlier. It was a powerful expression of his spiritual commitment.

Our struggle is not easy. Those who oppose our cause are rich and powerful, and they have many allies in high places. We are poor. Our allies are few. But we have something the rich do not own. We have our own bodies and spirits and the justice of our cause as our weapons.

When we are really honest with ourselves, we must admit that our lives are all that really belong to us. So it is how we use our lives that determines what kind of men we are. It is my deepest belief that only by giving of our lives do we find life.

I am convinced that the truest act of courage, the strongest act of manliness is to sacrifice ourselves for others in a totally nonviolent struggle for justice. To be a man is to suffer for others. God help us to be men![6]

Over the years Chávez engaged in many other fasts, each for a specific purpose. His followers soon learned the depth of his commitment to the principle of nonviolence, so that to violate that code was personally to affront Chávez. For the most part, his followers respected their leader's philosophy and abjured violence in deference to Chávez's moral authority.

In the late spring of 1969 the grape harvest was about to begin. To rally support for the strike and boycott, Chávez decided to organize a march through the heart of the Coachella and Imperial valleys to the U.S.–Mexican border as a way to call attention to the growers' use of undocumented immigrants from Mexico as strikebreakers. On 10 May 1969, Chávez began the march with an outdoor mass celebrated in a labor camp in Indio. As in the 1966 march to Sacramento, the Coachella pilgrimage proved a tremendous organizing tactic. Hundreds of farm workers and supporters joined in the colorful procession, which included the Reverend Ralph Abernathy, who joined the march on the eighth day and pledged the support of the Southern Christian Leadership Conference; Senator Walter Mondale; famous Hollywood actors; and Chicano student activists. The march dramatized the strike to hundreds of Mexican workers who were in the fields as the marchers passed. In the evening, masses, speeches, and theater performances educated them about the issues involved. The march lasted nine days and ended in Calexico, the border town across from Mexicali, in Baja California, where Chávez gave a speech calling for Mexican workers to join the strike and support the UFWOC.

By 1969 Chávez had expanded the boycott to include all California table grapes. All over the country volunteers were picketing supermarkets that sold grapes. Shipments of California table grapes to the cities of Boston, New York, Philadelphia, Chicago, Detroit, Montreal, and Toronto practically stopped. Grape sales fell and millions of pounds rotted in cold storage sheds. In reaction, the growers filed a lawsuit charging that they had lost more than $25 million since the beginning of the boycott. In desperation, they turned to the Teamsters and held meetings to try to work out a contract that would bring peace to the fields. But the Teamsters were leery of entering the fields again, given their previous experience: the growers had reneged on a sweetheart deal when the pressure had become too great.

Despite the support of the U.S. Department of Defense for grape purchases, the boycott pressures became unbearable for the growers. In the late spring of 1969 some influential growers in the Coachella Valley signed contracts with the UFW. By June 1970 the majority of table grape growers who were still resisting unionization were in the Delano area. Finally, through the efforts of a committee organized by the National Conference of Catholic Bishops, twenty-three companies, including the Guimarra Corporation, agreed to begin negotiations to recognize the UFW.

On 29 July 1970, twenty-six Delano growers filed into Reuther Hall on The Forty Acres to sign contracts. The contracts raised the workers' wages to $1.80 per hour. In addition, the growers agreed to donate 10 cents an hour to the

Robert Kennedy Health and Welfare Fund. The contract provided for all hiring to be through the union hall and for the protection of workers from certain pesticides. The victory in Delano meant that almost 85 percent of all table grape growers in California were under a union contract. This was a victory without precedent in the history of American agriculture. Never had an agricultural workers' union managed such a sweeping success.

Following the UFW triumph, a new and formidable challenge to the farm workers arose, this time from the Teamsters and growers in the Salinas Valley, who were conspiring to undercut the UFW's newly won recognition. The Teamsters organization had several times before threatened to expand its operations to organize fieldworkers. In 1970 the Teamsters and the UFW were both members of the AFL-CIO, so this announcement by the Teamsters amounted to a raid on the UFW's jurisdiction. The Teamsters had signed sweetheart contracts giving the vegetable growers almost all that they wanted, while sacrificing workers' benefits. Evidence of collusion abounded. The Teamsters had signed the contracts without even negotiating wage rates for the workers.

Quickly, Chávez moved to counter. He and the rest of the UFW staff moved the headquarters of the union to Salinas and began organizing a strike. He traveled to the AFL-CIO convention in Chicago and attempted, with no success, to get the national organization publically to condemn the Teamsters. Throughout the month of August, Chávez worked to keep the pressure on the growers with Teamster contracts by selective picketing of the largest corporations. Yet about 170 vegetable growers stubbornly refused to switch from the Teamsters to the UFW. Chávez called for a general strike.

During this struggle with the Teamsters, Chávez also led the union to fight against a newly passed farm labor law in Arizona that outlawed the boycott and limited strikes, much as had been advocated by the Nixon administration. To raise people's awareness of the necessity to repeal the law and recall the governor who had signed it, Chávez began a fast. For twenty-four days he fasted and directed the recall campaign from a small room in Saint Rita's Center in a Mexican barrio of Phoenix.

That fall the California growers tried to pass similar legislation to hamstring the farm labor movement. They sponsored Proposition 22, an initiative that would outlaw boycotting and limit secret-ballot elections to full-time, nonseasonal employees. In California, Chávez followed the strategy he had adopted in Arizona of getting citizens registered to vote as well as informing them about the proposition's threat to workers. During the fall the "No on 22" campaign gathered momentum through the use of human billboards. On 7 November 1972, Proposition 22 was soundly defeated by a margin of 58 percent. The UFW, through its boycott strategy, had proved that organized farm workers were a serious political force.

Meanwhile, the lettuce boycott and struggle with the Teamsters continued. On 15 April 1973, grape growers in the San Joaquin Valley announced that they had signed contracts with the Teamsters. Chávez immediately called for a strike and pulled most of the UFW workers from the fields. The Teamsters recruited goons, and soon violence exploded, with two union members being killed. Finally, on 1 September, the UFW called off the strike and resumed the boycott, which now included Gallo Winery after it had signed a contract with the Teamsters. The decision to abandon the strike was motivated in part by Chávez's desire to avoid future violence but also by his deeply felt conviction that the boycott would be more effective than a strike. The strategy worked. The Teamsters finally gave up their campaign to organize fieldworkers and take over UFW contracts late in 1974. Nevertheless, the grape and vegetable growers had contracts in place that would not expire for several years. Until then Chávez had to decide on a strategy to keep his union together.

In 1975 Chávez decided to intensify the boycott against Gallo. The AFL-CIO had agreed to support the UFW lettuce and grape boycotts if the union dropped the secondary boycott of Safeway and A&P supermarkets. Gallo, which had signed a Teamster contract after its UFW contract had expired, was highly vulnerable to a boycott. On 22 February, Chávez organized a 110-mile march from San Francisco to Modesto, home of Gallo Wineries. More than 15,000 supporters ended the march a week later. The tremendous turnout proved again that the UFW enjoyed much popular support.

The message was not lost on the newly elected governor of California, Jerry Brown, a son of former Governor Edmund Brown, whom some considered almost an antipolitician, a perfect type to be successful in the post–Watergate era. Brown had supported the farm workers' cause and had marched with them in the Coachella Valley. As California's secretary of state in 1972, he had helped the UFW challenge Proposition 22. His election to the governorship in November 1974 signaled a new opportunity for the UFW to shape public policy regarding labor relations in the state.

Late in 1974 Chávez and the UFW proposed a state agricultural law they hoped might help reverse the decline of the union's strength, provided the law guaranteed the rights to boycott and to strike, and for seasonal workers to vote in union elections. Initially, the growers opposed all of these conditions, but by 1975, after the years of strikes, jurisdictional violence, and boycotts, they were willing to concede these points. After considerable political maneuvering, the California Agricultural Labor Relations Act was passed in May 1975, the first such law in the continental United States to govern farm labor organizing (farm workers in Hawaii had a similar law). The law gave the UFW what it wanted— secret-ballot elections, the right to boycott, voting rights for migrant seasonal workers, and control over the timing of elections. The growers were convinced that the law would end boycotts and labor disruptions that had cost them millions of dollars in profits.

The struggle with the Teamsters for representation of farm workers continued under the supervision of the state agency. Governor Brown supported Chávez and the UFW by appointing a pro-UFW majority to the Agricultural Labor Relations Board (ALRB), the body that was to oversee the elections and rule on complaints. A major controversy arose over the access rules for unions. The UFW wanted unlimited right to enter ranches and farms to talk to workers about the union, whereas the growers wanted total control over access, giving preference to the Teamsters. Another problem was funding. The ALRB ran out of money at the beginning of 1976 and suspended operations for five months, until the legislature could vote for a regular appropriation.

Chávez attacked the issues of funding and access by appealing directly to the voters. In politics, as in union organizing, he preferred grassroots and populist methods. In a massive initiative campaign, the UFW sent out its workers and gathered over 700,000 signatures in only twenty-nine days. The UFW-sponsored initiative, known as Proposition 14, provided for guaranteed funding for the ALRB and assured union organizers access to workers. Because of an advertising campaign funded by oil companies and agricultural corporations, Proposition 14 lost by a two-to-one margin in the November 1976 elections. The public seemed to have been convinced that the funding of the ALRB was already a moot point and that the access provision was a threat to property rights.

Some observers regarded the defeat of Proposition 14 as a turning point in Chávez's ability to mobilize public support for the farm workers and their union. The promise of the ALRB as a means to help organize farm workers rapidly disappeared. The ALRB was increasingly controlled by Republican pro-grower interests, who consistently ruled against the many grievances that were brought before it by the union.

There were some victories. One was the result of years of lobbying and complex legal maneuvers: the abolition of *el cortito*, the short-handled hoe, in 1975. For decades the growers had required fieldworkers to use this tool, which forced them to bend over while working long hours. Thousands of farm workers permanently damaged their backs and spent the rest of their lives in disabling pain. Chávez and the UFW had opposed the use of *el cortito* because of its damaging effect on the worker's health. Together with attorneys for California Rural Legal Aid (CRLA), they won its abolition.

In terms of union building, the period following the passage of the California Farm Labor Act was one of growth in membership and contracts. The UFW had won almost two-thirds of the elections after 1975, and in March 1977, admitting that they were beaten, the Teamsters said they would not contest future elections. The dues-paying membership of the UFW soared to over 100,000 by 1978.

It would seem that the union had attained a degree of organizational success. But there were troubling signs that all was not well. A number of long-time staff members left the union, some expressing their unhappiness with Chávez's leadership and others admitting to being burned out by working long hours for almost no pay. In March 1979, Jerry Cohen, the UFW's chief attorney, left after the executive board defeated his proposal to allow his staff to be paid salaries rather than in-kind benefits. A few months later, Marshall Ganz, who helped organize the lettuce strike, and Jim Drake, another long-time organizer, left the union, along with a number of other union leaders from the Salinas area, over a dispute having to do with union policy. The newspaper and journal reactions to these resignations was to magnify them as signaling the end of the Chávez-led union.

Chávez had decided to reorganize the union, and some staff members left because they disagreed with his strategies. In late 1975 he called for a conference to discuss ideas for modernizing the union and invited several management consultants to union headquarters for staff training sessions. As part of the modernization drive, the union began computerizing all its records and purchased a microwave communications system so that it would not be dependent on public telephones.

Despite these measures, the UFW lost momentum. In 1984 only fifteen of the seventy grape growers in the Delano area were under a UFW contract. The union was winning fewer and fewer elections: in 1976 it had won 276, but in the years since, it had won only 56. Union membership dropped to less than 12,000 active members in the mid-1980s. There were fewer and fewer strikes, and the UFW reduced the number of organizers in the fields, hoping to encourage more local leadership and initiative.

Chávez blamed the decline on the ALRB, which was firmly in the hands of the grower interests. He believed growers used the Board to stifle unionization. The ALRB took an average of 348 days to settle disputes over contested elections and about half as long to render a decision on whether to litigate an unfair labor practice. As of 1984, the ALRB had not rendered any award for violation of the labor law. Under such circumstances, Chávez reverted to the boycott as the best weapon to force the growers to sign contracts. On 12 June 1984, the UFW launched a new grape boycott, but its objective was unclear and public support was erratic. The UFW had sponsored more than fifty boycotts over the years, leaving the public confused as to what was and wasn't still being boycotted. For the new, or any, boycott to succeed, the union needed to undertake a tremendous educational campaign.

At the same time, the UFW expanded its interests to environmental concerns, an issue increasingly important to the nation's middle class. The UFW produced a movie, *The Wrath of Grapes*, with graphic footage showing the birth defects and high rates of cancer that pesticide poisoning produced among farm workers and consumers. In 1987 and 1988, Chávez traveled to Midwestern and Eastern cities, where grapes were viewed as a luxury item and where union support had always been strongest. To call attention to pesticide use, Chávez began a fast at mid-night on 16 July 1988. The fast went largely unnoticed by the public until the children of Robert Kennedy visited Chávez to lend their support. Finally, on Sunday, 22 August, Chávez gave up his water-only fast. As an expression of support, Jesse Jackson, a presidential candidate, and actors Martin Sheen and Robert Blake vowed to continue the fast for three days, to keep alive the ''chain of suffering.'' Thereafter, for several months, individuals joined three-day mini-fasts to demonstrate their support for the union.

During the thirty-six-day fast, Chávez issued a statement that summarized his commitment to the union and the boycott:

As I look back at this past year, I can see many events that precipitated the fast, including the terrible suffering of farm workers and their children, the crushing of farm worker rights, the denial of fair and free elections and the death of good-faith bargaining in California agriculture. All of these events are connected with the great cause of justice for farm worker families.

Until his death in 1993, Chávez had the same qualities of character that had brought victory in the earlier boycott. Most of all, he remained tenacious in his leadership, despite an apparent change in the activist mood of the country. He believed that the modern boycott could be won with an alliance among Latinos, blacks, and other minorities, plus allies in labor and the Catholic Church. He also had faith that for the generation of activists from the 1960s and 1970s, the boycott would become a social habit. By 1991, statistics on grape consumption seemed to bear out his optimism. During the crucial period from May to August 1990, grapes delivered for sale declined in twelve major cities. In New York City grape consumption was down 74 percent; it declined by 37 percent in Los Angeles and by 36 percent in San Francisco. The UFW could cite official statistics showing that the growers were selling grapes at a loss.

Chávez was confident about the ultimate success of the UFW struggle and remained so until his unexpected death in Yuma, Arizona, on 23 April 1993. He had been coordinating the boycott and fighting legal battles against the growers, traveling to raise money, and fasting for spiritual enlightenment. The tremendous outpouring of condolences and support that followed his death bore testimony to his importance as a leader who touched the conscience of America.

Admirers correctly identified Chávez as a civil rights leader as much as a labor leader. Indeed, his crusade had been part of a worldwide commitment to human and civil rights, and its strategy and appeal had been borrowed from, and had informed, the American civil rights movement. Chávez knew and communicated with many of the leaders of the civil rights movement. The emphasis on nonviolence within the farm workers' movement was reinforced by the civil rights struggle in the South. The fight for labor rights, Chávez reminded supporters, was a fight to enlarge the rights of all workingmen and workingwomen.

Chávez's strength derived from principles he espoused and practiced: self-sacrifice for others, struggle despite overwhelming odds, respect for all races and religions, nonviolence, belief in a divine soul and a moral order, rejection of materialism, faith in the moral superiority of the poor, and a central belief in justice. He embodied the struggles of a people, *la raza*, to achieve a better life in America. Through the UFW and his own example, he made the nation aware of the plight of Mexican Americans and the sufferings of farm workers. However diminished the union has become in numbers and in negotiating power, the memory of the man and the continued force of the movement that he, more than anyone else, had founded attest to the power of collective action in expanding the nation's social consciousness.

NOTES

1. Jacques E. Levy, *César Chávez: Autobiography of La Causa* (New York, 1975), 99, 102.
2. Ronald Taylor, *Chávez and the Farm Workers* (Boston, 1975), 136.
3. Levy, *César Chávez*, 196.
4. Ibid., 273.
5. Ibid., 285.
6. Ibid., 286.
7. *Los Angeles Times*, 23 August 1988.

BIBLIOGRAPHY

Day, Mark. *Forty Acres: César Chávez and the Farm Workers*. New York, 1971.
Dunne, John. *Delano, Story of the California Grape Strike*. New York, 1967.
Fusco, Paul, and George D. Horowitz. *La Causa!: The California Grape Strike*. New York, 1970.
Kushner, Sam. *The Long Road to Delano: A Century of Farmworker Struggle*. New York, 1975.
Levy, Jacques E. *César Chávez: Autobiography of La Causa*. New York, 1975.
London, Joan, and Henry Anderson. *So Shall Ye Reap: The Story of César Chávez and the Farm Workers' Movement*. New York, 1970.
Matthiessen, Peter. *Sal Si Puedes: César Chávez and the New American Revolution*. New York, 1969.
Meister, Dick, and Anne Loftis. *A Long Time Coming: The Struggle to Unionize America's Farm Workers*. New York, 1977.
Nelson, Eugene. *Huelga: The First Hundred Days of the Great Delano Grape Strike*. Delano, Calif., 1966.
Taylor, Ronald. *Chávez and the Farm Workers*. Boston, 1975.

Barry Commoner
and Environmentalism

DOUGLAS H. STRONG

A stylized portrait of Barry Commoner graced the front cover of *Time* magazine early in 1970. Sun streamed onto verdant fields next to one side of his face; gloomy clouds hovered over smokestacks and polluted water on the other side, depicting the threat to America's land, air, and water. *Time* hoped that "a tiny band of ecologists" could enlighten the public about the plight of the environment and singled out Commoner, who, it stated, "has probably done more than any other U.S. scientist to speak out and awaken a sense of urgency about the declining quality of life." The magazine called him the "Paul Revere of Ecology," "a professor with a class of millions," and a person who put his faith in people's ability "to reform when confronted by compelling facts."[1]

The year 1970 represented the high-water mark of environmentalism. Biologist Victor Scheffer stated succinctly that its goal is "to preserve the diversity and wondrous beauty of our world while recognizing that billions must steadily draw upon its substance for survival."[2] Environmentalism grew out of "conservation," the earlier efforts to preserve and use natural resources wisely. Although traditional "conservation" continued, it did not address the emerging threats to the global biosphere, such as explosive population growth and the poisoning of the air and water.

The year 1970 also marked the peak of Commoner's influence as a scientist and educator. He first gained national attention through his efforts to end atmospheric testing of nuclear weapons during the late 1950s and early 1960s. As a result of this experience, he called for fuller disclosure of scientific information by scientists and governments so that the public could make informed judgments on which technologies to pursue and which to avoid. In *The Closing Circle* (1971), he argued that technologies developed since World War II posed the principal threat to natural ecological cycles. Commoner blamed this problem on the single-minded, short-term pursuit of profit and expressed the belief that it could be solved through "democratic socialism," a system in which social rather than private investment decisions prevail.[3] Although he failed in his bid to establish a new political party in the 1980 presidential election, he remained dedicated to finding ways to meet human needs while minimizing damage to the environment.

Commoner was born on 28 May, 1917 to Isidore and Goldie Yarmolinsky Commoner, hardworking Russian immigrants. He grew up in a poor neighborhood in Brooklyn, New York.[4] An uncle and his poet wife who lived with Commoner's family for a time often invited their literary friends to visit. When Commoner researched a school assignment on Cotton Mather, his uncle provided access to the stacks of the New York Public Library, where he was chief of the Slavonic division. He also gave him a microscope. On weekends while in high school, Commoner explored Brooklyn's Prospect Park, collecting plant specimens to study.

Commoner worked his way through Columbia University, graduating in 1937 with honors in zoology. Next he entered Harvard, and in 1941 received his doctorate. The year before, when only twenty-three, he had launched his academic career as an instructor at Queens College in New York. World War II intervened, however, and Commoner spent the next four years on active duty in the U.S. Naval Reserve. After his military service, he served briefly as associate editor of *Science Illustrated*, where he honed his writing skills. He then accepted a position as professor of plant physiology at Washington University in St. Louis.

Trained as a cellular biologist, Commoner pursued biochemical and biophysical research on free radicals and the tobacco mosaic virus. He later startled many of his colleagues by arguing that DNA's role as a determinant of heredity had been exaggerated and that those who focused their research on molecules neglected the study of the "natural complexity of biological systems." His defense of "classical biology" and a holistic approach eventually contributed to his identification as an ecologist, a person who studies the relationship between organisms and their environment.

An event far from his academic laboratory, the atmospheric testing of nuclear weapons, first alerted Commoner to a growing environmental crisis. The Atomic Energy Commission (AEC), created in 1946, had been placed in charge of developing military and peaceful uses of atomic and nuclear energy. Because of the secrecy that surrounded weapons testing, the public heard little from the government except assurances that all tests were harmless and restricted to remote sites. But in the spring of 1953, physicists near Troy, New York, reported highly radioactive fallout that apparently had come to earth in a rainstorm after drifting across the country from a nuclear test site in Nevada. In 1954 fallout from an American H-bomb test in the Pacific Ocean fell on and eventually killed several crewmen of the *Lucky Dragon*, a Japanese fishing boat. Three years later, the AEC carried out a series of sixteen nuclear tests in Nevada. At one called "Smoky," over 1,000 infantrymen took positions in trenches about 5 miles from a tall tower on which a forty-four-kiloton bomb was exploded. Ninety minutes after the blast, the troops waged a mock battle next to ground zero. One of the soldiers, Paul Cooper, described the site as "cherry hot." Twenty years afterward, he died of leukemia. Commoner commented later, "The AEC turned me into an ecologist."[5]

As the dangers of nuclear testing became apparent and the curtain of government secrecy fell away, Commoner turned activist. In 1956 he provided information on fallout for a letter from a group of scientists to presidential candidate Adlai Stevenson, who incorporated the issue into his campaign. In the same year, Commoner initiated a petition to protest nuclear testing that was circulated among scientists at home and abroad. Two years later he helped form the St. Louis Committee for Nuclear Information (CNI), a citizen organization that pioneered public education about fallout and other scientific issues of public concern. "I was making speeches in every church and hall in St. Louis," Commoner noted, "describing the facts of atmospheric testing."[6]

The fallout issue raised moral questions about the responsibility of scientists. Commoner reflected some years later:

If we are concerned with the human meaning of science, its social usefulness, and the usefulness of the technology that it generates, we have to look past the gaudy circus of space spectaculars, past the boasts of unparalleled military force, past the claims that every human ill can be cured by some new chemical, some marvel of electronics, or some biological sleight of hand. Instead, we need to ask why, despite all the new marvels of science, the heavens reek, the waters below are foul, children die in infancy, and we are all threatened with nuclear annihilation. Having asked these questions, we need to seek answers that will restore the power of science to the service of man.[7]

Because it affected every person on earth as well as those to be born for generations to come, nuclear fallout posed a unique problem in the history of humanity. The sustained efforts of citizens and scientists like Commoner contributed to the Nuclear Test Ban Treaty of 1963, in which the United States and the Soviet Union agreed to stop atmospheric testing of nuclear weapons. Commoner later labeled this the first victory "in the campaign to save the environment—and its inhabitants—from the blind assaults of modern technology."[8]

From Commoner's perspective, because science had the potential for greatly improving human life as well as for endangering it, social agencies had to determine the best use of scientific knowledge. Accordingly, the scientist had the responsibility to inform people about the facts and the possible results of proposed actions. Then the people should make the value judgments about which avenues to pursue. In a democracy, he stated, these judgments belonged not in the hands of experts but "in the hands of the people and their elected representatives."[9]

In 1966 Commoner summarized his conclusions in his first book, *Science and*

Survival. Written in a clear, nontechnical style, it reached a wide audience. He noted that humans pay a price for every intrusion into the natural environment, and that continued unchecked pollution of the earth would "eventually destroy the fitness of this planet as a place for human life."[10] Generations living in the nineteenth century had launched a "greedy assault" upon the nation's natural resources. Now, he argued, "we are stealing from future generations not just their lumber and their coal, but the basic necessities of life: air, water, and soil. A new conservation movement is needed to preserve life itself."[11]

The scientific community, Commoner complained, failed to provide the information needed for environmental reforms. Government contracts directed scientific investigation to defense-oriented projects, and secrecy discouraged free inquiry and collaboration among scientists. The government's focus on applied research and development resulted in emphasis on the physical sciences and neglect of the biological and social sciences. Within biological research, Commoner noted increasing inattention to the natural complexity of biological systems; scientists studied cells and molecules isolated from the living organisms of which they were a part. He believed that scientific research had become fragmented and overspecialized.

In 1966, in an effort to address these issues, Commoner founded the Center for the Biology of Natural Systems at Washington University. The staff, drawn from such diverse fields as biophysics, sanitary engineering, anthropology, and economics, focused on practical problems that needed solutions. These included pollution of water supplies in Illinois by farmland wastes and the contamination of Lake Erie by nitrates and phosphates dumped into its waters. Commoner championed a holistic approach and the solution of "real problems in the real world."

These efforts to solve environmental problems continued a tradition of conservation in the United States that dated back to colonial times. Even during the height of American expansion and settlement in the nineteenth century, a few writers and scientists—such as Henry David Thoreau, Frederick Law Olmsted, and George Perkins Marsh—had promoted the idea of conservation. Thoreau demonstrated the value of living simply and close to nature, Olmsted helped initiate urban parks and planning, and Marsh revealed how severely people had altered the land.

After the Civil War, private citizens experimented with tree planting and commercial fish cultivation. A new breed of sportsmen, who hunted and fished for pleasure rather than out of economic necessity, helped to launch a movement to protect resources and improve opportunities for outdoor recreation. Urban dwellers countered mounting health hazards through smoke abatement ordinances and construction of sewerage and waterworks systems. Citizen conservation associations, such as the Appalachian Mountain Club, the Boone and Crockett Club, and the Sierra Club, took the lead in asking the government to reverse its traditional policy of placing control of the public domain in private hands. Congress responded by establishing the first national parks and gave the president authorization to set aside forest reserves, which were later renamed national forests. By the turn of the century, John Muir had emerged as the leader of preservationists, who advocated the protection of scenic and recreational land in its natural state as parks, and Gifford Pinchot championed utilitarian conservation, the wise management and use of natural resources.

During the presidency of Theodore Roosevelt, scientists in government bureaus warned of the depletion of the nation's timber and water supplies. This helped lead to federal management of public lands based on the principle of wise, efficient, and equitable use. The first national conservation movement peaked at the Governors' Conference in 1908, where Roosevelt spoke of the danger of exhaustion of natural resources and called conservation "the weightiest problem now before the Nation."[12]

After World War I and the business-oriented 1920s, concern for conservation revived during the New Deal in the 1930s. Secretary of the Interior Harold Ickes blamed shortsighted and unchecked greed for "denuded forests, floods, droughts, a disappearing water table, erosion, a less stable and equable climate, a vanishing wildlife."[13] The administration of Franklin D. Roosevelt began to rehabilitate the land nationwide, creating new conservation agencies and services and directing large appropriations into new programs. During the first days of the New Deal, both the Tennessee Valley Authority (TVA) and the Civilian Conservation Corps (CCC) gained congressional approval. Soil conservation and reforestation became important priorities, and more land was set aside for wildlife, recreation, and aesthetic purposes.

The conservation programs of the New Deal largely ended with the outbreak of World War II and then gave way to an era of consumption and wasteful resource use after the war ended. Gross national product grew at an unprecedented rate, and prosperity appeared to have no limits. Secretary of the Interior Douglas McKay spoke for many Americans of the 1950s when he stated, "It took human initiative and ingenuity which could prosper only under a free system to take hold and make something out of the land and its resources."[14]

Most Americans supported the existing economic system; their livelihoods depended on it. As they moved in growing numbers to the suburbs, they welcomed the construction of freeways and shopping centers. The federal government funded an interstate highway system but paid little attention to air and water pollution. Oligopolies dominated steel, oil, and automobile production, and advanced technology permitted construction of huge oil rigs, supertankers, and petrochemical plants. America's automobile society counted on an endless supply of cheap energy. By the mid-1950s, the United States, with 6 percent of the world's population, produced almost half its goods. Why, in the midst of such economic abundance, did Americans launch the "environmental movement?"

Historian Samuel P. Hays, in his book *Beauty, Health, and Permanence* (1987), argues that the movement reflected the emergence of new values. Affluent middle-class Americans, better educated than earlier generations, wanted more than the necessities and conveniences that had satisfied their forefathers. Many Americans, with leisure time and the security of a dependable income, cared increasingly about the quality of their daily lives. They protested having chemicals dumped into waterways and released into the air, and were concerned about the threat of pollution to the health of their families and communities. They desired outdoor recreation in unsullied natural settings, urban neighborhoods with clean air and water, and a life of physical and mental wellness.

Hays suggests that the environmental movement was composed of divergent strands, each of which followed a somewhat independent course. First came an interest in the protection of the natural environment from the mid-1950s through the 1960s. This stage witnessed the epic battles to protect Dinosaur National Monument and the Grand Canyon from proposed dams, passage of the Wilderness Act in 1964, and major expansion of the national park system. Second, from the mid-1960s into the early 1970s, legislation emerged to help control pollution, especially of air and water. Third, in the early 1970s, a concern for human health arose as toxic chemicals threatened life itself. Jogging, health-food stores, organic gardening, and holistic medicine experienced a rapid rise in popularity; smoking in public increasingly came to be viewed as an antisocial act. Americans recognized that their health depended on the health of the environment in which they lived, and more and more of them questioned the standards by which corporations and government agencies determined safe levels of pollutants. The contaminated environment was being linked to cancer, heart disease, genetic and reproductive problems, and deteriorating immune systems.

The environmentalism of the 1960s differed markedly from earlier conservation movements. Whereas the older movements depended on the federal administration for leadership, the new movement had its origin and strength at the grassroots level. An amalgamation of groups, loosely allied, championed a variety of causes, such as consumerism, scientific responsibility, holistic health, birth control, and population stabilization. People organized to protect open space in their communities and to prevent such major intrusions as strip mining and construction of high-megawatt power stations. ''Ecology'' became a widely used (and misused) term as students learned of carbon cycles and the intricacies of an ecosystem.

The movement reached its peak in 1969–1970 with Earth Day, the passage of the National Environmental Policy Act (NEPA), the creation of the Environmental Protection Agency (EPA), and the growth of citizen environmental associations. Earth Day, celebrated on college campuses across the nation, proved a catalyst for environmental awareness and legislation. The NEPA required federal agencies to prepare statements on the impact of all federal projects that might have significant environmental consequences and to consider alternatives that would minimize damage. It also provided for a Council on Environmental Quality to advise the president. The regulation of environmental quality became institutionalized with the creation of the EPA, and Congress passed important legislation to clean up the nation's air and water.

The Environmental Defense Fund, the Natural Resources Defense Fund, Friends of the Earth, and Environmental Action represented a new breed of environmental associations in the early 1970s. At the same time, older established associations (the Sierra Club, the National Audubon Society, and others) enjoyed dramatic increases in membership. Environmental activism found a home in many new endeavors, including environmental education and environmental law.

Although *Time* magazine gave special recognition to the role of Barry Commoner for the rise of environmentalism, several others deserved special credit. Rachel Carson, in her best-selling book *Silent Spring* (1962), had launched a campaign to control the use of insecticides and herbicides. She asked how supposedly intelligent human beings could "seek to control a few unwanted species by a method that contaminated the entire environment and brought the threat of disease and death even to their own kind." She added, "If the Bill of Rights contains no guarantee that a citizen shall be secure against lethal poisons distributed either by private individuals or by public officials, it is surely only because our forefathers, despite their considerable wisdom and foresight, could conceive of no such problem."[15] Carson warned:

We still talk in terms of "conquest"—whether it be of the insect world or of the mysterious world of space. We still have not become mature enough to see ourselves as a very tiny part of a vast and incredible universe, a universe that is distinguished above all else by a mysterious and wonderful unity that we flout at our peril.[16]

Carson was not alone in calling public attention to threats to the environment. René Dubos, a microbiologist, noted the ignorance of those who proposed eliminating all insect pests and unwanted germs. Eradication, he explained, could not succeed; humans needed greater humility and acceptance of coexistence with nature—germs included. Paul Ehrlich, a young Stanford University biology professor, argued that the explosive growth of world population was at the root of the environmental crisis. In *The Population Bomb* (1968), he warned of a catastrophe if the rate of world population growth were not curbed. Ehrlich called for an aggressive "family planning" movement, beginning in the United States, and draconian measures if all else failed. Another California biologist, Garrett Hardin, argued that people needed to restrict access to the "commons" (air, water, and so on) through "mutual coercion, mutually agreed upon."[17]

Commoner offered a different explanation of the environmental crisis in his influential book *The Closing Circle* (1971). He called Americans "unwitting" victims of ignorance. We had become dependent on the automobile long before we understood the health hazards of smog in our cities. We had given up soap in favor of detergents before we recognized that the latter pollute our water supplies. We had developed insecticides only to discover that they threaten more than the lives of pests. In a series of technological changes, synthetics replaced cotton and wool, trucks displaced railroads, and chemical fertilizers were substituted for animal manure. Such changes reflected a shift from natural to synthetic, from energy-conserving to power-consuming, and from reusable to disposable.

Commoner stated that we had "broken out of the circle of life." He concluded that the chief reason for the environmental crisis that had engulfed the United States was the "sweeping transformation of productive technologies since World War II."[18] While recognizing that increased population and greater affluence affected the level of pollution, he argued that productive methods developed since 1946 accounted for 80 to 85 percent of the total output of pollutants. New products, such as synthetic fibers and plastics, were not assimilated in natural environmental cycles and thus became pollutants. High-compression engines caused nitrogen and oxygen to combine as nitrogen oxides, the key ingredients in smog. Likewise, large electric power plants created sulfur dioxide and nitrogen oxides. And new farm technologies upset natural cycles: insecticides disrupted the balance between pests and their predators, and excessive amounts of inorganic fertilizer contributed to water pollution.

The negative impact of these new forms of pollution was borne by society, not by those who produced them. Commoner concluded that the economic system needed to be based on social goals rather than private gain, and that ecological considerations should guide economic and political decisions. The costs to clean up the environment and convert to ecologically sound technological practices would be enormous—hundreds of billions of dollars—and would absorb the resources and capital of the nation for at least a generation. In Commoner's view, the United States had two options: "rational, social organization of the use and distribution of the earth's resources, or a new barbarism."[19]

Commoner had little sympathy with those who advocated restricting people's choices through some form of coercion or who argued that saving the environment depended on severe restrictions of economic growth. In particular, he criticized two influential studies of the early 1970s: *Blueprint for Survival*, the work of a group of prominent British scientists, and the computer-based study *Limits to Growth*, commissioned by an international group of industrialists, economists, and scientists. Both argued for a transition from economic growth to global equilibrium in order to save the environment. Commoner countered optimistically that existing technologies could provide a high quality of life for a growing population and allow economic expansion at the same time. He also maintained that the earth is not a closed system with a fixed resource base. Rather, he believed that limits on economic growth depended on the rate at which renewable solar energy could be captured and used.

Commoner leveled his sharpest criticism at Ehrlich, who, he thought, had a fixation on the need for population control. To Commoner, controlling population growth meant some measure of political repression, and he abhorred the idea of involuntary or state-imposed birth control. He agreed that developing countries faced both immediate and long-term threats because of overpopulation, but argued that the solution was economic development rather than stringent population-control measures. A believer in the theory of demographic transition, Commoner thought that developing countries, with high rates of births and deaths, could follow the population trends of industrialized countries, where an increase of wealth led to reduced mortality and a willingness by couples to have fewer children. He blamed high birthrates on poverty and cited colonial exploitation and the uneven distribution of wealth as the root of much of the problem.

As Commoner put it later, "the world population crisis, which is the ultimate outcome of the exploitation of poor nations by rich ones, ought to be remedied by returning to the poor countries enough of the wealth taken from them to give their peoples both the reason and the resources voluntarily to limit their own fertility."[20] Addressing the Environmental Forum at the United Nations Conference on the Human Environment at Stockholm in 1972, he concluded that to solve the environmental crisis, humanity must first solve the problems of "poverty, racial injustice and war." In brief, "a peace among men must precede the peace with nature."[21]

Commoner pointed to what he considered a fundamental flaw in American society—the design of the country's economic system. The private-enterprise system failed to meet such essential social needs as renewable and nonpolluting energy and resources; efficient and minimally harmful technologies in agriculture, transportation, and manufacturing; and production processes that allow for safe and rewarding jobs while requiring limited capital. He attributed these failures to the desire to maximize profits regardless of the costs in energy, capital, or environmental health. The petrochemical industry, he believed, revealed what had gone wrong: this most capital-intensive and labor-saving of major manufacturing industries had remained profitable to private investors precisely because the public had absorbed such externalities as pollution, unemployment, and danger in the workplace.

Commoner advocated conversion to renewable resources, particularly solar energy, which he believed was environmentally safe and, in the long run, inexpensive. Although the transition to a renewable resource base would take several decades, such feasible and well-known practices and developments as organic farming and electrified railroads could be pursued immediately. Natural gas would be a safe transition fuel because a heating system that burned it could also burn methane produced from organic matter. Cogeneration (the use of electricity and waste heat) would produce major savings, and solar electrical cells (photovoltaics) could become economically attractive.

It galled Commoner that the federal government continued to subsidize the nuclear and synthetic-fuel power industries. In 1976, speaking on the nuclear-power industry, he complained, "It is a lopsided partnership between the private and public sectors, in which the rewards have been private and the huge risks— the hazards to life, the waste of billions of dollars, the rising cost of power, the impending collapse of the nuclear-power program, and the ensuing economic chaos—have been assigned to the public.''[22]

Increasingly, Commoner saw solar conversion as more a political than a technical or an economic problem. Solar energy was feasible now, if the government would give it a helping hand. He argued that big oil companies, electric utility companies, and the two major political parties stood in the way of such a policy. He joined with other dissidents to form the Citizens' party, described by *Newsweek* as an ''antibusiness amalgam of environmentalists, consumerists, antinuclear activists and minority-rights advocates.''[23]

In April 1980, 262 delegates from some 30 states gathered in a Cleveland hotel for the founding convention. According to one account, several well-groomed executives ''watched with bewilderment as shabbily dressed delegates—some barefoot, others in Indian garb, some carrying backpacks, children or bags of fast food—emptied from rusting vans and marched into the hotel lobby.''[24] The founders of the party had no illusions about winning at the national level, but they dreamed that their presidential candidate, as an initial step, might achieve credibility by gaining 5 percent of the vote, thus qualifying the party for matching federal funds. The first task was to decide on a strategy and qualify candidates for the ballot in as many states as possible.

Party members believed strongly in internal democracy and an ideology that combined populism and social democracy. They submitted position papers and resolutions to form the basis of a party platform to be voted on by the entire membership through mail ballots; Commoner later described this as ''an insane idea, which utterly failed.''[25] The Citizens' party stood for public control (but not necessarily ownership) of energy industries, an end to nuclear power plants, the use of solar energy and conservation practices, sharp and immediate reductions in defense spending, active support for human rights at home and abroad, employment for anyone who wanted it, the establishment of stable prices for necessities such as food, housing, fuel, and medical care, and limitations on the power of corporations.

Commoner, who agreed to be the party's presidential nominee, argued that owners of capital made major decisions for American society based ''on the sole criterion of maximizing profit.''[26] Someone needed to look after the welfare of the people, the creation of jobs, the protection of the environment, and the conservation of energy. His effort to gain attention from the national media failed, however, and he attracted fewer than 250,000 votes. Nevertheless, he hoped that ''green'' party politics had gained a foothold in America.

In spite of continued support from many sectors of American society, the environmental movement had encountered growing resistance. Long lines at gasoline stations during the oil embargo of 1973–1974, recession, inflation, and the ''jobs versus environment'' controversy dampened enthusiasm. Business interests lobbied to blunt enforcement of environmental legislation. In the contest over complex and technical issues, corporations and government agencies had considerably more political and economic clout than environmental associations.

Ronald Reagan's election to the presidency in 1980 initiated an acrimonious debate over environmental issues. The new president pledged to "take government off the people's backs and turn the great genius of the American people loose once again."[27] To strengthen the economy, he gave private interests greater freedom to develop the land as they saw fit. His administration appointed policymakers with strong ties to extractive industries, reduced environmental standards and regulations, drove many conservation-oriented people from public service, and used the Office of Management and Budget to control the actions and policies of federal environmental agencies. When environmentalists protested, they found the doors of federal agencies closed to them.

In 1981 Commoner moved his Center for the Biology of Natural Systems to Queens College. New York City offered opportunities to confront the environmental and energy problems of urban dwellers, especially the poor. Here, he and his staff launched a flurry of activities, including the study of environmentally safe methods of disposing of municipal garbage, the development of a neighborhood energy cooperative using cogenerators to provide both heat and electricity to row houses, the organization of workshops to train people on optimum weatherization techniques, and the creation of a computer network on environmental and energy issues for use in public education. The Center remained dedicated to solving the "real problems" of urban and rural communities.

Now in his seventies, Commoner took the opportunity of the twentieth anniversary of Earth Day in 1990 to assess what the environmental movement had accomplished. At home, the United States had spent more than $1 trillion to control environmental pollution, but the results, he concluded, were "minimal."[28] Globally, chemical pollutants were destroying the ozone layer, and rising levels of carbon dioxide in the atmosphere threatened to result in global warming. The task ahead, Commoner noted, was formidable:

We must recognize that the assault on the environment cannot be effectively controlled but must be prevented; that prevention requires transforming the structure of the technosphere, bringing it into harmony with the ecosphere; that this requires a fundamental redesign of the major industrial, agricultural and transportation systems; that such a transformation of the systems of production conflicts with the short-term profit-maximizing goals that govern investment decisions under capitalism; and that, accordingly, politically suitable means must be developed that bring the public interest in long-term environmental quality to bear upon these decisions. Finally, because the problem is global and deeply linked to the disparity between the development of the planet's Northern and Southern hemispheres, what we propose to do in the United States must be compatible with the global task of closing the economic gap between the rich North and the poor South—and indeed must facilitate it.[29]

Commoner did not know how to implement such a program, but he did offer a few suggestions on how to help foster such a transition. The U.S. government, which earlier had stimulated research and commercial development of the computer chip, could do the same to encourage such things as smogfree engines, disposal of trash through recycling, and organically grown fruits and vegetables. Consumers could boycott environmentally harmful products. Environmentalists could find common ground, particularly about the choice of production technologies, with consumer groups, labor unions, churches, civil rights defenders, women, minorities, and peace advocates. He never explained, however, how these groups could compete successfully with the two major political parties within an electoral system in which the winner takes all.

The main environmental successes since 1970, Commoner pointed out, had resulted from eliminating a pollutant altogether: "If you don't put something into the environment, it's not there."[30] Air emissions of lead had declined by 86 percent because much less lead had been added to gasoline. Similarly, environmental levels of DDT, PCB, mercury in surface waters, and strontium 90 had dropped sharply. Commoner did not insist on government control of all facets of production, only the "crucial ones" in which the social interest in environmental quality came first.

Outspoken and opinionated, Commoner criticized those with whom he disagreed, including his fellow environmentalists. He thoughtthat those who believed in the intrinsic value of nature (such as "deep ecologists") and those who advocated reform through ecologically defined regions (such as "bioregionalists") failed to recognize the heart of the environmental problem: the private governance of production technologies. He took issue with older mainstream environmental organizations, such as the National Wildlife Federation, the Sierra Club, and the National Aububon Society, which he saw as too prepared "to adjust the goals of environmentalism to the reality of Washington politics."[31] He believed that they naively placed their trust in legislation and litigation to ameliorate environmental degradation, a kind of band-aid approach.

In contrast, Commoner praised the actions of local grassroots organizations that took the "hard political path." The grassroots movement, exemplified by the response at Love Canal, in New York State, worked to prevent pollution in neighborhoods, "directly challenging the corporation's exclusive power to make decisions that threaten the community's health."[32] He commended the work of the Citizens' Clearinghouse for Hazardous Wastes, the National Toxics Campaign, Greenpeace, and Ralph Nader's Public Interest Research Groups (PIRGs).

Although Commoner worked at the grassroots through his Center for the Biology of Natural Systems, he believed increasingly that a long-term solution to environmental problems depended on "social governance" of capitalism.[33] Although he never clearly explained the meaning of "social governance," he meant some form of democratic decision making that placed social interests ahead of private gain. Critics thought "social governance" would entail greater regimentation and government control, which would be contrary to Commoner's belief in personal freedom, equality, and human rights. They railed that he could not have it both ways, suggesting "socialistic" practices while opposing centralized controls. They argued that there was no evidence that a socialist system would treat the environment any better than had capitalism, and that Commoner was naive, utopian, and a "peddler of political panaceas."

Some of these criticisms had merit. Commoner lacked the expertise in economics and political science needed to set forth an integrated plan of action for the future. Nevertheless, he argued that the urgency of the environmental crisis obliged both economists and environmentalists "to take the risk of reaching across the boundaries of their disciplines and to accept the consequent criticism as something to be borne, cheerfully if possible, as a social duty."[34] He would have had greater success had he exhibited greater tact and skill at consensus-building. For example, he could have acknowledged the ideas of others that paralleled or complemented his own, such as Lewis Mumford's criticism of modern technology, the "soft energy" path of Amory Lovins, and the "small is beautiful" concepts of E.F. Schumacher. He dismissed Ehrlich's population thesis too readily, failing to recognize how a growing population would contribute to many of the technological changes he opposed. Moreover, he largely ignored a number of environmental issues of primary concern to others, such as animal rights, endangered species, wilderness, and preservation of natural landscapes.

No one person could integrate all knowledge about the environment, bridge the differences in values held by a growing diversity of environmentalists, and set forth a workable solution to the environmental crisis. Commoner deserves credit for being in the forefront of the environmental movement in the 1950s and 1960s, when Americans began to question their faith in science, business, and politics. His belief that scientists have a moral responsibility to inform the general public about the state of the environment and his argument that the environmental crisis resulted from new production technologies stirred a healthy debate.

Barry Commoner, as much as anyone, educated this country's citizens about the plight of the environment in the post–World War II era. As a scientist dedicated to informing the public and as a citizen willing to enter politics, he helped to raise the environmental awareness and political consciousness of Americans.

NOTES

1. "Fighting to Save the Earth from Man," *Time* 95 (2 February 1970): 56–63.

2. Victor B. Scheffer, *The Shaping of Environmentalism in America* (Seattle, Wash., 1991), 197.

3. Barry Commoner, "Economic Growth and Environmental Quality: How to Have Both," *Social Policy* 16 (1985): 24.

4. Portions of the text below are based on pages in Douglas H. Strong, *Dreamers and Defenders: American Conservationists*, copyright 1988 by the University of Nebraska Press, and the author's introduction to Hans Huth, *Nature and the American: Three Centuries of Changing Attitudes,* copyright 1990 by the University of Nebraska Press. Used by permission of the University of Nebraska Press. All rights reserved.

5. Barry Commoner, "Beyond the Teach-in," *Saturday Review* 53 (1970): 51; "Hiroshima at Home," *Hospital Practice* 13 (1978): 58; and "The Fallout Problem," *Science* 127 (1958): 1023–1026.

6. Alan Anderson, Jr., "Scientist at Large," *New York Times Magazine*, 7 November 1976, p. 60.

7. Barry Commoner, "Science and the Sense of Humanity," *The Humanist* 30 (1970): 10

8. Barry Commoner, *The Closing Circle* (New York, 1971), 56.

9. Ibid., 198.

10. Barry Commoner, *Science and Survival* (New York, 1966), 122.

11. Ibid., 127.

12. *Proceedings of a Conference of Governors in the White House, Washington, D.C., May 13–15, 1908* (Washington, D.C., 1909), 3.

13. Harold L. Ickes, *The New Democracy* (New York, 1934), 19.

14. Gladwin Hill, "M'Kay Emphasizes U.S. Lands Policy," *New York Times*, 3 November 1953, p. 25.

15. Rachel Carson, *Silent Spring* (Boston, 1962), 8, 12–13.

16. Rachel Carson, "Of Man and the Stream of Time," graduation address delivered at Scripps College, Claremont, Calif., 1962, p. 8.

17. Garrett Hardin, "The Tragedy of the Commons," *Science* 162 (1968): 1247.

18. Commoner, *The Closing Circle*, 177.

19. Ibid., 296.

20. Barry Commoner, *Making Peace with the Planet* (New York, 1990), 168.

21. Barry Commoner, "The Meaning of the Environmental Crisis," paper presented 5 June 1972 (MS, Box 138, Barry Commoner Papers, Library of Congress, Washington, D.C.).

22. Barry Commoner, *The Poverty of Power* (New York, 1976), 120.

23. "Dr. Ecology for President," *Newsweek* 95 (21 April 1980): 48.

24. Joseph L. Wagner, "New Party Picks Candidates," *Washington Post*, 14 April 1980, p. 2.

25. Frank Smallwood, *The Other Candidates: Third Parties in Presidential Elections* (Hanover, N.H., 1983), 217.

26. Ibid., 212.

27. Quoted in C. Brant Short, *Ronald Reagan and the Public Lands: America's Conservation Debate, 1979–1984* (College Station, Tex., 1989), 42.

28. Commoner's pessimistic assessment can be debated. As a sociopolitical movement, environmentalism is stronger than ever. But it remains to be seen whether it can attain its goal of protecting the environment. See Riley E. Dunlap and Angela G. Mertig, eds., *American Environmentalism: The U.S. Environmental Movement, 1970–1990* (Philadelphia, 1992), 1–10.

29. Barry Commoner, "Ecosphere vs. Technosphere: Ending the War Against Earth," *The Nation* 250 (30 April, 1990): 589–590.

30. Barry Commoner, "Environmental Democracy Is the Planet's Best Hope," 40 *Utne Reader* (July/August 1990): 61.

31. Commoner, *Making Peace with the Planet*, 175.

32. Ibid., 179.

33. Commoner, "Economic Growth and Environmental Quality," 24–26.

34. Commoner, *The Closing Circle*, 251.

BIBLIOGRAPHY

Anderson, Alan, Jr. "Scientist at Large." *New York Times Magazine,* 7 November 1976,
    pp. 58–75.
Borelli, Peter, ed. *Crossroads: Environmental Priorities.* Washington, D.C., 1988.
Chisholm, Anne. *Philosophers of the Earth: Conversations with Ecologists,* 122–139.
    London, 1972.
Commoner, Barry. *The Closing Circle: Nature, Man, and Technology.* New York, 1971.
———. *Making Peace with the Planet.* New York, 1990.
———. *Conservators of Hope: The Horace M. Albright Lectures.* Moscow, Idaho, 1988.
Dowie, Mark. *Losing Ground: American Environmentalism at the Close of the Twentieth
    Century.* Cambridge, Mass., 1995.
Dunlap, Riley E., and Angela G. Mertig, eds. *American Environmentalism: The U.S.
    Environmental Movement, 1970–1990.* Philadelphia, 1992.
Fleming, Donald. "Roots of the New Conservation Movement." In Donald Fleming and
    Bernard Bailyn, eds., *Perspectives in American History,* vol. 6, 7–91. Cambridge,
    Mass., 1972.
Hays, Samuel P. *Beauty, Health, and Permanence: Environmental Politics in the United
    States, 1955–1985.* New York, 1987.
Krier, James E. "The Political Economy of Barry Commoner," *Environmental Law* 20
    (1989): 11–33.
Scheffer, Victor B. *The Shaping of Environmentalism in America.* Seattle, Wash., 1991.
Sills, David L. "The Environmental Movement and Its Critics." *Human Ecology* 3
    (1975): 1–41.
Strong, Douglas H. *Dreamers and Defenders: American Conservationists.* Lincoln,
    Nebr., 1988.

Dorothy Day
and the Catholic Worker Movement

ANNE KLEJMENT

"We were just sitting there talking and people moved in on us," explained Dorothy Day about the origins of the Catholic Worker movement, which was dedicated to caring for the poor and promoting nonviolent revolution.[1] Day's self-deprecating wit highlighted the role of ordinary people as agents of social change. By doing his or her small part, each person hastened the day of revolution. A traditional Catholic, devout and loyal to church authority, Day challenged the social and political orthodoxies of several generations of social activists, including New Dealers, Old Leftists, the New Left, charity volunteers, credentialed experts, and welfare bureaucrats.

The Catholic Worker movement began in 1933 with a monthly paper, the *Catholic Worker*, edited and published by Day, a Catholic journalist with ties to Greenwich Village radicals, anarchists, and Communists. Next came hospices for the homeless, begun on the initiative of a few enterprising people, guests and volunteers alike, who shared a pot of coffee, a kettle of soup, a few donated beds, and, all too often, vermin. Then came the farming communes, where the urban unemployed could adopt a self-sufficient and morally healthy way of life, independent of bosses, plutocrats, and unstable market forces.

The paper, the unique experience of community life, and informal programs on Catholic social thought educated people from all walks of life about the need for Gospel-based social justice and nonviolent revolution. In all of these endeavors, Dorothy Day and the Catholic Worker movement connected traditional Catholic spirituality (the mass, sacraments, prayer, fasting, works of mercy) to American radicalism. By taking the Gospel seriously, by loving even enemies, the Catholic Workers' revolution of the heart aimed to change society from the bottom up.

A winding path led Dorothy Day to Catholic social radicalism and nonviolent revolution. Born on 8 November 1897 in Brooklyn, New York, she was the third of five children of John and Grace Satterlee Day. The comfort and security of her birth into the middle class proved illusory. Before her nineteenth birthday, she and her family had crisscrossed the United States, following the lofty ambitions of her newpaperman father and escaping from downward plunges that were the result of natural and economic disasters.

The protective parents attempted the impossible task of shielding their children from the harshness of life. While living in Oakland, California, the Days survived the 1906 San Francisco earthquake but suffered an enormous financial reverse, losing both home and income. Starting anew in Chicago, they slowly recovered, only to fail again through no fault of their own.

''First in violence, deepest in dirt,'' according to reformer Lincoln Steffens, Chicago left a lasting imprint on young Dorothy. The precocious and introspective child related the sights, sounds, and smells near the family's tenement to her reading. The social realism of socialist novelists Upton Sinclair and Jack London, whom she surreptitiously read, graphically portrayed the abuses of capitalism suffered by the working class. These favorite authors advocated systemic change coming not from the tinkering of Progressive reformers but through socialism, through a redistribution of power and wealth. Day's brother Donald was employed by the *Day Book*, a Socialist paper unencumbered by capitalistic advertisements. Copies of the paper that he brought home reinforced the radical message of the novels his sister read. Dissatisfied with the nominal Christianity of her parents at about the same time she was forming her social conscience, Day joined the Episcopal Church.

At the age of sixteen, Day entered the University of Illinois on scholarship. She became disillusioned with the failure of Christians to challenge social injustice, and on campus she joined a club for aspiring writers and briefly attached herself to a campus Socialist forum, where she heard provocative speakers like Rose Pastor Stokes and Scott Nearing. Finding all but her literature courses dull, Day left after two years without a degree and rejoined her family in New York City.

Armed with a few published articles, she sought employment in journalism against the wishes of her conservative father, who opposed careers for women. An editor at the *New York Call*, a Socialist daily, was beguiled into hiring Day. Working for a pittance, she launched her career in journalism with a colorful human interest series on working women that was based on her own experiences. Within a few months, she was promoted to covering a wide variety of causes dear to Socialist hearts: poverty, labor protests, peace activism, bread riots, and birth control. Often, while researching her articles, which reflected the Socialist creed of her editors, she joined in the protests that she was covering.

Two events of 1917, the Russian Revolution and the American entry into World War I, informed Day's consciousness for a lifetime. At a rally in Madison Square Garden, Day celebrated the power of common people to shape a socialist future. Soon war clouds overshadowed the joyous event. The United States entered World War I, and Day and a handful of radicals and pacifists refused to cooperate. Day objected to the war's benefits to capitalist arms merchants and its division of the international working class into soldiers who fought each other. Watching helplessly as the suppression of dissent resulted in the arrests of friends and the closing down of the radical press, she opposed the draft and wartime government censorship.

Day spent her first night in jail in 1917, but not for antiwar activity. Having traveled to Washington with militant women's suffragists, she and her companions were charged with blocking traffic near the White House. At the notorious Occoquan Workhouse in Virginia, Day scuffled with her jailers over their denial of her basic human rights. Conservative critics, horrified by the prospect of an increase in women's political activity, noticed the antiwar attitudes of the militant suffragists, some of whose signs referred to ''Kaiser Wilson.'' Day later wrote that she had intended to support political prisoners in Washington. Although she was leading the life of a new woman, independent in spirit, career-oriented, and open to free love, she was no suffragist. Impatient with politics, the young revolutionary Socialist preferred mass action to balloting and compromise.

Upon her return to New York, Day found herself unable to earn a living as a radical journalist. Recently an assistant editor at the chic and naughty *Masses*, the ''awkward and charming young enthusiast, with beautiful slanting eyes,'' as her boss Floyd Dell described her, had remained at that radical magazine long enough to edit a couple of issues that attracted the attention of postal censors.[2] The senior editors of the *Masses* twice faced sedition charges and twice won acquittal. But the magazine was dead, one of the many literary casualties of the war, replaced by a tame (and to Day unappealing) pretender, the *Liberator*.

From 1918 through 1923, Day lived a life that evoked an embarrassed silence in her autobiography. Weary of overbearing editors and government repression of writers and activists, she studied nursing and worked at menial jobs while continuing to write. A tempestuous love affair, an abortion, a failed marriage, and an apparent suicide attempt suggest her faltering sense of purpose and disenchantment with radical activism.

By 1924 Day had managed to turn her life around. Publication of *The Eleventh Virgin*, a heavily autobiographical novel of disillusionment, and its sale to Hollywood brought Day modest financial security. Shortly thereafter, she settled contentedly into a domestic partnership with Forster Batterham, brother of a friend. The birth of a daughter, Tamar, in March 1926, sparked a crisis. Since childhood Day had from time to time yearned for a rich spiritual life. Now she could no longer suppress the desire. The birth of her daughter, her blissful partnership, and Batterham's infectious appreciation of nature focused her thoughts on God. Drawn to Catholicism, she was forced to choose between Batterham, an adamant nonbeliever, and the church, which could not bless their irregular union. After hesitating, Day was baptized a Catholic in December 1927.

Conversion addressed complex needs in Day's life. Tired of her moral drift, Day was still attracted to the cause of industrial workers although her activism had diminished. She naturally turned to the church of workers and immigrants. The conversion, however, did not bring instant comfort. Anguished by the loss of her partner, Day was also troubled by the social conservatism of church leadership, the smug self-satisfaction of bourgeois Christians, and their practice of charity without social justice. "I loved the church," she admitted, "for Christ made visible. Not for itself, because it was so often a scandal to me."[3]

Finding a career suited to a radical Catholic single mother took time. During the winter of 1932–1933, five years after her conversion, Day was beginning to grasp her new calling. Using her radical connections, she gained entry to a protest in Washington organized by the Communist-influenced Unemployed Councils, then reported about the concerns of workers and farmers for readers of two Catholic magazines.

At least one reader, fifty-five-year-old Peter Maurin, an immigrant from rural France, was captivated by the accounts of the demonstrations. Rooted in European Catholic culture, the Gospel, and agricultural life, Maurin could often be found proclaiming his message of social change and spiritual renewal from a soapbox in Union Square or handing out mimeographed copies of his free verse social thought. Like Day, he took Christ's teaching of love for one's neighbor seriously.

In contrast to Day, the quintessential urbanite, Maurin gloried in the rural ethos, which he had experienced as a child in southern France. He called for a green revolution, a return to the soil minus high technology and a marketplace mind-set. In place of city life and capitalism, he imagined a simple Christian cooperative society. Skilled craftsmen—he did not advance the cause of women workers—would create useful items. Each craft would be regulated by its own guild. Farmers, formed into communes, need not fear the perils of profit and loss. Shared surpluses would eliminate want. Maurin's utopia meant an escape from such evils as worker alienation, low industrial wages, the impersonality and corruption of cities, rugged individualism, secularism, dependency, class warfare, and the extremes of capitalism and state communism. Work, Maurin taught, should support basic human needs rather than create profits for the few and poverty for the masses. Hospitality would be the work of every individual, following the Christian code of love. Those in need would be cared for by their neighbors, not by an impersonal bureaucracy.

To encourage people to organize themselves to effect a nonviolent social revolution, Maurin wanted to implant his ideas in enthusiastic followers. He could reach a few people from his soapbox and with his leaflets, but in the midst of the Great Depression, Maurin imagined that more people than he could personally reach would be interested in the green revolution. Having sensed a kindred spirit in Day's writing, he sought out the author.

Under his tutelage in Catholic social thought, Day became cofounder of a new radical Catholic movement and editor and publisher of its newspaper. She was a perfect complement to Maurin. Deeply religious and committed to revolution, Day wrote powerful articles about social issues. Native-born and respectable, but with a dash of bohemianism from her Greenwich Village past, she could reach a larger group of potential disciples than Maurin. Never before a leader in the radical movement or in the church, Day already displayed great energy and enthusiasm, self-discipline, deep spirituality, and can-do optimism. With Maurin's encouragement, she would shape the Catholic Worker movement.

In order to hear Maurin's message, Day ignored his eccentricities of demeanor, dress, and personal hygiene. Her new platonic friend convinced her of the urgency of meeting human needs and the ability of lay Catholics to undertake programs without special permission from the church hierarchy. Day moved forthrightly to promote the works of mercy, nonviolent revolution, and spiritual renewal. Since the idea of editing her own paper was so appealing, the Catholic Worker movement started with the distribution of an eight-page, tabloid-style penny paper.

At the same time the New Deal was attempting to restore public confidence in government and in the economy, Day launched the *Catholic Worker* with small donations, including $2 from a nun, and small loans. Religious faith reinforced her radical values. She expected capitalism to be crushed by the depression. Its failure, she believed, would hasten a nonviolent revolution leading to a cooperative Christian society. Mistrustful of centralized power, Day was still grounded in the experience of wartime repression in 1917–1918 and the excesses of the Red Scare. Still influenced by her youthful radicalism, she thought that the state, its laws, and its enforcement agencies were unnecessary. In decentralized Christian communities the Gospel spirit of love would be supreme, not the letter of the law. Surveying the lives of ordinary folk around her, Day found abundant evidence of human need: evictions, hunger, and joblessness were among the most obvious problems. Rather than treating symptoms without eradicating the causes, or working for revolution while ignoring present human needs, Day believed that a program founded on the daily practice of works of mercy, such as feeding the hungry and sheltering the homeless, combined with nonviolent direct action—Maurin's program met the test—was the surest path to social change and the most direct route to social revolution.

The paper made an unforgettable impression. Priced at a penny a copy, the *Catholic Worker* advocated Gospel values over profit. Volunteers wrote stories; helped to edit, address, bundle, mail, and hawk the paper; and cared for the poor. The paper and the movement survived on small donations, which, Day pointed out, kept the movement humble and its following large. At a modest twenty-five cents a year for a subscription, most readers could afford an offering above the cost of the paper. By operating without corporate sponsors (the paper was advertisement-free) or grants from foundations, and by deliberately avoiding legal incorporation as a charity, Day kept her editorial and investigative freedom without fear of offending a corporate sponsor or the government.

Peter Maurin had anticipated a paper devoted solely to his writings and ideas, but Day prevailed, producing a high-quality paper of wider interest. Besides Maurin's didactic verses and her appealing column, eyewitness accounts of injustice; major theological treatises; lively essays on labor, farming, race relations, liturgy, calligraphy, and other subjects; and letters from Catholic Workers throughout the country attracted a remarkably diverse readership. Day wrote most of the unsigned copy in the early years and invited articles from great minds. Social critics Eric Gill and Lewis Mumford, liturgist Virgil Michel, philosopher Jacques Maritain, and sociologist Paul Hanly Furfey shared their thoughts in the early years. Later the paper published the poetry of Claude McKay and William Everson (Brother Antoninus), and the writings of social justice advocates Michael Harrington, Thomas Merton, and Daniel and Philip Berrigan. Belgian-born Ade Bethune, who depicted saints as workers, was the first of many exceptional artists to offer her work to the paper. Others were Fritz Eichenberg, Rita Corbin, and Robert McGovern.

Measured by any standards, the paper was a success. Low in cost, high in quality, original in viewpoint, and aesthetically pleasing, it attracted a large readership. Volunteers hawked the paper on New York streets, sometimes calling out "Read the *Catholic Worker* daily!" in good natured verbal competition with Communists selling copies of the *Daily Worker* nearby. Day herself urged readers to "[p]ass your copy of THE CATHOLIC WORKER *[sic]* on to a friend—that's how our circulation has grown from 2,500 to 20,000 in six months!"[4] By 1938 circulation peaked with 190,000 copies, many of which were sent in bulk orders to parish priests. Day's insistent pacifism during World War II led to a slump in subscriptions. At the war's end, slightly more than 50,000 copies of each issue were circulated. But Day's reputation, the movement's unflagging advocacy of the poor, and its consistent Christian ethic led to a rebirth of the movement and the paper by the 1950s. During the 1980s and early 1990s circulation of the *Catholic Worker* usually hovered between 90,000 and 100,000 copies per issue.

Volunteers and supporters were attracted to the movement largely by its principles and work, the *Catholic Worker* paper, and Day's charismatic personality. Art student Ade Bethune helped out after hearing from a classmate about two women (Day and volunteer Dorothy Weston) sleeping on the floor, whenever necessary, to shelter the poor. Joseph Zarrella, recalling that at the time he "wasn't particularly a good Catholic," volunteered after encountering Catholic Workers selling the paper in Union Square. He was "captured" by the "excit[ement]" generated by the movement.[5]

As critical as ideas and leadership were, Day knew that action was essential. "We start to write about justice, about changing the social order," she stated, "and we are overwhelmed by those coming to claim our pity and our sharing."[6] Following the example that Day set throughout her life, *Catholic Worker* editors engaged in direct action; picketed for organized labor; attended meetings and marches in support of housing, labor, peace, and other causes; educated themselves and others about social issues; committed civil disobedience; and shared their lives and goods with the poor.

Voluntary poverty was a cornerstone of the movement's nonviolent revolution. As Day explained in one of her columns, "Love of [others] means voluntary poverty, stripping one's self . . . denying one's self. . . . It also means non-participation in those comforts and luxuries which have been manufactured by the exploitation of others."[7] If everyone took less, she calculated, then fewer would be in need.

In her writing, on the picket line, in court, and in jail, Day supported the right of laborers to unionize, to be paid decently, and to work in conditions that protected their health and safety. The immigrant Catholic Church of the late nineteenth and early twentieth centuries was a church of manual laborers. First a few Catholic leaders, then the collective voice of the Catholic hierarchy, supported workers' rights. Day built on their efforts.

More than a generation before Day joined the church, Catholics like Terence Powderly of the Knights of Labor and James Cardinal Gibbons supported organized labor at a time when many Catholics, including members of the hierarchy, feared that the Vatican had targeted them when it denounced secret and anti-Catholic groups. Gibbons defended the Knights of Labor, convinced Rome to tolerate labor organization, and reassured American Catholics that blanket condemnation of unions had been based on an erroneous view of these groups. After World War I, the most visible Catholic guardian of labor was John A. Ryan, a priest who advised both the bishops and New Dealers. A committed reformer, Ryan used orthodox theological method to sanctify Progressive reform and workers' rights.

Day founded the Catholic Worker movement to address the immediate concerns of workers. A cooperative apartment kept low-paid women workers off the streets. From the 1930s, the movement sided with union militants, sharecroppers, and migrant farm workers. Its breadline fed the unemployed and unemployable. Dedicated to unionism, the movement nonetheless challenged the materialist ethos of workers and even suggested during World War II that defense industry jobs compromised Gospel pacifism.

The meager resources of the Catholic Worker movement were generously expended on workers attempting to unionize. In 1936–1937, when seamen decided to organize the National Maritime Union in New York, Day responded with publicity and material aid. Throughout the strike period, the paper ran articles sympathetic to the unionists. The Catholic Worker movement even added a branch near the docks so that the seamen would have a place to eat and relax. When the victorious strikers shipped out, Day was left with a sizable debt for their food and rent. The movement typically supported labor with boycotts and picketing. For Day, picketing was a spiritual discipline, "a form of supplicatory procession such as the Church has always through the ages upheld."[8] At the age of seventy-five she was arrested for the final time, picketing with César Chávez's United Farm Workers in California's vineyards. Given the

limited resources of the movement, the aid rendered to labor activism was significant. Such help made a difference—for example, when the *Catholic Worker,*
writing of the low wages earned by workers at the National Biscuit Company
during the 1930s, convinced readers to sell their shares of Nabisco in protest.

On labor issues, Day sometimes asserted her independence from the bishops
and Peter Maurin. During the 1930s she supported a proposed child labor
amendment, whereas the Catholic bishops, anxious about government intrusion
into family issues, opposed it. A defender of strikes, Day early on found herself
in opposition to Maurin, who hoped workers would exchange their machines
for plowshares. Both Maurin and Day, however, agreed to support sitdown
strikes, which were emblematic of a radical restructuring of the workplace.

Day's antistatist tendencies (she preferred self-organization at the community
level to a strong nation-state) made her suspicious of government initiatives.
Critical of liberal reform for its failure to get to the root of social problems,
Day nonetheless believed that in an emergency, government should provide
economic assistance to the needy. Thus, she praised some New Deal programs
while criticizing others.

The new cooperative Christian social order advocated by Day and the Catholic
Worker movement would come about through a nonviolent personalist revolution. Borrowing from French philosopher Emmanuel Mounier, Day advocated
personalism, an individual's free initiative to take responsibility for others, to
change the world by the cumulative effect of the humble efforts of serious
Christians. In this way, nonviolent revolution could come one day, and the profit
motive would no longer drive the economy, create class divisions, fuel racism,
or dominate politics.

The Catholic Worker movement was an intentional community in which activists who shared a hunger for spiritual growth, service to the poor, and social
revolution could support each other. Members took no vows. Some, like seventeen-year-old Stanley Vishnewski, who came to help, stayed for a lifetime.
Many of the young remained until marriage. Several married couples persisted
in the work. Dorothy and Bill Gauchat of Avon, Ohio, for example, cared for
handicapped children. Others, perhaps repelled by the literal truth in Day's view
that "poverty is lice," left quickly.

To end her "long loneliness" outside the Catholic Church, Day had desired
spiritual community as a convert. But even as a Catholic, she found that few of
her coreligionists totally shared her emerging vision of love, peace, revolution,
and voluntary poverty. Thus, Day created her own community within the church.
The paper, the intellectual ferment, the house of hospitality, and the farming
communes drew like-minded people into the movement. Communal life also
resolved, albeit somewhat inadequately from Day's point of view, one of her
major difficulties. Ever anxious about her parenting, Day was helped by members of the movement as she juggled her conflicting roles as single parent and
activist journalist.

When she was not at boarding school, Day's daughter lived at the Catholic

Worker hospice or farm and enjoyed the company of the young volunteers and neighbors, who shared responsibility for her care. But a childhood spent in a hospice was hardly carefree. The shy little girl had to deal with the odd and aggressive behaviors of unbalanced guests, some of whom could not be restrained from destroying her toys. The uneasy mother entrusted her daughter to a spiritual parent—Mary, the mother of Christ—to compensate for her maternal deficiencies. As Tamar neared adulthood and an early marriage, Day took her only sabbatical from the movement, in part so she could spend more time with her daughter.

Before the first Catholic Worker hospice opened, poor folks depended on a network of kin, friends, churches, charities, shelters, and public relief, all of which were stretched to their limits by the magnitude of need during hard times. Catholics had begun to coordinate charitable efforts by 1910 with the National Conference of Catholic Charities, which worked with the dioceses to provide regulated and professional charity as well as to unite against conservative and anti-Catholic opposition. Catholic charitable work, however, was largely directed by religious orders, leaving the laity with the task of funding these efforts.

For Dorothy Day, the New Testament command to love one's neighbor suggested a personal responsibility for others. Christ's commandment was unburdened by restrictive clauses; the law of love applied to all. To do the church's social work, Day tapped the talents of the underutilized laity. She reminded Catholics that they are the church, layperson and religious, male and female, rich and poor, educated and unschooled alike. Eager volunteers crossed gender, class, and race lines as they pitched in to provide relief and to agitate for social revolution. Women's domestic work was elevated to a high spiritual value and, in response to the Gospel, men and women cooked, cleaned, and cared for others. Women could escape domestic work at the soup kitchen to edit the paper, write, speak in public, and picket. Finally, the spiritual leadership of the Catholic Worker movement fell to Dorothy Day, despite her occasional disclaimers.

Catholic Worker hospitality was influenced by contemporary theology. Day popularized a papal theme of the 1930s, the unity of the Mystical Body of Christ and the dignity of each individual member of that body. Each person had a unique place and duty. Because Christ was within all people, the "ambassadors of Christ," as the poor were known in the Catholic Worker movement, were all deserving of help.

Catholic Worker hospitality offered an alternative to the rigidity of the detested "turnstile charity." To maintain the human dignity of those receiving aid, Catholic Workers provided necessities with no questions asked and with no red tape. Guests and volunteers ate the same food, slept in the same dormitory, and wore the same donated clothing. Unlike the situation in public shelters and private charities, where professionals ministered to their charges, Day's movement blurred social distinctions. Guests sometimes became volunteers. And, as Day realized, guests were not the only ones who benefited from association with the movement. Volunteers shared in the largesse that fed, clothed, and sheltered the homeless and reaped spiritual gain.

What began as a small local effort rapidly matured into a loose national (and later international) network of houses and farms influenced by the New Testament. By the end of the 1930s, this community included hospices and agrarian communes stretching from Boston to Houma, Louisiana, and from the District of Columbia to Seattle.

If the Catholic Worker movement in the city meant hospices, in the country it meant a farming commune. Advocated by Peter Maurin, the farming commune idea came to life with the publicity, initiative, and gifts generated by Day. A small plot of land and a house on Staten Island became the first garden commune. By 1936 a more spacious farm was purchased near Easton, Pennsylvania.

These agrarian communities proved taxing to operate. Poorly capitalized, the farms were sometimes no better than rural slums. Resistance to the use of technology and untrained farmhands hindered efficiency and kept production low. Innocent of farming, the New York Catholic Workers purchased the Easton property before anyone noticed the lack of water. One of the more serious tests of Day's leadership and the movement's principles was a dispute during the 1940s involving a group of disgruntled rural Catholic Worker families with their own alternative understanding of farming communes and spirituality; it was resolved by Day's decision to cede land to the dissenters, sell the remainder of the Easton farm, and buy new land elsewhere. Problems aside, the farming communes were an integral part of the Catholic Worker movement. Besides feeding Catholic Workers in the cities, the rural communities provided opportunities for work and functioned as spas for tired volunteers, sanatariums for the ill or unbalanced, and conference centers for spiritual renewal and intellectual growth. By promoting harmony with nature, the Catholic Worker movement appreciated divine creation and foreshadowed the environmentalism of more recent times.

Harmony with creation was also expressed in the Catholic Workers' pacifism. As a Catholic, Day's absolute pacifism was rooted in the gospel of love. Again relying on contemporary themes in theology and philosophy, Day synthesized personalism and Mystical Body theology with an unusual thought for Catholics at that time: biblical pacifism. In so doing, she reached the conclusion that all war was evil. ''As long as [people] trust to the use of force,'' she wrote, ''only a superior, a more savage and brutal force will overcome the enemy.''[9]

Once a Socialist opponent of war, as a Catholic pacifist, Day no longer approved of class warfare. But she sprinkled some of the antiwar ideas of her radical youth into her Christian writings. Her criticism of war profiteering, whether by arms merchants or imperialistic governments, was evidence of the lingering influence of her radical past.

By the 1930s, Day advocated absolute nonviolence, recommending prayer and reception of the sacraments to spiritually overpower armies. Once an opponent of war on political and social grounds, she believed that to follow in

Jesus' footsteps, one must love one's enemy. The same Gospel command that had led to the founding of houses of hospitality and to advocacy of the poor and workers lent authority to Day's controversial religious pacifism. For Day, "a disarmament of the heart" meant active resistance to war and injustice by using spiritual weapons such as prayer, fasting, and love.

Catholic Workers did not invent pacifism. Until the Christianization of the Roman Empire under Constantine, early Christians had refused to engage in war. To defend the Christian state, the teachings of Augustine and Thomas Aquinas set conditions under which war was morally defensible. Pacifism entered into the modern era from a few smaller Protestant sects. In the United States, the Catholic Church normally found its country's wars to be just. But after World War I, when public opinion reflected revulsion with war and disillusionment, elite Catholics sought peaceful alternatives to armed conflict.

The Catholic Association for International Peace (CAIP), founded in 1927, supported international organization and collective security. Adhering to a just war rationale rather than to Gospel pacifism, the CAIP concluded that the United States fought just wars. Unlike the Catholic Worker movement, the CAIP exercised its muscle through its high-level lobbying and educational efforts, avoiding the visible antiwar activism of Dorothy Day and Catholic Worker pacifists.

By the late 1930s, Catholic Workers promoted pacifism in editorials and articles, and established the peace group PAX. Catholic Worker representatives, including Day, testified vigorously but unsuccessfully against a peacetime draft measure before Congress in 1940. When war came, Day remained firmly pacifist, although the movement was divided by the issue of war.

Day tolerated supporters of World War II in the movement so long as they did not block open discussion of pacifism. She lent crucial emotional and financial support to Catholic conscientious objectors in the Civilian Public Service camps. But Day's preferred response to war was complete noncooperation or radical pacifism. She took the precaution of signing a petition against extending the draft to women, refused to pay war taxes, and advocated refusal to register for the draft or to work in war industry.

The Catholic Worker movement was one of the pacifist groups that built the foundation for the antinuclear movement. Day condemned the annihilation of the civilian populations of Hiroshima and Nagasaki with atomic bombs as a "colossal slaughter of innocents," reminding all that " '[t]he Son of Man [Christ] came not to destroy souls but to save.' He said also, 'What you do unto the least of these my brethren, you do unto me.' "[10] The enormous power of governments in the nuclear age reconfirmed Day's mistrust of the state.

Neither domestic political witch-hunting nor fear of international communism during the 1950s curtailed Catholic Worker antinuclear activism. Joining with other radical pacifists, Day and several Catholic Workers were repeatedly arrested and jailed for violating mandatory Civil Defense air-raid drills. By the early 1960s the drills were discontinued, and the federal government urged citizens to construct home bomb shelters.

As a pacifist group, the Catholic Workers were early critics of the Vietnam War. In 1954, when French forces were on the brink of defeat, Day rejected the need for American military involvement in Southeast Asia. And Catholic Workers were burning their draft cards before the Gulf of Tonkin Resolution of 1964 guaranteed extraordinary powers to the president in order to repel any threat to the U.S. military overseas. Slowed down by a heart condition, Day still supported young pacifist noncooperators and lent her name to the newly organized Catholic Peace Fellowship, which provided draft counseling for young men, used the spiritual weapons of prayer and fasting for peace, and gave thoughtful consideration to the merits of the draft board raid movement led by the priests Daniel and Philip Berrigan.

Day's pacifism was premised upon nonviolent resistance to state authority and economic hegemony, and on obedience to the laws of God over human decrees. Rejecting the standard view of ''rendering to Caesar the things that are Caesar's,'' Day argued that God's claims to human obedience superseded those of the state when in conflict with the Gospel.

Although the Catholic bishops moved slowly in condemning the Vietnam War and guaranteeing the right of conscience to oppose war during the 1960s, by the 1980s they denounced the stockpiling of arms and celebrated Day's nonviolence. Some of them, including Maurice Dingman of Des Moines and Raymond Hunthausen of Seattle, advocated noncooperation and engaged in acts of resistance on their own.

Day died in New York City on 29 November 1980, at the age of eighty-three. Although a few critics question whether the movement still lives up to her ideals, Day's influence is strongly felt both inside and outside of the Catholic Worker movement. Her writings awaken consciences, keeping her revolutionary spirit alive in a conservative age. Catholic Worker hospices and farms throughout the United States, Canada, Europe, and Australia provide relief.

Some supporters of Dorothy Day have launched a campaign for her canonization as a saint. However, many of her closest followers refuse to support her formal canonization, honoring instead Day's belief that ''[a]ll are called to be saints. Not to do the extraordinary—if sanctity depended on doing the extraordinary, there would be few saints.''[11] Day wanted to set an example requiring no heroic feats, only simple acts of feeding, sheltering, and clothing those in need; a spiritual life drawing from the rich Christian heritage; and a willingness to live nonviolence.

The Catholic Worker spirit of personalism, or individual responsibility for one's community, has countered an emphasis in the modern American reform tradition to seek redress for economic, social, and political inequality from the federal government. ''We are not denying the obligations of the State,'' Day explained. ''But . . . we must never cease to emphasize personal responsibility.''[12]

The Catholic Worker principles anticipated Catholic renewal during the Second Vatican Council of the 1960s. A pilgrim in Rome during part of the council,

Day used spiritual tools—prayer, fasting, and education—to reassert what she believed was the early church's pacifist ethic. Although the bishops fell short of condemning the possession of nuclear weapons and continued to rely on ''just war'' theology over absolute pacifism, they did uphold the right of conscientious objection and endorsed economic and social justice throughout the world.

Catholic Worker stands on economic justice, social equality, the rights of political prisoners, and peace seemed similar to the positions of the Left. Admirers of the movement, such as the Communist Elizabeth Gurley Flynn, who bequeathed her modest estate to the movement, and Yippie leader Abbie Hoffman, who viewed Day as the first hippie, understood the utter authenticity of Day's radicalism. Unlike these sympathetic radicals, Day insisted on an explicit spiritual grounding for the movement, an appreciation of the Catholic heritage. When a few young Catholic Workers of the early 1960s whose beer blasts, free sexuality, and uninhibited expression (they printed the magazine *Fuck You!* on the *Catholic Worker*'s press) displayed their preference for a bohemian lifestyle over service to the poor, Day demanded that they leave, an incident known humorously as the ''Dorothy Day Stomp.''

Both a traditional Catholic and a dedicated lifelong radical, Day possessed a genius for synthesis. Without compromising her social radicalism, she joined the Catholic Church. By fortifying herself with a spiritual shield, Day built a nonviolent revolution from daily service to the poor and agitation for change. Dedicated to building a new heaven on earth, she understood that the poor ''are not put in our way to be judged, only that we may purchase heaven from them.'' Love, prayer, and works of mercy were for Day the ''holy force'' leading to revolution and salvation.[13]

NOTES

1. Dorothy Day, *The Long Loneliness* (New York, 1952), 285.

2. Floyd Dell, *Homecoming: An Autobiography* (New York, 1933), 296.

3. Day, *Long Loneliness*, 149–150.

4. *Catholic Worker* 1 (November 1933): 2.

5. Rosalie Troester, ed., *Voices from the Catholic Worker* (Philadelphia, 1993), 5–6.

6. Dorothy Day, ''Here and Now'' (1949), in Robert Ellsberg, ed., *By Little and by Little: Selected Writings of Dorothy Day* (New York, 1983), 101.

7. Dorothy Day, quoted in Stanley Vishnewski, ed., *Meditations: Dorothy Day* (New York, 1970), 48.

8. An anonymous author covered the spirituality of picketing in ''Orbach and Klein Violate NRA Codes and Jail Pickets,'' *Catholic Worker* 2 (February 1935):1, 6.

9. Dorothy Day, ''Editorial—CW Stand on the Use of Force'' (September 1938), quoted in Thomas C. Cornell and James H. Forest, eds., *A Penny a Copy: Readings from the Catholic Worker* (New York, 1968), 36.

10. Day's much-quoted jeremiad first appeared in the *Catholic Worker* in September 1945, and is reprinted in Ellsberg, ed., *By Little*, 266–269.

11. Dorothy Day, quoted in William D. Miller, comp., *All Is Grace: The Spirituality of Dorothy Day* (Garden City, N.Y., 1987), 102.

12. Dorothy Day, *House of Hospitality* (New York, 1939), 258.

13. Dorothy Day, quoted in Miller, comp., *All Is Grace*, 134, 93.

BIBLIOGRAPHY

Catholic Worker. 1933–.

Coles, Robert. *Dorothy Day: A Radical Devotion.* Boston, 1987.

Cornell, Tom. ''Dorothy Day Remembered.'' *Sign* 60 (June 1981): 5–11, 54.

Coy, Patrick, ed., *A Revolution of the Heart: Essays on the Catholic Worker.* Philadelphia, 1988.

Day, Dorothy. *The Eleventh Virgin.* New York, 1924.

———. *From Union Square to Rome.* Silver Spring, Md., 1938.

———. *House of Hospitality.* New York, 1939.

———. *The Long Loneliness.* New York, 1952.

———. *Loaves and Fishes.* New York, 1963.

Ellsberg, Robert, ed., *By Little and by Little: The Selected Writings of Dorothy Day.* New York, 1983.

Klejment, Anne, and Alice Klejment. *Dorothy Day and ''The Catholic Worker'': A Bibliography and Index.* New York, 1986.

Klejment, Anne, and Nancy L. Roberts, eds. *American Catholic Pacifism: The Influence of Dorothy Day and the Catholic Worker Movement.* Westport, Conn., 1996.

McNeal, Patricia. *Harder Than War: Catholic Peacemaking in Twentieth-Century America.* New Brunswick, N.J., 1992.

Merriman, Brigid O'Shea. *Reaching for Christ: The Spirituality of Dorothy Day.* Notre Dame, Ind., 1994.

Miller, William D. *A Harsh and Dreadful Love: Dorothy Day and the Catholic Worker Movement.* New York, 1973.

———. *Dorothy Day: A Biography.* San Francisco, 1982.

———, comp. *All Is Grace: The Spirituality of Dorothy Day.* Garden City, N.Y., 1987.

Murray, Harry. *Do Not Neglect Hospitality: The Catholic Worker and the Homeless.* Philadelphia, 1990.

O'Brien, David J. *Public Catholicism.* New York, 1989.

Piehl, Mel. *Breaking Bread: The Catholic Worker and the Origin of Catholic Radicalism in America.* Philadelphia, 1982.

Roberts, Nancy L. *Dorothy Day and the ''Catholic Worker.''* Albany, N.Y., 1984.

Troester, Rosalie, ed., *Voices from the Catholic Worker.* Philadelphia, 1993.

Eugene Victor Debs
and Radical Labor Reform

SCOTT MOLLOY

The American left has produced many leaders who have battled the abuses of big business, government, and other institutions of authority and power since the 1890s. Despite the romantic appeal and dramatic flair of their underdog crusades, few have graced even the footnotes of mainstream history textbooks. Furthermore, many of those eligible for historical attention have been victims of character assassination by left-wing organizations whose fraternal goodwill stopped abruptly at any divergence of opinion. The only personality to transcend these internecine conflicts and maintain a vestige of radical support and public popularity is Eugene Victor Debs. Labor leader, Socialist, reformer, antiwar activist, and five-time presidential candidate, Debs has been the one folk hero on the left to struggle from the margins to the center of history.

Debs's appeal filtered through almost the entire left prism during his life and after his death. Arthur Schlesinger, Jr., hailed him as a great American liberal; the United Auto Workers lionized him as a mainstream progressive during arguments before Congress to restore his citizenship in the 1970s; and the Communist party featured him posthumously in several pamphlets that idealized his life of struggle.

America's radical phalanx has always strained for respectability and never achieved it. Debs, an indigenous supporter of socialism, shielded the movement to some extent with his folksy Hoosier charm. He translated Marxist tenets into homespun attacks on industrial capitalism in language his listeners could understand. He went to jail in 1894, in a bold challenge to national railroad interests. A quarter of a century later he went to prison for opposing World War I, a stand that enhanced his reputation in the 1920s, when the nation retrospectively criticized American involvement in the Great War. In fact, when Debs was imprisoned at age sixty-five, the sentence was widely preceived as a death sentence because of his age and health. His death, a few years after his early release, enshrined him in the eyes of many as a martyr for the cause. His integrity, courage, and commitment to true democratic principles, eschewing all underground and violent tactics, won him a popular following and provided a protective canopy for the rest of the left.

Debs seemed an unlikely candidate for such canonization. He was born in Terre Haute, Indiana, on 5 November 1855. His parents, Jean and Marguerite Debs, were French immigrants who raised six children. They named their third child, Eugene, in honor of the progressive French authors Eugene Sue and Victor Hugo. Debs's father operated a grocery store and raised his family in a middle-class environment that reflected the parents' comfortable upbringing in Alsace. Although he had a head start in life over his working-class companions in Terre Haute, Debs left high school after one year to find his fortune in the workplace.

At the age of fourteen, he began earning fifty cents a day as a locomotive paint scraper. Debs graduated to the position of locomotive fireman, a job that took him across the state to drink at the ''Fountain Proletaire,'' as he later put it. At night he attended business school. The Horatio Alger lifestyle he charted temporarily detoured when the Panic of 1873 left him unemployed. With his father's assistance, however, Debs went to work in a wholesale grocery store.

He also joined the local lodge of the Brotherhood of Locomotive Firemen and was elected recording secretary. As he straddled Terre Haute society with one foot in the blue-collar camp and the other in the white-collar one, Debs toiled to become a model citizen acceptable to all classes. His mother, a Catholic, had been a mill worker at his Protestant grandfather's textile factory in France. Because the family refused to approve his parents' marriage, young Debs seemed sensitized to religious and class discrimination. He sought acceptance in a more tolerant America. He attended literary and cultural events, kept the union's minutes, and seemed to fulfill the Gilded Age's expectations of political manhood and civic responsibility. He reveled in Terre Haute's postbellum booster spirit and hitched his own promising career to the town's seemingly prosperous future.

Somewhat insulated from the era's financial dislocation, Debs enjoyed his third decade of life. His conservative deportment dovetailed nicely with the respectable demeanor of the railroad lodge that increasingly took up his time. His clerical skills served him well as local secretary and official correspondent to the officers and the monthly journal of the Locomotive Firemen. At the time, the various railroad unions divided train workers into very specific craft categories. The brotherhoods doubled as mutual benefit associations for their members and as premium hiring halls for railroad owners. The unions imposed craft standards and personal qualities as strict as any demanded by management.

During the 1877 railroad strike that convulsed the nation, Debs refused to endorse the walkout or accept the trainmen's excuse that the steady wage reductions caused the controversy. He intimated in the union's magazine that members needed to square their lifestyle with the age's ideal in order to be successful, regardless of the destructive crosswinds that buffeted society during economic downturns. ''We feel ourselves in duty bound,'' he wrote, ''to give to railway corporations a class of sober and industrious men. A class of men who are not only satisfied with having performed the ordinary functions of their situations, but men who will be in the direct interest of their employers.''[1] Debs believed in a social compact between citizen and society that required a moral contribution by all, regardless of station in life. The cream would rise to the top, he reasoned, and the purity of one could emulsify the rest.

Weaned on the folklore of the founding fathers and the patriotism of the American Revolution, Debs had difficulty finding blemishes in the mosaic of entrepreneurial success in the United States. He studied the same patriotic and moralistic schoolbooks as did future business leaders like Henry Ford, but at home his parents read the French classics to their children. Throughout his life Debs often reread Victor Hugo's blistering novel *Les Miserables*, in the original French, for personal inspiration. When the Gilded Age transformed captains of industry into robber barons, Debs entered in the period's class conflict and drew on the heritage of the French Revolution. For the time being, however ironically, he directed his wrath at strikers and demonstrators who undercut his idealistic vision of a labor movement and disrupted the class harmony that served as a linchpin for societal stability. He assailed the 1877 railroad strike, the Molly Maguires, and the Haymarket martyrs. After his transformation to American radical, Debs altered his autobiography to show that he had supported these milestone labor events.

Debs ran for local political office in Terre Haute and climbed the Brotherhood of Locomotive Firemen's ladder of success. He was elected city clerk in 1879 and became a state representative in 1884. His political appeal transcended social class and brought him victory in city wards of various socioeconomic statuses. Debs married Katherine Metzel in June 1885. He became editor of the Locomotive Firemen's monthly journal in 1880 and five years later was chosen the Brotherhood's national secretary-treasurer. Debs's brand of self-improvement was paying personal dividends. This double helix of civic and vocational achievement reinforced his conservative philosophy despite the industrial maelstrom stirred by the rank and file in the Noble and Holy Order of the Knights of Labor during the mid-1880s.

Debs missed involvement with the Knights by only a few years but borrowed liberally from their organizational structure and political outlook. Their mission, to create a cooperative commonwealth and an interlocking directorate between skilled and unskilled workers, was a hallmark of his vision in the 1890s. Although the Knights of Labor had been established in 1869, the group remained secretive and virtually unknown until it electrified the nation with an organizational and strike victory against Jay Gould's Wabash Railroad in 1885. Skilled members of the various railroad brotherhoods cheered from the sidelines despite the Knights' egalitarian and quasi-industrial form of organization. Debs opposed any participation by the Brotherhood of Locomotive Firemen, but the Knights' stunning victory and the power of railroad corporations forced him to take another look at America's industrial power relations.

Debs's worldview, formed by his own personal prosperity, obscured the larger reality of growing corporate strength. Even Grover Cleveland, the era's only Democratic president, complained about the iron heel of business influence. Debs remained unsure of an antidote. He feared unbridled labor mobilization because it might interfere with individual freedom, liberty, and mobility—and produce evidence of a class struggle. He felt comfortable criticizing robber barons who misused their privilege to interfere with democratic values by forming pools, cartels, and monopolies. Some legislative adjustments, Debs thought, might solve the problem; but any direct rebuke of the system was still out of the question. He embraced the Democratic party as labor's standard-bearer for any political changes. As his official responsibility for the members of his own union increased, so did his questioning of what made the world go round. The Knights' meteoric success and failure speeded this process.

In February 1888, Debs's Locomotive Firemen did the unthinkable: they struck the Chicago, Quincy, and Burlington Railroad. The walkout, ostensibly called to settle long-standing grievances, involved a fierce clash of personalities, union policy debates, and competition from the Knights of Labor. Debs vigorously endorsed the strike and assisted as second in command. The railroad's two-year campaign to avoid resolution of formal complaints embarrassed the Firemen and pushed Debs over the edge. Court injunctions, disunity, and strike-breaking, however, enfeebled the brotherhood.

Debs was far too earnest to undergo an instant metamorphosis. Nor could he easily forsake an orderly bureaucratic system that, whatever its faults, restrained the many ills he saw bubbling just below society's surface. But once liberated from the views learned in his childhood, Debs quickly sought workable ways to curb the growing corporate abuse that he now viewed as the chief impediment to equal opportunity in the United States. The labor movement had to balance the industrial equation—but what kind of labor movement? Debs borrowed from the Knights of Labor, who had unified miners and trainmen employed by the same railroad owners. But the rank and file would have to be restrained in order to prevent violent outbreaks that would destroy public confidence in unions. Debs took the Knights' federation tactic and transformed it into a strategy. He debated the particulars for four years, experimenting with a loosely drawn organization of railroad firemen, switchmen, and brakemen.

Debs did not invent industrial unionism, in which one labor organization represents all workers in a single establishment, regardless of skill. He did choose the historical moment to unveil his scheme after reaching the painful decision that his cherished Locomotive Firemen and the other jealous brotherhoods were not the vehicle for such reform. Debs resigned as secretary-treasurer of the brotherhood at the 1893 convention and then followed that personal decision with an organizational one. He established the American Railway Union (ARU) that same year, accepting any and all white trainmen as members, as well as any ancillary workers—miners and longshoremen—who received a paycheck from a railroad. (Although Debs argued strenuously for inclusion of black rail workers, delegates at the first convention, like their brethren in the brotherhoods, voted in favor of the color bar—albeit by a narrow margin. The union offered to support any separate black organization.) The ARU offered all the perquisites of the brotherhoods for a $1 initiation fee. Announced inauspiciously at a small meeting of rail workers at Chicago in June 1893, the industrial arrangement became a holy grail to trainmen and an immediate nemesis to management in the ensuing financial panic of that year.

The timing turned the federation idea into a material force. Individual members of the brotherhoods affiliated behind the ARU's collective shield; unskilled laborers joined the only union sympathetic to them; and growing numbers of unemployed workers sought any hope of improvement. In 1894 Debs, infused with energy and excitement, orchestrated a strike against the Great Northern Railroad and its shrewd owner, James J. Hill. Economic depression often quenches the human spirit's ability to struggle against adversity; in this case, rail workers sensed an opportunity and followed Debs. They rallied together in an eighteen-day walkout against wage reductions. Debs employed his diplomatic skills and split Hill from his customers, especially the grain magnate Charles Pillsbury, who feared the imminent spoilage of his produce. Hill agreed to arbitration, and a judge rescinded the cuts in May 1894.

In one of the nineteenth century's bleakest economic years, the ARU made industrial unionism a force to be reckoned with in both management and labor circles. Debs discovered the means to push back selfish corporate power and open the way for working-class opportunity. The victory, as momentous as the Knights' stunning defeat of Jay Gould in 1885, catapulted Debs and the ARU onto the national stage.

Debs's calculated boldness aroused unreasonable expectations among unsophisticated new members who stampeded into the organization. The ARU membership quickly surpassed that of the combined brotherhoods, peaking at approximately 150,000. Debs envisioned a judicious use of the strike and boycott to pressure employers to recognize the union and deal with labor on an even collective bargaining plane, a visionary labor-management scenario unattainable until the end of World War II. "An era of close relationship between capital and labor is dawning," he wrote at the time, "one which I feel will place organized labor on a higher standard. When employer and employee can thoroughly respect each other, I believe, strikes will be a thing of the past."[2] He expected to isolate and punish the occasional titan who might challenge this new labor juggernaut. The damage inflicted on any challenger would serve as a warning to others and help preserve peace in the workplace. This reformist scenario mutated into a revolutionary drama as capitalism grew bolder and Debs grew wiser.

Such a strategy required a disciplined rank and file educated to the sophisticated ways of the organization. The membership, buoyed by the Great Northern victory and inspired by the novel solidarity of industrial unionism, expected an immediate transfer of power from owners to workers. Two decades of wage reductions, management insults, and deteriorating working conditions incited an understandable lust for revenge. A strike over grievances at the Pullman Car Works outside of Chicago during the spring of 1894 offered a chance to test the union's mettle even further. George Pullman, like Henry Ford after him, was part utopian and part exploiter. He manufactured luxury sleeping cars for the nation's railroads, leasing the vehicles to ensure a steady income. He established a model company town for his workers but offended their sense of propriety with his petty tyranny. When times turned hard, he cut wages but not rents and utility costs. The dismissal of a group of employees who brought their complaints to management initiated a walkout on 11 May 1894.

Debs unofficially aided the strikers but was afraid that the ARU was not ready to embrace production workers, whose relationship to railroad corporations was tentative. He mobilized reform elements of Chicago society to help the Pullman employees, trying to duplicate the wedge he had driven between James Hill and public opinion the year before. As fate would have it, the ARU had scheduled its first national convention in Chicago a month after the strike began. Pullman workers lobbied the delegates and found sympathetic listeners concerned about workplace oppression everywhere. The ARU voted to boycott all trains that carried Pullman sleepers and, in effect, endorsed a national strike. Like Terence Powderly and some of the brotherhood chieftains before him, Debs agonized over the membership's decision. Another year or two of education and training, and perhaps they would have been ready. A selective strike here and there against a vulnerable line could work. But a climactic showdown with too many untrained members against a unified rail system seemed suicidal. A year earlier the conservative railroad workers were not ready for Debs's militancy when he quit the Locomotive Engineers; now Debs was unprepared for their belligerence. He reluctantly accepted his associates' decision to strike.

The boycott began on 25 June 1894. Although the membership faced a gargantuan task, they did not shrink from the battle. The first few days resembled the railroad showdown in 1877, when strikers had paralyzed train service nationally for the first time. In 1894, however, railroad management had prepared a counterattack. Unlike the regional Great Northern contest, the Pullman conflict imposed a unity of will on the railroad corporations, which put aside petty jealousies and banded together in the General Managers Association. Although the ARU decisively halted most rail traffic initially, the union was not prepared for federal intervention. U.S. Attorney General Richard Olney, in a blatant conflict of interest, orchestrated legal and military challenges against the ARU despite being a member of the General Managers Association and serving on the boards of major rail lines. He falsely accused the union of interfering with mail cars and interstate commerce. He then sent federal troops into Chicago, precipitating the violence that Debs knew would undermine the union effort.

In an atmosphere that hummed with the possibility of a general strike and even insurrection, Debs had to backpedal in the face of injunctions, martial law, and the arrest of his entire executive board in July 1894. The American capitalist system that he had toiled so hard to vindicate and humanize turned with a revolutionary fury to protect one of its own—George Pullman—and to put down the upstart workers' federation. Ironically, the authorities almost engendered the class conflict they were trying to prevent. In November 1894, Debs was sentenced to six months in prison for contempt of court, for violating Olney's strike injunction. A federal judge decided the case without a jury. At the time, Debs harbored no secret agenda to overthrow the government or the system. His simple reform impulse, although radical for the times, might have saved the business community more than four decades of subsequent industrial strife. Debs's vision of labor-management relations was so advanced that he eventually sought a different solution that reached beyond the confines of the labor population.

Debs served his six months in prison in 1895. After a decade of frenetic activity, he probably found the sentence a respite from his hectic regimen. Allowed to carry on his business by a friendly warden, he reflected on American life, corresponded voluminously, received visitors, and read. Legend would have it that he left prison a socialist. Certainly Debs reset his political compass after half a year of philosophical debate with himself. Reading Marx's *Das Kapital* opened up a new world of political thought, but he remained confused about society's direction. Soon after his release Debs claimed that the liberal American voters could "sweep away trusts, syndicates, corporations, monopolies and every other abnormal development of the money power, designed to abridge the liberties of workingmen and enslave them by the degradation incident to poverty and enforced idleness, as cyclones scatter the leaves of the forest."[3] Later in life he interpreted the lessons of Pullman differently: "in the gleam of every bayonet and the flash of every rifle *the class struggle was revealed.*"[4]

If Debs was unsure of his political direction, there was little doubt about his bright future. At age forty he was America's first national working-class hero; 100,000 supporters greeted him in the rain upon his release from prison. He barnstormed the country, attacking corporate treachery. A young Harvard student recalled going to hear "the monster" out of curiosity. In two hours Debs turned that listener and a cold audience into glowing admirers. A brilliant orator who gave an estimated 6,000 speeches during his lifetime and called himself "the tongue of the working class," Debs did not want to lead his followers down any garden path. He flirted with populism, a colonization scheme, and a social-democratic grouping before joining the precursor of the Socialist party during the Spanish-American War.

Debs's brand of socialism crossed America's class boundaries—filling political voids in middle-class nooks and professional crannies that mocked the vocational molds of European Marxism. Debs made his pragmatic appeals in patriotic vernacular but flavored them with snippets of Marxism. This working-class party in the United States probably counted as many members outside the ranks of the proletariat, as well as a large contingent of foreign-speaking immigrant workers. The industrial and populist upheavals frightened a growing middle class squeezed between corporate monopoly and leftist militancy. In a way, Debs and the Socialist party played midwife to the Progressive era by making moderate reform appear as a reasonable alternative to the anarchist bite and the reactionary sting.

In 1900 Debs embarked on the first of five campaigns for president. As the Socialist party (SP) matured and developed an impressive number of local political machines that cranked out a variety of sophisticated publications, Debs's vote total climbed from 100,000 in 1900 to about 1 million in 1912. (The SP tallies were probably underreported.) Debs campaigned from a train nicknamed the Red Special. Although popular Socialist platforms nudged both mainstream parties to the left, neither Debs nor the Socialist party overcame the contradictions between reform and rebellion in America. Many leftists believed they could vote the revolution into office and dismantle bourgeois society from within. Hundreds of local candidates were indeed elected, and Victor Berger from Milwaukee and Meyer London from New York City became members of the U.S. Congress. Honest city administrations that curbed business and utility graft provided a lease on life for some Socialist mayors long after the party's eclipse. To a more sophisticated and militant left wing, such successes were electoral fool's gold, a lure to trap Socialist energies in a reformist political system that would never yield to a radical victory regardless of its democratic nature. Such cynicism found confirmation during the postwar red scares when some Socialists were arbitrarily expelled from elected offices by Democrats and Republicans.

Debs, and many members at both ideological ends of the Socialist party, often ran the gamut on the revolution–evolution continuum, depending on external circumstances. Debs was no doctrinal hairsplitter and preferred to be an agitational mouthpiece for the party. He avoided internal discord but found himself stretched between the dialectical poles of reform and revolt. This contradiction was particularly acute in the United States, which has perpetually confounded Marxist theorists. American exceptionalism, the doctrine that the United States is different from the Old World and thus requires a different revolutionary plan of action, bedeviled Socialist planners on both sides of the Atlantic. Marxists faced a country with liberal voting privileges, widespread social mobility, and a national labor federation that embraced class consciousness but not class struggle. Whereas class was the essential factor in understanding European social structure, race, religion, and ethnicity were more relevant for understanding the American experience. Debs pragmatically smothered this incongruity by rolling all single issues around the Socialist party spool. He spliced the black question, woman's suffrage, and political elections into a pragmatic socialism that avoided the fragmentation of progressive issues.

As befitted his role of a broad propagandist, Debs shied away from offering microeconomic solutions to systematic problems. Instead, he attacked American capitalism with heavy verbal artillery. The Socialist party, on the other hand, compiled itemized reform packages that appealed to different and competing interests, from agrarian measures to zoning regulations. At times Debs peppered his talks with references to such reforms, but he seldom spelled them out. Most seekers can find some affirmation of traditional Progressive themes in Debs's long career. There are passages and pages that endorse women's rights, African–American liberties, and even birth control. Debs also focused on prison reform. The party published his slender volume, *Walls and Bars*, a year after his death. The book chronicles his incarceration with *les miserables* and indicts capitalism for all crimes. Only one chapter, however, vaguely suggests how Debs would change the prison system.

The advent of World War I opened a new window of opportunity for an old cause. When the U.S. government drifted toward a policy of rescuing its European financial allies, the Socialist party tried to rally antiwar sentiment. That nonintervention message attracted support outside the party's usual membership orbit until U.S. troops physically participated in the war. Once American dough-boys landed on European soil, the public accepted the government's propaganda. Socialist appeals not to register for the draft now seemed unpatriotic. Federal, state, and local authorities orchestrated red scares to discredit all left-wing organizations. The Bolshevik Revolution's stated intent to export revolution legitimized these fears.

As socialist parties in the warring countries of Europe eventually endorsed World War I on nationalist grounds, the American party held firm against the conflict. Speakers continued publicly to denounce the killing of workers in the name of commercial profit. The passage of the Espionage Act, which outlawed criticism of the war effort, invigorated Debs and his colleagues for one last sally. In June 1918 federal agents arrested him for a mild antiwar speech in Canton, Ohio. Debs used the incident to indict the system. His speech to the jury is still powerful, but the brilliantly delivered oratory served more as a literary legacy than as a call to arms. Several months after the armistice was signed, Debs was sentenced to ten years in prison. The agitator scratched the nation's conscience one last time when he ran for president from his jail cell in 1920, garnering 1 million votes, as he had in 1912.

During his trial, Debs provided many memorable passages on social justice. He knew that the socialist moment in America had passed. His defense was a legacy to a more sympathetic posterity. He offered his followers a vision of the future:

When the mariner, sailing over the tropic seas, looks for relief from his weary watch, he turns his eyes toward the Southern Cross, burning luridly above the tempest-vexed ocean. As the midnight approaches the Southern Cross begins to bend, and the whirling worlds change their places, and with starry finger points the Almighty marks the passage of Time upon the dial of the universe; and though no bell may beat the glad tidings, the look-out knows that the midnight is passing—that relief and rest are close at hand. Let the people take heart and hope everywhere, for the cross is bending, the midnight is passing, and joy cometh with the morning.[5]

Like the Southern Cross, Debs and the Socialist party bent under the weight of American exceptionalism. President Warren G. Harding displayed an example of this when he pardoned the unrepentant revolutionary on Christmas Day, 1921. By this time the centrifugal force of the Bolshevik Revolution had pulled most of the world's leftists to itself. Before his death Debs would condemn Soviet chauvinism and conspiratorial revolution, wanting no part of any stifling statism. He died, childless, on 20 October 1926, at Lindlahr Sanitarium near Chicago.

The Socialist juggernaut would never be the same. Debs, unwittingly, *was* the party in the eyes of the nation, just as Samuel Gompers *was* the American Federation of Labor. Long association with the organization since its inception indelibly linked leader and cause. Debs's physical decline and death paralleled the party's eclipse after World War I and the red scares. Even Norman Thomas never escaped the long shadow of his predecessor. At the height of the SP revival during the Great Depression, Thomas could muster only 800,000 votes for president, less than Debs a generation earlier. Historians now refer to the party's halcyon period as the era of Debsian socialism, when an ''un-American'' movement created an American legend. Earlier in his career Debs wrote his epitaph in a tribute to the nineteenth-century labor journalist John Swinton: ''He knew that the masses for whom he did everything, and gave up everything, would never—at least in his own lifetime—understand or appreciate him, and this thought harrowed his sensitive soul and gave him unutterable pain.''[6]

History, however, has been kinder, as Debs speculated it might. A corpus of printed material—biographies, anthologies, interpretative essays, and even a 1991 three-volume collection of his letters—has provided notoriety and divergent but respectful judgments about him. Liberals, Socialists, and Communists have all claimed him for their cause.

Debs was not a genetic radical with insurrectionary chromosomes charting a predetermined course to social rebellion. Rather, he learned from his own mistakes. He admitted once that early in his career he had overlooked revolution because ''I was too deeply absorbed in perfecting wage-servitude.''[7] Debs toiled diligently to overcome that mistake and to overthrow the system he had once embraced. Although he could applaud various reforms and reformers as representing short steps in the march toward socialism, Debs believed that real reform hinged on society's ownership of the means of production. Ironically, the other major parties nibbled away at the Socialists' practical suggestions, sanitized them, and claimed the credit. The Democrats and Progressive Republicans took over the Socialist message to such an extent that they drained off its distinctiveness. In the 1930s Franklin Roosevelt incorporated standard Socialist planks into the New Deal. Social Security, workers' compensation, and a host of other institutional reforms reflected Debs's platforms since the turn of the century.

The social ferment of the 1930s proved hospitable to a legion of CIO labor organizers who spread Debs's message of industrial unionism during America's most sustained organizing drive ever. The dream of the ARU finally became a reality. Debs's picture graced the offices of many a labor leader in that period.

Another generation later, disaffected students rediscovered Debs as a champion. His vision of a society acting collectively in its best interests while maintaining individual perspectives was appealing in the 1960s. Although the lanky old man in the grainy photographs seems more grandfatherly than revolutionary now, in his time Eugene Victor Debs led a movement that inspired dread in corporate boardrooms and political backrooms, and offered a vision of a better world.

NOTES

1. Nick Salvatore, *Eugene V. Debs: Citizen and Socialist* (Urbana, Ill., 1982), 30.
2. Ibid., 124.
3. Eugene Debs, "The Genius of Liberty," in *Law, Labor and Liberty* (Tennessee City, 1896), 10.
4. Stephen Reynolds, ed., *Debs: His Life, Writings and Speeches* (St. Louis, 1908), 82.
5. Ronald Radosh, *Debs* (Englewood Cliffs, N.J., 1971), 84.
6. Frank Harris, ed., *Eugene V. Debs: Pastels of Men* (New York, 1919), 45.
7. Reynolds, *Debs*, 81–82.

BIBLIOGRAPHY

Brommel, Bernard. *Eugene V. Debs: Spokesman for Labor and Socialism*. Chicago, 1978.
Cannon, James P., ed. *Eugene V. Debs Speaks*. New York, 1972.
Constantine, Robert J., ed. *The Letters of Eugene V. Debs*. 3 vols. Urbana, Ill., 1991.
Debs, Eugene V. *Walls and Bars*. Chicago, 1927.
Ginger, Ray. *The Bending Cross: A Biography of Eugene Victor Debs*. New Brunswick, N.J., 1949.
Radosh, Ronald. *Debs*. Englewood Cliffs, N.J., 1971.
Reynolds, Stephen, ed. *Debs: His Life, Writings and Speeches*. St. Louis, 1908.
Salvatore, Nick. *Eugene V. Debs: Citizen and Socialist*. Urbana, Ill., 1982.

John Dewey and Pragmatic Education

GEORGE B. COTKIN

Writing in the mid-twentieth century, historian Henry Steele Commager noted that philosopher John Dewey had been "the guide, the mentor, and the conscience of the American people: it is scarcely an exaggeration to say that for a generation no major issue was clarified until Dewey had spoken."[1] Whether or not this was an exaggeration, Dewey managed by the force of his ideas to become the leading public spokesman for a progressive ideal of educational reform for the entire first half of the twentieth century. Even if many of his ideas, in the end, were not adopted, he demanded that Americans scrutinize the basic intellectual underpinnings of educational theory and practice. Only from such critical examination could needed reforms in education be initiated.

At first glance, John Dewey seemed an unlikely candidate to define the course of American thinking about educational reform. Dewey was born 20 October 1859, in Burlington, Vermont, to Archibald S. and Lucina Rich Dewey. His father was a grocer of sparkling wit but limited ambition; his mother was deeply religious, demanding strict moral codes and evangelical fervor. Thus Dewey's initial environment was small-town, rural, and traditionally Protestant. Dewey never abandoned these values. As someone remarked on the occasion of Dewey's ninetieth birthday in 1949, on "meeting him [Dewey], one would imagine oneself talking with a Vermont countryman."[2] Painfully shy and often reticent in public, Dewey delivered college lectures that consisted of sometimes mumbled, spontaneous, impenetrable, but also brilliant thinking out loud about difficult philosophical and social issues. His writing style did not help: his prose lacked punch and meandered endlessly. But what Dewey lacked in background and charisma was more than made up for by the force of his ideas and his tireless devotion to reforming educational thinking and institutions. Most intriguingly, although he came from a small-town, rural atmosphere, he spent most of his long life (he died in 1952) in big cities, always open to the diversity of people and problems in urban centers. And as education had been the vehicle that carried Dewey into a wider, more exciting world of ideas, so he was convinced that education would enable all Americans to experience the world around them in a more beneficial manner.

Dewey's ideas about education were forged in the context of the social dislocation at the end of the nineteenth century. Living in Baltimore, Chicago, and New York City, he saw firsthand, with an always perceptive eye, that the complications of industrial civilization (horrible working and living conditions; periodic depressions; racial, ethnic, and gender strife—the list could be expanded ad infinitum) demanded that old methods of education be revised in the light of new conditions. If progress were to be achieved, if better and more fulfilling lives were to be possible for the next generation of Americans, then change was required. Although educational progress might not always be as immediate in its results as legislation regulating working conditions or reforming corporate abuses, he maintained that a good education could transform the individual, presenting him or her with the conceptual and vocational skills to confront present and future problems. As Dewey summed it up in "My Pedagogic Creed" (1897): "I believe that education is the fundamental method of social progress and reform."[3]

Dewey was a philosopher and psychologist. He originally turned to philosophical study for religious reasons, seeking a perspective that would unite the diversity of phenomena, that would fit the particular into a meaningful whole. Such a desire was not unusual for late-Victorian era Americans who remembered, or imagined, an earlier age of unity and certitude but who increasingly confronted a world of apparent chaos and ceaseless change. Under the direction of George Morris at Johns Hopkins University, Dewey emulated his mentor's enthusiasm for Hegelian philosophy. By the 1890s, Dewey was slowly dropping the language of Hegel and coming to favor scientific rhetoric. Yet he never abandoned the original desire to overcome dualisms (mind and body, man and nature, meaning and action) and to relish both the particular and the general.

Along with many other educational and social reformers at the turn of the century, Dewey was tremendously influenced by the psychological theories of William James, who taught at Harvard University, and by the tremendous implications of the Darwinian revolution in science. Dewey was awed at the naturalistic, Darwinian, and empiricist approach that James employed in his monumental *Principles of Psychology* (1890). Darwinian and Jamesian ideas offered Dewey an approach to psychological and philosophical problems that recognized change (also central to Hegelianism) without jettisoning continuity. As he later phrased it in an important essay, "The Influence of Darwinism on Philosophy" (1909): Darwinian evolution had upset "the sacred ark of absolute permanency." In the process, it celebrated "the principle of transition, and thereby freed the new logic for application to mind and morals and life."[4] Thus, out of the crucible of scientific and psychological research came the intellectual weapons that reformers like Dewey could wield in their fight to transform existing institutions and achieve social progress.

Armed with this evolutionary, reformist perspective, Dewey crafted a philosophical system that started with a rejection of a passive view of adaptation. He contended that in the process of adapting to the given environment, the organism changed the nature of the environment. Dynamism replaced dualism, activism supplanted passivity. Mind, as Dewey explained it in a manifesto proclaiming a ''New Psychology,'' ''is content to get its logic from this [realistic not abstract] experience, and not . . . by forcing it to conform to certain preconceived abstract ideas.'' In sum, the ''New Psychology,'' as conceived by Dewey, ''bears the realistic stamp of contact with life . . . [and] lays large stress upon the will . . . as a living bond connecting and conditioning *all* mental activity.''[5] These essential principles, first enunciated in 1884, recur throughout the extensive corpus of Dewey's philosophical and psychological writings, and they form the foundation for his work in pragmatic education.

''Since one of the main offices of education is the training of mind,'' wrote Dewey in 1908, ''a changed view of the nature and purpose of mind carries with it a very great change in educational ideas and practices.''[6] This is a key to understanding the importance of pragmatism not simply to Dewey's general philosophical perspective but also to how it became his intended method of reforming American education and American society at large.

Instrumentalism was the name that Dewey employed for his brand of pragmatism. Ideas were conceived as instruments that allowed an individual to pursue ends. Unlike his friend William James, who sometimes equated the efficacy or truth of ideas with the satisfactions that they brought to the individual, Dewey took a more cautious attitude. He claimed that the instrumental truth of an idea generally resided in the long rather than the short term and in its social more than its individual effects. Truth was, in essence, nothing more than ''warranted assertibility.'' In addition, Dewey's epistemological stance questioned all absolutes or foundational theories of knowledge that posited a representational view of truth as a simple correspondence between concept and thing. For some, this was a shattering thought, undermining certitude and leaving the individual and society adrift without firm moorings. For Dewey, however, it was liberating, forcing old truths to be reexamined, tested, revised, and reconstructed. Freed from the dead weight of the past, philosophy and education might undergo a renaissance of immense proportions.

Dewey maintained that change was ubiquitous and that new conditions required new adaptations, which created ever new conditions and challenges. Experience must be closely examined, and it was never narrow or stagnant. Dewey's pragmatic sensibility demanded intelligent recognition that in the last century society had undergone a massive transformation, and that old ways of thinking about the individual or of viewing education as a rote method of learning no longer usefully served either the individual or society. A new approach was needed to allow for a maximum of adaptation to and improvement of the new conditions of the twentieth century. Even without absolute foundations or confidence in conventional wisdom, Dewey exuded optimism: progress was possible so long as individuals took responsibility for their freedom and chose to act in a concerted and intelligent manner to improve society.

Dewey believed that the American mentality of frontier individualism was no longer relevant to the conditions of an interdependent, urban America. For him, a valuable, modern individualism acknowledged that the individual and the community were interconnected, working together to confront problems. A confirmed liberal, Dewey believed that government had a central role to play in organizing and directing economic and social life. In this perception, he was in the mainstream of much of twentieth-century progressivism. Although government and experts would play a greater role in the liberal ideal of state and society, Dewey did not seek to undermine either individuality or the private sphere. He simply emphasized that the public sphere must not be allowed to suffer the claims of individual rights and responsibilities that no longer applied in complex, interdependent modern society. Moreover, he realized that only by having an activist, reformist government could the ideal of the individual be reinvigorated, freed from the often debilitating and numbing effects of unplanned and harsh economic realities.

Dewey was a thoroughgoing empiricist. He avoided abstractions and refused to confine himself to the book-lined study to contemplate a perfect system. Instead, he sought to experience life. Dewey had, for a brief time in the late 1870s and early 1880s, following his graduation from the University of Vermont in 1879, taught in high schools in Oil City, Pennsylvania, and his native Vermont. The little evidence available suggests that Dewey was a less than successful teacher. Perhaps determined to find a better way of approaching educational problems, and at the behest of his talented wife, Alice Chipman, an educational reformer he had married on 28 July 1886, Dewey examined firsthand the problems that modern industrial society presented for the process of education. In the scientific spirit, he determined to test his philosophical perspectives in a laboratory setting. Out of these experiments and in keeping with his instrumentalist philosophy, Dewey built the basis for his pragmatic philosophy of education. In a short time, he began to gain both disciples and enemies as his ideas became more and more central to debates about educational theory and practice in the twentieth century.

In 1894 Dewey was hired to teach philosophy at the University of Chicago (he earned his Ph.D. at Johns Hopkins University in 1884). The university, with ample endowment from John D. Rockefeller, wanted to attract the finest minds to its campus and to have the university play a role in the community. Such an imperative was at one with Dewey's desires: for him, school and society were forever linked. He immersed himself in the rich reformist life of the polyglot city, becoming associated with the settlement house work of reformer Jane Addams. Dewey did not limit himself to teaching philosophy. As professor of pedagogy, and with the help of his wife and other educational reformers, in

1896 he established the Laboratory School on the campus of the University of Chicago as a place where the educational process might be studied scientifically with problems resolved through experimentation and observation.

The Laboratory School attempted, in the manner of Progressive era educational practices, to create an environment where teachers could observe the natural and social instincts of children and discover how to relate the education of children to the industrial and urban civilization that surrounded them. In this sense, the Laboratory School and Dewey's influential writings on education were never to be isolated from the problems of society at large. Indeed, the entire point of the educational observation at the Laboratory School was to develop and refine techniques that would make teachers more effective in supporting children's natural capacities to learn and in attempting to direct their instincts into areas of study that would better fit them to cope with the modern world. One historian describes the activities of the Laboratory School:

Six-year-olds built models of community life on a sand table, seven-year-olds practiced culinary chemistry in the kitchen. . . . The participants and their activities brought together an extended community of reformers, academics and parents who shared Dewey's commitment to ''democratic'' education. . . . Beginning with home life, the instructors gradually expanded the children's social universe to include more diverse occupations, other cultures, and other historical periods, all the while encouraging them to investigate the subject matter collectively.[7]

Out of his work with the Laboratory School and within the crucible of Chicago's civic life, Dewey burst forth as a major theorist of education in the United States by 1900. Beginning most importantly with a series of lectures to parents of children attending the university elementary school, *The School and Society* (1899), later codified in his *Democracy and Education* (1916), Dewey laid out the essentials of pragmatic education. His vision of the importance of education was well suited for his historical era. Although some of his ideas have not worn well over the years, his primary emphasis upon creativity and democracy in the process of education remain important ideals.

Dewey did not consider himself a radical renovator of education. He rejected some Progressive era educational reformers who thought it best to allow the child's instincts free reign without supervision. He also fought against traditionalist approaches that stressed rote memorization and training in the classics. Dewey's middle-ground position recognized that successful education must engage the child's natural inclinations and curiosity. The teacher's role was to build upon this base with necessary interventions. Dewey was not opposed to classical knowledge as such, but he questioned the relevance of traditional subject matter, especially when its supporters claimed that it was valuable for abstract reasons or for its presumed ability to discipline young minds. For Dewey, emphasis upon disciplining the child's mind through boring and nonutilitarian exercises seemed a prescription for educational irrelevance and disaster.

Dewey's ideal classroom facilitated the exercise of the child's imagination. Innate curiosity was to be tied to relevant and timely subject matter and complex learning experiences. Thus, for example, educational activities must be intimately connected with the world that surrounded children. Children learned through active experience, a crucial concept in Dewey's lexicon of pragmatic education. Successful education combined the natural playfulness, creativity, and interest of the child with the ideals of a common task, social efficiency, and even scientific experimentation. Yet the onus for learning remained with the student. In a typical Dewey educational experience, children might learn gardening skills. Dewey did not want them to worry about mastering techniques or mechanics of gardening or to perceive the exercise in narrowly vocational terms. The value of gardening as an educational exercise was in how well it

affords an avenue of approach to knowledge of the place farming and horticulture have had in the history of the race and which they occupy in present social organization. Carried on in an environment educationally controlled, they are means for making a study of the facts of growth, the chemistry of soil, the role of light, air, and moisture, injurious and helpful animal life, etc. There is nothing in the elementary study of botany which cannot be introduced in a vital way in connection with caring for the growth of seeds. . . . it will then belong to life, and will find, moreover, its natural correlations with the facts of soil, animal life, and human relations. As students grow mature, they will perceive problems of interest which may be pursued for the sake of discovery, independent of original direct interest in gardening—problems connected with the germination and nutrition of plants, the reproduction of fruits, etc., thus making the transition to deliberate intellectual investigations.[8]

To continue Dewey's metaphor, the acorn grows into the tree of education and life. First, the child's natural curiosity is inspired in a project. Second, the child works with other children in a process of trial and error, of experimentation under the watchful but not intrusive eye of the teacher. Third, by working with other children, the individual child becomes part of a larger community and learns the elementary basics of democratic participation. Fourth, the specific lessons learned in a particular chore such as gardening are studied not as ends in and of themselves, but as vital elements of historical development and current social needs. Fifth, interest beckons the child toward more abstract knowledge and further experimentation. Thus, for Dewey's pragmatic ideal of education, the school and society, the task and results, the individual and the group, the student and teacher are all mutually implicated in the process of learning, experimenting, and developing.

Similar ideas have been held by many reformers throughout history, but they were especially popular during the Progressive era. Dewey's stature as a philosopher of note, along with his constant stream of publications explaining and extolling the possibilities of pragmatic education, transformed him into an important figure in educational circles. But Dewey's ideas were not sui generis. He learned as much from Jane Addams's social reform experiments at Hull

House in helping immigrants adjust to a new environment as she did from his particular theories. Dewey's genius was in being open to the rich experimentation already going on around him—for example, the work of teacher and district superintendent Ella Flagg Young in Chicago's public schools—as well as in his ability to summarize, theorize, and present a coherent educational philosophy. His success in social and educational reform lay not only in recognizing the tempo and demands of the historical moment but also in actively seeking to stretch the essential assumptions of the society without breaking them.

Yet Dewey's ideas probably had a limited immediate effect on educational thinking and practice. It is perhaps even more difficult to determine whether his educational philosophy actually benefited the child, the school, and the society. Ideas often take on a life of their own. In the hands of self-appointed disciples, the original intentions of Dewey became mere shadows, sometimes dark ones, that undermined the original imperatives. The history of Dewey's educational reform is as much a product of his theory as a function of his disciples' practices.

In a book with his daughter, Evelyn, titled *Schools of To-Morrow* (1915), Dewey attempted to survey the landscape of progressive schools, institutions that were employing theories and practices similar to those that he had outlined in his writings. Dewey recognized resistance on the part of school administrators and parents to progressive education principles. He also chided some of his followers for deemphasizing the importance of direction, discipline, and teacher involvement in the process of education. Surveying experimental schools in places as diverse as Gary, Indiana, Fairhope, Indiana, New York City, and Chicago, Dewey uncovered a new spirit of experimentation, an unwillingness on the part of many progressive administrators and teachers to stand pat with conventional methods and assumptions. The hope remained that progressive schools, enlightened by the pragmatic educational ideals of John Dewey, were ''showing how the ideal of equal opportunity for all is to be transmuted into reality.''[9] Thus, in the near future progressive schools might still transform education, reconstruct society, and reinforce democracy.

Dewey's most brilliant disciple, Randolph Bourne—who later broke bitterly with Dewey over the latter's support for World War I—captured some of this initial excitement in his *The Gary Schools* (1916). In Gary, under the direction of progressive educator William A. Wirt, the school system was closely integrated with the community. Education in Gary stressed vocational training and attempted to socialize a largely immigrant population to American values. Bourne found much to praise in the experimental nature of the Gary school system, which seemed to be following Dewey's imperative to recognize the reality of industrial civilization and to organize schools accordingly. Indeed, the publicity that Bourne gave to the Gary experiment made its assumptions more widely known and furthered attempts to apply the model to the New York City school system.

Yet, as Bourne later realized, behind the reforms lurked dangerous assumptions and goals. After all, at what point—in the minds of cost-conscious administrators wanting to produce students ready and able to enter the work force—did Dewey's emphasis upon vocational training transform the school into nothing more than a publicly funded conduit to funnel young people into the capitalist world of work? Was Dewey's ideal of education even capable of instilling values, or was it only able to emphasize technique and ends? The reaction of Jewish parents at the notion that New York City's schools might be reorganized under Gary principles brought forth torrents of protest. These parents wanted the schools to give their children the skills, culture, and sensitivity to make better lives for themselves; they did not want them to help their children "adjust" to the industrial discipline and realities of sweatshop and factory. Industrial training and the Progressive era emphasis on the Americanization of immigrant students, as Bourne eventually understood, too often failed to respect the particular contributions that diverse cultures brought to America. Indoctrination, even in the name of a utilitarian and unifying Americanization, augured less of experimentation and growth, of openness and diversity, than it did of the imposition of discipline and values at once narrow and condescending.

Thus, from the start, the reforms that Dewey proposed as a means toward freedom and democracy were put through a wringer, often forcing him to respond to critics as well as to overzealous supporters. He always firmly maintained that the point of pragmatic education was to open the field to experimentation, democracy, and growth. Although Dewey never jettisoned his belief in the benefits of vocational education, in *Experience and Education* (1938) he realized that "Overemphasis upon activity as an end, instead of upon *intelligent* activity, leads to identification of freedom with immediate execution of impulses and desires."[10] Rather, for Dewey, through scientific method and intelligent activity, students gained skills to deal with the complexities of modern, democratic America.

In the early years of Dewey's educational theorizing, the hubbub seemed to be much ado about nothing. Most schools in America continued training their students in a traditional manner with only the slightest concern for Dewey's theories. His initial impact was mostly confined to progressive schools and to the lower grades in public schools. His ideas met great resistance from administrators and teachers responsible for high school students. One study of Dewey found that his initial works in education, although popular among philosophers and psychologists, failed to gain influence among educators and the public. Even within the National Educational Association meetings before World War I, there was almost no sustained discussion of his ideas. In part because Dewey's prose was prolix and his ideas often quite radical, many educators before the 1920s seemed unwilling or unable to follow his advice.

There were exceptions to this rule. In 1919 Dewey visited Japan to deliver lectures later published as *Reconstruction in Philosophy.* Soon after, at the behest of some of his Chinese students, he visited China, where he discussed educational reform. In both China and Japan, his ideas on philosophy and education—with his pragmatic emphasis on thought as process, on the dual import of democracy and the scientific frame of mind, and on the role of education in national progress—won him many followers and an enduring reputation as an educational innovator.

Dewey's influence spread more slowly into American schools and into the minds of educational leaders. His success was greatly aided after World War I, when pragmatism became popular as part of the rhetoric of liberal or cosmopolitan idealism. Even if the reform spirit of the Progressive era was relatively quiescent in the 1920s, the general philosophical underpinnings of it, as expressed in the corpus of Dewey's philosophy, became part of the conversation of American intellectual life. Such disciples as Will Durant, Irwin Edman, and Sidney Hook popularized Dewey's principles, along with the belief that pragmatic philosophy might result in the valuable social and intellectual reconstruction of American society. Within educational circles, Dewey's influence continued to grow. In 1904 he moved to Columbia University's Teachers College, thus gaining additional disciples to take his message to the public and to train a new generation of educators in his philosophy.

Still, no complete consensus developed regarding the precise application of Dewey's ideas. Although nearly all of Dewey's disciples joined with their mentor in celebrating the essentials of pragmatic education—allowing the child's interests free play, learning by doing, experimentation and scientific method, the importance of intelligence in the process of social reconstruction—they differed, especially in the politically charged late 1920s and 1930s, about what role the school and teacher should actually play in hastening and directing the process of social reconstruction. In the face of the Great Depression and subsequent world war, the notion that the school and society must be closely linked struck some of Dewey's disciples as both a banal truism and a dangerous fact. If school and society were one, then the class, economic, race, and gender inequities within society might be replicated or supported within the school system. If Deweyan education, with its emphasis on vocational training, served administrators as a means of socializing children to become more willing tools of capitalist oppression, then the original reform ideals of John Dewey might now be viewed as the property of the forces of reaction rather than of reformation.

In the minds of Dewey's more radical critics, reform was part of the problem. Schools must be transformed into vehicles to reconstruct the foundations of society in radical fashion, upon a more equitable, noncapitalist basis. Teachers, according to educator George S. Counts, who in the 1930s preached a much more radical brand of educational reform than Dewey, must take a leadership role, recognizing that the American tradition of competition and pecuniary gain was antagonistic to social progress. Once they had accepted this insight, Counts demanded that teachers become committed to educating students to the only two realistic alternatives for the present age: communism or fascism. Deweyan calls for attention to the interests of the child were now called irrelevant. The crisis of the historical era demanded action and radical transformation. True teaching, in Counts's view, necessitated presenting the students with the correct alternative vision to bourgeois democracy.

Dewey responded to Counts's proposals with a reiteration of his reformist educational ideals. Dewey preferred a middle-of-the-road response. He was unwilling to surrender his faith in choice over dictation, in democracy over totalitarianism. At the same time, Dewey's response revealed unresolved problems at the heart of his pragmatic educational theory. Dewey agreed with Counts that competitive individualism was not a useful response to the environment of depression and worldwide political upheaval, but he saw no reason why students should be indoctrinated into either Communist or fascist ideology. Instead, Dewey believed that the proper role for teachers was to help students learn how to think in an open and experimental manner. This method empowered students to choose among diverse ideological possibilities without determining at the outset which options were most beneficial. The abstract truths of communism or fascism, presumed at the outset by their devotees, too often determined the outcome of the educational process. In Dewey's democratic mode of education, the only values that the students and teachers needed were openness of mind and critical acumen, attained by a process of sustained questioning and examination. In essence, Dewey simply repeated the educational ideas that he had outlined decades earlier in *School and Society*. Ever the reformer, never the revolutionary, he admitted that his method of education did not predetermine the results to be discovered, nor did it proceed rapidly: "But it may make up in sureness what it lacks in speed."[11]

There were hidden assumptions, indeed ideological predicates, in Dewey's educational agenda quite as much as in his opponents' openness to Marxian social planning. Dewey presumed that the presentation of material could proceed in an open and objective manner. He struggled to achieve this goal by fighting for academic freedom for teachers and for minimal administrative interference in education. But Dewey never questioned the value of experimentation or democracy as ends in and of themselves. They were the foundations of his entire pragmatic theory of education. Although he realized that he might be criticized for having his own essential presumptions that he sought to impose on the students, Dewey dismissed such criticisms as "purely dialectical" quibbles. In the end, he held that "the value which is prized is that of permitting and encouraging each student to do his own observing and reflecting and arrive in the end at his own scheme of valuations."[12]

Pragmatic education in Dewey's formulation, then, was predicated upon this democratic, participatory, experimental ideal. It was not without values, if one accepts that a method of inquiry is in and of itself a value. But as Counts and other radicals in the 1920s and 1930s worried, the method did not assure the outcome. In following their interests in a society that was organized according to certain principles, students might not necessarily be able to consider alternatives fairly. The power of the dominant ideology might actively reinforce presumptions, now sanctioned through an educational system that proclaimed conclusions were reached through open discussion and experimentation.

In this sense, Dewey was naive about the transformative powers of the educational experience. Yet, at the same time, he must be praised for refusing to yield on the values that he believed must be part of education: the natural interests of the child, the responsibility of the teacher, the potential gains through pragmatic modes of approaching problems, and the necessity of freedom. Upon such principles rest the success and relevance of Dewey's reputation as a reformer and as someone who still demands our attention. Nowhere did he more succinctly summarize his educational ideals than in the address "Philosophy and Education" (1930):

For the ultimate aim of education is nothing other than the creation of human beings in the fulness of their capacities. Through the making of human beings, of men and women generous in aspiration, liberal in thought, cultivated in taste, and equipped with knowledge and competent method, society itself is constantly remade, and with the remaking the world itself is recreated.[13]

Dewey died on 1 June 1952 in New York City. He is perhaps best understood as a child of the nineteenth century, always wanting to hold onto progress as a possibility and believing in change as beneficial if humans endeavored to make it so. Such thinking did not necessarily render him a star-struck optimist, but it did define the contours of his personality, commitment, and philosophical perspective. Throughout his life he remained earnest, rational, and enlightened, even in the face of the horrors of the modern world he lived long enough to witness.

NOTES

Initial research for this essay was made possible by a National Endowment for the Humanities Fellowship for College Teachers.

1. Henry Steele Commager, *The American Mind* (New Haven, 1950), 100.

2. Irwin Edman, quoted in George Dykhuizen, *The Life and Mind of John Dewey* (Carbondale, Ill., 1973), 1.

3. John Dewey, "My Pedagogic Creed," in *John Dewey: The Early Works, 1882–1898*, 5 (Carbondale, Ill., 1972), 93.

4. John Dewey, "The Influence of Darwinism on Philosophy," in *John Dewey: The Middle Works, 1899–1924*, 4 (Carbondale, Ill., 1977), 3, 7–8.

5. John Dewey, "The New Psychology," in *John Dewey: The Early Works,* 1, (1969), 59–60.

6. John Dewey, "The Bearings of Pragmatism upon Education," in *John Dewey: The Middle Works,* 4:181.

7. Andrew Feffer, *The Chicago Pragmatists and American Progressivism* (Ithaca, N.Y., 1993), 119.

8. John Dewey, *Democracy and Education* (New York, 1916), 235.

9. John Dewey, "The Schools of To-Morrow," in *John Dewey: The Middle Works,* 8 (1979), 404.

10. John Dewey, *Experience and Education* (New York, 1938), 81.

11. John Dewey, "Discussion of 'Freedom,' in Relation to Culture, Social Planning, and Leadership," in *John Dewey: The Later Works, 1925–1953,* 6 (Carbondale, Ill., 1985), 145.

12. Ibid., 144.

13. John Dewey, "Philosophy and Education," in *John Dewey: The Later Works, 1925–1953,* 5 (Carbondale, Ill., 1984), 297.

BIBLIOGRAPHY

Bode, Boyd H. *Progressive Education at the Crossroads.* New York, 1938.

Bourne, Randolph S. *The Gary Schools.* Cambridge, Mass., 1970.

Brickman, William W., and Stanley Lehrer, eds. *John Dewey: Master Educator.* New York; 1959.

Childs, John L. *Education and the Philosophy of Experimentalism.* New York, 1931.

Cremin, Lawrence A. *American Education: The Metropolitan Experience, 1876–1980.* New York, 1988.

Cuban, Larry. *How Teachers Taught: Constancy and Change in American Classrooms, 1890–1980.* New York, 1984.

Dewey, John. *The Early Works, 1882–1898.* 5 vols. Carbondale, Ill., 1967–1972.

———. *The Middle Works, 1899–1924.* 15 vols. Carbondale, Ill., 1976–1983.

———. *The Later Years, 1925–1953.* 17 vols. to date. Carbondale, Ill., 1981–1995.

Dykhuizen, George. *The Life and Mind of John Dewey.* Carbondale, Ill., 1973.

Feffer, Andrew. *The Chicago Pragmatists and American Progressivism.* Ithaca, N.Y., 1993.

Gouinlock, James. *John Dewey's Philosophy of Value.* New York, 1972.

Hook, Sidney. *Education & the Taming of Power.* LaSalle, Ill., 1973.

Meiklejohn, Alexander. *Education Between Two Worlds.* New York, 1942.

Peters, R.S., ed., *John Dewey Reconsidered.* London, 1977.

Ryan, Alan. *John Dewey and the High Tide of American Liberalism.* New York, 1995.

Sleeper, Ralph W. *The Necessity of Pragmatism: John Dewey's Conception of Philosophy.* New Haven, 1986.

Tenenbaum, Samuel. *William Heard Kilpatrick: Trail Blazer in Education.* New York, 1951.

Westbrook, Robert B. *John Dewey and American Democracy.* Ithaca, N.Y., 1991.

Wirth, Arthur G. *John Dewey as Educator.* New York, 1966.

Zilversmit, Arthur. *Changing Schools: Progressive Education Theory and Practice, 1930–1960.* Chicago, 1993.

Dorothea Dix
and Mental Health Reform

ELISABETH LASCH-QUINN

"I am the Revelation," Dorothea Dix once wrote, "of hundreds of wailing, suffering creatures hidden in your private dwellings, and in pens, and cabins,— shut out, cut off from all healing influences, from all mind restoring cares."[1] Nineteenth-century reformer, author, teacher, and Civil War superintendent of nurses, Dix helped usher in a revolution in the way Americans thought of and treated those considered mentally ill. Incensed by her firsthand observations of the living conditions of the insane confined in her local jail, she began a lifelong project of examining such conditions and bringing them to public attention primarily through her memorials, which were presented for government action by members of the legislatures of the various states. These elaborate testimonials raised general awareness of the most shocking and tangible details of cruel treatment and confinement, and through the nineteenth-century reformer's method of moral suasion, Dix managed to compel legislatures to appropriate funds for the construction of new hospitals for the treatment of the insane and for improvements to extant ones, thus abetting the transition to institutionalization already under way. Dix's reform work struck her as the humanitarian imperative of her life: "I am the Hope of the poor crazed beings who pine in cells, and stalls, and cages, and wasterooms," she wrote.[2]

When Dix promoted institutions for the insane, she pictured benevolent hospitals in which treatment would be the province of enlightened doctors who saw madness as a disease, albeit one with a moral component. Far from the authoritarian and inhumane psychiatric hospital of the modern American cultural landscape—as depicted, for instance, in Ken Kesey's *One Flew over the Cuckoo's Nest*—or the overcrowded place of confinement, not cure, described by discouraged asylum superintendents, Dix's ideal asylum was a place of kindness, order, and decency. Part of a larger movement that sought to revise older ways of viewing insanity, Dix advocated the application of science and medicine to madness, which by the early nineteenth century was presumed to possess a discrete and unique character. Like many doctors, asylum superintendents, and reformers, she was outraged at what many mistakenly considered the colonial custom of mass confinement of all dependents, often in deplorable conditions. Confinement of the insane together with criminals, or the poor, came under constant attack in her memorials, as did forcible restraint of the insane more generally. She considered institutions for the insane an alternative to dehumanizing methods of confinement. Dix's writings on behalf of the insane offer remarkable testimony, as does her entire life of reform, to the rise of a new sensibility concerning insanity in the late eighteenth and early nineteenth centuries.

The notion that insanity was a unique condition that set its victims apart from the rest of the population replaced the colonial tendency to view it as part of life and to integrate the afflicted into the other structures of community life. During the interim between colonial methods of provision for the insane and nineteenth-century institutionalization, the heightened sensitivity toward insanity as a separate condition buttressed the emerging notion that the insane should be separated from society. Coupled with such forces of drastic social dislocation as population growth, industrialism, and urbanization, this sensitivity led to changes that included the passage of a law in Massachusetts in 1796 that required the confinement of those considered "furiously mad" in jail.[3] Once policies concerning the insane were initiated, and confinement began to appear appropriate, "the right to confine extended to all classes." According to Mary Ann Jimenez, "Insanity had now taken on an independent status, and the insane, whether paupers or not, were the object of policies designed especially for them."[4]

Driving the movement to institutionalize the insane was the belief that it was not only the violent insane that required confinement—a central irony of the work of reformers like Dix. While decrying the confinement of the insane in *"cages, closets, cellars, stalls, pens!"*[5] Dix promoted confinement in institutions, which entailed other forms of maltreatment. Reformers generally thought they were freeing the insane from abuses inherent in colonial custom, but actually, Jimenez writes, "those insane who suffered the difficulties of confinement in the beginning of the nineteenth century had been subject to a more insistent rationality that characterized the early Republic," when "the anxiety about madness apparently led to a new pattern of confining the non-violent insane."[6]

Unfortunately, the abuses prevalent in the period that witnessed the decline of colonial traditions became wedded in many people's minds with colonial traditions themselves. Those who considered themselves compassionate rejected earlier customs as a whole, without salvaging what was useful and beneficial to the community, such as the integration of nonviolent troubled individuals into family and community life. Practices that publicly singled out the insane for special attention only when they became dependent on the community protected the privacy and encouraged the self-reliance of anyone who managed to cope with the demands of daily life. This guideline, at its best, could keep the focus on the objective need for care and support instead of on subjective conceptions of normal behavior. Once judgments about normality began to be the criteria for insanity, the population considered insane mushroomed and therapeutic procedures eventually insinuated their way into the innermost realms of private life. Although it would be naive to idealize colonial custom as a whole, given that it veered off at times into witch-hunting or ostracizing misfits, many have erred in dismissing it as inhumane in all aspects. In the nineteenth century, partly because of reformers like Dix, the colonial failure to distinguish between insanity and other forms of dependency became associated with the most cruel forms of confinement, which were actually more prevalent in the early national period and all melded into one bogey—tradition. As a result of their faith in newness and progress, nineteenth-century asylum superintendents, prompted by conscientious reformers, perpetuated a shorter-lived practice whose particular flaws they tried to remedy but whose larger misdirection they overlooked—confinement.

Dorothea Lynde Dix was born on 4 April 1802, in Hampden, Maine (then part of Massachusetts), to Joseph and Mary Bigelow Dix. Her parents apparently did not provide a very stable, comforting, or inspiring environment for the young girl. Her father, Joseph Dix, began his studies at Harvard but dropped out to marry the impoverished Mary Bigelow, twenty years his senior, who was considered an unsuitable addition to the respected Dix family. Joseph's inability to provide for the family, which came to include two sons, combined with Mary's physical infirmities to put unusual burdens on young Dorothea. When Joseph turned to the itinerant Methodist ministry, she spent her days sewing his tracts. Her life contrasted markedly with the order and plenty of the elegant Boston estate of her grandparents. On visits there, until he died when she was seven, Dorothea was inseparable from her grandfather, whom she loved to accompany on walks around his gardens, on drives to historical Boston sites, and on outings to his place of work.

At age twelve Dorothea ran away from her parents to live with her grandmother, Dorothy Dix, the widow of Elijah Dix, a prosperous physician, chemical manufacturer, and land promoter. When her grandmother, a strict disciplinarian, tried to educate Dorothea in proper decorum and other social skills, she encountered a headstrong girl with ideas of her own, formed by the demands of frontier life. Dorothea was sent to live with her great aunt in Worcester, where she found a more congenial environment in a home filled with children. At age fourteen, she set up a little school in a vacant building and became a "school marm," dressing severely to appear older than she was. In the course of teaching "reading, writing, manners, and sewing," she proved herself a harsh disciplinarian, whipping her pupils for misbehaving and making one walk to and from school with a sign on her back reading "A Very Bad Girl Indeed."[7]

Dorothea returned to her grandmother's house in Boston and pursued her own education with the help of her grandfather's substantial library and private tutors. Driven by the need to support her mother and two younger brothers and to become financially independent, she soon opened a school with a special section for needy children that was inspired by the work of Hannah More in England. Dorothea became engaged to a cousin, Edward Bangs, but as her work expanded to fill her waking hours, the engagement was broken off. A key figure in her emotional life stepped in; Ann Heath, who then lived with her family in Brookline, became a lifelong friend and confidante. Dorothea did not participate in social events—ignoring her grandmother's encouragement to enter society as an eligible young lady—not even those arranged around intellectual and reformist endeavors. One biographer wrote:

In her nature there lodged an intensity, a search for perfection, an awful seriousness, dwelling there side by side with an unyielding reserve, that made for a deportment considered old-fashioned, ultra-ladylike, even in those days of gentle manners. It is not hard to see that this young woman of unbending dignity and serious purpose might have been a damper on any assemblage not committed to improvement of the human lot.[8]

From an early age, Dorothea avoided frivolity in attire, preferring dark, simple dresses and wearing her hair parted down the middle of her head and stretched across her ears to a tight knot in back, and expressed a conscious dislike for "fashionable dissipation."[9] Perhaps it was the unreliability of her parents and the contrasting model of order and respectability provided by her grandparents that steered her toward a heightened sense of purpose, order, seriousness, and self-control. She mentioned to friends that she had always to counteract an innate tendency to avoid work; such self-criticism seemed to ensure that little of her life would be spent in relaxation.

In her twenties Dix wrote a science text titled *Conversations on Common Things* (1824), a book of poems titled *Hymns for Children* (1825), and numerous other works for young people. From early on, however, she thought teachers had the responsibility to inculcate in children a self-critical moral awareness, as illustrated by her book, *American Moral Tales for Young Persons* (1832), and by previous students' comments about the strict decorum she required and a curious technique she had of soliciting quasiconfessions from her students. In her grandmother's house, where she ran a boarding school for young women, Dix kept a large shell, "a sort of ear of God,"[10] in which she asked her students to place daily letters spelling out the results of constant self-examination. Dix wrote extensive replies, encouraging students to forsake greed and vanity, and on Saturday evenings discussed their shortcomings with them in individual consultations.

Dix's teaching, writing, and studying occupied nearly all her waking hours. Lack of rest, combined with physical ailments, resulted in periodic infirmity, including a full-scale collapse in 1836 and numerous other battles with illness throughout her life. To recuperate, she traveled to Liverpool, England, and, through William Ellery Channing's introduction, stayed with a Unitarian merchant and philanthropist, William Rathbone. While living with Rathbone and his family, she may have met—and certainly became acquainted with the ideas of—one of the leading reformers of conditions for the insane in England, Dr. Samuel Tuke, son of William Tuke, a Quaker who founded the York Retreat in 1792. Upon her return to America, Dix traveled, avoiding teaching because of the potential strain. In 1841, at the age of thirty-nine, she taught a Sunday school for women at a prison in East Cambridge, Massachusetts. There she encountered mentally ill women confined in an unheated section of the jail. Horrified at both the inhumane living conditions and the confinement of prisoners and the insane together, she launched a career in the reform of conditions for the mentally ill in America.

Dix began her life's work by conducting an intensive survey of all Massachusetts jails, almshouses, and houses of correction. Finding atrocious conditions, she spelled them out in detail and used them as a basis for a moral appeal to the Massachusetts legislature in the form of an 1843 memorial written by her and presented by Samuel Gridley Howe. Along with Charles Sumner and Horace Mann, Howe supported Dix's efforts and championed her cause, taking public stands against those who accused her of sensationalism and inappropriateness. The result was a triumph for Dix—the appropriation of more funds for Worcester State Hospital. Drawing on this experience, she went on to conduct surveys of Rhode Island and New York, and then many other states, presenting numerous memorials. Her inspections entailed thousands of miles of traveling in often grueling conditions. At times, she participated in other reforms, as when she conducted research on prison conditions and published the results in *Remarks on Prisons and Prison Discipline in the United States* (1845).

In 1848 Dix had Senator John A. Dix of New York present a different kind of memorial—one asking Congress to set aside millions of acres of public land as a perpetual trust, the income from which would fund the treatment of the insane. For six years she lobbied Congress to pass the bill, but when both the House and the Senate finally did vote in favor of it, President Franklin Pierce vetoed the measure on the grounds that the responsibility for public welfare rightly belonged to the states. Nevertheless, Dix's agitation for better treatment of the insane resulted in the allotment of state funds for new or improved facilities. In the 1850s, she continued her work abroad in Scotland, Italy, France, Turkey, and Russia.

During the Civil War, Dix served as superintendent of nurses for the Union. Before undertaking this role, she tried to continue her efforts on behalf of the insane without speaking out about slavery, for fear it would close all doors to her reform work in the South. But when the war broke out, she immediately boarded a train for Washington, in order to volunteer for nursing duty. She was assigned the responsibility of hiring nurses and placing them in military hospitals, along with other duties. The idea that one woman could perform such work, which derived from misconceptions about the war's duration and seriousness, was mistaken. In addition, Dix's experience in reform work had taught her to be independent and to answer only to her own high standards of morality and organization. Faced with the exigencies of war and administration, which called for practical solutions, compromises, and cooperation with other workers, she sought much more single-handed control than was possible. Even her friends spoke of the difficulties she encountered working with others, the impossibly high level of ''pure consecration to duty'' she demanded of her nurses, and her inability to tackle effectively the problems at hand with her usual tone of moral righteousness. She sought out abuses, fought with surgeons, and ''tried to stand over the sick and wounded soldiers as the avenging angel of their wrongs,'' as a biographer put it.[11]

Observers like Elizabeth Blackwell and Louisa May Alcott thought Dix a difficult or arbitrary administrator, and she was formally reprimanded by removal of the ultimate authority over nurses from her hands. In spite of her unsuitability for the work and her unpopularity in this position, she never took a day's vacation during the war. She spent the duration organizing nurses, arranging for medical supplies, inspecting hospitals, and exposing poor conditions in them. Undoubtedly Dix's efforts led to the saving of many lives. Nevertheless, looking at her Civil War work, she said, ''This is not the work I would have my life judged by!''[12]

After the Civil War, Dix again visited hospitals and prisons, particularly those in the South, lamenting the decline in conditions. She came to symbolize the movement to institutionalize the insane, and worked in concert with the Association of Medical Superintendents of American Institutions for the Insane, founded in 1844. At least partly because of her efforts, by 1850, 123 hospitals for the insane existed in the United States (in 1843 there were only thirteen); Dix had helped found thirty-two of them and had inspired many more. She was particularly proud of the New Jersey State Hospital for the Insane in Trenton, New Jersey, which she called ''my first-born child.''[13]

Lobbying for the establishment of this hospital, Dix had her memorial concerning conditions in New Jersey presented to the state legislature by Joseph S. Dodd. It stressed that the asylum was the only viable alternative to physical restraint of the insane at home, indicating that it was not only the indigent who were treated in that manner. One well-known former judge, lawyer, and member of the state legislature, Dix said, had fallen from a place of ''honor and trust'' to one of loneliness and despair because he had lost his wealth through economic ''fluctuations'' and his mind had begun to drift with age.[14]

Behind the scenes, Dix worked from before dawn to late night, writing letters and editorials, meeting with legislators individually and in small groups, in attempts to influence those who did not favor increasing taxes in order to finance the building of a hospital for the insane at Trenton. She wrote to a friend: ''You cannot imagine the labor of conversing and convincing.''[15] Viewing her endeavor as a purely humanitarian one, Dix approached her political maneuvering

as a missionary cause, as is evident in her description of her conversation with
one doubting Thomas:

The last evening, a rough country member, who had announced in the House that the
"wants of the insane in New Jersey were all humbug," and who came to overwhelm
me with his arguments, after listening an hour and a half with wonderful patience to my
details and to principles of treatment, suddenly moved into the middle of the parlor, and
thus delivered himself: "Ma'am, I bid you good-night! I do not want, for my part, to
hear anything more; the others can stay if they want to. *I am convinced*; you've conquered
me out and out; I shall vote for the hospital. If you'll come to the House, and talk there
as you've done here, no man that is n't [*sic*] a brute can stand you; and so, when a man's
convinced, that's enough. The Lord bless you!"—and thereupon he departed.[16]

When the vote was finally taken, on 14 March 1845, the bill for the establishment of the New Jersey asylum passed into law, as did many others that Dix
was to initiate. Her desires for a homey place of order and pleasantness were
seemingly fulfilled; she visited the asylum on numerous occasions and returned
there to spend her last years. She died there on 18 July 1887.

Although it might be tempting to view Dix as inaugurating drastic social
changes nearly single-handedly, her work can be understood only in the context
of nineteenth-century social conditions and cultural transition. Stirred by the
reform fervor of the period, particularly strong in Boston in the 1830s, Dix
responded to particular circumstances when she decided to devote her life to
altering the ways that the insane would be treated. She was one of a small but
growing number of women, for instance, who fashioned an expanded female
sphere from the imperatives of the emerging "cult of true womanhood," with
its emphasis on the superiority of women in the moral and domestic sphere and
its view of the inherent differences between men and women. Although she
criticized politicians for their petty partisanship and disputes driven by self-
interest, she was as politically active as it was possible for a woman to be, given
the lack of the right to vote, the capacity to hold public office, and approval for
speaking in public. In fact, Dix was not known to speak to a group of more
than about a dozen people at a time throughout her life.

Although Dix had sympathy for the cause of women's rights, she criticized
the extremism of some reformers, drawing on notions of "respectable womanhood" to advance her cause. She asserted that her femininity compelled her to
bring to the attention of the public the horrifying details of conditions in prisons
and almshouses. She called on the "Men of Massachusetts": "I beg, I implore,
I demand, pity and protection for these of my suffering, outraged sex."[17] At the
same time, she apologized for stepping out of the modest reserve of ladylike
behavior to convey the abuses she witnessed: "I shall be obliged to speak with
great plainness, and to reveal many things revolting to the taste, and from which
my woman's nature shrinks with peculiar sensitiveness. But truth is the highest
consideration."[18] Like Catharine Beecher, Frances Willard, and others, Dix used

her femininity to argue, as moral guardian, for a political goal she thought transcended traditional politics:

Fathers, Husbands, Brothers . . . .Here you will put away the cold, calculating spirit of selfishness and self-seeking; lay off the armor of local strife and political opposition; here and now, for once, forgetful of the earthly and perishable, come up to these halls and consecrate them with one heart and one mind to works of righteousness and just judgment. Become the benefactors of your race, the just guardians of the solemn rights you hold in trust. Raise up the fallen; succor the desolate; restore the outcast; defend the helpless; and for your eternal and great reward, receive the benediction . . . .''Well done, good and faithful servants, become rulers over many things!''[19]

Dorothea Dix also belonged to a generation of reformers who interpreted their religious views as a mandate for social reform. Although she criticized revivalists as succumbing to an ''age of impulse,'' Dix partook of that aspect of reform Christianity that rejected determinism and emphasized the possibility for earthly perfection through ideal, man-made institutions. In addition, her agitation for federal land that would provide a fund for care of the insane made her part of the longer-term movement to expand the realm of the federal government into public welfare that came to fruition in the twentieth century. It was, however, the successful movement for the appropriation of federal land for internal improvements that laid the immediate groundwork for Dix's demand.

Most crucial for understanding Dix's life and role in the movement on behalf of the insane is, of course, the major transformation in attitudes toward madness already under way by the time Dix became involved in furthering such change at age thirty-nine. The debate over the ultimate significance of this transformation has centered on basic differences over how reformers, self-appointed humanitarians, philanthropists, and other do-gooders should be understood.

Some scholars have stressed the humanitarian motives of reformers, viewing the results of their efforts as advancements from an inferior set of arrangements to a rational order more conducive to the needs of beneficiaries. Others have criticized this progressive view, citing the class interests and ulterior motives of reformers as evidence that behind the eleemosynary expressions lurked a desire to control the poor and deviant, to rein in the disorder they appeared to cause. Others see reformers as seeking to impose their middle-class morality in order to discipline the work force, and as representing a larger shift in attitudes that included the families of the insane as well as the insane themselves. The asylum, in sum, symbolizes a fundamental change in American culture. It marks the shift from local, familial, and community arrangements for the care and control of those who failed to function as fully in society as their neighbors, to centralized, bureaucratized solutions that subjected to scrutiny the most private preserves— the body and the mind—in order to classify individuals as either insane or sane. In order to explain the nature and significance of Dorothea Dix's reform work, it is important to place it in its larger context—the rise of new institutional forms that accompanied a wholesale shift in sensibility about insanity.

A radical change in social policies and popular attitudes toward the insane occurring in America at the end of the eighteenth and beginning of the nineteenth century resulted in the erection of asylums. In the colonial period, families who could afford to do so cared for their own members, allowing them to participate in family life to the degree of their capacity. In the case of the dependent, colonists aimed primarily to mitigate the individual's economic stress; they did not single out the "distracted" as having public needs different from those of paupers. The primary rule governing the care of the poor was that communities should shoulder responsibility for the support of their resident needy. In *The Discovery of the Asylum* (1971), David Rothman writes that "poor relief was a local system, towns liable for their own, but not for others."[20] Colonial adherence to local care translated into practices such as bidding-out, contracting, warning-out, and confining the insane in an almshouse. Laws absolved towns of responsibility for nonresident dependents. Warning-out, a practice consisting of warnings or forceful removal, enabled residents to rid their towns of the burden of illegitimate dependents, who had no choice but to move on.

In the case of resident paupers, communities arranged for their care locally. Towns gave donations raised from taxes to support at home those individuals requiring only partial aid. In the case of total dependents, towns auctioned them off to the lowest bidder, that is, to the person who offered to house and support the dependent for the least cost to the town. Contracting, basically a system of labor, hired out a group of paupers to a single household for a fixed price. Bidding-out and contracting usually took place yearly, thus exacerbating the insecure, volatile living conditions of the poor. According to David Rothman, the last alternative was the almshouse, which provided the cheapest answer to the problem of the poor. Workhouses provided yet another deterrent to outsiders by threatening them with hard labor.

These methods allowed towns on the brink of survival to devote their limited resources to caring for their residents. They also grew out of the Elizabethan poor laws, which, in response to the perceived increase of vagrancy and vagabondage, assumed the existence of two kinds of poor—the deserving poor and the shiftless. Bidding-out and contracting represented the belief that the deserving poor should receive aid. Warning-out gave communities the right to make the distinction. Although these customs left much to be desired when applied to the insane, especially for unclaimed dependents, they rested on the notion of family and community responsibility. At their best, they led to the integration of the insane as much as possible into the regular life of the community, rather than placing them in special institutions at a remove from society, as Dix and others later favored.

A variety of demographic, economic, intellectual, and social changes prepared the ground for the growth of asylums and other Jacksonian reforms. An increase in population and in population density occurred in the new republic and magnified the visibility of the insane. Historian Gerald Grob indicates that most large urban areas built almshouses before 1800 because of population growth and its destructive effect on other local solutions. Geographic mobility and population increase rendered obsolete old forms of poor relief; communities could no longer solve the problem on an individual basis because of expense and impracticality. Almshouse incarceration presented a cheaper, though least desirable, alternative.

Another condition setting the scene for the appearance of asylums was the intellectual impact of the Enlightenment. According to Grob, social reform movements developed from a new intellectual stance.

The new outlook stressed the desirability of innovation, condemned stagnation and sought a greater application of human intelligence to social problems. The result was a widespread conviction not only that the conquest of disease was merely a matter of time, but that many of the perennial dilemmas of humanity—including poverty, vice and ignorance—could be minimized if not abolished altogether.[21]

Rationalist activism invaded all aspects of life, including attitudes toward the deviant. Whereas insanity appeared to be folly or ''demoniacal possession'' to colonists, Americans increasingly considered it not only a disease with definite somatic causes but also one more curable than most diseases. The Second Great Awakening, with its message of individual conversion and regeneration as the means of establishing a good society, added impetus to reform as well as a moralistic mission of eradicating impurities from society. Thus science and religion became intertwined in the crusades of reformers like Dix.

Institutions for the confinement of paupers, the insane, and criminals had provided a solution for the homeless or burdensome dependents since the seventeenth century in Europe. Almshouses and jails increasingly served this purpose in America. The novelty of nineteenth-century institutionalization was that it pointed to the asylum as the preferred solution to the plight of the insane and singled out the insane for separate curative treatment. By the end of the eighteenth century, partly because the early hospices brought about an unhealthful and undesirable amalgam of the diseased, the criminal, and the indigent, reformers perceived a need to separate these groups.

Associationist philosophy, a dominant strand of medical thought at the time, underpinned the belief that insanity was a medical problem. Charles Rosenberg sums up this school of thought as rooted in a metaphor of the body as ''a system of dynamic interactions with its environment.'' Associationism embodied the tenets that each part of the body was related to every other, that the body was ''a system of intake and outgo,'' and that ''equilibrium was synonymous with health, disequilibrium with illness.'' Madness was the culmination of both physical and moral afflictions, all part of one disease, for ''just as man's body interacted continuously with his environment, so did his mind with his body, his morals with his health.''[22] This interpretation of insanity paved the way for a system of active therapeutics including the regulation of a system's intake and outgo, usually through drugs, as well as active treatment of the nonsomatic causes and symptoms of insanity.

"Moral treatment," the primary treatment employed for the nonphysical aspects of madness, occupied center stage in the era of the founding of American asylums. This entailed sequestering a patient from the environment producing or aggravating the disorder, and placing him or her in an atmosphere completely dedicated to therapy. This environment was to resemble a well-ordered family and to instill disciplined behavior through the example of the superintendent, the staff, and the well-behaved patients. Classification of patients by sex and by type and extent of illness created a ward system in which patients could proceed to convalescent and privileged wards as a reward for good behavior. As the father of the asylum family, the superintendent was to exert the kind but strict authority he might use in bringing up his own children. Treatment enlisted the active participation of the patient, who was to acknowledge his or her disease and learn self-control in order to overcome it. The success of moral treatment thus required a sort of conversion experience on the part of the patient.

This treatment assumed the existence of a genre of curable insanity that later acquired the title "moral insanity," for a long time a catchall for any form of insanity in which the intellect survived intact but the moral sense was impaired. English physician James Pritchard defined it in 1835 as any affliction that left the intellect untouched but injured "the state of feelings, temper or habit."[23] Patients with moral insanity primarily lost inhibition; they proved "incapable of conducting [themselves] with decency and propriety."[24] In other words, this disease indicated a loss of moral intuition and was the diagnosis for individuals who "had lost their ability to accept society's judgments about what constituted moral behavior."[25]

The notion of moral insanity caused an expansion of the boundaries of insanity, for it encompassed not only the indigent and helpless "feebleminded" but also members of any social class who had difficulty abiding by society's moral code. Moral treatment thus took root in a belief that asylums could restore lost moral sense to individuals. Moral treatment, based on the concept of moral insanity, thus relied on the superintendent and the asylum to restore patients to a semblance of self-control.

Moral treatment had grave implications for what the asylum was to become. It established physicians as guardians of the moral order within the asylum and endowed them with a large share of the responsibility for defining that moral code. They did not possess absolute power, however, for families and neighbors played a large part in deciding who required moral education. Asylum officials ultimately had the authority to determine whose moral sense had been regained enough to merit that person's return to society.

Moral treatment came to the awareness of American reformers like Dix through the ideas of William Tuke and Philippe Pinel, both of whom stressed the need for a combination of kindness and authoritarianism. Pinel deemed the asylum a laboratory for studying mental illness as well as a place for humanitarian treatment, "a mode of care that made an institutional setting a sine qua non." He believed that the treatment of the insane demanded the creation of a separate environment and that insanity "was a curable disease, given understanding, patience, guidance, and proper treatment." Although Pinel is best known for the image of removing female lunatics from chains at the Bicêtre in Paris in 1793, he also believed in a highly authoritarian approach to the care of the insane. Institutionalization was necessary because only within walls could a physician establish himself as the dominant influence in the patient's life and thus instill "an appreciation of normal behavior."[26] The relationship between doctor and patient took on a paternalistic character, and the successful physician would achieve the "happy effects of intimidation, without severity; of oppression without violence; and of triumph, without outrage."[27] To an extent, moral treatment assumed that a departure from social norms consisted of willful misbehaving, lack of discipline, or ignorance of social hierarchies of authority. Moral treatment applied psychological force with the goal of triumphing over behavior and thought considered immoral or abnormal.

Another figure who influenced Americans was William Tuke, who helped found the York Retreat in 1792, a model for American asylums. Founders of this Quaker hospital perceived the need to mitigate the corrupting influence of other patients' unclean or unacceptable behavior on convalescing or well-behaved individuals. Therapy aimed to "develop patients' internal means of self-restraint and self-control" with humane rather than cruel or harsh punishments. Instead of corporal punishment, Tuke applied the "principle of fear" and fostered the "desire for esteem."[28] Tuke likened this treatment to the indoctrination of children. Moral treatment as defined by Pinel and Tuke came to Americans as a fully formed justification for establishing asylums. To Dix, whose moral righteousness seemed to equal her sensitivity to abuse, both humanitarian and authoritarian treatment might have appeared logical and legitimate explanations for institutionalizing the insane.

In assessing the results of these drastic changes in the way the insane were viewed and treated, historians differ over the reasons for the emergence of the asylum in early nineteenth-century America, and their interpretations in turn color their view of its subsequent history. In short, those who deem the mental institution a positive invention believe it emerged from advances in medical opinion inspired by Enlightenment optimism and rationalism. Grob and other scholars who share this view understand the widely proclaimed failure of asylums by the late nineteenth century to deliver on their promises of ideal therapeutic environments and high cure rates as having resulted from parsimonious state legislatures and inexorable demographic forces that caused overcrowding and derailed the best intentions of reformers and physicians.

Critical of the notion that asylums resulted from a humanitarian impulse and a progressive medical profession, other scholars stress reformers' concern for combating the forces of social disorder they feared would burst the seams of

early nineteenth-century American society. Historians who emphasize motives
of social control, such as David Rothman, contend that reformers anticipated
that the patient population would be largely lower class, and consider their
reforms a conscious effort to control what the reformers saw as the chaos and
dangerous excitement of workers and the poor, as well as an attempt to restore
traditional social structures, which they thought were threatened by urbanization
and social mobility.

Structuralist historians trace this concern for disorder to reformers' class interests. Some write that reformers, doctors, and other asylum advocates sought
to instill the discipline of a well-ordered family in order to develop the regular
work habits needed in an industrial labor force. Michel Foucault emphasized
the rise of a new bourgeois ideology that legitimized the imperatives of capitalism. The middle class's growing sensitivity to harsh public punishment helped
to foster the acceptance of separate institutions and to discourage tolerance of
the association of people of a wide range of capabilities, classes, and behaviors.
The possibility of exerting psychological rather than physical restraint in a controlled, separate environment best suited this new middle-class sensibility.

The abuses of asylum treatment revealed in the late nineteenth century were,
in this view, natural outgrowths of an oppressive regime. Christopher Lasch
argued that asylums and other institutions of confinement represented the growing class consciousness of the middle class, which brought with it ''a decline
in the sense of collective responsibility'' and an urge to avoid ''the spectacle
of suffering and depravity'' and ''the contamination of the lower orders.''[29]
Drawing on the theory of ''total institutions'' articulated by Erving Goffman
and Gresham M. Sykes, Lasch asserted that asylums developed according to
their own internal, bureaucratic needs; healing was sacrificed to administrative
efficiency. Ironically, the ''humanizing of the asylum'' set this new machine in
motion: ''Once therapy became the object of confinement, however, and once
therapy had been defined as learning to submit to moral discipline, efficient
administration came to be so closely identified with treatment that in practice
the distinction between them was almost impossible to maintain.''[30]

This kind of institution thus resulted less from a vanguard of reformers than
from a basic shift in thinking about the place of the insane in the social order.
Richard Fox, for instance, has shown that families willingly committed their
members to psychiatric hospitals. Patient records show, further, that the mentally
ill sometimes volunteered themselves for admission, finding the institution pref-
erable to the world outside. This evidence correlates with the testimony of numerous people who wrote to Dix, thanking her for the work she did on their
behalf. Any view of Dix must take into account that many of her contemporaries,
well and unwell, praised her efforts. They were not so much participating in
their own oppression as agreeing that current methods of confinement required
serious change, and that some better form of care was needed. Hindsight suggests that this dire set of circumstances, and the limited notion of what could
be done to remedy it, resulted from the decline of older customs and the rise

of a new sensitivity to, and even terror of, insanity. Because of the change in sensibility, older customs that benefited communities were abandoned along with the unsatisfactory, even brutal ad hoc measures resulting from the breakdown of traditions. Out of this strange blend came a belief in engineered therapeutic environments, the need for intense personal scrutiny of others for signs of madness, confinement of the insane away from the rest of society, and the use of insanity as a way of classifying people and segregating communities.

The portrait of reformers like Dix has tended to be oversimplified; the most basic versions of the social control and progressive views have reigned, failing to take into account the much more illuminating interpretations that illustrate the role of both long-term structural changes and more precise short-term shifts in cultural practices. On the one hand are the many biographies full of praise for Dix as a great humanitarian crusader, quoting her contemporaries' view of her as ''the chosen daughter of the Republic,'' ''the angel of mercy,'' or ''the apostle of humanity.''[31] On the other hand are a number of psychology texts that question the ultimate benefit of her work. Critics focus on her embrace of institutionalization, blaming her for helping to usher in custodialism. Both views simplify the significance of Dix's life by portraying her as either a saint or Nurse Ratched in disguise; neither image can suspend disbelief.

The depiction of Dix as an agent of social control or custodialism fails to appreciate the depth of her commitment to what she considered better treatment, the energy she devoted to exploring actual conditions and exposing desperate neglect to the public eye, and her example of a life dedicated to moral principle. Poet John Greenleaf Whittier, among many others, wrote letters of admiration to Dix, lamenting how far short he fell when he measured himself against her model of generosity and devotion toward those less fortunate. On the other hand, the glorified portrait of Dix as a superhuman champion of the downtrodden, a compassionate samaritan whose moral sense placed her apart from her contemporaries, takes her completely out of the context of her times. She is better understood as one of many reformers who, for a number of reasons based on her personal circumstances and the tenor of her society, decided to devote her considerable moral energy to a reform already under way by the early nineteenth century.

Dix undoubtedly drew attention to a vital subject—the abusive practices that prevailed in the treatment of the insane in her time. She did so by traveling thousands of miles in the United States and abroad, examining such treatment firsthand and exposing it through her persuasive testimony. She lobbied furiously at a time when women were largely shut out of the political system and achieved many concrete political objectives, securing funds to establish numerous new asylums and to expand ones already in existence. Dix influenced mental health reform by helping ally it with other humanitarian causes, persuading many that increased appropriations for the insane was a moral imperative. But far from the simple matter of moral righteousness that she considered it, the treatment of the insane she favored was only one of the possible alternatives.

Dix's moral appeals on behalf of the insane underpinned her particular view that institutions provided the best treatment, that the state and the national government should assume responsibility for matters of individual welfare, that the treatment of the mentally ill rightly fell to the medical establishment, and that asylums could provide the benefits of a well-ordered family. The persuasiveness of her appeals, the extensiveness of her own fieldwork, and the tirelessness of her lobbying efforts made a huge impact on the direction of mental health reform. The securing of funds from the state would have been met with much fiercer resistance had not Dix disarmed the opposition with her stature, argument, and unassailable moral stance. Above all, perhaps, her life was devoted to defining decent treatment of troubled individuals as a moral issue; indecent treatment that later emerged in many contexts, including in the asylum, did so in spite of her efforts.

In sum, Dorothea Dix helped usher in a major shift in public opinion that designated insanity as the special province of asylum superintendents and doctors, a discrete condition requiring special and humane treatment, and an affliction best treated in institutions apart from society. Her shortcomings and those of the movement for mental health reform lay in the belief that their plans for change needed to entail a wholesale rejection of earlier customs as well as their failure to distinguish colonial custom from early national practice.

Dix and fellow reformers were blind to the possibly devastating effects of the larger movement toward incarceration even of the nonviolent insane, the subsequent expansion of the population considered insane, the invasion of the psychological realm necessitated by the new institutions and treatment, and the replacement of individual, family, and community obligations with governmental and institutional responsibility. Unquestioning faith in the new forms and a certain righteous impatience helped complete a revolution in the way Americans thought about madness. Thus were buried the best along with the worst customs of long past generations—to the detriment of future ones.

NOTES

1. Dorothea Lynde Dix, ''Memorial to the General Assembly of North Carolina'' (1848), quoted in Helen Marshall, *Dorothea Dix: Forgotten Samaritan* (Chapel Hill, N.C., 1937), 15.

2. Ibid.

3. Mary Ann Jimenez, ''Madness in Early American History: Insanity in Massachusetts from 1700 to 1830,'' *Journal of Social History* 20 (Fall 1986): 35.

4. Ibid., 36.

5. Dix, ''Memorial to the Legislature of Massachusetts'' (1843), in Dix, *On Behalf of the Insane Poor: Selected Reports* (New York, 1971), 4.

6. Jimenez, ''Madness in Early American History,'' 36.

7. Gladys Brooks, *Three Wise Virgins* (New York, 1957), 14.

8. Ibid., 18.

9. Ibid.

10. Marshall, *Dorothea Dix*, 45.

11. Francis Tiffany, *Life of Dorothea Lynde Dix* (Boston, 1891), 339.

12. Ibid.

13. Dorothy Clarke Wilson, *Stranger and Traveler: The Story of Dorothea Dix, American Reformer* (Boston, 1975), 336.

14. Tiffany, *Life of Dorothea Lynde Dix*, 111, 110.

15. Ibid., 115.

16. Ibid.

17. Dix, ''Memorial to Massachusetts,'' 24–25.

18. Ibid., 3.

19. Ibid., 25.

20. David Rothman, *The Discovery of the Asylum: Social Order and Disorder in the New Republic* (Boston, 1971), 5.

21. Gerald Grob, *Mental Institutions in America: Social Policy to 1875* (New York, 1973), 38–39.

22. Charles Rosenberg, ''The Therapeutic Revolution: Medicine, Meaning and Social Change in Nineteenth-Century America,'' in Morris J. Vogel and Charles Rosenberg, eds. *The Therapeutic Revolution: Essays in the Social History of Medicine* (Philadelphia, 1979), 5–10.

23. Eric T. Carlson and Norman Dain, ''Moral Insanity in the United States, 1835–1866,'' *American Journal of Psychiatry* 118, no. 9 (1962): 795–801.

24. Eric T. Carlson and Norman Dain, ''Psychotherapy in the Hospital: 1740–1840,'' *Current Psychiatric Therapies* 2 (1962): 219–225.

25. Grob, *Mental Institutions in America*, 10.

26. Ibid., 42.

27. Philippe Pinel, quoted in ibid.

28. Samuel Tuke, quoted in ibid., 44.

29. Christopher Lasch, ''Origins of the Asylum,'' in his *The World of Nations: Reflections on American History, Politics, and Culture* (New York, 1973), 13.

30. Ibid., 12.

31. Marshall, *Dorothea Dix*, 122.

BIBLIOGRAPHY

Beach, Seth Curtis. *Daughters of the Puritans: A Group of Brief Biographies*. Repr. Freeport, N.Y., 1967.

Brooks, Gladys. *Three Wise Virgins*. New York, 1957.

Carlson, Eric T., and Norman Dain. ''Moral Insanity in the United States, 1835–1866.'' *American Journal of Psychiatry* 118, no. 9 (1962): 795–801.

———. ''Psychotherapy in the Hospital: 1740–1840.'' *Current Psychiatric Therapies* 2 (1962): 219–225.

Deutsch, Albert. *The Mentally Ill in America: A History of Their Care and Treatment from Colonial Times*. New York, 1949.

Dix, Dorothea Lynde. *On Behalf of the Insane Poor: Selected Reports*. New York, 1971.

Foucault, Michel. *Madness and Civilization: A History of Insanity in the Age of Reason*. New York, 1965.

Fox, Richard. *So Far Disordered in Mind: Insanity in California, 1870–1930*. Berkeley, Calif., 1978.

Gollaher, David L. *Voice for the Mad: A Life of Dorothea Dix*. New York, 1995.

Grob, Gerald. *Mental Institutions in America: Social Policy to 1875*. New York, 1973.

Jimenez, Mary Ann. ''Madness in Early American History: Insanity in Massachusetts from 1700 to 1830.'' *Journal of Social History* 20 (Fall 1986): 25–44.

Lasch, Christopher. ''Origins of the Asylum.'' In his *The World of Nations: Reflections on American History, Politics, and Culture*. New York, 1973.

McGovern, Constance M. ''The Myths of Social Control and Custodial Oppression: Patterns of Psychiatric Medicine in Late Nineteenth-Century Institutions.'' *Journal of Social History* 20 (Fall 1986): 3–24.

Marshall, Helen E. *Dorothea Dix, Forgotten Samaritan*. Chapel Hill, N.C., 1937.

———. ''Dorothea Lynde Dix.'' In Edward T. James, Janet Wilson James, and Paul S. Boyer, eds. *Notable American Women, 1607–1950: A Biographical Dictionary*. Vol. 1. Cambridge, Mass., 1971.

Rosenberg, Charles. ''The Therapeutic Revolution: Medicine, Meaning and Social Change in Nineteenth-Century America.'' In Morris J. Vogel and Charles Rosenberg, eds., *The Therapeutic Revolution: Essays in the Social History of Medicine*. Philadelphia, 1979.

Rothman, David. *The Discovery of the Asylum: Social Order and Disorder in the New Republic*. Boston, 1971.

Schlaifer, Charles, and Lucy Freeman. *Heart's Work: Civil War Heroine and Champion of the Mentally Ill, Dorothea Lynde Dix*. New York, 1991.

Tiffany, Francis. *Life of Dorothea Lynde Dix*. Boston, 1891.

Viney, Wayne, and Karen Bartsch. ''Dorothea Lynde Dix: Positive or Negative Influence on the Development of Treatment for the Mentally Ill.'' *Social Science Journal* 21 (April 1984): 71–82.

Wilson, Dorothy Clarke. *Stranger and Traveler: The Story of Dorothea Dix, American Reformer*. Boston, 1975.

W.E.B. Du Bois, the NAACP, and the Struggle for Racial Equality

CARY D. WINTZ

In 1903, W.E.B. Du Bois opened his essay, "Of the Dawn of Freedom," with prophetic words: "The problem of the twentieth century is the problem of the color-line,—the relation of the darker to the lighter races of men in Asia and Africa, in America and the islands of the sea."[1] Du Bois was thirty-five years old when he published these words, and already established as the preeminent African-American academician of this period. He was on the verge of abandoning the academy and embarking on a career that would place him at the forefront of the struggle for racial justice in the United States. For the next quarter century Du Bois played a major role in the efforts of black and white reformers to define a solution for America's racial problems. He was a leader in the effort to move beyond Booker T. Washington's leadership and racial strategies, and was a prime mover in the establishment of the National Association for the Advancement of Colored People (NAACP) in 1909. By 1920 he had used his post in the NAACP, especially his role as editor of *Crisis*, to position himself as the dominant figure in black America.

During the period of his ascendancy, Du Bois represented several diverse themes in the ideology and politics of race in the United States. To one degree or another, he advocated racial equality and integration; championed pan-Africanism, nationalism, and racial pride; and argued that economic and social justice could be attained only through a poorly defined (and, until the late 1920s, a non-Marxist) system of social democracy. His strengths were as an intellectual—a theorist, writer, and editorialist. He proved much less successful as a political organizer or power broker, and he never attained the oratorical skills of his adversaries such as Washington and Marcus Garvey. Du Bois's political and social ideas continued to evolve throughout his career. By the mid-1930s his increasingly Marxist and nationalist philosophy led to a rift with the more conservative NAACP leadership. In 1934 Du Bois resigned as editor of *Crisis*, and his influence on American race and politics diminished in the years that followed.

During the first three decades of the twentieth century, Du Bois epitomized realities that race in American life imposed on a black intellectual. He, more than any other individual of the period, focused attention on racial injustice and defined the parameters of the African-American reaction to this injustice. He accurately perceived the centrality of race to American culture; likewise, he recognized the necessity for directly confronting racial injustice (and understood the limits that African Americans faced in this confrontation). If his racial philosophy and his tactics for reform seemed at times inconsistent, this inconsistency reflected the difficulty of coming to terms with the complexities of race in the United States and the difficulty of defining an effective strategy for African Americans to adopt in their struggle both for survival and for racial justice.

William Edward Burghardt Du Bois was born in Great Barrington, Massachusetts, on 23 February 1868. His father Alfred deserted the family shortly after he was born and his mother was an invalid during much of his childhood, but Du Bois's early years were happy though economically impoverished. He excelled in the public schools of Great Barrington and associated rather freely with middle-class white children. As adolescence approached, Du Bois became increasingly aware of race and the difficulties that his racial identity presented to him, even in the relatively enlightened environment of Massachusetts. If Mary Silvina Burghardt Du Bois could provide her son with little else, she was determined that he receive the best possible education. With the assistance of his high school principal, Du Bois took the college preparatory course. In 1885, a few months following his mother's death, with a scholarship provided by the local community, Du Bois left Great Barrington and enrolled at Fisk University.

At Fisk, and especially during the summers of 1886 and 1887, which he spent teaching in rural Tennessee, Du Bois discovered black Southern life—a culture far removed from what he had known in Massachusetts. These experiences, as well as confrontation with the racism of Southern whites, molded his early racial philosophy. These early views, expressed in published and unpublished materials written while he served on the editorial staff of the *Fisk Herald*, combined Booker T. Washington's optimism that interracial cooperation was possible, and that it was imprudent for blacks to "demand social equality or amalgamation," with a strong condemnation of lynching, a demand for "those civil rights which pertain to our manhood," and a militant belief in black pride.[2] Du Bois's Southern experiences left him with a deep distrust of and antipathy toward whites.

In June 1888, Du Bois received his B.A. from Fisk. That fall he entered Harvard University as a junior. At Harvard, he studied under the best minds of late nineteenth-century America—William James, Josiah Royce, George Santayana, and Albert Bushnell Hart. He continued his record of academic success, receiving his B.A. cum laude in 1890 and his M.A. in history in 1891. Intellectually, Harvard reinforced his commitment to scholarship and his conviction that intellectual and scientific study were essential in countering racial prejudice and dispelling racial myths. Socially, his years at Harvard reinforced his sense of isolation from whites. Du Bois remained sensitive to racial slights and spent most of his free time in Boston's black community.

In 1892, with a scholarship from the Slater Fund for the Education of Negroes, Du Bois left the United States for two years of graduate study at the University of Berlin. This period was crucial in his intellectual development. First, his European experiences broadened his understanding of race and prejudice. The rarity of overt bigotry in regard to his racial identity forced Du Bois to reassess his attitude toward whites, and his encounters with anti-Semitism and prejudice against ethnic groups in the Austro-Hungarian Empire and in occupied Poland caused him to see racism in a broader perspective that included the oppression of national minorities in Europe and colonial peoples in Africa and Asia. Second, Du Bois's involvement with the German Social Democratic Party introduced him to a non-Marxist socialism. Finally, the University of Berlin broadened his education as he interacted with such faculty members as the young sociologist Max Weber, the liberal professor of German politics Rudolph von Gneist, and the anti-Semitic and racist historian Heinrich von Treitschke. Du Bois returned to the United States in 1894 determined to wage war against racism and the color line, using as his weapons the analytical tools of social science, and armed with a broad understanding of the global implications of American color prejudice.

In 1894 Du Bois accepted a position on the faculty of Wilberforce College in Ohio, beginning a sixteen-year career as a university professor and researcher. Although he was not particularly happy at Wilberforce, Du Bois's two-year stay there was productive and eventful. He completed his dissertation, ''The Suppression of the African Slave-Trade to the United States of America, 1638–1870,'' and received his Ph.D. from Harvard in 1895; he published his dissertation in 1896 as the first volume in the Harvard Historical Studies series; he courted and married one of his students, Nina Gomer; and he met Alexander Crummell and was deeply influenced both by the man and by his black nationalist and Pan-Africanist views. In the summer of 1896, DuBois left Wilberforce and moved his small family to Philadelphia, where, with the rank of assistant instructor at the University of Pennsylvania, he conducted an eighteen-month research project on the black community in Philadelphia. He published the results of this project in 1899 as *The Philadelphia Negro: A Social Study*. Du Bois's growing reputation as a scholar earned him an appointment as professor of history and economics at Atlanta University in late 1897, a position he held until August 1910.

The Atlanta years represented a major turning point in Du Bois's life. Scholarship gradually gave way to politics, and Du Bois moved from being an ally and supporter of Booker T. Washington to being one of his most outspoken critics. Du Bois came to Atlanta prepared to continue his scholarly research into black life in America. The results were impressive. He initiated a series of studies on black communities throughout the South. In the process he almost single-handedly defined the parameters of black sociology. Augmenting this research were the annual Atlanta University conferences and the publications that resulted from them. Du Bois transformed the conferences into focused, systematic, scholarly investigations of the problems confronting African Americans. Although he failed to achieve the ambitious goals that he envisioned, the conferences and their accompanying publications established his reputation as the leading African-American social scientist.

While continuing to function as a productive scholar, Du Bois moved, somewhat hesitatingly, into the public arena. This move is understandable, given the worsening race relations characterized by the increase in segregation, the deterioration of black political rights, and the growth of racial violence in the United States at the turn of the century. In March 1897, a few months before he arrived in Atlanta, Du Bois had participated in the first formal session of the American Negro Academy, an organization for black intellectuals founded by Crummell. At that meeting, Du Bois attracted much attention with the presentation of a riveting and controversial paper, ''The Conservation of Races.'' In this paper he developed two themes that characterized his work for the next thirty years. First, he argued that each race had its distinctive characteristics and must maintain its separate identity in order to fulfill its destiny. African-American destiny, he asserted, was linked to that of other peoples of Africa or of the African diaspora, and could not be realized by assimilation or absorption into white culture. Second, Du Bois addressed the dualism of African-American identity, insisting that blacks were Americans by birth, citizenship, political ideals, language, and religion, but beyond that they were the awakening vanguard of the vast Negro race.

Five months later, Du Bois published a more developed version of these thoughts for a national audience in the *Atlantic Monthly*:

[The American Negro] does not wish to Africanize America, for America has too much to teach the world and Africa; he does not wish to bleach his Negro blood in a flood of white Americanism, for he believes—foolishly, perhaps, but fervently—that Negro blood has yet a message for the world. He simply wishes to make it possible for a man to be both a Negro and an American without being cursed and spit upon by his fellows, without losing the opportunity of self-development.[3]

Du Bois, at this point in his career, embraced cultural pluralism, a position between that of the nationalists and of the integrationists; he also deemphasized immediate demands for civil or political rights. On the subject of Pan-Africanism, he likewise took a moderate position that rejected emigration to Africa as impractical and undesirable. He proposed instead that African Americans take the lead in undertaking social science research projects in Africa, and that they work to promote cultural exchanges and trade among blacks on both sides of the Atlantic.

Du Bois initially embraced most of the racial program developed by Booker T. Washington, who argued that the future of African Americans was directly linked to that of white Southerners. He did not oppose civil rights and higher education, stressing that full economic and civil rights would come naturally, after the economic development of the black community. To that end, he insisted that the appropriate education for the black masses was in institutions, like Tuskegee, that stressed industrial education. While Washington worked diligently behind the scenes to fight segregation, disfranchisement, and racial violence, his public image was that of a moderate who avoided direct confrontation with racist America. Washington outlined much of his philosophy in his 1895 speech that opened the Atlanta Exposition. This speech propelled him to a position of leadership within the African-American community (especially in the eyes of white Americans) that he did not wholly relinquish until his death in 1915.

Du Bois initially applauded the Atlanta speech. He wrote: ''Let me heartily congratulate you upon your phenomenal success at Atlanta—it was a word fitly spoken.''[4] Du Bois then captured the spirit of the Atlanta speech in his address to the American Negro Academy in 1897, when he advocated not integration but parallel development, ''not such social equality between these races as would disregard human likes and dislikes, but such a social equilibrium as would, throughout the complicated relations of life, give due and just consideration to culture, ability, and moral worth, whether they be found under white or black skins.''[5] Cooperation between Du Bois and Washington continued into the early twentieth century. In 1900 Washington tried to bring Du Bois to Tuskegee, and Du Bois asked Washington to support his candidacy for the post of assistant superintendent of colored schools in Washington, D.C. In August 1899, Du Bois defended Washington against attacks by militants at the National Afro-American Council meeting; and four months later the two worked in concert trying to defeat a measure to limit black suffrage in Georgia. From 1900 to as late as 1904, Du Bois and Washington cooperated on several projects in behind-the-scenes efforts to combat the spread of segregation in the South.

In spite of their common interests, friction between Du Bois and Washington intensified in the early twentieth century. There were two principal causes of this friction. First, as the racial situation in the United States worsened in the early twentieth century, Du Bois moved to the left. Specifically, he began to have serious reservations about the policy of accommodation and cooperation with Southern white leadership, and with the effectiveness of the behind-the-scenes manipulation that Washington relied on so extensively. In taking this position, Du Bois abandoned his earlier moderate views on segregation and began to advocate full civil rights for blacks. At the same time, he grew increasingly dissatisfied with Washington's emphasis on industrial education—a strategy that potentially undermined Du Bois's work at Atlanta University. The second cause of the rift was Du Bois's dissatisfaction with the power that Washington wielded in both black and white America, and especially his opposition to the way Washington used this power to undermine his political enemies and reward his friends. Du Bois himself believed that his failure to get the assistant superintendent position in Washington, D.C., was the result of Washington's manipulation of his powers of patronage.

Two events in 1903 brought the conflict between Washington and Du Bois into the open. The first was the publication Du Bois's best-known book, *The Souls of Black Folk*, with its chapter "Of Mr. Booker T. Washington and Others." In his assessment of Washington, Du Bois acknowledged that he was the "most distinguished Southerner since Jefferson Davis, and the one with the largest personal following."[6] Furthermore, Du Bois insisted that he sincerely valued Washington's achievements and recognized the political realities in the South that forced moderation. However, he sharply criticized Washington for perpetuating the alleged inferiority of blacks through his educational system and for counseling blacks to give up temporarily their claims for political power, civil rights, and higher education. The most damning indictment of the Washington program, Du Bois maintained, was that during the ten years that it had dominated black thought, blacks indeed had been disfranchised, had been legally segregated in a distinct and inferior civil status, and had witnessed the steady withdrawal of funds from liberal arts programs at black colleges.

The second event that deepened the split between Du Bois and Washington was the so-called Boston Riot. On 30 July 1903, as Washington addressed 2,000 listeners in Boston, a small group of dissidents led by William Monroe Trotter disrupted the speech, and police were called in to restore order. Several of the hecklers were arrested; among them was Trotter, who spent a month in jail. Although Du Bois had no direct involvement in the disturbance, he spent time as a guest in the Trotter home later that summer, and he criticized his host's having been sent to jail. This criticism convinced Washington that Du Bois was behind the riot and prompted Washington to launch a campaign to discredit his opponent and to punish him by denying him access to funding and by threatening his employer with a loss of funds. These two events intensified the philosophical differences between Washington and Du Bois, crystallized the growing split in the black intellectual community, and propelled Du Bois to the forefront of the anti-Washington faction.

Although Du Bois and Washington maintained a surface cordiality, and continued to correspond on various projects for several more years, there was, after 1903, a deep distrust between the two men. A clear sign of this distrust was Du Bois's anger and frustration over Washington's control of political power, especially his influence over the African-American press. Du Bois launched an attack on this aspect of Washington's power in a January 1905 article, "Debit and Credit," which charged the Tuskegeean with making cash payoffs to buy the support of the black press, and in a 24 March 1905 letter to Oswald Garrison Villard (editor of the *New York Post*, grandson of the great abolitionist, and supporter of black rights) detailing the charges against Washington. Although much of the evidence supporting the charges was circumstantial, the publication of the accusation, along with increased attacks on Washington's policies, escalated the conflict between the two men.

As Du Bois turned away from Washington and his program, he began the development of his own political agenda. He based his approach on several firm convictions that he began to enunciate in the first decade of the twentieth century. He outlined the areas of his concerns in an essay on the conflicts that had emerged among black leaders, published in 1904. "The points upon which American Negroes differ as to their course of action," he wrote, "are the following: First, the scope of education; second, the necessity of the right of suffrage; third, the importance of civil rights; fourth, the conciliation of the South; fifth, the future of the race in this country."[7] In putting together his political agenda, Du Bois addressed each of these questions.

First, Du Bois argued that blacks needed a well-educated leadership to direct the uplifting of the race. To accomplish this, black colleges and universities should not focus their efforts exclusively on industrial education but should continue to offer a strong liberal arts program to produce the class of teachers and professionals necessary to carry out this task. Du Bois had no objections to practical education in the industrial arts (so long as it did not perpetuate skills that were becoming obsolete in industrial America), but he warned that it would be dangerous to ignore classical education because ultimately it would be the educated elite, the "talented tenth," who would bring culture and progress to the race. As Du Bois put it, "If we make money the object of man-training, we shall develop moneymakers but not necessarily men; if we make technical skill the object of education, we may possess artisans but not, in nature, men. Men we shall have only as we make manhood the object of the work of the schools— intelligence, broad sympathy, knowledge of the world that was and is, and of the relation of men to it—this is the curriculum of that Higher Education which must underlie true life."[8]

In addition to challenging Washington's ideas about education, Du Bois attacked his political tactics. Rejecting the moderate tone that he had sounded in his 1897 speech to the American Negro Academy, Du Bois now insisted that protest, not conciliation of the South, was the only viable way for blacks to secure their civil and political rights. He argued that blacks could never gain self-respect until they fought for their rights; they could never secure and defend their position as property owners until they achieved and exercised the right to vote. Du Bois now refused to accept segregation on even a temporary or short-term basis. Instead, he argued that "separate but equal" was never equal; rather, it was a system designed to foster inequality and perpetuate the subordination of blacks. Although he urged blacks to develop their own businesses and to patronize the businesses of other blacks, and he acknowledged that integration might undermine the economic development of the black community, he insisted that the evils of segregation more than offset its short-term economic advantages. Within this context, racial pride and racial solidarity ceased to be ends in themselves; they became weapons to protest disfranchisement and segregation and to win the struggle for civil rights.

Du Bois also responded directly to the argument that the heritage of slavery and the deeply ingrained racial bigotry of white Americans made it impossible for blacks ever to achieve equal rights in the United States. He explained:

To this I answer simply: I do not believe it. I believe that black men will become free American citizens if they have the courage and persistence to demand the rights and treatment of men, and cease to toady and apologize and belittle themselves. The rights of humanity are worth fighting for. Those that deserve them in the long run get them. The way for black men to-day to make these rights the heritage of their children is to struggle for them unceasingly, and if they fail, die trying.[9]

Du Bois's new militant tone contrasted not only with Washington's conciliatory public comments but also with the tone that Du Bois himself had used in the past.

Thus far the differences between Du Bois and Washington, though substantial, were in degree rather than in substance, in means rather than in ends. Both men were committed to uplifting their race, instilling racial pride, and securing political and civil rights. However, Du Bois, the greatest black intellect of the prewar period, constantly explored concepts that were alien to the more conservative Washington. In 1910, for example, he shocked many moderates of both races when he condemned the prohibition of interracial marriage (although he qualified his stand with the observation that, given current social conditions, a ''wholesale intermarriage of races . . . would be a social calamity.'').[10] He also continued his interest in black nationalism and professed the belief that there were inherent differences between the races and that strong ties existed between American blacks and other colored peoples. Du Bois also examined socialism and attempted to explain racial discrimination in terms of class conflict. In 1911 he joined the Socialist party, and by the end of the decade he had become convinced that the ultimate solution of racial problems would be found through the elimination of class antagonisms and a union between black and white workers. Although Du Bois remained a moderate on the issue of Pan-Africanism (he continued to be cool to the idea of mass emigration to Africa), he did become increasingly involved in the organized Pan-African movement. He served as a delegate to an international Pan-African conference in London in 1900 and was selected to direct the American branch of the Pan-African Association. His other obligations and interests kept his commitment to Pan-Africanism in the background until after World War I.

The most tangible result of Du Bois's evolving political philosophy was the role he played in the organization of the Niagara Movement in the summer of 1905 and of the NAACP in 1910. In July 1905, Du Bois and twenty-eight other black leaders, impatient with accommodation, met in Fort Erie, Ontario, to organize a more militant civil rights organization. The resulting Niagara Movement selected Du Bois as its general secretary and dedicated itself to universal manhood suffrage, declared that "any discrimination based simply on race or color is barbarous," and pledged that "the voice of protest of ten million Americans must never cease to assail the ears of their fellows, so long as America is unjust."[11] The major target of the Niagara Movement was Booker T. Washington's domination of black America; in turn, Washington used his control of the black press to discredit the organization and his political influence and prestige to sabotage the careers of its organizers. Du Bois recognized that the Niagara Movement needed its own national publication if it wanted to get its message across. He served as editor of *Moon: Illustrated Weekly*, which failed in less than a year, and of the only slightly more successful *Horizon*. Faced with Washington's relentless opposition, its inability to establish a broad base of support within even the middle-class black community, and divisions within its leadership, the Niagara Movement began to self-destruct in mid-1908. One reason for the failure was Du Bois's ineffectiveness as a political leader. Another problem was that the Tuskegee machine prevented the organization from acquiring much white support. Quite simply, although it directly addressed the racial issues of its day, the Niagara Movement never gained sufficient funds or enough influence to achieve much success. It disbanded in 1909.

The failure of the Niagara Movement and the emergence of a small group of liberal-to-radical white progressives concerned about race in America led to the development of a biracial civil rights movement. The event that precipitated the actual creation of such an organization was the Springfield, Illinois, race riot of 1908. Although this was neither the only nor the worst race riot of this period, the image of Lincoln's hometown torn apart by racial violence as the nation prepared to honor the centenary of Lincoln's birth disturbed a number of liberal whites. In the aftermath of the riot a call went out to recapture the spirit of the abolitionists and launch a new social movement committed to racial equality and full civil rights for black Americans. To lay the groundwork for this movement, Mary White Ovington, with support from Oswald Garrison Villard and one or two other white Progressives, sent out a call to black and white liberals to meet in New York to discuss the racial situation. White participants included Jane Addams, William Dean Howells, Florence Kelley, andJohn Dewey. They represented the liberal Progressives and moderate Socialists. Some, like Villard, were former supporters of Washington who had grown impatient with his leadership; most, though, had little knowledge or understanding of the black situation. Washington was invited to attend but, fearing another Niagara Movement, convinced most of his supporters to boycott the conference. Consequently, the black attendees were mostly former Niagaraites, many of whom attended despite their reservations about the reliability of Villard and the other white liberals.

The result of this conference was the selection of a biracial steering committee to continue the organizational process. No one was particularly satisfied with its composition. The anti-Washington faction felt that too many radicals were excluded and too many Bookerites were appointed. The Tuskegee machine, meanwhile, tried to discredit the process. Many blacks felt that their interests were betrayed by their white friends. Du Bois emerged as a major force during the conference and the deliberations that followed. His reason and restraint impressed many of the whites, as did his eloquent argument that economic progress and the exercise of political rights were intrinsically linked.

Within a few months the steering committee reached a consensus to establish a permanent civil rights organization, the National Association for the Advancement of Colored People. At a second conference in May 1910, the first slate of national officers was elected. Except for Du Bois, all officers and board members were white. Liberal reformer Moorfield Storey became president, Socialist William English Walling (who first conceived the need to respond to the Springfield riots) became chair of the executive committee, liberal Republican John E. Milholland became national treasurer, and Villard became distributing treasurer. Du Bois was named director of publicity and research. Although there was no formal merger of the defunct Niagara Movement and the NAACP, most of the Niagaraites joined the new organization, making that group the dominant black element in the NAACP from the outset. Most important, the NAACP succeeded where the Niagara Movement had failed. As a biracial organization that was dominated by whites during its first two decades, it was strong enough and sufficiently funded to withstand Washington's attacks and, after his death in 1915, succeeded in at least temporarily reconciling and uniting most factions in the black community.

The creation of the NAACP was a turning point in Du Bois's life. With some hesitation, he left academia, moved to New York City, and began working full-time as a political and civil rights activist for the new organization. The move to New York was a courageous step for Du Bois. His job at the NAACP was not well defined, and the future of the new organization was uncertain. However, his position in Atlanta had become increasingly tenuous because of his political activities and growing pressure on the university from the Tuskegee machine.

Du Bois and his family arrived in New York City on 1 August 1910. During his first four years at the NAACP, he engaged in a struggle with more conservative board members to define his role and his authority. For once in his career, Du Bois functioned effectively within a highly politicized organization. Indeed, his success was remarkable. First, with no specific authority to do so, he founded *Crisis*, the NAACP's monthly journal. Du Bois then established his independent control over *Crisis* and its editorial content. Finally, he engaged in a successful power struggle with conservative white board members.

From the moment he assumed his position at the NAACP, Du Bois was determined to create a NAACP journal as a successor to *Horizon*, which had ceased publication six months earlier. He put his plans in motion without requesting the permission of the other members of the NAACP board and against the advice of many friends and associates. He simply moved ahead, preparing text for the first issue, selecting a name for the publication (actually the name was suggested by Walling, the chair of the executive committee), and ordering the printing of 1,000 copies. In the first issue (November 1910), Du Bois defined his vision for both *Crisis* and the NAACP in two short editorials. In the first, he announced that "the object of this publication is to set forth those facts and arguments which show the danger of race prejudice, particularly as manifested to-day toward colored people."[12] In the second, he affirmed his commitment to political agitation:

The function of this Association is to tell this nation the crying evil of race prejudice. It is a hard duty but a necessary one—a divine one. It is Pain; Pain is not good but Pain is necessary. Pain does not aggravate disease—Disease causes Pain. Agitation does not mean Aggravation—Aggravation calls for Agitation in order that a Remedy may be found.[13]

Amazingly, *Crisis* was a financial success, at least until the late 1920s. By the fourth issue Du Bois was printing 4,000 copies; circulation reached 15,000 in July 1911, and 70,000 by the end of World War I. This success created problems for Du Bois. A financially successful journal gave Du Bois an independence that troubled some members of the NAACP board. The problem centered on the dual nature of Du Bois's relationship to the NAACP—he was both a board member and, as editor of *Crisis*, an employee. The problem also involved a political clash between conservatives and radicals over the racial philosophy of the organization, and it involved race. The conflict surfaced when Villard attempted to shift editorial control over *Crisis* from Du Bois to the board. In March 1913, as chairman of the board of the NAACP, Villard ordered Du Bois to print a list of major crimes committed by blacks as a companion to the annual list of blacks who had been lynched. Du Bois refused. In January 1914 Du Bois again angered Villard by printing an editorial that argued against any racial restrictions on whom individuals could marry. He took the position that as a board member, he was the equal, not the subordinate, of Villard; he further argued that Villard had no experience dealing with a black man as his equal, and certainly was not used to having a black say no to him. He also contended that Villard wanted to subvert the original radical platform of the NAACP. In January 1914, Villard resigned as chairman of the board to protest Du Bois's actions; in April 1914 he attempted, without success, to convince the board to limit Du Bois's editorial authority. In January 1916, Du Bois could claim victory when the executive committee voted to grant him full authority over *Crisis* editorials.

Du Bois's victory in these struggles meant that until he resigned from *Crisis* in 1934, he had a forum from which he could express his ideas on the issues of the day. He used this position to push a fairly militant, fairly radical political agenda. It also meant that Du Bois made *Crisis,* and to a lesser extent the NAACP, the vehicle for his personal political philosophy.

During his first decade at *Crisis,* Du Bois tended to react to almost all issues in terms of how they affected African Americans. For example, his position on both woman's suffrage and labor was colored by the racial component of these issues. Although Du Bois generally sympathized with the expansion of the suffrage to women (and ultimately supported woman's suffrage), he criticized the antiblack statements of Carrie Chapman Catt and several other suffragettes. Both because of his sociological studies of working-class blacks and because of his Socialist sympathies, Du Bois believed that ultimately the welfare of African Americans was linked to that of all working-class Americans, and that most racial problems would fade away when white workers recognized their common interests with black workers. However, Du Bois also recognized the racial policies of many labor unions. In a July 1912 editorial he affirmed that "the CRISIS believes in organized labor," then warned against the prejudice and discrimination practiced by many American unions:

So long as union labor fights for humanity, its mission is divine; but when labor fights for a clique of Americans, Irish, or German monopolists who have cornered or are trying to corner the market on a certain type of service, and are seeking to sell that service at a premium, while other competent workmen starve, they deserve themselves the starvation which they plan for their darker and poorer fellows.[14]

In 1918 he went even further when he felt forced to acknowledge that union behavior in East St. Louis demonstrated that "in the present Union movement, as represented by the American Federation of Labor, there is absolutely no hope of justice for an American of Negro descent."[15]

It is important to note that on several significant political issues Du Bois took a moderate position during his first decade at *Crisis*. For example, in 1912 he resigned from the Socialist party in order to endorse Woodrow Wilson's presidential candidacy. Six years later he refused to join with other radicals in opposition to World War I. In one of his best-known and most controversial editorials, he urged African Americans to "Close Ranks," to put aside their "special grievances" and stand "shoulder to shoulder with our own white fellow citizens."[16] During the course of the war, Du Bois did not protest segregated military units—indeed, he lobbied for an expansion of the segregated officer corps.

At the end of World War I, Du Bois stood at the peak of his power and influence. He had just turned fifty, he held a position of power in the dominant civil rights organization in the United States, and, as editor of *Crisis*, he controlled a platform from which he could broadcast his political and racial philosophy across the country. Ironically, the 1920s was not a successful period for Du Bois. He saw his views and leadership challenged from both the right and the left; he seemed to be stranded on the periphery as major developments transformed the black community. As his personal political views became more radical and more international in outlook, he found himself out of step with the more traditional leadership of the NAACP.

The 1920s began with Du Bois abandoning the patient, moderate view he had voiced in "Close Ranks" and returning to a militant demand for equal rights and justice. Provoked by the wave of racial and political violence that swept across the United States after the war, Du Bois warned returning black soldiers that they were coming home to a country that lynched, disfranchised its black citizens, encouraged their ignorance, stole from them, and insulted them. His prescription for this situation was blunt:

By the God of Heaven, we are cowards and jackasses if now that the war is over, we do not marshal every ounce of our brain and brawn to fight a sterner, longer, more unbending battle against the forces of hell in our own land.

> *We return.*
>
> *We return from fighting.*
>
> *We return fighting.*

Make way for Democracy! We saved it in France, and by the Great Jehovah, we will save it in the United States of America, or know the reason why.[17]

This renewed militancy set the stage for Du Bois's political shift to the left in the 1920s.

Du Bois's political evolution in the 1920s was characterized by a reawakened interest in Pan-Africanism and in socialism. The war and the subsequent Bolshevik Revolution convinced him that these two ideologies would dominate the rest of the twentieth century. Although Du Bois first had become interested in Pan-Africanism in the late nineteenth century, the opportunities offered by the fluid world situation in the postwar period convinced him to devote more time and energy to this cause. In late 1918 he traveled to France to arrange the Pan-African Congress that would present the views of Africa and all peoples of African lineage at the upcoming peace conference. With no support from the United States, and only reluctant permission from the French, the 1919 Pan-African Congress convened at Paris in February. Political squabbling among British and French colonial factions undermined the conference. Rather than calling for African self-determination, as Du Bois proposed, the Congress forwarded to the peace conference the much more modest proposal that former German possessions in Africa be turned over to an international body, and advocated vague political and economic reforms for the rest of colonial Africa. The Congress's proposals had little impact on the peace conference.

Du Bois returned to the United States convinced that the struggle for political rights in the United States was linked to the rights of blacks around the world. At the second Pan-African Congress in London, Brussels, and Paris in 1921, Du Bois was a spokesman for the radical faction that wanted to force the colonial powers either to integrate the colonial peoples into their societies, granting them full political and civil rights, or to grant them the right of self-government. Once again, moderates undermined Du Bois's position. The 1921 meeting marked the high point for Pan-Africanism in the 1920s. The movement declined rapidly during the rest of the decade. Its permanent secretariat quickly closed its doors for lack of funding, and the 1923 Congress failed to attract the participants or publicity of the earlier meetings. Du Bois also failed to draw much support for Pan-Africanism in the United States. Although *Crisis* reported extensively on African issues, neither the black middle class nor the NAACP expressed any real interest in Pan-Africanism.

Du Bois also had a long interest in socialism that was based upon his belief that the unity of the working class would eventually undermine racial divisions. In the early 1920s he hoped that a reinvigorated socialism might become a viable political choice for African Americans. However, Du Bois was troubled by the organized socialist parties in the United States. He continued to criticize the American Socialist party for its refusal to agitate for racial justice, and he dismissed the Communist party for advocating violent revolution, which he believed was both impractical and impossible in the United States. Du Bois advocated evolutionary socialism, such as that represented by the British Labour Party.

Du Bois's moderate socialism made him a subject of scorn among black radicals. A. Phillip Randolph, who was coeditor of *Messenger* and a supporter of the Russian Revolution and Soviet communism, led the leftist attack on Du Bois. The *Messenger* had been sharply critical of Du Bois's "Close Ranks" policy during the war; in a series of articles and editorials following the war, it labeled Du Bois a representative of the old Negro leadership, ignorant of the needs of the black masses. It further denigrated him as a political opportunist who lacked intelligence and courage, and as a reactionary who refused to recognize the accomplishments of Soviet Russia. These charges were echoed by other radical blacks, such as the poet and writer Claude McKay, and Cyril V. Briggs, founder of the militant African Blood Brotherhood.

Du Bois's style of leadership was coming under attack during the 1920s, much as Booker T. Washington's had been challenged two decades earlier. Although Du Bois had become a virtual institution for most younger blacks, several black intellectuals ten to twenty years his junior were less willing to accept his leadership. As early as 1920, William H. Ferris suggested that Du Bois was "too aristocratic and hypercritical, too touchy and too sensitive, too dainty and fastidious, too high and holy to lead the masses of his race." Furthermore, he argued that Du Bois was too eager to "referee" the work of other blacks in an effort to dictate " 'who was who' in the Negro race."[18] Ferris's criticism was shared by three prominent black scholars: Carter G. Woodson, founder of the Association for the Study of Negro Life and History and editor of the *Journal of Negro History*; Alain Locke of Howard University; and sociologist Charles S. Johnson of the Urban League.

In addition to the growing criticism of his leadership, Du Bois also found himself out of touch with the two major movements that influenced black America in the decade following the war: Marcus Garvey and his Universal Negro Improvement Association (UNIA) and the Harlem Renaissance. Garvey arrived in the United States in 1916 for the purpose of raising funds and support for his Jamaica-based UNIA. The potential wealth and power represented by the American black masses convinced Garvey to remain in the United States; the war, the black migration to Northern cities, and the turmoil of the "Red Summer" that followed the war presented him with the opportunity to build a mass movement among African Americans. Garvey established his base of operations in New York City and used his considerable skills as an organizer and orator to build his movement. His message was militant black pride, Pan-Africanism, and black nationalism, with a touch of Tuskegeean self-help. He promoted himself as the leader of the world's 400 million blacks, promised to realize the liberation of Africa, organized black businesses and enterprises, and planned a mass migration of black Americans to their African homeland.

Even though there was sufficient common ground in their racial and political programs to make Du Bois and Garvey allies, the two men never got along. Garvey began his attacks on Du Bois even before he arrived in the United States. He saw Du Bois as a man who had sold out to white leadership and abandoned the interests of the common man. He was particularly critical of Du Bois's trip to Paris in 1918 and his involvement in the Pan-African Congress of 1919, charging that the *Crisis* editor had been sent to Europe in the pay of the U.S. government to undermine the interests of blacks. Du Bois's initial reaction to Garvey was restrained. He published a balanced assessment of Garvey's accomplishments and weaknesses in *Crisis* in December 1920 and January 1921. However, Du Bois also became increasingly critical of Garvey. He personally investigated the acquisition of ships for Garvey's ill-fated Black Star Line and denounced rumored links between Garvey and the Ku Klux Klan. Finally, in 1924, when Garvey was facing a federal prison term for his illegal business dealings related to the Black Star Line, Du Bois editorialized: "The American Negroes have endured this wretch all too long with fine restraint and every effort at cooperation and understanding. But the end has come . . . this open ally of the Ku Klux Klan should be locked up or sent home."[19] Although Du Bois's censure of Garvey was appropriate, Du Bois nevertheless missed an opportunity when he failed to connect with the Garvey movement. He never enjoyed the support of the black masses that Garvey was able to generate.

Du Bois also failed to relate effectively to the Harlem Renaissance. This is somewhat puzzling because in many ways the Harlem Renaissance epitomized Du Bois's vision for the black intelligentsia. It was in a real sense the flowering of Du Bois's talented tenth. The literary movement certainly reflected much of his political agenda: black pride, a commitment to racial equality and equal rights, with a tinge of black nationalism, socialism, and Pan-Africanism.

Du Bois's own literary interests made him an early supporter of black art and literature. He greeted with enthusiasm the early stirrings of the Harlem Renaissance, and he opened the pages of *Crisis* to the poems and stories of the young black writers. Basically, however, Du Bois's literary tastes were too conservative for much of the Harlem Renaissance, and he was too wrapped up in his political agenda to recognize that literature and art needed intellectual freedom to flourish. With a heavy hand, he attempted to channel black literature in directions that would serve his political agenda. This meant that art must subordinate itself to political propaganda, a view that he outlined in a 1926 *Crisis* article. "All Art is propaganda," he wrote, "and ever must be, despite the wailing of the purists. I stand in utter shamelessness and say that whatever art I have for writing has been used always for propaganda . . . I do not care a damn for any art that is not used for propaganda."[20] These sentiments—and, indeed, the very attempt to define the appropriate nature of black literature—offended many young writers. Claude McKay described it as the attempt of that NAACP crowd to turn itself into a "Ministry of Culture for Afro-America." The dissonance between Du Bois and the Harlem Renaissance reflected Du Bois's growing alienation from the black intelligentsia, with whom he should have been most involved.

In many ways, Du Bois seemed out of step in the 1920s, challenged on all sides and failing to react effectively to opportunities that presented themselves. In the early 1930s these failures, combined with new problems, undermined his position within the NAACP. In the late 1920s, Du Bois moved to the left politically. In 1926 he visited the Soviet Union and returned to the United States impressed with the accomplishments of the Bolshevik Revolution. Between 1927 and 1934, Du Bois published a series of articles and editorials in *Crisis* favorable to the Soviet Union. His trip to Russia also stimulated his interest in Marxism. As his new leftist political leanings distanced him from the more moderate leadership of the NAACP, the situation within the NAACP also changed. In the late 1920s *Crisis* began losing money on a steady basis. The onset of the Great Depression worsened the financial problems of *Crisis* and the NAACP. With *Crisis* no longer financially self-sufficient, Du Bois's autonomy as editor once again came under review by a board that was increasingly uncomfortable with his leftist politics.

In 1931 Walter White became the secretary of the NAACP. White was very critical of Du Bois's political beliefs. Specifically, he ardently opposed segregation and Marxism, and had little interest in Pan-Africanism. Furthermore, he differed sharply with Du Bois's criticism of the Harlem Renaissance. White believed that the *Crisis* editor was "not in harmony with contemporary issues and trends," and that his pro-Soviet, pro-Marxist political stance was "dangerous to the progress of the NAACP."[21] NAACP president Joel Spingarn concurred with White's assessment that Du Bois was becoming too radical. Between 1932 and late 1933, White maneuvered to reduce Du Bois's power. His success came when he thwarted Du Bois's efforts to gain control of the NAACP board by dominating the process of nominating new board members.

Du Bois precipitated the final confrontation with White and the NAACP board in January 1934 when he wrote an editorial challenging the NAACP's antisegregation position. He argued that discrimination, not segregation, was the source of racial injustice in the United States, and that although segregation and discrimination usually went hand in hand, this was not always the case. In fact,

Du Bois argued that as long as prejudice existed, voluntary segregation and cooperation were essential for black progress. "It is the race-conscious black man," he concluded, "cooperating together in his own institutions and movements who will eventually emancipate the colored race."[22] In taking this position Du Bois was coming to terms with the fact that in a racist society it is better to have segregated schools and hospitals than to have no schools or hospitals; it is also usually better to have segregated facilities than to be discriminated against, mistreated, or provided poor service in integrated facilities. Du Bois was also aware that the black community, everywhere in America, would not survive without separate churches, schools, fraternal and social organizations, and businesses. Abolishing all segregated facilities might be an ideal, but it was an ideal that would not be realized in 1934 or any time near that date.

Du Bois's assessment of segregation was realistic, but it differed from NAACP policy. It also led to a broad-based attack on Du Bois in the black press. One problem was that his arguments in defense of segregation seemed reminiscent of Washington's arguments thirty or forty years earlier. As criticism of Du Bois mounted, the NAACP came under intense pressure to clarify its position. White, Spingarn, and other NAACP board members printed antisegregation articles in the March issue of *Crisis*, and the board published its official position on segregation in the April issue. In May, the NAACP board passed a resolution stating that no salaried officer could criticize the policy, work, or officers of the NAACP in *Crisis*. Du Bois resigned.

In the fall of 1934, Du Bois returned to Atlanta University, where he became chairman of the Department of Sociology. Du Bois was sixty-six when he left the NAACP. Most of his colleagues assumed that in Atlanta he would drift quietly into retirement. Few imagined that his career would continue for almost three more decades. The ten years that Du Bois spent at Atlanta University in the late 1930s and early 1940s were anything but a retirement. His scholarly output certainly belied his age. He published four books, including the groundbreaking *Black Reconstruction*; founded and edited the journal *Phylon*; and wrote several hundred newspaper articles, including columns for the *Pittsburgh Courier* and Harlem's *Amsterdam News*. Politically, Du Bois continued his leftward drift. His socialism merged into Marxism, he became increasingly infatuated with and supportive of the Bolshevik experiment in the Soviet Union, and he persisted in his belief that segregated black institutions and organizations were an appropriate response to the American racial situation. Despite his impressive record of scholarship, Du Bois's independence and his outspoken radicalism were too much for the administration at Atlanta University. The institution's board of trustees forced him into retirement, effective 30 June 1944. Ironically, just as he was completing his last semester at Atlanta, Du Bois received an invitation from Walter White and the board of the NAACP to rejoin their staff as director of special research. It is likely that White expected the seventy-six-year-old Du Bois to be more of a figurehead than an active participant in NAACP policymaking. However, Du Bois's leftist political beliefs quickly alienated him from NAACP leadership and rekindled his conflict with White. His employment in the NAACP ended in 1948.

In the late 1940s and early 1950s, Du Bois became deeply involved in Socialist politics and opposition to the Cold War and American foreign policy. In 1950 he ran for a U.S. Senate seat from New York on the American Labor party ticket, and he participated in the organization of the leftist Peace Information Center. This latter activity resulted in his indictment, trial, and acquittal on federal charges that he was an unregistered foreign agent. Although he prevailed in the trial, Du Bois had his passport seized and lost his access to the mainstream press during the McCarthy hysteria.

Du Bois believed that the aftermath of World War II (like the years following World War I) provided a new opportunity for the destruction of colonialism and the creation of an effective Pan-African movement. In the late 1940s he participated in the revival of the Pan-African Congress. A decade later the independence of Ghana began the process of African liberation that Du Bois long had championed. In 1960 he accepted Ghanian President Kwame Nkrumah's invitation to direct work on a monumental scholarly project, the *Encyclopedia Africana*. The following year he moved to Ghana. In February 1963, Du Bois became a citizen of Ghana; six months after that, on 27 August 1963, as several hundred thousand Americans prepared to demonstrate for civil rights in the March on Washington, Du Bois died in Accra in his adopted country, at the age of ninety-five.

Du Bois was the dominant African-American intellectual in the first third of the twentieth century. More than any other American of his generation, he studied, grappled with, and attempted to define solutions to the dilemmas that race placed on American culture. His ideas continued to evolve during his long career. When he separated from the NAACP, it was not because he had become conservative or intellectually rigid as he entered the seventh decade of his life; rather, it was because he had become more radical. In many ways, Du Bois's life presaged the increasing radicalism of the modern civil rights movement and the insistence on "black nationalism" that grew from that movement during the 1960s. While the NAACP provided the legal talent and persistence in challenging segregation in the courts, Du Bois provided the historical vision necessary to combat discrimination and to encourage self-worth among blacks everywhere.

NOTES

1. W.E.B. Du Bois, *The Souls of Black Folk* (Chicago, 1903), repr. in W.E.B. Du Bois, *Writings* (New York, 1986), 372.

2. W.E.B. Du Bois, "Open Letter to the Southern People," in Herbert Aptheker, ed., *Against Racism: Unpublished Essays, Papers, Addresses, 1887–1961* (Amherst, Mass., 1985), 4; and Manning Marable, *W.E.B. Du Bois: Black Radical Democrat* (Boston, 1986), 11.

3. W.E.B. Du Bois, "Strivings of the Negro People," *Atlantic Monthly* 80 (August 1897): 195.

4. W.E.B. Du Bois to Booker T. Washington, 24 September 1895, in Herbert Aptheker, ed., *The Correspondence of W. E. B. Du Bois*, 1 (Amherst, Mass., 1973), 39.

5. W.E.B. Du Bois, "The Conservation of Races," repr. in *Writings*, 825.

6. Du Bois, *Souls of Black Folk*, 393.

7. W.E.B. Du Bois, "The Parting of the Ways," *World Today* 6 (April 1904): 521–523, repr. in Herbert Aptheker, ed., *Writings by W.E.B. Du Bois in Periodicals Edited by Others*, vol. 1 (Millwood, N.Y., 1982), 200.

8. W.E.B. Du Bois, "The Talented Tenth," in *The Negro Problem: A Series of Articles by Representative Negroes of To-Day* (1903), repr. in *Writings*, 842.

9. Du Bois, "The Parting of the Ways," 202.

10. W.E.B. Du Bois, "Marrying of Black Folk," *The Independent* 69 (13 October 1910): 812–813, repr. in Aptheker, ed., *Writings in Periodicals Edited by Others*, vol. 2, 34.

11. "The Niagara Movement: Declaration of Principles, 1905," repr. in Herbert Aptheker, ed., *Pamphlets and Leaflets by W.E.B. Du Bois* (White Plains, N.Y., 1986), 57.

12. "The Crisis," *Crisis* 1 (November 1910): 10.

13. "Agitation," *Crisis* 1 (November 1910): 11.

14. "Organized Labor," *Crisis* 4 (July 1912): 131.

15. "The Black Man and the Unions," *Crisis* 15 (March 1918): 217.

16. "Close Ranks," *Crisis* 16 (July 1918): 111.

17. "Returning Soldiers," *Crisis* 18 (May 1919): 14.

18. William H. Ferris, "Review of *Darkwater*" [June 1920], repr. in Theodore G. Vincent, ed., *Voices of a Black Nation: Political Journalism in the Harlem Renaissance* (San Francisco, 1973), 342–348.

19. "A Lunatic or a Traitor," *Crisis* 28 (May 1924): 9.

20. W.E.B. Du Bois, "Criteria of Negro Art," *Crisis* 32 (October 1926): 294.

21. Marable, *Du Bois*, 139.

22. "Segregation," *Crisis* 41 (January 1934): 20.

BIBLIOGRAPHY

Aptheker, Herbert, ed., *The Correspondence of W.E.B. Du Bois*. 3 vols. Amherst, Mass., 1973–1978.

———. *Writings by W.E.B. Du Bois in Non-Periodical Literature Edited by Others*. Millwood, N.Y., 1982.

———. *Writings by W.E.B. Du Bois in Periodicals Edited by Others*. 4 vols. Millwood, N.Y., 1982.

———. *Against Racism: Unpublished Essays, Papers, Addresses, 1887–1961*. Amherst, Mass., 1985.

Du Bois, W.E.B. *The Souls of Black Folk: Essays and Sketches*. Chicago, 1903.

———. *Dusk of Dawn: An Essay Toward an Autobiography of a Race Concept*. New York, 1940.

———. *The Autobiography of W.E.B. Du Bois: A Soliloquy on Viewing My Life from the Last Decade of Its First Century*. Edited by Herbert Aptheker. New York, 1968.

———. *Writings*. New York, 1986.

Foner, Philip S., ed., *W.E.B. Du Bois Speaks: Speeches and Addresses*. 2 vols. New York, 1970.

Lewis, David Levering. *W.E.B. Du Bois: Biography of a Race, 1868–1919.* New York, 1993.

Marable, Manning. *W.E.B. Du Bois: Black Radical Democrat.* Boston, 1986.

Meier, August. *Negro Thought in America, 1880–1915: Racial Ideologies in the Age of Booker T. Washington.* Ann Arbor, Mich., 1966.

Rudwick, Elliot M. *W.E.B. Du Bois: Propagandist of the Negro Protest.* New York, 1969.

Wintz, Cary D. *Black Culture and the Harlem Renaissance.* Houston, 1988.

———. ed., *African-American Political Thought, 1895–1935: Washington, Du Bois, Garvey, and Randolph.* New York, 1995.

Mary Baker Eddy
and Theological Reform

MARY FARRELL BEDNAROWSKI

''Reformer'' may be too moderate a term to apply to Mary Baker Eddy although, like many other founders of religions, she began her theological work
with the intention of reforming rather than departing from the New England
Calvinist tradition in which she had been raised. When it became clear to her
that the established Christian churches were hostile to her message, she started
a church of her own. The *Manual of the Mother Church*, the small book that
elaborates the structure and governance of Christian Science, quotes Eddy's
motion at the 12 April 1879 meeting of the Christian Science Association: ''To
organize a church designed to commemorate the word and works of our Master,
which should reinstate primitive Christianity and its lost element of healing.''[1]
This somewhat traditional-sounding statement of intent masks the reality that
Mary Baker Eddy founded a distinctive religious tradition offering a new interpretation of Christian theology and a healing method based on a radically spiritual metaphysics.

   During her nearly lifelong search for physical and emotional health, Mary
Baker Eddy became convinced that sickness, suffering, and death were caused
by a false understanding of God and the nature of reality. Her frustrating jour-
neys through both ''regular,'' or allopathic, medicine and numerous alternative
medical therapies available in the nineteenth century moved her, finally, not
toward medical reform but in the direction of theology. She wanted to strip
Christianity of what she saw as erroneous understandings of God and creation
that had accrued over centuries. In her opinion, these had produced destructive
hierarchies—''priestcraft,'' as she called it—and a doctrine of God that presented believers with the insuperable dilemma of having to reconcile the biblical
assurance of God's goodness and mercy with the reality of human suffering.
The result was the loss of what Eddy considered the central message of Chris-

tianity: that sin, sickness, suffering, and death could be overcome through a healing of the separation between God and humankind.

One way, then, to interpret the life and work of Mary Baker Eddy is to describe her as a theologian, one who saw her primary task as offering new responses to old questions of an ultimate nature. What is God like? Who are we as human beings? Why do we get sick, and what makes us well? How must we live our lives? How should a church be organized and governed, if it sufficiently reflects the true nature of God and reality? Seen in this context, she offers a compelling case study of the theologian as a kind of artist, the creator of a cultural construct akin to a painting or a novel or a sculpture. And just as a work of art can be the source of provocative perspectives on the conflicts and questions of a particular time in history, so can a theological system be seen as a creative response to those most pressing problems of an ultimate nature that are present in any culture.

Out of the experiences of her life, Eddy's primary mode of expression came to be theology, although the first half of that life does not offer many clues that she would be the founder of a new religious movement. She was born on 16 July 1821 into a New Hampshire farm family, the last of Mark and Abigail Baker's six children. Her secular education was not unusual for her time, gender, class, and rural location—one-room district schools, a year or two of "academy," and occasional tutoring by her brother Albert, home on vacation from Dartmouth College. Her attendance was sporadic due to frequent illness and emotional anxiety. Her theological education was of the informal kind, acquired through church attendance and a family devotional life that emphasized prayer, Bible reading, study of the Westminster Catechism, and intense theological discussion. Eddy's memory of the formational aspects of her childhood include the opposing pieties of her parents: her father a rigid Calvinist and her mother the proponent of a gentler kind of religion that emphasized God's love. Early on, she seems to have made a connection between physical illness and particular doctrines of God.

In *Retrospection and Introspection*, an autobiographical account published when she was seventy, Eddy recounts a childhood experience of being stricken with fever caused by fear and doubt about the doctrine of predestination. "I was unwilling to be saved," she said, "if my brothers and sisters were to be numbered among those who were doomed to perpetual banishment from God." Her father sought to win her away from heresy by a "relentless theology" that "emphasized belief in a final judgment-day, in the danger of endless punishment, and in a Jehovah merciless towards unbelievers." It was Eddy's mother who advised her daughter to lean on God's love and seek guidance in prayer. The fever was relieved, and the " 'horrible decree' of predestination—as John Calvin rightly called his own tenet—forever lost its power over me."[2] What Eddy sought to convey nearly sixty years after the event was her experience, more intuited at the time than articulated, that one model of God made her sick and another made her well.

Eddy remained at home until her marriage to George Washington Glover in 1843. In six months she was a widow, pregnant, without financial resources, and in physical and emotional distress. Except for a little money she earned by writing, Eddy was dependent on relatives for shelter and sustenance, and required extensive assistance in caring for her only child, a son born in 1844. By 1851 he was placed in the care of foster parents who eventually moved to Minnesota, and Eddy did not have contact with him again until 1861. In 1853 Eddy entered a twenty-year, mostly unhappy marriage to Daniel Patterson, an itinerant dentist. Poverty, frequent moves, and Patterson's unreliability and extended absences caused Eddy to seek a separation in 1866 and a divorce in 1873.

During all these years Eddy's ill health persisted, and so did her attempts to seek relief. She was diagnosed by her regular physician as having "dyspepsia," accompanied by spinal and gastric pain. She tried both traditional medicine and various kinds of alternative healing, including the Graham system of diet, hydropathy, and homeopathy, without much effect. Her search for medical relief took place within a world that had not yet had the advantage of Pasteur's and Koch's discovery of the role of microorganisms in causing disease. In the first three-quarters of the nineteenth century, regular medicine had few disease-specific therapies, and treatment proceeded on the basis of general assumptions about the relationship of the body to its environment. According to medical historians, it did not offer significant advantages over alternative therapies and was often more dangerous. As Robert Fuller points out. "The therapeutic arsenal at his [the physician's] disposal consisted of drugs and various invasive techniques that could influence a patient's ability to assimilate or excrete fluids. Bleedings, sweating, blistering, and the use of drugs aimed at inducing either vomiting or diarrhea were the most common therapeutic techniques."[3] Given the state of regular medicine, then, Eddy was not likely to be cured by alternative therapies, but she may have been in less danger of harm from them. The point is that she was helped by neither regular nor alternative medicine, and she was motivated over and over again to ask why that was so.

If alternative therapies like homeopathy and hydropathy did not cure Eddy, they nonetheless led her more and more to think about a mental theory of disease—suffering caused by the patient's state of mind and, as a consequence, susceptible to relief by a change in that state. Thus, she was predisposed to the therapy offered by Phineas Parkhurst Quimby of Portland, Maine, a mesmeric healer to whom she turned in 1862 upon finding ineffective the water cure she was undergoing at the Vail Hydropathic Institute in Hill, New Hampshire. Quimby had expanded mesmerism's assumption that health depended upon the unblocked flow of magnetic fluids throughout the body to a conviction that it was a patient's positive beliefs or attitudes that regulated the flow of this fluid in a way that ensured good health. Eddy reported her health improved under Quimby, but she experienced relapses, apparently related in part to the return of Dr. Patterson and the resumption of her difficult marriage. She returned to

Quimby's care periodically until his death in January 1866, an event that caused Eddy emotional distress and fear for her health.

In February 1866, a month after Quimby died, Eddy fell on the ice in Lynn, Massachusetts. There is some debate about the extent and seriousness of her injuries, but she experienced a "spontaneous healing" that occurred while she was reading an account of one of Jesus' healings in the Gospel of Matthew. Although it must be seen within the broader context of her whole life and work, this injury and subsequent healing became the obvious and pivotal catalyst for the development of Christian Science theology, and it started Eddy on the path to constructing a system of spiritual healing based on a new model of God.

She compared what she experienced to Newton's discovery of gravity: "My immediate recovery from the effects of an injury caused by an accident, an injury that neither medicine nor surgery could reach, was the falling apple that led me to the discovery how to be well myself, and how to make others so."[4] What Eddy termed a "discovery" came to be articulated as the Christian Science Scientific Statement of Being, still read at every Sunday service: "There is no life, truth, intelligence, nor substance in matter. All is infinite Mind and its infinite manifestation, for God is All-in-all."[5] This radical understanding of the ultimate nature of reality—that it is spirit, not matter—gave Eddy the key to formulating a new model of God and a healing method different from any proposed by traditional medicine, orthodox Christianity, or the available alternative therapies that she had tried.

It was to be a scientific religion based on principles and laws rather than on beliefs and creeds—a theology whose efficacy could be demonstrated (thus the frequent use of the term "demonstrate" in Christian Science) by the healing it brought about. At the same time it was to be *Christian*. "I named it *Christian*," she said, "because it is compassionate, helpful, and spiritual."[6] And it was at its foundation scriptural because, as Eddy explained it:

The Bible was my textbook. It answered my questions as to how I was healed; but the Scriptures had to me a new meaning, a new tongue. Their spiritual significance appeared; and I apprehended, for the first time, in their spiritual meaning, Jesus' teaching and demonstration, and the Principle and rule of spiritual Science and metaphysical healing— in a word, Christian Science.[7]

None of these elements of Christian Science was so evident to Eddy in 1866 as they were in retrospect. It was 1875 before the first edition of *Science and Health* elaborated her ideas in published form. Eddy spent the intervening time in poverty and dependence on the charity of others while she wrote out the implications of her new interpretation of Christianity and attempted to distinguish her system of healing from that of mesmerists, including Quimby. In 1870 she set up residence in Lynn, Massachusetts, where she lived for the next twelve years. She engaged in healing work, taught small groups of students about her new method of healing, and formed a partnership with Richard Kennedy, a young former student who had worked in a box factory. In 1872 Eddy broke with Kennedy over disagreements about her resolve to abolish any kind of physical contact from her healing method. This was to be a pattern until the end of her life: a teacher–student relationship that flourished in the beginning but ended in rupture, usually over issues of authority emerging from conflicts about the nature of Christian Science healing. Many of those students—among them Clara Choate, Emma Curtis Hopkins, Ursula N. Gestefeld, and Augusta Stetson—went on to form rival healing practices based in great part on Christian Science teachings.

Eddy's healing method, as it emerged more clearly during the second half of her life, was distinctive because she was constructing what she saw as a new model of God. She did not use the language of ''models,'' by which contemporary theologians signal their awareness of the constructed nature of various doctrines of God, but she made it clear in her voluminous theological writings that the interpretation of deity she had inherited from Calvinism was inadequate for purposes of healing and did not coincide with her own experiences of a loving God. She became increasingly convinced that suffering and sin persisted in the world because of a cosmic misunderstanding about what God is like.

If there was any issue that concerned Eddy above all others in her many years of seeking health, it was the ancient question of theodicy: why is there suffering in the world, and what does God have to do with it? Her response came to be this: God has nothing at all to do with the suffering of the world. God did not create the material world, which therefore has no ultimate reality. Neither did God create or intend the pain that occurs there. If we truly understood God as ''incorporeal, divine, supreme, infinite, Mind, Spirit, Soul, Principle, Life, Truth, Love,''[8] and the creation, including ourselves, as a reflection of God, we would cease to believe in the ultimate reality of matter and its power over us. All suffering in the form of illness, pain, and death caused by belief in matter would cease. We would, in other words, be healed of both sin and sickness.

In the process of revisioning the Christian doctrine of God and separating the deity from all connection to the material world, Eddy did not go so far as to abandon the traditional attributes of God or the notion of God's absolute sovereignty. God, she said, is ''omnipotent, omniscient, and omnipresent Being, and His reflection is man and the universe.''[9] In this sense, she retained the heritage of her Puritan ancestors. Eddy saw her task as interpreting her heritage in a new way. She did go so far, however, as to suggest that God, although not anthropomorphic in nature, could nonetheless be thought of in personal terms as ''Father–Mother,'' a term she said ''is the name for Deity, which indicates His tender relationship to His spiritual creation.''[10]

Eddy did not leave behind the biblical conviction that humankind is made in the image and likeness of God. But the severing of God from the creation of the physical world—the world of matter and bodies—required a new doctrine of human nature. There was no way, in Mary Baker Eddy's worldview, that the body could be considered the temple of the Holy Spirit, for the physical body has no ultimate basis in reality. "Man is not matter," she said in *Science and Health*. "He is not made up of brain, blood, bones, and other material elements."[11] And if the human person is not made up of matter, then the five senses are of no use in informing us about true human nature. In fact, reliance on the five senses—the "corporeal senses," as Eddy called them—can only lead us astray. "Corporeal sense defrauds and lies,"[12] she wrote. How, then, to talk about the human person if not in the traditional way, as an entity made up of both body and spirit? Eddy responded: "Man is spiritual and perfect; and because he is spiritual and perfect, he must be so understood in Christian Science. Man is idea, the image, of Love; he is not physique."[13]

Eddy was well aware that in spite of the claims of her theology, women and men experience themselves as finite creatures who sin and suffer and die. Thus, on the surface, her insistence on humankind as spiritual and perfect seems overly optimistic if not ludicrous, as many of her critics pointed out. Eddy worked at clarifying her doctrine of human nature by distinguishing between "real man," the perfect reflection of a perfect God, and "mortal man," the false understanding of the human person as made up of both body and spirit, and thus finite and susceptible to suffering and death. It is mortal man who is detected by the five senses, who is treated by traditional medicine, and who is ministered to by the established religions that insist that humankind is not perfect but sinful and finite. It is mortal man who sins and suffers and dies. Eddy did not deny, as many of her critics claimed, that humankind experienced suffering as real. She denied, instead, that such suffering was inevitable or necessary.

To be healed in Christian Science means to know oneself as "true man," not "mortal man." It is to know oneself as the perfect reflection of a perfect God. The entire apparatus of Christian Science, including the role of the practitioner, is set up to ensure that this insight into the true nature of reality can be realized and in turn bring about healing. It is the obligation of the individual to pray and to engage in daily reading and study of *Science and Health* and the Bible in order to comprehend this truth. This healing method evolved as one that does not make use of the laying on of hands or of any kind of physical manipulation. It is instead a spiritual healing that requires the individual to deny the reality of matter and its effects, and to open one's mind to the perfection of spiritual and physical health that has already been granted. "People want healing," says Robert Peel, "but even more they want the truth . . . .Healing for the Christian Scientist is more than a rescue from pain or disability; it is a revelation, in some degree of what Jesus meant when he said, 'I am the way, the *truth*, and the life' (John 14:6)."[14] The relationship between the knowledge of God and healing in Christian Science is reciprocal. To understand God's true nature is to be healed, and to be healed is to understand the truth about God, human nature, and reality. Thus, one is healed not only of sickness but also of error, not only of suffering but also of sin.

Healing is possible not only for the individual but also for the world, according to the Christian Science perspective, although Eddy did not assume that this spiritual healing process would occur any time soon. In this sense, in fact, she was not at all optimistic. "Far from seeing human experience in optimistic terms," writes historian Stephen Gottschalk, "she maintained that general dislocation and suffering would continue and even increase until humanity awakened from the fundamental error of belief in existence separate from God."[15]

Eddy was not a systematic theologian in the traditional, academic meaning of that term. Her theological work, as she saw it, was meant to bring about healing rather than to offer a totally coherent, logically irrefutable set of theological or philosophical claims. But she was aware that she needed to enlarge upon the implications of the denial of the reality of matter for other aspects of Christian theology. Otherwise, Christian Science would have no way to offer its insights to other Christians. Thus, Eddy's new understandings of God, reality, and human nature required a creative reconstruction of many other categories of Christian theology, including the Bible, Jesus, the atonement, sin and evil, prayer and miracles, and the church.

Eddy never abandoned the primacy of the Bible in her theology. Instead, she claimed it for Christian Science, insofar as she held that her discovery of the unreality of matter made clear the true meaning of the Bible—its spiritual significance. The first tenet of Christian Science is this: "As adherents of Truth, we take the inspired Word of the Bible as our sufficient guide to eternal life."[16] But Eddy had her own idea of what was meant by the term "inspiration." As Gottschalk points out, "She did not regard all of the Bible as inspired nor even the inspired portions of it as equally inspired."[17]

In the chapter-long exegesis of Genesis in *Science and Health*, Eddy differentiates between the first and second creation accounts. The first she sees as compatible with Christian Science. But the second, beginning with "But there went up a mist from the earth, and watered the whole face of the earth" (Gen. 2:6), she considers as "mortal and material." She is not reluctant to point out that it is erroneous. This second account, says Eddy, contains a "material view" of God. It is too anthropomorphic, in her opinion, and pantheistic as well in its reference to humankind as created from the dust of the earth. She asks, "Is Spirit, God, injected into dust, and eventually rejected at the demand of matter? Does Spirit enter dust, and lose therein the divine nature and omnipotence? Does Mind, God, enter matter to become there a mortal sinner, animated by the breath of God?"[18] To all of these questions Eddy implied an emphatic "No!"

For Eddy, the Bible was meant to be practical. It was to be read every day along with passages from *Science and Health*. Eddy saw the Bible at its core as a record of healings, particularly the New Testament, and believed its deepest meaning opened the way to the healing of spiritual and physical ills. She did not accept the Bible as literally true, word for word, but she did believe it was inspired by God and true in a spiritual sense in its entirety. Contemporary Christian Scientists echo Eddy's conviction about the practical aspect of the Bible.

The Jesus of the Bible in Christian Science theology becomes the Scientist par excellence, the human person who most fully demonstrated the spiritual nature of reality and the possibility of healing sin, suffering, and death. Eddy described Jesus of Nazareth as "the most scientific man that ever trod the globe. He plunged beneath the spiritual surface of things, and found the spiritual cause."[19] According to Eddy, the healings he performed were not miracles in the traditional sense of the word. They were not interventions in the workings of the natural world; they were demonstrations of spiritual science. "Jesus walked on the waves," she said, "fed the multitude, healed the sick, and raised the dead in direct opposition to material laws."[20] As Eddy saw it, Jesus did not need to interfere in the laws of the natural world, because he knew that they did not exist in the first place. He overcame the illusion of the reality of their existence and invoked instead the spiritual laws that govern the universe in order to heal.

In several ways Eddy's understanding of Jesus mirrored other nineteenth-century interpretations of him as a totally self-actualized human being, an exemplar, one with capacities that anyone had the potential to develop. The particular Christian Science perspective is that Jesus knew more fully than any other person in history that the ultimate nature of reality is spirit. It was out of this knowledge that he healed sin and suffering and overcame the illusion of death, as he demonstrated by his resurrection. Because Christian Science does not subscribe to an understanding of human nature as "fallen," and therefore in need of salvation from a sinful state, Jesus' saving work is that of demonstrating the truth. Jesus was also the Christ because he so completely demonstrated his knowledge of "true man." But he was not divine in any sense that the rest of us do not have the potential to be divine. The healings he performed can be imitated by people today. In Christian Science theology the Christ principle is available to all.

Within the framework of this worldview there was a need for new interpretations of the crucifixion and the atonement. Christian Science claims that through the crucifixion Jesus showed the way for others to overcome the illusion that death and matter are real. He demonstrated his at-one-ment with God. But he did not do this on behalf of all other human persons—this was not a vicarious atonement. Instead, he showed them how to do it for themselves. "While we adore Jesus," said Eddy, "and the heart overflows with gratitude for what he did for mortals . . . yet Jesus spares us not one individual experience, if we follow his commands faithfully; and all have the cup of sorrowful effort to drink in proportion to their demonstration of his love, till all are redeemed through divine love."[21]

As Robert Peel points out, Eddy did not neglect to emphasize the suffering of Jesus. Chapter II of *Science and Health*, "Atonement and Eucharist," is full of references to "agony," the "earthly cup of bitterness," and "mockery, desertion, and torture." But this is not suffering imposed on Jesus by God. It is the suffering that comes in attempting to throw off the error of believing in the reality of matter.[22] Jesus' resurrection, which Eddy accepted as a historical event, as she did the Virgin Birth, was his demonstration for the rest of humankind that the illusion of death can be overcome. In a sense, Jesus dematerialized by means of his certain, hard-won knowledge that matter was not real, and the illusion of a fleshly body could not fetter spirit.

New meanings for old concepts included the need to reinterpret "prayer," "heaven," and "hell." The first chapter of *Science and Health* is devoted to prayer. The purpose of prayer in Christian Science is to bring one into unity with the thoughts of God—to understand reality as it truly is. It did not make sense to Eddy to petition God to take away suffering that did not exist and that God did not create. God is not influenced, said Eddy, by human petitions to do what God has already accomplished: "Who would stand before a blackboard and pray the principle of mathematics to solve the problem?" she said. "The rule is already established, and it is our task to work out the solution."[23] Petitionary prayer goes against the understanding of God in Christian Science.

"Heaven" is described as a state of mind in Christian Science theology, "a divine state of Mind," not a place. Insofar as one understands the true nature of reality as spiritual, this divine state of mind is possible. Hell is that state in which belief in the reality of matter blinds one to Truth. To be in hell is to be captive to Mortal Mind, a term Eddy used to convey a false consciousness, an erroneous way of thinking, about the nature of reality. In Eddy's theology there is no Judgment Day, at which time individuals are sent either to heaven or to hell. Judgment, as she understood it, is a constantly occurring process, "For the judgment-day of wisdom comes hourly and continually, even the judgment by which mortal man is divested of all material error."[24] Almost all Eddy's language is familiar to those acquainted with Christianity. "Mortal Mind" is an exception along with "Malicious Animal Magnetism," a term she used to denote human thoughts that were meant to inflict harm rather than healing (also called mental malpractice).

Eddy's reinterpretation of tradition extended likewise to new understandings of what "church" meant, on the assumption that ecclesiology and polity must reflect theology. She spent the last third of her life constructing her church as an institution that would protect the integrity of Christian Science and her own authority over it, distinguish it from rival healing systems, and foster spiritual healing. Eddy did not want a church organization with an elaborate hierarchy or a complex bureaucratic structure. In the words of Stephen Gottschalk, "The distinguishing feature of this church lies in its emphasis on spiritual experience over religious tradition, denominational adherence, creedal confession and public worship."[25]

In the years after the publication of *Science and Health*, what would become the institution of Christian Science began to emerge, but not without trial and error. The 1880s saw the beginnings of an institutional church, but at the end of that decade came the dissolution of what had been put together. In 1879 Eddy and several followers formed the Church of Christ, Scientist, and that same year she and Asa Gilbert Eddy, whom she had married in 1877, moved to Boston. In 1881 the Massachusetts Metaphysical College was chartered for the training of Christian Science practitioners, with Eddy as the president and only teacher.

In 1883 the first issue of the bimonthly *Journal of Christian Science* was published. But Eddy was dissatisfied with what she had created. By 1890 the Massachusetts Metaphysical College had been dissolved, even though it was attracting many students, the church was formally disorganized, and the National Christian Science Association was adjourned for three years. Eddy had resigned the pastorate of the church and left Boston, and was living in Concord, New Hampshire.

Very quickly the rebuilding began. In 1892 the Mother Church in Boston was reorganized and reestablished, and in December 1894, the first service was held in the new church building. Mary Baker Eddy now served as pastor emeritus, having ordained not a person to replace her but the Bible and *Science and Health*, in order to prevent personal preaching from distorting the message of Christian Science as put forth by Eddy. In 1895 the *Manual of the Mother Church* was published; it serves to this day as the repository of Christian Science organization and polity. Eddy continued to revise the *Manual* until her death in 1910.

Christian Science polity, as outlined in the *Manual of the Mother Church*, makes provisions for the structure and operation of the Mother Church in Boston and its relationship to the branch churches. The church is governed by a self-perpetuating, five-person board of directors. Because the major act of piety in Christian Science might be described as "study," there is much attention to various forms of education, including the training of practitioners and teachers, and vehicles for public information. There are also sections on membership and discipline. In addition, the *Manual* contains the order of service for Sunday morning and Wednesday evening worship, the latter primarily a time of testimonials on healings. In place of a sermon, Sunday services include the reading of the lesson-sermon composed of selected passages from *Science and Health* and the Bible, prepared in Boston at the Mother Church for use in all the branch churches. There is no clergy in Christian Science. Practitioners and teachers are considered lay people, as are the first and second readers of the Mother Church and the branch churches. The *Manual* performed the sociological function of moving the church from a charismatic to a bureaucratic institution, a transition that many new religious movements do not survive. Through the institution she constructed, Eddy made possible the continuation of the movement after her death. She also institutionalized the perpetuation of her theological and political authority in the same document, and her name remains the only one attached in any prominent and public way to the Church of Christ, Scientist.

By the last decade of her life, Mary Baker Eddy had achieved financial security and fame as the founder of Christian Science. She spent no time at the Mother Church in Boston but directed its proceedings from Pleasant View, the farm near Concord to which she had moved in 1892. In 1907, at the age of eighty-six, she experienced the difficulty of what came to be called the "next friends" suit. Her son, George Glover, and several others sought control over her affairs, contending that she was no longer able to manage them. The case was dismissed when court-appointed representatives found her obviously competent. In 1908 Eddy founded the *Christian Science Monitor* as a vehicle for expressing social concern within the Christian Science context. The *Monitor*'s reputation for outstanding news coverage has persisted, and only one page of each issue is devoted to Christian Science teaching. Eddy died 3 December 1910, in Brookline, Massachusetts. At that time Christian Science membership was close to 100,000.

The church that Mary Baker Eddy founded has survived more than a century. A majority of its members come from the educated professional and managerial middle class—the per capita income of Christian Scientists is among the highest of any denomination. Since its beginnings it has drawn a disproportionately large number of women as members and as practitioners. Church officials at present acknowledge a declining membership and aging population but point to similar trends in mainline Protestant denominations. Christian Science does not make membership statistics available, but estimates range from 250,000 to 500,000 (the latter number seems optimistic) in the United States. There are 2,600 branch churches throughout the world. The spiritual healing practiced by Christian Science, which involves prayer rather than drugs, therapy, mental healing, or the laying on of hands, is accepted to the extent that the financial costs of practitioners and nursing homes (of which there are thirty-two in the United States, Canada, and England) are covered by insurance.[26] In many states there is legislation giving parents the legal right to use spiritual healing for their children rather than traditional medicine.

In spite of its persistence in American religious life and its middle-class constituency, the church founded by Mary Baker Eddy is nonetheless controversial—mostly due to court trials involving the deaths of children who were treated by Christian Science healing. In their defense, parents who are obviously devoted to their children offer theological reasons for their use of Christian Science healing rather than traditional medicine, generally in combination with testimonials of multigenerational family histories of successful healings. While Christian Scientists are not prevented by church doctrine from using traditional medicine if they choose, Christian Science healing is considered incompatible with traditional medicine, because it is based on a radically different worldview. Christian Science healing proceeds on the assumption that there is no ultimate reality in matter. Traditional medicine, on the other hand, is a "material science," perceived by Christian Science as intensifying the error that has caused the illness in the first place, and thereby further endangering the ill person. Thus, if Christian Scientists choose traditional medicine for their children, as they sometimes do, they are no longer practicing Christian Science. The crisis of conscience generated by this conflict is well documented in court trials and publications. Thoroughly mainstream in most respects, Christian Science asks its members to make a radical departure from American cultural practice in responding to illness.

Christian Science, like any other religious tradition, has had to contend with internal conflict. Brief mention has already been made of Eddy's difficulties with students who left to form their own healing systems and religious movements. These began in the 1870s and persisted in various ways almost to the time of her death. Augusta Stetson, for example, was excommunicated in 1909.[27] In the years since Eddy's death other teachers and practitioners have tangled with the board of directors and have been disciplined in various ways. Internal governance also has been a source of difficulty. A major dispute between the board of directors of the Mother Church and the board of the Christian Science Publishing Company over issues of authority and money had its beginnings even before Eddy's death. Called the Great Litigation, it was resolved by decision of the Supreme Judicial Court of Massachusetts in favor of the board of directors in 1921. In the 1990s there was another controversy in Christian Science, again involving the authority of the board of directors in relation to the *Manual* and charges of financial mismanagement. A group of church members sued the board of directors over the spending of $325 million on a cable TV station that was subsequently shut down, concealing the financial condition of the church, and publishing with church approval *The Destiny of the Mother Church*, issued privately in 1947 by Bliss Knapp, a Christian Science practitioner and teacher. Publishing the Knapp book made the church eligible for a $98 million bequest from the estate of Knapp, his wife, and his sister-in-law.

Critics, church historian Stephen Gottschalk among them, charged that Knapp's comparison of Eddy to Jesus contradicts Christian Science theology in a way that Eddy called sacrilegious and that the church was selling out ''for a mess of pottage.'' Church officials claimed that Knapp's comparison is not entirely clear and the appropriate response to internal conflict is prayer rather than ''media manipulation.'' At the heart of the controversy were theology, polity, and the church's interpretation of Eddy's identity. Church members and scholars alike assessed the conflict, which continues in 1995, as serious enough to cause a schism.[28] If the history of the movement is any lesson, it may be the case that the group that holds the board of directors at fault will split off and form another movement. On the other hand, internal reform may also take place. Or perhaps both will occur.

More than a century after the founding of Christian Science and eighty-five years after her death, Mary Baker Eddy remains an enigmatic and challenging figure in American religious history. She has been praised excessively as well as caricatured, dismissed as theologically insignificant and castigated as a heretic and a fraud. She has been described as a mind healer, an exponent of the religion of healthy-mindedness, a positive thinker, and a harmonialist. These categories tend to overemphasize the optimistic dimensions of her theology, obscure its complexity and its debt to Calvinism, and place Eddy in the company of those from whom she tried to distinguish herself. Scholars of religion may do better to treat Eddy as the founder of a distinct religious tradition, one that overlaps with many theological trends in nineteenth-century America but does not fit easily into any one category. As Stephen Gottschalk has put it, Christian Science is Christian but not Protestant—and, one would add, not Catholic. In recent years Christian Scientists have become more willing to engage in dialogue about the distinctiveness of Christian Science theology in comparison with other Christian theologies. This process is likely to increase knowledge of Christian Science teaching and practice and to make it easier to assess its place in American religious history.

Mary Baker Eddy and the religion she founded offer compelling arenas of inquiry in many areas. As a female founder of a religious movement that has survived beyond the first generation, she is a rare phenomenon. Whether that makes her a feminist reformer has been the subject of debate in recent years as scholars have worked to interpret patterns in the ways women have been both present and absent in American religious history. It would be difficult to argue that women's rights were Eddy's primary concern, even though she favored economic equality and the right to vote. She was fairly traditional in her understanding of male and female social roles and did not make it easy for other women to assume positions of authority. Whatever the assessment of her feminism, there remains the opportunity to explore how Eddy's experience as a woman in nineteenth-century America shaped the theology she constructed and the church she founded.

Christian Science and its founder also have contributions to make to scholarship in the area of church–state relations in a plural society and the issues that emerge when one way of healing is perceived by the state as more conducive to the common good than another. In this matter ethicists, theologians, legal scholars, and jurists enter the arena of different kinds of moral discourse and conflicting narratives. Christian Science testimonies of healing, some of them validated by medical examination, tell one story. Those for whom Christian Science healing has failed tell another, and the conflict sometimes has to be adjudicated in the courts.

Finally, Eddy and Christian Science offer a compelling example of how the repository of theological ideas in American religious history can be expanded beyond the mainstream in order to respond to pressing issues in both church and culture. Mary Baker Eddy's medium of expression was theology, the primary locus of her creativity, even though her intent was to formulate a system of spiritual healing rather than a systematic theology. In her search for physical and emotional health, she reinterpreted the categories of traditional Christian theology to formulate a doctrine of God that absolved God of complicity in the suffering of the world or helplessness in the face of it. This was a God whose reality could be apprehended by demonstrable, pragmatic, scientific means: healing. Eddy formulated her new model of God in the late nineteenth century, at a time when science was emerging as the new arbiter of ultimate truth; the religious faith of many, Protestants particularly, appeared to be waning; and the therapeutic techniques of established medicine frequently offered more pain than relief. For Eddy and her followers, Christian Science offered the means to respond positively to all these realities.

NOTES

1. Mary Baker Eddy, *Manual of the Mother Church* (Boston, 1980), 17.

2. Mary Baker Eddy, *Retrospection and Introspection* (1891), in *Prose Works Other Than Science and Health* (Boston, 1925), 13–14.

3. Robert Fuller, *Alternative Medicine and American Religious Life* (New York, 1989), 14.

4. Eddy, *Retrospection and Introspection*, 24.

5. Mary Baker Eddy, *Science and Health with Key to the Scriptures* (Boston, 1934), 468. First published in its final form in 1910. Hereafter referred to as *S & H*.

6. Mary Baker Eddy, ''The Great Discovery,'' in *Retrospection and Introspection*, 25.

7. Ibid.

8. *S & H*, 465.

9. Ibid., 466.

10. Ibid., 332.

11. Ibid., 475.

12. Ibid., 488.

13. Ibid., 475.

14. Robert Peel, *Health and Medicine in the Christian Science Tradition: Principle, Practice, and Challenge* (New York, 1988), 54.

15. Stephen Gottschalk, ''Christian Science and Harmonialism,'' in Charles H. Lippy and Peter W. Williams, eds., *Encyclopedia of the American Religious Experience*, vol. 2., *Studies of Traditions and Movements* (New York, 1988), 915.

16. *S & H*, 497.

17. Stephen Gottschalk, *The Emergence of Christian Science in American Religious Life* (Berkeley, Calif., 1973), 19.

18. *S & H*, 524–525.

19. Ibid., 313.

20. Ibid., 273.

21. Ibid., 26.

22. Peel, *Health and Medicine in the Christian Science Tradition*, 61.

23. *S & H*, 3.

24. Ibid., 291.

25. Stephen Gottschalk, ''Christian Science Polity in Crisis,'' *The Christian Century* 110 (3 March 1993): 242.

26. Some of the most reliable and to-the-point sources of information about Christian Science theology, healing practice, organization, and membership can be found in depositions submitted for trials involving Christian Science parents whose children have died while undergoing spiritual healing. See, for example, the affidavit of Nathan Talbot, at the time manager of Christian Science Committees on Publication, sworn on 20 December 1989: *State of Minnesota* v. *William Lisle McKown, Kathleen Rita McKown, and Mariano Victor Tosto*, District Court, 4th Judicial District.

27. Stetson presents a somewhat unusual case, because even after her excommunication and Eddy's death she persisted with the expectation of vindication to profess loyalty to Eddy. See Augusta Stetson, *Vital Issues in Christian Science* (New York, 1914) and *Reminiscences, Sermons and Correspondence 1884–1913* (New York, 1926).

28. See Stephen Gottschalk, "Honesty, Blasphemy and *The Destiny of the Mother Church*," *The Christian Century* 108 (6 November 1991): 1028–1031; "Christian Science Turmoil," *The Christian Century* 109 (1 April 1992): 330; Stephen Gottschalk, "Christian Science Polity in Crisis," *The Christian Century* 110 (3 March 1993): 242–246; "Members Group Sues Christian Scientists," *New York Times*, 2 January 1994, p. 7Y.

BIBLIOGRAPHY

Ahlstrom, Sydney. "Eddy, Mary Baker." In Edward T. James, et al. eds., *Notable American Women*, Vol. 1, 1971, 551–561. Cambridge, Mass.

———. *A Religious History of the American People*. New Haven, 1972.

Bednarowski, Mary Farrell. "Outside the Mainstream: Women's Religion and Women Religious Leaders in Nineteenth-Century America." *Journal of the American Academy of Religion* 48 (1980): 207–231.

———. *New Religions and the Theological Imagination in America*. Bloomington, Ind., 1989.

Braden, Charles S. *Christian Science Today: Power, Policy, Practice*. Dallas, 1958.

Braude, Ann. "The Perils of Passivity: Women's Leadership in Spiritualism and Christian Science." In Catherine Wessinger, ed., *Women's Leadership in Marginal Religions: Explorations Outside the Mainstream*. Urbana, Ill., 1993.

Cather, Willa, and Georgine Milmine. *The Life of Mary Baker Eddy and the History of Christian Science*. Lincoln, Nebr., 1993.

John, DeWitt. *The Christian Science Way of Life* with *A Christian Scientist's Way of Life*, by Erwin Canham. Englewood Cliffs, N.J., 1962.

Eddy, Mary Baker. *Manual of the Mother Church*. Boston, 1895.

———. *Science and Health with Key to the Scriptures*. Boston, 1906.

———. *Retrospection and Introspection*. In *Prose Works Other Than Science and Health*. Boston, 1925.

Gottschalk, Stephen. *The Emergence of Christian Science in American Religious Life*. Berkeley, Calif., 1973.

———. "Christian Science." In Mircea Eliade, ed., *The Encyclopedia of Religion*, 442–446. New York, 1986.

———. "Christian Science Today: Resuming the Dialogue." *The Christian Century* 103 (1986): 1146–1148.

———. "Mary Baker Eddy." In Mircea Eliade, ed., *The Encyclopedia of Religion*, 29–31. New York, 1986.

———. "Theodicy After Auschwitz and the Reality of God." *Union Seminary Quarterly Review* 41 (1987): 77–91.

———. "Christian Science and Harmonialism." In Charles H. Lippy and Peter W. Williams, eds., *The Encyclopedia of the American Religious Experience*, 901–916. New York, 1988.

———. "Spiritual Healing on Trial: A Christian Scientist Reports." *The Christian Century* 105 (1988): 602–605.

———. "Honesty, Blasphemy and *The Destiny of the Mother Church*." *The Christian Century* 108 (1991): 1028–1031.

———. "Christian Science Polity in Crisis." *The Christian Century* 110 (1993): 242–246.

Knee, Stuart. *Christian Science in the Age of Mary Baker Eddy.* Westport, Conn., 1994.

Leishman, Thomas L. *Why I Am a Christian Scientist.* New York, 1958.

Lindley, Susan Hill. ''The Ambiguous Feminism of Mary Baker Eddy.'' *Journal of Religion* 64 (1984): 318–331.

McDonald, Jean A. ''Mary Baker Eddy and the Nineteenth-Century 'Public' Woman: A Feminist Appraisal.'' *Journal of Feminist Studies in Religion* 2 (1986): 89–111.

Melton, J. Gordon. ''Emma Curtis Hopkins: A Feminist of the 1880s and Mother of New Thought.'' In Catherine Wessinger, ed., *Women's Leadership in Marginal Religions: Explorations Outside the Mainstream.* Urbana, Ill., 1993.

Peel, Robert. *Mary Baker Eddy: The Years of Discovery.* New York, 1966.

———. *Mary Baker Eddy: The Years of Trial.* New York, 1971.

———. *Mary Baker Eddy: The Years of Authority.* New York, 1977.

———. *Health and Medicine in the Christian Science Tradition.* New York, 1988.

Robbins, Pam, and Robley Whitson. ''Mary Baker Eddy's Christian Science.'' *Sign* 59 (1980): 16–21.

Schoepflin, Rennie B. ''Christian Science Healing in America.'' In Norman Gevitz, ed., *Other Healers: Unorthodox Medicine in America.* Baltimore, 1988.

Simmons, Thomas. *The Unseen Shore: Memories of a Christian Science Childhood.* Boston, 1991.

Twain, Mark. *Christian Science.* New York, 1907.

Charles G. Finney
and the Evangelical Reform Impulse

NANCY A. HARDESTY

Charles Grandison Finney was an evangelist, pastor, professor of theology, and college president whose preaching and teaching formed a central impulse in the whirlwind of nineteenth-century reform. Finney's thrust was in perfect harmony with American activism and the democracy of the Jacksonian age. He grasped the genius of the church as one among many voluntary organizations, applying the ideas of moral agency and immediate conversion to the reform of the world, the implementation of the kingdom of God on earth.

Finney was born on 29 August 1792 to Sylvester and Rebecca Rice Finney in Warren, Connecticut, an area of Litchfield County first known as East Greenwich. Two years afterward his family moved to Oneida County, New York, and later to Hanover, on the shores of Lake Ontario. Finney attended Hamilton Oneida Academy in Clinton, southwest of Utica, for two years, and then the Warren Academy for four years. There, he learned the New Divinity propounded by Yale University graduates, a modified Calvinism that put less stress on predestination and original sin, and more emphasis on human ability.

After a stint as a schoolteacher, Finney returned to Adams, in Jefferson County, New York, and began to study law. Courting the local belles and playing cello at the Presbyterian church, he was beginning to take his place in local society when revivalist Jedediah Burchard arrived. Stirred by Burchard's preaching, Finney says in his *Memoirs*, ''I made up my mind that I would settle the question of my soul's salvation at once.'' It was ''the 10th of October, and a very pleasant day.'' Finney spent it reading the Bible and praying in the woods. Late in the afternoon, he found that ''all sense of sin, all consciousness of present sin or guilt had departed.''[1] He had been converted.

Finney returned to Adams and announced that he was forsaking the legal profession. He began to read theology with Presbyterian pastor George W. Gale.

He was admitted to the St. Lawrence Presbytery on 25 June 1823 and was given a preaching license in December. He was ordained 1 July 1824.

His first pastoral assignment, made on 17 March 1824, was as a missionary to Jefferson County, supported by the Female Missionary Society of the Western District of New York (founded in 1806 by the women of First Presbyterian Church, Utica). In October, Finney married Lydia Andrews of Whitestown, Oneida County. Several days after their marriage, he traveled to Evans Mills, in Jefferson County, promising to return for her within the week. But revival broke out throughout the area, and after six months he finally sent a church elder to fetch her.

Revival spread like wildfire as Finney moved from LaRayville to Rutland, Western, and Rome. He spent the winter of 1825–1826 in Utica. From there Finney moved on to Auburn, to which he returned in spring 1831. In the fall of 1826 he began conducting services in Troy.

Finney's "new measures" stirred loud criticism from fellow evangelists Asahel Nettleton and Lyman Beecher. The two sides met at New Lebanon, New York, on 18 July 1827 to debate the issues. Finney's pattern was to go into churches at the invitation of a pastor or of sympathetic laypeople. He would hold protracted meetings every day for several months. His preaching was colloquial, using illustrations from common life and urging listeners to respond, rather than giving exegesis of a text, as his opponents thought more proper. Preaching meetings were accompanied by daily prayer meetings in homes and in churches. People were prayed for by name; opponents felt this constituted coercion. Those under "conviction" or concerned about the state of their souls were invited publicly to admit their concern by attending "anxious meetings" following the services or by sitting up front on the "anxious bench." In Finney's meetings women were allowed to pray aloud and testify to their own religious experiences in "promiscuous" (or mixed) assemblies, which was considered a grave breech of etiquette (Presbyterian and Congregational women, unlike some "uncultured" Methodist women, were expected to be quiet, sedate listeners during religious exercises).

Nettleton, Beecher, and their supporters were particularly upset at the way Finney and his backers denounced clergy who did not support revivals. Discussion proceeded for days. Finney agreed to tone down his criticism of other clergy, and understandings were reached on most of the new measures—except for the issue of women praying and testifying. On that, the two sides could not agree. Beecher would not condone women's participation, and Finney would not silence them.

Eventually many of the same practices would be incorporated into reform. Reformers gave fervent lectures in hopes of converting the unconverted. They denounced "sinners" who owned slaves, frequented prostitutes, or sold liquor. Women were allowed to participate as equals and eventually as superiors, because they were considered more "holy."

Finney moved on to meetings in Pennsylvania and New York City in 1830.

There he met philanthropists Anson G. Phelps and Arthur and Lewis Tappan. The Tappans had attained great wealth from their silk-importing business. Along with others, they had formed the Association of Gentlemen to further various social reform causes.

The high point of Finney's revival crusades began on 10 September 1830 in Rochester, New York. The meetings continued through 6 March 1831. From Rochester, Finney moved on to Auburn, New York, Buffalo, Providence, and then Boston. As an itinerant evangelist, Finney followed in the footsteps of George Whitefield and set the standard for Dwight L. Moody, Billy Sunday, and Billy Graham.

Exhausted by ten years as a revivalist, suffering from recurring respiratory illness, and in need of a home for his growing family, Finney in 1832 agreed to become pastor of the Second Free Presbyterian Church in New York City, better known as the Chatham Street Chapel. The Tappans had converted a theater into a church facility large enough to accommodate the annual "anniversary meetings" of the "Great Eight" benevolent societies held during the first two weeks of May each year. At Chatham Chapel in 1835, Finney preached his *Lectures on Revivals of Religion* and allowed them to be published in *The New York Evangelist* to boost its circulation, which had fallen because of the outspoken antislavery sentiments of its editor, Joshua Leavitt. Later in 1835 Finney became pastor of the Sixth Free Church or Broadway Tabernacle, built to his specifications by the Tappans. He resigned from the more conservative Presbyterian Church in 1836 and adopted the freedom of Congregationalism.

In 1835 Finney moved his family to Ohio and became professor of theology at Oberlin College. For a number of years, he divided his time between Ohio and New York. Oberlin, founded in 1833, was the first college in the United States to enroll men and women, blacks and whites, together in a collegiate program. The college's founder, the Reverend John Jay Shipherd, had been impressed by Finney's Rochester revival (Shipherd's father was a pastor in Troy), and invited Finney to Oberlin.

Finney became president of Oberlin in 1851. Lydia had died in 1847, and he had married a Rochester widow, Elizabeth Ford Atkinson, in November 1848. She began to speak publicly during the Finneys' wedding trip to England. Finney seems to have taken pride in her efforts, mentioning them in his *Memoirs.* Together they held revival meetings throughout New England and the British Isles during the 1850s and early 1860s. Finney resigned the presidency of Oberlin in 1866 but continued as pastor of the Congregational church in Oberlin until 1872. He died in Oberlin on 16 August 1875.

Social reform became a part of Finney's life and work in various ways. He first included temperance issues in his Rochester revival in 1830–1831. Finney encouraged Theodore Dwight Weld to supplement his own preaching with lectures on temperance. Weld so stirred the city that many converts vowed to have nothing to do with the liquor trade, and merchants poured their stores of ardent spirits into the Erie Canal. Temperance became an obsession in this grain-processing town where once a number of distilleries had flourished.

The American Temperance Society (founded in 1826) was one of the Great Eight national groups that met annually at Chatham Chapel. The others were the American Board of Commissioners for Foreign Missions (founded in 1810), the American Education Society (1815), the American Bible Society (1816), the American Society for Colonizing the Free People of Color in the United States (often called simply the American Colonization Society, 1816), the American Sunday School Union (1817), the American Tract Society (1826), and the American Home Missionary Society (1826). These national societies—built on the base of innumerable local and regional groups, often divided by gender and age, as well as many other organizations devoted to prison reform, the uplifting of prostitutes, the keeping of the Sabbath, and numerous other causes—formed the mass of evangelical social concern that coalesced around Finney in New York.

Arthur and Lewis Tappan and their Association of Gentlemen supported all of these causes and more. In spring of 1830, just after Finney's first New York City revival, a young Princeton divinity student, John R. McDowall, arrived as a summer missionary for the American Tract Society. Women converts from Finney's crusade helped him with Sunday school classes in prisons and alms-houses in the notorious Five Points area. He also began to work with prostitutes. Arthur Tappan, who had visited a Magdalen Asylum in London, wanted to duplicate the British efforts. He hired McDowall as superintendent of the Magdalen Society of New York and persuaded the Association of Gentlemen to underwrite an ''Asylum for Females who have Deviated from the Paths of Virtue.''

With the instincts of a social worker, McDowall tackled the problem. Within a year he published a graphic report that elicited cries of shock and outrage from the city fathers. Even Tappan was shaken when the presbytery charged McDowall with being an irresponsible scandalmonger for pointing the finger not at the moral weakness of the women but at the men of wealth and status who patronized them. Tappan quietly closed the ''House of Refuge,'' but McDowall refused to back down. When he issued a second report, Tappan denounced him and formed the Society for Promoting the Observance of the Seventh Commandment, which would provide no asylums.

Disgusted with the Association of Gentlemen, McDowall turned to a more understanding group. On 12 May 1834, a group of women had met at Chatham Chapel to form the Female Moral Reform Society. Lydia Andrews Finney was its first ''directress,'' and Finney encouraged their work at the December meeting. The final issue of *McDowall's Journal*, dated 28 January 1835, contained rebuttals to all charges that had been made against him by the Association of Gentlemen and a ''will,'' leaving his paper, his work, and all its assets to the women. They renamed *McDowall's Journal* the *Advocate of Moral Reform*. By 1837 the *Advocate* had 16,000 subscribers, the majority of them in the ''burned-over'' district of western New York where Finney's revivals had sensitized people to reform.

The group tried to improve the economic status of prostitutes through job retraining, child care, and cooperative workshops. They also tried to shut down brothels by putting them under surveillance and printing the names of customers. In many ways the crusade for moral reform radicalized ordinary churchwomen, raising quite modern feminist questions. All agents for the society, and even its typesetters and printers, were women.

Slavery was, of course, the major concern of Finney's day. One of the converts of Finney's Utica revival was Theodore Dwight Weld. He and Henry Brewster Stanton, deputy county clerk, journalist, and convert during Finney's Rochester meetings, became members of Finney's ''Holy Band'' of assistants. Finney expected them to become evangelists; instead, both became antislavery lecturers. The Tappans had moved to found the New York City Anti-Slavery Society in October 1833 at Chatham Street Chapel and shortly thereafter organized the American Anti-Slavery Society, committed to the principle of immediate abolition. In 1834 Finney barred slaveholders from taking communion at Chatham Chapel.

Finney's Holy Band was looking for a seminary in which to train for the ministries opening up at ''Presbygational'' churches in the West. They settled on Lane Seminary in Cincinnati, Ohio, which had just hired Lyman Beecher as president. The seminary, founded in 1828, subscribed to the ''manual labor principle,'' meaning that students were required to do the manual labor necessary to run the school. The Tappans had hired Weld to promote this educational ideal.

Beecher was a leader in the American Colonization Society, which was committed to gradually freeing the slaves and relocating them in Liberia. Most of the Lane students initially shared their president's sentiments, associating immediate abolition of slavery with the fanaticism of William Lloyd Garrison. However, Weld and Stanton shared the Tappans' vision and had been quietly praying and trying to change their fellow students' minds. In February 1834 the students asked Beecher for permission to discuss the issues in public, and he agreed. For eighteen nights, more in the spirit of a protracted revival than of a formal debate, the students prayerfully considered their responsibilities to people of color. The meetings began by considering the question ''Ought the people of the slaveholding states to abolish slavery immediately?'' The arguments for ''gradual emancipation, immediately begun'' were presented by a Southern student. The group also heard testimony from other Southern students and a former slave. Weld closed the presentations. A vote on the ninth evening was unanimous in favor of immediate abolition.

The next nine evenings were devoted to a discussion of the American Colonization Society: Should Christians support it? Catharine Beecher presented her father's plan for uniting the efforts of abolitionists and colonizationists. No one defended it. Instead, the students read the society's *African Repository* and pamphlets and heard a report on conditions in Liberia. In the end they voted down colonization and formed an antislavery society. They began to work to better the lot of free blacks in Cincinnati. President Beecher was upset, and the seminary trustees were divided.

Eventually a large block of students, led by Weld and Lane trustee Asa Mahan bolted from Lane and agreed to relocate at Oberlin College on two conditions: Mahan, a Presbyterian minister, must become president, and Finney should be their professor of theology. The Tappans pledged substantial financial support.

Chatham Chapel continued to be a center of abolition activity even though Finney preferred to segregate black parishioners to the back and resisted "amalgamation," the nineteenth-century term for social interaction and mingling of blacks and whites. The Tappans and Weld encouraged amalgamation. The "Seventy" (see Luke 10) abolition lecturers were trained there in November 1836 by Weld and Stanton. Among the "Seventy" were the Grimké sisters, Sarah and Angelina, of South Carolina. Their fervent evangelism on behalf of freeing the slave provoked the first public debate over women's rights to participate in public ethical and religious debate. The Finneyite wing of the American Anti-Slavery Society favored political action (Garrison did not) and eventually participated in the formation of the Liberty and Republican parties.

In order to promote revivals, Finney declared that "the church must take right ground in regard to politics." He listed temperance, moral reform, and the abolition of slavery as issues on which it must take a positive stand. He consistently equated slavery with sin, declaring "The fact is that slavery is, pre-eminently, the *sin of the church.*" He denounced the church's resistance to reform on "any question involving human rights."[2] In 1846 he wrote:

No generation before us ever had the light on the evils and wrongs of Slavery that we have; hence our guilt exceeds that of any former generation of slave holders; and, moreover, knowing all the cruel wrongs and miseries of the system from the history of the past, every persisting slave-holder endorses all the crimes and assumes all the guilt involved in the system and evolved out of it since the world began.[3]

However, although Finney encouraged reform, his commitment was always to revival. This caused tension and eventual alienation between him and the Weld-Tappan coalition. As Theodore Weld wrote to an angry Lewis Tappan:

The truth is Finney has always been in revivals of religion. It is his great business, aim and *absorbing passion* to promote them. He has never had hardly anything to do with the Bible, Tract, missionary, Education, Temperance, moral Reform and anti-slavery societies.[4]

Finney felt that reform would follow revival. Because sin was at the core of all injustice, conversion was needed first. A nationwide revival would best prepare the country to eliminate its evils, including slavery. He wrote to Weld:

Is it not true, at least do you not fear it is, that we are in our present course going fast into a civil war? . . . How can we save our country and affect the speedy abolition of slavery? This is my answer. . . . Now if abolition can be made an append[a]ge of a general revival of religion all is well. I fear no other form of carrying this question will save our country or the liberty or soul of the slave.[5]

Finney tried to convince his "Holy Band" of young men of the validity of this strategy, but most of them turned their revivalist skills to the cause of abolition. Nevertheless, Finney and Mahan were the first to put their signatures on the constitution of the Oberlin Anti-Slavery Society at its formation in 1835. On the issue of abolition Finney tried to steer a moderate course between commitment and fanaticism.

Although Finney apparently never publicly endorsed woman's rights, the movement grew up around him. Elizabeth Atkinson Finney's public preaching and Finney's vision of reform indirectly influenced women's reform in several ways. Elizabeth Cady, for example, who claimed to be a convert at his Troy revival, eventually married Finney lieutenant and abolitionist lecturer Henry Stanton. She was radicalized when she attended the World's Anti-Slavery Convention in London and sat with Hicksite Quaker preacher Lucretia Mott, who had been elected as a delegate by the American Anti-Slavery Society but denied access because she was a woman. They called the first woman's rights convention at Seneca Falls, New York, in 1848. Significantly, though, Elizabeth Stanton later denounced Finney for his timidity and, especially, for what she regarded as his manipulative attempts to convert young people.

At Oberlin, Finney was surrounded by strong women. As Lucy Stone once said, "Men came to Oberlin for various reasons; women because they had nowhere else to go."[6] She had sat in the balcony of the West Brookfield (Massachusetts) Congregational Church in 1837 when the General Association of the Congregational Churches of Massachusetts drafted their *Pastoral Letter* against the "abolition agitation" of the Grimké sisters. She had read Sarah Grimké's defense of woman's rights in her *Letters on the Equality of the Sexes and the Condition of Women*. Stone had enrolled at Mary Lyon's Mount Holyoke Seminary in 1839 but withdrew after Lyon was disturbed because Stone left copies of Garrison's *Liberator* in the parlor and turned her missionary mite box into one for the American Anti-Slavery Society. She came to Oberlin in 1843. Upon graduation she, like her classmate Sallie Holley, became an antislavery lecturer. Later Stone became a founder of the American Woman Suffrage Association.

Stone's closest friend at Oberlin was Antoinette Brown, whose father had been converted during Finney's Rochester campaign. Brown felt a call to the ministry. After completing the ladies' course in 1847, she enrolled in the theology course, completing it in 1850. Not even Stone encouraged her, but Brown reported that "When President Finney heard me give my reasons for wanting to become a minister he said that some women had been called to preach and I might be of that number."[7] President Mahan encouraged Brown, while still a student, to publish her exegesis paper on 1 Corinthians 14 and 1 Timothy 2 in the *Oberlin Quarterly Review*. She was ordained 15 September 1853 by the First Congregational Church of Butler and Savannah, Wayne County, New York. Active in the woman's rights movement, defending such rights on the basis of the Bible, Brown eventually became a Unitarian minister.

Many early women students at Oberlin were active in abolition and woman's rights. One of its first graduates, Betsey Mix Cowles, founded the Ohio Woman's Rights Association. Hannah Conant Tracy was able to attend for only one year, 1847–1848, but she readily imbibed the spirit of reform. Her first husband was killed while aiding escaped slaves; she later became matron of the Ohio Deaf and Dumb Asylum. Frances Willard was not a student at Oberlin, but she vividly remembered the excitement of being there when her father and mother were students in the late 1840s. It prepared the way for her own devotion to reform, particularly temperance and woman's rights. A number of the early woman's rights conventions were held in Ohio and/or chaired by Oberlin women. Although Finney had no hand in such proceedings, and perhaps even doubted their efficacy, his own general interest in reform and the congenial reform environment at Oberlin during his tenure there encouraged woman's rights, and other, reforms.

Finney approached evangelism more as a lawyer than as a Presbyterian or Congregational minister. He often remarked, "I came right from a law office to the pulpit, and talked to the people as I would have talked to a jury."[8] He was a firm believer in the abilities of human reason. Despite the Calvinism of his mentor George Gale, Finney declared that to say human beings do not have free will "slanders God . . . charging him with infinite tyranny, in commanding men to do that which they have no power to do." "Conversion," said Finney, "consists in the right employment of the sinner's own agency."[9] In conversion, the sinner simply apprehends the truth and wills to obey it, turning from selfishness to benevolence.

Finney ridiculed those who told sinners to just "wait on God" to see if they were among the elect. "Religion is something to *do*, not something to *wait for*," he declared. "*Religion is the work of man*. It is something for man to do." He told sinners that their " 'cannot' consists in their unwillingness, and not in their inability. . . . We, as moral agents, have the power to obey God, and are perfectly bound to obey, and the reason we do not, is that we are unwilling." A sinner's problem was not hardness of heart but stubbornness of will: "It is not a question of *feeling* but of *willing* and *acting*. . . . WILLING to obey Christ is to be a Christian."[10]

With this view of conversion, Finney eventually coupled a view of sanctification that came to be labeled Oberlin Perfectionism. Although he had read John Wesley's *Plain Account of Christian Perfection* and knew Holiness leader Phoebe Palmer personally, he formulated his own teaching on the subject (Mahan was more Wesleyan in his views). Finney's and Mahan's quest grew out of a question asked by a student during a revival prayer meeting at Oberlin in

October 1836. Many students were familiar with the writings and activities of John Humphrey Noyes as well as with Methodist views.

Finney and Mahan spent the winter of 1836–1837 in New York City, pondering the question of perfection. Mahan felt that he experienced a second work of grace; Finney did not enter into the experience until 1843, but he began preaching it immediately. His first two sermons on the topic, given at Broadway Tabernacle, were reprinted in his *Letters to Professing Christians*. His text was Matthew 5:48: ''Be ye therefore perfect, even as your Father which is in Heaven is perfect.'' Both men also published essays in the *Oberlin Evangelist*, which first appeared on 1 November 1838.

Finney and Mahan argued that although all people have a sinful nature (all inevitably sin), their wills are not totally depraved (we have free will and we do not sin by necessity). Humans have a choice; they can will to be converted and to be perfect. The human dilemma is that they generally will things contrary to the will of God. For Finney, perfection consisted in right willing rather than perfect living. It was ''perfect obedience to the law of God . . . perfect disinterested, impartial benevolence, love to God and love to neighbor.''[11] God's grace and Christ's power enable humans to will correctly. Finney also spoke of perfection as perfect obedience to the moral law; again his emphasis was on human ability almost to the exclusion of God's enabling.

Finney decried the fact that ''many professed Christians hold that nothing is needful but simply faith and repentance, and that faith may exist without real benevolence, and consequently without good works.'' No ''mistake'' could ''be greater than this,'' according to Finney. The ''grand requisition which God makes'' upon humans is that they become ''truly benevolent,'' that is, that they exhibit ''compassion like God's compassion.''[12] In a word, Christians must become *useful*; they must ''stand their ground and do their duty.'' ''If filled with the Spirit, you will be useful. You cannot help being useful.''[13] He advised converts to

set out with a determination to *aim at being useful in the highest degree possible*. They should not rest satisfied with merely being useful, or remaining in a situation where they can do *some* good. But if they see an opportunity where they can do more good, they must embrace it, whatever may be the sacrifice to themselves.[14]

Thus, the spirit of the Christian was ''necessarily that of the reformer,'' said Finney. ''To the reformation of the world they stand committed.''[15] In a set of ''Letters on Revivals,'' published in the *Oberlin Evangelist*, Finney decried ''The Pernicious Attitude of the Church on the Reforms of the Age.'' He asserted that ''the great business of the church is to reform the world—to put away every kind of sin. The church of Christ was originally organized to be a body of reformers.'' Its job was the ''universal reformation of the world,'' and it should aggressively ''reform individuals, communities, and governments, and never rest until . . . every form of iniquity shall be driven from the earth.'' He vehemently denounced the clergy for "neglecting or refusing to speak out and act promptly and efficiently on these great questions of reform." Such actions, said Finney, grieve and quench the Holy Spirit, making revivals impossible.[16]

Revivals were the first evidence, Christian perfection the second, and reform the third indication for Finney that the millennium was at hand. A postmillennialist, he believed that it was the church's duty to institute the kingdom of God on earth and to prepare the earth for Christ's thousand-year reign of peace and prosperity. Christians must "stand their ground and do their duty."[17] If the church issues the cry "*to the work* . . . let us have the United States converted to God," then "the millennium may come to this country in three years."[18] In the initial issue of the *Oberlin Evangelist*, the editors declared that one reason for its publication was "to call the attention of Christians to the fact the Millennium is to consist in the entire sanctification of the church." The church must take up arms against the forces of evil and purge society of all ills. If Christians would only "feel as the heart of one man, and be agreed as to what ought to be done for the salvation of the world, the millennium will come at once."[19] In fact, said Finney, "If the whole church as a body had gone to work ten years ago, the millennium would have fully come in the United States before this day."[20]

Charles Grandison Finney was one of America's most important national evangelists. He set the standard in his theology, his style of preaching, and his organization of revival worship. His *Lectures on Revivals of Religion* continue to be the yardstick for evangelicals today. Although Finney always considered his primary task to be evangelism, a number of his emphases encouraged social reform: his understanding of human ability in conversion, Oberlin perfectionism, his insistence that Christians must be "useful," and his emphasis on the millennium. Unlike many contemporary revivalists, however, Finney integrated an understanding of and commitment to progressive reform. He felt that converted people could and should change the world for the better.

The key difference was undoubtedly his eschatology. Most fundamentalists and evangelicals today subscribe to the dispensationalist notion that the world will become worse and worse until Christ snatches all true believers up to join him in the clouds (the "Rapture"). Finney believed it was the job of Christians to institute the kingdom of God on earth, in the hope that Christ would soon come to rule.

NOTES

1. Charles G. Finney, *Memoirs* (New York, 1876), 18, 12, 18.

2. Charles G. Finney, "A Seared Conscience," *Oberlin Evangelist*, 28 April 1841.

3. Finney, *Oberlin Evangelist*, 4 February 1846, as quoted in Keith J. Hardman, *Charles Grandison Finney, 1792–1875: Revivalist and Reformer* (Syracuse, N.Y., 1987), 370.

4. Theodore Weld to Lewis Tappan, 17 November 1835, in Gilbert H. Barnes and

Dwight L. Dumond eds., *Letters of Theodore Dwight Weld, Angelina Grimke Weld and Sarah Grimke, 1822–44* (New York, 1934), vol. 1, 243.

    5. Finney to Weld, 21 July 1836, in ibid., vol. 1, 318.

    6. Elinor Rice Hays, *Morning Star: A Biography of Lucy Stone, 1818–1893* (New York, 1961), 33.

    7. Antoinette Brown Blackwell, ''Reminiscenses of Early Oberlin,'' February 1918, Blackwell Family Papers (Radcliffe College, Schlesinger Library, Cambridge, Mass.), p. 5 (handwritten).

    8. Finney, *Memoirs*, 168.

    9. Charles G. Finney, *Lectures on Revivals of Religion*, ed. William G. McLoughlin (Cambridge, Mass., 1960), 207, 318.

    10. Ibid., 207, 209, 107–108, 372, 374.

    11. Charles G. Finney, *Lectures to Professing Christians* (New York, 1878), 341.

    12. Charles G. Finney, *Sermons on Gospel Themes* (Oberlin, Ohio, 1876), 328.

    13. Finney, *Lectures on Revivals*, 242–243, 118.

    14. Ibid., 404.

    15. Charles G. Finney, *Lectures on Systematic Theology* (New York, 1878), 450.

    16. Reprinted by Donald W. Dayton in *Discovering an Evangelical Heritage* (New York, 1976), 20–24.

    17. Finney, *Lectures on Revivals of Religion*, 243.

    18. Ibid., 305–306, 404–405.

    19. Ibid., 328.

    20. Ibid., 305–306.

BIBLIOGRAPHY

Abzug, Robert H. *The Passionate Liberal: Theodore Dwight Weld and the Dilemma of Reform.* New York, 1980.

Barnes, Gilbert Hobbs. *The Anti-Slavery Impulse 1830–1844* (New York, 1933; repr. New York, 1964).

———, and Dwight L. Dumond, eds. *Letters of Theodore Dwight Weld, Angelina Grimké Weld, and Sarah Grimké, 1822–44.* New York, 1934; repr. Gloucester, Mass., 1965.

Cross, Whitney R. *The Burned-over District.* New York, 1950.

Dayton, Donald W. *Discovering an Evangelical Heritage.* New York, 1976.

Drummond, Lewis A. *Charles Grandison Finney and the Birth of Modern Evangelicalism.* London, 1983.

Finney, Charles Grandison. *Lectures on Revivals of Religion.* Ed. William G. McLoughlin. Cambridge, Mass., 1960.

———. *The Memoirs of Charles G. Finney: The Complete Restored Text.* Ed. Richard A. G. Dupuis and Garth M. Rosell. Grand Rapids, Mich., 1989.

Hardesty, Nancy A. *Women Called to Witness: Evangelical Feminism in the Nineteenth Century.* Nashville, Tenn., 1984.

———. *''Your Daughters Shall Prophesy'': Revivalism and Feminism in the Age of Finney.* New York, 1991.

Hardman, Keith. *Charles Grandison Finney, 1792–1875: Revivalist and Reformer.* Syracuse, N.Y., 1987.

Hendricks, Tyler O. ''Charles Finney and the Utica Revival of 1826.'' Ph.D. diss., Vanderbilt University, 1983.

Hewitt, Glenn A. *Regeneration and Morality: A Study of Charles Finney, Charles Hodge, John W. Nevin, and Horace Bushnell.* New York 1991.

Johnson, James E. ''The Life of Charles Grandison Finney.'' Ph.D. diss., Syracuse University, 1959.

Lesick, Lawrence T. *The Lane Rebels: Evangelicalism and Antislavery in Antebellum America.* Metuchen, N.J., 1980.

Mattson, John. ''Charles Grandison Finney and the Emerging Tradition of 'New Measures' Revivalism.'' Ph.D. diss., University of North Carolina, 1970.

Rosell, Garth Mervin. ''Charles Grandison Finney and the Rise of the Benevolence Empire.'' Ph.D. diss., University of Minnesota, 1971.

Smith, Timothy. *Revivalism and Social Reform: American Protestantism on the Eve of the Civil War.* New York, 1957.

Sweet, Leonard I. *The Minister's Wife: Her Role in Nineteenth-Century American Evangelicalism.* Philadelphia, 1983.

Vulgamore, Melvin L. ''Social Reform in the Theology of Charles Grandison Finney.'' Ph.D. diss., Boston University, 1963.

Wyatt-Brown, Bertram. *Lewis Tappan and the Evangelical War Against Slavery.* Cleveland, Ohio, 1969.

Betty Friedan
and the National Organization for Women

BARBARA McGOWAN

Feminism and concern for the rights of women have been a continuing but not always particularly strong theme in American history since the founding of the Republic. The first visible women's rights movement, associated with the fervor of reform in antebellum America, was symbolized by the Seneca Falls convention and declaration of 1848. The second push for women's equality coincided with the Progressive era and resulted in ratification of the Nineteenth Amendment in 1920. What can be described as the third identifiable wave of American feminism emerged in the early 1960s.

One of the signal events in the third wave of American Feminism was the publication in 1963 of *The Feminine Mystique* by Betty Friedan. Friedan—born Betty Naomi Goldstein on 4 February 1921 in Peoria, Illinois, the third child of Harry and Miriam Goldstein—was a Westchester County, New York, housewife with an impressive educational background (Smith College summa cum laude, 1942, followed by a year of graduate work in psychology at the University of California at Berkeley) and some journalistic experience. The book, which drew on findings from a survey of Smith alumnae in the late 1950s, described "the problem that has no name," Friedan's term for the discontent experienced by millions of American women who wanted roles beyond the socially prescribed ones of wife, mother, and homemaker.

Friedan's book traced the roots and dimensions of the domestic role, blaming its limits and frustrations on such factors as Freudian psychology, functionalist sociology, and media images of acceptable female roles. She demonstrated how Freudian psychology hurt women by convincing them and their spouses that female fulfillment could be achieved only through deep personal acceptance of the culture's definitions of wife and mother roles. Functionalist theories on social organization harmed women by suggesting that society worked most efficiently when men exercised public, political, and economic power, and women restricted themselves to domestic concerns. Friedan condemned advertisers for encouraging American women to be housewife consumers. The book sold three million copies. In addition, excerpts ran in both *Good Housekeeping* and the *Ladies Home Journal*, magazines which normally celebrated and promoted the feminine mystique that Friedan criticized. The book and its reception made Friedan a visible and controversial figure, and provided her with a career as a lecturer, a writer, and eventually an organizer for feminist causes.

At the same time that Friedan's book was prompting intense reaction from the American public, more traditional and institutionalized supporters of women's rights were benefiting from the policies of a new administration in Washington. In 1960 John F. Kennedy was elected president with the active support of women like Esther Peterson, longtime activist in trade union movements, educational organizations, and the Democratic party. Peterson, who was appointed head of the Women's Bureau at the Department of Labor, suggested to the new president that he consolidate his position with her branch of the party by naming a National Commission on the Status of Women.

The resulting reports from the National Commission and various similar state commissions documented widespread discrimination against women and made specific recommendations, most having to do with federal action on equal pay and job equity. Service on the commissions brought together many skilled and determined women who were willing to go beyond traditional women's organizational tactics to bring about change. In 1964 the oldest surviving branch of the suffragist movement, the National Women's party, was instrumental in obtaining an ambiguous but welcome victory when the 1964 Civil Rights Act was amended to bar employment discrimination against women as well as racial minorities. Eventually this amendment, and the federal government's reluctance to enforce it, served as the catalyst that caused Friedan and a group of ''middle-aged, middle-class women'' to found the National Organization for Women (NOW) in 1966.[1]

But Friedan and NOW would never have had the opportunity to change the lives of American women if they had not been the beneficiary of larger demographic and economic changes. By the mid-1960s, a number of social trends were altering the lives of American women and challenging traditional sex roles, no matter what the ideological inclinations of individual women and men. Increased numbers of women were in the work force, including women with young children. American women, especially middle-class women, were increasingly well educated but still faced persistent discrimination in the workplace and especially in admission to professional schools and training programs. Middle-class women, because of their high levels of education but low chances for high-paying, professional careers, felt the relative deprivation that can be a powerful base for reform movements. In addition, longer female life spans, better contraceptive technology, and more household conveniences were making motherhood and homemaking both less of a full-time job and less of a lifetime occupation. Another source of strength for the burgeoning women's movement was the New Left activism that had its roots in the civil rights and anti-Vietnam War movements. Many younger women, most of them students at elite colleges and universities, had become disillusioned with the demeaning attitudes toward women expressed by male movement leaders and were more than willing to transfer their organizing skills and revolutionary fervor to a renascent feminist movement.

The NOW organization actually emerged in October 1966, when longtime activists within the government and their sympathizers, many of them members of state Commissions on the Status for Women, failed to persuade the Equal Employment Opportunity Commission to take job discrimination against women seriously. Frustrated, these "very reluctant women," in Friedan's words, organized the National Organization for Women, "to take the actions needed to bring women into the mainstream of American society, now, full equality for women, in fully equal partnership with men."[2] Friedan drafted the statement of purpose, and it was accepted as she wrote it with one interesting exception. Friedan wrote that women had the right to choose—to control her own childbearing—meaning access to birth control and abortion. Her fellow founders deemed this stand too controversial.

The statement is an important document because it shows that Friedan was well within the American liberal tradition calling for equality of opportunity and freedom of choice for women on the basis of their rights as individual Americans and as human beings. As was subsequently noted by many of her more radical critics, Friedan criticized the American educational and employment systems only for their discrimination against women; otherwise, she seemed fully to support their social and economic aims. Although Friedan and NOW later were also taken to task for ignoring the needs of working mothers, the original statement averred: "We do not accept the traditional assumption that a woman has to choose between marriage and motherhood, on the one hand, and serious participation in industry or the professions on the other. . . . True equality of opportunity and freedom of choice for women requires such practical and possible innovations as a nationwide network of childcare centers." Nor did Friedan's statement ignore the role of men within the family, unwittingly laying the groundwork for the "superwoman" charge that was later made against the liberal, "individualistic" founders of NOW. (When men took on more duties in the home, thus freeing women *to pursue careers*, women often felt they had to overachieve in both career and home to justify their place in each.) She wrote: "We believe that a true partnership between the sexes demands a different concept of marriage, an equitable sharing of the responsibilities of home and children and of the economic burdens of their support."[3]

From the beginning, NOW, with Friedan as its founder and first president, relied heavily on media publicity to communicate its message and achieve specific objectives. At first, the organization reflected the relative sophistication and professionalism of its charter members and concentrated on approaches and goals that fit their generally middle-class orientation. One of NOW's first actions was to fight sex-segregated help wanted ads and age discrimination against airline stewardesses. Their tactic was to hold small demonstrations against the Equal Employment Opportunity Commission (EEOC) and invite the national television networks to cover them. The ploy worked, and in both cases the commission was forced to change its rulings in favor of nondiscrimination. NOW also sent a strongly worded and lengthy letter to President Lyndon Johnson, one tangible result of which was an executive order barring discrimination against women by federal contractors.

Looking back on this period of NOW's existence, Jo Freeman, an activist coming out of the student-oriented New Left, claimed that the organization was too elitist and inaccessible: "I first read of the National Organization for Women—with feelings of delight and relief—early in 1967 in a newspaper interview. My letter to the interviewee was never answered. Nor were any of the other five letters I wrote during the next year. . . . Clearly something was happening, but I couldn't find it.''[4] Friedan's perception, reflecting her own temperamental distaste for prolonged meetings and procedural disputes, was that "all we wanted was enough organization to keep women in touch with one another.''[5] Being at the center of the organization, Friedan obviously felt "in touch,'' and she was clearly bored by organizational issues relating to the development, leadership, and autonomy of local branches and chapters of NOW.

Soon NOW was both bolstered and challenged by women from Freeman's generation and sharing her perspective. Ironically, though, the first dissent within the organization came from moderates rather than radicals. The United Auto Workers (UAW) women were forced, temporarily, to withdraw their support from NOW because their union would not allow them to work for an organization that supported the Equal Rights Amendment (ERA). (The union still subscribed to the idea that women workers benefited more from protective legislation based on gender difference than from full legal equality.) In the second year, a small group of women, concerned by NOW's decision to support abortion rights and wary of Friedan's controversial public image, broke off to found the Women's Equity Action League (WEAL), an organization that concentrated on legal approaches to gender equality in education and employment.

From that point on, the conflicts within NOW and the women's movement, and the criticism directed at Friedan, came much more from the left than the right. NOW was not a monolithic organization and was becoming, by the late 1960s, a complex structure with a national board but also with local branches that exercised considerable autonomy. There were numerous board members, local chapter heads, and task force members.

NOW welcomed younger, often more radical women but also encountered problems with them. For example, Ti-Grace Atkinson, president of the New York chapter of NOW, began to advocate separatism from men, told a joint NOW-National Conference of Christians and Jews meeting that the only honest woman was a prostitute, and smuggled the SCUM (Society for Cutting Up Men) manifesto out of Valerie Solanis's hospital room (Solanis was confined in a mental hospital after she shot pop artist Andy Warhol in the stomach). On a less dramatic level, Atkinson denounced the NOW leadership structure as hierarchical and called for rotation of decision-making positions by lottery. Her proposals were rejected, and Atkinson left to found an extremely radical group called The Feminists. Friedan described this controversy as "short-lived." She later lamented, however, that "the media continued to treat Ti-Grace as a leader of the women's movement, despite its repudiation of her. And her kind of thinking has from time to time crept up again to disrupt the women's movement in the years that followed."[6]

Whereas the Atkinson incident clearly demonstrated the potential for conflict between the liberal mainstream feminist movement (organizations like NOW were characterized by sociologists as women's rights organizations or bureaucratic organizations) and more radical feminists (these were described by the same sociologists as women's liberationist organizations or collectivist rather than bureaucratic), the strong stance taken by NOW on the abortion issue brought temporary unity to the movement. Friedan was extremely active in the fight for abortion rights, and in 1970 the movement won a key victory when New York State made abortion available on demand.

In 1970, according to Friedan, NOW had about 3,000 members in 30 cities. At that time, for political and personal reasons, she decided to step down as president of NOW. As a farewell gesture, she proposed a strike for 26 August 1970, to commemorate the fiftieth anniversary of the Nineteenth Amendment and to call attention to "the unfinished business of women's equality."[7] The NOW convention supported the idea, but incoming president Aileen Hernandez, who was afraid the strike would fail, joined with other board members to insist Friedan take full responsibility for the strike.

The Strike for Equality was the largest demonstration ever held for women's rights. It marked the beginning of the women's movement as a mass movement, because after the strike, polls showed 80 percent of American adults were aware of the women's movement. The strike made women and the public conscious of the tremendous potential for power inherent in an organized women's movement. The strike also created a false sense of unity, for by the summer of 1970, the women's movement was deeply divided and NOW was obviously implicated in those divisions.

Friedan's own assessment of the period is pessimistic. Looking back on events in 1976, Friedan wrote: "It has been said that the women's movement had three golden years, in which we discovered ourselves, that 'sisterhood is powerful.' But after August 26th 1970, the day that made the power visible to the world, the women's movement became the target—the vulnerable, even willing victim—of others' political and economic ripoffs and of women's own hunger (greed or desperate need) for a personal taste of that power and its economic payoffs." In her statement Friedan alluded to her feeling that many people in the movement, particularly in NOW, felt hostile toward her because of the success of the strike. But they also felt hostile toward her because she used the strike's success to urge NOW to take the leadership ''in organizing a permanent, ongoing political coalition of women based on the diverse elements we had brought together.'' Friedan wanted to draw on the support of women who were probably not theoretical feminists but supporters of the practical benefits offered by the expansion of work and educational opportunities for women, equal pay for equal work, and better child-care options.[8]

NOW's reaction to Friedan's proposal revealed further the growing rift between the organization and its founder and most prominent member. Discussing why she stepped down from leadership of NOW in 1970, Friedan gave a variety of reasons: ''I'd been spending virtually full time as an activist. Divorced myself now, I had to go back to my writing and otherwise pay the rent.'' Friedan also mentioned the availability of Aileen Hernandez, a former EEOC commissioner and minority group member, to serve as president and conceded that ''a black woman—and a good administrator—could be right for NOW at this time.'' In addition to these reasons, Friedan also confessed that she ''didn't want to be a 'straight woman' fronting for a lesbian cabal.''[9]

Although Friedan clearly overstated the presence, if not the influence, of lesbians in NOW in 1970, most observers seem to agree that the issue of sexual preference was a real and divisive one. By December 1970 it threatened to split the movement apart. Kate Millet, author of *Sexual Politics*, publicly declared her bisexuality, thereby winning the enthusiastic support of feminists like Gloria Steinem and Flo Kennedy and the extreme disapproval of Friedan, who feared the public discussion of lesbianism would cause a backlash against the women's movement. While conceding that Friedan was correct in seeing the lesbian issue as causing conflict, Friedan's critics, then and now, argue that by denigrating lesbianism and denying its connection to feminism, Friedan cut herself off from the women's movement, lost all right to leadership in the movement, and became increasingly irrelevant to many feminists. This is an arguable point, but it is certainly true that Friedan's influence within NOW declined after the summer of 1970.

In the 1970s, Friedan's relationship with NOW was a troubled one. In many ways, Friedan became a critic, as well as a supporter, of the women's movement. Organizationally, she concentrated her energies on the National Women's Political Caucus (NWPC), which was founded to increase women's participation in conventional politics. The NWPC won an early and lasting victory when it convinced the Democratic National Committee to mandate basically equal representation for women at Democratic party conventions. The NWPC also played an instrumental role in winning Senate ratification of the ERA in March 1972. It proved particularly effective during the Nixon, Ford, and Carter administrations in identifying possible female candidates for federal positions and ensuring their appointment.

But from the outset the NWPC was divided by disputes between Friedan and more radical members led by New York Democratic Congresswoman Bella

Abzug and *Ms.* magazine founder Gloria Steinem. The conflict was between Friedan's vision of the organization as bipartisan, broadly based, and essentially interested in women's issues, and, in Friedan's words, "attempts to narrow the appeal, to take positions and stands couched in radical jargon that was okay for the East Village in New York or counterculture San Francisco, but not for the breadth of women throughout America wanting their own political voice. It wasn't the same voice. (Women from Middle America were not that interested in lesbianism, for instance.)"[10] The infighting within the NWPC became so bitter that after Friedan lost a disputed, possibly fraudulent election for a seat on its board in 1974, she withdrew from the organization.

Friedan once described her life in the 1970s as a retreat undertaken "to try to come to new terms with the political as personal, in my own life." For a while in the early 1970s, she wrote for *McCall's*, a mass-circulation women's magazine, and in her columns expressed her doubts about the direction of the women's movement. She attacked the belief that "the conditions we are trying to change are caused by a conspiracy for the social and economic profit of men." She reassured her middle-American readers that feminism "does not mean class warfare against men, which denies our sexual and human bonds with men, nor does it mean the elimination of children, which denies our human future."[11]

In 1973 Friedan attended the NOW national convention in Washington, D.C. She gave a speech that she believed warded off moves to "disavow equality with men and partnership with men as purposes of NOW—and even to eliminate men as members of NOW." Still, she came away from the meeting concerned that the "organized women's movement was caught up in the rage and exhilaration, of uncovering, defining, confronting all the ways women had been oppressed and exploited in every profession and local community across the country." Friedan was also upset that "the major pre-occupation of the media, and many of the delegates, seemed to be lesbianism."[12]

One of Friedan's few positive contacts with NOW in the 1970s involved her addressing a conference called by the NOW Task Force on Marriage and Family. In that speech, Friedan combined the appealing, common-sense descriptions of reality with prescriptions for action that had made her so effective a decade earlier. She noted that "divorce has increased 1,000 per cent in the last few years" but cautioned, "Don't blame the women's movement for that—blame the obsolete sex roles on which our marriages were based." She called for immediate televised hearings by state legislatures nationwide to discuss basic reforms of marriage and divorce laws. Among the reforms she suggested were payroll deductions for child support, marriage and divorce insurance, and financial compensation to divorcing wives who had put their husbands through college and professional schools.[13]

The occasion was also noteworthy because it was one of the few times in the 1970s that Friedan referred to her 1969 divorce from Carl Friedan, an advertising executive whom she had married in 1947 and with whom she had three children. Obtaining a divorce was a wrenching experience for Friedan, raising fears that it would hurt both her personal career and the women's movement. As she put it: "I was warned by my publisher, editor, agent, and my dear husband that I would be ruined, I would be destroyed, if I got divorced—that my whole credibility, my ability to write in the future about women and the credibility of the movement would be destroyed—and I didn't dare say boo. At the time I did not know personally a single woman who had gone through the experience. . . . And then somehow the women's movement began to give me the strength. . . . And I said, I don't care, I have to do something about my own life."[14]

While Friedan was alternately retreating and speaking out through a variety of public forums, NOW in the 1970s was experiencing bitter internal struggles interspersed with some very real accomplishments in the public arena. The problems within NOW were as much structural as ideological. By 1973 NOW had over 600 chapters, 27 national task forces, and countless ad hoc committees and continuing committees at the national, state, and local levels. Communication between the national board and the state and local branches was imperfect, a situation constantly exacerbated by personal and philosophical differences at each level of the organization.

In 1974 the differences became more visible to the public when there was an open contest for the presidency of NOW. The winner, Karen DeCrow, characterized herself as a radical, but by 1975 her successful reelection bid was marked more by dubious tactics than by radical actions. The organization did not regain its focus until 1977 with the election of Eleanor Smeal and the embracing of ERA ratification as the primary goal of NOW. Although the ERA campaign ultimately failed, the organized efforts for its ratification brought NOW new membership, favorable media coverage, and some unity for the first time since the Women's Strike for Equality in 1970.

Despite these problems, NOW, in concert with other organizations, especially NWPC and WEAL, continued to achieve breakthroughs at the national level. Acting as an interest group directly lobbying Congress, by the mid-1970s they managed to obtain minimum wage for domestic workers, educational equity, access to credit, female admission to military academies, job protection for pregnant workers, and funds for the observance of the International Women's Year. Lawyers working for the organized women's movement brought *Roe v. Wade* to the Supreme Court, winning a landmark decision establishing basic abortion rights.

In assessing the relationship between Betty Friedan and NOW throughout the 1970s, a number of points can be made. Perhaps the primary consideration explaining the relationship was the personality, temperament, background, and ambitions of Friedan herself. Unlike many of the other founding NOW members, she was not a lawyer, nor had she worked for the government or a lobbying group. She had no experience with any of the other older-line feminist groups or much political experience beyond voting. Her original ambitions, which had been thwarted after college graduation when she left Berkeley to pursue a romantic relationship, centered on research psychology. Friedan was an extremely well-educated woman with some journalism experience who had written a best-selling book describing a problem. Only after its publication was she drawn into political and social activism.

From the beginning, Friedan was intolerant of organizational detail and planning. Ideologically, she was a liberal pragmatist who had arrived at her controversial conclusions about women's lives through analysis of her own life and the lives of similarly placed women as revealed by a survey of fellow Smith College alumnae. What Friedan wanted for herself and other women was full participation in the American public arena. As long as NOW remained focused on goals related to fuller participation for women in the political and economic system, she was satisfied. But when the infusion of younger, more radical women into the organization in the late 1960s brought with it a tendency to dwell on male oppression and female self-expression, particularly lesbian sexuality, combined with a basic questioning of the existing social system, Friedan grew uneasy.

Actually, for most of the 1970s NOW was an umbrella organization able to contain within its ranks radical and liberal members, younger and older women. Although its rhetoric was sometimes heated—in the late 1970s NOW declared itself to be out of the mainstream and into the "Revolution"—most of its policies and strategies remained compatible with the original aims of liberal feminism.

This perspective on NOW and Friedan is much more easily arrived at from a distance. It also fails to take into account the possibility that Friedan was at least partially correct in her opinion that NOW, by openly discussing and dwelling on issues like lesbianism, did hurt the women's movement in the 1970s, narrowing its appeal and opening it to media ridicule and criticism. Although NOW did increase its membership in the 1970s and did win some significant victories, the organization and the women's movement as a whole suffered some real setbacks. The most notable defeat was the failure to secure ratification of the ERA. In assessing that defeat, it is very possible to accept an analysis that lends credence to Friedan's fears about the impact of feminists' attack on such institutions as the family. In many ways, campaigners for the ERA were not able to separate support of the amendment from the rhetoric of the women's movement nor to differentiate it from such controversial issues as lesbianism. Thus, negative public images of feminists and their attacks on traditional family life and conventional sexual arrangements and morality in the end helped defeat the ERA. Friedan made much the same observation when she stated: "The sexual politics that distorted the sense of priorities of the women's movement during the 1970s made it easy for the so-called Moral Majority to lump ERA with homosexual rights and abortion into one explosive package of licentious family threatening sex."[15]

The beginning of the 1980s presented a confused picture of progress and retreat. On the one hand, female participation in the workforce reached 51.5 percent of all adult women working, including 45 percent of women with children under the age of six. Twenty-five percent of medical school graduates were female, as were 30 percent of law graduates. The percentage of women office-holders on both the national and local level had more than doubled, and in 1984 the Democratic party nominated a woman for the vice presidency. On the other hand, Ronald Reagan had been easily elected president on an antiabortion, anti-ERA platform, and the organized antifeminist movements were attracting millions. For example, the antiabortion National Right to Life Committee claimed 11 million members. (NOW, at its height in the early 1980s, had 220,000 members.) One possible interpretation of these realities was that American women wanted to work outside the home or were forced to do so for economic reasons, but outside employment, even in a professional career, did not necessarily mean a commitment to a feminist agenda. Another possibility was that employment was creating, as well as solving, problems for American women.

Friedan, who now criticized feminists for creating a new ''feminist mystique'' just as damaging as the old ''feminine mystique,'' responded to these changing realities in her book *The Second Stage* (1981). First, she described what she saw as the problem: ''What worries me is 'choices' women supposedly have, which are not real. How can a woman 'choose' to have a child when her paycheck is needed for the rent or mortgage, when her job isn't geared to taking care of a child, when there is no national policy for parental leave, and no assurance that her job will be waiting for her if she takes off to have a child?'' Then she stated her belief that solutions to these problems could come only when feminists and all women admit that they have dual needs: the first, a need for ''power, identity, status and security'' through work, and the second, a need ''for love and identity, status, security and generation through marriage, children, home, the family.'' Friedan labeled as reactionary those feminists who denied the female need to love and nurture, which she viewed as usually expressed through family life. She saw a need for personal accommodations and national policies that acknowledged the realities of motherhood.[16] Although Friedan's concerns distanced her still further from NOW, they were reflected in the works of other respected commentators such as economist Sylvia Hewlett (*A Lesser Life*), sociologist Arlie Hochschild (*Second Shift*), and philosopher Jean Bethke Elshtain (*Public Man, Private Woman*).

NOW's reluctance to accept this new family-oriented definition of feminism was symbolized by its position on *California Federal Savings and Loan Ass'n. v. Guerra* in 1986. In this case NOW, sticking to its position of gender-blind equality, argued against maternity leave on the grounds that such benefits should be extended to all workers and that limiting maternity leave to women unfairly favored women over men. Friedan disagreed, pointing out that ''there has to be a concept of equality that takes into account that women are the ones who have the babies.''[17]

Another point of friction between Friedan and the organized women's movement in the 1980s was the fight against pornography. Whereas many feminist groups, including NOW, supported legislation prohibiting pornography as a form of sex discrimination and a violation of civil rights, Friedan saw the concern as irrelevant to most women and expressed the civil libertarian view that laws prohibiting explicitly sexual material were, in the words of a former NOW leader and lawyer, "far more dangerous to women than the most obscene pornography."[18]

Aside from such criticisms and comments, Friedan shifted direction in the 1980s to concentrate on the research and writing of a new book on aging. Meanwhile, NOW struggled throughout the decade to find effective leadership, defining issues, and attractive strategies. Judy Goldsmith succeeded the charismatic Eleanor Smeal in 1982 and was blamed for the fact that during her term of office membership fell to 185,000 and debt exceeded $1 million. Smeal returned to head NOW in the mid 1980s and promptly became involved in a very public fight with the Catholic Church (Smeal was a Catholic) over birth control, abortion, and women in the priesthood. Her successor, Molly Yard, angered many feminist groups by calling for a third political party devoted to feminist issues. Members of the NWPC and the National Abortion Rights Action League were quoted as calling the idea "silly" and "narrowing."[19]

In the 1990s, Betty Friedan and NOW are no longer connected, except, perhaps, in the public mind. Friedan immersed herself in a new role as an advocate for innovative approaches to aging. Her book *The Fountain of Age* (1993) was a conscious effort to transfer her basic insight about the lives of women in the 1960s—that the culture was not describing or confronting women's problems and potentialities with any degree of accuracy—to a discussion of old age in late twentieth-century America. In much the same way that she searched for new roles and patterns for women, Friedan now looked for creative possibilities in love, work, and play for older Americans.

Meanwhile, NOW continued its tradition of public controversy accompanied by assiduous lobbying for particular pieces of legislation, such as public funding of abortions. Both Friedan and NOW members still viewed themselves as feminists, and in their similarities and differences demonstrated the depth and diversity of the movement. But in the mid-1990s their contributions and activities were being supplemented and occasionally challenged by an inchoate movement labeled Feminism's Daughters. These women, mostly under thirty years of age and many literally the daughters of 1960s activists, were introducing new issues and new perceptions. They appeared to be interested in causes ranging from eliminating harassment in the workplace to ending women's poverty. Although she disagreed with some of their specific approaches, Friedan realized the historical import of the continuing movement, saying in 1993 that "Young Women are true daughters of feminism; they take nothing for granted and are advancing the cause with marvelous verve. If they keep doing what they're doing, 30 years from today we may not need a feminist movement. We may have achieved real equality."[20]

Future historians, assessing the significance of Betty Friedan, NOW, and the many changes that took place in women's lives between the early 1960s and the 1990s, will have to consider some provocative questions. First, how important was the organized women's movement in enabling women to break down barriers to their educational and occupational advancement? Was the women's movement really "responsible" for later age at marriage, increased female participation in the workforce, and a declining birth rate—or did those developments cause the women's movement? Were the disputes between Friedan and NOW basically the result of personal animosities, or did they reveal deep, continuing fissures within the feminist movement? Also, how does one define and describe a "movement" that at certain times and on various issues involved literally millions of women and at other points attracted the support of only a handful of activists? These are all important questions that should be explored and answered. Yet there is a certain simplicity and truth in Friedan's statement that for her, and countless other women, "it [the movement] changed my life."

NOTES

1. Betty Friedan, *It Changed My Life* (New York, 1976), 75–91.
2. Ibid., 87.
3. Ibid., 90.
4. Jo Freeman, *The Politics of Women's Liberation* (New York, 1975), xi.
5. Friedan, *It Changed My Life*, 106.
6. Ibid., 109.
7. Ibid., 142.
8. Ibid., 155.
9. Ibid., 140–141.
10. Ibid., 175.
11. Ibid., 245.
12. Ibid., 258.
13. Ibid., 325.
14. Ibid., 324.
15. Friedan, quoted in *Current Biography Yearbook* (New York, 1989), 190.
16. Betty Friedan, *The Second Stage* (New York, 1981), 23, 95.
17. Friedan, quoted in *Current Biography Yearbook*, 191.
18. Betty Friedan, "How to Get the Women's Movement Moving Again," *New York Times Magazine*, 3 November 1985, p. 28.
19. "Taking Issue with NOW," *Newsweek* 114 (14 August 1989): 21.
20. "Feminism's Daughters," *U.S. News and World Report* 115 (27 September 1993): 71.

BIBLIOGRAPHY

Atkinson, Ti-Grace. *Amazon Odyssey*. New York, 1974.
"Betty Friedan." In *Current Biography Yearbook*, 188–192. New York, 1989.
Blow, Richard. "Don't Look NOW," *New Republic*, 11 April 1988, pp. 11–12.
Bunch, Charlotte. *Passionate Politics*. New York, 1986.
Carden, Maron Lockwood. *The New Feminist Movement*. New York, 1974.

Cassell, Joan. *A Group Called Women: Sisterhood and Symbolism in the Feminist Movement*. New York, 1977.

Elshtain, Jean Bethke. *Public Man, Private Woman*. Princeton, 1981.

Evans, Sara. *Personal Politics: The Role of Women's Liberation in the Civil Rights Movement and the New Left*. New York, 1979.

———. *Born for Liberty: A History of Women in America*. New York, 1989.

"Feminism's Daughters." *U.S. News and World Report* 115 (27 September 1993): 68–71.

Ferree, Myra, and Beth Hess. *Controversy and Coalition: The New Feminist Movement*. Boston, 1985.

Filene, Peter G. *Him/Her Self: Sex Roles in Modern America*. Baltimore, 1974.

Freeman, Jo. *The Politics of Women's Liberation*. New York, 1975.

Friedan, Betty. *The Feminine Mystique*. New York, 1963.

———. *It Changed My Life*. New York, 1976.

———. *The Second Stage*. New York, 1981.

———. "How to Get the Women's Movement Moving Again." *New York Times Magazine*, 3 November 1985, pp. 26–28, 66–67, 84–89, 98 106, 108.

———. *The Fountain of Age*. New York, 1993.

Gelb, Jean, and Marion Lief. *Women and Public Policy*. Princeton, 1982.

Hewlett, Sylvia. *A Lesser Life*. New York, 1986.

Hochschild, Arlie. *The Second Shift*. New York, 1989.

Hoff-Wilson, Joan, ed. *Rights of Passage: The Past and Future of the ERA*. Bloomington, Ind., 1986.

Klein, Ethel. *Gender Politics*. Cambridge, Mass., 1984.

Kopkind, Andrew. "NOW Redux." *Nation* 245 (August 1987): 76–77.

Mansbridge, Jane. *Why We Lost the ERA*. Chicago, 1986.

Rosenberg, Rosalind. *Divided Lives: American Women in the Twentieth Century*. New York, 1992.

Rupp, Lelia J., and Verta Taylor. *Survival in the Doldrums: The American Women's Rights Movement, 1945 to the 1960's*. New York, 1987.

"Taking Issue with NOW." *Newsweek* 114 (14 August 1989): 21.

Wandersee, Winifred D. *On the Move: American Women in the 1970's*. Boston, 1988.

Wickenden, Dorothy. "What NOW?" *New Republic* 194 (5 May 1986): 19–25.

William Lloyd Garrison
and Abolitionism

MERTON L. DILLON

"A Johnny-come-lately to the antislavery movement." With those dismissive words, a modern critic denied the importance of William Lloyd Garrison, the founder and for thirty years editor of *The Liberator* and the best-known of all American abolitionists.[1] Not surprisingly, the effort to demote Garrison failed, if only because a personage whose significance has been acknowledged for so long a time is not easily dislodged from history. Yet the "Johnny-come-lately" charge does suggest a major truth about the antislavery movement: Garrison and *all* the men and women who worked against slavery in the 1830s and afterward were building upon—not originating—a campaign for racial justice that started long before any of them were born.

Garrison and his coworkers inherited, extended, and invigorated the opposition to American slavery that began sometime early in the seventeenth century. As others have noted, the first opponents of slavery were those imported Africans who resisted their enslavement, perhaps by refusing to obey their owners' commands, perhaps by running away to nearby woods and swamps. Such response was to be expected as expression of a natural desire for autonomy. Less predictable was the sympathy shown by Americans of European origin for the Africans' plight. Slaves early discovered that certain white Americans would help them escape their owners' control and would side with them in their struggles.

The motives that led to this subversive activity cannot be fully known to us. But among them surely was revulsion against the scenes of cruelty and oppression that were inseparable from slavery. For Quakers and members of other pietistic sects, religious teachings and their own painful experience with prejudice and misused power reinforced such sympathies. From first to last, whether in the colonial period or in Garrison's day, antislavery thought and action were inseparable from observation of slavery and awareness of its implications. Opposition to slavery threaded through all of American history from its introduction in 1619 to its abolition in 1865. At no period is that opposition to be explained solely by changes in American culture, society, and economic structure, although its varying intensity and form may be.

By the time Garrison was born—12 December 1805, to Abijah and Frances Lloyd Garrison in Newburyport, Massachusetts—slavery had ended in the North, but it remained an integral part of the economic and social structure of the nation's tobacco- and rice-growing regions and was about to gain vast additional import as cotton production spread westward. Its political role in the new nation and its political advantage for the South had been assured when the framers of the Constitution decreed that three-fifths of the slave population would be counted in determining representation in Congress. Further, as Southerners at the time understood and appreciated, the decentralized nature of the new government made outside interference with state and local institutions difficult if not impossible. None of these developments, it should be noted, took place without incurring sustained, heartfelt opposition—from humanitarians who deplored the suffering of their fellow human beings; from egalitarians who objected to the emergence of a new, slave-based aristocracy; from persons who regretted the spirit of despotism they believed slavery fostered; from prophets who warned that slavery must some day explode in a bloody war for liberation; from those who found the presence of large numbers of persons of different cultural and racial background menacing and disagreeable; and from Northeastern interests jealous of the enhanced political power that slavery gave to the South. These formed the essential ingredients of antislavery until the institution ended.

Although as a child Garrison spent an unpleasant year and a half apprenticed to a shoemaker in Baltimore, slavery made no recorded impression on him at that time. He was absorbed with his own problems—his wastrel father had abandoned the family, throwing his poverty-stricken wife and children on their own meager resources. Later, as apprentice to the editor of the *Newburyport Herald*, his concern was politics rather than social issues. As a youth, Garrison showed little interest in black people or in antislavery activity either by them or by white reformers. Nevertheless, such activity constantly took place, though often obscurely, and Garrison soon built his reform career upon its heritage.

In 1794 delegates from antislavery societies in New York, Pennsylvania, New Jersey, Delaware, and Maryland, together with representatives from Connecticut and Virginia, met in Philadelphia to hold the first of a series of American Conventions for Promoting the Abolition of Slavery and Improving the Condition of the African Race. Its members were respected white humanitarians whose main goals were to persuade state legislatures to enact gradual emancipation laws, to protect free blacks from reenslavement, and to help them become self-supporting, respectable citizens. At the same time, free blacks themselves were organizing, usually through their churches, for similar purpose. None of these efforts, by either whites or African Americans, accomplished anything substantial toward the ending of slavery, useful though they otherwise were.

The issues of slavery and race would not go away. In 1816 a group of distinguished white men organized the American Colonization Society (ACS) at Washington, D.C. Their ultimate goal, so they claimed, was the gradual end of slavery; their immediate purpose, however, was to deal with what many then thought a troublesome social problem: the rapidly growing free black population. Slaveholders worried about their destabilizing influence on slaves, and city dwellers in both the North and the South considered their ever more conspicuous presence disruptive to good order. Even people who sincerely sought the end of slavery believed that the question of what was to become of freed slaves in a racially biased society severely impeded emancipation prospects. In view of all this, it is not surprising that the ACS's plan to send blacks to Africa met widespread approval from the white population.

The 1820s, the decade in which Garrison reached maturity, was the period of the ACS's greatest prominence. As soon as he began to think seriously about slavery and race—subjects impossible for a politically aware editor long to ignore—Garrison, like many others who later became full-fledged abolitionists, endorsed the colonizationists' deportation program, impractical and morally dubious though it was. Free blacks, however, with great unanimity, rejected the prospect of removal to Africa. America was their land as much as it was the whites', they argued, and they had no intention of abandoning their kindred in bondage by leaving it. By the end of the 1820s Garrison had adopted the free blacks' position as his own. Owing in part to their prompting, he condemned the ACS as the chief enemy of abolition and inaugurated a successful propaganda campaign against it.

The proposal to admit Missouri as a slave state in 1819—well before Garrison showed much interest in such matters—precipitated national debate over the wisdom and morality of extending slavery into the Louisiana Purchase. Most of the arguments—economic, social, religious, and political—that ever would be raised against slavery were voiced at that time. Although the controversy subsided with the political Compromise of 1820, it never entirely disappeared. In the person of the Quaker reformer Benjamin Lundy and in the forum offered by his newspaper, *The Genius of Universal Emancipation*, the antislavery cause continued to be agitated throughout the 1820s. It occasionally flared into national attention, as in 1824, when a resolution from Ohio's state legislature urging Congress to support the colonization of free blacks provoked Southern outrage, and in 1828–1829, when an accelerated petition drive—which Garrison endorsed—called for abolition in the District of Columbia.

By that time Garrison had shifted his editorial focus (he was then editing the Burlington, Vermont, *Journal of the Times*) from near single-minded concern for the fortunes of the doomed Federalist party to examination of a variety of reform causes, including antislavery. Like many another incipient abolitionist, he had first invested much of his energy in the temperance movement; but when

Lundy visited Boston in 1828 and the two men met, Garrison's attention turned to slavery above everything else. Obviously, he held no patent on such concern, nor was its source to be found exclusively in religion and the moral code. Slavery and the Southern political influence that it made possible already had become irritants for New Englanders uncertain of their status in the rapidly developing nation.

In 1829 Garrison accepted Lundy's invitation to join him in Baltimore as coeditor of *The Genius*. Garrison brought to *The Genius* the sense of urgency that was then being expressed by a new, energized phase of the venerable antislavery movement. Slavery, a growing number of Northerners now believed, had become a grave national problem that demanded immediate attention. To those reformers, no existing effort seemed adequate to the need. In the months just before his move to Baltimore, Garrison undertook an intensive study of the American Colonization Society. He concluded that immediate emancipation *without* colonization was correct policy, and that this goal could be achieved only if white Americans first renounced their racial bias and resolved to accept African Americans as their equals.

In espousing these unconventional ideas, Garrison was encouraged by conversations with similarly impatient reformers, including African Americans whom he met in Philadelphia and Boston, and especially by reading *The Book and Slavery Irreconcilable,* a biblically based condemnation of slavery and a fervent call for its immediate end written by the Reverend George Bourne, an English-born Presbyterian who had been censured by his church and forced to leave Virginia on account of his radical antislavery positions. Close association with free blacks in Baltimore reinforced Garrison's commitment to these points and convinced him that they formed the only correct basis for an antislavery movement.

Meanwhile, in western New York the Reverend Charles G. Finney had been conducting a religious revival whose grand purpose, besides the saving of souls, was cleansing the earth from sin in preparation for the millennium. Finney exhorted his converts to contribute to this endeavor. The stimulus thus given to reform efforts of all sorts energized the movement against slavery as never before, bringing dozens of able recruits into its service and imbuing them with evangelical fervor. The evangelists' call for the immediate abandonment of sin differed little from Garrison's demand for the immediate end of slavery. Garrison did not participate in the Finney revivals, but as a devout Baptist he shared much of their spirit. For him, as for scores of other young men and women in the 1830s, abolitionism became an urgent, God-inspired duty, and abolitionism became the near equivalent of a religion.

Garrison and Lundy's coeditorship of *The Genius* did not last long. Patronage for the newspaper, never generous, declined still further, and Garrison found himself jailed for libel—he had published a bitter attack on a Massachusetts ship captain, Francis Todd, for his alleged participation in the coastal slave trade. After Arthur Tappan, the wealthy New York reformer, paid his fine, Garrison returned to New England. He had no regrets about departing Baltimore. "Of southern habits, southern doctrines and southern practices, I am heartily sick," he wrote. "The first are loose; the second disorganising; the last oppressive. There is nothing which the curse of slavery has not tainted. It rests on every herb, and every tree, and every field, and on the people, and on the morals."[2]

In 1834 Garrison married Helen Benson, member of a Quaker family with venerable antislavery credentials. The marriage appears to have been one of extraordinary felicity. In their domestic relations the Garrisons and their children lived in an atmosphere of harmony and tranquillity, in welcome contrast to the acrimony and contention that marked his public career.

In Boston, on 1 January 1831, Garrison began publication of *The Liberator* with financial aid from Arthur Tappan and a few others, including the Boston lawyer Ellis Gray Loring, and the printers Stephen Foster and Isaac Knapp, and with advance subscription fees collected by African-American agents, especially by James Forten of Philadelphia. *The Liberator*'s finances always were shaky. But in times of crisis such friends as Loring, Samuel May, Jr., Wendell Phillips, and the English reformer Elizabeth Pease could be counted on to come to the aid of both the newspaper and the Garrison household.

As abolitionist and editor, Garrison's was no ordinary determination. In *The Liberator*'s first issue appeared the stirring editorial pledge that would echo through the antislavery movement as none other ever did: "I will be as harsh as truth and as uncompromising as justice. . . . I am in earnest—I will not equivocate—I will not excuse—I will not retreat a single inch—AND I WILL BE HEARD."

Garrison's choice of Boston as his publication site marked an epoch in the development of the antislavery movement. Until then antislavery had been perceived as a national rather than a sectional enterprise. Even as late as the mid-1820s antislavery opinion was nearly as likely to be voiced in the slaveholding states of the upper South as in the North. The declining support for *The Genius* in Baltimore and Garrison's move to Boston signified momentous change. Save for a few beleaguered exceptions remaining in the upper South, antislavery henceforth would be almost exclusively Northern. The founding of *The Liberator* signaled a major step in the developing sectionalism that three decades later would end in civil war.

Garrison's influence in inspiring and mobilizing hostility to slavery was immense. Ready material was at hand. Some persons in the modernizing North found slavery a glaring anachronism that, aside from its unclothed cruelties, clashed with every value the new age espoused. A slave labor system appeared to them to have no place in an economy increasingly dedicated to individualism and capitalistic enterprise. According to their understanding, the corruption and licentiousness and tyranny bred by slavery threatened ruin for the entire nation.

For many, that conclusion was not the result solely of abstract speculation. By the early 1830s, sensitive young Northerners were witnessing slavery for the first time. Slavery in the North had disappeared a generation earlier, but now improved means of travel and communication brought Northerners into ever closer contact with the institution in its fully developed form, and some shrank from what they saw. At about the same time, settlement in the North—especially in Ohio, Indiana, and Illinois—of Southerners whose discomfort with life in a slaveholding region had led them to leave their section introduced an additional element from which ''islands of abolitionism'' could be formed.

Garrison's impassioned call for enlistment in a religious and patriotic crusade against what he saw as a fatal blot on the national character brought enthusiastic response from a cadre of young men and women eager to commit themselves to so elevated and urgent a cause. *The Liberator* and Garrison's pamphlet exposé of the racism of the ACS, *Thoughts on Colonization* (1832), found sympathetic readers in widely dispersed locations and of widely varying circumstance. Not surprisingly, Northern free blacks, welcoming both publications as eloquent expressions of their own beliefs and goals, generously supported *The Liberator* in its first months of publication, before many others did. Garrison reciprocated by offering his columns to their correspondence and reports. Thus was formed a mutually supportive relationship that lasted for the rest of Garrison's life. Garrison displayed few of the traces of racism that marked the majority of Northerners and even many abolitionists. Yet, despite genuine sympathies, a gulf developed between him and African-American abolitionists, principally because the Garrisonians remained to the end moral reformers who concerned themselves mostly with abstractions, whereas most black leaders sought immediate, practical goals that might most readily be attained by the political action that Garrison opposed.

The abolitionists were a diverse lot in social origin and economic status. Garrison grew up in deprivation and came from what now is termed a broken home. In contrast, Theodore Dwight Weld, one of the leading Western abolitionists, had two supportive parents who held respected positions in their community. Although some of Garrison's followers had origins as humble as his, others—of whom Wendell Phillips, one of the greatest antislavery orators, is a striking example—belonged to Boston's elite. After calling the roll of abolitionists, one may conclude from their diversity that no social profile that fits all of them can be devised. But however strikingly they otherwise differed, they were united by hatred of slavery, agreement that it must be abolished, and, above all, conviction that they themselves must work to accomplish that end. They were not willing to trust the slow processes of history to blot out so great an evil. Thus, they rejected gradualism and colonization and joined Garrison in his stentorian call for immediate emancipation.

But how to reach so difficult and controverted a goal was less easily agreed upon. Quakers, an important component of Garrison's adherents, long had relied on appeals to conscience as the means to end slavery. In the eighteenth century they rid their own sect of all connection with slavery, and missionaries among them (of whom Lundy was a late example) traveled in slaveholding regions to sow an antislavery gospel. In contrast, members of the early constituent societies of the American Convention for the Abolition of Slavery expected to achieve their goals less by changing opinion, and thereby altering behavior, than by petitioning state legislatures and Congress for antislavery legislation. Similarly, the American Colonization Society did not appeal to individual conscience but claimed that its program of sending freed slaves to Africa would encourage manumissions for pragmatic reasons, and thereby eventually lead to the end of slavery.

Garrison and the evangelically minded who responded to his message followed the Quaker example because they, too, in effect were a religious, not a secular, group. Slavery and the prejudice that supported it, they held, were sins and, like other sins, must be repented and renounced. They relied on appeals to individual, rather than to corporate or social, responsibility. The securing of converts to the abolitionist gospel became their immediate purpose. Thus they made public testimony and condemnation central to their campaign. They expected the coercive force of public opinion, rather than of law, to bring the end of slavery. In their hands the antislavery movement became an overwhelmingly verbal campaign dominated by denunciation of slavery and exposure of its cruelties and of the iniquities of slaveholders and their minions. No one among the abolitionists was more skilled in the use of such weapons than Garrison.

Like reformers in most other causes of the day—temperance and peace were prominent examples—Garrison planned to organize his followers into societies in the interest of both fellowship and efficacy. He found this more difficult to accomplish than might be expected. When he called an organizational meeting in Boston in November 1831, only nine of the fifteen of his white friends who attended were willing to join a society committed to immediate emancipation. Of the seventy-two names eventually affixed to the constitution of the New England Anti-Slavery Society, approximately a quarter were those of African Americans. Immediate emancipation, it appeared, would not be an easy policy for white Northerners to accept.

Despite this inauspicious beginning, Garrison, together with abolitionists in New York City and Philadelphia, went forward with plans to form a comprehensive society that could be considered national or, more exactly, Northern in scope. They felt obliged to delay doing so, however, when they encountered evidence of deepening sectional discord and of slave unrest to which they feared a new antislavery organization might contribute. South Carolina's defiance of federal authority and its threats of nullification, even of secession, suggested that they be cautious even as such acts provoked their resentment at the arrogance of what they would soon be calling "the slave power." More alarming still was Nat Turner's slave rebellion in Southampton County, Virginia, in August 1831. Although this horrific event demonstrated to abolitionists the urgency of emancipation, it also warned them to do nothing that might encourage further bloody and fruitless uprisings. The wisdom of forbearance seemed proved when Southerners charged that through *The Liberator*, Garrison had provoked Nat Turner to rebel. They called upon public officials in Massachusetts to suppress the newspaper and even to send Garrison to the South for trial.

In the long run, however, caution would not be the hallmark of the antislavery movement. It never was Garrison's. His merciless condemnations fell on recalcitrant Northerners as well as slaveholders, and apparently without thought of consequence—except for the progress toward abolition such condemnation might bring. Conciliation seems not to have been in his vocabulary.

In December 1833, sixty-two delegates, including women and African Americans, most of them from New England, New York, and Pennsylvania, met in Philadelphia to form the American Anti-Slavery Society. Although all could agree on the central purpose of immediate emancipation, the New York group in particular felt misgivings about a point on which Garrison insisted—full implementation of the principle of racial equality. From the onset the unity of the antislavery movement was strained by tension between (1) those who worried that adherence to policies the majority of Americans regarded as extreme—and racial equality certainly was one of these—would inhibit the movement's growth and (2) those radicals like Garrison who disdained to cater to the opinions of a public they considered corrupt. Garrison was never willing to curry favor at the price of making concessions to what he regarded as error.

One of Garrison's early converts, the Reverend Beriah Green, presided over the new society's organizational meeting, and Garrison himself, the best-known of all the delegates, played a major role in its proceedings. Indeed, Garrison was chiefly responsible for drafting the new organization's Declaration of Sentiments, its platform throughout its existence and statement of the principles essential to the definition of abolitionism.

Immediate, uncompensated emancipation without colonization was its central plank. All present could agree on that. Garrison then added, in defiance of prevailing prejudice and the doubts of moderates within the movement, that the organization also would work ''to secure to the colored population of the United States, all the rights and privileges which belong to them as men and as Americans.'' Abolitionists, then, called not only for the end of a major American institution but also for a revolution in social relationships. It is this aspect of their movement that warrants placing them among the very few genuine American radicals. Contemporaries recognized this fact, for to the abolitionists'egalitarian goal is to be ascribed much of the enormous hostility that their agitation provoked.

If their program appeared extreme, their methods were less so. According to Garrison, abolitionists renounced ''all carnal weapons for deliverance from bondage.'' They sought ''the destruction of error by the potency of truth—the overthrow of prejudice by the power of love—and the abolition of slavery by the spirit of repentance.'' They intended no encouragement to potential Nat Turners.

Although this was to be primarily a campaign of moral suasion, Garrison did not altogether exclude political action. All laws supporting slavery, he declared,

stood ''before God utterly null and void.'' He conceded that within the states
the institution lay beyond congressional interference, but Congress did have
unquestioned power to end the domestic slave trade and to abolish slavery in
the territories and in the District of Columbia. Thus was left open a vast arena
for the exercise of electoral antislavery politics, although Garrison himself came
to shun that means of action.

After establishing these general principles, Garrison set forth the abolitionists'
mode of operation. They intended to persuade citizens of the free states to work
for the end of slavery ''by moral and political action.'' They would organize
antislavery societies ''in every city, town, and village in our land.'' They would
send out antislavery lecturers and circulate antislavery tracts and periodicals.
They would especially target preachers and editors, the molders of public opinion.

In particular, abolitionists would ''aim at a purification of the churches from
all participation in the guilt of slavery.'' Under abolitionist guidance, the national evangelical denominations, which were at least as prominent in the South
as in the North, would be transformed into agencies of abolitionism too powerful
for their slaveholding communicants to resist. The churches' endorsement of
abolitionism would virtually ensure the end of slavery.

Despite abolitionists' considerable success in gaining religiously oriented converts, they failed to win the churches to their cause. No major denomination
unambiguously endorsed abolitionism. This reluctance had profound consequences for the course of the antislavery movement. It helped push Garrison
and others into taking militant anticlerical stands (thereby confirming common
opinion that they were dangerous radicals), and it encouraged a portion of the
movement in the later 1830s and 1840s to resort to electoral politics rather than
continue to rely solely on moral suasion, and, it followed, increasingly to focus
on secular concerns.

Abolitionist efforts to flood the South with printed material met generally
successful resistance. At Charleston in 1835 a mob invaded the U.S. Post Office
and destroyed the offending items before they could be delivered. Elsewhere,
state legislatures criminalized circulation and possession of antislavery literature.
Although disappointing, such hostile reaction did not surprise those who had
planned the postal campaign. Southern hostility had the effect, however, of raising the tone of abolitionist rhetoric to even shriller heights, for it demonstrated,
so abolitionists believed, the depths of oppression to which slavery had sunk
the South. Garrison and his followers never altogether abandoned hopes of
Southern conversion and welcomed evidence of antislavery sentiment wherever
it appeared, but such evidence in regions south of Kentucky and the mountains
of east Tennessee was rare indeed.

Northern reaction to the Garrisonian message was not much more favorable.
Mobs assailed abolitionist lecturers who had placed their trust in moral suasion
(''the potency of truth—the power of love—the spirit of repentance''). Criticism
of the American Colonization Society and advocacy of racial equality brought

howls of protest wherever they were voiced. Racial prejudice, strong and age-old, had to be confronted everywhere. There might be common recognition in the North that slavery clashed with proclaimed American principles; that it did not fit with the emerging free labor, capitalist economy, and on that account would someday have to end; but such recognition did not mean that many Northerners welcomed the prospect of African-American equality or approved proposals calling for immediate, contentious change. Further—and this was of momentous import—the flourishing American economy had produced close and profitable financial, mercantile, and manufacturing relationships between Northern and Southern interests. Antislavery agitation threatened to disrupt all these valued ties. In many quarters, abolitionists discovered, avarice, as well as complacency and self-satisfaction, ruled. Many Northerners, it appeared, were as implicated in slavery, even if unwittingly, as were slaveholders themselves. The changes Garrison advocated would revolutionize the North as well as the South.

It is not to be wondered, then, that waves of mob violence in the 1830s nearly drove the American Anti-Slavery Society's lecturers from the field. A mob led Garrison through the streets of Boston with a rope tied around his body; Henry B. Stanton, lecturing in Ohio and Pennsylvania, estimated he had faced mobs seventy times; mobs in Alton, Illinois, destroyed three of Elijah P. Lovejoy's presses before finally murdering him as he defended a fourth. The surprising thing is not that abolitionists faced rabid opposition but that antislavery and anti-Southern sentiment grew throughout the 1830s, 1840s, and 1850s in spite of the fact that abolitionists demanded disruptive institutional change and insulted white Americans by branding one of their most deeply held folk beliefs as sin.

As Garrison understood, the explanation for the evident growing opposition to slavery and to slaveholders was not to be found solely in counting conversions to the platform he had set forth in the American Anti-Slavery Society's Declaration of Sentiments. There can be no doubt that persons who declared themselves abolitionists, especially those close to Garrison and within his circle, were dedicated both to the immediate end of slavery and to the admittance of African Americans to all the privileges of citizenship. But the number of persons capable of making that difficult moral commitment and willing to undergo the obloquy such commitment commonly provoked was severely limited. They were too few to account for the antislavery force that by the 1840s began to stir the Northern electorate and, it followed, the Congress.

Southern efforts to protect slaveholding interests against the abolitionist campaign did at least as much to provoke anti-Southern and antislavery attitudes as did the campaign itself. Northerners found themselves defending civil rights against what they came to call "the slave power." They were put in this position in part because of the multitude of mobs that attempted to silence antislavery lecturers and editors, but an equally powerful influence was the infamous gag rule enacted by Congress in 1836 and in force until 1844. Antislavery petitions, Congress ruled, henceforth would be received but not read. By this means, the political parties thought to save themselves from the stress of debate over slavery, certain to be sectionally divisive, and Southern representatives would be spared the embarrassment of hearing their institutions condemned within the halls of Congress. This effort to perpetuate sectional harmony did not work. Abolitionists resolved to redouble their petitioning efforts. Congress was deluged with mountains of petitions that had been circulated throughout the North, especially by women. Not even the most adroit parliamentarian could stifle completely the controversy the gag rule provoked. The bonds of national unity weakened as the political parties began to lose their cohesiveness. Abolitionist leaders at the New York headquarters of the American Anti-Slavery Society had engineered the petition campaign. Although Garrison welcomed it, his interest then, as always, lay more in formulating and proclaiming doctrine than in managing extensive, essentially political enterprises.

Many who signed the petitions to Congress were not technically abolitionists and probably did not consider themselves to be such. Nevertheless, they had come to feel that slavery was wrong and should not be extended by such means as the annexing of Texas, as was proposed in 1836, nor should it be protected by enforcement of fugitive slave laws, a persistent and, after 1850, a growing irritant. Even more potent in promoting antislavery, anti-Southern views was the conviction, slowly arrived at, that Southern interests controlled Washington, if not the entire nation, at the expense of Northern welfare. Nothing, many Northern voters decided, should be allowed to strengthen that control. Herein lay the material from which a political movement against slavery could be built. Antislavery sentiment was about to be tied to political power.

Just at the time an influential part of the antislavery leadership awakened to this appealing possibility, Garrison began to proclaim increasingly radical positions on a host of sensitive issues other than slavery. He offended the conventionally religious by lashing out at clergymen who proved resistant to abolitionist influence, and then outraged them by questioning the legitimacy and authenticity of revealed religion itself. He enthusiastically endorsed the incipient women's rights movement at a time when most thought it a scandalous departure. He identified himself with such unfamiliar doctrines as perfectionism (the theological view that sinlessness is possible in this earthly life) and nonresistance, each of which appeared heretical and bizarre. *The Liberator* began to give all these startling views nearly as much attention as it gave to abolition. Abolitionism, as construed by Garrison, thus became linked with what many shunned as anarchy and fanaticism. His reckless course threatened to alienate thousands of Northern voters who seemed about to endorse central parts of the abolitionist program.

The dispute that erupted within the ranks of organized abolitionism in the late 1830s was essentially between persons like Garrison, who believed that society needed radical change—that slavery was only one manifestation of deranged values—and others who considered the nation fundamentally sound though requiring reform. The antislavery movement definitively split in 1840 when its more evangelically oriented and ideologically conservative members left the American Anti-Slavery Society and formed the American and Foreign Anti-Slavery Society.

Garrison held fast to his positions, mercilessly flaying the Protestant establishment when most Americans remained conventionally Christian, and denouncing the Constitution as a ''Covenant with Death, An Agreement With Hell'' at a time when most Northerners were intensely patriotic. He opposed the move to form, in turn, the Liberty, Free Soil, and Republican parties, on the ground that a resort to electoral politics would tempt abolitionists to dilute and compromise their program in the interest of electoral victory. Not political action but continued agitation was needed, Garrison insisted, because the Northern electorate, antislavery and anti-Southern in sentiment though it now appeared to be, was prepared to punish the South and diminish its power for essentially self-serving and vindictive reasons. There was as yet no consensus that slavery and prejudice were sins to be repented and atoned for. If slavery should in some way be ended before that change of heart occurred, little would have been gained. The freed African Americans would suffer from oppression much as before.

Garrison continued to proclaim these views even as antislavery political organization went forward and elections were won. He welcomed every evidence of electoral success while relentlessly criticizing the flagrant shortcomings that accompanied it. When secession finally came in 1860–1861 and war ensued, he took the lead in formulating the abolitionists' critique of Lincoln's policies, finding them insufficiently turned toward emancipation. But as soon as the war for the Union metamorphosed into a war against slavery, Garrison endorsed Lincoln's leadership. In an uncharacteristic warping of perspective, he saw emancipation as the consummation of his life's work, despite a dearth of evidence that it proceeded from the revolutionary transformation in spirit that he had always held essential.

The dramatic shift brought reward. Popular and official approval marked his advancing years. Above all else, Garrison in his turnabout construed events as progress and lauded emancipation as testimony to the generation's beneficence and as prophecy of swelling national grandeur. The radical had become a reformer, and a self-congratulatory one at that. With scarcely a qualm, he allowed himself to be absorbed into the consensus.

The crusade that Garrison did so much to promote and shape at last had achieved its most obvious goal, and Garrison was hailed as the architect of the victory, a view of his career that he fully shared. Yet, as he had tirelessly warned might happen but now chose to ignore, the victory came by force and not as a consequence of the moral regeneration he had always called for and insisted was essential. Emancipation resulted from the use of coercive power without being accompanied by that change in values that would have given it more fundamental, lasting significance.

On 29 December 1865, Garrison set the type for the final edition of *The*

Liberator and, at about the same time, wrote privately that "My vocation as an abolitionist is ended."[3] His interest in reform and public affairs did not cease, however, as his many articles in the *New York Independent* indicate. He opposed President Andrew Johnson's leniency toward the South and supported the more stringent policies of President U.S. Grant and the Radical Republicans. In his later years Garrison concerned himself especially with education for the freedmen and favored integrated schools. He deplored the persistence of racial prejudice and the mistreatment of Indians and Chinese immigrants. He continued to advocate women's rights, although his support of the postwar movement for woman's suffrage was tempered by his dislike for Elizabeth Cady Stanton and Susan B. Anthony, its leading proponents.

Garrison died on 24 May 1879, in New York City, an inspiration to those who would continue his uncompromising call for equality and lauded as the personification of the nation's highest ideals even by many who once opposed his abolitionism.

NOTES

1. Quoted in Dwight L. Dumond, *Antislavery: The Crusade for Freedom in America* (Ann Arbor, Mich., 1961), 87.

2. William Lloyd Garrison to Harriet Farnham Horton, 12 May 1830, in Walter M. Merrill and Louis Ruchames, eds., *The Letters of William Lloyd Garrison*, 6 vols. (Cambridge, Mass., 1971–1981), vol. 1, 92.

3. Quoted in James Brewer Stewart, *William Lloyd Garrison and the Challenge of Emancipation* (Arlington Heights, Ill., 1992), 193.

BIBLIOGRAPHY

Aptheker, Herbert. *Abolitionism: A Revolutionary Movement.* Boston, 1989.

Barnes, Gilbert Hobbs. *The Antislavery Impulse, 1831–1844.* New York, 1933.

Davis, David Brion. *The Problem of Slavery in the Age of Revolution, 1770–1823.* Ithaca, N.Y., 1975.

Dillon, Merton L. *The Abolitionists: The Growth of a Dissenting Minority.* DeKalb, Ill., 1974.

———. *Slavery Attacked: Southern Slaves and Their Allies 1619–1865.* Baton Rouge, La., 1990.

Dumond, Dwight Lowell. *Antislavery Origins of the Civil War in the United States.* Ann Arbor, Mich., 1939.

———. *Antislavery: The Crusade for Freedom in America.* Ann Arbor, Mich., 1961.

Fladeland, Betty L. "Who Were the Abolitionists?" *Journal of Negro History* 49 (April 1964): 99–115.

Friedman, Lawrence J. *Gregarious Saints: Self and Community in American Abolitionism, 1830–1870.* Cambridge, England, 1982.

Garrison, William Lloyd, and Francis P. Garrison. *William Lloyd Garrison, 1805–1879.* 4 vols. New York, 1885–1889.

Haskell, Thomas L. "Capitalism and the Origins of the Humanitarian Sensibility." *American Historical Review* 90 (April 1985): 339–361 and (June 1985): 547–566.

Huston, James L. "The Experiential Basis of the Northern Antislavery Impulse." *Journal of Southern History* 56 (November 1990): 609–640.

Kraditor, Aileen. *Means and Ends in American Abolitionism: Garrison and His Critics on Strategy and Tactics, 1834–1850.* New York, 1969.

McKivigan, John R. *The War Against Proslavery Religion: Abolitionism and the Northern Churches, 1830–1865.* Ithaca, N.Y., 1984.

Merrill, Walter M. *Against Wind and Tide: A Biography of Wm. Lloyd Garrison.* Cambridge, Mass., 1963.

———, and Louis Ruchames, eds. *The Letters of William Lloyd Garrison, 1805–1879.* 6 vols. Cambridge, Mass., 1971–1981.

Stewart, James Brewer. *Holy Warriors: The Abolitionists and American Slavery.* New York, 1976.

———. *William Lloyd Garrison and the Challenge of Emancipation.* Arlington Heights, Ill., 1992.

Thomas, John L. *The Liberator: William Lloyd Garrison, a Biography.* Boston, 1963.

Henry George
and Utopia

GEOFFREY BLODGETT

Most nineteenth-century Americans, when they thought about a better world than the one they lived in, learned to think about the future. Henry George, in contrast, thought about the past. Whereas so many of his contemporaries looked forward to a kinder time ahead, fueled by benign national growth, collective enterprise, and the rewards of hard work, George conjured up a golden age in memory, back before the progress he idealized for productive individuals was scarred by poverty and injustice among them. In *Progress and Poverty* (1879) he offered Americans a compelling utopian vision that was firmly grounded in the preindustrial values of the eighteenth century, where men labored on the land where they lived. He then provided his converts with a tactical proposal for restoring that vision. That proposal—a single tax to eliminate monopoly landownership—would never be implemented, but his vision endured among his followers long after his death in 1897.

Utopian dreams of one sort or another had flourished among Americans from the outset of their history, beginning most famously with John Winthrop's call to his fellow Puritans to build a "city upon a hill" in the New England wilderness of the 1630s and thus inspire their English motherland with a model of religious purity. Thereafter, repeated efforts to create utopian models, both religious and secular, punctuated the process of continental occupation as small bands of like-minded true believers, recoiling from what they felt to be the cramped and corrupting arrangements of conventional society, strove to fashion alternative communities where, by themselves, they might try out reformist innovations in labor, dress, diet, sexual and family relations, ownership, and worship. Examples included Shaker settlements among the celibate followers of English-born Mother Ann Lee, beginning in the 1770s; German-American pietist communes like those founded at Ephrata, Pennsylvania, in 1732 and Zoar, Ohio,

in 1817; the quasi-socialist community organized by the Welsh industrial reformer Robert Owen in 1825 at New Harmony, Indiana; the perfectionist Oneida
community of John Humphrey Noyes in upstate New York, launched in 1848;
and the various utopian phalanxes inspired by the French social theorist Charles
Fourier. Brook Farm, outside Boston, the most celebrated utopian venture of the
pre-Civil War era, became a Fourierite phalanx three years after its founding by
Transcendentalists in 1841.

The swift expansion of a competitive market economy in antebellum America,
and the widespread urge to elude its constricting grip, propelled thousands of
sensitive men and women into utopian community experiments during the
1830s, 1840s, and 1850s. These decades traditionally have been regarded as the
heyday of communitarian model building in America, but recent scholarship has
demonstrated that such pilot efforts continued to punctuate utopian reformism
nationwide across the Gilded Age and into the next century. One example linking the communitarian impulse to Henry George was Fairhope, Alabama, a
single-tax community founded by a cluster of his acolytes in 1894.

George's utopian vision, however, sprang from sources quite independent of
communitarianism, and its appeal proved to be vastly more far-reaching, even
global, in its range. George was born to Richard and Catherine George on 2
September 1839 in Philadelphia. He grew up in a neighborhood of lower-
middle-class worker families. His family's home environment mixed his parents'
earnest Episcopalian religiosity with his father's Jacksonian Democratic politics,
two faiths that tinged his social attitudes throughout his life. In his maturing
mental set, the Jacksonian class resentments against the idle rich, which he
picked up as a boy along with the lessons of the Bible, ultimately validated his
millennial hope for God's kingdom of perfect justice, a hope encouraged by the
Social Gospel mood of his final years. Meanwhile, the repeated frustrations that
blocked his headstrong search for personal fulfillment gave a sharp autobiographical edge to his indictment of the imperfect world he moved through.

George left school at age fourteen to go to work, and two years later, in 1855,
set sail as a mast boy on a merchant ship bound for Melbourne and Calcutta.
This adventure brought his first shocks over extremes of human inequality, captured in his diary account of watching dead bodies float past the riverside dry-
docks and palatial homes of Calcutta's imperial Englishmen. On his return to
Philadelphia he worked briefly setting type in a printshop—a classic nineteenth-
century alternative education for bright boys—and then went off to sea again
in 1857, this time headed for America's burgeoning post-gold rush Pacific Slope.
After two failed tries to make his own fortune in the gold fields, George fell
back on work as a newspaper typographer in San Francisco. In 1861 he joined
five fellow printers to launch their own daily, the *Evening Journal*. The paper
soon collapsed for lack of access to the Associated Press monopoly on news
traveling over the new transcontinental telegraph.

Now in his early twenties, in love with the woman who soon became his
wife, George fretted at his inability to be successful in what had seemed the

wide-open promise of California. Disappointed at every turn, virtually penniless, and nagged by self-doubt, he confessed to his sister Jennie a dream of utopian escape: ''Sometimes I feel sick of the fierce struggle of our high civilized life, and think I would like to get away from cities and business . . . and find some place on one of the hillsides, which look so dim and blue in the distance where I could gather those I love, and live content with what Nature and our own resources would furnish.'' Then, as he contemplated the human potential for natural communion on the open land, the dream expanded: ''How I long for the Golden age, for the promised Millennium, when each will be free to follow his best and noblest impulses, unfettered by the restrictions and necessities which our present state of society imposes upon him—when the poorest and meanest will have a chance to use all his God-given faculties, and not be forced to drudge away the best part of his time in order to supply wants but little above those of the animal.''[1]

But for George the worst was yet to come. In December 1861 he married Annie Fox—a love match that brought him some emotional solace but also family obligations, the first of their three children being born within a year. George drifted from one short-term printer's job to the next in San Francisco and Sacramento during the Civil War years, which were depression years in California, bringing his new family to the shabby edge of destitution. At one point, his wife pregnant again, George found himself begging money from a stranger on the street. Finally, at war's end his situation brightened as he turned to writing articles on current events and then landed his first paying job as a reporter and editorialist for the *San Francisco Times.*

The experience of poverty left scars. Years later, in his greatest book, George described it from memory: ''Poverty is the open-mouthed, relentless hell which yawns beneath civilized society. . . . it means shame, degradation; the searing of the most sensitive parts of our moral and mental nature as with hot irons; the denial of the strongest impulses and the sweetest affections; the wrenching of the most vital nerves. You love your wife, you love your children; but would it not be easier to see them die than to see them reduced to the pinch of want in which large classes in every highly civilized community live?''[2] Few nineteenth-century witnesses caught more movingly the elemental fear and self-hatred that poverty set loose among them.

As George finally began to establish himself as a journalist and essayist of some note in postwar California, the recollection of the shame he and his family had struggled through inspired a search for social and economic, rather than personal, reasons for the blight of poverty. What was happening all around him in California gave him a glimpse of an answer. In its frenzied population growth since the war with Mexico and then the gold rush, California was fast recapitulating the developmental history of the nation as a whole. Once open, bountiful, and free, the Golden State was now filling with aggressive land-grabbers who carved up its space with claims of ownership, closing off access to resources to those less favored by the fortunes of growth. And as the technology of economic development, electric wires and steel rails reached westward to the coast, the historical process accelerated.

In 1868, with the transcontinental rail line to San Francisco nearing completion, George pondered its consequences in an article for the *Overland Monthly*, "What the Railroad Will Bring Us." The arrival of the iron horse promised brisker business and yet another population surge—"more people, more houses, more farms and mines, more factories and ships."[3] But George mistrusted this kind of progress. He feared it would sharpen inequalities between the rich and the poor, between concentrated ownership and a growing army of hired hands. All the fine amenities of advancing civilization could not mask the grim prospect of pinched opportunities for working people. "The locomotive is a great centralizer," he warned. "One millionaire involves the existence of just so many proletarians."[4] What he saw while walking the streets of New York City late in 1868 confirmed his anxiety about the future awaiting the younger San Francisco—a "shocking contrast between monstrous wealth and debasing want."[5] It was now apparent to George that this contrast was a reality of national dimensions, but its precise causes remained elusive.

Back in California, George entered the state's political controversies, aligning himself with the Democratic party (to his father's satisfaction) and committed to free trade, free homesteads, opposition to federal land subsidies to railroads, and protest over rising Chinese immigration, which he perceived as both a cultural and an economic threat to beleaguered American workingmen. His stance on each of these issues reflected his guiding Jacksonian fear that headlong growth was stratifying the region's population between the House of Have and the House of Want. He yearned for the key to recovering the lost Eden of earlier times, a natural order that in his mind glowed with agrarian innocence. "On the land we were born," he would put it later on, "from it we live, to it we return again—children of the soil as truly as is the blade of grass or the flower of the field."[6]

Years later George recalled with unforced melodrama the moment the revelation came to him how Eden had been lost. On horseback one day, riding in the pleasant open foothills outside Oakland, he chanced to ask a passing stranger about the local price of land and was stunned to learn that it was selling for a thousand dollars an acre. "Like a flash it came upon me that there was the reason for advancing poverty with advancing wealth. With the growth of population, land grows in value, and the men who work it must pay for the privilege. I turned back, amidst quiet thought, to the perception that then came to me and has been with me ever since."[7] He understood now how the natural order was abused: the rising price of land charged by those who owned it drained the income of those who wanted to apply their labor to it. The key applied everywhere, George concluded in a pamphlet on land policy published in 1871: "And thus we see it, all over the world, in countries where land is high, wages are low, and where land is low, wages are high."[8] George spent the rest of his life elaborating on these themes.

During the 1870s George was editor of the reformist *San Francisco Evening Post* and later was state inspector of gas meters, a Democratic party patronage job that gave him spare time for sustained study. He immersed himself in the literature of political economy, a field still open to inventive amateurs as it evolved slowly toward academic rigor and complexity. The giants of the English liberal tradition from Adam Smith to John Stuart Mill came under his scrutiny, as well as the work of American economists Henry C. Carey and Francis Amasa Walker. George was conscious of his relative isolation from the wellsprings of conventional economic wisdom. "I am on the outskirts, intellectual as well as geographical," he acknowledged to tariff reformer David A. Wells.[9]

In a guest lecture at the University of California at Berkeley in 1877, George asserted his outsider's status by announcing his scorn for academic economics in its current state. Its professors wasted their energies in "intellectual hair-splitting and super-refinements," he said, to give the field "an air of repellent abstruseness and uncertainty." Worse, their timid deference to powerful mon-eyed interests prevented serious attention to pressing practical problems in the working economy or any sympathy for the efforts of workers to improve their lot. The professors had reduced their subject to a learned justification of the status quo, which "seems but to justify injustice [and] canonize selfishness." A true political economy should provide remedies, George argued—"Not in wild dreams of red destruction nor weak projects for putting men in leading-strings to a brainless abstraction called the state, but in simple measures sanctioned by justice."[10] If economics could be merged with the golden rule of basic human morality, the riddle of wretchedness in the midst of wealth, dramatized by the hard times currently gripping the country, could be solved.

In the fall of 1877, suffering from debt and meager income, George undertook the writing of *Progress and Poverty*. Nineteen months later it was complete. He told a friend: "I have tried to make a book which would be intelligible to those who have never read and never thought on such subjects before, and to do that in such a way as to get the primary truths firmly established in their minds." His motive, he added, was an "earnest, burning desire to do what I might to relieve human misery and make life brighter."[11]

The subtitle of the book revealed his aim: *An Inquiry into the Cause of Industrial Depressions and of Increase of Want with Increase of Wealth*. The inquiry took him back to Adam Smith's eighteenth century to start a fresh exploration of the ground covered by Smith's misguided successors. In historian John Thomas's striking words, George "set out through the enemy territory of the classical economists in search of utopia."[12]

He began his search by noting that "the great enigma of our times," the phenomenon of spectacular economic progress generating widespread poverty, was apparently implacable, as if a huge, malign wedge were being steadily driven through society, separating those elevated by progress from those crushed by it.[13] The goal of *Progress and Poverty* was to show readers how to understand the momentum behind this unnatural split, stop the momentum, remove the wedge, and thus ensure a more natural and equitable distribution of wealth. Otherwise, George warned, the structure of modern society was headed for catastrophe.

George next set out to overcome the arguments of earlier authorities in the "dismal science" who had concluded that poverty and inequality were a natural and unavoidable economic condition. These included Thomas Malthus and David Ricardo. George flatly denied the Malthusian assertion that poverty sprang from the world's population outrunning its own food supply. To refute Ricardo's theory that a fixed wage fund, drawn from the hard-won capital resources of employers, limited the wages that could be paid to workers, George asserted the primacy of productive labor in generating capital. Rather than being locked in combat over the rivalry of wages and profits, labor and capital ideally formed a working partnership, collaborating to draw production from the resources of the land, the ultimate source of wealth. (George made a careful distinction between legitimate and "spurious" capital. The latter, represented by the Astors, Vanderbilts, and other millionaire monopolists, depended not on productivity but on the power of what he vaguely called "bad social adjustments.")[14]

The main adversary of both labor and capital was the monopolistic landowner. Private ownership allowed voracious, unproductive landlords to profit unfairly from the rent they charged to productive landusers. Rent depleted the net returns of labor and capital alike. The blight of rent on the fruits of productivity, moreover, spread in ratio with society's economic development and population growth, which drove land values up and wages down. Landowners, after securing possession of the best land, the richest resources, and the most valuable urban sites, creamed off this rising value through rising rent, whether they improved the land with productive facilities (factories, mines, housing) or not. The profits of rent—what George called the unearned increment—were pure robbery. They were the overriding cause of social injustice inflicted on producers. The most alarming result was an impoverished class of yeomen and artisans, stripped of their natural liberties, and clinging to an animal existence of constant want, their poverty in the midst of plenty an imminent threat to society's stability and survival.

What to do? Before turning to his own solution, George dismissed as inadequate or unrealistic a number of other antidotes for poverty: governmental regulatory intervention, socialism, unionization, cooperative production, graduated income taxation, the confiscation and redistribution of land. Although sympathetic with the goals of most of these projects, he concluded that no one of them could dissolve the wedge between rich and poor.

After some 360 dense pages of vivid prose, George revealed his favored remedy, breathtaking in its conceptual simplicity: a single tax on ground rent. A tax on owners equal to the value of the ground they owned (irrespective of improvements on it) would draw off the unearned increment and make ownership without use—absentee ownership—no longer profitable. In this way the principle of private property might remain intact, but the unjust privilege of mere ownership would disappear. Let landowners continue, if they wished, to retain title to their land, George wrote. "Let them buy and sell, and bequeath and devise it. We may safely leave them the shell, if we take the kernel. *It is not necessary to confiscate land*," he stressed; "*it is only necessary to confiscate rent.*" This single confiscatory tax would stimulate the breakup of big tracts into smaller parcels and their sale to those who wanted to live on the land, put it to productive use, and share the tax costs of functional ownership. The result would be a huge increase in the numbers of actual working landowners and a more even distribution of land resources among them. The benefits of this re-arrangement, as George imagined them, would bring a dazzling social, political, and cultural renaissance. It would "abolish poverty, give remunerative employment to whoever wishes it, afford free scope to human powers, lessen crime, elevate morals, and taste, and intelligence, purify government and carry civilization to yet nobler heights."[15] Utopia!

Moreover, the single tax would render all other taxes unnecessary. Its proceeds would be ample enough to fuel a transformation of governance. Relieved of its stern regulatory functions, the government would become a benign agency of social and cultural services for its people, providing public transportation and communication facilities as well as museums, libraries, theaters, universities, parks, and playgrounds to a contented interactive population. "We should reach the ideal of the socialist," George promised, "but not through governmental repression."[16] Most alluring among the prospects opened by the single tax was a demographic transformation—a return to a more natural balance between rural and urban growth as compacted cities released their trapped inhabitants to spread across the land and restore vitality to the life of small farms, villages, and gardened suburbs. Here lay the great appeal of George's utopia to so many Gilded Age Americans, farmers and city dwellers alike, for whom the headlong pace of urban crowding and stratification provoked strong misgivings. His promise of a renewed fusion between ownership and productive labor among small proprietors in the common country landscape, once the rent wedge between rich and poor had been removed, resonated with a central value of the Jeffersonian democratic tradition.

George concluded *Progress and Poverty* by forcing his readers to an urgent choice. A fateful turning point in human history confronted them. They must avert catastrophe or experience it. By seizing his remedy, they could save their civilization now and restore its finest virtues. By drifting passively into a future of widening inequalities, they would ensure its swift collapse. "The civilized world is trembling on the verge of a great movement," he warned. "Either it must be a leap upward, which will open the way to advances yet undreamed of, or it must be a plunge downward, which will carry us back toward barbarism."[17] At the end was a call to conversion. The City of God on earth was within grasp, but only if Americans were willing to reach. Convinced by his own vision, George prepared to become its prophet.

The career of *Progress and Poverty* got off to a rocky start. George's chosen publisher, D. Appleton of New York, found the manuscript "very aggressive," rejected it, and finally published it only after George supplied the page plates.[18] Sales of the Appleton edition were modest. The publisher later estimated that fewer than 18,000 copies were sold over the next twenty years. Cheaper paperback editions in the United States and Europe reached a much wider audience, but claims that the book became a best-seller second only to the Bible seem generous. Most initial American reactions to the book, including reviews in the *Nation* and the *New York Times*, were wary or downright hostile. Even the social reformer Henry Demarest Lloyd dismissed George as a quack. The country's most prominent Social Darwinist, William Graham Sumner of Yale, condemned the book for its "fallacies and errors" in attempting "to recreate society."[19] When Sumner proceeded to reiterate his familiar fatalistic warnings against misguided social tinkering, George was stung to reply in a series of popular magazine articles. These later were included in a book, *Social Problems* (1883), which rejected Sumner's "blind conservatism," elaborated George's evangelical call for reform, and aimed his single-tax remedy more clearly at the cancerous malaise of America's swollen cities.[20]

George moved to New York City in 1880. There he connected his cause with American supporters of the Irish Land League. The long history of Irish tenant oppression under absentee landlords struck George as a paradigm of the problem he had exposed. He agreed to travel to Ireland and report his findings for the New York newspaper *Irish World*. The journey extended to England and brought him into contact with the growing circle of English socialist intellectuals, who found his message appealing but not altogether persuasive, especially when measured against the overshadowing wisdom of London's Karl Marx. Marx himself acknowledged that *Progress and Poverty* was a significant departure from economic orthodoxy but denounced it as "utterly backward," a disguised effort to "save capitalist domination" by diverting attention to land problems.[21]

George returned to Britain four more times for lecture tours between 1882 and 1890. Among his rapt listeners was the young George Bernard Shaw, who later wrote: "Some of us regretted that he was an American, and therefore necessarily about fifty years out of date in his economics and sociology from the point of view of an older country, but only an American could have seen in a single lifetime the growth of the whole tragedy of civilization from the primitive forest clearing." Shaw dated the kindling of his Fabianism from this encounter. "When I was thus swept into the great Socialist revival of 1883, I found that five sixths of those who were swept in with me had been converted by Henry George."[22]

Shaw's double-edged testimony summed up two salient ambiguities in George's utopian appeal. On the one hand, many readers and listeners on both sides of the ocean wondered about the technical adequacy of George's economic analysis and his specific remedy; on the other hand, his passionate exposure of social injustice opened their minds to a broad spectrum of reform possibilities, from free trade to socialism. These ambiguities swirled around George's public career for the rest of his life.

The crowds he attracted abroad enhanced George's political reputation back in New York. Irish-American workingmen lionized him; Terence Powderly, head of the Knights of Labor, befriended him; Manhattan's liberal Catholic priest, Father Edward McGlynn, allied with him. In 1886 the city's Central Labor Union asked him to run for mayor. Attracted less by the office than by the chance to build a political constituency for his views, George plunged into the contest on a United Labor party platform that aimed his tax theories at the city's tenement slums and called for public ownership of railroads and telegraph. He waged a campaign as lively as any the city had ever witnessed, and brought together in his cause an excited coalition including such incongruous supporters as trade unionist Samuel Gompers, future Marxist Daniel DeLeon, and religious activists like Father McGlynn and the Baptist Social Gospeler Walter Rauschenbusch. George came in second on Election Day, running ahead of the Republican candidate, young Theodore Roosevelt, but behind the Democrat Abram Hewitt, whose support from Tammany regulars sealed the outcome. Convinced that voting fraud had done him in, George promptly added the secret ballot to his reform agenda.

His hope that the United Labor party might become a new force in American politics was shattered within a year; doctrinal factionalism, the constant nemesis of left-wing third-party politics, blew the volatile coalition of 1886 apart. George himself hastened the collapse by supporting a purge of socialists from party ranks. Thereafter, his following no longer included many workingmen and was grounded mainly in his broad middle-class readership, which he reached through the pages of the new single-tax journal, *The Standard*. His followers now seemed more attuned to brisk, focused argument about solutions than to mass agitation about conditions. "I think by the way that the single tax men are doing good work in stirring up the entire tax question," a Chicago tariff reformer wrote, "and they are an exceedingly bright, earnest and wholesome lot of people."[23] Men of wealth and professional status became more prominent among George's devotees. These included New York lawyer Thomas G. Shearman and the Cleveland millionaire Tom Johnson, who became one of the country's outstanding Progressive mayors in the early twentieth century.

Meanwhile George's rhetoric veered toward a more centrist and libertarian mood, more appealing to promoters of progress than to victims of poverty. "What we want to do is not merely to impose a certain kind of tax," he wrote for *The Standard*, "but to get rid of other taxes. Our proper name, if it would not seem too high flown, would be 'freedom men,' or 'liberty men,' or 'natural order men,' for it is on establishing liberty, on removing restrictions, on giving natural order full play, and not on any mere fiscal change that we base our hopes for social reconstruction." He went in with language that would become familiar in the vocabulary of twentieth-century business conservatism: "We want as few taxes as possible, as little restraint as is conformable to that perfect law of liberty which will allow each individual to do what he pleases without infringement of equal rights of others.''[24] He also explicitly renounced trade unionism and strikes.

These libertarian attitudes set George apart from more radical voices speaking to the pervasive sense of impending economic crisis that shadowed late nineteenth-century American thought. Rival utopian musings of that era, including those of Lawrence Gronlund, Edward Bellamy, Ignatius Donnelly, and Henry Demarest Lloyd, anticipated a future governed by more collectivized political and economic arrangements than George desired. Gronlund, a Danish-American immigrant, offered in *The Cooperative Commonwealth* (1884) a popularized Marxist message about the socialist transformation needed to overcome class exploitation and bring industrial equity. The outlines of his commonwealth bore a striking resemblance to the fictional environment laid out in Bellamy's *Looking Backward* (1888), the most famous utopian novel written by an American. In contrast to George, Bellamy seized on both the technological advances and the spreading monopolistic trends in the country's economy to project a thoroughly nationalized society of the future, purged of competitive strife, social insecurity, political dissonance, and governed, like Gronlund's socialist utopia, by a bland paternal bureaucracy.

A more feverish and pessimistic vision of the coming century informed the pages of Donnelly's *Caesar's Column* (1891), a novel in which utopian longings are overmatched by relentless capitalist greed and ultimate revolutionary catastrophe. Donnelly's complex career in Minnesota politics and literary fantasy reached a notable climax when he joined forces with the prairie populism of the Middle West and wrote the preamble to the Populist Omaha Platform of 1892, an arresting assertion of agrarian radicalism that distilled the apocalyptic warning in *Caeser's Column*. And Lloyd, a Chicago lawyer and journalist, completed *Wealth Against Commonwealth*, a stern indictment of industrial monopoly, in 1894. That same year his utopian essay, ''No Mean City,'' imagined a reformers' paradise springing up from the abandoned White City of the Chicago World's Fair of 1893. For the real world, Lloyd favored an incremental program of governmental ownership through ballot box politics and tried hard to forge a farmer-labor alliance behind a collectivized Populist agenda.

For all the variety in their diagnoses and cures, Gronlund, Bellamy, Donnelly, and Lloyd were unanimous in doubting the adequacy of George's single tax. George's own political stance, together with a minor stroke suffered in 1890, left him poorly prepared to respond to the radical political turmoil that rocked the United States in the decade following his mayoral campaign of 1886. Although many of his converts, including Hamlin Garland, whose powerful short story ''Under the Lion's Paw'' dramatized George's critique of absentee landownership, welcomed the Populist agitation of the early 1890s, George himself mistrusted Populist collectivism and opposed Lloyd's efforts to achieve a political merger between agrarians and urban wage workers during the depression of 1894. During these years George found himself drawn back to the Democratic party. He supported the tariff reform initiatives of Grover Cleveland, and in 1896 wound up backing the party's presidential nominee, William Jennings Bryan. A year later, physically worn out at age fifty-eight, he agreed to run for the New York City mayoralty once again, on a Bryanite splinter ticket. He died on 29 October 1897, a week before the election.

The strands of Henry George's legacy, though frayed and indeterminate, remained discernible well into the twentieth century. Testimony to the impact of his writing came from both the famous and the obscure. Leo Tolstoy, Sun Yat-sen, and a former American president, Rutherford B. Hayes, counted themselves among his admirers. So did future historian and diplomat Claude Bowers, who as a precocious Indiana schoolboy wrote two weeks after George's death: ''My man was Henry George—I admire the stirring eloquence of his burning pages. Rhetoric and compact reasoning united as in his works are quite rare to me. I am sometimes tempted to fall down and worship his theory. After all the land *is* God's, and God despises monopoly.''[25]

George's leading biographer, Charles Barker, has carefully tracked the influence of George's ideas on political leaders of the Progressive generation down through the presidency of Woodrow Wilson. Despite the withering critique of George's version of political economy by academic economists Francis Amasa Walker, Alfred Marshall, and E. R. A. Seligman, his single-tax remedy continued to reach a large Progressive audience through the sponsorship of the Fels Fund created by the Fels-Naptha soap magnate Joseph Fels. Later the Robert Schalkenbach Foundation underwrote the *American Journal of Economics and Sociology*, launched in 1940 to foster interdisciplinary inquiry along lines first broached by George. The philosopher John Dewey, yet another admirer, lent his prestige to this scholarly venture, which remains active over half a century later.

But perhaps the most durable afterglow of George's utopian vision may be detected, as John Thomas suggests, in the continuing twentieth-century debate over efforts to effect a happier balance among the patterns of urban compaction, metropolitan sprawl, and rural decay in modern population trends. The Garden City proposals of the English planner Ebenezer Howard, published at the turn of the century and supported by, among others, his fellow social radical Bernard Shaw, sprang in part from Howard's sympathy for George's critique of lopsided urbanization. Howard's remedy called for the creation of small, decentralized city clusters through cooperative planning, his alternative to the single tax. The Garden City dream fed into American efforts at suburban and regional planning over succeeding decades, and in the 1930s was forcefully revived in the grand decentralizing projections of Frank Lloyd Wright's Broadacre City. Wright explicitly acknowledged his intellectual debt to Henry George, used ''rent'' as a virtual synonym for exploitation, and endorsed the single tax in his antiurban arguments for demographic reform through decentralized landownership. The New Deal's greenbelt cities program for urban relocation was yet another expression of this reform impulse during the Great Depression. A generation later, in the 1960s, rivalry between the urban prospects defined by Lewis Mumford and Jane Jacobs marked a new phase in the long debate over urban crowding, and again suggested the lasting resonance of George's concerns about land use.

Meanwhile, the historical realities he had identified almost a century earlier as obstacles to utopian harmony—technological momentum, lurching economic growth, spectacular human inequalities, and accumulating governmental measures for social control—continued their clattering coexistence.

NOTES

1. Henry George to Jennie George, 15 September 1861, as quoted in John Thomas, *Alternative America: Henry George, Edward Bellamy, Henry Demarest Lloyd, and the Adversary Tradition* (Cambridge, Mass., 1983), 14.

2. Henry George, *Progress and Poverty: An Inquiry into the Cause of Industrial Depressions, and of Increase of Want with Increase of Wealth* (New York, 1879), 411.

3. Quoted in Thomas, *Alternative America*, 49.

4. Quoted in Charles A. Barker, *Henry George* (New York, 1955), 103.

5. Quoted in ibid., 121.

6. George, *Progress and Poverty*, 266.

7. Quoted in Thomas, *Alternative America*, 52.

8. Quoted in ibid., 67.

9. Henry George to David A. Wells, 19 September 1871, David A. Wells Papers (Library of Congress, Washington, D.C.).

10. Henry George, ''The Study of Political Economy,'' *Popular Science Monthly* 16 (March 1880): 601–612.

11. Henry George to Charles Nordhoff, draft, 21 December 1879, Henry George Papers (New York Public Library).

12. Thomas, *Alternative America*, 106.

13. George, *Progress and Poverty*, 8, 9.

14. Ibid., 174.

15. Ibid., 364 and passim.

16. Ibid., 410.

17. Ibid., 488.

18. D. Appleton to Henry George, 9 April 1879 and 22 September 1879, George Papers.

19. *Scribner's Monthly* 22 (June 1881): 312–313.

20. Henry George, *Social Problems* (Chicago, 1883), 18, 264–296, 316–324.

21. Quoted in Daniel Bell, *Marxian Socialism in the United States* (Princeton, 1967), 28.

22. George Bernard Shaw to Hamlin Garland, 29 December 1904, in Dan H. Laurence, ed., *Bernard Shaw: Collected Letters, 1898–1910* (New York, 1985), 476–478.

23. Franklin MacVeagh to Horace White, 21 August 1890, Horace White Papers (Illinois State Historical Library, Springfield).

24. *The Standard*, 2 March 1889, as quoted in Arthur N. Young, *The Single Tax Movement in the United States* (Princeton, 1916), 261.

25. Claude Bowers to William Everett, 15 November 1897, William Everett Papers (Massachusetts Historical Society, Boston).

BIBLIOGRAPHY

Aaron, Daniel. *Men of Good Hope: A Story of American Progressives.* New York, 1961.

Andelson, Robert V., ed. *Critics of Henry George: A Centenary Appraisal of Their Strictures on Progress and Poverty.* Rutherford, N.J., 1979.

Barker, Charles A. *Henry George.* New York, 1955.

Cord, Steven B. *Henry George: Dreamer or Realist?* Philadelphia, 1965.

Egbert, Donald D., and Stow Persons, eds. *Socialism and American Life.* Princeton, 1952.

Fishman, Robert. *Urban Utopias in the Twentieth Century: Ebenezer Howard, Frank Lloyd Wright, and Le Corbusier.* New York, 1977.

Fogarty, Robert S. *All Things New: American Communes and Utopian Movements, 1860–1914.* Chicago, 1990.

———, ed. *Dictionary of American Communal and Utopian History.* Westport, Conn., 1980.

George, Henry. *Progress and Poverty: An Inquiry into the Cause of Industrial Depressions, and of Increase of Want with Increase of Wealth.* New York, 1879.

———. *Social Problems.* Chicago, 1883.

Horton, Joseph, and Thomas Chisholm. ''The Political Economy of Henry George: Its Ethical and Social Foundation.'' *American Journal of Economics and Sociology* 50 (1991): 375–384.

Lause, Mark. ''Progress Impoverished: Origin of Henry George's Single Tax.'' *The Historian* 52 (1990): 394–410.

Nicklason, Fred. ''Henry George: Social Gospeller.'' *American Quarterly* 22 (1970): 649–664.

Rose, Edward J. *Henry George.* New York, 1968.

Ross, Steven J. ''Political Economy for the Masses: Henry George.'' *Democracy* 2 (1982): 125–134.

Starr, Kevin. *Americans and the California Dream.* New York, 1973.

Thomas, John L. *Alternative America: Henry George, Edward Bellamy, Henry Demarest Lloyd and the Adversary Tradition.* Cambridge, Mass., 1983.

Young, Arthur Nichols. *The Single Tax Movement in the United States.* Princeton, 1916.

Washington Gladden
and the Social Gospel

JACOB H. DORN

Few Protestant clergymen in American history have enjoyed greater stature or wider influence than Washington Gladden. One of the first ministers to call upon the churches to address the issues of a rapidly industrializing and urbanizing society in the Gilded Age, he lived to see his ideas gain currency through a revitalization movement known as the Social Gospel and to influence many of the reforms of the Progressive era.

The Social Gospel was not the only perspective on Christian social responsibility to emerge in the new urban-industrial age. Many Protestants worked to alleviate the burdens of the poor and needy, without offering much criticism of the social system as a cause of those burdens. In sharp contrast, a small but vocal group of socialists insisted that applying the message of Jesus to modern conditions required a thoroughgoing reconstruction of American institutions. The Social Gospel represented a middle option. While offering ministries to individuals, its practitioners were also deeply committed to institutional change. They believed that American institutions were essentially sound, however, and worked for reform, not radical change. Although proponents of the Social Gospel were prone to stress the novelty of their movement, it had important continuities to the past—in particular, to antislavery and other moral and social reforms for which pre–Civil War Protestants had worked through a "benevolent empire" of extradenominational societies.

Washington Gladden's life and ministry grew from the same middle ground of Christian concern and antebellum reform that bred the Social Gospel. Born on 11 February 1836, to Solomon and Amanda Daniels Gladden, in Pottsgrove, Pennsylvania, and reared there and in Owego, New York, Gladden experienced religious conversion in the context of evangelical abolitionism. When in 1853 he joined Owego's Congregational church, the product of an antislavery secession from the local Presbyterian church, it was not, he later wrote, "an individualistic pietism" that attracted him but "a religion that laid hold upon life with both hands, and proposed, first and foremost, to realize the Kingdom of God in this world."[1] For the young Gladden, such a religion entailed loyalty to both the temperance movement and the newborn Republican party.

There were important differences between the Social Gospel and the evangelical reformism of Gladden's youth, three of which deserve emphasis. First, the issues changed. Whereas Protestant activists in the earlier period gave little attention to economic issues, from the 1870s on, industrialization focused attention on labor-management conflicts and the legitimacy of unions. Second, as Protestant thinkers responded to the realities of a more complex social system and to intellectual trends in the natural and social sciences, they gradually became sharply critical of the individualism that had permeated antebellum thought. Third, in contrast to antebellum reformers who worked through single-issue organizations outside the denominations, Social Gospel leaders brought public issues into the arena of denominational life.

Despite these differences, Protestant social reforms in both periods are best understood as stages in the venerable quest for a "Christian America"—a righteous, just, and democratic society guided by Protestant ideals toward a unique destiny in world history. Given the separation of church and state, Protestants could mold such a society only through persuasion and voluntaristic methods. So strongly did they identify Protestant values and beliefs with the advance of American civilization, however, that they assumed a prerogative to speak for the nation and to define its interests. A core group of denominations—Episcopal, Presbyterian, Methodist, Congregational, Baptist, at least—were a kind of American establishment. They were not established legally, but their members had a sense of cultural priority and authority, and exerted considerable influence in politics, education, business, journalism, and the arts.

The nineteenth century was one of expansion and success for American Protestants—and consequently one of confidence and expectation. Forces that would undermine their hegemony were already at work by the end of the century, but Protestants were more buoyant than defensive. The Social Gospel was especially attractive to members of the middle class, for whom belief in progress, translated by their preachers into a coming kingdom of God on earth, seemed reasonable. As for the clergy, social status and cultural presumptions varied widely, but many Social Gospel figures led prominent urban churches and were respected personages in their communities. Far from being drawn to reform in order to reverse a decline in the social status of the ministry, they worked from a long-standing expectation that it was their right and responsibility to use their influence to perfect a Christian civilization.

Gladden's career mirrors the history of the Social Gospel from its emergence in the 1870s to its institutionalization in denominational and ecumenical organizations in the decade before World War I. After graduating in 1859 from Williams College, where he received a conventional education in Common Sense moral philosophy and laissez-faire economics, he taught briefly in Owego before seeking more satisfying work in the ministry. He first encountered the urban world during a pastorate in Brooklyn, New York, in 1860–1861. Forced by a nervous breakdown to take up a more relaxed charge in the village of Morrisania, where he remained until 1865, he attended classes at the Union Theological Seminary but never completed a seminary education.

Except for several years (1871–1874) as religious editor of *The Independent*, the most widely circulated Protestant paper in the nation, Gladden spent the rest of his life in three pastorates: at the Congregational Church of North Adams, Massachusetts (1866–1871), the North Congregational Church of Springfield, Massachusetts (1875–1882), and the First Congregational Church of Columbus, Ohio (1883–1914). Although his churches in Massachusetts were important locally, the one in Columbus was uniquely positioned to give him a base for civic leadership and even national recognition. It was situated downtown, across the street from Capitol Square, and its members were generally well educated and prosperous. Numerous business leaders belonged to Gladden's church, as did two successive principals of the Central High School and the directors of three state asylums situated in the city. According to a survey in 1902, 32 of 130 faculty members at the Ohio State University were members of or attended the First Church. Gladden had his hands in a wide variety of public and private activities; when he died on 2 July 1918, he was widely acclaimed as ''the first citizen of Columbus.''

There was no theological uniformity among Social Gospelers. Commonly they belonged to the liberalizing party within Protestantism that tried to accommodate the higher criticism of the Bible and evolutionary scientific thought to the Christian faith. Theological liberalism and social liberalism were not necessary correlates, however. Henry Ward Beecher, one of the Gilded Age's most popular preachers, heralded his acceptance of evolution and a critical historical analysis of the Bible while articulating a deeply conservative social ethic. Conversely, prior to the coalescence of militant fundamentalism after World War I, theological conservatives often worked for political, economic, and social reforms scarcely distinguishable from those advocated by Social Gospelers.

In Gladden's case, theological and social liberalism were inseparably joined. Although several British and American theologians influenced him, he considered Horace Bushnell his theological emancipator. Bushnell's emphasis on the limitations of language nurtured Gladden's distrust of creeds and confessions to convey adequately the reality of God. A leading participant in intramural Congregational battles in the 1870s and 1880s, Gladden rejected Calvinist doctrines of election and damnation that, in his judgment, presented God as immoral and unloving. He also began in those decades to interpret Charles Darwin's work and biblical higher criticism as aids, not threats, to faith. Such books as *Burning Questions of the Life That Now Is and of That Which Is to Come* (1890), *Who Wrote the Bible?* (1891), *Seven Puzzling Bible Books* (1897), *How Much Is Left of the Old Doctrines?* (1899), and *Present Day Theology* (1913) were intended to popularize an intellectually open faith.

With only minor variations but with great rhetorical force and a complex array of arguments and illustrations, Gladden reiterated his core ideas over four decades. Not unique to him, these ideas were common currency within the Social Gospel. Scripture and evolution both taught that God was immanent in nature and human experience, and God's presence made all of life sacred and guaranteed the final triumph of good over evil. The central themes of Jesus's Gospel, which completed an evolving biblical revelation, were that God is best understood as a loving parent, that all people are God's children, and that the familial relationship is therefore normative for human life. Personal and social salvation were thus linked in the realities of the Fatherhood of God and the brotherhood of man: the individual could not truly receive God's love and love God in return without loving God's other children.

Moreover, the end toward which God was working in history—and thus the end toward which Christians should bend every effort—was a social order in which a perfected humanity would dwell in peace, harmony, and justice. The coming of God's kingdom on earth was both a spiritual and a social reality: it was registered in the inner life of individuals and in social mores, customs, institutions, cultural expression, and relationships between racial, national, religious, and economic groups. Because of the kingdom's dual nature, no social blueprint could define it. It meant transformed character and social reform: not one or the other, and not one before the other, but both concurrently. "If you ask which of these must take the precedence," Gladden wrote, "I answer neither; they must be held together."[2] As Lyman Abbott, pastor of Brooklyn's Plymouth Church and editor of *Outlook*, defined Gladden, he was not "a preacher of the Gospel *and* a moral reformer" but "a preacher of a Gospel that is a moral reform."[3]

In the light of such ideas, it is not surprising that the Social Gospel was, first and foremost, a movement of reform *within* the churches. As Gladden put it, "In order that the church may be fitted for its work a reformation of the church itself is called for, no less radical than that of the sixteenth century."[4] For Gladden, the relationship between religion and social reform was vital. Religion must flow into social life, and society must have the aspiration and ideals of religion.

In one of his fullest addresses on the subject, "The Church and the Kingdom," he argued against seeing the church as an end in itself, but also against blurring its distinct identity and functions. The church is to the kingdom what the brain is to the body. The kingdom is "the whole social organism so far as it is affected by divine influences"; but the church, as "the seat of thought and feeling and motion," is its "most central and important" organ. The church must recognize its organic relationship to society. When it withdraws "to set up a smug little ecclesiasticism, with interests of its own, and a cultus of its own, and standards and sentiments of its own, and enjoyments of its own,"

Gladden declared, it becomes "dead and accursed; it is worse than useless; it is a bane and a blight to all the society in which it stands."[5] Yet his was not a low view of the church, for he assigned it a unique role as teacher, inspirer, and guide. Addressing future ministers at the Yale Divinity School in 1902, he proclaimed:

I do not, for my own part, expect to see any radical or permanent cure discovered for poverty or pauperism, for grinding monopoly or municipal corruption, for bribery or debauchery or crime, except as men's minds and hearts are opened to receive the truths of the spiritual world; except as they are brought into conscious and vital relations with things unseen and eternal. There can be no adequate social reform save that which springs from a genuine revival of religion; only it must be a religion which is less concerned about getting men to heaven than about fitting them for their proper work on earth.[6]

One implication of such a view of religion was that the pulpit must make explicit connections between religious ideals and public life. Thus, as a reform in church life, the Social Gospel brought about a significant broadening of the American preaching tradition. Though unusually systematic, Gladden was symptomatic of the Social Gospel clergy as a whole. He considered preaching central to his vocation as pastor and crafted his sermons with such care that many of them became articles and books with little revision. By the early 1880s he was devoting most Sunday evening sermons to social subjects. An inventory of his sermons is a guide to the events, ideologies, literature, and public issues of his day. Socialism, contemporary fiction, municipal elections, strikes, diplomatic crises, race relations, poor relief, settlement houses, the concentration of wealth—such subjects were regular fare at the First Church. This preaching incidentally helped Gladden draw large audiences at a time when the evening service was becoming problematic for some churches. For Gladden, however, it was not a gimmick. Rather, he probed "secular" topics because he believed the teachings of Jesus had a bearing on them.

The Social Gospel utilized many parachurch organizations to motivate and educate both the clergy and the Protestant public. These included the Chautauqua Institution in New York, where in 1893 Gladden, the economist Richard T. Ely, and others organized an American Institute of Christian Sociology; the "Schools of the Kingdom" held at Iowa (Grinnell) College in the 1890s under the dynamic leadership of George D. Herron; and, after 1898, Josiah Strong's American Institute of Social Service with its many publications, industrial exhibits, Social Gospel Sunday school lessons, and speakers' bureau.

Social Gospel fiction was another instrument for motivating Protestants to reform. The most famous such work, Charles M. Sheldon's *In His Steps* (1897), was a runaway best-seller. It follows the pastor and key members of the First Church in "Raymond" after they promise to ask, before every decision, "What would Jesus do?" That question is shot through with social implications and consequences. The hundreds of other Social Gospel stories include William

Dean Howells's *A Traveler from Altruria* (1894), William Allen White's *A Certain Rich Man* (1909), and Winston Churchill's *The Inside of the Cup* (1913).

Gladden contributed two works to the genre, both based on his own experience and intensely practical. *The Christian League of Connecticut* (1883) is a story of religious cooperation to improve local religious life and alleviate social problems. In it, the churches of New Albion conclude that they are really one church with several branches, united not by creedal tests but in a common mission. Their experiment gradually spreads across the state and is on the verge of expanding further as the story ends. Gladden captured both the Social Gospel's view of the churches' social task and the ecumenical spirit that would be among its legacies. His second work, *The Cosmopolis City Club* (1893), involves cooperation to end municipal corruption.

One other example of how some advocates of the Social Gospel tried to inspire and educate the Protestant public is the Men and Religion Forward Movement of 1910–1912. Beginning as a mass evangelical campaign among men and boys, this enterprise was not initially linked with the Social Gospel. It did include a department of social service, however, and the work of this department unexpectedly attracted the greatest interest in many of the seventy cities in which mass meetings were held. Social Gospel leaders who were involved exploited this opening and gave to the Men and Religion Forward Movement a reformist thrust that linked personal religious decisions with projects for community betterment and reform. Gladden served on the movement's social-service commission, spoke at its concluding congress in New York, and pronounced it "the most salutary influence which has visited the churches of this country since my ministry began."[7]

As a reform of church life, the Social Gospel meant more than inspiring and educating the churched. It also meant reexamining the relationship between the church and its neighborhood and, thus, devising new forms of parish ministry, including aid to those outside the church's own membership. Many churches engaged in such reexamination and adopted social-service programs for their neighborhoods from motives quite distinct from the Social Gospel. Survival in radically changed neighborhoods, which their members had abandoned when poorer, immigrant, and non-Protestant populations had moved in, was often the central consideration. If Social Gospel ideas were not the driving force behind all new urban ministries, however, they dovetailed nicely with efforts to rejuvenate urban Protestantism.

The best-known ministries were those of so-called institutional churches: St. George's Episcopal in New York, the Baptist Temple and Bethany Presbyterian in Philadelphia, Morgan Memorial Methodist in Boston, and others in most large cities. The most comprehensive programs included gymnasiums, free baths, medical dispensaries and nursing services, boys' and girls' clubs, savings banks, and classes in English, citizenship, and housekeeping. Except for their religious services, churches with such extensive programs might be hard to distinguish from social settlements. Numerous settlements, in fact, operated under explicitly

Christian auspices. At least three—Andover (later South End) House in Boston, the Chicago Commons, and New York's Union Settlement—were started by seminaries. Even settlements without religious affiliations were suffused by the Social Gospel ethos of Christian service.

The work of institutional churches and settlements exemplified Gladden's conception of the church's mission in advancing the kingdom of God. In a widely used textbook on pastoral theology, he defined the church as an ''army of occupation'' rather than an ''Ark of Safety.''[8] Familiar with settlements through visits in 1888 to Toynbee Hall and Mansfield House in London, and through personal acquaintance with such American settlement pioneers as Graham Taylor and Jane Addams, he considered them ''one of the most beautiful and noble agencies yet devised for the promotion of the Kingdom of God.''[9]

Gladden's ideal church was an inclusive body transcending barriers of class, ethnicity, and race. Disappointed that relatively few wage earners were part of congregations like his, he wrote that it was ''a monstrous thing even to conceive that a church of Jesus Christ could exist as a class institution, with the largest social class in the community outside of it.''[10] The question of the ''alienation'' of the working class was for him and for the Social Gospel a spur to numerous surveys and attempts at rapprochement. His soundings in the 1880s suggested two reasons for the situation: wage earners resented their ''inability to dress well enough to appear in a place as stylish and fashionable as the average church,'' and they felt a ''sense of injustice'' over their treatment by employers, who were conspicuous in those churches.[11]

Anxiety about working-class alienation reflected the social isolation of elite congregations and pastors. Large numbers of churchgoing Protestants, both in the mainline denominations and in the Holiness and Pentecostal movements that took shape in the period 1880–1920, worked for little income in factories and mines and in agriculture. American Catholic parishes were made up predominantly of working-class folk. These Christians, outside bourgeois circles of privilege and power, met social needs in their own ways, without the distinctive orientation and rationale that informed Gladden's work.

Although Gladden tried to create a democratic atmosphere in his church, he was never able to attract many industrial workers to its membership. He was, however, able to use his members' financial resources, leadership skills, and energies to fulfill Social Gospel objectives in Columbus. He helped start Congregational churches, at least one of which offered institutional programs, in several working-class neighborhoods. For many years the First Church conducted a Sunday afternoon school for children in a poor neighborhood nearby, and for a while it employed a city missionary to work with those children's families. Most important, in 1905 it launched what was to become Columbus's most important settlement, the West Side Social Center (renamed the Gladden Community House in 1920). Although the center's quarters west of downtown were cramped and unattractive, it offered a kindergarten, library and reading room, district nursing service, domestic science classes, music and drama clubs, and gymnastics. Gladden called it the most important enterprise the First Congregational Church had ever undertaken.

The Social Gospel, academic social science, and social work were closely linked in these years. Social Gospelers looked to the social sciences for guidance in understanding social problems and applying Christian principles efficiently to their solution. Many social scientists, active in Protestant church life, saw their academic work in a reformist framework that placed it in alliance with the Social Gospel. Although professionalizing at a rapid pace, social workers still owed much to nineteenth-century religious philanthropy. Because of the functions they were taking upon themselves, churches received considerable attention in social-scientific and social-work circles. An entire issue of the *Annals of the American Academy of Political and Social Science* in 1907 was devoted to "The Social Work of the Church." It was not unusual that Gladden should address the National Conference of Charities and Corrections in 1911, on the churches and social service. An important regional group, the Southern Sociological Congress, gave a high profile to cooperation between churches and other social agencies at its first meeting in 1912.

The Social Gospel had a powerful impact on denominational structures and on Protestant ecumenical ventures. In these settings, too, Gladden was a pioneering and influential figure. What the Social Gospel did to the denominations it touched most strongly was win acceptance for the systematic consideration of social issues in their official proceedings and for social education and advocacy through permanent church agencies. In contrast to the nineteenth-century pattern, in which religious reformers had to work through voluntary societies outside the denominations, the denominations now acknowledged a corporate responsibility for the social welfare. That acknowledgment remains a permanent legacy of the Social Gospel, despite many subsequent shifts in the religious and social contexts of denominational life.

In the late nineteenth century, social questions occasionally arose at denominational gatherings. Gladden spoke on "Christian Socialism" at the National Congregational Council in 1889; and when that council met again in 1892, in the aftermath of the Homestead strike, he was appointed chairman of a committee to investigate the causes of industrial unrest. Other church bodies reacted to strikes, unions, and industrial violence in a similar sporadic manner, without continuity or commitment to a course of action.

The pattern began to change in the twentieth century. Although impressionistic evidence suggests that much of the laity remained theologically and socially more conservative than the clergy and lay elites, Social Gospel leaders were well enough positioned to gain the sanction of a number of denominations. Their work in the Episcopal, Congregational, and Northern Methodist, Baptist, and Presbyterian denominations was especially significant.

In 1901 the Episcopalians and Congregationalists set up committees to investigate labor questions and submit reports at their next triennial meetings. Those committees were reappointed in 1904 and made permanent in 1907.

Northern Presbyterians took unprecedented action in 1903 by appointing Charles Stelzle, a "son of the Bowery" who had been a machinist before entering the ministry, to "a special mission to workingmen." His multifaceted work to build bridges between churches and unions was buttressed in 1906 when he was put in charge of a new Presbyterian Department of Church and Labor. The Northern Baptist Convention, organized in 1907 around a number of autonomous Baptist societies, established a Commission on Social Service within its first year. The Methodist Federation for Social Service, created in 1907, though only an "unofficial" organization, was pivotal among Northern Methodists. Nomenclature, mission statements, and reporting relationships sometimes changed, but each of these denominational entities soon achieved both bureaucratic security and high visibility.

Gladden played a key role in his denomination's institutionalization of the Social Gospel. His writings and addresses at colleges and seminaries gave him a following among younger ministers. Through loyal support of a wide range of Congregational educational and mission enterprises, he gradually rose to national prominence among Congregationalists, and his rise meant increasing recognition of the things he stood for. He chaired the denomination's first Committee on Capital and Labor, appointed in 1892, and served continuously on the Committee on Labor, created in 1901, until several years after its reorganization as the Commission on Social Service in 1913. As moderator of the National Council of Congregational Churches from 1904 to 1907, he spoke to Congregational audiences across the country and gave the Social Gospel a prominent place on the agenda for 1907. In 1917, when he stood to speak at his final council, on "The Range of the Social Demand of the Gospel," the audience rose in his honor.

Although it arose from many influences besides the Social Gospel, the modern American ecumenical movement represents the Social Gospel's impact as a reform movement without the churches. Inasmuch as many advocates of the Social Gospel were theological liberals with a deep aversion to creedal tests and sectarian controversy, they were naturally attracted to the ideal of Christian cooperation. Ecumenicity was also appealing because of their action-oriented understanding of the Christian faith. If its mission was to advance the kingdom, the church must devote its energies to social progress, and not to perpetuating theological and ecclesiastical differences. Cooperative effort struck a responsive chord among Social Gospelers, moreover, because it promised greater effectiveness. Admiring the scientific method, and expecting it to reduce duplication and waste when applied to social problems, advocates of the Social Gospel were modernizers who shared in the Progressive era's celebration of efficiency.

A strong orientation to social mission was apparent in the Open and Institutional Church League, organized in 1894 as a network and clearinghouse for urban ministries, and its successor, the National Federation of Churches and Christian Workers, founded in 1901. The latter organization was the principal agent in arranging the Inter-Church Conference on Federation in 1905, from which emerged the Federal Council of the Churches of Christ (FCC) in 1908. A supporter of the Open and Institutional Church League and the Columbus and Ohio federations of churches, Gladden presided one day at the Inter-Church Conference in 1905.

Unlike earlier voluntary interdenominational organizations, the FCC was an official body created by and representative of denominations. Initially it included thirty-three communions with about 17 million members. Its stated purposes included increasing the churches' influence over moral and social conditions and promoting the application of Christian motives and values to all human relationships—both Social Gospel objectives. To those ends, the FCC in 1908 created the Commission on the Church and Social Service and adopted the "social creed" just approved by the Northern Methodist General Conference. Dedicated to the goals of "equal rights and complete justice" for all, this manifesto called for the regulation of female and child labor, one day's rest in seven, protection against dangerous machinery and occupational diseases, improved wages, and other industrial reforms. Revised in 1912 to incorporate a broader range of reforms, the creed paralleled the social and industrial planks of the Progressive party platform adopted later that year. It was not changed again until 1932. The FCC's social service commission, on which Gladden served, was its most active unit for several years. It linked the work of denominational social-service offices and collaborated with secular organizations—including the American Federation of Labor, National Civic Federation, National Consumers' League, National Child Labor Committee, Association for Labor Legislation, and American Public Health Association—whose goals it shared. Significantly, every president of the FCC from 1908 to 1920 was a Social Gospel leader.

With the outbreak of World War I, the FCC quickly created the Commission on International Justice and Goodwill to promote an arbitrated peace. Despite the noninterventionist perspective of many of its leaders, it supported the American war effort in 1917–1918. In fact, the war broadened its Social Gospel agenda and created an exhilarating sense of opportunity and progress, much as it did for other Progressives. Through its General War-Time Commission of the Churches, the FCC represented the denominations' interests in such matters as chaplaincy, public hygiene, social and religious conditions among servicemen, and the welfare of women and African Americans in industry.

As a reform of Protestant church life (and of the beliefs and conduct of the Protestant public), the Social Gospel was also a movement to reform American society. Although impossible to measure precisely, the contribution to a great number of Progressive era reforms made by people working from Social Gospel assumptions was considerable.

Gladden's attempts to influence the public sector, though exceptional in range and duration, well represent the Social Gospel as a reform outside the churches. His many interests included unemployment, business regulation, race relations, child and female labor, temperance, and international arbitration. None better illustrate his combination of pulpit rhetoric and public activity, however, than the issues of labor organization and municipal government. In both instances, he used his persuasive powers and leadership skills to help create a climate of opinion conducive to Progressive reforms.

Although an important early Social Gospel work, Gladden's first systematic treatment of labor issues, *Working People and Their Employers* (1876), displayed a superficial understanding of the causes of depression and of working-class conditions. Gladden urged the unemployed to accept any work that was available, or even go back to farming, and to avoid expenditures on clothing, amusements, and, above all, "strong drink." He approved unions but judged their leaders harshly and advised that strikes were often unnecessary, if not actually counterproductive. Locating the solution to labor's problems in a more benign stewardship by employers, he urged them to take greater personal interest in their workers' moral, physical, and intellectual welfare and to overcome class differences through experiments in profit sharing.

Within the next decade, Gladden's perspective underwent a profound change. He continued to favor profit sharing as a means of joining the interests of workers and owners, as well as of giving workers a fairer share of what they produced. By 1886, when he wrote *Applied Christianity: Moral Aspects of Social Questions*, however, he was largely disabused of his trust in employer benevolence. Sadly applying the imagery of war to contemporary industrial relations, he attributed much of the violence associated with strikes to employers' determination to break up unions, which workers correctly saw as necessary for self-defense. War was reprehensible, but it was not the greatest of evils: "The permanent social degradation of the people who do the world's work would be a greater evil," he concluded. "If war is the order of the day, we must grant to labor belligerent rights."[12] For there to be justice in industry, workers must possess countervailing power to that of employers, and especially to that of large corporations.

This remained Gladden's basic stance in numerous subsequent sermons and such books as *Tools and the Man* (1893) and *Social Facts and Forces* (1897). Preaching to Columbus's Retail Grocery Clerks' Union in 1901, he wished "that all the working men in every trade were included in the union representing that trade, and that all the bargaining were collective bargaining."[13]

Gladden's final comprehensive utterance on industrial relations, *The Labor Question* (1911), reflected his awareness of the campaign that such employers' groups as the National Association of Manufacturers had begun waging against unions and his own experience during a streetcar strike in Columbus in 1910. The strike was especially disillusioning because the company obdurately rejected all his efforts to bring matters to arbitration and thus defeated the union. The issues, he wrote, were more than economic; they were deeply moral. Industrial arrangements, which he characterized as "feudal," must be democraticized, and that necessitated collective bargaining. In a remarkable statement to his congregation and readers of his book, he said, "My own mind is clear upon the proposition that if I were a wage-worker in any trade I should feel under obligation to join the trade-union."[14]

Gladden's philosophical and theological commitments presupposed a fundamental harmony of social interests. Thinking of society as an organism and believing that the model of familial love could be extended to society, he implicitly rejected Marxism or any other analysis predicated on conflict. As a middle-class spokesman, moreover, he always presented himself as impartial, an interpreter of each side to the other, a reconciler. That he viewed industrial conflict through cultural filters that vitiated his claims to objectivity is not remarkable. What is remarkable is that his defense of unions and condemnation of employers had both clarity and force despite his organicist idealism and social position.

The problems produced by the transformation of the United States into an urban society were many, and few of them escaped Gladden's notice. His efforts to improve municipal government are especially noteworthy. The Social Gospel was not free of a strain of antiurbanism, but that strain could not be dominant in the light of the biblical image of the kingdom of God as a city. Gladden's accent, for example, was on his belief that a clean, harmonious, prosperous, and culturally rich urban civilization was possible, rather than on disappointment over urban failings. The city was a holy entity, a part of the process of social salvation, he frequently observed.

Like other urban ministers, Gladden engaged in campaigns to crack down on vice, gambling, and drinking. Lenient administrations in Columbus looked the other way as saloons stayed open beyond legal hours, prostitutes walked the downtown streets, and boxing matches and horse races drew noisy crowds. Crusades to enforce a Puritan-pietist public morality involved, at one level, a cultural clash between native-born Protestants and immigrants. Although Gladden rarely used nativist phraseology, his role in such crusades did align him with one group's attempt to impose its values on another.

To secure consistent law enforcement, Gladden threw himself in the 1890s behind the "federal plan" for municipal government. In place of a council whose members shared (and thus avoided) responsibility for overseeing city departments, this plan located executive responsibility in a strong mayor. Gladden brought Brooklyn's mayor Seth Low to Columbus to endorse the plan, marshaled the Board of Trade (whose Committee on Municipal Affairs he chaired), and contributed significantly to its adoption in 1893. He helped popularize the plan nationally through his story "The Cosmopolis City Club." A founder of the National Municipal League in 1894, Gladden continued to seek improvements in city government. In 1896 he brought Theodore Roosevelt to Columbus to speak about his experiences as police commissioner in New York City.

Gladden's agenda for reform included more than a clean administration enforcing the laws. Long before the muckraker Lincoln Steffens investigated the corrupting influence of companies that provided municipal services, Gladden had concluded that they posed a greater threat than working-class lawbreaking. Contracts and franchises for streetcar lines, water plants, gas and coal, street lighting, and public construction were lucrative indeed; and the entire community was at the mercy of the businessmen who received them. In the 1890s Gladden began arguing that cities should own and operate public services that were "natural monopolies." When such "municipal socialism" was impossible, he demanded full publicity about municipal contracts.

The epitome of Gladden's role as a politically active minister occurred in 1900–1902, when he served as an independent alderman. His term coincided with the administrations of Samuel M. Jones in Toledo and Tom L. Johnson in Cleveland, and reforms in the three cities marked the coming of age of Ohio's Progressivism. As chairman of the Committee on Gas and Electricity and a member of the committees on the waterworks, fire department, railroads and viaducts, and sewers and drainage, Gladden demonstrated a penchant for mastering technical issues and realism about goals. Translating Social Gospel ideals into council policies, he worked successfully for a streetcar franchise renewal that gave a significant financial return to the city and low fares to riders, for expansion of the municipally owned electrical plant, and for a new gas contract that protected consumers' interests.

Gladden continued after this experience to be highly visible in the expanding reformist politics of the period. Believing that the cities needed greater authority and flexibility, he promoted municipal home rule until it was endorsed by the Ohio Constitutional Convention in 1912, and thereafter worked, unsuccessfully, to get Columbus's voters to adopt the commission plan.

If Gladden's personal involvement in secular politics was exceptional among the Social Gospel clergy, it was exceptional in degree rather than in kind. In fact, he illustrates the convergences that existed between the Social Gospel and Progressive reforms. Reform-minded people in charitable and settlement circles were often receptive to Social Gospel ideals, as were such politicians as Seth Low, Samuel M. Jones, and Tom L. Johnson at a local level, and Theodore Roosevelt, Woodrow Wilson, and William Jennings Bryan at the national level. They saw Gladden as their counterpart in the ministry, and he saw them as practitioners of an applied Christianity. Both he and they were joined in a social crusade, nourished by religious ideals, to perfect America.

Despite biting indictments of corruption, complacency, and selfishness, and despite positions that were sometimes ahead of public opinion, Gladden was one of this crusade's preeminent moderates. Some of his colleagues in the Social Gospel, such as Francis Greenwood Peabody, who pioneered in social ethics at Harvard Divinity School, were more sanguine about the nation's capitalist direction and championed a more modest reform agenda. Others, such as the Baptist historian and theologian Walter Rauschenbusch, offered a more thorough analysis of the significance of social class, brooded more deeply about collective and institutionalized evil, and saw greater promise in the socialist movement than did Gladden. Like Gladden, Peabody and Rauschenbusch were pragmatists who sought social reconciliation, believed in progress, and adopted gradualistic methods. However, differences in life experiences, temperament, ideology, and social position produced variations in diagnosis, prescription, and style among them and other Social Gospelers.

The optimistic mood and idealistic temper of the Social Gospel—and of Progressivism—did not survive much beyond World War I. Generous hopes for a socialized nation and a democratized, peaceful world, both guided by Christian values, found expression at war's end in the Interchurch World Movement, a brash effort to raise hundreds of millions of dollars for Social Gospel purposes. The movement collapsed in 1920, the victim of postwar financial troubles and a conservative backlash against its pro-union report on the recent steel strike. American Protestants faced novel conditions in the 1920s. Many churches experienced a decline in both members and revenues by mid-decade. Northern Baptists and Presbyterians, and to a lesser extent several other denominations, were riven by theological struggles. Middle-class support for reform suffered erosion, as the pro-business culture of "normalcy" replaced the earlier muckraking spirit. Rightist reaction, manipulated by superpatriotic organizations and conservative business groups, discouraged causes that had seemed respectable a few years before.

The Social Gospel survived, but in truncated form. It had its continuing voices in denominational and ecumenical bureaucracies and in pulpits and lecture halls, and it even took up new causes. But it was no longer the movement it had been when Theodore Roosevelt could launch a political party with a "Confession of Faith" and speak of "standing at Armageddon" and "battling for the Lord." That particular ethos, with its high optimism and moralism, would never be recaptured.

NOTES

1. Washington Gladden, *Recollections* (Boston, 1909), 63.
2. Washington Gladden, "Christianity and Socialism," *Chautauquan* 30 (1899): 140.
3. "Washington Gladden," *Outlook* 82 (27 January 1906): 154–155.
4. Washington Gladden, sermon, "The New Reformation," quoted in *Ohio State Journal*, 7 September 1907.
5. Washington Gladden, *The Church and the Kingdom* (New York, 1894), 6, 13.
6. Washington Gladden, *Social Salvation* (Boston, 1902), 30.
7. "Men and Religion," *Outlook* 100 (30 March 1912): 714–715.
8. Washington Gladden, *The Christian Pastor and the Working Church* (Edinburgh, 1898), 416.
9. Washington Gladden, sermon, 5 October 1897, Washington Gladden Papers (Ohio Historical Society, Columbus).
10. Washington Gladden, *The Church and Modern Life* (Boston, 1908), 146–147.
11. Washington Gladden, *Applied Christianity: Moral Aspects of Social Questions* (Boston, 1886), 155–157.
12. Ibid., 124–125.

13. ''Washington Gladden, sermon, ''Strengths and Weaknesses of Organized Labor,''
28 April 1901, Gladden Papers.

14. Washington Gladden, *The Labor Question* (Boston, 1911), 140.

BIBLIOGRAPHY

Abell, Aaron I. *The Urban Impact on American Protestantism, 1865–1900.* Cambridge, Mass., 1943.

Brown, Ira V. *Lyman Abbott: Christian Evolutionist.* Cambridge, Mass., 1953.

Dorn, Jacob H. *Washington Gladden: Prophet of the Social Gospel.* Columbus, Ohio, 1967.

Ernst, Eldon G. *Moment of Truth for Protestant America: Interchurch Campaigns Following World War One.* Missoula, Mont., 1974.

Gladden, Washington. *Recollections.* Boston, 1909.

Gorrell, Donald K. *The Age of Social Responsibility: The Social Gospel in the Progressive Era, 1900–1920.* Macon, Ga., 1988.

Handy, Robert T., ed. *The Social Gospel in America: Gladden, Ely, Rauschenbusch.* New York, 1966.

Hopkins, Charles Howard. *The Rise of the Social Gospel in American Protestantism, 1865–1915.* New Haven, 1940.

Hudson, Winthrop S., ed. *Walter Rauschenbusch: Selected Writings.* New York, 1984.

Luker, Ralph E. *The Social Gospel in Black and White: American Racial Reform, 1885–1912.* Chapel Hill, N.C., 1991.

McDowell, John Patrick. *The Social Gospel in the South: The Woman's Home Mission Movement in the Methodist Episcopal Church, South, 1886–1939.* Baton Rouge, La., 1982.

Magnuson, Norris. *Salvation in the Slums: Evangelical Social Work, 1865–1920.* Metuchen, N.J., 1977.

May, Henry F. *Protestant Churches and Industrial America.* New York, 1949.

Meyer, Donald B. *The Protestant Search for Political Realism, 1919–1941.* Berkeley, Calif., 1960.

Miller, Timothy. *Following In His Steps: A Biography of Charles M. Sheldon.* Knoxville, Tenn., 1987.

Minus, Paul. *Walter Rauschenbusch: American Reformer.* New York, 1988.

Piper, John F., Jr. *The American Churches in World War I.* Athens, Ohio, 1985.

Sanford, Elias B. *Origin and History of the Federal Council of the Churches of Christ in America.* Hartford, Conn., 1916.

Sharpe, Dores R. *Walter Rauschenbusch.* New York, 1942.

Wade, Louise C. *Graham Taylor: Pioneer for Social Justice, 1851–1938.* Chicago, 1964.

White, Ronald C., Jr. *Liberty and Justice for All: Racial Reform and the Social Gospel (1877–1925).* New York, 1990.

White, Ronald C., Jr., and C. Howard Hopkins, eds. *The Social Gospel: Religion and Reform in Changing America.* Philadelphia, 1976.

Samuel Gompers and the American Federation of Labor

BRIAN GREENBERG

In a debate arranged by the United States Commission on Industrial Relations in 1914, Samuel Gompers, president of the American Federation of Labor (AFL), squared off against Morris Hillquit, a leader of the Socialist party. In the give-and-take of this debate, the two men identified many of the essential differences between the apparently ad hoc pragmatic trade unionism most associated with Gompers and the radical (egalitarian) political and economic transformation of American society pursued by the Socialists. "The intelligent, comprehensive, common-sense workmen" who comprised the membership of the AFL, Gompers lectured Hillquit, preferred "to deal with the problems of today . . . rather than to deal with a picture and a dream which has never had, and I am sure never will have, any reality in the affairs of humanity." But was not the AFL guided by some "general social philosophy," Hillquit challenged Gompers, or did it simply "work blindly from day to day?" As to whether the AFL had "ultimate ends," Gompers responded that in looking to improve the condition of working people, the labor movement was "guided by the history of the past, drawing its lessons from history, to know of the conditions by which the working people are surrounded and confronted. . . . You have an end; we have not."[1] By the time of this debate, history had left Gompers with little patience for all "isms"; as he saw it, the principal task of American trade unions was to achieve better wages and conditions for workers within the existing order.

The stirring clash between Gompers and Hillquit—the former's powerful appeal to American individualism versus the latter's clarion call to collective action and solidarity—represented fundamental differences on aims and methods that had long challenged the American labor movement. Over a century earlier, urban workers had begun organizing collectively both to defend their craft and to secure economic benefits as customary work relations started to change. Although trade unions originated in the impulse to gain better material conditions for individual members, they were, in fact, part of a more broadly based labor reform movement that rallied the "producing classes" against "wage slavery" or the growing fear that wage labor would become a fixed condition in the United States. Many early union leaders doubted that laboring people could preserve their dignity and independence by organization alone. The foremost labor leader of the Civil War era, William Sylvis, hoped to achieve a permanent solution to the problem of labor and capital through reforms such as the eight-hour workday, the greenback movement, and cooperative workshops. By the time of his death in 1869, Sylvis had concluded that workers must stand together at the ballot box as well as in the workplace.

The Knights of Labor, which began in Philadelphia in 1869 as a small craft union of garment cutters, had by the 1880s become the leading alternative labor association to the AFL. Unlike the national craft unions that comprised the AFL, the Knights welcomed all wage earners regardless of skill, race, or gender, and urged workers from different trades and industries to join together in local and district assemblies. Under the leadership of Terence V. Powderly, a machinist who also served as mayor of Scranton, Pennsylvania, the Knights insisted that workers' posture toward the existing order was "necessarily one of war." But rather than engage in unrelenting economic battle forever, the Knights sought to establish a new, more cooperative, industrial society in America.

Gompers repudiated the more communal conception of the producing classes that underlay such nineteenth-century labor movements as the Knights of Labor and the National Labor Union, in which Sylvis had played a prominent role. From the outset of his career in the labor movement, Gompers insisted that trade union membership be restricted to wage workers who shared a similar work experience. His faith in the efficacy of trade unions so constructed as the representative agency for American workers was the one constant of his life as a labor leader. With Gompers leading the way, American trade unions developed the institutional scaffolding that put them on a more permanent and businesslike basis. Expressing the conviction that partisan politics would divide workers, Gompers eschewed what he called "labor partyism," the formation of independent political movements by labor. Gompers thought of trade unions as "voluntary associations of wage-earners" that best served workers' interests by fostering individual initiative and discouraging reliance on the actions of government. Opposition by the labor movement to the concentration of corporate economic power in the United States, he came to believe, was futile. To be effective, workers had to fashion trade unions as counterorganizations capable of dealing with capital on an equal footing. This would not happen, in his view, until they centralized authority and developed a practical administrative system as well as focused on winning tangible benefits for members. Only when trade unions achieved a balance of power with capital could they, through collective bargaining, secure members' material needs: higher wages, shorter hours, and better working conditions.

In his young manhood Gompers, who had been influenced by Marxian and radical ideas, had embraced an ambitious concept of class struggle, one that assumed that the economic interests of the employing class and those of the working class were in conflict, and that a fundamental change in American society was needed if workers were ever to achieve economic justice. Initially, in common with other nineteenth-century labor leaders, Gompers associated unionism with the basic restructuring of society in America. In 1889, during the Brooklyn street-railway workers' strike, he had written to a correspondent that the mission of unions was to be ''the remnant which saves society from demoralization and preserves the liberties of people.''[2] By the beginning of the new century, however, Gompers was the acknowledged symbol of a pure-and-simple trade unionism operated along business principles. In his view, the organization of labor, once an agency to maintain ''past achievements and further our advancement and our civiliza[tion],'' had become the saving remnant, a vehicle for achieving ''more,'' not for the mass of workers but for a privileged segment of the working class—largely white, male, craft workers who were either native born or from ''old'' immigrant groups.[3] Left out were black and female wage earners as well as most unskilled workers in mass-production industries.

Gompers's evolution as a trade union leader was not a steady progression from radical youth to conservative elder statesman. Gompers upheld the basic tenets of pure-and-simple trade unionism throughout his life. But early in his career his labor philosophy was leavened with contradictory, often more radical, impulses. What would change was Gompers's conception of what constituted labor's best interests. Essentially, his point of view moved from one that was relatively open and inclusive to one that was doctrinaire and narrowly focused. Gompers's involvement in Henry George's 1886 United Labor party mayoralty campaign in New York City is a case in point. In an interview with a reporter from *The Leader*, a newspaper associated with the George campaign, Gompers seemed unaware of the paradoxical nature of what he was doing. On the one hand, he expressed agreement ''with most advanced thinkers'' in the ultimate objective of abolishing the wage system; on the other, he evinced little regard for single-tax reform, the core of George's social ideas. Gompers also had no problem reconciling his long-standing opposition to labor's involvement in partisan politics with the active role he was playing in this campaign. In comparison, there is a greater uniformity to the ideas that he articulated later in life. By the time of his debate with Hillquit nearly thirty years later, Gompers hewed to a more dogmatic, pure-and-simple trade unionism.

The eldest child of Dutch-Jewish immigrant parents—Solomon and Sarah Rood Gompers—Samuel Gompers was born 26 January 1850, in Spitalfields, a poor silk-weaving district in East London. The family's poverty forced him to leave school at age ten. After a brief apprenticeship to a shoemaker, Gompers began working for a cigarmaker, his father's trade. The family's economic circumstances continued to deteriorate, and they decided to emigrate to the United

States, where they had friends and relatives and where the cigar trade was expanding. With help from an emigration fund created by the Cigarmakers' Society of England, the Gompers family set sail on 10 June 1863 for New York on the *City of London*.

It must have been difficult for Gompers to believe that immigration to America had improved the family's prospects. The family settled into the ethnically diverse Lower East Side of Manhattan; their first home faced a slaughterhouse across the street and had a brewery at its back. Although the Gompers family would move frequently over the next two decades, each time "seeking some little improvement in comfort or rent," they would always live in packed tenements within this notoriously overcrowded and squalid part of New York.[4]

Sam began making cigars in the workshop his father set up in the front room of their first apartment. Eighteen months later, at age sixteen, he left to work in a nearby cigarmaking shop where he apparently became a shop leader, called on to present the workers' grievances to their employer. Both he and his father belonged to Cigarmakers' Local Union No. 15. Yet young Sam had joined, he later wrote, more out of a sense of obligation than of conviction. Gompers recalled his early days fondly: "I loved the freedom of that work . . . .Often we chose someone to read to us who was a particularly good reader . . . .The reading was always followed by discussion, so we learned to know each other pretty thoroughly."[5]

During this time Gompers met and married Sophia Julian, who, like him, was a London-born émigré. Sophia, who stripped tobacco leaves in the same shop as Sam, was only sixteen years old when they married. In his *Autobiography*, Gompers makes it appear that their decision to embark on matrimony was something of a lark. After being married by a justice of the peace at City Hall in Brooklyn, the newlyweds went to a "cheap" restaurant for "a bite to eat as our wedding supper." They then attended a play, after which Sam took Sophia to her home and returned alone to his. A decidedly public man, Gompers, in his *Autobiography*, devotes only one chapter of forty-seven to what he calls "Things Personal." When Sophia is mentioned, she is described as a "helpmate" who, like the other "wives of men who have devoted themselves to the labor movement," is esteemed for having endured sacrifice and hardship without complaint.[6]

However much Gompers enjoyed his work, during the 1860s and 1870s the craft of cigarmaking was undergoing a transformation. At first, cigarmaking in New York had been dominated by small craft shops, each with from one to four workers. But as cigar smoking became more popular among Americans, the industry expanded dramatically. Larger firms became more common, and new equipment such as cigar molds and power-driven bunching machines was introduced. The transition from craft to industrial production devalued the skill of the individual cigarmaker and led to the hiring of cheap labor, especially women and recent European immigrants from regions such as Bohemia. By the first decade of the twentieth century, large-scale production had spread to the point that huge firms, some with more than a thousand workers, had virtually replaced the smaller shops in Manhattan.

Into the 1870s most immigrant cigarmakers in New York affiliated with their fraternal or mutual aid societies rather than with Local 15. In 1872 Gompers joined with a fellow cigarmaker, Adolph Strasser, a German-speaking Hungarian immigrant who had only recently come to America, and others to bring new leadership to the city's cigarmakers' labor movement. Initially, they tried to organize an independent union of cigarmakers; in 1875 they affiliated with Local 144, Cigar Makers' International Union of America (CMIU). Striving to be inclusive, Gompers advocated bringing "all elements working in our trade into one Organization, for the wrongs heaped upon one element today are merely the precursor for another to morrow."[7] At the same time, however, Gompers and Strasser were promoting measures, such as high dues and the elimination of separate foreign-language sections, that would likely be barriers for the workers they targeted. A similar compromise of principle occurred at the 1880 Chicago convention of the CMIU. There Gompers spoke in favor of a proposal that "No local union shall permit the rejection of an applicant for membership on account of sex, color, or system of work." But when opposition to this legislation arose, he allowed the issue to be left to the discretion of the local unions.[8]

Strasser became president of the CMIU in 1877. Both he and Gompers introduced reforms to transform the CMIU from a "combination of local unions, very loosely connected" into a disciplined and centrally directed national union.[9] The preamble to the union's new constitution, adopted in 1879, offers evidence of the sort of practical trade unionism that Gompers advanced throughout his life. As "the capital of the country becomes more and more concentrated in the hands of the few," so must labor unify and focus its efforts. Labor's "only hope" lay in organization, and the cigarmakers had to organize as quickly as possible: "We are no theorists," and the plan that we offer "is no visionary plan, but one that is eminently practicable." Charging uniform dues, providing travel benefits for members seeking employment, and each quarter equalizing the funds held by local unions were among the necessary tangible benefits that would put trade unions on a "permanent basis." Once assured of permanence, trade unions would be ready to cope with the conditions brought on by modern industrialism.[10]

Practical benefits served the cause of permanence by binding members to the organization. In 1888 Gompers argued in favor of the CMIU's adopting an out-of-work benefit as part of the union's protective and benevolent plan. Rather than losing members in "dull times," the union would be sustained by such benefits because members would "lose too much by leaving the union and [so] don't leave."[11] Or, as one member expressed it, cigarmakers' benefits had a "tendency to create a fraternal and binding effect on us."[12] Both Strasser and Gompers were skeptical of any claim for an inherent class feeling among American workers. Instead, the CMIU's leadership believed that a system of tangible benefits encouraged the formation of bonds among union members based on mutual self-interest.

Gompers's effort to imprint the CMIU with his businesslike, straightforward trade unionist ideas did not go unchallenged. During the early 1880s Strasser and Gompers launched a Local 144-sponsored legislative drive to get a bill passed in the New York State legislature forbidding the manufacture of cigars in tenements. In New York City, families of cigarmakers made cigars by the piece in tenement apartments that they rented from cigar manufacturers, who supplied them with the tobacco. To gain public support, Gompers made a personal survey of the tenements in which cigars were made and reported the deplorable conditions that he found. After two years of vigorous political lobbying and of helping elect sympathetic legislators and defeat those opposed, Local 144 saw its efforts rewarded in 1883 when the state legislature approved a law regulating the manufacture of cigars in tenement houses. However, the legislative victory was not enough, for this law, like another one passed the following year, was declared unconstitutional by the state's courts.

Gompers called Local 144's campaign against tenement labor "a cigar makers' issue, pure and simple, in behalf of which we intend to use our political influence."[13] The decision of the union's leaders to seek legislation that would outlaw tenement work, rather than to organize the industry's largely immigrant and female labor force, exacerbated a developing factional struggle within the union. Cultural and political differences led to the formation in 1882 of the Cigar Makers' Progressive Union (CMPU). Already critical of the English-speaking leadership of Local 144, the CMPU, composed of a diverse group of socialist workers of German and Bohemian backgrounds, also censured Gompers and Strasser for their failure to support the formation of an independent labor party. This sectarian struggle continued until 1886, when the CMPU, facing an attempt by the Knights of Labor to dissolve its separate organization, rejoined the CMIU.

The moral the CMIU leaders drew from the antitenement campaign was that trade unions should seek to accomplish "through economic power what we had failed to achieve through legislation."[14] Stymied by the courts, the CMIU attempted to harass cigar manufacturers into abandoning the tenement manufacturing system. Nevertheless, when cigar production in tenement houses eventually ended, it was more as a consequence of technological change than of the union's actions.

In supporting economic over political action, as in their committed opposition to trade union involvement in a labor party, Gompers and Strasser were joined by a small group of like-minded trade unionists who had come together in the mid-1870s to create a semiofficial association that called itself the Economic and Sociological Club (also referred to as the "No. 10 Stanton Street group"). Members of this club, Gompers observed in his *Autobiography*, expressed their common opposition to subordinating trade unions to any "ism" or political "reform." They regarded trade unions as "the fundamental agency through which we could achieve economic power, which in turn would give us social and political power.'' Pure-and-simple trade unionism was, they declared, a movement especially well suited to the political and economic environment of the United States.[15]

Another member of the Economic and Sociological Club who, like Strasser, had a critical influence on Gompers was Karl Ferdinand Laurrell, an early shop-mate of Gompers and something of a mentor. Laurrell introduced Gompers to the works of Marx, Engels, Ferdinand Lassalle, and other prominent German economic writers. The Marx embraced by Gompers, Laurrell, Strasser, and the others of their circle maintained that American workers had first to develop class organizations based on economic struggle before they could secure political power. Inspired by these ideas, Laurrell would gently remind Sam, ''Study your union card, Sam, and if the idea doesn't square with that, it ain't true.'' Thus, Gompers recalls, ''My trade union card came to be my standard in all new problems.''[16]

Gompers rejected the idea that conciliation between capital and labor was possible until workers were as organized as their employers. After the ''Great Uprising,'' the national railroad strikes of 1877, many public officials across the United States expressed alarm that the growing rift between capital and labor might be permanent. Arbitration appealed to them as a rational alternative to strikes and a means of restoring social harmony. ''Arbitration,'' Gompers told a Senate committee investigating the relations between capital and labor in August 1883, ''is only possible when the workingmen have, by the power of their organization, demonstrated to the employers that they are the employers' equal.''[17] For Gompers, workers must be better organized before they could be ''in a position to defend and protect their rights.'' Only then could arbitration be considered.[18]

In the aftermath of the setback to the CMIU's campaign against tenement labor, Gompers saw the need to concentrate on ''organization work'' instead of legislative efforts. Nevertheless, he led the effort in 1881 to establish the Federated Organization of Trades and Labor Unions (FOTLU). Greatly influenced by the British Trade Union Congress, 69 American organizations sent 107 delegates to a meeting in Pittsburgh on 15 November 1881 to launch, as Gompers later wrote, some kind of ''national amalgamation'' of trade unionists to replace the National Labor Union (NLU). According to the plan of organization adopted by these delegates, the federation's ''objects are to encourage and form trade and labor unions, and secure legislation in the interest of labor.''[19] The new organization's Declaration of Principles called for laws permitting trade unions to be chartered and recognized as legal bodies, the compulsory education of all children, laws prohibiting employment of children under the age of fourteen in any capacity, the establishment of a bureau of labor statistics, the imposition of protective tariffs, and the abolition of tenement manufacture of cigars.

From his key position as head of the FOTLU's Legislative Committee, Gompers sought to shape the program that the federation would follow. Most important to him was "to keep this new organization free from taint" by excluding "all political partisan action" from FOTLU deliberations. In his *Autobiography*, Gompers cites the conviction of "our No. 10 Stanton Street group" that trade unions had to concentrate on the development of economic power and that political discussion would simply dissipate organizational energy.[20]

Gompers was disappointed by the FOTLU. By mid-decade he had become convinced, as had others, that "We needed a consolidated organization . . . .As year by year we learned the inadequacy of our program we tried to revise our constitution to authorize action in the economic field. Now the time had come to stop patchwork and rebuild."[21] With these goals in mind, the American Federation of Labor (AFL) emerged out of the 1886 FOTLU congress.

Whereas the FOTLU had been meant to function mainly as a labor lobby, the AFL was developed as an organization of trade union groups. The AFL's constitution called for the formal chartering of federation affiliates and the "strict recognition of the autonomy of each trade."[22] Conscious of the administrative shortcomings of the old federation, the AFL-affiliated unions established a stronger financial system, replacing the FOTLU's annual assessment with a monthly per capita tax, as well as providing for a full-time president, at an initial annual salary of $1,000, to administer the organization. Elected in 1886 as the AFL's first president, Gompers remained in office, except for a brief "sabbatical" in 1895, until his death almost forty years later.

Reflecting on the AFL's founding in his *Autobiography*, Gompers compared the organization to a "rope of sand and yet the strongest human force—a voluntary association united by common need and held together by mutual self-interest."[23] But discovering how to foster unity and build a secure organization without violating craft autonomy—the commitment to member unions' "self-government within their particular trade"—was Gompers's first and ongoing test as president of the AFL.[24] More than just reform of the FOTLU's administrative structure was needed. Gompers settled on an AFL-led eight-hour campaign to do the job. Knowing that, whatever their ethnic or political differences, most workers supported this reform, Gompers hoped to use the eight-hour campaign to unify the membership as well as to publicize and promote the AFL's program.

Gompers's confidence in the enthusiasm of AFL's members for an eight-hour workday was well founded. Throughout the nineteenth century, American workers had repeatedly joined in demands for a shorter workday. Ira Steward, a Boston machinist and the father of the eight-hour movement in the mid-1800s, saw the shorter workday as a critical first step to workers' political and economic independence. Still, despite some success prior to the 1880s, most notably an 1868 federal eight-hour law covering government employees (which was, at best, irregularly enforced), shortening the workday had proved to be an elusive goal.

Gompers had helped draft a FOTLU resolution that set 1 May 1886 as the date for general adoption of eight hours as a day's work. Left unsettled, however, was how to implement this demand. Whereas the exact proportions of what took place on 1 May remain unclear, there was unmistakably a massive outpouring of support for the eight-hour day. According to one recent estimate, some 90,000 demonstrators marched through the streets in most major cities across the United States, and 30,000 to 40,000 workers struck on behalf of eight hours. Gompers, speaking before a reported crowd of 10,000 in Union Square in New York City, celebrated the day's events as a complete success. Three days later, at the end of a mass rally called in support of an eight-hour strike in Chicago, a bomb exploded in Haymarket Square, initiating a wave of anti-radical hysteria that effectively brought to a close this phase of the eight-hour movement.

Despite Haymarket, Gompers urged the AFL to take on the issue. In response, the 1888 AFL conference fixed 1 May 1890 as the day "upon which working-men will demand that eight hours constitute a day's work."[25] The federation also called for a series of mass meetings (on Washington's Birthday, Independence Day, and Labor Day), and authorized publication and wide distribution of pamphlets and other materials to educate and elicit public support. Gompers wrote to the secretary of the AFL, P. J. McGuire, that in developing publicity for the eight-hour campaign, the AFL should not lose "the opportunity to get something out that will live in history."[26]

Even with the nearly thousand public meetings that Gompers reported as being held in 1889 alone, the AFL's campaign for an eight-hour day never developed into a cohesive mass movement. Led by its Executive Council, the AFL adopted a conservative strategy of limiting its activity on behalf of a shorter workday to one or two trades each year. Having optimistically launched the eight-hour campaign as a means of creating organizational unity, Gompers found himself facing member insistence on craft autonomy. And, as usual when caught between contradictory forces, Gompers allowed his pragmatism to overrule his principles.

In March 1890 the United Brotherhood of Carpenters and Joiners of America was chosen by the Executive Council to lead the way on eight hours. Although the Carpenters and Joiners' campaign produced some concessions, the AFL-led movement ended abruptly when the next standard-bearer, the United Mine Workers of America, failed to take up the issue. After this debacle, the AFL no longer played any significant role as an organization in the movement to secure a shorter workday.

As his high hopes for the AFL's eight-hour campaign faded, Gompers began recasting his arguments favoring this reform. At first he articulated a view of eight-hour reform in accord with the ideals expressed by Ira Steward. Testifying at the 1883 hearings of the Senate Committee on Education and Labor, Gompers, citing Steward, told the politicians that "if you wish to improve the condition of the people, you must improve their habits and customs." Like Steward, Gompers linked the opportunity for greater leisure afforded by a shorter workday to the raising of workers' standard of living. Only when workers had sufficient time for rest and contemplation could they fully appreciate their condition and make the necessary demands to change it. The general reduction of the daily hours of labor to eight would, Gompers anticipated, "create a better spirit in the working man; it would make him a better citizen. . . . A man who works the eight hour day possesses more independence both economically and politically." Gompers concluded, "The reduction of the hours of labor reaches the very root of society."[27]

Through the 1880s, Gompers continued to connect the moral and intellectual advantages afforded workers by a shorter workday to the possibility of fundamental economic and social change. Yet even as he articulated a vision of eight-hour reform compatible with Steward's, he retained the pragmatic notion that for the AFL the essential utility of this campaign was as a rallying cry uniting workers behind the new organization: "Eight hours is the cry which can unite all forces at least for the present and will check the indifference and want of confidence too prevalent today."[28] Nor had Gompers, whether he was speaking of eight-hour reform in terms of Steward's ideals or in terms of its more immediate tactical value to the AFL, abandoned his faith in voluntarism. Having adopted an eight-hour law, the federal government should see that it was "faithfully executed." However, the government's role did not extend to "private employments"; eight hours was a question best settled between "ourselves and our employers."[29]

In the 1890s Gompers began to emphasize reducing the workday as a means of spreading employment. In August 1894 he complained to a federal judge that the introduction of machinery was "turning into idleness thousands faster than new industries are founded." Should workers, he asked, "sit idly by and see the vast resources of nature and the human mind be utilized and monopolized for the benefit of the comparatively few?" Of course not. They must learn that "only by the power of organization and common concert of action can either their manhood be maintained, their rights to life (work to sustain it) be recognized and liberty and rights secured."[30] Organization was always foremost among Gompers's priorities.

Gompers never tired of proclaiming his faith in trade unions as the "legitimate outgrowth of our system." A dominant fact of that system, "the unity of Capital," the AFL Executive Council concluded in 1888, demanded "the unity of Labor." These facts of modern industrial society were forced upon the consciousness of wage workers, they continued, and "we must recognize these facts or the facts will crush us."[31] Gompers obviously agreed, and by the mid-1890s, he had clearly returned to the more comfortable ground of promoting trade unions as pure-and-simple counterorganizations to concentrated capital.

Gompers's rededication to achieving immediate and tangible results through trade union organization was not solely a result of the member unions' lack of enthusiasm for a broad-based eight-hour campaign by the AFL. Beginning with the Haymarket riot, a series of frequently violent labor confrontations, often ending with the forceful intervention of government troops, reinforced not only

Gompers's antistatism but also his sense of the power and commitment of the forces arrayed against labor. In his memoirs he referred to the iron- and steelworkers' 1892 Homestead strike as the AFL's "first big struggle with a modern industrial corporation" and concluded that "this was the beginning of the policy of antagonism to trade unions followed by the Steel Corporation, which included maintenance of an excessive working force, the majority of whom were recent immigrants and hostile to organized labor."[32] What stood out in the Homestead strike was the sheer determination of the steel masters to break the union.

Two years later, while the nation was in the midst of an industrial depression, organized labor again found itself confronting employers in a major industry— the railroads. In 1894 Pullman Company workers belonging to the American Railway Union (ARU), which had been organized as an industrial union (in contrast to the existing railway craft brotherhoods), went out on strike. The ARU battled both George Pullman and the General Managers Association (GMA), a trade group of twenty-four lines serving Chicago, to a standstill until the GMA connived to get federal troops sent in to break the strike. Shortly afterward, Gompers convened a conference of labor organizations at the Briggs House in Chicago to consider how to respond. Rejecting an appeal for a general strike from Eugene Debs, a founder of the ARU and the recognized leader of the Pullman strike, the assembled labor leaders in a public statement asked rhetorically, "Against this array of armed force and brutal moneyed aristocracy would it not be worse than folly to call men out on general or local strikes in these days of stagnant trade and commercial depression?"[33] Wary of getting unions caught up in mass movements, Gompers concluded from the antilabor onslaughts in the 1890s that what the AFL needed to do was hold the line. What this meant in practice was that the AFL must maintain its unwavering support for the primacy of economic over political action and encompass an increasingly narrowly defined craft unionism.

Gompers's view of what was best for organized labor and the AFL under the conditions imposed by modern industrial society provoked opposition, led by Socialist members. The question of independent political action was the main issue on the agenda at the 1894 AFL convention in Denver. Debate centered on a resolution, supported by the Socialists and fought by Gompers, that would have committed the AFL to the organization of an independent labor party. Believing that partisan politics had in the past only distracted and not advanced the labor movement, Gompers, in his presidential address, urged the delegates to "steer our ship of labor safe from that channel whose waters are strewn with shattered hopes and unions destroyed."[34] Although Gompers surmounted this challenge to his leadership, he did not emerge unscathed. At this convention his opponent for president was John McBride, president of the United Mine Workers Union; when the ballots were counted, Gompers had been defeated. Thus began what Gompers would refer to in his *Autobiography* as "My Sabbatical Year."

From the organization's beginnings, socialist trade unionists, in varying guises, attempted to liberate the AFL from Gompers's control. At the 1890 convention the conflict between federation members affiliated with the Socialist Labor party (SLP) and the AFL came to a head. At this time Gompers responded that "the man who would accuse me or charge me with being anti-Socialist, simply says that that [*sic*] he don't know anything about, he does not know Sam Gompers. I say here broadly and openly that there is not a noble hope that a Socialist may have that I do not hold as my ideal. There is not an inspiring and ennobling end that they are striving for that my heart does not beat in response to. But our methods are different."[35] The difference over methods in terms of trade union policy was critical, and Gompers succeeded at this convention in excluding SLP representatives from membership in the AFL.

In response to largely the same events of the late 1880s and early 1890s that had deeply affected Gompers, Eugene Debs, after the Pullman strike, helped found the Social Democracy of America, a political party endorsing socialism. On 1 January 1897, in an open letter to the membership of the ARU, Debs proclaimed: "The issue is Socialism versus Capitalism. I am for Socialism because I am for humanity. . . . The time has come to regenerate society—we are on the eve of universal change." Indicting corporate capital for its "revolutionary transformation of American society," Debs hoped to inspire a trade union revolution for all workers rooted in this country's democratic traditions.[36]

In contrast, Gompers, after being reelected as president of the AFL in 1895, began a process of accommodation with corporate realities in America by making a clean break with his socialist and radical past. Writing of the founding convention of the Social Democracy of America in an editorial in the *American Federationist*, the AFL's official journal, Gompers stated that he saw nothing "new or novel" in this gathering and predicted that only "defeat, hopes deferred, aspirations destroyed and courage frozen" would be the result of this movement. All such efforts to find "a 'shorter route' out of the industrial miasmic atmosphere into the haven and elysium of social happiness" lose sight of the incontrovertible fact that "modern industry and commerce admits of no side show or small competitor. The struggle for the attainment of labor's rights, for justice to the toilers, must be waged *within* modern society and upon the field of modern industry and commerce." This must be the struggle of the labor movement, according to Gompers, and though progress might be slow, it was yet "fastest, truest" and most successful when conducted by trade unions.[37]

At the AFL's 1903 convention in Boston, Gompers's break with the Socialists reached "a sort of climax." The Socialist members of the AFL introduced ten different resolutions that aimed to bring about "some phase" of the cooperative commonwealth. To this effort Gompers responded: "I want to tell you, Socialists, that I have studied your philosophy; read your works upon economics . . . studied your standard works. . . . I know, too, what you have up your sleeve. And I want to say that I am entirely at variance with your philosophy. I declare to you, I am not only at variance with your doctrines, but with your philosophy. Economically, you are unsound; socially you are wrong; industrially you are an impossibility.''[38] Unlike Debs, Gompers had come to view the power of large-scale corporations as inescapable, and he committed the AFL to winning acceptance from business for trade unions as a legitimate agency within modern industrial America.

In his *Autobiography*, Gompers declared that having successfully met the many challenges of the 1890s, the AFL "had developed discipline as an essential of trade unionism. With discipline the movement emerged from confusion of thinking and practice to a definite trade union philosophy."[39] In defining this philosophy Gompers observed, "I saw no reason why it was not just as practical for employes to mobilize and control their economic power as a counter-move. The force of such economic organization would interpose a protecting barrier against arbitrary employers who failed to understand that those who supplied human labor for industries were human beings, and thus make possible the development of constructive methods."[40] Capital was organized, and to be effective, so must labor be. But it must be organized along principles of the strictest pragmatism. According to Gompers, collective bargaining did not mean wage-earners control of industry: "It proposes that employees shall have the right to organize and deal with the employer through selected representatives as to wages and working conditions."[41] Gompers's prescription for trade unionism in America consisted of, in equal measures, a practical business administrative system that enabled unions to sustain contractual relations with employers and an adherence to voluntary principles and nonpartisan political practices.

The organization that Gompers entrusted with enabling the labor movement to fill this prescription was the National Civic Federation (NCF). A tripartite conservative reform association founded by financial and corporate leaders in 1900, the NCF brought these business leaders together with representatives of trade unions and the public. Gompers was named vice president at the founding of the NCF and held this position until his death on 13 December 1924. He maintained that the NCF accepted the trade union as a "legitimate" social organization, the equal of the church and of business in American life. The Gompers who debated Hillquit had come to see the solution of the wage system in America as more wages. Trade unions, by continually striving for "more," for practical improvements, were, in his view, the "natural" organization for workers in America.

Gompers wanted more than simply to earn respectability for workers. What he sought from capital, and eventually from government, was acceptability. Despite Gompers's reluctance for labor to have an active partisan political role, in the twentieth century both the AFL and he personally became more rather than less involved in the political arena. Because Gompers's antistatist voluntarism meant that unions must never seek "at the hands of government what they could accomplish by their own initiative and activities," during the Progressive era the AFL opposed legislation that would have provided workers with government-funded unemployment compensation and social security benefits. But in the early 1900s, in the wake of numerous court decisions that aided an open-shop drive by employers by severely proscribing union activities, Gompers was forced to seek political allies. This led him to forge an alliance with Woodrow Wilson, an association that helped produce sympathetic labor legislation, particularly the Clayton Anti-Trust Act (1914). But this act was certainly not "Labor's Magna Carta," as Gompers would claim; unions had failed to secure legal recognition of their collective bargaining rights and still faced repeated use of injunctions against them. Gompers's desire to stake out a legitimate role for labor had involved him in the activities of the NCF before World War I. During the war, this quest led him to serve on the National War Labor Board and afterward to participate in the peace conference at Versailles.[42]

Initially, Gompers's accommodationist program appeared to pay off. Between 1897 and 1903 union membership increased fourfold, reaching 2 million. Of greater consequence, AFL membership became concentrated in the nation's smaller firms and actually declined in the larger industries at the center of the economy. With the ascendence of William Green to the federation's presidency in 1924, the organization remained true to Gompers's legacy of business unionism. The AFL under Green's leadership willingly offered to collaborate with employers in implementing scientific management and measures promoting industrial efficiency. But corporate employers, especially those in basic industries, had other ideas. Under what was called the "American Plan," they led an assault on labor, forming company unions and providing their employees with the tangible benefits—such as pension plans, bonuses, and improved working conditions—that had long been goals of the AFL. Unorganized workers remained unorganized as total untion membership declined during the 1920s to its lowest level since World War I. Hardest hit were the United Mine Workers (UMW), the International Association of Machinists (IAM), and other AFL affiliates in the more modern basic industries. More and more, the AFL came to represent a steadily shrinking segment of the industrial workforce.

As the "lean years" of the 1920s turned into the "turbulent years" of the Great Depression, an alternative to the AFL emerged in the form of the Congress of Industrial Organizations (CIO). Led by insurgents from within the AFL, especially John L. Lewis, president of the UMW, and by militant and frequently radical workers in mass production from outside the federation, the CIO organized the vast numbers of workers whose gender, race, or skill had barred them from the older federation. But even these "new unionists" of the CIO willingly traded an active role in management for the more immediate material gains brought by seniority rights and grievance procedures. Moreover, after 1935, with the implementation of the Wagner Act, the relation of capital and labor, or of employer and employee, was increasingly defined by collective bargaining, which had been Gompers's long-held aspiration. A relatively brief period of grudging acceptance of unions by employers followed the end of World War II. Since the early 1970s, however, management has reverted to the open-shop stance (shorn of much of its paternalism) that had characterized its approach to labor during the 1920s. Evoking Hillquit's challenge to Gompers during their

1914 debate, former president of the United Auto Workers (UAW), Douglas Fraser, admonished the labor movement "to get basic protection not only under the collective bargaining agreement but under the laws of the land."[43] To accomplish this objective, the labor movement must recapture the sense of social mission that is its birthright.

NOTES

1. Leon Litwack, *The American Labor Movement* (Englewood Cliffs, NJ, 1962), 37–42; Gerald Emanuel Stearn, ed., *Gompers* (Englewood Cliffs, NJ, 1971), 52–58; Morris Hillquit, Samuel Gompers, and Max J. Hayes, *The Double Edge of Labor's Sword* (New York, 1971); Bernard Mandel, *Samuel Gompers: A Biography* (Yellow Springs, Ohio, 1963), 328–30; Daniel Bell, *Marxian Socialism in the United States* (Princeton, 1952), 35. Alice Kessler-Harris, "Trade Unions Mirror Society in Conflict Between Collectivism and Individualism," *Monthly Labor Review* 110 (August 1987): 32–40, greatly aided my understanding of the duality of labor's heritage.

2. Stuart B. Kaufman, et al., eds., *The Samuel Gompers Papers*, vol. 2, *The Early Years of the American Federation of Labor, 1887–90* (Urbana, Ill., 1987), 196.

3. Ibid.

4. Stuart B. Kaufman, et al., eds., *The Samuel Gompers Papers*, vol. 1, *The Making of a Union Leader, 1850–86* (Urbana, Ill., 1986), 4.

5. Samuel Gompers, *Seventy Years of Life and Labor*, 2 vols. (1925; repr. New York, 1967), vol. 1, 45.

6. Ibid., 35–41, 479, 493–516.

7. *The Samuel Gompers Papers*, vol. 1, 77–78.

8. Gompers, *Seventy Years of Life and Labor*, vol. 1, 169.

9. As quoted in *The Samuel Gompers Papers*, vol. 1, 72.

10. Ibid., 71–73, 140–142; Stuart B. Kaufman, *Samuel Gompers and the Origins of the American Federation of Labor* (Westport, Conn., 1973), 93, 95, 117–118.

11. *The Samuel Gompers Papers*, vol. 2, 144–145.

12. Patricia A. Cooper, *Once a Cigar Maker: Men, Women, and Work Culture in American Cigar Factories, 1900–1919* (Urbana, Ill., 1987), 98.

13. *The Samuel Gompers Papers*, vol. 1, 171.

14. Gompers, *Seventy Years of Life and Labor*, vol. 1, 194–197.

15. Ibid., vol. 1, 207–210; Kaufman, *Samuel Gompers and the Origins*, 132–133.

16. Gompers, *Seventy Years of Life and Labor*, vol. 1, 75.

17. *The Samuel Gompers Papers*, vol. 1, 349.

18. Ibid., vol. 3, 192, 303–304.

19. Gompers, *Seventy Years of Life and Labor*, vol. 1, 224.

20. Ibid., vol. 1, 229–230.

21. Ibid., 264.

22. *The Samuel Gompers Papers*, vol. 1, 468.

23. Gompers, *Seventy Years of Life and Labor*, vol. 1, 333.

24. *The Samuel Gompers Papers*, vol. 1, 468; vol. 2, 119, 122.

25. Ibid., vol. 2, 163–173.

26. Ibid., 188.

27. Ibid., vol. 1, 315–318.

28. Kaufman, *Samuel Gompers and the Origins*, 176.

29. *The Samuel Gompers Papers*, vol. 1, 322–323.

30. Ibid., vol. 3, 556.

31. Ibid., vol. 2, 121–122.

32. Gompers, *Seventy Years of Life and Labor*, vol. 1, 338–340.

33. *The Samuel Gompers Papers*, vol. 3, 535–538.

34. Ibid., xxi, 419–421.

35. Ibid., vol. 2, 400–401.

36. Nick Salvatore, *Eugene V. Debs: Citizen and Socialist* (Urbana, Ill., 1982), 134, 151–156, 161–162.

37. Stuart B. Kaufman, et al., eds., *The Samuel Gompers Papers*, vol. 4, *A National Labor Movement Takes Shape, 1895–98* (Urbana, Ill., 1991), 360–362.

38. Gompers, *Seventy Years of Life and Labor*, vol. 1, 396–397.

39. Ibid., vol. 1, 375.

40. Ibid., vol. 2, 1–2.

41. Charles C. Heckscher, *The New Unionism: Employee Involvement in the Changing Corporation* (New York, 1988), 20.

42. James R. Green, *The World of the Worker: Labor in Twentieth-Century America* (New York, 1980), 48–49.

43. Kessler-Harris, ''Trade Unions Mirror Society,'' 35.

BIBLIOGRAPHY

Bell, Daniel. *Marxian Socialism in the United States*. Princeton, 1952.

Commons, John R., et al. *History of Labor in the United States*. 4 vols. New York, 1919–1935.

Cooper, Patricia A. *Once a Cigar Maker: Men, Women, and Work Culture in American Cigar Factories, 1900–1919*. Urbana, Ill., 1987.

Diggins, John P. *The American Left in the Twentieth Century*. New York, 1973.

Dubofsky, Melvyn. *Industrialism and the American Worker, 1865–1920*. New York, 1975.

Gompers, Samuel. *Seventy Years of Life and Labor*. 2 vols. 1925; repr. New York, 1967.

———. *Seventy Years of Life and Labor: An Autobiography*. Edited by Nick Salvatore. Ithaca, N.Y., 1984.

———. *The Samuel Gompers Papers*. Edited by Stuart B. Kaufman et al. 4 vols. Urbana, Ill., 1986–1991.

Hattam, Victoria C. *Labor Visions and State Power: The Origins of Business Unionism in the United States*. Princeton, 1993.

Heckscher, Charles C. *The New Unionism: Employee Involvement in the Changing Corporation*. New York, 1988.

Hillquit, Morris, Samuel Gompers, and Max J. Hayes. *The Double Edge of Labor's Sword*. New York, 1971.

Kaufman, Stuart. *Samuel Gompers and Origins of the American Federation of Labor, 1848–1896*. Westport, Conn., 1973.

Laslett, John H. M. ''Samuel Gompers and the Rise of American Business Unionism.'' In Melvyn Dubofsky and Warren Van Tine, eds. *Labor Leaders in America*. Urbana, Ill., 1987, 66–88.

Laurie, Bruce. *Artisans into Workers: Labor in Nineteenth-Century America*. New York, 1989.

Litwack, Leon, ed. *The American Labor Movement*. Englewood Cliffs, N.J., 1962.

Livesay, Harold C. *Samuel Gompers and Organized Labor in America*. Boston, 1978.

Mandel, Bernard. *Samuel Gompers: A Biography*. Yellow Springs, Ohio, 1963.

Roediger, David R., and Philip S. Foner. *Our Own Time: A History of American Labor and the Working Day*. Westport, Conn., 1989.

Rogin, Michael. ''Voluntarism: The Political Functions of an Anti-Political Doctrine.'' In David Brody, ed. *The American Labor Movement*. New York, 1971, 100–18.

Salvatore, Nick. *Eugene V. Debs: Citizen and Socialist*. Urbana, Ill., 1982.

Stearn, Gerald Emanuel, ed. *Gompers*. Englewood Cliffs, N.J., 1971.

Tomlins, Christopher L. *The State and the Unions: Labor Relations, Law, and the Organized Labor Movement in America, 1880–1960*. New York, 1985.

Sylvester Graham
and Health Reform

VINCENT J. CIRILLO

Orthodox medicine in Jacksonian America had relatively little to offer in the way of effective therapeutics. Vigorous treatment with heroic doses of drugs that were dangerous and of unproven value was to Oliver Wendell Holmes the major crime of his profession: "I firmly believe that if the whole materia medica, *as now used*, could be sunk to the bottom of the sea, it would be all the better for mankind,—and all the worse for the fishes."[1] With few exceptions, there were no cures. The role of medicine was to assist and nurse the sick, and to alleviate their suffering to some degree. Medical intervention (e.g., aggressive bloodletting and purging) sometimes resulted in more harm than good. The most common diseases were infectious, but the germ theory, which provided a rational basis for contagion and its prevention, lay in the future. Thus, it is not surprising that the public was skeptical of the benefits of conventional medicine and turned to health reformers whose various diets and regimens promised them longer and healthier lives. Right living, not doctors and drugs, was the certain means to good health.

The passion for health reform was influenced as much by an intense moralism derived from Christian revivalism as by medical science. Health was thought to depend on a proper symbiotic relationship between nature, society, and the individual, and disease was interpreted as resulting from pernicious behavior. Thus, the reformer's role was to discover the factors governing health and to disseminate these findings for the commonwealth.

Sylvester Graham, the quintessential proponent of "Christian Physiology," became one of the most prominent and influential antebellum health reformers. He believed that Americans were suffering in unprecedented numbers from debility, skin and lung diseases, headaches, nervousness, and weakness of the brain—all of which were induced by their ruinous habits. Graham was convinced that good health was rooted in a simple and inexpensive system that anyone could adopt. He urged Americans to eat vegetables, fruits, and coarse, unbolted wheat bread (dubbed Graham bread), and to abstain from meat, spices, coffee, tea, and alcohol. Sexual excess was soon added to his list of forbidden indulgences.

Sylvester Graham, the youngest of seventeen children sired by the Reverend John Graham, Jr., was born in West Suffield, Connecticut, on 5 July 1794. Sylvester's father died when he was only two years old, and his mother, Ruth King Graham, ill and without income, was unable to care for her seven children by John's second marriage. The family disintegrated, and young Sylvester was sent to live with a succession of neighbors and relatives who neglected his schooling and health. Little is known about his youth, except that he was a melancholy child who suffered from dyspepsia and consumption.

After a series of false starts, Graham entered Amherst Academy in Massachusetts, at the late age of twenty-nine, to prepare for the ministry, but he was expelled after only one quarter because of problems related to his arrogant and forceful personality. This episode foreshadowed his lifelong difficulty in dealing with people. In later life, Graham was described by many supporters as conceited, abusive, self-righteous, and insufferably long-winded—attributes that kept people from joining and remaining with his health crusade. After leaving Amherst, he chose to settle, for reasons now unknown, in Little Compton, Rhode Island, where he experienced a nervous breakdown. He was nursed back to health by two daughters of a sea captain named Oliver Potter Earl, and on 19 September 1824 he married Sarah M., the older sister. She brought him a dowry of approximately $1,300.

Still interested in the ministry, Graham studied privately with the Reverend Emerson Paine, the Presbyterian minister who had officiated at his wedding, and was granted a license to preach. In November 1827 he took the pulpit in Belvidere, New Jersey, where he preached until February 1829, when he became the supply minister of the Presbyterian church in Bound Brook, New Jersey. He served in this capacity until 5 May 1830, when the Reverend Ravaud K. Rodgers was installed as the seventh pastor of the church. Apparently Graham was a vegetarian at this time; there are no butcher's bills listed in his private journal of expenses. His records also show that he purchased sacks of wheat flour and wheat meal from local millers, suggesting that the family preferred homemade whole-wheat bread to commercially available white bread.

From 1 October 1825 to 28 April 1826, Graham recorded expenditures for rum, brandy, wine, and gin—"all used by my wife and child while Mrs. G— was nursing my little daughter [Sarah S.?], in spite of my continued remonstrances Mother said it must be."[2] It appears that Sarah Graham was an independent soul who was indifferent to her husband's doctrines. The journal also contains a touching reminder of the tenuousness of life in a laconic remark penned on 8 February 1830: "Paid for Lead Coffin for Little George."[3]

In the summer of 1830 Graham was hired as a lecturer by the Pennsylvania

State Society for the Suppression of the Use of Ardent Spirits (mercifully renamed the Pennsylvania Temperance Society). This was to prove the defining event of his life. Graham immediately put his furniture in storage and moved to Philadelphia, the preeminent city in American medicine. It was famous for the Pennsylvania Hospital (1751), the University of Pennsylvania Department of Medicine (1765), the College of Physicians (1788), Jefferson Medical College (1825), outstanding physicians, excellent clinical facilities, and unsurpassed libraries. During his residence in the City of Brotherly Love, Graham became acquainted with the latest medical concepts, which, combined with his own philosophy, shaped his future career as a health reform lecturer. Physiology provided the scientific basis for his ideas, and the temperance movement enabled him to articulate and develop his theories.

Graham derived his physiological principles from the Paris school of medicine, which greatly influenced the Philadelphia medical profession during the antebellum period. Specifically, the works of the French vitalists Marie-François-Xavier Bichat, an anatomist at the Grand Hospice d'Humanité, and François-Joseph-Victor Broussais, a pathologist at the Val de Grâce, underlay Graham's beliefs in the importance of the gastrointestinal tract in health and disease, the necessity for healthful foods, and the control of passions.

Enlightenment theories of vitalism purported that the phenomenon of life was not explainable simply in terms of chemistry and physics. Animal tissues were imbued with special qualities (e.g., irritability) that did not exist in inanimate forms. An immaterial property—an *anima* or vital principle—distinguished living from nonliving matter. This *causa vitae* inhabited every part of the organism and prevented its spontaneous putrefaction. Early nineteenth-century French vitalists objected to a single ultraphysical force, postulating instead an ensemble of vital properties: sensibility, excitability, and contractility. One of the most striking vital powers was the ability of organisms to respond to environmental stimuli. There were drawbacks, however. Overstimulation caused excessive excitation, producing irritation and inflammation.

In what are probably his most famous words—certainly they were memorable to Graham—Bichat began his *Recherches physiologiques sur la vie et la mort* (1800) with "La vie est l'ensemble des fonctions qui résistent à la mort"(Life is the sum of the functions that withstand death).[4] Thus, the primary purpose of vitalistic laws was to resist destruction. Furthermore, Bichat proposed that the body consisted of separate and autonomous vital systems called animal life and organic life. Wholly internal functions were "organic" (later termed vegetative); the operations by which the body perceived and responded to the external world were termed "animal." Organic life functions included digestion, respiration, circulation, and secretion. Animal life functions included the five senses, voluntary muscles, and the intellect. Although seated in the organic life, the passions (e.g., anger, joy, and sorrow) could modify the actions of animal life. Bichat used the example that fear could precipitate locomotion, anticipating by a century Walter Cannon's adage, "fright, fight or flight." Reproduction was a combination of organic and animal life functions.

Broussais hypothesized that gastroenteritis was the basis of all pathology. Disease was caused by overstimulation by "ingesta" (e.g., food and alcohol) or "percepta" (e.g., moral influences), and the stomach irritation could spread via anastomoses of the thoracic and abdominal ganglionic nerves of organic life to other organs, which would, in turn, experience irregularities of function. Broussais's monistic system of pathology was eventually overturned by Théophile Laennec and Pierre Bretonneau. To his contemporaries, however, Broussais was a progressive thinker, and his work won him many supporters in America.

Graham's reliance on Bichat and Broussais was reinforced by the involvement of Philadelphia's medical profession in the crusade against alcohol abuse. John Bell, a prominent physician with the temperance society who helped Graham construct his physiological theories, aided in the publication in 1826 of the English translation of Broussais's *Traité de physiologie appliquée à la pathologie* (1822). Bell's introduction to this volume was a succinct exposition of Graham's future philosophy of health.

Graham's journal shows that he bought Broussais's *Treatise on Physiology* on 26 January 1831. Over the next three years, he purchased many important medical works on diet, anatomy, and physiology, including William Beaumont's *Experiments and Observations on the Gastric Juice, and the Physiology of Digestion* (1833). Graham applied his newly learned physiological principles in his temperance lectures in order to lend a scientific verisimilitude to his pronouncements on the evils of drink. Overstimulation, so threatening to Christian morality, was now shown to be equally dangerous for the body. Alcohol irritated the stomach, he argued, causing the gastrointestinal mucosa to become inflamed and the circulation to malfunction. The skin did not perspire, and muscles contracted irregularly. Unlike other prominent temperance reformers, such as Lyman Beecher of Connecticut, Graham never discussed the addictive properties of alcohol, for he was concerned solely with its physiological effects.

A lively and impassioned speaker, Graham soon attracted large and enthusiastic audiences, numbering in some instances as many as 2,000 people. His lectures had the characteristics of sermons rather than secular addresses. As public interest increased, Graham's ego swelled and he grew more confident about the validity of his theories. The temperance ideal began to evolve into a more comprehensive theme of sensible living and good health. In January 1831, Graham severed his ties with the temperance society and began lecturing on chastity, courtship and marriage, and diet reform.

Graham moved in 1832 to New York City, where his lectures on the then raging cholera epidemic made him a national figure. Asiatic cholera was a terrifying disease that served as a potent catalyst for public interest in health reform. His followers—who became known as Grahamites—were not in a position to know the facts and believed that Graham's ideas were original. Graham encouraged this belief by stating that his theories were not founded on the opinions of others. The evidence is clear, however, that he borrowed dietary and scientific concepts without acknowledging their source. His indebtedness to Bichat and Broussais is evident throughout his *Lecture on Epidemic Diseases Generally, and Particularly the Spasmodic Cholera* (1833). Graham even began his book in a manner reminiscent of Bichat's when he wrote, "Life is a temporary victory over the causes which induce death."[5] Graham ruled out pestilential essences or living organisms in the etiology of cholera. Instead, he argued that the disease was dependent on human agency and resulted from pernicious dietary and bodily habits. Radical changes in nutrition and sexual behavior were the only effective antidotes to cholera.

All undue excitements and exercises of the mind, and of the passions; all excessive indulgences of the appetites; improper qualities and quantities of food . . . and worst of all, the habitual use of artificial stimulants, such as . . . irritating condiments . . . and particularly . . . alcoholic substances;—all act upon the stomach to disturb its functions, and to impair the health of its nervous and muscular tissues.[6]

Cholera, Graham opined, was a morbid irritation of the alimentary tract caused by intemperance, overindulgence in stimulating food, and venereal excess. Lewdness explained why the cholera epidemic in Paris carried off prostitutes by the hundreds.

When a healthy gastrointestinal tract became irritated, Graham continued, the body relieved the irritation by a mild form of diarrhea. The response to cholera was similar, except more violent, because the body was attempting to purge itself of poisonous impurities. In short, cholera was not the cause but the consequence of poor health. To preserve health and prevent disease, Graham recommended moderation, self-restraint, and a bland diet based on bread made from unbolted wheat. Meat was not totally abandoned at this stage of his career. A small portion of beef or mutton once a day was permissible. Pure water was the only fitting drink. Impure water should be boiled, especially when cholera was prevalent.

Graham contended that no disease was contagious to anyone whose conduct produced a perfectly healthy organic life. That is, the propagation of disease depended less on some exogenous factor than on the predisposition of the human system. Cholera was a symbolic event, an example of America's vulnerability to new forces. Fundamental changes had taken place in society since Graham was a boy. By the 1830s America was becoming more urbanized, commercialized, and materialistic. Health reformers were alarmed over the moral perils of a hostile environment that alienated man from nature and threatened the individual with destruction. The city represented poverty, pollution, crime, and the decline of morality. Such a perception was not necessarily pessimistic. Health reformers, after all, believed in the infinite worthiness of humanity, and that reform would lead to perfection. Only self-control could minimize the impact of this new and frightening world. Mastery of diet and sexual behavior meant mastery over one's destiny.

After 1832 Graham expanded his lectures to include the problems of sexual excesses. He reasoned that temperance should not be limited to drink. Men were intemperate in other ways that violated nature's physiological laws. Subsequently, he published *A Lecture to Young Men* (1834), the first and most influential of the nineteenth-century antimasturbation tracts. It went through many editions and was translated into a number of languages.

Graham condemned sexual activity because its intensity had disastrous individual and social consequences. Natural functions were disrupted, which in turn led to moral, intellectual, and physical degeneracy.

The convulsive paroxysms attending venereal indulgence, are connected with the most intense excitement, and cause the most powerful agitation to the whole system, that it is ever subject to. The brain, stomach, heart, lungs, liver, skin—and the other organs—feel it sweeping over them with the tremendous violence of a tornado . . . .—and this violent paroxysm is generally succeeded by a great exhaustion . . . lassitude, and even prostration.[7]

Masturbation, or self-pollution, was the worst form of venereal indulgence. It provoked gastric irritation, which had profound effects on the other viscera. Graham attributed a farrago of afflictions—including dyspepsia, apoplexy, diabetes, tuberculosis, tooth decay, suppurating blisters, hemorrhoids and insanity—to this solitary vice. The senses were adversely affected, too. Eyesight was enfeebled, smell was impaired, taste and touch were blunted, and "the ear grows dull and hard of hearing . . . and distressing ringing, like the knell of ruined health . . . is the only music which occupies it."[8] Graham further imposed on the reader's credulity when he wrote that self-pollution could lead to the "still more loathsome" crime of homosexuality.

The causes of excessive self-pollution were improper diet and a lack of exercise. Medical science with all its stimulants, tonics, and specifics, however abundantly prescribed, could effect no cure. For relief, the sufferer must scrupulously avoid meat, intoxicating liquors, tobacco, coffee, tea, pepper, ginger, mustard, horseradish, and peppermint. In essence, all kinds of stimulating substances that reduced the vital powers of the nerves of organic life were taboo. It was in his *Lecture to Young Men* that Graham first advocated in print the absolute vegetarianism that became the capstone of his physiological principles.

Farinaceous food, properly prepared . . . and good bread, made of coarsely-ground, unbolted wheat . . . are among the very best articles of diet that such a person can use. . . . No animal food, therefore should be used, in any quantity . . . and no other liquid but pure, soft water . . . should ever be drank [*sic*].[9]

A young man should sleep on a hard mattress, rise early in the morning, take a shower or bath with cold water, and exercise vigorously before breakfast.

Wedlock was no protection. The popular view that any libidinous act was permissible within the marital bonds was erroneous. Sexual excesses within the marriage would result in a similar liability for disease. Here, too, only a proper diet and strict regimen could subdue a carnal appetite, restore constitutional powers, and lengthen life. In general, according to Graham, healthy and robust married men should have sexual intercourse no more than once a month. William Andrus Alcott, a vigorous proponent of health reform and a prolific author of many advice manuals, felt that limiting the frequency of coition was a doctrine ''so utterly at war with the general habits and feelings of mankind'' that it ''excited the public hatred and rendered his name [Graham] a by-word of reproach.''[10]

Not unexpectedly, most male health reformers paid little attention to female sexual excesses. In their eyes, the majority of women were bereft of sexual feelings of any kind. William Acton, a physician, remarked:

What men are habitually, women are only exceptionally. . . . There can be no doubt that sexual feelings in the female is in the majority of cases in abeyance, and that it requires positive and considerable excitement to be roused at all: and even if roused (which in many instances it never can be) it is very moderate compared with that of the male.[11]

The young, rootless, urban male was the symbol of the sexual temptations that endangered the order and structure of society.

Around 1835, Graham ceased lecturing on sex because of its controversial nature and began promoting sound nutrition. He considered this change to be a natural consequence of his discoveries, in view of the fact that a proper diet could mollify sexual desire. At the time, Americans consumed large quantities of meat, especially pork and beef, because of the widespread belief that animal flesh was essential for strength and stamina. Vegetables were overcooked, and bread was saturated with grease. These heavy foods were eaten rapidly and washed down with an assortment of alcoholic beverages. The lack of fresh fruits and vegetables in the cities, resulting from the difficulty in supplying perishable products to urban markets, compounded America's dietary woes. Graham's panacea was the ideal food: bread. Bread made from unbolted wheat meal, coarsely ground (Graham bread), was the health reformer's *deus ex machina* for the salvation of man.

In *A Treatise on Bread and Bread-Making* (1837), Graham lamented that the production and consistency of bread had changed, and that urbanites had become consumers rather than producers of bread. Bread constituted the universal article of prepared food among the ancients. Hippocrates recommended unbolted wheat bread, and Greek athletes ate only this kind of bread in order to strengthen their limbs. According to Graham, the best bread was made of top-quality wheat from which the bran had not been removed. It was to be baked in a brick oven, then allowed to stand on a clean, airy shelf for twenty-four hours before it was eaten. Following these simple rules would ensure a bread of unusual sweetness and richness.

Graham denounced commercial bakers for compromising the public's health by adulterating bread for profit.

Alum, sulphate of zinc, sub-carbonate of magnesia, sub-carbonate of ammonia, sulphate of copper, and several other substances have been used by public bakers in making bread . . . with very great success in the cause of their cupidity . . . even chalk, pipe clay and plaster of Paris, have been employed to increase the weight and whiteness of their bread.[12]

Commercially made bread was inferior to homemade bread. Unscrupulous bakers used old, spoiled flour and harmful additives, and honest ones used superfine flour (with the bran removed). In either case, the result was an unwholesome product that was unpalatable and injurious to the consumer's health. According to Graham, diarrhea, bilious colic, fits, convulsions, and worms could be traced to the use of superfine flour and could be alleviated by switching to coarse, whole-wheat bread.

I have seen cases of chronic diarrhoea of the most obstinate character . . . yielding entirely under a proper general regimen, in which this bread was the almost exclusive article of food, and not a particle of medicine was used.[13]

Graham felt that bakers would never be motivated to make the best bread, because they had no interest in the physical, intellectual, and moral well-being of their customers. Where should one look for such sensibility?

[It] is the wife, the mother only . . . who loves her husband and her children as woman ought to love, and who rightly perceives the relations between the dietetic habits and physical and moral condition of her loved ones . . . she alone [has] the indispensable attributes of a perfect bread-maker.[14]

In the tradition of early Federal days, the mother was depicted as watching the loaf bake as anxiously as she would the cradle of a sick child. Graham idealized a mother he never had.

The *Treatise on Bread* precipitated trouble. In the winter of 1837, a mob inspired by outraged bakers and butchers threatened to attack Graham during a lecture at the Marlborough Hotel in Boston. The constabulary being unequal to the task, Graham's followers subdued the crowd by shoveling slaked lime on them from the upper-story windows. Thereafter the subject of much chaffing, Graham was nicknamed the ''Peristaltic Persuader'' by the press, and tagged ''the prophet of bran bread and pumpkins'' by Ralph Waldo Emerson.

In his magnum opus, *Lectures on the Science of Human Life* (1839), Graham examined a sensation even more insatiable than sexual desire: hunger. Hunger, he wrote, is a true instinctive indication of the alimentary needs of the body. Yet "there cannot be a blinder guide, in regard to quantity of food, than appetite."[15] A morbid appetite, caused by habitual overeating, is no more reliable as a signal for safe eating than a drunkard's thirst is to drinking. Graham considered excessive alimentation as one of the greatest sources of morbidity. Thus, he made a reduction in food consumption a cardinal principle of his system.

Every individual should, as a general rule, restrain himself to the smallest quantity, which he finds from careful investigation and enlightened experience and observation will fully meet the alimentary wants of the vital economy of his system, knowing that whatsoever is more than this is evil![16]

Just as a wife aroused less intense desire and excitement than a mistress, so vegetable foods provoked a more moderate hunger than animal foods. Meat eaters generally ate too much. Craving for meat, like craving for sex, was an unnatural habit. A diet based on meat caused overstimulation, gastric irritation, and debilitation. Vegetarianism reduced destructive sexual urges by depriving the body of overstimulating foods. To Graham's mind, biblical history and scientific evidence proved conclusively that "man is naturally frugivorous and granivorous, or a fruit and vegetable-eating animal."[17]

At that time, the prevailing view was that the anatomical structure of human teeth indicated that humans were omnivorous. John Hunter, the celebrated Scottish anatomist who held that structure was the ultimate expression of function, wrote that human teeth "are fitted for the conversion of both animal and vegetable substances into blood. . . . [Man] ought, therefore, to be considered as a compound, fitted equally to live upon flesh and upon vegetables."[18] The implication was that the vital economy was best served by a mixed diet of meat and vegetables. Further, in 1833 army surgeon William Beaumont published his famous observations on digestion in a patient named Alexis St. Martin, a French-Canadian voyageur suffering from a gunshot-induced gastric fistula. After examining the effects of gastric juice in situ on different foods, one of the most important contributions ever made to practical dietetics, Beaumont concluded that meat was more easily digested than vegetables.

Graham and his disciples could live with such anatomical claims, since tooth morphology indicated only what humans could eat, not what was necessary for good health. On the other hand, they could not ignore Beaumont's findings. Determined to reassess the validity of Beaumont's results, the American Physiological Society, an organization established on 11 February 1837 by laymen devoted to promoting Grahamism, made inquiries concerning the possibility of bringing St. Martin to Boston for "more perfect" investigations. In his tactful reply, dated 29 August 1837, Beaumont noted that although it had always been his desire to have his patient studied by other physiologists, St. Martin

has always refused and positively declared that he would never submit to be experimented upon by any other person or persons than myself, and has ever declined all offers and inducements from individuals and societies to engage him for that purpose.... He is capriciously and foolishly obstinate in that respect, and has always been.[19]

According to Graham, Beaumont's physiological data were imperfect, because the digestibility of food should be measured by the expenditure of vital force, not time. Experience showed that the body was weakened more by meat than by vegetables, because a vegetable diet was less stimulating. Not surprisingly, Graham approved of Beaumont's comments on the injurious effects on the stomach of tea, coffee, and alcohol, and that dyspepsia was due to overeating—all of which supported Grahamism.

Not all scientific data were seen as damaging; some supported vegetarianism. It had been demonstrated in the late 1830s that all tissue nitrogen was obtained from food. Therefore, a nourishing diet had to contain a large amount of nitrogenized foods. The distinguished German chemist Justus von Liebig argued in his pathbreaking *Die Thierchemie oder die Organishe Chemie in ihrer Anwendung auf Physiologie und Pathologie* (1842) that plant and animal proteins were composed of identical fundamental units (termed amino acids about 1850). On 28 June 1841, Liebig wrote to his friend Friedrich Wöhler:

I have been working on the legumin of leguminous plants and have obtained the remarkable result that it is casein [milk protein] in all its properties and its composition. We have therefore a complete analogy, we have plant albumin, plant fibrin, and plant casein, all three identical with each other and with the animal proteins that bear their names.[20]

Grahamites were ecstatic; Liebig's work indicated that a vegetarian diet was nutritionally superior to meat—that is, nitrogen could be absorbed more efficiently from plants than from meat, which originally was formed from plant proteins. Herbivores ate plants, and carnivores ate herbivores, assimilating plant proteins into their blood and tissues. For humans, it was more natural to get nitrogen directly from vegetables than indirectly, after a contaminating passage through an animal's body.

Fired with admiration for the healing power of nature, Graham urged his followers to avoid doctors and drugs. Conventional medicine was the problem rather than the solution. Instead of replacing heroic therapy with milder medicines, Graham rejected drugs altogether, as evil. His solution for health problems was diet, personal hygiene, and sexual continence. Living in accordance with natural laws established by a benevolent God would counterbalance the effects of urban civilization and restore the organic life.

In contrast to the popularity of his previous books, *The Science of Human Life* was not received favorably, and sales were poor. It was too long, too tedious, and too repetitive. To make matters worse, Graham's lectures were no longer drawing crowds. Fellow reformers such as William Andrus Alcott were stealing the day. In addition, in 1840 the American Physiological Society ceased to exist, and the *Graham Journal of Health and Longevity* (founded in April 1837), a magazine of testimonials to the beneficial effects of Grahamism, was absorbed by Alcott's *Library of Health.* Believing that he was a failure, Graham suffered a second nervous breakdown and retired to Northampton, Massachusetts. There he cultivated his vegetable patch, composed melancholy poetry, and became increasingly misanthropic. He never found the inner serenity he praised so often. Sometime toward the end of 1850 he became ill and was treated by an eclectic doctor in a manner that violated Graham's own physiological doctrines. His health failed, and he died on 11 September 1851 after submitting to stimulants, a dose of Congress water, and a tepid bath. Graham was survived by his wife and two children, Sarah S. and Henry Earl. He was predeceased by two children who died young, George and Caroline Elizabeth.

Antediluvian longevity was assumed to be the norm from which the human race had degenerated. Thus, it followed that anyone who obeyed the divinely ordained physiological laws would be rewarded with a patriarchal life span. Imagine how it must have shocked Graham's disciples when their hero died at the relatively early age of fifty-seven. They quickly closed ranks in defense of the virtues of a vegetable diet. Graham, they emphasized, had inherited a frail constitution and had occasionally strayed from his own teachings.

Graham's ideas did not die with him. Vegetarianism, which became an independent hygienic movement, was dominated by his philosophy. Grahamite principles were incorporated into phrenology and hydropathy, and became part of the rituals of the Shakers and Seventh Day Adventists. In the 1860s, Russell Trall's Hydropathic and Hygiene Institute in lower Manhattan sold what was probably the earliest version of the modern graham cracker. Graham boardinghouses were established in many cities; their routine revolved around a strict schedule of meals, exercise, and sleep. Water was the exclusive drink. Tea, coffee, chocolate, fermented malt, distilled liquors, and tobacco were prohibited. The daily fare consisted mainly of graham bread, fruits, and vegetables; some meat (except goose and duck flesh) was grudgingly allowed at lunchtime.

In 1876 the Seventh Day Adventists, who thirteen years earlier had adopted Grahamism following one of Sister Ellen White's revelations, hired a twenty-four-year-old physician named John Harvey Kellogg as the superintendent of their health institute in Battle Creek, Michigan. Kellogg turned the twenty-bed spa into the famed Battle Creek Sanitarium, then the health mecca of the world. The sanitarium's regimen was based on Graham's tenets to such a degree that it has come to be viewed as an epic version of a Graham boardinghouse. Within two years, Kellogg began manufacturing Granula (renamed Granola in 1881), the first cold breakfast cereal, which was made from a mixture of water and Graham flour baked into thin sheets, ground into small pieces, and baked again. A patent dispute with James Caleb Jackson, the inventor of Granula, led Kellogg to develop new foods (e.g., peanut butter and nut-based meat substitutes) and cereals that he marketed through a separate company, the Sanitas Food Company. By 1902 Kellogg had invented cornflakes, and the modern American breakfast cereal industry was born.

What kind of people espoused Grahamism? Judging from those who patronized the boardinghouses, joined the American Physiological Society, and wrote testimonials for the *Journal,* such converts were generally men who shared certain traits: a weak constitution, bad habits, and a diminished vitality approaching semi-invalidism. When their condition was realized, they renounced self-indulgence and sought hygienic truth. Contemporary accounts depicted boarders as "lean-visaged, cadaverous" radicals, and American Physiological Society members were described as feeble, chronically ill individuals. "Not a few joined . . . as a last resort, after having tried everything else, as drowning men are said to catch at straws."[21]

Outside of the short-lived American Physiological Society, Grahamites never organized or attempted to enact new legislation or change existing state and federal laws. Because of critical differences in philosophy, they never joined forces with the public health movement led by orthodox physicians. Professional rivalry also played a part, as physician-activists shunned their "amateur" predecessors. This bifurcation had a significant impact on the nature of modern American public health activities. Health departments focused on the identification and treatment of major diseases while minimizing the importance of moral, social, and environmental influences. In short, health reform became sharply distinguished from benevolence. Grahamite philosophy, in contrast, stressed that the mind, body, and society continuously interacted and influenced each other. By the early 1900s, this romantic conception of health reform, which was private and individualistic in theory, was all but forgotten.

Was Sylvester Graham a charlatan? Did he and his followers contribute to American health reform? Graham "was undoubtedly honest and sincere in sustaining [his theories]."[22] He hated capitalism and was motivated by a concern for the welfare of humanity. As he himself pointed out, he had nothing to sell, and he certainly never profited from Graham boardinghouses or the sale of Graham health foods. At a time when Americans ate and drank to excess, rarely bathed or exercised, and often lived in crowded, poorly ventilated, unsanitary conditions, Grahamism promoted personal hygiene, frequent bathing, loose clothing, fresh air, sunlight, daily exercise, leafy vegetables, fruits, rough cereals, and pure drinking water. Americans were encouraged to modify their habits in ways that are considered quite healthful today. Graham's principles had broad appeal and in time were largely accepted by the medical profession. By the 1840s Americans had become more concerned with their diets. Over the next four decades per capita alcohol and meat consumption declined, and the use of wheat products, fruits, and vegetables increased. All of this, of course, was not attributable solely to the efforts of the Grahamites. But the fact remains that they did contribute substantially to the success of the popular health movement. Health reform principles reached a huge audience through Graham-inspired books, magazines, advice manuals, lectures, and the phrenology and hydropathic movements. Graham and his supporters were the first and most influential group in mid-nineteenth-century America to advocate sound eating habits. Although most Americans probably rejected limited sexual activity and strict physiological vegetarianism, they did accept the notion of better personal hygiene, exercise, and a balanced diet.

Sensing that he belonged to history, Graham had predicted that a huge monument would mark his grave and that pilgrims would flock there. This was pure rhetoric. No obelisk was erected, and no converts came. If Graham is remembered at all today, it is only in connection with the proverbial cracker. Whereas the names of other reformers "appear on many a pedestal . . . Graham's is still relegated to the grocery store."[23]

NOTES

1. Oliver Wendell Holmes, *Medical Essays 1842–1882* (Boston, 1883), 203.

2. Sylvester Graham, "Journal of Expenses," 1823–1850 (Somerset County Historical Society, Van Veghten House, Bridgewater, N.J.), 75.

3. Ibid., 141.

4. Sir William Osler, *The Evolution of Modern Medicine* (New Haven, 1921), 201, 203.

5. Sylvester Graham, *A Lecture on Epidemic Diseases Generally, and Particularly the Spasmodic Cholera* (New York, 1833), 2.

6. Ibid., 10–11.

7. Sylvester Graham, *A Lecture to Young Men* (Providence, R.I., 1834; repr. New York, 1974), 20.

8. Ibid., 55.

9. Ibid., 72.

10. James Reed, *From Private Vice to Public Virtue. The Birth Control Movement and American Society Since 1830* (New York, 1978), 24.

11. John S. Haller, Jr., and Robin M. Haller, *The Physician and Sexuality in Victorian America* (Urbana, Ill., 1974), 98.

12. Sylvester Graham, *A Treatise on Bread and Bread-Making* (Boston, 1837), 44–45.

13. Ibid., 56.

14. Ibid., 105.

15. Sylvester Graham, *Lectures on the Science of Human Life*, 2 vols. in 1 (New York, 1858), 581.

16. Ibid.

17. Ibid., 491.

18. John Hunter, *The Natural History of the Human Teeth: Explaining Their Structure, Use, Formation, Growth, and Diseases*, 2nd ed. (London, 1778), pt. I, 120.

19. Jesse S. Myer, *Life and Letters of Dr. William Beaumont. Including Hitherto Unpublished Data Concerning the Case of Alexis St. Martin* (St. Louis, 1912), 244.

20. Joseph S. Fruton, *Molecules and Life. Historical Essays on the Interplay of Chemistry and Biology* (New York, 1972), 97.

21. Hebbel E. Hoff and John F. Fulton, "The Centenary of the First American Phys-

iological Society Founded at Boston by William A. Alcott and Sylvester Graham,'' *Bulletin of the Institute of the History of Medicine* 5 (1937): 696.

22. Obituary, *New York Times*, 18 September 1851, p. 2.

23. Richard H. Shryock, ''Sylvester Graham and the Popular Health Movement, 1830–1870,'' *Mississippi Valley Historical Review* 18 (1931): 183.

BIBLIOGRAPHY

Ackerknecht, Erwin H. *Medicine at the Paris Hospital 1794–1848.* Baltimore, 1967.

Carpenter, Helen Graham. *The Reverend John Graham of Woodbury, Connecticut and His Descendants.* Chicago, 1942.

Carson, Gerald. *Cornflake Crusade.* New York, 1957.

Coleman, John P. ''Casting Bread on Troubled Waters: Grahamism and the West.'' *Journal of American Culture* 9 (1986):1–8.

Graham, Sylvester. *A Lecture on Epidemic Diseases Generally, and Particularly the Spasmodic Cholera.* New York, 1833.

———. *A Lecture to Young Men.* Providence, R.I., 1834; repr. New York; 1974.

———. *A Treatise on Bread and Bread-Making.* Boston, 1837.

———. *Lectures on the Science of Human Life.* 2 vols. in 1. New York, 1858.

Hoff, Hebbel E., and John F. Fulton. ''The Centenary of the First American Physiological Society Founded at Boston by William A. Alcott and Sylvester Graham.'' *Bulletin of the Institute of the History of Medicine* 5 (1937):687–734.

Naylor, Mildred V.''Sylvester Graham, 1794–1851.'' *Annals of Medical History,* 3rd ser., 4 (1942): 236–240.

Nissenbaum, Stephen. *Sex, Diet, and Debility in Jacksonian America: Sylvester Graham and Health Reform.* Westport, Conn., 1980.

Shryock, Richard H. ''Sylvester Graham and the Popular Health Movement, 1830–1870.'' *Mississippi Valley Historical Review* 18 (1931): 172–183.

Sutton, Geoffrey. ''The Physical and Chemical Path to Vitalism: Xavier Bichat's *Physiological Researches on Life and Death.*'' *Bulletin of the History of Medicine* 58 (1984): 53–71.

Whorton, James C. *Crusaders for Fitness: The History of American Health Reformers.* Princeton, 1982.

Martin Luther King, Jr., and the Modern Civil Rights Movement

RALPH E. LUKER

After the Montgomery, Alabama, bus boycott of 1955 and 1956 drew Martin Luther King, Jr., out of obscurity, he became the most powerful spokesman for social justice in mid-twentieth-century America. King was deeply rooted in the faith and style of the Southern African-American church. In Northern white schools, he learned the language of Walter Rauschenbusch's Social Gospel, Boston University's theological personalism, Reinhold Niebuhr's tempered political radicalism, and Mahatma Gandhi's nonviolent social protest. Yet King remained most at home with a Southern black congregation. That tells us much about the origins and composition of the movement he led and his role at its dynamic center. From there, until his assassination in 1968, King challenged the nation to live up to the values of its biblical religion and liberal political heritage.

Born on 15 January 1929, in Atlanta, Georgia, King was the second of three children of Martin Luther King, Sr., the pastor of Ebenezer Baptist Church, and Alberta Christine Williams King. His maternal grandfather, Adam Daniel Williams, had been pastor of the Ebenezer congregation and a founder of Atlanta's branch of the National Association for the Advancement of Colored People (NAACP). Thus, King was born into a family whose memory, institutional loyalties, and civil rights activism extended over several generations. He was the fourth of five generations of men in the King family to bear the initials M. L. His father's side of the family tree is difficult to trace. It bears the scars of dislocation and discontinuity that were too often the bitter fruit of slavery. When there was little else that could be handed from one generation to the next, however, the initials could carry a mother's or a father's desire for continuity.

More important, King and his brother, Alfred Daniel, were the fourth of five generations of black Georgia Baptist preachers. He was first, last, and always a preacher. It is a serious mistake to forget it. Black preaching is an oral tradition, at most only secondarily literary and academic. That tradition has important implications for how one learns to do what one does. Listening and borrowing, reshaping material first used by someone else to one's own style, is essential to the process. And King was a Baptist preacher. For over a century, about half of African Americans have been Baptists. Since 1895 the National Baptist Convention has been the largest African-American organization in the United States. For longer than that there have been more black Baptists in Georgia than in any other state in the country. By the 1840s, as far back as one can trace the King family, black Baptists outnumbered white Baptists in Augusta and Savannah by five to one and eight to one, respectively. King's roots, then, were in the rich mother lode of the African-American tradition.

Like his grandfather, Adam Daniel Williams, and his father, Martin Luther King, Sr., before him and his brother, A. D., after him, King served as pastor of Atlanta's Ebenezer Baptist Church. The first two occupied its pulpit continuously for eighty-three years. The weave between family and church was such that the church was extended family. For King, institutional loyalties extended beyond the church to Atlanta's black public schools and Baptist colleges. He was a verbal child. As a first-grader, he told his mother "I'm going to get me some big words."[1] And surely he did. But the words were for oral presentation. He was singing in public at six and preaching at fifteen. Pushed by an ambitious father, a doting mother, and accommodating teachers in Atlanta's public schools, King skipped several grades in the city's black schools to enter Morehouse College at fifteen, with an eighth-grade reading level and spelling skills that never reached beyond that.

At Morehouse, King majored in sociology and matured under the influence of President Benjamin Mays and professors George D. Kelsey, Samuel Williams, and others who were models of the black intellectual as Christian social critic. As a black student among black students of black professors, King's academic record was mediocre. But he was listening, borrowing, reshaping, and learning from others how to evoke an appropriate response from an audience, whether it was a professor or a congregation. King was ordained at Ebenezer and graduated from Morehouse in 1948. He was the third of four generations of men in the Williams–King family to graduate from Morehouse. His sister, Willie Christine King, who graduated from Spelman College in the same year, was the third of four generations of women in the Williams–King family to graduate from Atlanta's Baptist college for African-American women.

At nineteen, King went north to Crozer Theological Seminary in Chester, Pennsylvania. He was attracted to the liberal evangelical theology of Crozer's faculty and thrived there academically. He served as president of the student body in his senior year and graduated with highest honors in 1951. Entering Boston University for graduate study in theology later that year, he absorbed Boston's insistence upon the sacred worth of human personality as the immanent manifestation of the transcendent Person. King was, said his adviser, one of his top five students. Too much of his image has been created out of those years in white academic institutions, perhaps to the neglect of his family, church, and Atlanta's schools. But his academic accomplishments in Atlanta and in the North were largely achieved by synthesizing material and learning to tell an audience what, in some very real sense, they already believed.

In his first year at Boston, King met and began dating Coretta Scott, a student at the New England Conservatory of Music. His only serious academic difficulties in graduate school were in the first semester of his second year, and they were resolved shortly after the King family agreed to their son's marriage to Coretta Scott. They were married on 18 June 1953 in the yard of her family's home in Perry County, Alabama, and settled into the King family's Atlanta home for the rest of the summer. In the fall, they returned to Boston for a final academic year, in which Coretta finished her program in music education and King took his comprehensive doctoral examinations and prepared to write his dissertation. On 24 January 1954, he preached a trial sermon, "Three Dimensions of a Complete Life," at Dexter Avenue Baptist Church in Montgomery, Alabama; six weeks later he was invited to become its pastor. In September 1954, the Kings moved from Boston to Montgomery. During his first year in Montgomery, King completed work on his dissertation and was awarded his doctorate by Boston University in June 1955. King's professors had taught him to use language that he knew they would approve. Like his earlier academic papers, the dissertation was marred by extensive borrowing without proper attribution.

When Rosa Parks was arrested for refusing to give up her seat on a Montgomery bus to a white passenger on 1 December 1955, the city's black leaders organized the Montgomery Improvement Association (MIA) and chose King to lead a bus boycott. Although initially reluctant to accept the responsibility, King was a good choice for its public spokesman. The articulate, well-educated pastor of the city's most prestigious black congregation, he had no enemies in the African-American community and no obligations to the city's white establishment. After a successful one-day boycott on 5 December, King persuaded black Montgomery to pursue its nonviolent Christian protest until the bus company agreed to offer courteous treatment to all passengers, hire black drivers on some bus routes, and adopt a less offensive form of racial segregation on the buses. Negotiations failed, however.

The black community prepared for a lengthy boycott, and the city retaliated with a "get tough" policy. On 26 January 1956, King was arrested for driving thirty miles per hour in a twenty-five miles per hour zone. It was the first of fifteen arrests in his life. Late the next night, King received a telephone call: "Listen, nigger, we've taken all we want from you." The caller threatened to blow up his house and kill him if he did not leave Montgomery. The threat led to a personal crisis. "I discovered then that religion had to become real to me, and I had to know God for myself," King later recalled. Then he heard "the voice of Jesus saying still to fight on. . . . He promised never to leave me, never to leave me alone."[2]

Three days later, as King was leading a mass meeting, a bomb was tossed onto the front porch of his home. It tore a hole in the floor, shattered windows, and filled the house with smoke, but Coretta, another woman, and the Kings' infant were unhurt. Seeing that his family was safe and that the gathering crowd was restless, King sought to calm the people. "We are not advocating violence," he told them.

We want to love our enemies. I want you to love our enemies. Be good to them. . . . I want it to be known the length and breadth of this land that if I am stopped, this movement will not stop. . . . For what we are doing is right. What we are doing is just. And God is with us.

After city officials added assurances of police protection for his family, King addressed the angry crowd. "Go home and don't worry," he said. "Be calm as I and my family are. We are not hurt . . . and remember that if anything happens to me, there will be others to take my place."[3]

The breakdown of negotiations, the city's rejection of the MIA's modest demands, police harassment of its volunteer drivers, and the violent retaliation convinced the MIA to open a legal challenge to bus segregation. On 1 February 1956, it filed a lawsuit testing the constitutionality of Montgomery's bus segregation ordinances in federal court. Three weeks later, on 20 February, a Montgomery grand jury indicted nearly a hundred leaders of the bus protest—the largest mass indictment in the country's history—on charges of violating a state law against boycotts. The prosecution focused the trial of 19–22 March on charges against King, the judge pronounced him guilty as soon as the summations were complete, and he was given a $500 fine or a year at hard labor. After his conviction, however, crowds outside the courthouse cried "Hail the King!" That night, he was introduced to a mass meeting at Holt Street Baptist Church with the words "Here is the man who today was nailed to the cross for you and me."[4]

Early in June, a panel of federal judges ruled that Montgomery's bus segregation ordinance was unconstitutional. The U.S. Supreme Court confirmed the lower court's decision on 13 November. Montgomery's buses were desegregated on 21 December 1956, when King and others boarded and sat near the front of a bus. As president of the MIA, King exerted leadership of a nonviolent local mass protest movement against racial discrimination that won him a position as a force among civil rights leaders. The boycott inspired local civil rights protests across the South and drew international attention to him and the cause. Yet the resolution of the Montgomery bus boycott was full of irony. It was the NAACP's characteristic strategy of litigation that brought the victory the MIA claimed. In that resolution, the inept tactics of the city's white leadership guaranteed that the MIA received none of the things that it had originally sought. Years later, the MIA was still seeking courteous treatment of all passengers and black drivers on some bus routes. It had won the one thing that it had not asked for: Montgomery's buses were desegregated.

On 10 January 1957, African-American pastors who sought racial justice through peaceful means in key Southern cities organized the Southern Christian Leadership Conference (SCLC) at Atlanta's Ebenezer Baptist Church. King became its first president. As president of SCLC, he wove a network of socially active black clergymen across the South—Atlanta's William Holmes Borders, T. J. Jemison of Baton Rouge, C. K. Steele of Tallahassee, Mobile's Joseph E. Lowery, and Birmingham's Fred Shuttlesworth—who added nonviolent methods of social protest to the civil rights movement's strategic arsenal for attacking institutionalized racism. In May 1957, SCLC joined other civil rights organizations in a prayer pilgrimage to Washington. It gathered at the foot of the Lincoln Memorial on 17 May 1957. There King stressed the importance of school desegregation and voting rights for black Southerners. His refrain—"Give us the ballot"—captured the headlines. *Ebony* and New York's *Amsterdam News* claimed that the prayer pilgrimage had made King the "number one" leader of black America.

In 1958 King published his autobiographical account of the Montgomery bus boycott, *Stride Toward Freedom*, which won the Ainsfield-Wolf Award. Subsequent critical attention has found some ghostwriting and plagiarism in its composition. Perhaps because the book was addressed primarily to a Northern, liberal white audience, its self-portrait may have exaggerated the influence of Northern, liberal white influences on King's intellectual development. While autographing copies of *Stride Toward Freedom* in September 1958, King was stabbed, almost fatally, by a black woman who was later found insane. On trips to Africa in March 1957 and to India in February 1959, King affirmed the solidarity of the American civil rights movement with the Third World's struggle against imperialism and deepened his own commitment to Gandhian nonviolent resistance to oppression.

In January 1960, King left Montgomery to became copastor with his father of Ebenezer Baptist Church and give closer attention to business at SCLC headquarters in Atlanta. "History has thrust something upon me from which I cannot turn away," he told a crowd of well-wishers before leaving Montgomery. He supported the sit-in movement that began in February. "If there is one lesson experience has taught us," he told a mass meeting of demonstrators in Durham, North Carolina, "it is that when you have found by the help of God a correct course, a morally sound objective, you do not equivocate, you do not retreat—you struggle to win a victory."[5]

In mid-April, SCLC acting director Ella Baker convened a meeting of student activists at Raleigh, North Carolina, to organize the Student Nonviolent Coordinating Committee (SNCC). It became a separate student organization, uncontrolled by any established civil rights group. Older leaders, like King, participated only in an advisory capacity. Baker wrote appreciatively and knowledgeably of an alternative style of leadership and decision-making that emerged among the student activists. Their "inclination toward *group-centered leadership*, rather than toward a *leader-centered group pattern of organization*," she said, "was refreshing indeed to those of the older group who bear the scars of the battle, the frustrations and the disillusionment that come when the prophetic leader turns out to have heavy feet of clay."[6]

In October, during the closely fought presidential contest between Vice President Richard Nixon and Senator John F. Kennedy, King was sentenced to four months in a state prison for violating probation on a charge of driving without a Georgia driver's license. King's family and closest allies were deeply concerned that he might be badly injured or killed in the hostile environment at Reidsville State Prison. Democratic presidential candidate John Kennedy intervened to help win his release on bail. Kennedy's action may have shifted enough black voters to the Democratic party to provide him with the critical margin of victory in key states such as Illinois, Michigan, New Jersey, Pennsylvania, and the Carolinas.

King's alliance with the Kennedy administration, however, was at best fragile. Shortly after John Kennedy's inauguration, leaders of the Congress of Racial Equality (CORE), a Northern, biracial organization founded by black and white social activists from the pacifist Fellowship of Reconciliation, organized the first Freedom Rides to test the desegregation of interstate bus transportation. After riding through Virginia and the Carolinas without incident, the Freedom Riders dined in Atlanta with King, who told them that Alabama's white public mood was so mean that they would not get across the state without injury. As he predicted, the Freedom Riders were greeted by violent white mobs at Anniston, Birmingham, and Montgomery. King rejected Attorney General Robert Kennedy's call for a cooling-off period and demanded federal intervention to protect the Freedom Riders.

By the summer of 1961, King and SCLC were already at the vital center of an uneasy coalition of civil rights organizations that were poised to lead the movement. Ranged vaguely to their right were the older, largely middle-class, National Urban League and NAACP. Bound by a half-century of struggle to traditional methods of negotiation and litigation, they were proud of their records, skeptical of the newcomers, and jealous of their prerogatives and sources of financial support. To their left, committed to nonviolent civil disobedience, were CORE, with its base of support in the Northern left, and SNCC, which drew its support from young black and white student activists. Based through its preachers in the folk Christianity of Southern black churches, SCLC and King could hope to mediate between the radically different partners in the movement and mobilize large numbers of people in critical moments.

That hope was tested in December 1961, when King was invited by leaders of the Albany Movement to assist their campaign to desegregate the southwest Georgia city. The Albany Movement was an uneasy alliance of the NAACP, SNCC, SCLC, and other local black organizations. King and its spokesman, Dr. William Anderson, led demonstrations through the summer of 1962, but they won no concessions from the city's white leadership. SNCC organizers expressed skepticism about King's charismatic leadership. Behind his back, they referred to the Baptist preacher as "de Lawd." The consensus in the news media was that King and the Albany Movement had been outmaneuvered by the cunning of Albany's police chief, Laurie Pritchett, who avoided obvious police brutality against civil rights demonstrators, and the relentless opposition of the city's other white leaders. By the end of the summer, King conceded that Albany had been a defeat for the civil rights movement.

By the end of 1962, King and SCLC were planning to implement lessons learned at Albany in a confrontation with racial segregation in Birmingham, Alabama. Rather than a broad-scale attack on all forms of segregation, King believed, it would be better to focus on a defined target, because the movement needed short-term victories in order to sustain a long-term campaign. Second, it was important to use the leverage of black economic influence by boycotting downtown merchants. SCLC sharply focused on an economic target to claim an early moral victory in Birmingham. In April 1963, King launched demonstrations at segregated lunch counters and a boycott of businesses in the downtown area. Arrested on Good Friday, 12 April, he addressed his "Letter from the Birmingham Jail" to local white clergymen, outlining their lack of leadership in race relations, the grievances of the black community, and his nonviolent protest for social change.

King was found guilty of criminal contempt, but the Birmingham campaign reached a climax only when children began demonstrating in large numbers and Commissioner of Public Safety Eugene "Bull" Connor ended a period of relative restraint. On 2 May, 900 children were arrested, and as demonstrators prepared to march the next day, they were attacked by police dogs and policemen wielding clubs and powerful fire hoses. Newspaper, and especially television, pictures of the police brutality against demonstrators in Birmingham galvanized national public sympathy for the movement, and the Kennedy administration sought to intervene. When police attacks provoked several thousand blacks to riot, Birmingham's black and white leadership negotiated a settlement. Although bombings led to another riot in Birmingham, the agreement survived, only to be narrowly interpreted by the city's white leadership.

Yet the Birmingham campaign was a major turning point. By mid-July, the city council repealed the city's racial segregation ordinances. The victory there set off new waves of civil rights demonstrations in cities across the country. In the next ten weeks, there were 758 demonstrations and 14,733 arrests in 186 cities. President Kennedy called for new federal legislation to desegregate public accommodations and promote equal employment opportunities. Finally, King's public position of leadership in the movement, threatened by the defeat in Albany and internal dissent, seemed to be restored.

On 28 August 1963, King joined other civil rights leaders in addressing 250,000 followers at the March on Washington. His speech repeated the biblical and democratic themes of his earlier sermons and speeches, but with unprecedented au-

thority and power. ''Go back to Mississippi; go back to Alabama . . . ,'' he urged
the crowd. ''Let us not wallow in the valley of despair.'' Despite all the difficulties, he said, ''I still have a dream.''

It is a dream deeply rooted in the American dream. I have a dream that one day this
nation will rise up and live out the true meaning of its creed—we hold these truths to
be self-evident, that all men are created equal.

The dream would seat ''the sons of former slaves and the sons of former slave-
owners'' in Georgia at the ''table of brotherhood''; it would transform Mississippi's ''sweltering heat of oppression'' into ''an oasis of freedom and justice'';
it would let his own children be judged not ''by the color of their skin but by
the content of their character''; in Alabama, it would allow little black boys and
girls to join hands with little white girls and boys ''as brothers and sisters. I
have a dream today!'' The dream lifted King from words of Amos to those of
Isaiah:

I have a dream that one day every valley shall be exalted, every hill and mountain shall
be made low, the rough places will be made plain, and the crooked places will be made
straight and the glory of the Lord shall be revealed and all flesh shall see it together.

This hope, this faith, said King, could ''transform the jangling discords of our
nation into a beautiful symphony of brotherhood.''
  With each cadence, the massive crowd lifted its approving roar. Then King
took up the first stanza of ''My Country 'tis of Thee'' to ring the bells of
freedom. He rang them from the hills of New Hampshire to those of New York,
from the mountains of Pennsylvania to those of Colorado and the ''curvaceous
slopes of California.'' He rang them from Georgia's Stone Mountain to Tennessee's Lookout Mountain, ''from every hill and molehill of Mississippi, from
every mountainside, let freedom ring.''

When we let freedom ring from every village and every hamlet, from every state and
every city, we will be able to speed up that day when all of God's children—black men
and white men, Jews and Gentiles, Protestants and Catholics—will be able to join hands
and sing in the words of the old Negro spiritual, ''Free at last, free at last; thank God
Almighty, we are free at last.''[7]

With that conclusion to his most powerful public address, King stepped aside.
  King's ''Letter from the Birmingham Jail'' and his ''I Have a Dream'' speech
rested his leadership of the civil rights movement on appeals to the Christian
democratic conscience of the nation. Subsequent events, however, convinced
more radical elements of the movement that appeals to conscience were inadequate. Two weeks after the March on Washington, on Sunday morning, 15
September 1963, dynamite shattered Birmingham's Sixteenth Street Baptist

church, killing four young black girls and wounding at least twenty other people. The Sunday bombing set off a new round of racial violence in the city. King called for dramatic intervention by the federal government to prevent "the worst racial holocaust this nation has ever seen." In Birmingham, on 18 September, 8,000 people, 800 of them black and white pastors of the city, crowded into and around the Sixth Avenue Baptist Church, where King offered the eulogy at a mass funeral for three of the four dead children. "At times, life is hard," he admitted to them, "as hard as crucible steel."[8]

At the year's end, King learned that *Time* would feature him on the cover of its New Year's issue as "Man of the Year." Reaching little beyond the public man for its insight, *Time*'s cover story referred to the "funereal conservatism" of King's preacherly black suits and, misled by his sober public demeanor, said that he had "very little sense of humor."[9] Hundreds of King's associates, both his admirers and his detractors, could have offered a more intimate portrait. His suits—and his pajamas—were commonly made of silk; and the sober public self disguised a lively private, often bawdy, sense of humor. Yet to be chosen "Man of the Year" was quite an honor for a thirty-four-year-old man, and it seemed to confer the status of mainstream politics on the movement he led.

In March 1964, King focused on an increasingly violent racial confrontation in St. Augustine, Florida, where some black people were arming to defend themselves against white terrorists and state troopers were sent into the city to maintain order. During March, over 200 demonstrators, including the wife of a prominent Episcopal bishop and Mrs. Malcolm Peabody, the mother of the Massachusetts governor, were arrested. Two months later, King and Ku Klux Klan leader J. B. Stoner went to St. Augustine to renew the confrontation. Early in June, King and nine leaders of St. Augustine's demonstrations tried to bring them to a climax by seeking service in a restaurant at the Monson Motor Lodge. Jailed by police in Jacksonville, King protested his treatment there. "I've been in fifteen jails," he said, "but this is the first time I have been treated like a hog."[10] Two days later, he was bailed out.

SCLC and a local grand jury neared an agreement to halt demonstrations in exchange for the establishment of a biracial committee to mediate local grievances. On 24 June, however, 200 SCLC demonstrators converged on a segregation rally at St. Augustine's slave market. Stirred by J. B. Stoner's rhetoric, the white crowd turned on the black demonstrators in a fury. When policemen tried to intercede, a three-sided pitched battle sent twenty injured people to the hospital. "I want out of St. Augustine," said King. "But I must come out of St. Augustine with honor . . . .I must come out of here with a victory."[11] Four days later, Florida's governor announced the appointment of two white and two black people to serve on a biracial committee. No committee had really been appointed and no one had agreed to serve on it, but state and federal authorities wanted to offer King an honorable way out of St. Augustine. Accepting the appearance of victory, SCLC halted demonstrations for two weeks. On 2 July, King left Florida to attend White House ceremonies at which President Lyndon

Johnson signed the newly passed Civil Rights Act of 1964 into law. As he did, St. Augustine businessmen asked local law enforcement authorities to sustain their agreement to abide by its provisions to desegregate public accommodations.

During the summer, King toured Mississippi to encourage black people there to support the Mississippi Freedom Democratic Party (MFDP) and its challenge to the all-white regular Mississippi delegation at the Democratic National Convention. With King's endorsement, the MFDP made a strong presentation of its case to the convention's credentials committee, but it could not match Lyndon Johnson's opposition to their challenge. With King lobbying in the MFDP's behalf and FBI agents monitoring his hotel room and MFDP headquarters to pass confidential information on to the White House, the administration used its power to win a compromise seating two at-large delegates from the MFDP and all members of the regular delegation who would sign a loyalty oath to support the nominee of the convention.

Senator Hubert Humphrey, Walter Reuther, Bayard Rustin, Roy Wilkins, Andrew Young, and Whitney Young urged the MFDP to accept the administration's offer as a gesture of goodwill committing the administration to continue to be friendly to the movement. King saw reasons to accept and to reject the offer. As a leader of the movement seeking administration support for future civil rights and voter registration efforts in the South, he favored accepting the offer, ''but if I were a Mississippi Negro,'' he told an MFDP delegate, ''I would vote against it.''[12] When Johnson administration forces ended negotiations, King joined in a halfhearted, last-minute appeal to MFDP delegates to accept the settlement. They rejected it, however, and he left the convention in a despondent mood. The defeat in Atlantic City sent a shock of cynical realism through younger civil rights activists that reinforced their growing doubts about American justice and King's leadership.

King's grueling public schedule put him in an Atlanta hospital for fatigue when word came in mid-October that he would receive the Nobel Peace Prize for 1964. He was the youngest person ever to receive that prize, and it brought an international endorsement to the movement he represented. Within a month, however, FBI Director J. Edgar Hoover attacked King as the ''most notorious liar'' in the country for suggesting that the FBI had been ineffective in protecting the civil rights of black people in the South.[13] King avoided public confrontation with Hoover.

The federal agency had been taping King's telephone and hotel room conversations for two years. Initially, the FBI focused on his relations with two aides, Stanley Levison and Jack O'Dell, who were suspected of having ties to the Communist party. As the wiretaps and bugging of hotel rooms picked up suggestions of an active extramarital sex life, the FBI increasingly focused its attention upon that. After the award of the Nobel Prize on 10 December 1964, King and his wife received a tape recording purporting to reveal his infidelity to her and an anonymous letter suggesting that the only way to avoid public humiliation was for him to commit suicide. They rightly suspected that the tape and the letter had come from the FBI.

In January 1965, King's attention turned to Alabama, where civil rights leaders sought a march on Montgomery to protest racial brutality and discrimination in Selma. They built up momentum by two months of local marches to protest the county's refusal to register black people to vote. After King was jailed in demonstrations on 1 February, Malcolm X visited Selma to address a mass meeting at Brown Chapel. "I didn't come to Selma to make [King's] job difficult," he told Coretta King. "I really did come thinking that I could make it easier. If the white people realize what the alternative is, perhaps they will be more willing to hear Dr. King."[14] Three weeks later, on 21 February, Malcolm X was assassinated in New York. The two men had met only once, and there were clear differences between them. Nevertheless, they respected each other, and after Malcolm left the Nation of Islam and King's analysis of American society became more sober, their ideological positions had begun to converge. King's telegram to Malcolm's widow condemned "the shocking and tragic assassination of your husband. While we did not always see eye to eye on methods to solve the race problem," said King,

I always had a deep affection for Malcolm and felt that he had a great ability to put his finger on the existence and the root of the problem. He was an eloquent spokesman for his point of view and no one can honestly doubt that Malcolm had a great concern for the problems we face as a race.

To reporters, he said: "It is even more unfortunate that this great tragedy occurred at a time when Malcolm X was re-evaluating his own philosophical presuppositions and moving toward a greater understanding of the nonviolent movement and toward more tolerance of white people."[15]

On 7 March 1965, a mounted posse of white volunteers and state troopers led by Colonel Al Lingo and Sheriff James Clark stopped a column of 500 demonstrators led by SCLC's Hosea Williams and SNCC's John Lewis at Selma's Edmund Pettus Bridge. Then they charged the line of marchers with cattle prods, clubs, and tear gas. Dramatic television coverage of the brutality reinforced national sympathy for the movement and brought hundreds of its supporters to Selma. Despite a federal court injunction and pressure from the Johnson administration, King led a similar march two days later. When confronted by troopers, he knelt with the marchers in prayer and then turned the line back toward Selma, a gesture that was widely criticized by black militants.

Addressing a joint session of Congress on 15 March, President Johnson denounced the violence in Selma, called for passage of a voting rights bill, and concluded that "We Shall Overcome." Two days later, a federal court authorized the march, and on 25 March 1965, King led 25,000 demonstrators into Montgomery and up Dexter Avenue to the state capitol. "Let us march on," King's litany summoned them: march on segregated schools, on poverty, on ballot boxes. The movement had seized the initiative, and although a "season of suffering" might lie ahead, there was no turning back. "How long will it take?" he asked.

> ... it will not be long, because truth pressed to earth will rise again.
>
> How long? Not long, because no lie can live forever.
>
> How long? Not long, because you still reap what you sow.
>
> How long? Not long, because the arc of the moral universe is long but it bends toward justice.
>
> How long? Not long, because mine eyes have seen the glory of the coming of the Lord.

Ending with two full stanzas of the "Battle Hymn of the Republic," King's speech brought roars of approval from his battle-weary army.[16] Six months later, he met other civil rights leaders at the White House where President Johnson signed the Voting Rights Act into law.

As winner of the Nobel Peace Prize and an internationally renowned spokesman for social justice, King began to press beyond the issue of racial discrimination to demand economic justice and peace among the nations of the earth. Yet King's closest white adviser, Stanley Levison, argued that the participation of a cross section of the nation's population in the Selma-to-Montgomery march indicated a significant change in the national mood between the Birmingham and the Selma demonstrations. It had elevated King to a powerful position of independent, transracial national moral leadership. Any radical action by him now would arouse fear among the complacent and could undermine the powerful coalition that he led. The national consensus for which King now spoke, said Levison, was "*militant only against shocking violence and gross injustice. It is not for deep radical change.*" Ironically, given the FBI's suspicions about his influence on King, Levison suggested that the movement might be "revolutionary" in its implications for the South, but that "in the north this movement is not revolutionary. It is a reform movement not unlike the essentially reform movement of the trade unions in the thirties." If it attempted to reach beyond that to radical structural changes, Levison warned, the movement would come apart. "The American people are ready to undertake some, and perhaps major, reforms," he said, "but not to make a revolution."[17]

In retrospect, Levison's admonition seems prophetic. In 1966, when King attacked racial discrimination in Chicago, he challenged the indifference of Mayor Richard Daley's regime, economic problems more complex than those of the deep South, and white mobs as hostile as any he had faced in the South. The Chicago campaign was interrupted when James Meredith was shot on a march from Memphis to Jackson, Mississippi. When King joined SNCC's Stokely Carmichael and CORE's Floyd McKissick to complete the march with a closing rally at Jackson, long-smoldering divisions within the movement became public. The NAACP's Roy Wilkins and the Urban League's Whitney Young refused to sign SNCC's ''massive public indictment'' of American society and left Memphis in anger. Struggling to hold the movement together and to mediate between increasingly irreconcilable positions, King signed the statement, but he balked at Stokely Carmichael's intonation of ''black power.''

Returning to Chicago, King led demonstrations at city hall and met with Mayor Daley. After a three-day riot in the city's West Side ghetto, his marches into Chicago's white neighborhoods to protest housing discrimination attracted hostile counterdemonstrators. Two days before a march into Cicero, King reached an agreement with the city's establishment to halt the demonstrations. The agreement was only a pledge by the white leadership to curb racial discrimination. King was increasingly aware of the tenacity of problems in Northern urban ghettoes and outspoken about the need for radical change in the social order.

After the Montgomery march, King grew more critical of the U.S. role in the Vietnam War and called for greater attention to the plight of the urban poor. The war offended his nonviolence and diverted important resources from domestic needs. His criticism of American foreign policy alienated King from the Johnson administration and from other civil rights leaders, but he was convinced by pictures of Vietnamese children burned by American napalm that he must condemn the violence of American foreign policy. Although he continued to argue that nonviolent methods could produce genuine social change, King was less optimistic in his expectations of white America. Increasingly, he told a reporter, he saw the futility of piecemeal reforms and the necessity of ''a reconstruction of the whole society, a revolution of values.''[18] The strain of internal dissent over a new agenda that attacked both the Vietnam War and poverty and racial discrimination in the urban North was undermining the civil rights coalition for which King spoke. His last book, *Where Do We Go from Here: Chaos or Community?*, reflected both King's growing sense of the necessity for radical change in American society and his increasing pessimism about the likelihood of accomplishing such a change.

In June 1967, when the U.S. Supreme Court upheld a contempt of court conviction stemming from the 1963 Birmingham demonstrations, King spent his prison sentence planning an interracial coalition of poor people to press for new antipoverty legislation. Plans completed in February 1968 called on poor white, black, Indian, and Hispanic Americans to march on Washington and demonstrate for federal legislation to guarantee jobs and a viable income to the poor and to end discrimination in education and housing. The campaign faced strong opposition from the Johnson administration and won little support from other civil rights groups. In March, King took time away from planning the Poor People's Campaign to go to Memphis, Tennessee, to lead a mass march in support of the city's striking sanitation workers. The demonstration was marred when some protesters began smashing windows and looting stores, but King returned to Memphis to lead a second march a month later. On 4 April, while he was standing on the balcony of his motel, King was shot in the head and died almost instantly. Two months later, James Earle Ray was arrested in London. In March 1969, after being charged with King's murder, Ray pleaded guilty.

For scarcely more than a dozen years, Martin Luther King and the civil rights movement led a largely successful assault on racial segregation and discrimination in American life. Summoning the nation to align its biblical and democratic values with its racial practices, King articulated a vision of the American dream that virtually destroyed the vestiges of de jure racial segregation by the time of his death. Yet as he turned to more entrenched problems of de facto segregation, poverty, and violence after 1965, his appeals to conscience were less successful. The coalition of forces for which he had spoken disintegrated, its left wing spinning off into self-destructive nihilisms or racial nationalisms that struck alliances with forces of political reaction. Exhausted by a dozen years of campaigning, and with his personal life increasingly the target of rumor mongers, King sensed that he might not "reach the promised land." Yet, he had seen it, told us about it, and urged us not to tarry over his death, but to go on.

NOTES

1. Jerry Talmer, "Martin Luther King, Jr., His Life and Times," *New York Post*, 8 April 1968, p. 37.

2. David J. Garrow, *Bearing the Cross: Martin Luther King, Jr., and the Southern Christian Leadership Conference, a Personal Portrait* (New York, 1986), 58.

3. Ibid., 60–61; and Taylor Branch, *Parting the Waters: America in the King Years, 1954–1963* (New York, 1988), 166.

4. Branch, *Parting the Waters*, 184; and Lawrence D. Reddick, *Crusader Without Violence: A Biography of Martin Luther King, Jr.* (New York, 1959), 145.

5. Garrow, *Bearing the Cross*, 125, 129.

6. Ella J. Baker, "Bigger Than a Hamburger," in Clayborne Carson, et al., eds., *The Eyes on the Prize Civil Rights Reader: Documents, Speeches, and Firsthand Accounts from the Black Freedom Struggle, 1954–1990* (New York, 1991), 121.

7. Martin Luther King, Jr., "I Have a Dream," in James M. Washington, ed., *A Testament of Hope: The Essential Writings of Martin Luther King, Jr.* (San Francisco, 1986), 217–220.

8. Garrow, *Bearing the Cross*, 292; and Branch, *Parting the Waters*, 892.

9. "Man of the Year: Never Again Where He Was," *Time* 83 (3 January 1964): 13–16, 25–27.

10. Garrow, *Bearing the Cross*, 331.

11. Ibid., 336.

12. Ibid., 349.

13. Ibid., 360.

14. Coretta Scott King, *My Life with Martin Luther King, Jr.* (New York, 1969), 256.

15. Clayborne Carson, ed., *Malcolm X: The FBI File* (New York, 1991), 83–84; and Garrow, *Bearing the Cross*, 393.

16. Martin Luther King, Jr., "Our God Is Marching On!" in Washington, *A Testament of Hope*, 227–230.

17. Garrow, *Bearing the Cross*, 420.
18. Ibid., 562.

BIBLIOGRAPHY

Branch, Taylor. *Parting the Waters: America in the King Years, 1954–1963*. New York, 1988.

Carson, Clayborne. *In Struggle: SNCC and the Black Awakening of the 1960s*. Cambridge, Mass., 1981.

———, et al., eds. *The Papers of Martin Luther King*. Berkeley, Calif., 1992–.

Fairclough, Adam. *To Redeem the Soul of America: The Southern Christian Leadership Conference and Martin Luther King, Jr.* Athens, Ga., 1987.

Farmer, James. *Lay Bare the Heart: An Autobiography of the Civil Rights Movement*. New York, 1985.

Garrow, David J. *Bearing the Cross: Martin Luther King, Jr., and the Southern Christian Leadership Conference, a Personal Portrait*. New York, 1986.

King, Martin Luther, Jr. *Stride Toward Freedom: The Montgomery Story*. New York, 1958.

———. *The Measure of a Man*. Philadelphia, 1959.

———. *Strength to Love*. New York, 1963.

———. *Why We Can't Wait*. New York, 1964.

———. *Where Do We Go from Here: Chaos or Community?* New York, 1967.

———. *The Trumpet of Conscience*. New York, 1968.

Meier, August, and Elliott Rudwick. *CORE: A Study in the Civil Rights Movement*. Urbana, Ill., 1975.

Morris, Aldon. *The Origins of the Civil Rights Movement: Black Communities Organizing for Change*. New York, 1984.

Norrell, Robert J. *Reaping the Whirlwind: The Civil Rights Movement in Tuskegee*. New York, 1985.

Ralph, James R., Jr. *Northern Protest: Martin Luther King, Jr., Chicago, and the Civil Rights Movement*. Cambridge, Mass., 1993.

Smith, Kenneth L., and Ira G. Zepp, Jr. *Search for the Beloved Community: The Thinking of Martin Luther King, Jr.* Valley Forge, Pa., 1974.

Van Deburg, William L. *New Day in Babylon: The Black Power Movement and American Culture, 1965–1975*. Chicago, 1992.

Washington, James M., ed., *A Testament of Hope: The Essential Writings of Martin Luther King, Jr.* San Francisco, 1986.

Wilkins, Roy, with Tom Mathews. *Standing Fast: The Autobiography of Roy Wilkins*. New York, 1982.

Rachel MacNair
and Feminists for Life

SUZANNE SCHNITTMAN

Equating feminism with a pro-life philosophy makes perfect sense to Rachel MacNair, president of Feminists for Life of America since 1984. "The ties of the feminist movement to a pro-abortion position are a fairly recent phenomenon, starting really in the last wave of the 1960s and 1970s," she once wrote. Therefore, she concluded, the current trend of identifying abortion defense with feminism is "only a short aberration in history," one that will fade as feminists rediscover their authentic roots and abandon the "recent idea that abortion is necessary to sexual equality," a belief that "actually sabotages equality."[1]

Rachel MacNair and the organization she heads occupy a unique position in the pro-life reform movement because they endorse full equality for women in all areas and the right of every baby to be born. They demand an end not only to abortion but "to all legal, social, and economic discrimination against women." Because they "recognize all people as individuals with equal rights, including the unborn," they "believe it is inconsistent to demand rights for ourselves and to deny them to the unborn." Feminists for Life find the roots of their philosophy and activities in the battle nineteenth-century feminists began more than 150 years ago when they fought for the rights of all oppressed, including slaves, women, and the unborn.

The same consistency that drove those reformers encouraged Rachel MacNair to devote herself to Feminists for Life. Her story resembles that of many women activists of the 1980s who journeyed a long way before they found a home in pro-life feminism. Civil liberties journalist Nat Hentoff characterizes them as "women who came out of the civil rights and antiwar movements and now work for what they call a 'consistent ethic of life.' " He portrays MacNair as the "lively" president of Feminists for Life, his "favorite activist group."[2] Her voice betrays a variety of hometown influences, but the Southern predominates.

MacNair was born 4 November 1958, in Rockford, Illinois; lived there until she was in third grade; then moved with her family to Memphis, Texas, where they spent the next three years. After her parents—Wilmer Everett and Dorothy Lois Kelso MacNair—were divorced, she, her brother, and her mother moved to Kansas City, Missouri.

MacNair described herself at thirteen as someone who "did teenager for a few months and that was enough." From then on, she considered herself to be an adult and enrolled in a local college course on nonviolence. The experience taught her about the horrors of the Vietnam War and led her to participate in antiwar demonstrations. Material on Gandhi, Martin Luther King, Jr., and Dorothy Day inspired a faith in nonviolence. Awareness of these leaders and their struggles helped her finally to make sense of the "racial violence" she had heard about in the media throughout her childhood.

The college course not only converted her to nonviolence, it exposed MacNair to the Quakers, who operated the Peace Center in Kansas City. Her parents had given MacNair permission to choose a religion when she reached the age of thirteen, so she was keenly interested in the many possibilities. Her experience with the philosophy and theology of the Society of Friends convinced MacNair to join the Quakers at the age of fourteen. Since her first encounter with this religion, it has had a significant influence on her life. She still participates in regular weekly meeting and observes Sunday for the "Lord's Day" and Saturday for the Sabbath, which "are very different from each other, you know."

Just as demonstrations against the Vietnam War launched other activists, so they inspired MacNair to lead a life of protest. Antinuclear actions, waged against both nuclear power and nuclear weapons facilities, replaced her antiwar actions in the mid-1970s. In high school she joined the Bendix Conversion Group, which used a variety of tactics to encourage the Bendix Corporation, located in Kansas City, to end its production of nuclear weapons parts. Higher education for MacNair was an opportunity to expand her knowledge about nonviolence. She earned a degree in peace and conflict studies at Earlham College in Richmond, Indiana.

The first time MacNair was arrested for acting on her dedication to nonviolence was for "disorderly conduct" at the Soviet consulate in New York City. In June 1978 the Mobilization for Survival had organized two groups to sit in at the American State Department and the Soviet embassy in Washington to advocate disarmament. MacNair wanted to avoid the "love it or leave it" advice given to Americans who criticized the United States, so she chose to carry her message to the Soviets. After her baptism in very mild waters, she went on to experience nine more arrests for antinuclear protests. At Seabrook, New Hampshire, authorities "legalized" the occupation staged by her group, which considered this a victory. At Black Fox, Wyoming, MacNair was arrested twice in what she calls "K-Mart" or "easy credit" arrests, which allowed demonstrators to escape with the promise to pay a moderate fine. At the Strategic Air Command in Omaha, Nebraska, she and a group spray-painted a military promotion billboard on the premises that read "Peace is Our Profession." The police watched them but made no arrests until the group went over the fence, then presented them with "ban and bar letters" that warned them not to do it again.

It was not until the early 1980s that MacNair exercised civil disobedience in the name of the pro-life movement. Like so many feminists, she had defended abortion and supported *Roe* v. *Wade* in the early 1970s because she was convinced that the ruling "put the back alley abortionists out of business." Within a few years her views changed significantly. The woman who turned MacNair's world upside down and inspired her pro-life feminism was Juli Loesch Wiley, who has had a similar effect on many people. Wiley, a native of Erie, Pennsylvania, has been an activist since the age of fifteen, when, like MacNair, she participated in anti-Vietnam War protests. Her initial exposure to civil disobedience and her first arrests came during the United Farm Workers grape pickers' strikes in Delano, California. In 1970 she left the Catholic Church (she later rejoined) and "immersed herself in feminism" and the "push for abortion reform."[3]

Wiley's conversion to pro-life feminism emerged from her study of nuclear radiation and its harmful effects on the unborn. After a speech in which she shared her findings, a woman asked her to compare the damage radiation inflicted on the fetus with that of a curette during abortion. Wiley had never considered the comparison, but the question compelled her to research further radiation's effects on prenatal development. This led her to think about the "inconsistency that I was concerned with what might happen accidentally [to a fetus] but not with what was being done deliberately through induced abortion." A report on the Three Mile Island nuclear power plant disaster in Pennsylvania that recorded "no deaths except through miscarriage" affected MacNair as well as Wiley. After "the antinuke movement radicalized" Wiley into an "antiabortion stand," she formed Prolifers for Survival to promote the consistency she was embracing.[4]

When Wiley came to Kansas City in 1979 to speak at the local Catholic Worker House, MacNair missed the talk but obtained a copy of the speech. She was attracted by Wiley's nonviolence as well as her belief in the "seamless garment philosophy," whose advocates opposed the taking of life through poverty, war, capital punishment, and abortion. Wiley's quick wit and tendency to speak forthrightly persuaded MacNair where her life must go. The speech, which called women and men to build structures that allow the powerless to live in harmony with the powerful, reminded feminists who see abortion as a right that they fail to recognize the pattern of domination they are repeating. How could women who feel oppressed by men demand the authority to oppress their children, she asked. The ideal society, she continued, could come about only through the creation of a community guided by feminist sexual ethics rather than through the availability of abortion.

For five years MacNair worked for these ideals as a member of Prolifers for Survival as well as the National Right-to-Life Committee. She widened her acts of civil disobedience to include rescues at abortion clinics, following Wiley's example. Her first of five arrests in protest of abortion was in January 1982. During the next summer MacNair was sentenced to sixty days for distributing pro-life leaflets inside an abortion clinic. She spent six weeks in jail after she refused probation, available only if she promised never to engage in civil disobedience over abortion again.

MacNair performed her last act of civil disobedience in 1985, just before her son was born. She believed the responsibility of motherhood took precedence over the risk of arrest, especially when a child will have only one parent. Such is the case with Matthew, who was conceived by artificial insemination by an anonymous donor. MacNair would not recommend single parenting to everyone, but for her it was appropriate. She settled in Kansas City with her mother and Matthew. From this city she ran the national office of Feminists for Life, having assumed the presidency in 1984.

By then the group had already experienced a colorful history. In 1972 its founders, Pat Goltz and Cathy Callaghan, had been radical feminists and members of the National Organization for Women (NOW). Their pro-life position on abortion was not popular in NOW, which by the early 1970s was ''single-mindedly focusing on abortion as its major concern.'' Goltz and Callaghan collaborated in an effort to change the direction of their NOW chapter in Columbus, Ohio, but its president challenged their opposition to abortion. After she ordered Goltz ''not to discuss abortion with any member of NOW at any time or place,'' the two women launched their own feminist organization.[5]

On 9 April 1973 Goltz and Callaghan convened American and Canadian women in Columbus to launch Feminists for Life. Their communication vehicle was *The Feminists for Life Journal*, later renamed *Sisterlife*. The women did not sever their ties to NOW and continued to press that organization to include a pro-life view. Goltz enlisted the help of former suffragist and pro-life feminist Alice Paul, who was distressed that promoters of the Equal Rights Amendment, which she had first introduced in 1923, were linking it to abortion. Finally, in 1974, NOW of Ohio expelled Goltz and Callaghan for what Nat Hentoff calls their ''heresy.'' This story continues to evoke distress from free speech advocates and to raise reactions from journalists who study the abortion issue. In a 1989 story about Feminists for Life, *Mother Jones* interviewer Pamela Erens noted the ''expulsion'' and the rift among feminists that continued fifteen years later. NOW's president at the time, Molly Yard, told Erens the pro-life feminists would meet the same fate in 1989 as they had in 1972: ''I don't know how someone can be a feminist if she's not for a woman's right to her own life.''[6]

Soon after the split with NOW, Feminists for Life had its first opportunity to present pro-life feminism to a large public forum, at the 1974 National Right-to-Life Convention in Washington, D.C. Its message was well received and brought other invitations to national meetings. Pat Goltz remained at the helm of the young organization, traveled widely, and helped establish Feminists for Life chapters in the United States, Canada, England, Mexico, and New Zealand.

By 1976 cofounder Catherine Callaghan had assumed a less active role, and Goltz moved the headquarters near her home in Tucson, Arizona. The next year Vice President Maggie Guenther, from Wisconsin, agreed to assume the presidency. Relocated in Milwaukee, the group abandoned its international perspective and changed its name to Feminists for Life of America. Under the leadership of Pam Circa, who assumed the presidency in 1981, the group held several widely attended national seminars on women's issues and pro-life feminism. The mailing list had grown to 1,500 by 1983, when Mary Ledbetter was elected president and moved the headquarters to Lincoln, Nebraska. When Ledbetter became seriously ill, Paulette Joyer, from Minnesota, took over most of her responsibilities.

In 1984 the Feminists for Life caucus at the National Right-to-Life Convention drafted Rachel MacNair as its new president "by default." Her effective two years in the group made her the obvious choice. The national office then moved to Kansas City, Missouri, where it is located today. Membership more than tripled by 1993, during which time MacNair gave Feminists for Life new direction as well as a strong base from which to communicate and to build.

MacNair sees two schools of thought on policy, that of the purists and that of the pragmatists. Purists argue that compromise on abortion (for example, allowing abortion in cases of incest or rape) is "immoral and detrimental in the long run." Pragmatists, on the other hand, are willing to argue for an "all or something" approach, and welcome any restrictions on abortion as steps in the right direction. MacNair suggests that most from the purist school belong to the American Life League. Its pragmatist counterparts are members of the National Right-to-Life Committee. Historical antecedents for such a split can be detected, for instance, in the temperance movement, in which purists demanded total abstinence and pragmatists allowed moderate drinking. Only when factions worked together were they able to obtain some reform. Even though drinking did not stop completely in the nineteenth century, the combination of moderation and abstinence campaigns reduced it drastically between 1830 and 1860.[7]

MacNair argues that a variety of policies strengthens the pro-life movement because "an all-or-nothing [approach] will probably end up achieving too much nothing." In short, "compromise can save lives and moves us closer to the goal [of outlawing abortion] than we were before." If we "let the pragmatists push and the purists pull, between the two of us, we'll get there faster than either one of us alone." Pro-life reformers disagree over tactics as well as policy, and align themselves in one of two divisions, which MacNair labels the "straight people" and the "street people." The straight people "believe respectability is important" and that "being outside the system is harmful to the cause." Street people favor "taking direct action immediately" and argue that it is "immoral to wait for normal legal channels." Straight people work within the structure for legislative change, often through legal channels. Street people perform rescues, do sidewalk counseling, and participate in civil disobedience. MacNair concludes that this "isn't a strict division, of course," because many people from both schools participate in legal demonstrations or cross over to the other side's tactics occasionally.[8]

A combination of tactics serves pro-life feminists well. To illustrate this, MacNair recalls a personal experience at a NOW convention she attended in Kansas. Outside the meeting of 50 people, 400 pro-lifers yelled, "Stop the killing NOW!" Several delegates to the convention turned to her as the "reasonable person to whom they could come and explain their sincerity." From this she "enjoyed some of the most productive dialogue that I have ever had at such a convention." MacNair believes that had she not been there, "the pro-life view would have been entirely dismissed as crazy." Also, without the picketers, she "would have had little opportunity for the matter to come up," and would not have been able to demonstrate the presence of feminists among the pro-lifers. In this movement, as in any other, she writes, "a good balance of respectable people wringing their hands over the tactics, while people in the street keep the issue hot, results in good progress."

MacNair has compared the conflict in tactics to that during America's fight for woman's suffrage nearly a century ago. The National American Woman Suffrage Association, the more respectable element, confined its efforts to petition drives and public speaking. Members of the National Woman's Party represented the street people because they chained themselves to public buildings and picketed Woodrow Wilson's White House for eighteen months. Only through a combination of tactics did women "win" the right to vote. MacNair believes the pro-life movement will succeed only through a combination of straight and street tactics practiced by purists and pragmatists.

Because Feminists for Life emphasizes pro-woman measures just as vigorously as it promotes pro-life measures, there is even more potential discord over its tactics than in traditional pro-life organizations. The group's argument that abortion is only one of many forms of violence against women, including poverty, assault, battering, and unjust wages, is perhaps most difficult to solidify and to convey. The two schools of thought on the connectedness of pro-woman and pro-life concerns pose a conflict that MacNair believes "gets the most Feminists for Life passion" flowing. Members disagree whether abortion should be a "single-issue" battle or an "everything's connected" contest. The compromise emerging in the early 1990s was toward a "single-issue, broadly defined" agenda. Feminists for Life would continue to direct its activities to "related issues like equal male responsibility for children, family leave, child care, rape, and childbirth choice," but steer clear of "issues like religion and the military." This would make it possible to "work in coalition with other groups concerned with these matters," which "does not dilute, but strengthen our ability" to work on abortion.[9]

MacNair is quick to point out feminism's long legacy of connecting pro-woman and pro-life philosophies. Not until the late 1960s did feminists advocate legal abortion. The nineteenth-century women's rights pioneers were also the pioneers of pro-life feminism, according to Feminists for Life, who see compelling parallels between the Victorian era and the 1980s and 1990s. Historians have called attention to the widespread availability of legal abortion in the United States during the nineteenth century. The earliest abortions were performed by "irregular physicians" as well as women whose recipes for home-brewed abortifacients were published in medical guides and health manuals. Frequently "regular physicians" were called upon to finish abortions begun by amateurs and save the lives of desperate women. Because no existing statutes addressed abortion, those who performed the procedure could never be held legally guilty of wrongdoing.[10]

Some historians suggest that before 1840 the community perceived abortion primarily as a desperate move, used especially by young women who feared the adverse reaction of society to their pregnancies. But after 1840 the social character of the practice changed. More women who had abortions were married, native-born, Protestant, and frequently from the middle or upper classes. In 1839 Professor Hugh L. Hodge of the University of Pennsylvania told a medical class "that abortion was fast becoming a prominent feature of American life." Twenty years later the Michigan State Medical Society declared that abortion "pervaded all ranks" in that state. One historian argues that abortion remained discreet before the Civil War but was not as rare as one might expect. Contemporary experts estimated that from 1800 to 1830 there was one abortion for every thirty live births; by 1850 the ratio had increased to one abortion for every six live births, even though some states had outlawed the practice by this time.[11]

With the rise of abortions in the nineteenth century, those who performed the procedure profited handsomely, a complaint echoed by pro-life feminists a century later. In the 1800s, women paid an average of $100 for an abortion (a very substantial sum in those days), but often more if doctors thought they could obtain it. Prices leveled off somewhat as the century advanced, but abortions remained profitable well into the 1870s. One historian notes that even during the most controversial periods of debate over abortion, most periodicals made no comment for fear of losing advertising revenues. Feminist publications like *The Revolution*, the newspaper Elizabeth Cady Stanton published with Susan B. Anthony, refused to run ads for patent medicines because these were frequently thinly disguised abortifacients. Victoria Woodhull and Tennessee Claflin, the notorious free-love advocates, held to the same policy in their weekly newspaper and exposed the most lucrative abortion practice in New York City. They insisted that "the rights of children as individuals begin while yet they remain the foetus [*sic*]."[12]

As abortion became a visible and significant nineteenth-century American phenomenon, opponents launched efforts to outlaw it. Physicians led the opposition, which was joined enthusiastically by Anthony Comstock, who lent his name to the legislation that finally outlawed abortion, birth control, and all other forms of "obscenity." The official position of the nation's feminists, who concurred with the opposition, was best stated by Elizabeth Cady Stanton. Writing in *The Revolution*, Stanton insisted in 1868 that "the murder of children, either before or after birth, has become frightfully prevalent''—evidence of the ''degradation of woman.'' She believed the ''remedy even for such a crying evil as [abortion]'' was the ''enfranchisement and elevation of women.'' Five years later she wrote to Julia Ward Howe: ''When we consider that women are treated as property, it is degrading to women that we should treat our children as property to be disposed of as we see fit.''[13]

Susan B. Anthony wrote in *The Revolution* that abortion was ''child murder'' that ''we want to prevent,'' not merely ''punish.'' She believed ''we must reach the root of the evil'' that was ''practiced by those whose inmost souls revolt from the dreadful deed.'' Her colleague in the suffrage movement, Matilda Gage, called abortion ''a subject that lies deeper down in woman's wrongs than any other.'' She asserted ''that most of the responsibility for this crime lies at the door of the male sex.''[14] Only one woman among all the well-known nineteenth-century feminist reformers, Angela Heyward, might have argued for legalized abortion.

Contrary to current assumptions, many nineteenth-century feminists supported birth control and saw the value both men and women placed on sex for pleasure and communication as well as procreation. Leaders of the woman's movement celebrated the unique contribution their gender made to society as mothers and nurturers who consistently supported the rights of all living beings. They simply carried their pro-life feminism to its logical extension. One historian finds it consistent that nineteenth-century women defined the sanctity of life from conception to death, which coincided with their movements against cruelty. They similarly advocated eliminating capital punishment, promoting peace, and abolishing torture and whipping for crimes.[15]

This consistency within the reform movement endured for more than seventy years after abortion was outlawed in 1873. Feminists of the early twentieth century did not fight to overturn this law, nor did abortion rights appear in the Equal Rights Amendments presented between 1923 and World War II. When the campaign to reform abortion law was finally initiated in the late 1960s, physicians, abortion's earliest opponents, led the movement, a development historians find difficult to explain. Abortion was not raised as a woman's issue until later, by which time repeal of the law against abortion replaced reform.[16]

When the National Organization for Women was launched in October 1966, it did not include abortion in its pledge ''to support claims for the equality for all deprived groups.'' It called for ''equal participation and treatment of women in employment, education, and government, for establishing new institutions to facilitate public roles for women, for true equality in marriage, and for destroying false images of women,'' but not for abortion. Only in NOW's second year did one faction make legal abortion a goal, ''redefine'' it as a ''women's issue,'' and add it to the convention agenda, after which ''serious divisions rose.'' Many members ''did not see abortion as a women's rights issue and they feared that NOW's stand would lose support for the young organization.'' In 1968 this and other differences caused various groups to leave NOW and form new women's organizations that would "avoid issues that polarize people." A major offshoot, the Women's Equity Action League, saw no role for abortion among its primary goals of employment, education, and reform.[17]

As NOW increased its identification with what came to be called the pro-choice position, it left few places for pro-life feminists, as demonstrated by the birth of Feminists for Life. Feminists for Life has benefited from many skilled and prolific writers who explain its positions. Besides Rachel MacNair and Juli Loesch Wiley, Sidney Callahan has been exceptionally effective not only in portraying pro-life feminism but also in making connections with other feminists. In a 1989 Pamela Erens said, "If anyone is trying to create a bridge between antiabortion and pro-choice feminists," it is Callahan, a psychology professor, who has brought a dispassion to the reform movement because to her "all sides seem good." In a 1986 ground-breaking article, Callahan established the philosophy of Feminists for Life, which insists that "abortion is a method of making society more masculine than feminine," and of "denigrating 'feminine' values of community and nurturance by subordinating them to the value of individual control ('choice')." The feminist ideal "that a woman has an inherent, inalienable worth loses meaning if a woman claims that another type of human life has value only if she bestows it."[18]

In her writing Callahan both recognizes the claims of fetal life and "offers a different perspective on what is good for women." In four parts she responds to the most "highly developed feminist arguments for the morality and legality of abortion." First, in answer to the "moral right to control one's own body," Callahan presents "a more inclusive ideal of justice." Women, who along with black people were once considered too different, underdeveloped, or "biological" to have souls or possess legal rights, today make the same assumptions about other unprotected life when they support abortion. It seems a "travesty of just procedures that a pregnant woman now acts as sole judge of her own case." A woman who defends abortion frequently resents the power men yielded and often still yield over her, but claims even a stronger power over the life of the child she carries.

Feminist historian Elizabeth Fox-Genovese expresses a similar concern in *Feminism Without Illusions*, in which she asserts that "the core of the argument for abortion lies in a defense of the rights of privacy." This defense "carries potentially unpalatable corollaries," especially the expectation that the state will intervene in a woman's privacy when men abuse her and her children, or will hold "men accountable for supporting" them, but should not intervene in the matter of pregnancy. Fox-Genovese's greatest criticism of the privacy argument is that it "reinforces the individualistic view of rights as essentially a form of property," which she calls one of the "illusions of feminism."[19]

In Callahan's second point, in which she responds to the argument for "the necessity of autonomy and choice in personal responsibility," she suggests an "expanded sense of responsibility." When a woman insists that individual rights take precedence over her unique obligation as a "human being embedded in an interdependent human community,'' she ''betrays a fundamental basis of the moral life.'' Fox-Genovese argues that the preoccupation women have with individual rights (like that of abortion) over community responsibilities and a spirit of sisterhood demonstrates a major source of the illusions of feminism. She believes that feminists who have abortion as a cornerstone do not recognize the collectivity's ''practical interest in the fate of children'' or the ''moral and political interest in the way in which we define and defend the right to life.'' Feminists lose credibility because they ''use feminist metaphors of motherhood and community'' in the same breath that they demand legal abortion as ''an absolute individual right.'' Like feminists of the nineteenth century, Fox-Genovese finds that ''the special sense of human connection and nurture that so many feminists attribute to women derives primarily from women's special roles as the bearers and rearers of children.''

She continues by suggesting that the wedding of feminism with legal abortion might be more pragmatic than theoretical because the ploy ''is drawing numerous fresh converts to feminist organizations, which had been having conspicuous difficulty in appealing to younger women.'' The argument that abortion is a woman's right may attract more followers, but Fox-Genovese contends that it ignores the difference between ''pregnancy and child rearing.'' The first is a biological function; the second ''relies on economic and social support.'' Because ''pregnancy itself does not long interfere with a woman's opportunity to live the life she chooses,'' a woman ''can afford to share her body . . . for nine months without serious consequences.'' Raising her child is ''another matter entirely''—one, she suggests, that ''drags women into poverty and keeps them there.''

In the third part of Callahan's thesis she addresses the heart of the biological function of pregnancy when she suggests that feminists move from the ''moral claim of the contingent value of fetal life'' to ''the moral claim for the intrinsic value of human life.'' When women decide to grant or deny their unborn children value (life), they assume that ''mere'' biological life has little meaning. Pro-life feminists argue that ''human life from the beginning to the end of development *has* intrinsic value,'' something mothers have no right to bestow or remove. It seems ''fallacious to hold that in the case of the fetus it is the pregnant woman alone who gives or removes its rights to life and human status.'' This sounds dangerously close to the power once assumed by the patriarch over his wife and children or by the master over his slaves.

Finally, Callahan notes that all feminists ''totally agree on the moral right of women to the full social equality so far denied them.'' When society in its acceptance pits women against their ''own offspring,'' however, it is morally, psychologically, and politically destructive. Rachel MacNair echoes the point: ''Women are told to regard our rights and the rights of our own children as being in conflict.'' Since it is common to feel ambiguous about a pregnancy in its first term, even for pregnancies that are well planned, ''it is especially vicious to then tell a woman that she and her child are in conflict.'' In fact, a male-dominated society "has created this conflict because it has made little room for the care and nurture of children." When a woman senses this conflict, the baby, being small and invisible, makes a perfect scapegoat.

MacNair carries Callahan's argument further. She believes that when women accept the idea that pregnancy and motherhood make them "disadvantaged," they buy the "patriarchal premise that nature made men superior and women (who are burdened with bearing children) inferior." When women believe that abortion is needed to keep them from being subjected to "the whims of nature," or from a crisis pregnancy, they agree with those who argue that pregnancy is the enemy. Accepting this premise "leaves women subject to more pregnancy discrimination." People who know they cannot get away with "anti-woman" remarks and feelings can be more subtle by "expressing hostility not to women but to pregnancy." In order to achieve equality, "women must be cruel to their own children." When a woman is advised to have an abortion, the overt message is that the baby does not have enough value to be worth the trouble of going through pregnancy. This implies that the woman does not have enough value to be worth that trouble either. Pro-life feminists believe "women are entitled to a better sense of our own value and to the right to make demands on behalf of ourselves and our children."

MacNair argues that when feminists focus most of their energy on obtaining legal abortion, a "macho approach to solving the problems of untimely pregnancy" works against getting the solutions mothers really need: good day care, job flexibility, comparable worth, and parental leave. When women and men assume the attitude that "motherhood is a voluntary project" rather than a precious privilege, "the demand for abortion overshadows the demand for ways to make parenting more feasible." The very cornerstone of pro-life feminism lies in MacNair's conclusion: "Abortion is an indicator of oppression; it is not a solution to the problem."

A reform movement like that of Feminists for Life has faced difficulties for many reasons, but the most fundamental has been the complexity of its motivations. The goal has been to restrict abortion, but the feminist approach to that achievement is new to contemporary society. Its leaders have been challenged to attract the attention of those who would not otherwise heed a pro-life message, who are willing to rethink long-held philosophies and to reassess the meaning of life and our control over it.

Historically, American reform movements were most successful when they not only commanded the attention of potential new followers but also delivered a credible message that promised a "new world" if their reform was realized. Pro-life feminists aim to demonstrate that an "abortion-free" America would be a place where women, especially pregnant women and their children, are valued and affirmed. This world would recognize that the difference between men and women lies primarily in the bearing of children. Its people and institutions would celebrate that difference, and make it popular and possible to welcome unplanned children just as it coped with other unplanned phenomena.

The challenge is to move society away from its devotion to the status quo and convince people, as the antebellum reformers did, that the world does not have to be the way it is and that individual efforts matter.

One historian notes that reform and radical movements arise from something more than the existence of real problems. Reformers emerge only when men and women declare something evil and provide the cure for it. Those who succeed combine old and new solutions, sometimes restoring order by applying traditional values to new situations. It remains to be seen if Feminists for Life and its leadership will rise to these challenges and establish a reform movement that makes a difference.[20]

A few lessons from the nineteenth century are instructive. One is that reform does not have to be coupled with legislation. Temperance began to spread before laws or government action, cutting the consumption of alcohol in half between 1830 and 1840. The leaders were often, but not always, church people. They changed the climate to make it unacceptable to drink as much as people did. Pro-life feminism has tried to make it more difficult to equate feminism with abortion and to remove legal abortion as the first demand of feminist activists. In such efforts, it has sought reform without legislation.

History also has demonstrated that reform can happen when a movement's leadership is small, if that leadership effectively captures sufficient public attention and sympathy. In the case of Feminists for Life, bringing the abortion debate to pages of scholarly journals has been an important first step in efforts to raise the profile and credibility of the group. The public has learned about the abortion controversy in short journalistic pieces whose authors often lack both the space and the ability to explore the historical process. Such treatment has been a disservice to both sides, presenting advocates as stereotypes. Historians can correct this situation and contribute the insight this issue demands, as Keith Cassidy has argued. Essential to that contribution is the story of organizations that participate in the movement but whose histories ''remain exceptionally weak.''[21]

To some observers, Rachel MacNair and Feminists for Life represent a position that feminists who make pro-choice the litmus test of their feminism could never embrace. To other observers, MacNair and Feminists for Life represent a set of beliefs that traditional pro-life reformers reject. The principal appeal of Feminists for Life has been its attempt to raise the issue of abortion in language that finds common ground between opposing forces. Insofar as Feminists for Life succeeds in sustaining a debate on abortion that allows varieties of feminists to find agreement on other issues, the movement will parallel the histories of earlier reforms that encouraged social change through persuasion rather than politics, agreement rather than acrimony. When the center of modern American feminism shifts from a preoccupation with reproductive rights to other matters, without women having sacrificed their individual priorities, Rachel MacNair and Feminists for Life will have emerged as a significant factor in redefining modern American feminism.

NOTES

1. Rachel MacNair, "Prolife Feminism," *Catholic Agitator* (December 1986): 6. All MacNair quotes that follow are from personal interviews conducted 26 October and 12 November 1993 and 21 January 1994.

2. Nat Hentoff, interview National Public Radio (April 1993); see also his "Pro-Choice Bigots: A View from the Pro-Life Left," *The New Republic* 207 (30 November 1992): 23–25.

3. Pamela Erens, "Anti-Abortion, Pro-Feminism?" *Mother Jones* (May 1989): 31. See the following by Juli Loesch Wiley: "Toward a Holistic Ethic of Life," *Blueprint for Social Change* 40 (March 1987): 1–7; "She's Come for An Abortion: What Do You Say," *Harper's Magazine* (November 1992): 46. See also Gail Grenier Sweet, ed., *Pro-Life Feminism: Different Voices* (Toronto, 1985).

4. Wiley, "Toward a Holistic Ethic," 4.

5. Cindy Osborne, "The History of Feminists for Life of America," in Rachel MacNair and Linda Naranjo-Hubel, eds., *Pro-Life Feminism Yesterday and Today* (New York, 1995), 120–125.

6. Ibid.; and Erens, "Anti-Abortion, Pro-Feminism?," 46.

7. Rachel MacNair, "Schools of Thought," in MacNair and Naranjo-Hubel, eds., *Pro-Life Feminism Yesterday and Today*, 206–216.

8. Ibid.

9. Ibid.

10. James Mohr, *Abortion in America: The Origins and Evolution of National Policy, 1800–1900* (New York, 1978), 241–243, 254, 275 n. 12.

11. Ibid., 250–254; Catherine Clinton, *The Other Civil War: American Women in the Nineteenth Century* (New York, 1984), 157; and Carl Degler, *At Odds: Women and the Family in America from the Revolution to the Present* (New York, 1980), 228, 229, 231, 232.

12. Mohr, *Abortion*, ch. 4; Clinton, *Other Civil War*, 157; Linda Gordon, *Woman's Body, Woman's Right: A Social History of Birth Control in America* (New York, 1977), 108; Mary Krane Derr, "Opposition to Abortion," *Sisterlife* (Summer 1993): 2; and *Woodhull's and Claflin's Weekly*, 24 December 1875.

13. *The Revolution*, 5 February and 12 March 1868; Elizabeth Cady Stanton to Julia Ward Howe, 16 October 1873, enclosed in Julia Ward Howe Diary (Harvard University Library, Cambridge); and Gordon, *Woman's Body*, 108. See also Keith Cassidy, "The Abortion Controversy as a Problem in Contemporary American History: Some Suggestions·for Research," *Journal of Policy History* 1 (1989): 440–460. On p. 442 he suggests that most writers who relate the nineteenth-century situation of abortion rely on Mohr, pp. 160–170, who "argued that doctors were motivated by a desire for greater professional status, fears about the decline of the native-born population relative to immigrants, concerns about the role of women, and a moral opposition to abortion as taking of a human life."

14. *The Revolution*, 8 July 1869 and 9 April 1868.

15. Theodore Stanton and Harriet Stanton Blatch, eds., *Elizabeth Cady Stanton as Revealed in Her Letters, Diary, and Reminiscences*, 2 vols. (New York, 1922), vol. 2, 10; and Degler, *At Odds*, 247.

16. Cassidy, ''The Abortion Controversy,'' 443; Kristin Lukor, *Abortion and the Politics of Motherhood* (Berkeley, Calif., 1984), 112–113, points out that ''the right to abortion, after all, was not always a central tenet of the feminist movement.''

17. Susan Hartman, *From Margin to Mainstream: American Women and Politics Since 1960* (New York, 1989), 119, 159, 161.

18. Erens, ''Anti-Abortion,'' 47; Sidney Callahan, ''A Case for Pro-Life Feminism: Abortion and the Sexual Agenda,'' *Commonweal* 113 (25 April 1986): 232–238.

19. Elizabeth Fox-Genovese, *Feminism Without Illusions: A Critique of Individualism* (Chapel Hill, N.C., 1991), 100.

20. Ronald G. Walters, *American Reformers, 1815–1860* (New York, 1978), x, xii, xiii, 3, 214.

21. Cassidy, ''The Abortion Controversy,'' 447.

BIBLIOGRAPHY

Bayles, Martha. ''Feminism and Abortion,'' *The Atlantic Monthly* 269 (April 1990): 79.

Callahan, Sidney. ''A Case for Pro-Life Feminism: Abortion and the Sexual Agenda.'' *Commonweal* 113 (25 April 1986): 232–238.

Callahan, Sidney, and Daniel Callahan, eds. *Abortion: Understanding Differences.* New York, 1984.

Cassidy, Keith. ''The Abortion Controversy as a Problem in Contemporary American History: Some Suggestions for Research.'' *Journal of Policy History* 1, no. 4 (1989): 440–460.

Degler, Carl. *At Odds: Women and the Family in America from the Revolution to the Present.* New York, 1980.

Erens, Pamela. ''Anti-Abortion, Pro-Feminism?'' *Mother Jones* (May 1989): 31.

Fox-Genovese, Elizabeth. *Feminism Without Illusions: A Critique of Individualism.* Chapel Hill, N.C., 1991.

Gordon, Linda. *Woman's Body, Woman's Right: A Social History of Birth Control in America.* New York, 1977.

Hentoff, Nat. *Free Speech for Me—But Not for Thee: How the American Left and Right Relentlessly Censor Each Other.* New York, 1992.

———. ''Pro-Choice Bigots: A View from the Pro-Life Left.'' *The New Republic* 207 (30 November 1992): 23–25.

Liias, Juergan W. ''The Internal Threat to Feminism.'' *New Oxford Review* 57 (October 1990): 4–8.

Lukor, Kristin. *Abortion and the Politics of Motherhood.* Berkeley, Calif., 1984.

MacNair, Rachel, and Linda Naranjo-Hubel, eds. *Pro-Life Feminism Yesterday and Today.* New York, 1995.

Mohr, James. *Abortion in America: The Origins and Evolution of National Policy, 1800–1900.* New York, 1978.

Sweet, Gail Grenier, ed. *Pro-Life Feminism: Different Voices.* Toronto, 1985.

Wiley, Juli Loesch. ''Toward a Holistic Ethic of Life.'' *Blueprint for Social Justice* 40 (March 1987): 1–7.

———. ''Why Feminists and Pro-Lifers Need Each Other.'' *New Oxford Review* 60 (November 1993): 9–14.

Wolf-Devine, Celia. ''Abortion and the 'Feminine Voice.' '' *Public Affairs Quarterly* 3 (July 1989): 81–97.
———. ''Is Support for Abortion Essential to Feminism?'' *New Oxford Review* 57 (November 1990): 11–14.

Horace Mann
and Common School Reform

WILLIAM W. CUTLER III

Education and reform constitute one of the most enduring partnerships in American history. Since the arrival of the first European settlers, it has been commonplace for Americans to believe that education is essential to individual and collective improvement. This association received the endorsement of Puritans and others in the seventeenth century and of their descendants who adopted the Declaration of Independence and ratified the United States Constitution. It certainly characterized the thinking of the generation of reformers who came of age in the thirty years before the American Civil War.

Antebellum reformers tackled many problems in American society. They sought to limit the use of alcoholic beverages or even drive them from the national scene. They refused to accept the growth of poverty, crime, and mental illness. Some attacked the institution of slavery. Others retreated to isolated locations, confident that, free from the influence of the unregenerate, they could discover or reveal the formula for individual or collective perfection. All these reformers believed in education. No matter what the flaw in American society, it could be controlled or even eradicated by proper enlightenment or training. Antebellum reformers possessed a powerful faith in what they called "moral suasion." By instilling Protestant values, they thought they could build the character of those at risk, rehabilitate the fallen, and make all Americans—men, women, and children—behave in a self-reliant, self-disciplined, and socially responsible way.

Given this belief in the efficacy of education, it was no accident that school reform became a special object of concern in antebellum America. Beginning in the 1820s, men and women like Horace Mann, Henry Barnard, Calvin Stowe, Caleb Mills, Emma Willard, and Catharine Beecher urged Americans to recognize the benefits of public education. They made this cause their own, acting as its promoters, publicists, and politicians. Inclined to believe in the possibility of human perfection, they were nonetheless so skeptical about the wisdom of their peers that they often found it difficult to resist the temptation to be paternalistic.

New England was the crucible of public education in America. It was there that reform of the common schools began in earnest. Its first and most famous champion was Horace Mann. Driven by a sense of duty that was nearly self-destructive, the militant Mann brought the mentality of a martyr to school reform in Massachusetts. His copious and careful writings on the subject combined passion for the cause with close attention to detail. He had no time for those who did not share his convictions or sense of dedication, and by 1850 his name had become synonymous with common school reform not only in New England but in many other parts of the United States as well.

Mann's friend and colleague, Henry Barnard, worked the same side of the street in Rhode Island and Connecticut. Even more than Mann, Barnard was single-minded and self-possessed; his life revolved around the cause of education. At the age of fifty-six he became the first U.S. commissioner of education. Despite such recognition, his reputation as a reformer never equaled that of Mann. He impressed too many people as an opportunist, confusing the advance of public education with the forward movement of his own career by promoting himself and the common school interchangeably. But as school reformers, Mann and Barnard had much in common; they shared many beliefs and objectives, perhaps the most important being their commitment to more systematic school organization. Not only would standardizing educational policy and centralizing its oversight be signs of progress in and of themselves; they would lead to other manifestations of educational, economic, and social progress as well.

As rising reformers, Horace Mann and Henry Barnard traveled in the same direction. Both graduated from college, the former from Brown in 1819 and the latter from Yale eleven years later. Both became attorneys, and then Whig politicians, serving in the state legislatures of Massachusetts and Connecticut, respectively. Between 1837 and 1848 Mann distinguished himself as secretary of the newly created Board of Education in the Commonwealth of Massachusetts. His annual reports quickly became required reading for anyone interested in school reform. Barnard assumed administrative responsibility for a similar government body in Connecticut in 1838. Unlike Mann, who survived a legislative attempt to dismantle his board and dismiss him in 1840, Barnard lost his public post in Connecticut when the state disbanded its Board of Commissioners of the Common Schools four years later. He made a lateral move, becoming the school agent for Rhode Island and subsequently its commissioner of public schools. In 1849 Barnard returned to Connecticut as the first superintendent of the state normal school.

Horace Mann was a far more complex and comprehensive reformer than his colleague to the south. Born 4 May 1796, in Franklin, Massachusetts, he learned to value cooperation and self-discipline on the family farm near Wrentham,

Massachusetts, where his parents, Thomas and Rebecca Mann, taught him and his four brothers and sisters to respect one another. As an adult, Mann joined the temperance movement, eventually becoming vice president of the Massachusetts Temperance Society. He took an active interest in the welfare of the defenseless, leading the way to the creation of the Worcester State Hospital for the insane and advocating the repeal of laws in the commonwealth that imprisoned those in debt.

On the subject of abolition Mann was at first cautious, perhaps even ambivalent. In principle, he opposed slavery unequivocally, but until 1850 he approached its elimination tentatively. The zealous tactics of such fellow Bostonians as William Lloyd Garrison and Charles Sumner nearly monopolized public discourse, threatening civic harmony as well as the prospects for success of other worthy causes. Elected to succeed John Quincy Adams in the U.S. House of Representatives, Mann openly opposed the Compromise of 1850. But he felt more at home in the world of education than of partisan politics. Beginning in 1853, he spent the last six years of his life presiding over Antioch College, a new coeducational institution in Yellow Springs, Ohio.

Driven to improve the management of education, Mann always took a special interest in the organizational structure and control of public schools. He believed that educational reform meant the development of uniform policies and common standards for schools. It meant systematic teacher training and centralized decision making. Above all, it meant the universal acceptance of a strong role for state government in the funding and supervision of elementary and secondary education.

In the United States, teacher education attracted considerable attention before the Civil War. Within a year of Mann's appointment as secretary of the Massachusetts Board of Education, three normal schools opened in the commonwealth. He devoted himself to their well-being, carefully selecting their leadership and impatiently monitoring their progress. Henry Barnard's support for teacher education was just as enthusiastic and almost as visible. He frequently addressed teacher institutes in Connecticut and elsewhere. While chancellor of the University of Wisconsin, he doubled as the agent for the state's normal schools. His *American Journal of Education* supplied teachers with educational data and professional advice for more than a generation.

But teacher education was not an end in itself. It was part of a larger scheme to develop a system of schooling in America. Each state should have a hierarchy of schools directed from above and managed by men and women well prepared to do so. Mann and Barnard pioneered the centralized collection and dissemination of information about education. They used the data that they gathered to encourage educational standardization and systematization. The school reform law adopted by Rhode Island in 1845, written by Barnard, established an educational chain of command from the state to the district level, headed by a strong commissioner. In his seventh annual report Mann articulated a similar vision for the schools of Massachusetts.

Outside New England the history of the reform of common schools illustrates the importance of men like Barnard and Mann. In the absence of such persistent reformers, legislation designed to encourage standardized procedures and organizational structure often failed to achieve these objectives. As early as the 1810s, lawmakers in New York and Michigan endorsed the concept of a comprehensive system of public education sponsored by state and local government. But this arrangement was unprecedented, and progress toward its implementation was far from universal and often slow in coming.

In colonial America fee and free schools predominated. A Quaker board of overseers, for example, educated both poor and paying students in Philadelphia. To promote the "more general diffusion of knowledge," Thomas Jefferson proposed legislation to establish a state system of education in Virginia. But many students still relied on academies, boarding schools, mechanics' institutes, and Sunday schools for training in basic skills long after Jefferson's time. Founded by well-to-do volunteers, charity schools offered the opportunity for a primary education to the children of the urban poor. In the cities of New York and Massachusetts more than a few parents transferred their children from private to public schools between 1800 and 1850. But much to the dismay of educational reformers, many others, rich and poor alike, neglected the formal education of their children, sending them to school infrequently or not at all. Establishing a system of public education was not the same as making it work.

During the first half of the nineteenth century, state governments gradually increased their presence in education. By 1850 most permitted local districts to levy taxes for schools, and many states required districts to raise revenue for basic education. Between 1848 and 1855 New York, Indiana, Illinois, and Wisconsin adopted such a mandate. The institution of slavery dampened enthusiasm for common school reform in the South; nevertheless, lawmakers in Virginia, North Carolina, and Georgia empowered towns and districts to levy school taxes if they chose. Some Southern legislatures even authorized the development of a statewide educational bureaucracy. The Alabama Free School Act of 1854 created the office of state superintendent, who was authorized to gather data about education, instruct teachers and school trustees on their duties, prescribe curriculum and texts, and oversee the state's educational finances. Virginia, on the other hand, waited until 1870 to create a Department of Public Instruction and appoint a state superintendent of schools. In the North and West, county school officials became commonplace in the middle years of the nineteenth century. They acted as intermediaries between the local teachers and the state board of education. Following the lead of Massachusetts, reformers in Ohio, Indiana, and Iowa tried to force the consolidation of district schools into township systems in the 1850s. But more often than not such administrative restructuring lacked rigor and discipline. It was not easy to remove the slack from the educational chain of command.

Support for the centralization of schooling came primarily from the urban middle class. Concerned about character formation, work discipline, and competent school management, many merchants, manufacturers, and professional men threw their support behind measures designed to make the delivery of educational services more efficient and systematic. But in the absence of good communication between the home and school, some parents resisted reforms of this nature that they might have been expected to accept. In 1837 school authorities in Boston faced determined parental opposition to a pupil redistribution plan intended to preserve gender segregation and relieve overcrowding in the city's elementary schools. In rural areas both parents and taxpayers often opposed state school leaders, classifying them as outsiders and their work as interference. In Massachusetts, Horace Mann could not count on the remote towns of the Berkshires to back him and the state Board of Education. As late as 1900 people in the American countryside were still resisting reforms aimed at any form of centralization. In both the South and the Midwest, parents fought to retain control over school taxation, teacher selection, schoolhouse location, and the length of the school term. Losing their grip on such matters would undermine the ideology of self-help and threaten the dignity that derived from being independent.

That reformers encountered strong resistance to the centralization and systematization of schools should not be taken as evidence of widespread disfavor for public education in the nineteenth century. Throughout the United States most people became convinced by 1850 that government should sponsor schools. Whether state or local authorities took primary responsibility, government had to be involved. In the face of rapid urbanization, accelerating immigration, and relentless westward expansion, the nation could not rely on private initiative either at home or in school. But until the middle of the century it was not clear where the boundary lay between the private and public sectors. Was the collective need for education satisfied merely by allocating public resources to schools regardless of who controlled them? Should parents be expected to pay for the education of their children? Was the state obliged to provide schooling for everyone or only for those who could not provide it for themselves? Should government schools be integrated by race, gender, or social class?

It took nearly fifty years to sort out the meaning of ''public'' in American education. In 1820 public education sometimes meant primary schools supported by the state for the education of the poor. Either private citizens or elected officials made policy for them. They could be free or supported in part by parental contributions. By the middle of the nineteenth century, the meaning of ''public'' in education had become universal. Public schools were those institutions of elementary education that were eligible for government support, subject to government control, free from tuition, and open to all white children, rich and poor alike.

Distinguishing the public from the private sphere was not restricted to the realm of education. In the first half of the nineteenth century, Americans confronted the need to differentiate more clearly between the individual and the common good in such disparate domains as business and moral reform. They debated the role of the state in the economy. Some said that government should encourage economic growth, while others believed in the wisdom of the marketplace. Americans also disagreed about the place of the polity in the lives of dependent, neglected, or undisciplined citizens. They reached no consensus about whether children and families were proper objects of public concern. But these were issues that affected everyone in an increasingly fragmented, complex, and diverse society. They cried out for action as well as attention.

Americans approached the concept of "public" in education with two different visions of the school's mission in mind. If the primary purpose of public education was to preserve the social and economic status quo, then public schools did not have to be accessible to all children. They could be only for those most likely to depart from established norms or upset the existing structure of American society. They could cater to the children of workers, immigrants, and the poor. It hardly mattered whether the state took charge of them or not. Since they would specialize in educating those outside the mainstream, elite volunteers could direct them as effectively as elected officials.

But there were many like Horace Mann who believed that the mission of public education should be more than merely social control. Public schools should honor both the future and the past. They should teach children to accept and direct economic growth while retaining their commitment to religious and political tradition. They should cultivate respect for capitalism, Protestantism, and republicanism. Such reformers favored a more inclusive concept of "public" in education. They thought that public schools should be not only supported and controlled by the state, but open and free to all white children as well. Their curriculum should be both basic and broad. Mann strongly opposed specialized trade training; it was not commensurate with the general purpose of public education. Defined in this way, common schools could meet the diverse needs of an expanding nation. They could satisfy the requirements of an aspiring people who were both attracted to and apprehensive about the consequences of change.

At the beginning of the nineteenth century, many state and local governments appropriated public money just for the education of the poor. The primary schools that opened in Boston in 1818 may have been accessible to any boy or girl, but their fundamental function was to rescue pauper children from lives of vice, crime, and ignorance. The welfare of such children had by then been the object of repeated attention in Philadelphia. As early as 1802 the Pennsylvania legislature passed a law providing for their education in private schools at public expense. Parents often derailed these plans by refusing to declare themselves indigent, and the city was forced to take an additional step. In 1809 it required its tax assessors to identify all children between five and twelve years of age whose families could not pay for their education. Such measures also proved to be inadequate. Led by the Quaker reformer Roberts Vaux, the Pennsylvania Society for the Promotion of Public Economy obtained legislation in 1818 establishing a free school system for the children of Philadelphia's poor.

When they supported education at all, Southern states aimed their aid at schools intended for the poor. Established by Virginia in 1810, the Literary Fund of the commonwealth confined its funding to pauper education until 1829, when individual communities received permission to apply state revenue to schools for white children irrespective of their parents' ability to pay. Not many districts chose to exercise this option before the Civil War. Georgia legally acknowledged the existence of pauper schools in 1818, and, except for a brief period in the late 1830s, its school fund existed exclusively for their support until 1858.

Such arrangements made good sense to those who thought of public education as a rearguard action. If the mission of the public school was merely to hold the line against unwanted social and economic change, then it could limit its reach to those at the margins of respectability. It did not have to be controlled by the polity. Nowhere was this concept of public education tested more fully and openly than in New York City. The Free School Society, founded in 1805, made basic education available to the poor children of the city. Although it relied on the state for the bulk of its funding, the Society remained largely independent of public control for nearly forty years. Men from the city's social and economic elite dominated its self-perpetuating board of trustees, setting educational policy that affected not only the poor but all New Yorkers before 1850.

In the 1820s the trustees of the Free School Society rethought the mission of their schools. They engaged in an open debate that called attention to the relationship between their schools and the state. This discussion raised many questions about the meaning of public education not just in New York but everywhere in the United States. Threatened by competition from denominational schools, the Society asked for exclusive rights to the city's share of the state school fund. In exchange it promised to open its schools to all children, regardless of their background. Although the Society never became the sole recipient of state school money in New York, it did open its schools to all in 1826. In recognition of this change in policy, the trustees secured the state's permission to rename their organization the Public School Society. They remained unconvinced, however, that public schools should be open and free to all. Mixing rich and poor threatened to make the Society's schools as unstable as New York City itself. Free schools reminded them too much of their own heritage as providers of charity education. Between 1826 and 1832 the Public School Society collected small tuition payments from parents who were willing and able to pay.

By 1832 the trustees of the Public School Society had discovered that they could not escape their reputation as educators of the poor. Far from attracting new pupils, tuition seemed to drive the old ones away. To eliminate any need for tuition, the trustees convinced the state legislature to authorize a property tax for basic education in New York City. It was a move that anticipated the policies of school reformers like Henry Barnard and especially Horace Mann. But when they scrapped tuition altogether in 1832, the trustees returned in practice to their original plan of providing free education for the children of the poor. After all, it was this segment of the population that still posed the greatest threat to the city's social and economic equilibrium. Still, the Public School Society's experiment with reform was not without significance or lasting meaning. Working in the nation's largest city, the Society's trustees had opened the door to a frank discussion of the concept of public education. Could public schools charge tuition? Did government support entail open admission?

The trustees' answers to these questions were not unambiguous. By 1832 they seemed certain only that public schools should not charge tuition. The children of the working class continued to comprise the vast majority of the Society's clientele. But over the next decade its pupils became more diversified; the sons and daughters of artisans and lawyers, merchants and clerks enrolled in at least some of its schools. The trustees did not turn such children away. Regardless of the special need to educate the children of the poor, public education in New York was beginning to mean something more comprehensive.

In 1840 the Society faced a new challenge to its concept of public education. Led by Bishop John Hughes, the Roman Catholic Church pressed the city and the state for money to maintain its denominational schools. It was not the first time that religious leaders in New York had asked the government to offset their educational debts. In fact, public support for denominational charity schools had been common before 1825. But the Catholic Church was interested in operating more than merely pauper schools. Unwilling to expose Catholic children to what it considered the Protestant bias of the Society's schools, the church demanded public money to educate them all in parish schools. In opposing the church, the Public School Society appealed to the principle of the separation of church and state. It was a persuasive argument, for in the end the church failed to obtain state aid for its schools. But the episode cost the Society its independence, calling attention to the anachronism of public support for education in the absence of public control. In 1842 New York adopted a complex system of local school committees. Based in each political ward, these committees reported to a central Board of Education whose ultimate authority the Society was forced to accept. Elected officials now superseded the Society's private board of trustees.

The New York Public School Society finally expired in 1853, the victim of its own obsolescence. Few expressed regret at its demise, but its trustees could look back with pride at some of their accomplishments. Like Horace Mann and Henry Barnard in New England, they brought some semblance of order and organization to education in New York. Their use of the monitorial system standardized expectations about the practice of teaching. The hierarchy of schools that they developed encouraged pupils to proceed from one level of education to another. The local school committees introduced in 1842 temporarily slowed the pace of educational centralization in New York. But the Society's efforts at systematization were not responsible for its failure to make a more enduring contribution to the history of American education. Instead, it was the trustees' preoccupation with social order and economic stability. Thinking in such conservative terms, they could be content with a narrow concept of public education. It need not be anything more than a basic service to acculturate the poor over which the elite would maintain strict control.

By the middle of the nineteenth century, many middle-class Americans conceived of education in their society differently. They imagined the United States as a self-reliant nation devoted to both progress and tradition, intelligence and virtue, freedom and morality. Only an inclusive system of education could reconcile such ideological opposites. Nothing less than a complex and comprehensive concept of the public school would do. It had to be a democratic institution, accessible to all. It had to be accountable, balancing the benefits of public support against the limitations of public control.

Many intellectuals and reformers accepted and articulated such a vision for education in America. The Baptist minister and college president Francis Wayland believed that both public morality and material progress depended upon improved education. His Unitarian colleague, William Ellery Channing, associated education with moral integrity and spiritual freedom. Together, he said, the mind and the soul would make Americans an independent yet responsible people. The educational reformers Frances Wright and Robert Dale Owen would not have disagreed. They believed that knowledge was indispensable to self-government. It was so important, in fact, that nothing about education could be left to chance. The state, said Owen and Wright, should take custody of all children, preparing them for the freedom of adulthood by isolating them in their formative years from all improper influences. It was a radical plan, yet one that was perfectly consistent with faith in the power of education. In the antebellum era it is not unreasonable to say, as one historian has, that many Americans believed in ''anarchy with a schoolmaster.''[1]

The leaders of the common school movement thought this way. Horace Mann took the position that more than any other public institution, common schools promoted both stability and progress. They instilled respect for freedom and authority. They were an engine of economic growth and a guarantor of equal opportunity. They were a source of shared values in an increasingly heterogeneous society. Above all, they taught civic virtue and social responsibility. A good education, Mann wrote in 1837, will raise the infant ''from his cradle into . . . manhood . . . possessed of all those qualities and attributes, which a being created in the image of God *ought to have*.'' Only the public school, he thought, could give Americans the capacity to be free and the will to resist when freedom turned in the direction of excess.[2]

In their efforts to transform the ideas of men like Horace Mann into legislation, school reformers often argued that public education was utilitarian; it would solve many practical problems. Common schools, they asserted, were the answer to crime and poverty. They built bulwarks against family breakdown and social decay. In his enthusiasm for public education, Mann conveyed the impression that common schools were a panacea. Without them the republic surely would fail to realize its promise. As Irish and German immigrants began to arrive in ever greater numbers, fears about the future multiplied. Advocates of public education responded by reminding their friends and neighbors of the importance of ideological uniformity. Every citizen, Mann insisted, should obtain a common core of cultural knowledge and political values. The destiny of America depended upon it, and the public school was the place to begin.

Although shared beliefs and expectations were essential to the future of America, the nation also needed disciplined workers and capitalists—men whose industry, judgment, self-reliance, and tolerance for risk would fuel economic development and prosperity. Such men would not appear automatically; they would have to learn the skills and values necessary to succeed. The public school was the key to economic growth. By teaching literacy, rewarding merit, and inculcating respect for work, common schools would both teach character and give children the tools they needed to contribute to economic expansion and the accumulation of wealth.

The ideology of the common school harbored many tensions and contradictions, but there also was a distinct bias to it. It favored middle-class aspirations and liberal, Protestant ideals: Individual character upheld public morality and propelled upward social mobility. There was nativism, too. Textbook after textbook portrayed Protestants as heroes and Catholics as villains. Ethnic and religious minorities complained about cultural discrimination in public education. German immigrants objected to the exclusive use of English in the common schools. Urban Catholics became so disenchanted with the Anglo-Protestant orientation of public schools that they diverted scarce resources to parish schools. Even many Protestants could not accept the common core approach to moral education that Horace Mann characterized as unobjectionable. Prayer in school and Bible reading "without note or comment" might seem beyond reproach. But some Calvinists thought the pan-Protestant ideology of the common school reformers placed altogether too much emphasis on human goodness and perfectibility, and many evangelicals took issue with the degree to which it seemed to disregard the hand of God in the affairs of men. The development of an independent system of Sunday schools in the nineteenth century may have helped advance the cause of public education by providing an outlet for sectarian education.

The expansion of schooling dovetailed with the agenda of the middle class. Common schools were not so much intended to prepare the working class for the factory as to enlarge economic opportunity for those in the best position to take advantage of a dynamic economy. Rather than being critics of public education, the working class more often proved indifferent to educational reform. Although some artisans in New York pushed for common schools, the enthusiasm of the labor movement for public education never went much beneath the surface of its leadership. Middle-class support for education and school reform did not depend upon industrialization. In Massachusetts, enrollment and attendance were more likely to be higher in towns engaged in commerce than in manufacturing. Local economic conditions affected the growth of public education. An expanding tax base made the proposals of men like Horace Mann appeal to voters and businessmen in ways that a stagnant economy never could.

Common school reformers could not ignore gender and race. Committed to the principle of education for all, they had to respond to the claims of women and blacks for access to public schooling. By 1860 it was clear that the experience of African Americans with public education would be very different from that of girls and women. Early and widespread acceptance of the practice of coeducation made equal access to public schools for boys and girls almost a matter of principle by midcentury. But when blacks had the chance to attend tax-supported schools at all, it was usually in segregated schools.

Formal education for girls was far from an established fact in the eighteenth century. Even in Massachusetts it was not uncommon for daughters to remain at home while their brothers went to school. Girls were excluded from the town schools of Boston and Northampton until the 1790s. But in colonial America family, church, and school were overlapping institutions with functions that were not sharply differentiated. It seemed perfectly natural for some women to assume responsibility for the care and training of other people's children. In New England they taught basic literacy to boys and girls at home, an informal practice that gradually evolved into publicly supported summer schools for young children. Operated by women, such schools established the idea that gender should not block the way to public education.

Between 1830 and 1860 many school reformers endorsed the principle of public education for women. It would improve their moral leadership at home, said Catharine Beecher, Emma Willard, and Mary Lyon, each the director of a well-known seminary for the advanced education of women. It would make them better able to teach their children the virtues of good citizenship, said Horace Mann and Henry Barnard. Taught together, boys and girls would learn from one another, the former acquiring some gentility while the latter gained a measure of self-assurance. But the case for gender equality in elementary education remained in doubt until the 1850s, when Americans discovered the savings that could be achieved by hiring female teachers. With women in charge, girls could not be excluded easily from public schools or relegated to separate facilities.

The South was slower to accept both public education and coeducation than any other region in the United States. The single-sex, private school sheltered Southern white girls from unruly boys or uncouth companions for most of the nineteenth century. African-American girls, on the other hand, did not require such delicate treatment. In the black public schools of the post-Reconstruction South, coeducation was the norm. But distinguishing between the education of whites and blacks was nothing new in the South or the nation as a whole. Although he opposed segregation, Horace Mann was unwilling to jeopardize the cause of public education by demanding racial justice in the common schools of Massachusetts. Elsewhere in the United States, African Americans rarely benefited from school reform to the same degree as whites.

Before the end of the Civil War, most Southern states made a concerted effort to keep blacks in ignorance. As early as 1740, South Carolina prohibited the education of blacks. Its lead was followed throughout the South during the first half of the nineteenth century. After Nat Turner led a slave insurrection in 1831, Virginia, North Carolina, and Alabama raised legal barriers to black education. In Northern and Western states, African Americans obtained access to public schools by 1860, but progress was slow and the way was marked by persistent discrimination.

Private schools gave free blacks their first opportunity for a formal education. Sponsored by churches and such secular organizations as colonization and abolition societies, pauper schools offered blacks a basic education. Quakers and Anglicans operated charity schools for African Americans, beginning in the eighteenth century. The New York Manumission Society opened its African Free School in 1787; it was followed by similar institutions in Boston, Philadelphia, New Haven, and Portland, Maine. In some places free blacks took responsibility for their own education. They organized day schools, Sabbath schools, and literary societies in Philadelphia, Albany, and New York City. Established by African Americans in 1846, the Society for the Promotion of Education Among Colored Children conducted two elementary schools in New York City but failed to generate enough support to maintain a high school for the city's black population.

Like the Public School Society, the Society for the Promotion of Education Among Colored Children received public money for its schools. Like its larger counterpart, it, too, lost this money when the Board of Education assumed control of all the public schools in New York in 1853. Still, public education was no panacea for African Americans. Public schools often were segregated, and black schools seldom received the same support as those for whites.

In the major Northern cities racial discrimination was commonplace in public education. Not one common school in Boston, New York, or Philadelphia was integrated before 1850. Blacks and whites in Brooklyn shared a building, but not classrooms, until local authorities erected a schoolhouse just for blacks in 1827. A combined primary and grammar school, the Lombard Street School was the largest and most important public school for African Americans in Philadelphia. Only a vigorous effort by the city's black community convinced school officials not to close it in 1841. Excluded from the city's new Central High School for boys, the alumni of the Lombard Street School could attend the private Institute for Colored Youth instead.

Legislation both hindered and advanced the cause of public school integration. An Ohio law, enacted in 1829, prohibited blacks' attendance at common schools. By midcentury blacks in Ohio could enroll in white public schools but only if they were few in number. The presence of twenty blacks in a school district constituted legal grounds for a separate school. Pennsylvania adopted a similar statute in 1854. A New York law, on the other hand, opened the state's public schools to all children, at least in theory, in 1841. Six years later the New York superintendent of education ruled that African Americans had the right to enroll with whites.

In Massachusetts school segregation became a public issue in the 1840s. Horace Mann showed his personal distaste for it when he refused to address a lyceum in New Bedford until the organization agreed to drop its policy limiting the audience to whites. In 1848 Mann and his second wife, Mary Peabody Mann, opened the spare bedroom in their new home to the first black admitted to the state normal school in West Newton, thereby offending many of their neighbors but making it possible for her to attend. The legality of public school segregation received a real test in the commonwealth between 1844 and 1855. Led by the black abolitionist William C. Nell, Boston's African Americans boycotted the all-black Smith School, sued the city unsuccessfully in the famous *Roberts* case, filed numerous petitions, and eventually persuaded the legislature to outlaw color as a criterion for admission to public school. Despite such advances, the practice of segregated education did not disappear entirely in Massachusetts or very much at all in the United States as a whole.

By the middle of the nineteenth century, Americans had drawn the outline of public education. Some regions of the country would fill it out more rapidly than others. Public schools were tax-supported and came under the authority of government officials. Any child could attend a public school, but not necessarily the one of his or her choice. Professional educators managed public education. They saw to it that the common schools taught both self-discipline and self-reliance in an orderly and efficient manner. They tried to reconcile the democratic tradition of local control with the practical advantages of centralized decision making.

Since the middle of the nineteenth century there have been many important changes in American education. School attendance has become compulsory. The high school is no longer a peripheral institution. Students with disabilities are now counted in the constituency of the public schools. Because of Progressive reformers like John Dewey, educators think differently about the relationship between teacher and learner; they believe that schools should adjust to students, not just the other way around. But modern education has not escaped the influence of men like Horace Mann. Even after his death on 2 August 1859, shortly after his retirement from the presidency of Antioch College, Mann lived on in the legacy of his ideas. By defining the common school as the only one entitled to receive public support, Mann, and others, set the terms by which Americans still debate the present status and future prospects of schooling in the United States. Contemporary reformers who favor giving parents public money to buy a private education, if they choose, find themselves sparring with the ideological legacy of Mann.

By stressing the benefits of professional school teaching and centralized leadership, the common school reformers shaped the way in which the politics of education would be construed for years to come. Educators in the Progressive era built upon the bureaucratic foundation laid by their predecessors. They extended the practice of centralized decision making and redefined the meaning of professional expertise. But it is not unfair to say that nineteenth-century school reformers such as Mann still cast their shadow over the organization and administration of schools today. Modern reformers who favor school-based management or more parental control must contend with assumptions that can be traced to the mid-nineteenth century. In school reform and public education, the more things have changed, the more they have remained the same. Once established and defined, public education became a remarkably enduring and steadfast institution in American life.

NOTES

1. Rush Welter, *Popular Education and Democratic Thought in America* (New York, 1962), 117–118.
2. Horace Mann, *Lectures on Education* (Boston, 1855; repr. New York, 1969), 16–17.

BIBLIOGRAPHY

Bowles, Samuel, and Herbert Gintis. *Schooling in Capitalist America: Educational Reform and the Contradictions of Economic Life*. New York, 1976.

Cremin, Lawrence A. *American Education: The National Experience, 1783–1876*. New York, 1980.

———. ed. *The Republic and the School: Horace Mann on the Education of Free Men*. New York, 1957.

Fuller, Wayne. *The Old Country School: The Story of Rural Education in the Middle West*. Chicago, 1982.

Glenn, Charles L., Jr. *The Myth of the Common School*. Amherst, Mass., 1988.

Jackson, Sidney L. *America's Struggle for Free Schools: Social Tension and Education in New England and New York, 1827–1842*. New York, 1965.

Kaestle, Carl F. *The Evolution of an Urban School System: New York City, 1750–1850*. Cambridge, Mass., 1973.

———. *Pillars of the Republic: Common Schools and American Society, 1780–1860*. New York, 1983.

Kaestle, Carl F., and Maris A. Vinovskis. *Education and Social Change in Nineteenth-Century Massachusetts*. New York, 1980.

Katz, Michael B. *The Irony of Early School Reform: Educational Innovation in Mid-Nineteenth Century Massachusetts*. Cambridge, Mass., 1968.

Katznelson, Ira, and Margaret Weir. *Schooling for All: Class, Race, and the Decline of the Democratic Ideal*. New York, 1985.

Mabee, Carleton. *Black Education in New York State from Colonial to Modern Times*. New York, 1970.

Macmullen, Edith Nye. *In the Cause of True Education: Henry Barnard & Nineteenth-Century School Reform*. New Haven, 1991.

Messerli, Jonathan. *Horace Mann: A Biography*. New York, 1972.

Ravitch, Diane. *The Great School Wars: New York City, 1805–1973*. New York, 1974.

Schultz, Stanley K. *The Culture Factory: Boston Public Schools, 1789–1860*. New York, 1973.

Tyack, David B. *The One Best System: A History of American Urban Education*. Cambridge, Mass., 1974.

Tyack, David, and Elizabeth Hansot. *Managers of Virtue: Public School Leadership in America, 1820–1980*. New York, 1982.

———. *Learning Together: A History of Coeducation in American Schools*. New Haven, 1990.

Welter, Rush. *Popular Education and Democratic Thought in America*. New York, 1962.

Russell Means
and Native-American Rights

RAYMOND WILSON

For nearly three decades, Russell Means has been a leading force in Native-American reform. "My ultimate aim," declared Means, "is the reinstitution of pride and self-dignity of the Indian in America."[1] Indeed, since the 1960s, Means has been involved in many of the dramatic demonstrations for Native-American rights, which demanded Indian self-determination, enforcement of treaties negotiated between tribes and the federal government, and better treatment of American Indians. Means addressed the significant issues facing Native Americans, but his inclination to resort to violence often weakened the objectives of the demonstration.

Until the early twentieth century, non-Indians dominated and headed Indian protest movements. Such organizations as the Indian Rights Association (1882) and the Lake Mohonk Conference of Friends of the Indian (1883) stressed assimilation of Indians into the mainstream society. Richard Henry Pratt, head of the Carlisle Indian School in Pennsylvania, emphasized the need to remold Indians into the white man's image.

It was not until 1911 that a group of educated Native Americans established the Society of American Indians, the first Indian reform organization run by Indians. Although this organization also encouraged assimilation through increased acculturation, it allowed Indians more of a voice in accepting or rejecting changes in their lifestyles. During the 1930s, Federal Bureau of Indian Affairs commissioner John Collier's Indian New Deal followed somewhat of a similar approach. And in 1944, the National Congress of American Indians (NCAI) was formed. Its Indian leadership focused on federal Indian policies. After World War II, the NCAI became a leading opponent of federal relocation and termination policies that threatened Indians' treaty rights and helped stimulate the Indian protest movements in the 1960s and 1970s.

This new Indian activism, which adopted methods used by African-American protest movements, demanded federal recognition of treaty rights and more political, economic, and educational rights for Indian people. Indian self-determination became the ultimate goal. Additional Indian-led organizations formed to give Indians more power included the National Tribal Chairmen's Association (1965) and the Council of Energy Resource Tribes (1975).

One of the most active and best-known of the protest organizations was the American Indian Movement (AIM), established in 1968. Much of AIM's activism can be associated with the actions of one of its leaders, Russell Means, who became a pivotal and controversial figure in Indian protest movements.

Russell Charles Means was born on the Pine Ridge Indian Reservation in South Dakota on 10 November 1939. He was the eldest of four sons (Ted and twins named Bill and Dale) born to Harold Means, a mixed-blood Oglala, and Theodora Means, a full-blood Yankton. After the outbreak of World War II, Harold Means, an auto mechanic and welder, moved his family to California and obtained work at the Mare Island Navy Yard near San Francisco.

Means received his childhood education at a reservation school and public schools in Vallejo, California. He earned good grades, enjoyed athletics, became a Catholic, and participated in the Boy Scouts. As an Indian attending white schools, Means faced discrimination, which intensified after he entered San Leandro High School. Such an unhealthy atmosphere took its toll on Means. His grades dropped and his involvement in sports suffered. Confrontations and fights became more common. Means became a juvenile delinquent and began to take drugs. In spite of these problems, he managed to receive his high school diploma.

After high school, Means drifted from place to place and from job to job. He went to Los Angeles, kicked his drug addiction, then became an alcoholic. In San Francisco, Means worked briefly as a ballroom dance instructor. Other jobs included laborer, farmhand, rodeo hand, and janitor. Although Means attended several colleges, such as the University of California at Los Angeles, Arizona State University, and Cleveland State College, he never graduated.

Within the framework of the 1960s, a decade of social rebellion and upheaval by minority groups who no longer passively accepted their mistreatment by the dominant society, Means took pride in his Indianness and engaged in activism. In 1964 he participated with other Indians in the initial, unsuccessful attempt to seize the abandoned federal prison on Alcatraz Island (a more coordinated occupation happened in 1969). The Indian demonstrators believed they had a right to take over the area because of a federal law that allowed abandoned federal property to revert to its previous owners. Symbolically, the demonstrators represented all Indians and hoped to win support for their demands for better treatment from the federal government.

Toward the end of the 1960s, Means became more active in issues involving Native-American rights. He worked briefly for the tribal council at Rosebud Indian Reservation in South Dakota. He then moved to Cleveland, Ohio, where he became director of the Cleveland American Indian Center, a government-funded operation. He showed promise as a skillful demonstrator, a trait that eventually brought him praise and criticism from both Indians and non-Indians. In 1969 Means met Dennis Banks, a Chippewa who had helped found the American Indian Movement (AIM), an Indian protest group started in Minneapolis, Minnesota, to protect urban Indians from harassment and violence in 1968. Impressed with AIM's objectives and tactics, Means founded the second AIM chapter, in Cleveland.

Indian activism continued and intensified in the 1970s, attracting more national attention to Indian matters and support from white liberals. Indian militancy increased, as shown by the number of events involving obstructive tactics such as "fish-ins" to protest violations of Indian treaty fishing rights and temporarily seizing places. On Thanksgiving Day, 1970, Means and other Indians took over the *Mayflower II* in Plymouth, Massachusetts, protesting, among other things, the terrible treatment of Indians by early white settlers; and in June 1971, he participated in AIM demonstrations that focused on Lakota claims to the sacred Black Hills, stolen from them in the 1870s, at Mount Rushmore. Both incidents focused on Indian demands for redress of past grievances, increased Means's stature as a spokesman for Indian people, and attracted media attention.

During the 1970s Means and Dennis Banks became well-known AIM activists throughout the nation. Means continued to attract the attention of the media and gained more support from non-Indian liberals. In September 1971, Means and about sixty Indians unsuccessfully attempted to occupy the Bureau of Indian Affairs (BIA) building in Washington, D.C. Means also filed a multimillion-dollar suit against the Cleveland Indians, declaring that its baseball mascot, Chief Wahoo, served as a symbol of racism directed against Indian people.

In February 1972, Means was involved in AIM's major intervention into the killing of Raymond Yellow Thunder, an Oglala from Pine Ridge Indian Reservation, by white men at Gordon, Nebraska. Two white brothers, who had boasted about roughing up an Indian, seized, beat, and publicly humiliated Yellow Thunder, who was later found dead in a truck on a used car lot on 20 February 1972. Too many times, Indian deaths resulted in minor punishments for the whites accused of killing them. Several hundred Indians took part in the protest and demanded that justice be served. Means and AIM forced the authorities to handle the case properly. In addition, Gordon officials agreed to form a board to hear Indian complaints. AIM's involvement in the incident and Means's declaration, "We've come here to Gordon today to secure justice for American Indians and to put Gordon on the map . . . and if justice is not immediately forthcoming, we'll be back to take Gordon off the map," enhanced their reputations among reservation Indians.[2]

By mid-1972, Means had resigned his position at the Cleveland Indian Center and returned to South Dakota. In July 1972, Means and other AIM members met at Rosebud Indian Reservation in South Dakota to plan a demonstration at the BIA building in Washington, D.C., in November, to coincide with the presidential election race between President Richard Nixon and George McGovern. Known as the Trail of Broken Treaties, the demonstration called upon Indians throughout the nation to organize caravans to the nation's capital to protest the numerous promises the federal government had made to Indian people and then broken.

Means was assigned to assemble a caravan in Seattle. He and Banks later met in San Francisco and headed east, stopping at several reservations to enlist additional participants. On 1 November the Indian caravans began to arrive at the nation's capital. Instead of adequate accommodations promised to them by government officials, the Indians found their lodging crowded and rat-infested. Equally disturbing was the group of government officials who met with the Indians. Their lack of sincerity and condescending attitudes enhanced the Indians' discontent.

As a result, Means and others staged a protest demonstration at the BIA. A confrontation ensued, which resulted in AIM occupying the building and renaming it the Native American Embassy on 2 November. Barricaded inside the building, the Indians destroyed and damaged furnishings and other items. The Nixon administration wanted to avoid excessive violence and decided to engage in negotiations, in which Means played a prominent role. The government agreed to look into AIM's twenty demands, which included reviewing treaty violations, increasing Indian sovereignty over Indian and non-Indian issues, and replacing the BIA with a new structure.

The Indian occupants withdrew on 9 November. The government promised limited amnesty and allocated $66,500 to transport the Indians home. Indian acts of destruction and vandalism could be prosecuted, however. Indeed, the occupation resulted in about $2 million worth of damages and a large number of missing documents. The highly publicized occupation of the BIA did more harm than good for the Indian movement because the acts of violence received more attention than the discussion of the Indians' grievances. Means argued, however, that documents he had procured definitively proved that the federal government had violated many of its promises to Indians. The Nixon administration later rejected the twenty demands, although Nixon did support Indian self-determination and other programs for Indian people.

Means returned to Pine Ridge, where he contested the leadership of Oglala Tribal Chairman Richard Wilson. He blamed Wilson for all the major problems on the reservation. A staunch opponent of AIM and Means, Wilson secured a tribal council resolution that prohibited AIM members from participating in meetings on the reservation. Wilson detested the divisiveness that AIM created at Pine Ridge and feared the threat that Means posed to his authority. Means planned to attend a meeting of the Oglala Sioux Landowners Association, in which he claimed membership, on 20 November 1972. Tribal police arrested and held him for several hours. After his release, Means held a press conference in Rapid City, declaring his rights had been violated. The stage was set for a major confrontation that pitted Indians against Indians: Means and other AIM members versus Wilson, his supporters, and a special guard of about forty men, whom Wilson's opponents called the ''goon squad.''

Means became involved in another AIM incident in Scottsbluff, Nebraska, in January 1973. Chicano activists invited AIM to participate with them in an united effort to expose similar discriminatory practices they encountered as minorities. One of the complaints involved police brutality. On 14 January 1973, violence broke out when the Scottsbluff police refused to talk to the activists. As a result, Means and others were arrested on a variety of charges that included intoxication, disorderly conduct, and carrying concealed weapons. An outraged Means declared, ''The frontier mentality of people in this area makes the Ku Klux Klan look like a Girl Scout troop.'' Means also contended that a loaded weapon was thrown into his cell, and he was ordered ''to make a break for it.''[3] Later, a U.S. District judge dropped all charges against Means and the other activists.

In February 1973, Means and other AIM members protested the second-degree manslaughter charge against a white man who had stabbed to death Wesley Bad Heart Bull in the small town of Buffalo Gap in Custer County, South Dakota. Means declared, ''I want to know why this white man who killed an Indian is charged with second-degree manslaughter instead of first-degree murder.''[4] At the Custer County Court House, discussions went nowhere, and a riot ensued in which several policemen and Indians were injured. Means, Banks, and other Indians were arrested. Means later served a thirty-day jail term for his involvement in this demonstration.

Political conditions at Pine Ridge continued to deteriorate in February. Means played an active role in the attempted impeachment charges brought against Chairman Wilson by some of the traditional chiefs; the Oglala Sioux Civil Rights Organization, a group that opposed the tribal chairman; and others. They accused Wilson of violating the tribal constitution and misusing tribal funds. All impeachment charges against Wilson were dismissed by the tribal council. According to Wilson's accusers, they did not have enough time to prepare their case adequately; moreover, they declared that Wilson exerted too much control over the tribal council proceedings against him. A few days later, Means attempted in vain to meet with Wilson to discuss abuses against Indians on and off the reservation. According to Means, he barely escaped a beating from Wilson's ''goon squad.'' The stage was now set for AIM's occupation of Wounded Knee.

After several strategy meetings, Means and approximately 200 followers, many of them armed, decided to occupy the hamlet of Wounded Knee on the Pine Ridge Indian Reservation on 27 February 1973. The well-known site was chosen because it symbolized the last major confrontation between the Sioux and the U.S. Army in 1890. The occupants declared they were the new traditional tribal government, demanded the removal of Wilson as tribal chairman, and requested a U.S. Senate investigation of treaty violations and of the BIA. Federal Bureau of Investigation agents, federal marshals, and BIA police swiftly established a perimeter around Wounded Knee. The standoff attracted mass media coverage, which Means and other AIM leaders skillfully exploited, for the next ten weeks. Firefights occurred, and two people were killed during the seventy-one-day siege. Wilson severely criticized Means and other AIM members for the seizure and their tactics.

Finally, in April, Means and other AIM leaders were permitted to go to Washington, D.C., to negotiate a settlement. Means had agreed to be taken to Rapid City, South Dakota, for arraignment. He was released under a $25,000 bond. The talks broke down, and Means was later held until the occupation ended. In May the federal government finally agreed to investigate the tribal government at Pine Ridge and the status of the 1868 Fort Laramie Treaty with the Sioux. The occupation officially ended on 8 May.

AIM's militant actions at Wounded Knee highlighted Indian grievances, but the violence was condemned by many Indians and non-Indians alike. AIM leadership was criticized for being dominated by urban rather than rural Indians. Even though the violent confrontations did not force the federal government to accept AIM's demands, Indian grievances and demands for more self-determination became major issues that the federal government subsequently addressed in the 1980s and 1990s. Means later observed that ''Wounded Knee was and is the catalyst for the rebirth of our self-dignity and pride in being Indians.''[5]

Means faced ten felony charges for his involvement at Wounded Knee II (as it has become known to distinguish it from the 1890 tragedy). If found guilty, he could receive a maximum sentence of eighty-five years in prison and $96,000 in fines. During the trial, Means challenged Wilson for the office of tribal chairman. He accused Wilson of not representing Indians and won the primary election by over 150 votes in January 1974. In the general election, however, Wilson retained his chairmanship by beating Means, 1,709 to 1,530 votes. Means appealed the results, citing threats, bribery, and ballot fraud by Wilson supporters. Although irregularities certainly existed, Wilson retained his position.

The trial of Means and Dennis Banks for their involvement at Wounded Knee II began on 8 January 1974 in St. Paul, Minnesota. The trial lasted for several months. Among the defense attorneys representing AIM were William Kunstler and Mark Lane, two lawyers who were quite effective in questioning the methods government officials used to gather evidence. The trial ended in September when federal judge Fred Nichol dismissed all charges against Means and Banks because of government misconduct that included lying under oath, illegal wire taps, and altered documents.

During and after the trial, Means continued his activism, some of which resulted in his sustaining bodily injuries through stabbing and shooting. For example, in April 1974 he was arrested for riot and assault at the courthouse in Sioux Falls, South Dakota. Means later served one year (1978–1979) in South Dakota State Penitentiary for his involvement in the courthouse riot. While in prison, he was stabbed by another inmate.

In March 1975, Means was present at a murder in a bar at Scenic, South

Dakota. Before the victim died, he declared Means did not kill him. In June a BIA policeman shot Means in the stomach during a bar incident at Fort Yates on the Standing Rock Indian Reservation in North Dakota. And in 1978, Means, before beginning his prison sentence, participated with other Indians in ''The Longest Walk,'' a protest march from Alcatraz in California to Washington, D.C., which at its peak attracted some 30,000 Indians, to protest anti-Indian legislation and other matters. Means even engaged in an exchange concerning Indian sovereignty and local and state laws with Senator Edward Kennedy, well known for his support of Indian causes.

After his parole in July 1979, Means resumed his activism. He became an advocate of environmental protection. Indians have long had a special relationship to the land. They continue to complain about its ruination and exploitation for profit. Means joined with other Indians and non-Indians in protesting dangerous environmental practices of certain corporate interests in South Dakota. He helped establish Camp Yellow Thunder (named after Raymond Yellow Thunder, who had been murdered in Gordon, Nebraska, in 1972) in the Black Hills. The camp was built as a spiritual and educational center, and in condemnation of the 1980 U.S. Supreme Court monetary settlement relating to the illegal seizure of the Black Hills by the United States. The Indians wanted the land back. And on 27 February 1983, the tenth anniversary of Wounded Knee II, Means again tried to become tribal chairman at Pine Ridge but was declared ineligible because he was a convicted felon.

For the remainder of the 1980s and into the 1990s, Means continued his efforts on behalf of Native-American rights. For example, he went to Nicaragua and to Canada to speak out against the mistreatment of native peoples. As the keynote speaker, on 28 March 1990, for Kansas State University's Native American Heritage Month, Means opposed the plan to expand Fort Riley and compared the expansion's impact of forcing farmers and ranchers to give up land to the taking of Indian lands by the federal government.

The redefinition of historical sites to recognize Indian perspectives emerged as an important spin-off from Indian activism in the 1980s. Means actively campaigned to rename Custer Battlefield National Monument as Little Bighorn Battlefield National Monument. He and others had long demanded the name change because it would better reflect the incident. The official ceremony that recognized the name change took place at the monument in November 1992.

Two other demonstrations in which Means participated concerned protests to end observance of Columbus Day in Denver, Colorado, and demands to eliminate racial discrimination against Indian students in the public schools in Rapid City, South Dakota. For several years, Means and AIM had opposed the celebration of Columbus Day, viewing it as an insult to Indian people. When in 1992, the quincentennary of the ''discovery'' of America by Christopher Columbus, groups throughout the United States planned special ceremonies to celebrate the event, a major confrontation was imminent because Indians viewed Columbus as more of a destroyer than a discover of a New World.

Means focused his attention on the planned ceremony in Denver, Colorado. The state of Colorado was the first state to have Columbus Day declared a legal holiday (in 1907), and for years Means had protested against the Columbus Day parade in Denver. He had been charged on previous occasions with such violations as disturbing the peace, obstructing a public street, and disobeying a police ordinance. Means argued that he was just exercising his constitutional right to protest.

Means and other AIM members tried to convince the Federation of Italian-American Organizations of Colorado to have as the main theme of their October 1992 parade the celebration of Italian-American culture and to eliminate all references to Columbus. Means insisted that the parade was "not an . . . Indian vs. Italian issue. It's an issue of racism."[6] The federation refused to exclude the name of Columbus from its parade but invited, as it had in the past, Indian activists to march with them. The Indians refused the invitation.

Denver authorities anticipated a violent confrontation between the two groups. Hundreds of police officers were assigned to arrest any person breaking the law. Means met with the Denver police chief and pledged that AIM would be nonviolent. "Now, if the police make it violent," continued Means, "then we will defend ourselves to the best of our ability."[7]

The Columbus Day parade was scheduled to begin at 10 A.M. on Sunday, 11 October 1992. At about 9:15 A.M., the parade organizers decided to cancel the event because of the potential risks. AIM protesters learned of the cancellation at 9:45. A jubilant Means declared, "We won. We abolished the holiday."[8] A shouting match later occurred between the protesters and Italian Americans on the capitol steps, where the latter gathered to hear speeches, to sing songs, and to dance. Such disputes between Indian groups, Italian Americans, and other organizers of Columbus Day programs throughout the United States continued in the 1990s and spilled over into efforts to strip Columbus's name from streets and public places. The struggle over memorializing Columbus involved views of history neither side was willing to concede.

Such concerns led to challenges to school curriculum and policy. In May 1993, Means was among the approximately 200 concerned parents who staged peaceful marches and rallies in an effort to convince the Rapid City Board of Education to adopt policies that would eliminate racism and bigotry. Means was particularly upset with the pushing, shoving, and verbal abuse directed against his two daughters by other students. A meeting took place between the protesters and the board. After serious discussion, the board agreed that racism would not be tolerated; students should not feel threatened in school. Indicative of a trend in American education, school officials promised to make curriculum and teaching more culturally oriented and less biased, and to include Indian representatives on the board and in the schools. Pleased with the outcome of the meeting, Means stated, "This is the first Indian community in the United States to stand up against racism."[9]

By the mid-1990s, Native-American activists could count several successes in redirecting the federal government's Indian policies. Examples include the restoration of Blue Lake to the Taos Pueblo; the settlement of Alaska natives' land claims; the restoration of tribal status to the Menominees; and the passage of laws strengthening Indian self-determination, religious freedom, education, child welfare, and loan and grant programs. Still, major problems continued, such as reservation unemployment, alcoholism, an alarming suicide rate, and the controversial issue of Indian gaming.

Means remained a significant voice for Indian America, fighting for the improvement of reservation conditions and other issues. He came to prominence during the turbulent 1960s, when Indian America, frustrated by injustices, neglect, and unfulfilled promises, could no longer stay silent. Indians rejected the forced assimilation programs to ''get the Indian out of the Indian.'' They demanded self-determination, which enabled tribes to have more decision-making functions, and the recognition of federal treaty obligations. Means was among Indian demonstrators who adopted the more militant protest methods and skillful use of mass media of some other minority groups. He attracted attention to major Indian causes, but his violent methods often alienated people and diverted attention from genuine Indian grievances.

Many Indians despised AIM and Means for their advocacy of violence. As time passed, critics of AIM and Means used the distinction between rural (reservation) Indians and urban Indians (AIM membership) to undermine AIM and Means, declaring they had lost touch with reservation issues. For example, one influential critic, Tim Giago, Lakota editor of *Indian Country Today*, a national Indian newspaper, condemned the radical methods used by Means and AIM, arguing that they had little support on reservations and insisting that AIM had become an urban Indian organization. Clyde Bellecourt, a founder of AIM, and Means had a falling out, each accusing the other of not truly representing Indian people and AIM.

Nevertheless, Means's distinctive looks and speaking abilities have served him well. To many, he stands as a symbol for Indian Americans. Recently, Means has used Hollywood as a medium to crusade for Indian causes, appearing in television documentaries, such as the highly acclaimed Home Box Office special on the Black Hills, and in movies, including the major supporting role of Chingachgook in *The Last of the Mohicans* (1992).

The year 1993 marked the twentieth anniversary of Wounded Knee II. Means reflected, ''We have survived the white man. We are alive.''[10] Indeed, Russell Means and other Indian reformers, in spite of some factionalism among them, continue to fight for federal recognition of treaty rights, environmental issues, and Indian sovereignty.

NOTES

1. ''Activist Turns to Acting,'' *Wichita Eagle*, 21 March 1993, p. 3C.
2. Ward Churchill and Jim Vander Wall, *Agents of Repression: The FBI's Secret*

Wars Against the Black Panther Party and the American Indian Movement (Boston, 1988), 122.

3. Rolland Dewing, *Wounded Knee: The Meaning and Significance of the Second Incident* (New York, 1985), 74.

4. Churchill and Vander Wall, *Agents of Repression*, 137.

5. "Means Reminisces," *Indian Country Today*, 25 February 1993, p. A1.

6. "Eyes on Denver as Parade Showdown Nears," *Rocky Mountain News*, 4 October 1992, p. 19.

7. Ibid.

8. "Protestors Succeed in Shutting Down Parade," *Rocky Mountain News*, 11 October 1992, p. 6.

9. "Rallies Generate Promises of Action Against Racism," *Indian Country Today*, 2 June 1993, p. A2.

10. "Tenacious Russell Means Holds Out for Sovereignty," *Rocky Mountain News*, 7 March 1993, p. 10.

BIBLIOGRAPHY

Note: Articles in such periodicals as *Akwesasne Notes, Denver Post, Indian Country Today* (formerly *Lakota Times*), *Indian Truth, Newsweek, Rocky Mountain News* (Denver), *Time*, and *U.S. News and World Report* contain valuable information on Means and AIM.

Burnette, Robert, and John Koster. *The Road to Wounded Knee*. New York, 1974.

Churchill, Ward, and Jim Vander Wall. *Agents of Repression: The FBI's Secret Wars Against the Black Panther Party and the American Indian Movement*. Boston, 1988.

Dewing, Rolland. *Wounded Knee: The Meaning and Significance of the Second Incident*. New York, 1985.

Josephy, Alvin M., Jr. *Now That the Buffalo's Gone*. New York, 1982.

Matthiessen, Peter. *In the Spirit of Crazy Horse*. New York, 1983.

O'Neil, Floyd A., June K. Lyman, and Susan McKay, eds. *Wounded Knee 1973: A Personal Account By Stanley David Lyman*. Lincoln, Nebr., 1991.

Weyler, Rex. *Blood on the Land*. New York, 1982.

Harvey Milk
and Gay Rights

R. LANE FENRICH

On 7 June 1977, after voters in Dade County, Florida, overturned that county's six-month-old gay rights ordinance, 5,000 lesbians and gay men marched through the streets of San Francisco in protest. Leading them, at the request of the police department, was the city's most talked-about gay leader, a former Wall Street analyst named Harvey Milk. After more than three hours of angry demonstration, the crowd rallied in Union Square, where Milk took aim at Anita Bryant, the former beauty queen who had spearheaded the repeal drive in Miami. As protesters hoisted a red flag proclaiming ''Gay Revolution,'' Milk declared: ''This is the power of the gay community. Anita's going to create a national gay movement.'' She did not, of course. Indeed, from her perspective, she was combating a movement that was already both national in scope and alarmingly successful, with antidiscrimination ordinances on the books in more than forty cities, gay rights legislation pending in Congress, and increasingly assertive gay communities in the nation's largest cities. Ironically, in attempting to turn back what seemed to her a tide of gay victories, Bryant helped solidify that movement, swelling its popular base and strengthening ties among loosely affiliated local groups. In California, Milk was the most visible symbol—and benefici-ary—of that solidification: an outspoken populist who mobilized gay and nongay voters alike in support of nondiscrimination. He would also be its most famous martyr.

It was no accident that the police turned to Harvey Milk for help that summer night. For nearly five years, Milk had worked to become the voice of San Francisco's gay community, especially that part of it concentrated in the city's Castro neighborhood. Indeed, even as he addressed the crowd in Union Square, Milk was running for a seat on San Francisco's Board of Supervisors, a position he had sought twice since moving to the city from New York in 1972. This time he would win, making him the first openly gay city official elected in the United States.* Moreover, he would do so not by courting the gay vote alone but by forging what seemed to many an unlikely coalition between gays, labor, small business owners, activists in many of the city's ethnic communities, and the dwindling number of nongay residents in the Castro—alienating much of the city's "gay establishment" in the process. His time in office, however, was tragically brief: on 27 November 1978, eleven months after taking office, Milk and San Francisco's mayor, George Moscone, were murdered by a disgruntled former colleague named Dan White. What the two men might have accomplished had they lived longer obviously can never be known. Long after his assassination, however, Milk's legacy was evident in the continued political power of San Francisco's lesbian and gay community.

To many who knew him before he moved to San Francisco, Milk's political career—and the politics on which he built it—came as something of a surprise. Born on 22 May 1930 to middle-class Jewish parents, William and Minerva Karns Milk, in Woodmere, New York, Harvey Milk played varsity sports, served in the Navy, and voted Republican. As late as 1964, the future Democratic maverick was an enthusiastic supporter of Barry Goldwater, the archconservative Republican who opposed Lyndon Johnson in that year's presidential campaign. At the same time, he shied away from the political activities of New York's Mattachine Society—a small, scrupulously moderate organization formed in the early 1950s to better the perception and treatment of homosexuals. With the help of sympathetic experts, the Mattachine challenged the prevailing image of homosexuals as maladjusted, immature, and probably dangerous, and advocated the repeal of sodomy statutes and other repressive legislation. Milk found such activities alarming—and intriguing—and although one of his early lovers joined the group and urged him to do the same, he steered clear of its efforts at reform. As was true for many gay men of his class and generation, the potential consequences of exposure as a homosexual—arrest, job loss, public humiliation—far outweighed the attractions of organized gay political activity. For the time being, at least, he would stay in the closet.

However closeted Milk may have been when it came to politics or on Wall Street, in other ways his life before he moved to San Francisco put him at the center of a burgeoning gay subculture. In New York and elsewhere such a subculture had flourished since at least the late nineteenth century. Since World War II, however, gay people had carved out vastly enlarged communities in the nation's major cities—especially port cities like New York and San Francisco, where military personnel underwent demobilization. Milk came of age in the midst of that transformation. Fifteen years old in 1945, he, like many other

---

*He was not, however, the first gay elected to office. In 1974, Elaine Noble had been elected to the Massachusetts House of Representatives after openly running as a lesbian. Soon after, Allan Spear, a member of the Minnesota Senate, publicly acknowledged his homosexuality.

young men in and out of the service, eagerly explored the sexual terrain of a city crowded with soldiers, a circumstance that both increased opportunities for homosexual encounters and rendered them relatively inconspicuous. Traveling into Manhattan for the day from his home on Long Island, Milk quickly learned the dimensions and codes of this new sexual space, enabling him not only to find willing sexual partners but also to deflect the suspicions of police and others when he did.

When the war ended in 1945, the sexual spaces created by mobilization changed in important ways. Having discovered possibilities for friendship and romance many had not previously thought possible, countless gay and lesbian service personnel—as well as thousands of civilians who had relocated to take jobs in war-related industries—staked out communities in New York, San Francisco, and other cities offering economic independence and relative anonymity. What such cities did not offer was freedom from harassment, arrest, or imprisonment. Indeed, as urban gay enclaves grew, local, state, and even federal authorities drew attention to the "threat" homosexuals and other "sex deviates" posed to American life. A series of journalistic exposés begun during the war warned that thousands of "inverts" had slipped into the military, undetected by the phalanx of psychiatrists marshaled to weed them out along with other "psychoneurotics." Compounding such warnings was biologist Alfred Kinsey's 1948 finding that homosexuals were "to be found in every age group, in every social level, in every conceivable occupation, in cities and on farms, and in the most remote areas of the country."[1] Not only that, Kinsey concluded, but there was no reliable way to tell the homosexual from anyone else.

Kinsey hoped his findings would change attitudes about homosexuality for the better. In an America gripped with fear of communism, however, reports of yet another invisible contagion spurred vigorous efforts to root out and punish its carriers, efforts that ranged from increased policing of bars, parks, and public toilets to the firing of workers suspected of homosexual activity. In 1947 Milk felt the force of those efforts when he was arrested for indecent exposure (he was sunbathing) in a gay section of New York's Central Park. Luckily, he was not charged. One close call, however, was more than enough for the frightened seventeen-year-old, and in the years that followed he took care to avoid repeating it.

After receiving his B.A. at the New York State College for Teachers in 1951, Milk spent four years in the Navy, eventually rising to the rank of chief petty officer on the U.S.S. *Kittyhawk*. The experience not only accorded with his politics at the time—he was a staunch Cold Warrior who supported the war in Korea as a fight against monolithic, global communism—but also provided him many of the same opportunities for friendship and romance enjoyed by gay people in World War II. Although he would later claim, falsely, to have been dishonorably discharged because of his sexuality, Milk successfully balanced his duties as an officer with an active social life. To be sure, as a homosexual he ran the risk of court-martial and expulsion if discovered. As it had been during World War II, however, that risk was tempered both by the military's manpower needs and by its concern for morale: simply put, more was to be gained by tolerating gay sailors (as long as they were ''discreet'') than by hounding them out, especially those as much liked by their men as Milk was.

After finishing his tour in the Navy, Milk returned to New York, taking a teaching job not far from his parents' home on Long Island. A year later, on a Long Island gay beach, he met his first lover, Joe Campbell, with whom he would live for the next six years. Biographer Randy Shilts characterized their relationship as ''a safe middle-class marriage,'' a haven from the riskier—and presumably more authentic—world of the bars.[2] Yet if Milk and Campbell avoided the bars, preferring the comfort of their lavishly decorated apartment and evenings at the opera, in other ways their ''marriage'' challenged the conventions that kept gay people in the closet. Although anxious to avoid the scrutiny of the police, for example, neither man avoided that of his family. Indeed, not only did Campbell attend dinner parties and holiday celebrations at the Milks's Woodmere home but the two men went so far as to visit Campbell's grandmother in Alabama—not the sort of decision calculated to preserve a low profile. That Milk in particular had a keen sense of limits seems clear, but that he also pushed those limits seems equally as clear.

In 1962 Milk's relationship with Campbell ended, and both men began new, although not entirely unrelated, phases of their lives. Always more interested in the bar scene than Milk, Campbell moved in and out of the coterie surrounding pop artist Andy Warhol. Similarly, after a brief romance with activist Craig Rodwell—who later founded the Oscar Wilde Memorial Bookstore, New York's first openly gay business—Milk became increasingly involved in New York's theatrical avant garde, a connection made when he met and wooed Jack McKinley, a young runaway then living with director Tom O'Horgan. McKinley soon moved in with Milk, and the three men became not only friends but collaborators, with McKinley working as O'Horgan's stage manager and Milk eagerly contributing advice and money to O'Horgan's increasingly ambitious productions. (He was also working as an analyst at a Wall Street investment firm.) In 1967 O'Horgan hit the big time with his first Broadway production, *Hair*, the opening number of which rhapsodized the joys of sodomy. When *Hair* went to San Francisco in 1968, McKinley and Milk went with it, the former becoming the production's stage manager and the latter taking a job in the city's financial district. McKinley soon returned to New York to stage manage O'Horgan's second hit, *Jesus Christ, Superstar*. Milk stayed in San Francisco, relishing its vibrancy as the capital of the counterculture and as the home of a vigorous, rapidly growing gay community.

Milk's decision to stay in San Francisco marked an ongoing shift in his lifestyle and political outlook. Although he would return to New York in 1971 as the associate producer of yet another O'Horgan production, he would scarcely be recognizable to those who had known him previously. As if living out the storyline of *Hair*, he let his hair grow, denounced the war in Vietnam, and gradually turned his back on middle-class respectability. A 1971 profile of O'Horgan and his associates described the new Milk as an "aging hippie with long, long hair, wearing faded jeans and pretty beads."[3]

The transformation was not simply physical. Living and working with the countercultural vanguard in both New York and San Francisco, Milk absorbed the language and emotion of the civil rights, women's, and antiwar movements—and after the Stonewall Riots of June 1969 (in which a police raid on a Greenwich Village gay bar sparked two nights of violent protest), the spirit of gay liberation. The combination was not coincidental. By 1969 the social movements of the day not only had demonstrated the possibility for resisting oppression but also had developed an analysis for describing it, an analysis that transformed a series of riots into a full-blown movement for gay liberation.

In the wake of those riots, dozens and then hundreds of groups proclaimed "Gay Power" and urged gay people to "come out" to their families, friends, and coworkers, a call Milk sounded throughout his career as an activist and politician. As important, gay liberationists distinguished their movement from the reform efforts of "homophile" organizations like the Mattachine Society, eschewing both their polite moderation and their reliance on nongay experts to legitimate their public presence. With Stonewall as their model, gay liberationists took to the streets in highly visible demonstrations and gleefully invaded gatherings their predecessors would scarcely have dared enter, from academic conferences to legislative assemblies to the newsrooms and editorial offices of antigay newspapers. Moreover, schooled as they were by other protest movements, many of those mobilized by Stonewall saw gay liberation as part of a larger movement that would liberate not only gay people but also African Americans, women, the poor, and other historically disadvantaged groups. Coming out—and coming of age politically—in the midst of this ferment, Milk exhilarated in talk of personal empowerment and social transformation, themes that he consistently developed in his later political rhetoric.

In 1972, when O'Horgan's play closed after a three-month run, Milk returned to San Francisco. He was soon followed by Scott Smith, his lover for the next four years. For months the two virtually dropped out of society. In early 1973, with the last of their savings, they opened a camera store in the Castro, a declining working-class neighborhood fast becoming the heart of the city's gay community. Six months later, Milk made his first bid for supervisor.

Although a newcomer to the city, Milk made an impressive showing in the 1973 supervisors' race, winning 17,000 votes and coming in tenth out of 32 candidates. Forty-three years old, a hippie, and gay, he was an unlikely political success story. He was also, however, surprisingly appealing, combining attacks on the city's downtown real estate interests with proposals for educational, health, and electoral reform, gun control, the legalization of marijuana, and the abolition of the vice squad. A vigorous campaigner, he won support from many of the city's liberal political groups—but few official endorsements. He did so by demonstrating both an understanding of and a willingness to work for a wide range of populist issues. In the midst of the campaign, for example, Milk persuaded gay bar owners to back a strike by the city's beer truck drivers and to boycott Coors when that company maintained its antiunion policies. The action won Milk the support—and in later campaigns the official endorsements—not just of the beer truck drivers but of the Teamsters, the Building and Construction Trades Council, and the city's firefighters—all unions that in other cities actively opposed gay rights.

Ironically, concerted opposition to Milk's campaigns came from longtime gay activists in the city's Alice B. Toklas Democratic Club, party loyalists with their own plan for gradual gay political advancement. In part, that opposition was a defense of political turf: a newcomer to the city, Milk had done nothing to prove his loyalty to the Democratic party or to win its loyalty in return. Moreover, the Toklas Democrats worried both that a gay candidate could not be elected and that an electoral defeat would undercut their efforts to enact gay rights legislation. Especially worrisome in that regard was the contrast between Milk's calls for reshaping a wide range of urban priorities and Toklas activists' more focused efforts to win gays a seat at the political table.

In some ways, the conflict between Milk and party regulars was not unlike the split emerging nationwide between those committed to ''gay liberation'' as part of a larger project of radical social change and those advocating equal treatment within the existing system, or ''gay rights.'' The Toklas Democrats clearly fell in the latter camp, as did most gay organizations formed after the heady days of early gay liberation. Milk, however, fit less easily into this schema: criticized by gay moderates as unrealistic and wild-eyed, he was denounced by radicals as a bourgeois assimilationist. In fact, Milk emerged as one of the few gay politicians who successfully bridged the reform-liberation gap: always openly, even defiantly a gay candidate, he advocated gay empowerment not as an end in itself but as part of a broader program for redistributing social and political power. From the standpoint of practical politics, the combination proved to be a tremendous success, winning the overwhelming support of the city's gay community as well as that of a wide range of nongay, progressive, and ethnic voters.

Buoyed by his electoral success, Milk became an enthusiastic community organizer, dubbing himself ''the mayor of Castro Street.'' From the summer of 1973 on, visitors to Castro Camera—whether drawn by Milk's political reputation or wanting to process their film—walked into what amounted to an unofficial aldermanic headquarters. Well aware of the margin he commanded among gay voters, Milk became a voter registrar and encouraged his supporters to do the same. He also took more direct action. When local merchants attempted to prevent a gay-owned antique store from opening, Milk formed the Castro Village Association (CVA) to champion the interests of the neighborhood's gay merchants and residents. Echoing the civil rights slogan ''Don't shop where you can't work,'' the CVA urged Castro residents to ''buy gay,'' soon demonstrating the community's growing economic clout. At Milk's prodding, the CVA also organized the first Castro Street Fair, an event so successful it became an annual event drawing people from around the country. Soon after the 1974 fair, when police arrested fourteen gay men and beat dozens of others for "blocking the sidewalk" outside a gay bar, Milk raised money for their defense and spearheaded community protest of continuing police harassment. The depth of the protest took police—and many gay people—by surprise, marking the increased confidence that grew out of larger numbers and the rhetoric of gay power. Milk did not create that confidence, certainly, but he did articulate it and to some extent focus it, forging a previously marginal population into an effective political base.

In 1975 Milk again ran for supervisor. He lost, but made an even more impressive showing than in 1973, coming in seventh behind the six incumbents in the race and once again carrying the gay neighborhoods by huge margins. The latter fact was obviously important. Because supervisors were elected at large rather than by ward or district, the city's minority neighborhoods found themselves virtually unrepresented: just as there were no gays on the board, there were also no Latinos, blacks, or Asians, all large communities in the city. In the aftermath of the 1975 election, a coalition of neighborhood and labor activists largely organized by Milk joined forces to pass an initiative providing for the election of supervisors by districts. In November 1976 the reform passed, forcing the sitting board to give up their seats and run again in 1977. In the meantime, newly elected Mayor George Moscone named Milk to a place on the city's Board of Permit Appeals, making him the first openly gay city official in the country. Milk's tenure on the Board was brief, however: five weeks after his appointment, he announced his candidacy for state assemblyman, provoking Moscone to fire him.

Moscone's decision to fire Milk grew out of a commitment he had made the year before to support another candidate, Art Agnos, a commitment that enabled Milk to depict himself as the opponent of a Moscone machine. In the end, the machine won: too much was at stake for too many of Milk's potential allies for them to risk alienating the liberal Democratic entente that controlled both the state assembly and the city's congressional delegation. Thus, with Milk unable to expand his base of support beyond those groups already in his camp, it was Agnos who went to Sacramento.

Having lost to the machine, Milk and his allies regrouped, concentrating their energies on winning voter approval for electing supervisors by district—a system that would favor candidates like Milk with reputations as neighborhood leaders. In addition, faced with continued opposition from the Toklas Democrats, Milk supporters formed the San Francisco Gay Democratic Club, dedicated not only to electing a gay candidate but also to claiming power equal to the community's growing size and cohesion. The club's manifesto proclaimed:

No decisions which affect our lives should be made without the gay voice being heard. We want our fair share of city services. We want openly gay people elected to city offices—people who reflect the diversity of our community. We want the schools of San Francisco to provide full exposure to and positive appreciation of gay lifestyles. We are asking no more than we deserve: We will not settle for less.[4]

Probably few of the Toklas Democrats would have disagreed with such a statement of principles. Neither, however, would they have made it the centerpiece of a political campaign, a difference in strategy and style that distanced them not only from Milk but also from the city's increasingly assertive gay electorate.

Judging by his three prior bids for office, Milk probably could not have lost the 1977 contest for supervisor. Running in the newly created District Five—encompassing not just the Castro but also Noe Valley and the Haight, neighborhoods with growing gay populations and strong populist affiliations—with the endorsement of the San Francisco Gay Democratic Club as well as various union locals, neighborhood organizations, and liberal interest groups, his popularity had never been higher. That he was opposed by longtime gay activist Rick Stokes, a stalwart in the local Democratic organization who lacked Milk's following in the Castro, scarcely made a difference. More important by far than Stokes or any of the fourteen other candidates in the race was a name that did not appear on the ballot: Anita Bryant.

In a way that even the most outrageous demonstrations and parades had not, the campaign to repeal Dade County's extension of civil rights protection to lesbians and gay men drew national attention to the issue of gay rights and the existence of a lesbian and gay movement. It did so as a direct result of efforts by the so-called New Right, an uneasy coalition of political conservatives and religious fundamentalists opposed to what they saw as a broad-based assault on traditional American values, particularly sexual values. In addition to gay rights, the New Right opposed pornography, legal abortion, sex outside marriage, and equal rights for women, all of which its organizers identified as threats to family life and individual morality. Bryant called on voters to "Save Our Children," forcing gay activists to fend off groundless but nonetheless highly charged images of sexual predation and vulnerability. Such images proved effective not only in rousing voter opposition to gay rights but also in winning a national constituency (and a voice in national politics) for New Right leaders like Bryant and the Reverend Jerry Falwell.

Ironically, in opposing nondiscrimination the New Right both focused public attention on the gains won by lesbian and gay activists in the previous five years and mobilized thousands of gay people who had not previously taken part in movement politics. In the years since Stonewall, lesbian and gay activists had worked with unprecedented success to alter repressive legal codes and professional and religious dogma about homosexuals. Between 1971 and 1976, activists had won the repeal of sodomy laws in seventeen states, making it possible for many lesbian and gay citizens to socialize without fear of going to jail. In 1973, after years of effort, long-time Washington activist Frank Kameny and others had persuaded the American Psychiatric Association to remove homosexuality from its list of mental disorders, a move with far-reaching legal as well as medical implications. In 1975 Kameny had won an eighteen-year fight to eliminate homosexuality as a bar to employment in the federal civil service, a fight that began with his dismissal as a government astronomer. In the same year, Democratic congressmen had for the first time introduced legislation mandating nondiscrimination on the basis of perceived sexual preference. All the while, gay and lesbian activists at the grassroots had worked for similar legislation, efforts that had paid off in more than forty cities before the uproar in Dade County. As that uproar made clear, much work remained to be done. Even so, for many gay people life had changed in important and positive ways, changes that made it all the more likely they would resist attempts by Bryant and others to turn back the clock and force them back in the closet.

Although it took many observers by surprise, the intensity with which gay people across the country reacted to the vote in Dade County indicated precisely the degree to which the ideology of Stonewall had transformed gay communal experience. Within hours of the vote, gay people in San Francisco and elsewhere mobilized in protest, demanding ''civil rights or civil war.'' For the rest of 1977 and throughout 1978, they repeatedly took to the streets as St. Paul, Minnesota, Wichita, Kansas, and Eugene, Oregon, joined Miami in overturning recently passed nondiscrimination ordinances. Californians faced their own antigay referendum: the day after the vote in Miami, state Senator John Briggs announced a campaign to bar homosexuals from teaching in the state's public schools, opposition to which occupied much of Milk's time as supervisor and won him a statewide and a national reputation. At the same time, like gay people across the country, Milk and his constituents faced a rash of violence fueled by the rhetoric of antigay crusaders. Two weeks after the vote in Miami—and five days before San Francisco's Gay Freedom Day celebration, marking the eighth anniversary of the Stonewall riots—four teenaged men attacked a gay couple they followed from a hamburger stand in San Francisco's Mission District. One of the men, Robert Hillsborough, died from multiple stab wounds. Many people, Milk among them, joined Hillsborough's mother in holding Anita Bryant responsible.

Coming only three weeks after the vote in Miami and less than a week after the Hillsborough murder, the 1977 Gay Freedom Day parade had an urgency then unmatched in the history of the event. To the consternation of city officials, many of whom, including Mayor Moscone, were downplaying their support for gay issues, the parade drew more than 200,000 marchers and onlookers from throughout the nation. Harvey Milk was ecstatic, choosing the day to announce his candidacy for supervisor. His speech included what had become familiar elements of his program, among them the need to control real estate speculation, to rebuild the city's neighborhoods, and to provide opportunities and services to the elderly and disadvantaged. It also addressed the moment, defying Bryant and others who assailed gay liberation and rebuking Moscone and other straight liberals who sought gay support but failed to speak out when gays were under attack. Empowerment, not just anger, was the theme: gay people could effect change, Milk contended, by organizing, by electing candidates, and, most important, by coming out.

On Election Day 1977, Milk was the undisputed victor in District Five, winning more votes than any other nonincumbent candidate in the city and beating his competitors by better than two to one. Elected with him were the city's first Chinese and Latino supervisors, an African-American woman, and a former police officer and fireman, all of them the beneficiaries of district elections. Milk quickly allied himself with the board's progressive minority and with Mayor Moscone—who had supported Rick Stokes in the District Five race. True to form, on his first day in office Milk proposed an ordinance banning discrimination on the basis of sexual orientation. He quickly followed it with proposals for a commuter tax, higher business taxes, and an antispeculation tax, issues he had emphasized since his first campaign in 1973. Much to the surprise of his detractors, he quickly proved to be a hardworking, well-informed, although not always diplomatic, supervisor with a legislative program geared to rebuilding the city's neighborhoods and empowering the relatively powerless.

Within weeks of the 1977 election, John Briggs qualified Proposition Six— an initiative barring lesbian and gay teachers from the classroom—for the November 1978 ballot. Notwithstanding his commitment to other issues, the struggle against Proposition Six occupied Milk as would no other. Ironically, that struggle helped assure passage of a gay rights bill in San Francisco, as politician after politician voiced support for nondiscrimination so as not to offend the city's gay electorate. Indeed, when the measure came up for a vote in March 1978, only one of the eleven board members, Dan White, voted against it. At Milk's urging, the board also voted to provide city funds for the annual Gay Freedom Day celebration, something it had long done for many of the city's other ethnic and neighborhood festivals. At the same time, in a move as popular with gay activists as it was unpopular with the Police Officers' Association, the city's police chief announced that the department would actively recruit gay and lesbian officers. With Milk a constant reminder of the growing political strength and savvy of the city's lesbian and gay community, San Francisco's leaders guided the city in directions then almost unthinkable elsewhere.

Outside San Francisco, the climate was far less hospitable. As late as August, polls showed California voters overwhelmingly in support of Briggs's initiative. In response, lesbian and gay activists undertook a massive grassroots campaign emphasizing the threat the legislation posed to civil rights generally and refuting Briggs's equation of homosexuality with child molestation and pornography— charges made familiar by Bryant's ''Save Our Children'' campaign in Florida. Approaching people in shopping centers, on the street, and on their doorsteps, opponents of Proposition Six took their case directly to the voters, personalizing the issues to a degree that activists in other states had not. Milk challenged Briggs to a series of public debates, a strategy that, week by week, turned public opinion against the proposed legislation. By November, what had seemed an unstoppable initiative drive had stalled, and such unlikely allies as Governor Jerry Brown, former Governor Ronald Reagan, and the California Teachers' Association had announced their opposition to its passage. On election day, 59 percent of those voting (75 percent in San Francisco) rejected Proposition Six. Milk received much of the credit.

By any standard, defeating the Briggs initiative was a major triumph for Milk and the movement he represented. From a national perspective, it was a triumph sweetened by the fact that on the same day voters in Seattle rejected a proposal to overturn that city's gay rights ordinance. For the time being, at least, the antigay tide seemed to be receding. In San Francisco, things had never looked brighter; some even discussed the possibility of electing a gay mayor. Less than three weeks later, however, Milk and Moscone were dead, murdered in their offices by then-former Supervisor Dan White.

The immediate reaction to Milk's death indicated both his tremendous personal popularity and his importance as a symbol of gay and lesbian power— and hope. The night of the murders, more than 40,000 people marched from the Castro to City Hall in what lesbian activist Sally Gearhart called "one of the most eloquent expressions of a community's response to violence" that she had ever seen.[5] Carrying candles and signs that read "Harvey Milk Lives," the marchers expressed not only their grief but also their sense of themselves as a community, a force that would survive Milk's death. By marching to City Hall, they also expressed their confidence—and their insistence—that Dan White would be punished for his crimes.

Five months after the assassinations, Dan White went on trial in what seemed to most people an open-and-shut case. On the day of the murders, an armed White—who had resigned his office two weeks before and then appealed, unsuccessfully, for Moscone to reappoint him—had sneaked into City Hall through an alley window; shot Moscone twice in the body, then twice more in the head; reloaded; walked across City Hall to Harvey Milk's office, and shot Milk five times, including twice in the head. He then fled City Hall, called his wife, and with her turned himself into the police. That much was admitted by White's attorney from the outset. Even so, the jury—an all-white group from which the defense had stricken not only homosexuals but also openly pro-gay heterosexuals—convicted White not of murder but of voluntary manslaughter, persuaded by the defense that the former police officer had acted under "diminished capacity" caused in part by a diet of junk food. White served five years in prison, received no psychiatric treatment, and later committed suicide.

The manslaughter verdict drew protests from throughout the city, including a forceful denunciation from Dianne Feinstein, who had become mayor after Moscone's assassination. It also drew praise from some, including many in the city's police force. Outraged by what they saw as a gross miscarriage of justice, however, more than 5,000 gay people marched on City Hall, mirroring the gathering that had followed the murders. This time, however, protest turned violent, the result not just of anger with the verdict but also of months of renewed police harassment and increasing attacks on the city's gay population, attacks White's jury seemed to be condoning. In what was later referred to as White Night, protesters smashed windows, set police cars on fire, and battled baton-wielding police. Late in the evening, after the rioters had dispersed, police waged a counterattack, wading into bars in the Castro and indiscriminately beating patrons. Once again, gay people fought back; only intervention by the chief of police kept the incident from turning into a pitched battle.

The events of White Night demonstrated both the heightened consciousness and the continued vulnerability of San Francisco's gay and lesbian community. Milk's assassination went to the heart of both. In killing Milk, Dan White had killed the single most visible gay person in California and indeed the nation, a man many gay San Franciscans had seen as the embodiment of their hopes as a community. Over the course of his political campaigns and during his short time in office, Milk had articulated a political vision that meshed with the lives of the post-Stonewall gay community, one that urged them to abandon the closet and claim the power that was their birthright. In voting for Milk, gay people had done just that, rejecting admonitions from gay and straight politicians alike to be patient and keep a low profile. White Night, too, signaled their willingness to do neither. That they were as a consequence increasingly exposed to attack—physical as well as rhetorical—was all too clear. And yet, where such attacks might once have gone unchallenged, they now met open resistance that in itself profoundly reshaped the political landscape.

Nationally, Milk's death coincided with an important shift in gay and lesbian politics, a shift in many ways exemplified by Milk's rise to prominence. In part, that shift was triggered by the emergence of the New Right as a well-organized, national opponent of gay rights and what it called "the gay lifestyle." Faced with a series of well-coordinated, well-publicized attacks on their very existence, lesbian and gay activists waged a highly visible, national campaign for gay rights and gay liberation. To be sure, grassroots organizations continued the push for change at the city, county, and state levels. At the same time, however, many advocated national strategies and called on national leaders to lead the fight for lesbian and gay equality. Speaking at the 1978 San Francisco Gay Freedom Day celebration, for example, Harvey Milk exhorted President Jimmy Carter, who had enshrined human rights as the centerpiece of his foreign policy, to speak out on gay rights as well. If Carter refused to speak, Milk told the crowd, he "call[ed] upon lesbians and gay men from all over the nation, your nation, to gather in Washington one year from now . . . on that very same spot where over a decade ago, Dr. Martin Luther King spoke to a nation."[6] In October 1979, a year after Californians rejected the Briggs initiative, the first such march took place, drawing nearly 100,000 people from across the country in an unprecedented demonstration of gay activism.

It was eight years before lesbian and gay activists organized a second march on Washington. In some ways, little had changed between the two marches. Conservatives still denounced "the gay lifestyle" as a threat to the family. Gay rights legislation still languished in Congress. Half the states still criminalized sodomy. And violence against lesbians and gay men was again on the rise. In other ways, of course, much had changed. Most important, the AIDS pandemic had ravaged gay communities across the nation, making health care and AIDS discrimination the top priorities for a vastly expanded pool of activists. With an unusually large and extremely well-organized gay community, San Francisco led the country in pioneering (and funding) AIDS services and in prohibiting discrimination against people with AIDS.

Reaction elsewhere was more complicated. Although evidence quickly mounted that the disease struck without regard for social status, many on the political right regarded it as confirmation that homosexuals were, by nature, diseased. Faced with the necessity of caring for a mounting number of sick and dying people, others, including many in local governments and religious organizations, distanced themselves from antigay rhetoric and turned to gay organizations for leadership in responding to the crisis. In providing that leadership, activists in the lesbian and gay and AIDS movements increasingly emphasized the ways class, race, gender, sexuality, and other social divisions intertwined in facilitating or blocking access to health care, research funds, and political power. However different the context, in other words, by the late 1980s a great many activists took for granted an understanding of politics not unlike Harvey Milk's, an understanding that saw gay rights, gay liberation, and AIDS as parts of an interrelated social whole. In that sense, at least, Harvey Milk lived.

NOTES

1. Alfred Kinsey et al., *Sexual Behavior in the Human Male* (Philadelphia, 1948), 627.

2. Randy Shilts, *The Mayor of Castro Street: The Life and Times of Harvey Milk* (New York, 1982), 20.

3. John Gruen, "Do You Mind Critics Calling You Cheap, Decadent, Sensationalistic, Gimmicky, Vulgar, Overinflated, Megalomaniacal?," interview with Tom O'Horgan, *New York Times Magazine*, 2 January 1972, 18.

4. Shilts, *Mayor of Castro Street*, 150.

5. Interview in *The Times of Harvey Milk* (Black Sands Production, 1984), Robert Epstein, director. (Academy Award-winning documentary; now available on videotape.)

6. Shilts, *Mayor of Castro Street*, 225.

BIBLIOGRAPHY

Adam, Barry D. *The Rise of a Gay and Lesbian Movement.* Boston, 1987.

Bérubé, Allan. *Coming out Under Fire: The History of Gay Men and Women in World War Two.* New York, 1990.

Chauncey, George, Jr. "The Postwar Sex Crimes Panic." In William Graebner, ed., *True Stories from the American Past.* New York, 1993.

————. *Gay New York: Gender, Urban Culture, and the Making of the Gay Male World, 1890–1940*. New York, 1994.

D'Emilio, John. *Sexual Politics, Sexual Communities: The Making of a Homosexual Minority in the United States, 1940–1970*. Chicago, 1983.

————. *Making Trouble: Essays on Gay History, Politics, and the University*. New York, 1992.

Duberman, Martin B. *Stonewall*. New York, 1993.

Epstein, Robert, dir. *The Times of Harvey Milk*. Black Sands Production, 1984.

FitzGerald, Frances. "The Castro." In her *Cities on a Hill: A Journey Through Contemporary American Cultures*. New York, 1987.

Katz, Jonathan. *Gay American History: Lesbians and Gay Men in the U.S.A.*. New York, 1976.

Marcus, Eric. *Making History: The Struggle for Gay and Lesbian Equal Rights*. New York, 1992.

Marotta, Toby. *The Politics of Homosexuality*. Boston, 1981.

Shilts, Randy. *The Mayor of Castro Street: The Life and Times of Harvey Milk*. New York, 1982.

A. J. Muste
and Pacifism

CHARLES CHATFIELD

Modern pacifism derives from two broad traditions: the total rejection of war, if not all social violence, and the organized effort to limit or eliminate warfare while justifying wars of defense. During and after World War I, a modern form of pacifism emerged as the rejection of war was merged with a concern for social justice and an orientation to political activism. No person could exemplify all the diverse currents of what has aptly been called "The Peace Reform."[1] Indeed, to pair any individual with a complex movement is to risk serious misrepresentation of its multiple leadership and dynamics, and there is a special risk when the individual is male, lest his gender be viewed as representative. With those caveats, though, the life of A. J. Muste (1885–1967) may be taken as an index or benchmark of the twentieth-century evolution of U. S. pacifism, and particularly of its activist element.

When *Time* magazine designated Muste as the "No. 1 U. S. pacifist" in 1937, it defined what it meant by the term: "A pacifist is a person who, on religious or moral grounds, objects to all wars, defensive or offensive. A conscientious objector is one who reserves to himself the right to decide whether to support his country in a particular war."[2] This is the tradition of nonresistance: violence, whether at the behest of political authority or in opposition to it, is rejected in favor of a nonviolent way of living. Pacifism in that absolute sense had a long lineage rooted in the early Christian church and the subsequent witness of isolated groups of Christians through the Protestant Reformation. It then attained a strong, even distinguishing position within the so-called peace churches: the Mennonites, the Society of Friends (Quakers), and the Brethren. Each of these sects, in the course of its own journey, carried the tradition to the New World.

Christian nonresistance in America had a few sturdy advocates outside the peace churches, notably in the peace societies first organized in 1815. From the outset, absolute pacifists contended with the prevailing view of peace advocates that warfare might sometimes be justified. In the 1840s William Lloyd Garrison and his followers joined nonresistance to the reform causes they espoused, but most of them refused to apply it to the American Civil War. Like Elihu Burritt, a handful of nonresistants rejected even that crusade, and absolute pacifism was threaded through the post-Civil War peace movement. It was a slender thread even for the peace churches, struggling to adapt to modern, nationalistic culture. It was, nonetheless, the nonresistant pacifist tradition that attracted A. J. Muste as he read incredulously of Europeans slaughtering one another in 1915–1916.

Muste had become by then, in the words of his biographer, Jo Ann Robinson, ''impatient with the orthodoxy of his native [Dutch Reformed] faith.''[3] Born on 8 January 1885 in Zierikzee, the Netherlands, at the age of six he had immigrated to the United States with his parents, Martin and Adriana Jonker Muste, who settled in Grand Rapids, Michigan. He grew up in the liberal, Americanized wing of the church, attended Hope College (graduating in 1905), taught briefly at a church academy in Iowa, and studied at New Brunswick Theological Seminary in New Jersey, graduating in 1909. After marrying Anna Huizinga in June 1909, Muste began his full-time ministry at the prominent Fort Washington Collegiate Church of New York City.

During his seminary years Muste took courses at New York University and Columbia University that brought him into direct contact with leading Progressive thinkers, and he became acquainted with the poverty of New York's Lower East Side. As a minister, he moved into the circle of Progressive, Social Gospel leaders, and in 1912 he earned his Bachelor of Divinity degree from theologically liberal Union Theological Seminary. Having moved leftward within the Dutch Reformed Church, he finally moved beyond it. In 1914 he resigned his pastorate, and the next year he became the minister of a Congregational church in Newtonville, Massachusetts. By then Europe was at war.

Muste had begun to read and study Christian mystics and to explore the Quaker insight of the ''inner light,'' the view that truth is revealed directly to the seeker. He avidly read the works of Leo Tolstoy. Nonresistance was an integral part of the Quaker heritage and the Tolstoyan life that Muste found increasingly attractive. Spiritual probing tapped an energy and focus for reform, and in 1916–1917 he edged fitfully toward antiwar activism and absolute pacifism. Increasingly uncomfortable in his Congregational parish, he resigned six months after the United States declared war. The following year he became the minister of a Quaker meeting, associated with absolute pacifists, and worked with conscientious objectors to military service.

In his own way, Muste shared the experiences of a generation of pacifist leaders like Jane Addams, John Nevin Sayre, Emily Greene Balch, Norman and Evan Thomas, Roger Baldwin, Devere Allen, Mildred Scott Olmsted, Kirby Page, Dorothy Detzer, and Frederick Libby. They were drawn largely from the Protestant mainstream and were oriented to Progressive politics. Social workers, clergy, educators, or publicists: they were all reformers. Many of them were familiar with Quaker thought and Tolstoy's writings. Most of them had been powerfully influenced by the twin convictions of the Social Gospel: that both sin and redemption have a societal dimension, and that Christian commitment involves a way of life. The outbreak of war in Europe clarified the meaning of that way of life: the new pacifists called it "love" or "reconciliation."

Absolute pacifists in wartime England founded the Fellowship of Reconciliation (FOR). Soon an American counterpart became a haven for pacifists who, like Muste, were increasingly isolated as militant patriotism gained ground. Meanwhile, the new pacifists were politically active. The core of women peace advocates, for example, were also active social reformers and suffragists. American women met with their European counterparts in 1915, appealed for an end to the war, elevated an internationalist vision, and urged Woodrow Wilson to mediate the conflict. From their initiative there evolved the postwar Women's International League for Peace and Freedom (WILPF). Some of the new pacifists formed the American Union Against Militarism to campaign against Woodrow Wilson's 1916 preparedness program, and in the spring of the next year they were joined by leading Socialists to fight U.S. intervention.

During wartime, pacifists constituted a small remnant of conscientious opposition to war. A few of them founded the National Civil Liberties Bureau (subsequently the American Civil Liberties Union) to defend dissenters, including conscientious objectors (COs) to military service. Quakers concerned for their own COs organized the American Friends Service Committee (AFSC), which evolved into an agency to promote peace and to serve war victims. Shortly after the war there emerged an American branch of the War Resisters International, a small movement that rejected war service in advance of military crises. World War I also elicited a nonresistant witness from Mennonites, Brethren, and others; but most important, it enlisted reformers who rejected war as an anachronistic and arbitrary social system. Their outlook was transnational in the sense that they were more concerned for common humanity than with sovereign nation-states. That and their commitment to social justice transformed nonresistance into action-oriented, organized pacifism that was liberal in the sense of seeking to break patterns of social violence through reform of the existing social and political system.

Ironically, the word "pacifism" derived from a second peace tradition. The term was coined in 1902 by Europeans who sought a positive image for their efforts to create alternatives to warfare, a cause earlier associated with Disiderius Erasmus, Jean-Jacques Rousseau, William Penn, and Immanuel Kant. Given the militant nationalism of the late nineteenth century, peace advocates were pushed to the political periphery and their patriotism was questioned. They hoped that "pacifism" would connote the so-called higher patriotism of resolving international conflict through reason under law.

During the nineteenth century, this kind of peace advocacy became an organized reform movement in Europe and the United States. The American Peace Society, which succeeded the original peace societies in 1829, promoted foreign policy reform through international organization, international law, and a system of arbitration treaties. In all of these causes Americans associated with Europeans. By 1914 there were hundreds of peace societies stretching around the northern hemisphere, together with several international peace organizations with fixed headquarters, staff, and programs. In the United States, well-funded groups such as the Carnegie Endowment for International Peace and the World Peace Foundation acquired leaders from the business and professional class. Within the foreign policy elite they advocated arbitration, peace education, cosmopolitan ideals, and international law. The outbreak of World War I raised the importance of international organization, which was promoted by the new League to Enforce Peace.

During the European phase of the war, U.S. internationalists steered a neutral course and focused attention on the terms of a peace settlement. When America intervened, the overwhelming majority of them supported the war effort, some working concurrently for military victory and a liberal, internationalist peace. World War I thus confronted internationalist peace advocates with both the importance of restructuring the nation-state system and the need for political action. Meanwhile, in wartime England and America, the word ''pacifist'' became narrowed to a pejorative, derisive name for those who would not support even this war to end wars—people like Muste and other liberal pacifists who valued political activism at least as much as did internationalist peace advocates.

During the interwar period, liberal pacifists were actively engaged with both foreign policy and domestic social justice issues. In both arenas they again faced the challenge of whether to sanction violence in a just cause. They also renewed their commitment to nonviolence as an ideal and as a form of action.

At the end of World War I, Muste felt that his calling was to live ''in the way of truth, nonviolence and love.''[4] In the atmosphere of the time, that could be interpreted as politically radical, a view that Muste confirmed by siding with textile strikers in Lawrence, Massachusetts. With his leadership and in the face of harassment and provocation, the workers remained cohesive and nonviolent, emerging successfully as the Amalgamated Textile Workers, with Muste as general secretary. Two years later he resigned to become educational director of Brookwood Labor College, a small institute at Katonah, New York, that trained labor organizers in analytical and rhetorical skills and exposed them to the literature on social issues and values. Under Muste's leadership, the faculty introduced peace issues into the curriculum. They endorsed proposals for disarmament, for international trade without nationalist barriers, for a stronger League of Nations and World Court, and for eliminating militarism from education. They identified war with capitalism and economic imperialism, and peace with the international workers' movement. They also supported the FOR-sponsored Committee on Militarism in Education, which campaigned effectively against military training in schools. Inevitably, Brookwood alienated the American Legion.

Other liberal pacifist groups—the FOR and WILPF, for instance—ran afoul

of the Legion and its Communist bogey: that was the price of political activism
in the 1920s. Several of them formed the independent National Council for
Prevention of War (NCPW), which developed the capacity to reach organized
constituencies of women, farmers, educators, labor, and church people. In effect,
it became their lobbying agent on foreign affairs. Founded in connection with
the Washington Conference of 1921–1922, the NCPW and its allied peace
groups urged the reconstruction of the international system and an active U.S.
role in it. They campaigned for disarmament, U.S. adherence to the World Court,
and the Kellogg-Briand Pact to outlaw war. Beyond political issues, pacifists
popularized a revisionist view of World War I and a moral view that, as Kirby
Page put it, "war is sin."⁵ A few pacifists, including Page, tried in vain to
coordinate the efforts of nonpacifist peace societies that were divided by competing priorities for the League of Nations, the World Court, and the outlawry
of war.

The situation changed rapidly when Japan invaded Manchuria in 1931.
Thenceforth the question of how to avoid war became increasingly urgent as
the great powers failed to respond effectively to Japanese aggression, to fascist
intervention in the Spanish Civil War, to Italian invasion of Ethiopia, and to
German rearmament and expansion. Those events set the stage for cooperation
in the mid-1930s between liberal pacifists and nonpacifist internationalists in the
United States.

For a brief time there was a common ground for a united peace front based
on programs to reform the international economic order, to support the League
of Nations, and to strengthen U.S. neutrality. The result was the organization of
the Emergency Peace Campaign (EPC), the largest peace effort to that time.
Liberal pacifists were able to seize the initiative in the EPC, given their ability
to raise funds, their experience, and the close working relationship of leaders in
the FOR, WILPF, NCPW, and AFSC. Their main agenda item was strict neutrality, which was embodied in the neutrality legislation of 1935–1937 that they
helped to write and pass. More clearly than in 1917, pacifists were faced with
the issue of whether to sanction war even in response to unjust, violent aggression. So long as that issue took the form of a possible second European war,
the idea of U.S. neutrality was popular.

Internationalists in the EPC found their agenda preempted by the pacifist
neutrality campaign as the threat of war accelerated. Explicitly favoring collective security, they formed the Committee for Concerted Peace Efforts, which
(under various names) campaigned against strict neutrality. Organized through
the League of Nations Association and led by Clark Eichelberger, the Committee
carried the issue of aid for Britain into a public debate that divided the country
from September 1939 to December 1941. Opposing them was the isolationist
America First Committee and the primarily Socialist Keep America Out of War
Committee, the latter organized by Norman Thomas. Pacifist groups initially
cooperated with Thomas, but as the nation geared up for war, they prepared to
defend conscientious objectors and civil rights, anticipating that political action

would be proscribed for the duration. In fact, during World War II the FOR and allied groups challenged the massive bombing of Axis civilian populations and the relocation of Japanese Americans, and they joined the massive campaign to win public support for the United Nations Organization. Still, most pacifist energy was consumed in the service of conscientious objectors. Muste was executive of the FOR by that time, having made a separate journey through the interwar years, a course that illustrated the liberal pacifist's concern for social justice.

Muste's biographer has observed that he directed "a partisan offensive on behalf of radically oriented labor education, using the Brookwood campus as his base."[6] Increasingly that brought him into conflict with the powerful, conservative American Federation of Labor. In 1929 Muste organized the Conference for Progressive Labor Action (CPLA), an instrument in the contest for workers' loyalty that claimed ever more of his energy. His ties to the FOR eroded, and his independent thrust split Brookwood, from which he resigned in 1933. Muste then transformed the CPLA into the American Workers party, which was designed to offer workers an alternative not only to the AFL but also to the Socialist and Communist parties. The erstwhile pacifist minister became ever more deeply involved in major strikes and radical factionalism. Eventually he was drawn into the orbit of the Trotskyists, who co-opted the American Workers party. At least implicitly, he accepted the principle of violence in the class struggle and in the cause of opposing imperialism, although he still opposed nationalist wars.

Muste was not alone in distinguishing the moral claims of national wars from those of social justice. Brookwood harbored other pacifists who opted to work with the labor movement, and the FOR invested heavily in the cause of labor, where it saw an opportunity to preempt violence through nonviolent activism. As the Great Depression deepened, ever stronger claims on worker loyalty came from unions and from radical parties such as Trotskyists, Socialists, and (Moscow-oriented) Communists. Given the breakdown of social order in central Europe, the question of violence in defense of a workers' movement became an ideological loyalty test for both radicals and pacifists. In a 1933 FOR referendum, an overwhelming majority of members voted to "hold to nonviolence in the class war as well as in international war," nearly half of them sanctioned political and economic coercion, and over three-quarters sided with the workers and underprivileged. The next year the same issue split the Socialist party, where pacifists around Norman Thomas wrote a statement of principles that advocated a general strike but no more violent action in a domestic crisis. Clearly, many pacifists in the FOR and the Socialist party were ready to combine nonviolence with direct action, the kind of approach with which Mohandas Gandhi was experimenting in India.

Exhausted, in 1936 Muste and his wife traveled to Europe, a region seething with the swirling currents of totalitarianism, militarism, and radical infighting. In Paris he experienced a mystical, revelatory conversion to what he interpreted as nonviolent revolution: absolute Christian pacifism joined to radical social concern. The following year, he found a pulpit from which to preach that vision. He became director of the Labor Temple, a Presbyterian agency serving immigrants in New York City and facilitating discussion of controversial issues. Muste also rejoined the FOR, becoming its executive secretary in 1940 at the urging of John Nevin Sayre, the Fellowship's mainstay throughout the years of Muste's independent journey.

During World War II, Muste fostered spiritual unity within the FOR and among various groups of absolute pacifists. The most divisive issue they faced was related to conscientious objectors. By law, conscripted pacifists were to be assigned to Civilian Public Service (CPS) camps, which were to be financed by the peace churches and FOR, and administered by the government in conjunction with the pacifist National Service Board for Religious Objectors (NSBRO). At first Muste supported the arrangement because, like others, he assumed that pacifists would share jurisdiction over the CPS with the Selective Service. As the NSBRO became ever more clearly subordinate to military administration, dissatisfaction infected the camps and Muste changed his mind. In spring 1943 he recommended that the FOR withdraw from the NSBRO, pressing the issue until he won majority support at the end of 1944.

The CPS was oriented to religious nonresistants, not to men who objected to military service on secular grounds, who rejected conscription itself, or who refused to cooperate with the system. These men often found themselves in federal prisons. Some of them engaged in work or hunger strikes to challenge prison practices such as racial segregation and mail censorship. At first critical of noncooperation, Muste increasingly supported the prisoners' initiatives. Conscription issues thus illustrated two dimensions of his wartime leadership: first, he tried to maintain pacifist unity under divisive wartime pressure, and second, he was receptive to the tactics of nonviolent direct action.

The latter approach was best illustrated by the Congress of Racial Equality (CORE), which Muste personally nurtured. Founded in 1942 by FOR worker James Farmer and other pacifists in Chicago, CORE spread across the country as interracial teams conducted sit-ins, bus rides, and similar actions against racial segregation during the 1940s. The organization received financial backing and administrative support from the FOR, and its early membership drew heavily from pacifist ranks.

Muste, like CORE's founders, regarded nonviolent direct action (sometimes simply called "nonviolence") as an American application of Gandhi's principles. As interpreted by Richard Gregg's *The Power of Nonviolence* and Krishnalal Shridharani's *War Without Violence* (the latter book published with Muste's help), Gandhi's *satayagraha* seemed to embody the vision of disciplined nonviolence and social revolution that had gripped Muste in 1936, reaffirming his 1919 commitment to social justice and pacifism. The development of active nonviolence, together with the 1930s neutrality campaign, suggest how far liberal, activist pacifism had come since its emergence during World War I.

At midcentury much of the world became polarized between two armed camps: states aligned with the Soviet Union and with the United States. That polarity framed the agenda for liberal pacifists and nonviolent activists for some forty years. During the balance of his life, Muste worked with both wings of pacifists, although he perhaps became best known for direct action.

At the end of World War II, veteran pacifist Kirby Page wrote, "If a third [and atomic] world war is to be averted, the American people and government must behave in ways that will reduce the suspicions and fears and enmities of the people and government of Soviet Russia," despite the fact that the Soviet Union was a ruthless, authoritarian state self-consciously engaged in an irreconcilable conflict with the West.[7] Page opposed appeasing the Soviets, but he advocated building mutual confidence based on global stability and international problem-solving—what thirty years later would be called détente. He recommended policies aimed at a much stronger international government, disarmament, economic stability, racial and social justice, the abolition of imperialism, the reconstruction of Germany and Japan as democratic societies, and the mobilization of people throughout the world (particularly Christians) for peaceful approaches to conflict. Page's analysis defined the political agenda of liberal pacifists throughout the Cold War.

In the aftermath of World War II, there was a brief surge of interest in world federation, stimulated by scientists who were horrified by the prospect of a nuclear arms race and by internationalists who were dissatisfied with the compromises on which the United Nations was formed. The world federalist movement was not a campaign of pacifists, although it attracted some of them, and it quickly succumbed to Cold War anxiety and McCarthyism. Internationalism became synonymous with U.S. worldwide influence. The field of peace activism was again left largely to liberal pacifists who were charged with being Communist sympathizers and fellow travelers. That was ironic, given pacifist experience with the factious and duplicitous politics of communism in the 1930s.

No one appreciated the reality of Communist politics better than Muste, but no one articulated better the danger of a foreign policy based on reflexive anticommunist ideology. Toward the end of World War II, he warned against trusting the future to the dominant powers. As those powers became polarized, and as U.S. foreign policy increasingly cast the containment of communism in military terms (including rearmament, a set of military alliances surrounding Russia and China, and the development of nuclear weapons), Muste and other pacifists challenged the wisdom of trusting the future to power itself, especially the power to wage nuclear war. With Page they believed that *"we have entered a new era of destructiveness and the old argument that war is a lesser evil is tragic delusion.* War has become totalitarian and totalitarian war is a combination of the worst evils that threaten the human race."[8]

In the book *Not by Might* (1947) and in shorter essays, Muste criticized the self-styled political realism often associated with the ethical analyses of Reinhold Niebuhr. He contributed to a major study conference, Church and War, in

1950. He was loaned by the FOR to the Church Peace Mission, a project (funded largely by the FOR, the AFSC, and the Brethren Service Committee) to carry the pacifist perspective to Christian leaders. In print and discussion, in America and internationally, through the Church Peace Mission and independently, Muste and his fellow pacifists challenged the realism of foreign policy predicated on nuclear war. Journalist James Reston observed of the campaign, which culminated with the 1955 AFSC pamphlet *Speak Truth to Power*, "For perhaps the first time in history reflective men have had to grapple with the pacifists' question: can national interests and human values really be served by waging a war with atomic and hydrogen weapons?"[9]

By the mid-1950s the hazard of fallout from testing nuclear weapons was an issue around which peace advocates could organize a massive public campaign. Adlai Stevenson, though defeated in his 1956 presidential election bid, advocated a test ban, which stimulated grassroots organizing. The following year the National Committee for a Sane Nuclear Policy (SANE) was formed as concerned scientists and internationalists joined liberal pacifists to challenge the government's assessment of nuclear risks, to provide public education on fallout and atomic weapons, and to mount a political campaign for an international treaty banning atmospheric testing. The American movement was part of a broad, international movement. In England the Committee for Nuclear Disarmament adopted a logo that featured a circle containing the semaphore signs for N and D, thus creating the now universally recognized "peace" symbol.

The strength of the campaign grew. In 1958 President Dwight D. Eisenhower preempted the issue to some extent by concluding a moratorium on testing with the Soviet Union, but new constituencies were added to the campaign: doctors organized Physicians for Social Responsibility; the Student Peace Union was formed; entertainment personalities lent their support; women mobilized against the arms race through Women Strike for Peace; and Reinhold Niebuhr, among other political realists, endorsed a comprehensive test ban. SANE opened a Washington office and, with a coalition of peace and religious groups, engaged in party and legislative politics. The campaign peaked in 1961–1962, responding to a new generation of weapons, the resumption of nuclear testing, and dramatic confrontations such as the construction of the Berlin Wall and the Cuban missile crisis. Largely in response to the threat of war they had created, President John F. Kennedy and Soviet Premier Nikita Khrushchev concluded a ban on atmospheric testing (1963), for which Kennedy explicitly called on the SANE network to help generate public support.

Muste, although he cooperated as fully as possible with the liberal peace wing and SANE (which he helped to form), played a pivotal role in nonviolent direct action against the nuclear arms race that was conducted by radical pacifists throughout the test ban campaign. In this respect, as historian Jo Ann Robinson noted, he moved "from dialogue and persuasion" to "protest and resistance."[10]

In 1955 Muste joined Catholic Worker pacifists refusing to cooperate with required civil defense drills. Two years later a broader field for action opened up with the formation of what came to be called the Committee for Non-Violent Action (CNVA). With fellow pacifists Muste held a vigil within sight of a Nevada atomic bomb test, illegally entered the test zone, and was arrested. Other actions followed. Protesters tried to sail into restricted Pacific testing areas, obstructed construction at a Wyoming missile base, engaged in civil disobedience at a Nebraska Air Force base, and challenged the construction of nuclear submarines in Connecticut. When he was not participating in nonviolent direct action, Muste was defending it, sometimes in court and often in discussions with skeptical pacifists.

He helped to internationalize the approach through the San Francisco to Moscow Peace March of 1960–1961, which witnessed for peace and nuclear disarmament on both sides of the iron curtain. He was instrumental in a nonviolent action on the border of Algeria to protest atomic testing by the French. That was followed by other international projects for nonviolent direct action or nuclear disarmament. In the wake of the Cuban missile crisis, Muste helped with a projected walk from Quebec to Guantánamo to protest the extension of the Cold War to Central America. The demonstrators encountered racist harassment in Georgia, which dramatized the conjunction of nonviolent direct action in the peace and civil rights movements.

When Martin Luther King, Jr., emerged as the leader of the Montgomery, Alabama, bus boycott in 1956, he received personal guidance from two pacifists experienced in nonviolent direct action: Glenn Smiley of the FOR and Bayard Rustin of CORE. In the early 1960s both organizations cooperated closely with the Southern Christian Leadership Conference and the Student Nonviolent Coordinating Committee. Significantly, the civil rights movement helped the peace movement by legitimating dissent, especially nonviolent direct action, but the drama of civil rights also vied with the test ban campaign for public attention and resources.

In any case, absolute pacifists had returned to the political arena. They had engaged political liberals, who began to question the terms of Cold War internationalism. They had challenged atmospheric testing and Cold War policy both through traditional action to influence public opinion and political policy, and through nonviolent direct action, including civil disobedience. In all these respects, they unknowingly had set the stage for the antiwar movement of the Vietnam era.

Muste was one of several pacifists and political liberals to warn against U.S. military involvement in Indochina before the Gulf of Tonkin incident in August 1964. At the outset, organized opposition to war in Vietnam built on existing pacifist and allied peace groups. Thus, a December 1964 demonstration against military intervention was supported by the War Resisters League, the Student Peace Union, the CNVA, the FOR, and the Socialist party (which is to say, Norman Thomas). In addition, the AFSC, SANE, and the WILPF lobbied on the issue, and the Women Strike for Peace and the recently formed Students for a Democratic Society (SDS) provided ready resources in the spring of 1965, when President Lyndon B. Johnson authorized sustained bombing of North Vietnam and committed ground troops to South Vietnam.

Public support for the president's policy, although initially strong, weakened during the following two years as casualties mounted without discernible results in winning the war. Organized opposition increased. Existing women's peace groups were supplemented by Another Mother for Peace, and students were mobilized for teach-ins, demonstrations, and political legwork. New constituencies were added to the antiwar coalition: church leaders organized in Clergy and Laity Concerned, professionals, artists, entertainers, labor unions, business executives, prominent Democrats in Americans for Democratic Action, elements of a youthful counterculture, organized draft resisters, and in 1967 civil rights leaders including Martin Luther King, Jr. There was no central direction of this eclectic coalition; its only common denominator was opposition to the war. Periodically cooperation was negotiated for specific demonstrations and political campaigns, but to a large extent each group worked on its own; in fact, the movement was mainly organized at the grassroots level.

Nonetheless, under the intense pressure of challenging national policy on moral and political grounds, two discernible groupings emerged within the antiwar movement. One wing aligned liberal pacifists and political liberals who focused on specific policy issues and sought change through the mainstream political process (SANE and the ADA, for example). The other wing comprised political radicals, elements of the so-called counterculture, and radical pacifists. It mounted multi-issue mass demonstrations and other direct action, including civil disobedience and draft resistance. Division constantly threatened the larger antiwar coalition and created special problems for groups like the FOR and AFSC, which spanned the spectrum of pacifism and war opposition.

The tensions within the antiwar movement explain why Muste became so pivotal in it. A man of good humor and complete integrity who was skilled in interpersonal relationships, he was trusted on all sides. Older leaders identified with his record of principled activism, and young people admired his spirit of innovation and his stamina (he completed an arduous trip to North Vietnam on his eighty-second birthday). Liberal pacifists remembered his work for labor in the 1920s, his opposition to Stalinist communism in the 1930s, and his efforts to penetrate the Cold War mentality through dialogue and persuasion in the 1950s. Radical pacifists knew him as a risk-taking Trotskyist in the 1930s, who subsequently endorsed civil disobedience and nonviolent direct action at home and abroad in campaigns against nuclear weapons. Here was an avowed Christian individualist who did not put down the counterculture; a leader who had long been associated with the FOR, had cooperated with the AFSC, WILPF, and War Resisters League, had helped organize or had provided crucial support for CORE, SANE, and CNVA, the Student Peace Union and SDS, one who knew the crucial importance of coalition politics in the quest for peace and justice.

Over his long career as a peace activist, Muste built and maintained connections with every dimension of pacifism—the religious nonresistance that antedated World War I, the liberal pacifism that became politically active between the world wars, and the radical pacifist experiments with nonviolent direct action in the civil rights and test ban campaigns. During the Vietnam War he extended those linkages. He personally made coalition politics work in the Fifth Avenue Parade Committee, which successfully put together antiwar demonstrations in New York City, and he repeatedly mediated differences between the radical and liberal wings of the movement on a national level. Where he did not intervene personally, he was an abiding symbol of cooperation for high purpose. His death on 10 February 1967 left a gap in the antiwar movement that was exacerbated by the extraordinary events of the following year.

In the wake of the 1968 Tet offensives, the Vietnam War became a political issue and President Johnson became a political casualty. Electoral politics engaged liberal opponents of the war, notably within the Democratic party, while the turmoil and violence of that year—riots following the murder of Martin Luther King, Jr., the assassination of Robert Kennedy, the Democratic National Convention—pushed political radicals toward extremism. By focusing on street demonstrations, confrontation, cultural deviance, and violence, television contributed to the image of antiwar protest as radical and un-American. That image was exploited by presidents Johnson and (even more explicitly) Richard M. Nixon, in their effort to push antiwar opposition to the political margin. Ironically, in the wake of the Democratic Convention in Chicago, the pacifist core of the antiwar movement organized to keep subsequent direct action disciplined and nonviolent, and liberal pacifists became ever more involved in electoral politics and lobbying, especially from 1972 to 1975. Pictured largely in radical terms, therefore, antiwar opposition lost visibility as it moved off the streets and into mainstream politics.

Pacifist organizations continued to be an integral part of the American peace movement after the Vietnam War. They provided critical resources and experience during the Nuclear Freeze campaign and the Latin American solidarity movement of the 1980s. Portrayed largely in terms of their absolute opposition to war, pacifists often were not appreciated for their peacetime role in challenging patterns of foreign policy through public education, political action, nonviolent direct action, or individual civil disobedience. Indeed, they were sometimes criticized for becoming involved in Cold War politics on the grounds that absolute pacifism is antithetical to citizen action in a world where force is a reality.

Muste would have found that assertion familiar. Given his own experience, he would have understood that it ignores the historical experience of modern pacifism. Muste did not represent all the dimensions of modern pacifism, but he came into contact with most of them. He valued both the nonresistant witness of absolute pacifists and the internationalist attempt to make the world less violent. He cooperated with liberal pacifists who challenged foreign policy, and he explored the activist side of pacifism in his personal experiments with nonviolent direct action and civil disobedience. Both seeking peace in the spirituality of his being and pursuing social justice through nonviolence, Muste relished the multifaceted character of modern pacifism.

NOTES

1. Charles DeBenedetti, *The Peace Reform in American History* (Bloomington, Ind., 1980).
2. "For Pacifists," *Time*, 10 July 1939, 36–37.
3. Jo Ann Ooiman Robinson, *Abraham Went Out: A Biography of A. J. Muste* (Philadelphia, 1981), 16.
4. Ibid., 25.
5. Kirby Page, *If War Is Sin* (Nyack, N.Y., 1935).
6. Robinson, *Abraham Went Out*, 36.
7. Kirby Page, *How to Prevent a Third World War* (La Habra, Calif., 1946), 36.
8. Ibid., 9.
9. The Reston comment is quoted in Robinson, *Abraham Went Out*, 158, where on p. 290, n. 49, it is attributed to a quotation in the pamphlet *Speak Truth to Power* (Philadelphia, 1955).
10. Robinson, *Abraham Went Out*. The quoted words are the apt titles for chapters 9 and 10, respectively.

BIBLIOGRAPHY

Alonso, Harriet Hyman. *Peace as a Women's Issue: A History of the U.S. Movement for World Peace and Women's Rights*. Syracuse, N.Y., 1993.
Brock, Peter. *The Quaker Peace Testimony 1660 to 1914*. York, U.K., 1990.
———. *Freedom from War: Nonsectarian Pacifism 1814–1914*. Toronto, 1991.
Chambers, John W., II, ed. *The Eagle and the Dove: The American Peace Movement and United States Foreign Policy, 1900–1922*. 2nd ed. Syracuse, N.Y., 1991.
Chatfield, Charles. *For Peace and Justice: Pacifism in America, 1914–1941*. Knoxville, Tenn., 1971.
———. *The American Peace Movement: Ideals and Activism*. New York, 1992.
Cooper, Sandi E. *Patriotic Pacifism: Waging War on War in Europe, 1815–1914*. New York, 1991.
DeBenedetti, Charles. *Origins of the Modern American Peace Movement, 1915–1929*. Millwood, N.Y., 1978.
———, ed. *Peace Heroes in Twentieth-Century America*. Bloomington, Ind., 1986.
DeBenedetti, Charles, with Charles Chatfield. *An American Ordeal: The Antiwar Movement of the Vietnam Era*. Syracuse, N.Y., 1990.
Divine, Robert A. *Second Chance: The Triumph of Internationalism in America During World War II*. New York, 1967.
———. *Blowing on the Wind: The Nuclear Test Ban Debate, 1954–1960*. New York, 1978.
Hentoff, Nat, ed. *The Essays of A. J. Muste*. Indianapolis, 1967. Includes Muste's "Sketches for an Autobiography," 1–138.
Herman, Sondra R. *Eleven Against War: Studies in American International Thought, 1898–1921*. Stanford, Calif., 1969.

Katz, Milton. *Ban the Bomb: A History of SANE, the Committee for a Sane Nuclear Policy, 1957–1985.* New York, 1986.

Kleidman, Robert. *Organizing for Peace: Neutrality, the Test Ban, and the Freeze.* Syracuse, N.Y., 1993.

Kraft, Barbara. *The Peace Ship: Henry Ford's Pacifist Adventure in the First World War.* New York, 1978.

Kuehl, Warren F. *Seeking World Order: The United States and International Organization to 1920.* Nashville, Tenn., 1969.

Marchand, Roland. *The American Peace Movement, 1887–1914.* Princeton, 1972.

McNeal, Patricia. *Harder Than War: Catholic Peacemaking in Twentieth-Century America.* New Brunswick, N.J., 1992.

Meyer, David S. *A Winter of Discontent: The Nuclear Freeze and American Politics.* New York, 1990.

Patterson, David S. *Toward a Warless World: The Travail of the American Peace Movement, 1887–1914.* Bloomington, Ind., 1976.

Robinson, Jo Ann Ooiman. *Abraham Went Out: A Biography of A. J. Muste.* Philadelphia, 1981.

Wittner, Lawrence S. *Rebels Against War: The American Peace Movement, 1933–1983.* 2nd ed. Philadelphia, 1984.

———. *One World or None: A History of the World Nuclear Disarmament Movement.* Stanford, Calif., 1993.

Wooley, Wesley T. *Alternatives to Anarchy: American Supernationalism Since World War II.* Bloomington, Ind., 1988.

Ziegler, Valarie H. *The Advocates of Peace in Antebellum America.* Bloomington, Ind., 1992.

Ralph Nader
and Consumer Politics

MARTHA MAY

Americans throughout the twentieth century have debated the benefits of governmental regulation of business. Despite serious disagreements over the extent of state restrictions, few Americans would deny that the average consumer today enjoys better protection from unsafe products, more information about product reliability, and greater availability of safety devices. Packaged food now carries a label giving information about nutritional quality and fat content. Automobile manufacturers vie for the right to claim the best safety equipment. Airlines boast about their reliability.

Consumer activism has allowed Americans to expect product safety and assume that dangerous items will be withheld or removed from the market by a federal agency. Ralph Nader, perhaps the most tireless and persistent consumer advocate of the twentieth century, has played a central role in creating new consumer protections and safeguards. The founder of over twenty organizations, Nader remains the champion of consumer rights whether the product is an automobile, an insurance policy, or a government service. His efforts have influenced how consumers understand their relationship to business and government. Whether consumers buy toys, trucks, or aspirin, they anticipate that a product will not harm them if it is used appropriately. This level of trust reflects both the success and the failures of the consumer rights movement of the 1960s and 1970s.

The consumer rights movement uprooted the "Business First" attitude of the 1950s, and replaced it with a new expectation among Americans that industries have an inherent obligation to produce safe products. Yet this movement has lacked the organizational form and the philosophical inclination to mount a more substantial challenge to the ability of business, rather than consumers or government, to control the marketplace. As a consequence, the political impact of consumer activism lessened through the 1980s as the movement focused on discrete aspects of consumer safety. Without an analysis broader than corporate obligation and consumer protection, what remains of a "movement" may well have encountered its own cross of gold. If Americans have increasingly relied upon consumer reports when making purchases, they also have grown more cynical about consumer organizations.

As political scientist Robert D. Holsworth suggests, the success of consumer politics in the 1970s and a subsequent reluctance among consumer activists to question the basic nature of a capitalist economy result largely from the skills and the limitations of leadership. Ralph Nader remains the most identifiable consumer activist in the United States after a career of thirty years. His tenacity, political sensibilities, and personal style have had a profound impact on consumer awareness and organization. Rangy and rumpled, Nader fought persistently to expose unsafe products, weak industrial standards, and corporate bias. He has been called a "Joan of Arc" by his admirers and condemned as a modern Savonarola by critics. In the 1970s, Americans regarded Nader as one of the nation's most admirable citizens. He founded or organized many of the organizations that still dominate consumer politics, such as the Center for the Study of Responsive Law and Public Citizen. By the mid-1990s, however, Ralph Nader commanded less open admiration, and the consumer movement he had spearheaded had fragmented. These shifts reflected both larger historical changes beyond the control of consumer advocates and the limits of Nader's control within the movement.

Consumer activism in the twentieth century has typically occurred in periods of heightened efforts to achieve social and political reform. Sociologist Robert Cameron Mitchell argues that during such periods, renewed interest in consumer politics has developed from demands for industrial regulation, deepened environmental concerns, and greater public distrust of big business.[1] These elements characterize the Progressive era and the New Deal. Consumer politics of the 1960s and 1970s remain unique, however, in its broader appeal and its achievements.

The rapid expansion of business by the end of the nineteenth century worried many Americans, from farmers organized in the Farmers' Alliance to skilled workers in the new American Federation of Labor. In the relatively brief life of the People's party, farmers had proposed producers' cooperatives and federal regulation of railways and telegraph. Their subtreasury plan called for a new relationship between agricultural producers and the government through price protection. Although largely a producers' movement, the Farmers' Alliance did articulate a politicized sense of farmers as the consumers, and the prey, of big business. Their insistence that the federal government acknowledge the small farmer's role as producer *and* consumer through federal intervention marked a significant shift from nineteenth-century laissez-faire.

Throughout the period between 1890 and 1920, various reformers insisted upon the need for some regulation of American business to protect workers and consumers. Progressive era social welfare workers in charities and settlement houses argued that widespread indigence in American cities stemmed as much from business indifference and low wages as it did from lax morals or personal deficiencies among the poor. In social surveys and sociological investigations, reformers documented the connections between inadequate legal supervision of business practices and high industrial accident rates, substandard housing, and poverty. Increasingly, a new generation of activists identified the human cost of laissez-faire policies, and called on state and federal governments to offer protection from the most outrageous abuses of business. Progressive era businessmen such as Edward Filene joined in advocacy for reform, and the National Civic Federation was organized in 1900 to pursue a moderate reform agenda.

Journalists were the most public advocates of government protection for consumers. In 1906 Upton Sinclair's novel *The Jungle* exposed outrageous conditions in the meatpacking industry. With its vivid descriptions of rotted meat and sickened children, *The Jungle* provided ammunition for reformers to win congressional passage of the Meat Inspection Act. Other muckraking journalists chronicled the abuses of other industries and the conditions of the cities. Lincoln Steffens's *The Shame of the Cities* (1904) revealed city corruption and patronage, and Ida Tarbell's investigation of Standard Oil in 1902 and 1903 described ruthless monopoly. The muckrakers heightened public awareness of business excesses and increased public support for reform. Through measures such as the Pure Food and Drugs Act and the Hepburn Railroad Regulation Act of 1906, the federal government asserted its ability to restrain corporate power.

The work of women reformers on what historians now label "maternal" issues—child health, widow's pensions, minimum wages, and industrial accident insurance, for example—contributed to the construction of consumer rights as well. By demonstrating the vulnerability of families within industrial capitalism, women activists such as Florence Kelley, Mary Simkhovitch, and Jane Addams politicized the role of the household in American society. Through the National Consumers League, Kelley campaigned for greater awareness of the connections between household consumption and industrial production. Addams, perhaps the preeminent woman reformer of her day, repeatedly spoke of the need for a practical recognition of the contributions of families to social well-being. Insisting that government acknowledge the importance of families to the life of the nation, Progressive reformers sowed the seeds of a more personal kind of movement, one directed not to citizens' political or economic status but to questions of satisfaction and security within the existing industrial order.

The professionalization of home economics through colleges and universities paralleled the political interest in family life. Leaders such as Ellen Swallow Richards argued that home consumption should be scientifically investigated and analyzed. Within the new field of sociology and the settlement houses, other investigators began to detail family budgets and critique consumption patterns. The idea that family purchases should be studied with the goal of improving consumer lives contributed to the later consumer movements.

The vigor of Progressive activism faded in the 1920s, but many elements of consumer politics remained intact. Throughout the decade, social scientists enthusiastically documented family budgets and determined "standards" of living. Home economists pursued scientific consumption through college classrooms and in popular magazines such as *Ladies Home Journal*. Articles such as "How to Survive on $25 a Week" not only taught frugality but also sharpened the notion that consumers should exercise some leverage in the marketplace.

The 1920s were, however, a decade of business. If the number of products available increased, consumers' control over industry lessened. While governmental regulation of consumer goods largely stalled, new sources of information for purchasers appeared. By the 1930s, *Consumers' Research Bulletin* addressed issues of safety. Its founder, Frederick Schlink, coauthored a study of product reliability in 1933—*100,000,000 Guinea Pigs: Dangers in Everyday Foods, Drugs and Cosmetics*—that became a best-seller. Another exposé of faulty products, Ruth De Forest's *America Chamber of Horrors*, contributed to growing public concern in 1938.

The federal government launched new consumer regulations during the New Deal. Although these were not extensive safeguards, federal action revealed the increasing importance of some form of consumer protection. Both the Consumer Advisory Board of the National Recovery Administration and the Consumers' Council within the Department of Agriculture provided new avenues through which consumers could seek information. More substantial protections from the government came in 1938, when renewed publicity about product safety contributed to the passage of a new Federal Food, Drug and Cosmetic Act. The 1938 Wheeler-Lea Amendment to the Federal Trade Commission Act of 1914 broadened federal regulations to prohibit deception as an element of unfair trade practices.

The postwar prosperity of the 1950s offered consumers a stunning array of products and governmental policies largely favorable to business. McCarthyism chilled critical social movements and encouraged conformity to the material vision of the American dream. Yet, even in this climate of abundance, new questions arose about the impact of a "consumer society" on national well-being. Sociologists such as David Riesman argued that alienation within the "lonely crowd" accompanied the new prosperity; economist John Kenneth Galbraith noted income disparities in *The Affluent Society* (1958). These challenges to business domination of culture were echoed by new critiques of advertising, including Vance Packard's *The Hidden Persuaders* (1957). In 1962 Rachael Carson identified the dangers unregulated industry posed to the environment in her pioneering work *Silent Spring*. These investigations did not undermine the pro-business attitudes of government officials and most American consumers during the 1950s, but they did begin to challenge the commonplace assumption that business expansion brought only benefits and better products. This skepticism grew deeper in the 1960s, when the cultural norm of conformity was replaced by a new rebelliousness and emphasis on the individual.

The new consumer movement of the 1960s and 1970s began with a proposed "Consumer Bill of Rights." In speaking to Congress in March 1962, President John F. Kennedy called for new standards of consumer protection. Consumer rights should include the right to safety, the president declared, and he enumerated additional guarantees: the right to information, to a choice of products, and to a fair hearing by government in the creation of consumer policy. Kennedy committed the government to two distinct courses of action. Business would be required to meet new production standards to ensure safety, and the government would mandate general safety standards for specific goods.

Tragedy rather than rhetoric prompted government action, however. A new drug named thalidomide was prescribed extensively in Europe to reduce rates of miscarriage. . . . In the United States, approval of thalidomide by the Food and Drug Administration (FDA) was blocked by one concerned physician, Frances Kelsey. As it became clear through congressional hearings in 1959 that thalidomide use caused serious birth defects, public concern about prescription safety grew. In 1962 the Kefauver-Harris Amendment to the Food, Drug and Cosmetic Act required new drugs to be tested for safety. The thalidomide disaster also deepened fears that the public was not yet protected from unreliable and dangerous products.

As the public began to consider the absence of product safety standards for all industries, Ralph Nader's first article on consumer safety, a discussion of automobile standards, appeared in *The Nation* in 1963. With the publication of *Unsafe at Any Speed* in 1965, Nader emerged as one of the nation's most articulate advocates of consumer rights. Yet the development of a consumer movement in the 1960s did not rest solely on Nader's persistence. The issues that troubled the nation in the 1960s—questions about individual freedom, a renewed sense of federal responsibility for the vulnerable and disadvantaged, cynicism about established institutions—led easily to consumer politics. The growing consumer movement required cultural acceptance of a particular notion of responsibility shared by citizen, government, and industry. Unlike the belief in laissez-faire of the nineteenth century, or the notion that a private citizen could contract, caveat emptor, with business, the new perspective of the twentieth century stressed the role of the government as a mediator between the power of business and the rights of citizens. Consumer rights activists demanded that federal and state authority be used to protect citizens through legislation, executive action, and court decisions.

As a lawyer, Ralph Nader excelled at using the existing avenues of legal reform. He also understood the need for new agencies for advocacy. Indeed, the construction of a network of consumer rights organizations remains his most enduring achievement. Beginning in 1968 with the establishment of the Center for the Study of Responsive Law, Nader rounded advocacy agencies ranging from the umbrella organization Public Citizen (1971) to the student-based Public Research Interest Group (1970). Other Nader organizations include the Aviation Consumer Action Project, the Center for Auto Safety, Congress Watch, the

Center for Responsive Law, and the National Insurance Consumer Organization. By 1995 over two dozen consumer organizations could trace their origins to Nader's efforts. In a study of testimony before Congress by consumer activists between 1970 and 1992, political scientists Ardith Maney and Lorree Bykerk concluded that Nader's agencies remained the dominant voice within the movement.

As the most public advocate of consumer rights, Ralph Nader has won plaudits and found vociferous enemies. Born in Winsted, Connecticut, on 27 February 1934, he grew up in a household known for a commitment to local politics. Nader's parents, Nathra and Rose Nader, had immigrated to the United States from Lebanon in 1925. After settling in Winsted, Nathra Nader operated a restaurant. Both parents encouraged their four children's interest in the community; Nader's older sister Laura eventually became a respected anthropologist and consumer advocate.

Whereas Nader later recalled a childhood of books and baseball, friends remembered him as studious and already something of an iconoclast. At Princeton, where he received his undergraduate degree Phi Beta Kappa and magna cum laude in 1955, Nader reportedly once wore his bathrobe to class. He entered Harvard Law School in 1955.

Nader later labeled Harvard a "high-priced tool factory" and initiated Harvard Watch, a consumer organization created to investigate the fair use of Harvard resources.[2] He began his consumer work while a student at Harvard Law School, focusing on the question of automobile safety in his research. He did not begin the career that led *Newsweek* to label him the "Consumer Crusader" immediately after receiving his law degree in 1958. Instead, Nader completed his six months of active duty in the U.S. Army Reserve, then worked for a short time at a law firm in Hartford, Connecticut. From 1961 until 1964, he traveled and worked as a journalist. In Scandinavia, Nader was particularly impressed by the use of an ombudsman for consumer complaints, but his efforts to secure similar legislation in Connecticut were unsuccessful. Nader also began work as a researcher and consultant on automobile safety for then Assistant Secretary of Labor Daniel P. Moynihan.

When Connecticut Senator Abraham Ribicoff, head of the Senate Subcommittee on Executive Reorganization, decided to hold public hearings on car safety, his staff turned to the knowledgeable Nader. The hearings began in March 1964, but remained unproductive and frustrating for the senator's aides. The climate changed in November, when Ralph Nader's investigation, *Unsafe at Any Speed*, revealed serious defects in the Chevrolet Corvair. Nader also documented General Motors' (GM) disregard for the car's inherent instability and its unwillingness to notify an unsuspecting public of the Corvair's problems. Nader demonstrated how GM had refused to remedy specific defects, such as a steering wheel with the potential to impale the driver upon impact. The intense young lawyer became the focus of national attention.

Senate hearings on automobile safety resumed in February 1966, with Nader as a major witness. By that time, he had become the object of surveillance by private detectives hired by General Motors to discredit him. Their attempts to interview Nader's friends, professors, and colleagues alerted Nader and Ribicoff's staff, and on 9 March 1966, GM acknowledged a "routine investigation." Senator Ribicoff responded with hearings on GM's actions, and the company admitted it had pursued Nader. Nader sued for invasion of privacy, and in August 1970, GM agreed to pay $425,000 in settlement to end the litigation. Admitting no wrongdoing, GM ironically ended up giving Nader the funds with which he created new consumer organizations. As Nader noted, GM was finally "financing their own ombudsman."[3]

Nader institutionalized his work for consumers by establishing the Center for the Study of Responsive Law in 1968. "Nader's Raiders," as they were dubbed by the press, directed their efforts at research and publicizing dangers for consumers. Staffed initially with graduates of Ivy League law schools, the Center drew praise for its tenacious explorations of air pollution, coal mine safety, and the food industry. Critics jumped quickly to condemn the lack of specific expertise on the Center's staff, labeling its work incompetent or naive. Such arguments had little effect on Nader or his raiders in the late 1960s and early 1970s; the movement grew rapidly, expanding under his auspices into the Public Interest Research Group, the Center for Auto Safety, the Corporate Accountability Research Group, the Clean Water Action Project, Buy Up, Essential Information, Inc., the Congressional Accountability Project, and others.

Public fascination with Nader as a person grew during this period. The GM investigation had turned up no scandal of any kind, and what the public saw through these discussions was an ascetic man devoted to a cause. Nader lived in a rooming house in Washington, D.C., socialized infrequently, and worked obsessively. The Consumer Crusader did not indulge in the material fruits of consumer society, rejecting material goods as a "potential trap." Nader refused to own a car, worried that it might limit a public perception of his objectivity.[4] Throughout his career, Nader has maintained this spartan lifestyle.

As Nader became the public focus of the growing consumer movement, two older organizations enjoyed a new climate for their advocacy. Consumers Union and the Consumers Federation of America became what one analyst called the "backbone" of consumerism. Including approximately 200 organizations, the Consumers Federation coordinated lobbying and provided publicity. Consumers Union offered information on specific products through testing and investigation, and published its findings in *Consumer Reports*.

Government response to increasing demands for consumer protection brought greater protection than at any time in American history. In 1964 President Lyndon Johnson appointed Esther Peterson to be the first special assistant for consumer affairs. Johnson's willingness to support consumer laws aided in the passage of new statutes, including, in 1966, the National Traffic and Motor Vehicle Safety Act; the Child Protection Act, prohibiting dangerous toys from interstate commerce; and the Fair Packaging and Labeling Act. Measures passed subsequently offered a wide range of safety standards, covering meat, flammable fabrics, consumer credit, child safety caps for medicines, and poultry inspection. In 1972 the Consumer Product Safety Commission was created to improve product safety and consumer redress.

By the late 1970s, however, the pace of legislation slowed. Although the 1976 Toxic Substances Control Act mandated testing of all chemicals prior to marketing, other consumer issues, such as airline safety and regulation of food additives, did not come to a legislative test. In 1981, when Nader turned control of Public Citizen over to a new director, Mark Green, the consumer movement entered a new and more difficult phase.

Historians and political scientists continue to debate the subsequent course of the movement. Clearly, on the national level consumer politics after 1980 lacked the strong direction it had maintained earlier. Yet local consumer groups flourished around the nation, and organizations such as the American Association of Retired Persons continued to fight for and win specific protections for their members. The most significant change in consumer politics lay not in the movement itself, perhaps, but in the return to conservative politics. The election of Ronald Reagan in 1981 brought into government a number of officials who were publically wary of consumer politics and environmental protection. President Reagan championed an ideal of government that did not regulate business, and throughout his administration executive agencies did not enforce or dropped consumer protections.

The Reagan administration's determination to withdraw from oversight or regulation of consumer industries forced consumer advocates to work to retain the achievements of the previous decade. The Center for the Study of Responsive Law, for example, documented less stringent inspection standards for meat and poultry by 1983, and Nader himself publicized the failures of the Occupational Safety and Health Administration (OSHA) to enforce workplace safety. Despite efforts to alert the public to the weakening of protections, consumer advocates were unable to undermine the flourishing pro-business attitude in government and in the nation. The 1980s became caricatured as the "greed" decade, a time when lavish spending and eliminating restraints were fashionable. In such a climate, consumer advocates turned from legislative initiatives to other goals. Public Citizen worked to advance consumer interests in public utilities, for instance.

Political scientists Maney and Bykerk note that business lobbies worked in concert to defeat many consumer bills. The National Association of Manufactures, the U.S. Chamber of Commerce, the National Federation of Independent Businesses, and the Business Roundtable, they report, allied in 1977 to defeat a proposed Agency for Consumer Advocacy. Vigorous opposition to consumer politics took other forms in the 1980s. In 1983 the College Republican National Committee launched a campaign against student consumer organizations such as the Public Interest Research Groups. Dan M. Burt, a persistent Nader critic, established the Capital Legal Foundation to lobby for what he termed a pro-business consumer policy.

The consumer movement faced additional obstacles in the 1980s. As the power of business grew, the ability of unions to secure adequate wages or better working conditions declined. Right-to-work campaigns reduced public sympathy for union claims, and by 1990 organized labor in the United States counted fewer members than at any time since the 1920s. Labor's decline further limited public criticism of business, a role that unions had previously shared with consumer activists. Increasingly through the 1980s, American consumers grew less wary of business dominance and more reluctant to accept the complaints of consumer groups. The reports of consumer advocates were sometimes lampooned for excessiveness, as when consumers were warned of the health risks of fried hamburgers, the fat content of Mexican food, or the dangers of fried rice.

At the same time, Americans voiced contradictory opinions of the relationships among business, government, and consumer groups. On the one hand, Americans expected to be protected from unsafe products, and sometimes expressed surprise to discover that they were not. By the same token, however, as media coverage of hazards grew, Americans became accustomed to what seemed to be a world of dangerous products on their lawns, in their driveways, in their kitchens, and even in their children's cribs. Scholars such as T. J. Jackson Lears and Todd Gitlin have noted the "numbing" effect of mass consumption, and to some degree the conflicting claims of advertisers and consumer activists, government officials, and watchdog agencies appeared to create apathy rather than action among American adults.[5]

Despite the difficulties faced by consumer organizations in the 1980s, some analysts have suggested that the movement itself must acknowledge its role in these difficulties. Nader particularly, as the most public figure in the movement, is sometimes cited as a chief reason for its failures. The most provocative critic in this regard has been political scientist Robert D. Holsworth, who has explored the liberal limits of consumerism and the role Nader has played in establishing them.

Nader's vision of consumer politics has not been revolutionary, Holsworth asserts, but a form of "defensive liberalism." Although Nader remains critical of corporate excess, the goal of his activism has been to make the existing economic system more responsive to the needs of citizens. He does not reject the premises of capitalism. Nader has described his work as "an attempt to preserve the free enterprise economy by making the market work better; an attempt to preserve democratic control of technology by giving government a role in the decision-making process as to how much or how little safety products must contain."[6] Nader told journalist Robert Buckhorn that he was "trying to tell people that if they just organize to make the establishment obey its own rules, they will have created a peaceful revolution of tremendous proportions. This is not radicalism."[7] Holsworth argues that in this approach Nader fails to challenge the economic divisions within American society, and he suggests that instead the reformer accepts the ideal that safe consumption, better consumption, could generate a satisfied nation.

Nader's work in the 1990s has demonstrated that the Consumer Crusader understands the limits of reform and the need for political action that addresses the structures of government. In 1992 Nader attempted a write-in candidacy during the New Hampshire presidential primary, and his focus on governmental programs, political corruption, and issues of access has increased. At times Nader's vocal criticism of new political initiatives has led him into strange company. In 1993 he joined conservative Pat Buchanan and millionaire Ross Perot in opposition to the General Agreement on Tariffs and Trade and the North American Free Trade Alliance. These efforts represent a new visibility for Nader in the post-Reagan era.

As Robert Holsworth notes, however, the success and failures of the consumer movement lie in its emphasis on citizens as consumers. By stressing the obligation of business to Americans, the consumer movement has made the public aware that it can, and should, have specific economic rights to safety. The inability of the consumer movement to move beyond the image of consumer-as-victim has meant that the factors that form the relationships of consumption receive inadequate attention. The agenda of consumer reform has remained incomplete, much as it had at the end of the Progressive era in the 1920s.

Whatever its limitations, however, that movement had gained significant new protections for Americans. As the central figure in reform, Ralph Nader remains the most important consumer advocate of the twentieth century, and one who seems unable to rest on past laurels. In 1994 Nader announced the formation of another consumer organization, a public interest law center named the Appleseed Foundation that will have branches through all fifty states. Nader was typically blunt about his ambition, defending his work with the belief that ''individuals still count; that they can generate a momentum for change; that they can challenge large and complex institutions; that there still is a very critical role for citizen action and for the development of citizenship that will improve the quality of life in the country.''[8] For the millions of Americans who on any day find protection in safe products, Nader's efforts have borne fruit.

NOTES

1. Robert Cameron Mitchell, ''Consumerism and Environmentalism in the 1980s: Competitive or Companionable Social Movements?'' in Paul N. Bloom and Ruth Belk Smith, eds., *The Future of Consumerism* (Lexington, Mass., 1986), 23–36.

2. Robert N. Mayer, *The Consumer Movement: Guardians of the Marketplace* (Boston, 1989), 42; Robert F. Buckhorn, *Nader: The People's Lawyer* (Englewood Cliffs, N.J., 1972), 39.

3. Buckhorn, *Nader*, 165.

4. Mayer, *The Consumer Movement*, 29.

5. T. J. Jackson Lears, *No Place of Grace: Antimodernism and the Transformation of*

American Culture 1880–1920 (New York, 1981), passim; and Todd Gitlin, ''Glib, Tawdry, Savvy and Standardized,'' *Dissent* 40 (Summer 1993): 351–356.

6. Robert D. Holsworth, *Public Interest Liberalism and the Crisis of Affluence* (Boston, 1980), 13.

7. Buckhorn, *Nader*, 49.

8. Ibid., 37.

BIBLIOGRAPHY

Asch, Peter. *Consumer Safety Regulation: Putting a Price on Life and Limb.* New York, 1988.

Bloom, Paul N., and Ruth Belk Smith, eds. *The Future of Consumerism.* Lexington, Mass., 1986.

Buckhorn, Robert F. *Nader: The People's Lawyer.* Englewood Cliffs, N.J., 1972.

Burt, Dan M. *Abuse of Trust: A Report on Ralph Nader's Network.* New York, 1982.

De Toledano, Ralph. *Hit & Run: The Rise—and Fall?—of Ralph Nader.* New Rochelle, N.Y., 1975.

Gorey, Hays. *Nader and the Power of Everyman.* New York, 1975.

Holsworth, Robert D. *Public Interest Liberalism and the Crisis of Affluence.* Boston, 1980.

Maney, Ardith, and Lorree Bykerk. *Consumer Politics: Protecting Public Interests on Capitol Hill.* Westport, Conn., 1994.

Mayer, Robert N. *The Consumer Movement: Guardians of the Marketplace.* Boston, 1989.

Nader, Ralph, ed. *Corporate Power in America: Ralph Nader's Conference on Corporate Accountability.* New York, 1973.

Nader, Ralph, and Kate Blackwell. *You and Your Pension.* New York, 1973.

Nader, Ralph, and Clarence Ditlow. *The Lemon Book: Auto Rights.* New York, 1990.

Nader, Ralph, and William Taylor. *The Big Boys: Power and Position in American Business.* New York, 1986.

Pertschuk, Michael. *Revolt Against Regulation: The Rise and Pause of the Consumer Movement.* Berkeley, Calif., 1982.

Rowe, Jonathan. ''It Happened in the Kitchen.'' *Christian Science Monitor*, 8 August 1991, 13.

Whiteside, Thomas. *The Investigation of Ralph Nader: General Motors vs. One Determined Man.* New York, 1972.

Margaret Sanger
and the Birth Control Movement

ELLEN CHESLER

Margaret Sanger went to jail in 1917 for distributing contraceptives to immigrant women from a makeshift clinic in a tenement storefront in Brooklyn, New York. When she died fifty years later, the cause for which she defiantly broke the law had achieved international stature. Although still a magnet for controversy, she was widely eulogized as one of the great emancipators of her time.

For more than half a century, Sanger dedicated herself to the deceptively simple proposition that access to a safe and reliable means of preventing pregnancy is a necessary condition of women's liberation and, in turn, of human progress. Although she encountered enormous resistance in her own lifetime and still invites criticism, Sanger popularized ideas and built institutions that have widespread influence today. Her leadership, though often quixotic, helped create enduring changes in the beliefs and behavior of men and women who perceive themselves as modern, not only in America but throughout the world.

Birth control and the promise of reproductive autonomy for women have fundamentally altered private life and public policy in the twentieth century. As the late psychologist Erik Erikson once provocatively suggested, no idea of modern times, save perhaps for arms control, has more directly challenged human destiny than has birth control, which may account for the profound psychic dissonance and social conflict it tends to inspire.[1]

Margaret Sanger was an immensely attractive woman: small, lithe, and trim. Her green eyes were flecked with amber, her hair a shiny auburn, her smile warm and charming, her hands perpetually in motion, beckoning even to strangers. As H. G. Wells once described her, she had a quick Irish wit, high spirits, and radiant common sense. She married twice and enjoyed the affection and esteem of both men and women, who provided her a lifelong network of emotional, financial, and organizational support. At the same time, she could be impossibly difficult, and those who dared to disagree with her quickly discovered her explosive temper.

Sanger was born Margaret Louisa Higgins on 14 September 1879, in Corning, New York, the sixth of eleven surviving children of Irish-born Michael Hennessy Higgins, a stonemason who earned a meager living carving cemetery monuments, and his wife, Anna Purcell Higgins. Margaret learned to dream at an early age from her father, a freethinker and religious apostate who squandered his talents and humane social vision on too much talk and drink. From her devout and resourceful mother she absorbed a powerful motivation to improve her lot and the self-discipline that made it possible to do so. One parent taught her to defy; the other, to behave. She struggled between the two but took from both a distinctive resolve to gain a better life for herself and for others.

From 1896 to 1898, Margaret attended the Claverack College and Hudson River Institute, a preparatory school located across the state in Columbia County. Her older sisters paid her tuition, and she earned room and board by working in the school kitchen. Lacking the funds to complete her degree, she returned to Corning to nurse her mother through the final stages of chronic tuberculosis. After Anna's death, Margaret enrolled in a nurse's training program at the White Plains Hospital in Westchester County. After completing two years of practical training, she met and married William Sanger, a New York City architect. Forced to chose between marriage and work, she left school without obtaining the registered nursing degree then required for work in hospitals, a fact she never admitted but always regretted. Weakened by a tubercular infection that lingered until finally cured by surgery many years later, and soon pregnant with the first of three children, Sanger settled down to a quiet life in Hastings-on-Hudson, New York, a community of young professionals. Her contentment with domesticity and suburban complacency was short-lived.

Eager for wider horizons, and overextended financially after a fire damaged their new home, the Sangers moved back to New York City in 1910. There Margaret helped make ends meet by working part-time as a visiting nurse and midwife in the immigrant districts of the city's Lower East Side. What she came to think of as an ''awakening'' allegedly occurred while tending a young Jewish immigrant woman named Sadie Sachs, whom she assisted through the complications of a self-induced septic abortion. Countless times throughout her career, Margaret would repeat the saga of Mrs. Sachs's broken plea for reliable contraception and the doctor's callous rejoinder that she tell her husband, Jake, ''to sleep on the roof.'' Returning several months later to find Mrs. Sachs dying of septicemia, Sanger resolved to abandon ''the palliative career of nursing in pursuit of fundamental social change.''[2]

Drugstore and mail-order remedies such as condoms, pessaries, and chemical douches had circulated widely in America in the nineteenth century, precipitating a dramatic decline in birthrates and a national preoccupation with moral and social purity. Ethnic and racial tensions in the wake of the Civil War helped fuel a conservative reaction to these developments, as well as to the changing dynamics of family life and the increasing independence of women in a rapidly modernizing society. During the 1870s, the federal government and almost every state adopted far-reaching obscenity statutes that criminalized contraception and abortion, and prohibited the distribution and sale of information or products intended to promote their use. Named after their principal architect and chief enforcer, Anthony Comstock, these laws did not succeed in suppressing the brisk traffic in contraception and abortion altogether, but they did push them farther underground, out of the jurisdiction of government bodies that might have regulated their price and quality. As a result, orthodox physicians, looking to consolidate their professional hegemony, defamed once common practices, and birth control became increasingly associated with medical charlatans. Despite these obstacles, middle-class birthrates continued to decline as the result of private arrangements. But the poor, especially the growing numbers of immigrant poor, could not afford contraception or understand the many popular subterfuges through which it was sold, such as feminine hygiene.

In New York, Sanger became active in local Socialist politics, first distinguishing herself as an organizer in the campaign for woman's suffrage and as the author of controversial columns on issues of health and sexuality for *The Call*, the Socialist party's daily newspaper. In 1912 she led an evacuation of the children of striking textile workers in Lawrence, Massachusetts. From her role she gained prominence as an organizer for the International Workers of the World (IWW) and as a romantic figure in the prewar cultural and political bohemia of Greenwich Village.

These were halcyon days before revolution, repression, and world war provided the century's more sober reality. The country seemed wide open with possibility. It was perhaps easier then than it has since become to believe in the potential of individual and social renewal—in the inevitability of human progress. Sanger teamed up with labor radicals and bohemians to organize strikes and pickets and pageants in the hope of achieving wholesale economic and social justice. ''No Gods, No Masters,'' the IWW's rallying cry, became her personal and political manifesto.

Inspired by Emma Goldman's forceful anarchist and feminist doctrines, even as the two women jousted for celebrity and quarreled over personal differences, Sanger in 1914 published *The Woman Rebel*, a radical feminist journal that encouraged personal and sexual autonomy for women through the use of birth control. ''Why the Woman Rebel?'' Sanger asked in the inaugural issue. Her answer: ''Because I believe that woman is enslaved by the world machine, by sex conventions, by motherhood and its present necessary childrearing, by wage-slavery, by middle-class morality, by customs, laws and superstitions.''[3] The paper never published explicit information about contraception, but Sanger was soon indicted for inciting violence and promoting obscenity. Facing the likelihood of conviction and a prison sentence in line with the harsh punishments routinely being given to agitators on the left, she jumped bail and fled under an alias to Europe. Once outside U.S. jurisdiction, she ordered the release of the pamphlet *Family Limitation* (1914), which provided concrete instruction on a variety of chemical and barrier contraceptive methods and counseled women to use them as weapons in the struggle for their emancipation.

In Margaret's absence, William Sanger was framed by a government agent to whom he handed a copy of the pamphlet. His arraignment was attended by Anthony Comstock. The case gave the birth control movement its first clear-cut challenge to the constitutionality of the Comstock prohibitions on birth control and its first major publicity. Middle-class women rallied alongside radicals as Bill Sanger was convicted and chose to serve a thirty-day jail term rather than pay a $150 fine.

When Margaret Sanger learned of these events, she decided to return and stand trial herself. Upon leaving her ship in lower Manhattan in October 1915, she stopped at a newsstand. There, by her own account, the words ''birth control,'' a phrase she had coined to give women a simple way of talking about the subject in public, now stared back at her from the headlines. Newspapers and magazines had quite suddenly turned their attention to the controversy. As Bill Sanger languished in a New York City jail, the prosecutors who had hoped to check birth control propaganda with his conviction achieved exactly the opposite effect. The tremendous public exposure given the issue substantially strengthened the rationale of Margaret Sanger's defense on free speech grounds. Who would be willing to punish her for initiating a debate that had since been conducted with impunity in major publications throughout the country? On 14 February 1915 all charges against Margaret Sanger were dropped, and the woman who had been a fugitive for more than a year was suddenly a celebrity.

The one casualty of these events was her marriage. When Sanger and her husband were finally reunited, he faced the reality of a callous and indifferent woman whose affections by then quite obviously lay elsewhere. He refused to grant her a divorce for several years, but she finally secured one in 1921, on grounds of desertion.

With her sophisticated understanding of the value of public relations over conventional political organization, Sanger devoted herself to gaining continued coverage of the birth control issue that helped destroy old taboos. She also took the opportunity to capitalize on her sudden fame by booking speaking engagements throughout the country; the fees helped support her children. Following her lectures she was often sought out in her hotel room by women eager to know of more effective birth control methods. Their intense hunger for personal communication and instruction convinced Sanger of the superiority of clinical distribution of contraception under scientific supervision, as she had seen demonstrated in Holland during her European sojourn. She was inspired to renewed militancy by the sudden and tragic death of her young daughter from pneumonia. Seeking to memorialize the child through a concrete achievement, she took a $50 contribution from a woman who had heard her speak in California and in 1916 opened the country's first birth control clinic behind the curtained windows of a tenement storefront on Amboy Street near the corner of Pitkin Avenue, in the Brownsville section of Brooklyn. Handbills advertising the location in English, Yiddish, and Italian promoted the benefits of contraception over abortion: ''Mothers! Can you afford to have a large family? Do you want any more children? If not, why do you have them? DO NOT KILL, DO NOT TAKE LIFE, BUT PREVENT.'' The women of Brownsville patiently stood in line for the service—there were 464 recorded clients during the several weeks the facility remained open.

On the ninth day a modishly attired woman identifying herself as ''Mrs. Whitehurst'' arrived, and immediately aroused suspicion. The following day she returned with three plainclothesmen from the police department's vice squad, who arrested Sanger and her coworkers: her sister, Ethel Byrne, a nurse on the staff of Mt. Sinai Hospital in New York, and Fania Mindell, a social worker. Byrne was tried first and sentenced to one month in the workhouse on Blackwell's Island, where she made more headlines with a hunger strike she and Sanger had modeled on the attention-getting exploits of the British suffragists. The normally sensation-shy *New York Times* ran Byrne's story on the front page for four consecutive days. Mindell was fined $50 for handing out illegal information. Sanger was charged with the more serious crime of actually fitting as a birth control device a Mizpah pessary, then commonly sold in pharmacies as a support for a prolapsed or distended uterus. Swathed in a spermicidal solution, it prevented sperm from entering the cervix and replicated the more reliable and comfortable rubber-spring diaphragm and spermicidal jelly that Sanger had observed in Holland.

Found guilty on these charges, but aware that her story was being crowded out of the newspaper headlines by the escalation of World War I in Europe, Sanger quietly served a month's sentence in the women's penitentiary in Queens County. By her own account, she passed her time reading to the illiterate prostitutes and drug addicts on her corridor, and lecturing them on sex and birth control over the protest of a resident matron, who claimed ''they knew bad enough already.''[4]

Appeal of the conviction established a medical exception to the New York State law prohibiting birth control. Doctors (though not nurses, as Sanger had hoped) were granted the right to prescribe contraception for health reasons. That constraint determined the future course of the birth control movement in United States. Independent, not-for-profit medical facilities became the model for the distribution of contraceptive services in the United States and throughout the world, a development that occurred largely in spite of leaders in American medicine, who remained shy of the subject for many years. The American Medical Association did not endorse birth control until 1937, well after Sanger's clinics had demonstrated the efficacy of the diaphragm-and-jelly regimen she endorsed.

During her year in Europe, Sanger had come under the influence of the renowned British physician and sexologist Havelock Ellis, who guided her conversion from conventional socialism to a Fabian faith in the ability of science and education to shape human conduct, and in the power of educated elites to enforce meaningful social change. Sanger had grown weary of the violence that had overtaken the labor movement in New York. She was ready to abandon the left in favor of an alliance with progressives, confident that capitalism might reform itself voluntarily and that bold public initiatives could be planned for human betterment. This philosophical shift was reinforced by H. G. Wells, who, like Ellis, became a lifelong mentor and intimate friend.

At the heart of this political transformation was the maturing of Sanger's consciousness as a feminist. She decided to invest in the collective potential of women. The victory for woman's suffrage had been achieved through the efforts of middle-class women who were oriented to activism and looking for a new cause. Sanger envisioned a united front of women who would claim the legalization of contraception, along with greater public candor about sexuality, as a fundamental right. Birth control, she argued, would enhance the opportunities of women beyond the promises of economic reformers, on the one hand, and of suffragists, on the other. It would be a tool for redistributing power fundamentally—in the bedroom, the home, and the larger community. Women would achieve personal freedom by experiencing their sexuality free of unwanted consequence. In taking control of the forces of reproduction, they also would lower birthrates, alter the balance of supply and demand for labor, and thereby accomplish the revolutionary goals of workers without the social upheaval of class warfare. Bonds of gender would transcend divisions of ethnicity, race, or class. Not the dictates of Karl Marx but the refusal of women to bear children indiscriminately would alter the course of history.

Through the 1920s and 1930s, Sanger divorced herself from her radical past, bested her competitors for leadership, and made her name virtually synonymous with the birth control cause. She had an uncanny feel for the power of a well-communicated idea in a democracy. Sanger wrote widely read books, published a journal, held conferences, gave lectures, and built a thriving voluntary social organization. In 1920 she published *Woman and the New Race*, which emphasized the relationship between birth control and women's rights and sold more than 250,000 copies. In 1921 Sanger incorporated and assumed the presidency of the American Birth Control League, a voluntary organization of middle-class women and male professionals whose objective was to educate public opinion and lobby for reform of the Comstock laws. The following year a second bestseller, *The Pivot of Civilization*, stressed birth control's economic, social, and eugenic dimensions. In the face of Sanger's appeal, the former suffragist Mary Ware Dennett, who was lobbying for total repeal of birth control prohibitions rather than a medical exception, closed down her competing organization.

Booked by agents in New York as ''the international champion of birth control''—or on another occasion as ''the outstanding social warrior of the century''—Sanger crisscrossed the country numerous times, addressing civic forums and women's groups and lending her support to the organization of local birth control federations. No matter how much she toned herself down, however, she remained a target of repression. A lecture at New York's Town Hall was raided and closed down by police ostensibly acting on orders of political authorities under pressure from the powerful Patrick Cardinal Hayes of New York. Her appearances in the heavily Catholic cities of Albany, Syracuse, and Boston were either canceled or interrupted; these incidents sustained her image as a daring and controversial figure, always on the edge of respectability. In 1929, when civic authorities in Boston refused her the right to speak at Ford Hall, she dramatically stood silent, with a band of tape across her mouth. The image emblazoned the front pages of newspapers around the world.

In 1923 Sanger had established the Birth Control Clinical Research Bureau (later renamed the Margaret Sanger Bureau) in New York City; it became the prototype for a network of facilities that developed with local sponsorship in major cities around the country. These pioneering clinics provided a range of preventive health care services for women including contraception, gynecology, sex education, marriage counseling, and infertility services to poor women and to many who could afford private doctors but preferred a sympathetic female environment. Under the best circumstances they became laboratories for Sanger's idealism, but, as often as not, the experiment failed, and Sanger grew disillusioned.

The birth control movement stalled during the Great Depression and World War II, stymied by the cost and complexity of the task of reaching women most in need, engulfed by internal dissension, and overwhelmed by the barrage of opposition it provoked. Timid politicians shied away from sexual controversy and refused to reform anachronistic obscenity laws. Birthrates plummeted in the face of economic crisis, precipitating a backlash against women, much like what had happened years earlier. Physicians feared the specter of socialized medicine that birth control clinics came to represent as the complexity and cost of providing quality clinical instruction in contraception became apparent.

Moreover, in the social sciences, eugenic concerns for the promotion of physical and mental fitness that had once been highly regarded by progressive proponents of social reform quickly deteriorated into an excuse for the control of "undesirables" on the straightforward basis of race and class. Sanger, among others, was forced to condemn them.

Along with a great many Americans in the 1920s—from ordinary workers and farmers to university professors, Supreme Court justices, and many on the left (including her dear friend, the perennial Socialist party presidential candidate, Norman Thomas)—Sanger had argued that sensible programs of social reform ought to address the manner in which heredity and other biological factors, as well as environmental ones, affect human health, intelligence, and opportunity. The idea of intervening to improve the quality of the human race became nothing short of a popular craze. It was not viewed as an alternative to progressive social reform but as an enhancement to it.

Trained in medicine, Sanger saw new possibilities in the idea of helping those most in need through a comprehensive program of preventive social medicine. She envisioned public health clinics for women and young children in every urban neighborhood and traveling caravans of nurses in rural areas. In the same vein, she endorsed prevailing views about society's obligation to prevent the transmission of hereditary defects such as mental retardation. Although she focused her principal efforts on the organization of voluntary birth control programs, she also supported controversial state statutes then under consideration that called for the forced sterilization of individuals in institutions for the "feebleminded," a commonly used term identifying individuals suffering from a variety of mental and physical defects thought to be inherited. Despite a scientific foundation that has proved largely specious and insupportable on moral grounds as well, eugenic interventions of this nature gained a broad constituency during these years. By 1927 Virginia's eugenic law was upheld in a nearly unanimous decision of the U.S. Supreme Court, *Buck* v. *Bell*.

Sanger comfortably courted eugenicists, whose stature at the time often helped blunt the attacks of religious and social conservatives against the then far less respectable birth control movement. As a propagandist, she continued to stress the relationship of birth control to economic and gender equality and to the promotion of healthier, happier families, but she got caught up in the eugenic zeal as well and accepted the support of individuals whose motivations were far less laudable than her own. On a number of occasions, she bemoaned the burden of the "unfit" on the productive members of the community and once spoke of investing in a "race of thoroughbreds," phrases that, lifted out of context, have been used to seriously misrepresent her intentions. Most eugenicists of the 1920s actually opposed birth control on the grounds that middle-class women should have more babies, not fewer. Sanger always disdained the idea that a "cradle-competition" existed between rich and poor, native and immigrant, or black and white. The initiative for individual and racial regeneration must "come from within," she wrote, "it must be autonomous, self-directive and not imposed from without."[5]

To this end, Sanger distinguished between individual applications of eugenic principles and cultural ones. She advanced social policies fostering universal mental and physical fitness and spoke out against immigration prohibitions and other measures that promoted ethnic or racial stereotypes with a biological rationale. She argued instead that America's essential public health challenge was to eliminate the potential of inherited defects among all. Having worked as a maternity nurse, she was particularly sensitive to the individual and social costs of diseases transmitted from mother to child during pregnancy as the result of inadequate nutrition and prenatal care. Sanger worked throughout her career to provide reproductive health care to poor women, irrespective of ethnicity or race, because she saw it as an essential tool of individual liberation and social justice, not of social control.

Sanger envisioned a society where birth control would be universally available, but in failing to repudiate supporters and adversaries alike who promoted its use to advance the interests of one group or one social class over another, she left herself vulnerable to attacks of racism and bigotry. By the 1930s, moreover, the perverse application of all eugenic principles under Nazi Germany's racial and genocidal policies had virtually discredited the American eugenics movement on all grounds, and the reputation of anyone associated with it—however tenuously.

Defaming Sanger's character as a way of undermining her message has long been an effective political strategy. By the 1930s, the alliance she forged with the country's establishment had turned into a political liability. She became the target of vicious personal attacks just as the votes of socially conservative Catholics in the cities and fundamentalist Protestants in the rural South became critical to the coalition that secured the presidential ambitions of Franklin Roosevelt.

Armed with the testimony of the needy and the endorsement of the powerful, Sanger mounted a diligent congressional lobbying campaign each year from 1931 through 1936. She even abandoned the term "birth control" for "family planning," a friendlier concept, and urged that it be incorporated into government programs. She tied her cause to the New Deal's enthusiasm for social and economic reconstruction and built a nationwide grassroots movement that mobilized constituencies as far-ranging as the Federal Council of the Churches of Christ in America, the YMCA and YWCA, the Socialist party, and other unlikely allies. But opposition from an increasingly politically powerful Catholic Church held sway on Capitol Hill and at the White House. Bending to political considerations, the New Deal denied birth control a place in America's progressive social welfare and public health agenda.

The issue lost ground, moreover, as a burgeoning trade in commercial contraception began to overwhelm the government's meager regulatory and enforcement capacity, leaving little chance that licensed druggists and physicians would be harassed. Even the Sears Roebuck catalog had begun to advertise "preventives." By 1935 the journal *American Medicine* was claiming that the mailing of contraceptive supplies and instruction was "as firmly established as the use of a gummed postage stamp," and a long-anticipated report of the American Medical Association found no actual evidence of interference with private medical practice by state or federal laws.[6]

Sanger's rationale for lobbying as a tool to educate public opinion was also undermined by the publication of polls showing that 70 percent of Americans, comprising at least a clear majority in every state, supported the legalization of birth control. From an educational standpoint, her campaign had done its work, even if the Comstock laws remained technically in force. In 1936, with Hannah Stone, M.D., medical director of the Birth Control Clinical Research Bureau in New York, Sanger prevailed in a federal appellate court decision in the case of *U.S.* v. *One Package*, which actually licensed physicians to import contraception and to use the federal mails for its transport. Although the ruling did not override remaining state prohibitions in Connecticut and Massachusetts, the courts had come close to achieving the objectives of federal legislative reform.

Rebuked in Washington but unwilling to concede defeat, Sanger quietly advanced a partnership with public health officials in the South, a region less vulnerable to Catholic influence and one where the need for services was acute because black Americans had substantially been left out of New Deal health and welfare entitlements administered by the states. She worked with the full support of the established leaders of the national black community—W.E.B. DuBois and Mary McLeod Bethune—and with the help of Eleanor Roosevelt, who in 1939 finally broke free of political constraints that had silenced her on the birth control issue during most of her husband's years in the White House, in order to assist on this Negro Project, as it was then called. It was advertised as ''a unique experiment in race-building and a humanitarian service to a race subjected to discrimination, hardship and segregation.'' ''Birth control, per se, cannot correct economic conditions that result in bad housing, overcrowding, poor hygiene, malnutrition and neglected sanitation,'' the statement of mission reads, ''but can reduce the attendant loss of life, health and happiness that spring [*sic*] from these conditions.''[7]

After 1937 Sanger lived in partial retirement in Tucson, Arizona, with her second husband, J. Noah Slee, whom she had married shortly after her divorce. A self-made industrialist, Slee invented and marketed 3-in-1 Oil, a household lubricant, and after selling his company, he helped bankroll his wife's charitable interests. In a private arrangement unconventional for its day, he had agreed that she would keep her own name professionally and in all respects maintain her freedom. Although they argued frequently over her many absences and her fierce commitment to her work, he held, however grudgingly, to this contract until his death in 1943.

Embittered by her failure to win support at home, and disenchanted with the increasing pronatalism of Americans after years of deferred fertility during the Great Depression and World War II, Sanger turned her attentions abroad. She had long ago planted the seeds of foreign diplomacy. In 1922 she carried the birth control message to Japan and China, leaving several small indigenous organizations in her wake. In 1927 she sponsored a World Population Conference in Geneva, Switzerland, that brought together internationally prominent social scientists and demographers. The conference failed to secure the attention of the League of Nations, as Sanger had hoped, but the initiative did result in the staffing of a small, London-based international population committee. Under its auspices Sanger toured India in 1936, again leaving behind rudimentary voluntary family planning advocacy and services. In 1948 she founded the London-based International Planned Parenthood Federation, an umbrella for national affiliates, which remains today the largest nongovernmental organization providing contraceptive services in the world.

Sanger's most exquisite triumphs were her last. She was past seventy when the world finally began to heed her concern for unchecked population growth. She was past eighty when the team of doctors and scientists she had long encouraged first marketed the oral, anovulant birth control pill that was developed by Dr. Gregory Pincus at a private research laboratory in Worcester, Massachusetts, after Sanger introduced him to Katherine Dexter McCormick, heiress to an agricultural equipment fortune, who provided the research funds. Sanger lived to see the realization of her repeated efforts as a litigant and a lobbyist through the landmark 1965 ruling of the U.S. Supreme Court in *Griswold* v. *Connecticut* that guaranteed constitutional protection to the private use of contraceptives by married couples. Seven years later, in *Eisenstadt* v. *Baird*, the Court extended that privacy to the unmarried.

Sanger died on 6 September 1966 of arteriosclerosis and heart failure at a nursing home in Tucson, just as Lyndon Johnson incorporated family planning into America's public health and social welfare programs—and committed at least a fraction of the nation's foreign policy resources to it. Thus was fulfilled her singular vision of how best to achieve peace and prosperity at home and abroad.

Since Sanger's death the rebirth of a vigorous feminist movement has given new resonance to her original claim that women have a fundamental right to control their own bodies. Her direct legacy endures in the international Planned Parenthood movement.

Since 1965 the rate of population growth has unexpectedly slowed in almost all countries in the world outside of sub-Saharan Africa, although absolute numbers still continue to grow precipitously in many regions. Moreover, extreme variations in reproductive behavior from one culture to another have reawakened interest in the comparative quality and impact of organized family planning intervention, and in the relationship between declining fertility and the status of women. At the third U.N. Conference on Population and Development, held at Cairo in 1992, many premises that have guided international population policy in the generation since Sanger's death were altered. The phrase ''population control'' was abandoned in the official literature of the United Nations in favor of more client-sensitive approaches intended to locate family planning within a comprehensive package of services to promote women's overall reproductive health. Gone as well from U.N.-endorsed policy is support for programs that may be coercive to women because they rely on fixed targets or quotas for fertility reduction.

Instead, agreement was reached on the principle that giving women adequate information and access to a wide menu of contraceptive options is most important, that under these circumstances they will most often assume the responsibility of having fewer children voluntarily. To this end, investments in the overall health, education, and welfare of the world's women have been declared a priority. For the first time, principles of gender equity were endorsed by international development and population policymakers.

In so doing, they have accepted Sanger's insistent view that individual women can be motivated to limit their fertility, even in the absence of wholesale economic and social change. It is now officially agreed that organized intervention works best when contraception is offered as part of a larger package of maternal and infant health care reforms delivered under paraprofessional auspices, much as Sanger and others pioneered. Prodded by contemporary feminists in the field, the United Nations has finally committed to invest in Sanger's vision of comprehensive preventive health care for women.

In 1935 H. G. Wells raised his glass in an affectionate toast. ''Alexander the Great changed a few boundaries and killed a certain number of men,'' Wells observed, ''but he made no lasting change in civilization. Both he and Napoleon were forced into fame by circumstances outside themselves and by currents of the time, but Margaret Sanger made currents and circumstances. When the history of our civilization is written, it will be a biological history, and Margaret Sanger will be its heroine.''[8] The words seem particularly well chosen in light of recent developments.

NOTES

1. Erik H. Erikson, ''Once More the Inner Space: Letter to a Former Student,'' in Jean Strouse, ed., *Women & Analysis: Dialogues on Psychoanalytic Views of Femininity* (New York, 1974), 386.

2. Margaret Sanger, *An Autobiography* (New York, 1938), 89–92.

3. *The Woman Rebel* 1 (March 1914): 1, cited in Ellen Chesler, *Woman of Valor: Margaret Sanger and the Birth Control Movement in America* (New York, 1992), 98.

4. Sanger, *An Autobiography*, 243.

5. Margaret Sanger, *The Pivot of Civilization* (New York, 1921), 22–23.

6. *Journal of the American Medical Association* 106 (1936); and *American Medicine* 41 (1935). Both cited in Chesler, *Woman of Valor*, 371.

7. Birth Control Federation of America, ''Birth Control and the Negro: An Analysis and Program'' (1939), cited in Chesler, *Woman of Valor*, 388.

8. Birth Control Information Center, London, ''Round the World for Birth Control,'' in Chesler, *Woman of Valor*, 361.

BIBLIOGRAPHY

Chesler, Ellen. *Woman of Valor: Margaret Sanger and the Birth Control Movement in America*. New York, 1992.

Cott, Nancy F. *The Grounding of Modern Feminism*. New Haven, 1987.

Degler, Carl N. *In Search of Human Nature: The Decline and Revival of Darwinism in American Social Thought*. New York, 1991.

Gordon, Linda. *Woman's Body, Woman's Right: A Social History of Birth Control in America*. New York, 1976.

Kennedy, David M. *Birth Control in America: The Career of Margaret Sanger*. New York, 1970.

Kevles, Daniel J. *In the Name of Eugenics: Genetics and the Uses of Human Heredity*. New York, 1985.

Moore, Gloria, and Ronald Moore. *Margaret Sanger and the Birth Control Movement: A Bibliography, 1911–1984*. Metuchen, N.J., 1986.

Piotrow, Phyllis Tilson. *World Population Policy: The United States Response*. New York, 1973.

Reed, James. *From Private Vice to Public Virtue: The Birth Control Movement and American Society Since 1830*. New York, 1978; rev. ed. Princeton, 1984.

Rosenberg, Rosalind. *Divided Lives: American Women in the Twentieth Century*. New York, 1992.

Sanger, Margaret. *Woman and the New Race*. New York, 1920.

———. *The Pivot of Civilization*. New York, 1922.

———. *An Autobiography*. New York, 1938.

Sen, Gita, Adrienne Germaine, and Lincoln C. Chen, eds. *Population Policies Reconsidered: Health, Empowerment and Rights*. Boston, 1994.

Ware, Susan. *Holding Their Own: American Women in the 1930s*. Boston, 1982.

Carl Schurz
and Radical Reconstruction

BROOKS D. SIMPSON

The waxing, then waning, of the commitment of white Northerners to Reconstruction is reflected in the career of Carl Schurz. An impassioned foe of slavery in the years leading up to the Civil War, Schurz pressed the Lincoln administration to move forthrightly against the peculiar institution once war broke out. In the immediate aftermath of Appomattox, Schurz unsuccessfully prodded President Andrew Johnson to take more decisive measures to protect the freed blacks and guard against a premature restoration of civil rule in the former Confederate states. These positions marked him as a committed spokesman for Radical Republicanism and an advocate of securing the fruits of emancipation. With the election of Ulysses S. Grant to the presidency in 1868, however, Schurz was drawn to new issues, notably civil service reform. Representing Missouri in the U.S. Senate, he gradually came to advocate reconciliation between the sections, spoke against measures to provide additional federal protection for the freed blacks, and broke with the Republican party in opposing Grant's renomination. During Grant's second term, Schurz continued to speak out against the administration's Reconstruction policy. In 1876 he rejoined the Republican party in the wake of Rutherford B. Hayes's nomination and was rewarded with a cabinet post. He supported Hayes's abandonment of intervention. It was only years later that he had second thoughts about the wisdom of his personal retreat from Reconstruction. Nevertheless, although Schurz expressed regrets about the status of African Americans in the South, his commitment to change and his vision of what change meant was limited, suggesting the boundaries of Reconstruction as reform.

Born near Bonn, Germany, on 2 March 1829, the son of Christian and Marianne Jüssen Schurz, Schurz emigrated to the United States in 1852 in the aftermath of his involvement in the 1848 revolution in Germany, followed by exile in London and Paris. He settled in Watertown, Wisconsin, and immediately became involved in public life as a lawyer and a journalist. Before long he entered political life as a supporter of the newly created Republican party. His hard work on behalf of Abraham Lincoln's presidential candidacy in 1860 earned him appointment as minister to Spain in 1861. But Schurz longed to see action on the battlefield. In 1862 he returned to the United States, received a commission as a brigadier general, lobbied for a command, and joined Union forces in the Shenandoah Valley on the heels of the concluding clash of Thomas J. ''Stonewall'' Jackson's masterful campaign. Eventually Schurz and his division were reassigned to John Pope's newly formed Army of Virginia and participated in Pope's ill-fated campaign against Robert E. Lee and the Army of Northern Virginia. At Second Bull Run (August 1862), Schurz performed creditably; in the aftermath of that Union defeat, his command became part of the Eleventh Corps of the Army of the Potomac.

As his men garrisoned the fortifications around Washington, Schurz redoubled his efforts at political intrigue, seeking to bolster the fading fortunes of a fellow German American, corps commander Franz Sigel. Before long, he took advantage of Lincoln's willingness to hear from him to offer some straightforward, if tactless, advice about the prosecution of the war. Cheered by news of Lincoln's decision to issue a proclamation of emancipation, Schurz, wanting more, told the president that Union military failure was due to the conservative political leanings of many of Lincoln's generals. Only Radical generals, with their commitment, enthusiasm, and energy, could win the kind of war envisioned by the Emancipation Proclamation. In a reply rare for its withering tone, Lincoln retorted that many prewar Democrats had contributed mightily to the Union war effort, and some of the most pronounced military failures of the war so far were Republican in their political affiliation. Unable to restrain himself, Schurz restated his charges, adding, ''I do not know, whether you have ever seen a battlefield. I assure you, Mr. President it is a terrible sight.'' This was the sort of sanctimonious claptrap that angered Lincoln; the president's searing response reminded the German general that ''there are men who have 'heart in it' that think you are performing your part as poorly as you think I am performing mine.''

What threatened to become a divisive quarrel was patched up only after Schurz paid a visit to the White House. Lincoln, having made his point, won Schurz over once more by detailing his own problems and perspective. All seemed forgotten. Several weeks later Schurz visited Lincoln on the evening before the president issued the Emancipation Proclamation, to offer encouragement and show his support for the administration. In later years Schurz seemed haunted by the tone of the president's reprimand. The episode failed to teach him how to offer advice to presidents without presenting a condescending lecture.[1]

Before long, Schurz needed to worry more about charging Confederates than about Democratic generals. The Eleventh Corps rejoined the Army of the Po-

tomac at Fredericksburg. Several months later, after more lobbying, Schurz secured his second star, but at Chancellorsville and Gettysburg his command was
overwhelmed by Confederate flanking assaults. Although Schurz preformed well
in holding Cemetery Hill at Gettysburg, he suffered heavy criticism; his German-
born soldiers were labeled ''the flying Dutchmen'' by others who hooted, ''I
fights mit Sigel and runs mit Schurz.'' The transfer of the Eleventh Corps to
Tennessee in September 1863 promised a respite from such remarks. At Chat-
tanooga, Schurz played a supporting role as Ulysses S. Grant broke the Confederate siege two months later. This was Schurz's last significant military
action. On leave during the critical campaigns of 1864, he scrambled for a
command, finally landing a position as chief of staff in the Army of Georgia in
the conflict's final month.

Schurz's relationship with Abraham Lincoln was an uneven one. The German's blunt persistence pushed the president into rare displays of temper and
sarcasm. Nevertheless, the president listened to Schurz, and Schurz in turn offered him what was intended to be constructive advice. An assassin's bullet
severed that relationship. Schurz, however, looked forward to working with Lincoln's successor, Andrew Johnson of Tennessee. He had met Johnson during
the war and had enlisted him in support of his quest for a command in 1864.
Now he offered his services to the new chief executive. ''So far he seems all
right,'' Schurz concluded after an early visit with the president; ''there are no
longer any traces of bad habits, and the hints he gives in regard to policy permit
us to hope from him on the whole an energetic and at the same time discreet
use of his executive powers.'' He told Senator Charles Sumner, the Massachusetts Radical whom he had befriended, that the new president's goals ''are all
the most progressive friends of human liberty can desire.'' Moreover, he approved what he believed to be Johnson's decision ''to bring about these results
practically without making them the subject of popular discussion in the shape
of an openly announced program.''[2]

Schurz soon took advantage of Johnson's suggestion that he write ''whenever
I had anything worthy of consideration to suggest.'' He advised Johnson on the
trial of those accused of involvement in Lincoln's assassination, the fate of
Jefferson Davis, and Mexican policy, convinced that the president would heed
his words. ''I am in a good way to acquire here a personal influence which, in
certain contingencies, may prove of great significance,'' he confided to his wife
Margarethe. Such assumptions suffered a setback, however, when Johnson ignored his recommendations for changes in the president's first proclamation
outlining the reconstruction process in North Carolina. Schurz had told Johnson
to strike a clause restricting the franchise to those eligible to vote in 1860 because it would bar blacks from voting; the president retained the clause. Disappointed, Schurz grumbled, ''I fear he had not that clearness of purpose and
firmness of character he was supposed to have.''[3] Convinced that Johnson was
still susceptible to advice, Schurz first suggested that Johnson allow blacks in
South Carolina to vote by allowing all loyal inhabitants ''without distinction''

to vote. Then he eagerly accepted Johnson's invitation to undertake an inspection tour of the South.

"The problem which remains for us to solve is in one respect more difficult than those problems already solved," Schurz told a friend. "To restore the Union in political form is a trifling matter. The former rebels are taking the oath of loyalty with pleasure and are eager to come back into the old rights of self-government under the constitution. But our aim is not fulfilled by that means. The Union must be reconstructed upon the basis of the results of the great social revolution brought about during the war in the South. A free labor society must be established and built up on the ruins of the slave labor society." Such a process would have to overcome the "proslavery sentiments" of most southern whites, who seemed determined to restore slavery as much as possible. Without federal intervention, "the development and promotion of a great social revolution would be confided to a population which is thoroughly hostile to the tendencies of this revolution."[4] A rapid restoration of civil government would be fatal to the freed blacks and free labor.

These premises shaped Schurz's accounts of the postwar South. He believed that by pleading his case with supporting documents, he could persuade the president to adopt his point of view. Johnson had asked him "to study the conditions and make reports and recommendations to him as to the policy that should be pursued," Schurz noted as he explained that his report "can perhaps be so shaped as to play a distinctive role in this weighty business."[5] He also planned to shape public opinion (as well as to defray his expenses) by writing columns for the Boston *Advertiser*. He embarked on his trip by sailing to South Carolina in July. From there he went to Georgia, then to Alabama, and by the end of August he was in Mississippi. At each stop on his trip he gathered reports from military officers, planters, and other observers about the state of affairs in the defeated South. In these he found plenty of facts to sustain his views.

Schurz observed that the attitudes of white Southerners toward the outcome of the conflict and its results depended upon their proximity to the field of military operations. Those whites who had seen war firsthand accepted reunion and emancipation, although they viewed it as the triumph of might over right. Whites in regions untouched by military operations were far more obdurate: only the arrival of Union occupation forces compelled them to abandon efforts to maintain slavery. Both groups looked eagerly to the restoration of civil rule, for then they would manage affairs in accordance with notions of white supremacy. Noting that most whites believed that blacks would not work except under coercion, Schurz argued that it would be some time before the principles of free labor would be firmly established. Even the most malleable of planters seemed reluctant to embrace the notion that the black man was now a free man and should be treated as such.

Surely the chaos attending the end of military conflict offered no fair trial for these principles: Schurz argued that the present period was better understood as a period of transition in which all Southerners, white and black, were adjusting to new roles and new relationships in the aftermath of emancipation. It was best for the time being, he thought, to delay a return to civil rule, for "the people are not yet in a fit condition to legislate." He had little faith in oaths of allegiance as sufficient guarantees of revived loyalty to the United States; indeed, "*I find that those who are most clamorous for the immediate restoration of civil government in these States* [are those] *who can least be trusted.*" Better to continue military supervision of affairs, he concluded. Schurz was aware that such advice ran counter to Johnson's own preferences. In an effort to win the president over, he recalled Johnson's own statement that "it is of the highest importance that the thing be started rightly," adding "then let it not be started at a time when a wrong start is almost inevitable."[6]

Much needed to be done to restore stability to the South and to establish the foundation for a new order. Johnson needed to clarify the status of property liable to confiscation; the Freedmen's Bureau required more personnel; the freed blacks wanted and needed opportunities for education; the president should seek "*real* union men" to fill offices rather than appoint former Confederates. Newspaper reports of resurgent loyalty were exaggerated and misleading; Schurz overheard the bitter remarks of many whites. Most disturbing were reports of violence against blacks and Union army personnel. In Atlanta, Schurz encountered blacks with gunshot wounds and heard reports of stabbings and poisonings; army officers in Selma, Montgomery, and Mobile, Alabama, furnished him with detailed descriptions of blacks who had suffered gruesome deaths or who had been maimed. Nor were civil officials prepared to right these wrongs. Several judges acted in the spirit of Roger B. Taney's declaration in *Dred Scott* v. *Sandford* that black men had no rights that white men were bound to respect. Schurz doubted that in Alabama it would be difficult to empanel a jury "prepared to find a white man who had killed a negro, guilty of murder, or another, who whipped a negro, guilty of assault and battery."[7]

The problem of violence was most vividly illustrated by an incident in Montgomery, Alabama, where a military commission convicted Dr. James T. Andrew of murdering a black man in a dispute over a horse. Citizens were petitioning for clemency in his case, citing his "kind treatment of negroes" in the past. In contrast, Schurz insisted "that unless the severest punishments known to the laws be visited upon white men killing negroes the Southern States will soon be a vast slaughter pen for the black race . . . .If such things can happen in broad daylight under the very eyes of the State Government and of the military forces of the United States, what may happen when there is no such check upon the brutal instincts of the masses? It seems to be that in such matters lenity is out of place." Military occupation would prevent such crimes; so would a more gradual restoration of civil authority. Black soldiers, despite problems with discipline, were most appropriate for occupation duty, for nothing would remind Southern whites that "the negro is a free man . . . than the bodily presence of a negro with a musket on his shoulder."[8]

Protecting blacks from violence; securing their basic civil rights; establishing a stronger Freedmen's Bureau; building the foundations of a free labor system—these measures all pointed to the need for a continued federal presence in the South. "I have come to the conclusion that the policy of the government is the worst that could be hit upon," he confided to his wife after arriving in South Carolina.[9] His fears were confirmed: Southern whites would opt for as little change as possible if left to their own devices. If Johnson wanted to build up a Union party in the South, his policy of distributing "power and patronage . . . into the hands of late rebels" would discourage "the true Union element."[10]

There were limits to Schurz's radicalism. Although he agreed that their ownership of land would promote the interest of the freed blacks, he said little about the confiscation of planters' lands and their redistribution to the freed blacks. Rather, he thought that economic circumstances would lead to the breaking up of plantation holdings. Like Salmon P. Chase, he justified extending suffrage to adult black males on the grounds that they were loyal citizens. However, in line with Thaddeus Stevens and Sumner, he forecast disaster should civil government be reestablished, ending whatever influence the federal government might exercise in promoting "the great social revolution" that would determine the meaning of emancipation.

The climax of Schurz's trip came when he arrived in Mississippi. Provisional governor William Sharkey, displeased with the performance of black occupation forces, had inaugurated measures for raising a white state militia to bring order to his state—an order that would include the intimidation of blacks and the subduing of their desire to exercise the rights of free people. Henry W. Slocum, Schurz's former commander and head of the military district of Mississippi, intervened to stop Sharkey. Schurz telegraphed Johnson in support of Slocum's directive. "Society is in a frightful state of demoralization, and the civil authorities present a lamentable picture of impotence and imbecility," he informed Secretary of War Edwin M. Stanton. "Take the military away and a brutal, savage mob will rule the whole concern." The president disagreed. Not only did he sustain Sharkey, he reprimanded Schurz, claiming that the envoy was supposed to help implement the president's policy, not to offer his own alternative. Schurz was nettled by the tone of Johnson's dispatch, but he had anticipated his response. "If the President persists in pursuing a false course he must not be surprised if, later, I bring into the field against him all the artillery I am assembling now."[11]

This row, plus the revelation of Schurz's being a newspaper correspondent, ended his mission for all practical purposes, although he filed additional reports from Louisiana. The president had no interest in receiving his final report. Schurz wondered what he had done wrong even as he eagerly prepared a document that would serve as a severe indictment of administration policy. As expected, the report claimed that the restoration of civil government was premature, that an extended federal presence was required to provide a lasting foundation for freedom, and that African Americans deserved not only civil but also political rights, including suffrage, and opportunities to gain an education as well as to be free laborers. Otherwise, the social revolution would remain incomplete, leading to serious complications and strife. It would be better to make sure that what was done, was done well rather than finished quickly.[12]

Johnson attempted to bury the report, but Sumner called for its publication. In order to offset the impact of Schurz's criticisms, the president paired his report with a much shorter one by Ulysses S. Grant that was based upon the general-in-chief's just-completed two-week swing through Virginia, the Carolinas, Georgia, and Tennessee. Grant's report was much more optimistic than Schurz's, although careful readers discerned that it was not the ringing endorsement of administration policy that Johnson claimed it to be. Radical papers praised Schurz's report as an accurate portrait of Southern conditions; critics mocked Schurz rather than grapple with his findings. Grant heeded Schurz's warnings about violence, directing his commanders to forward information about such acts to Washington. Before long, he told Schurz that his optimism about Southern whites had been misplaced and that he regretted the use Johnson had made of his own observations.

Republicans made good use of Schurz's heavily documented findings as they countered Johnson's policy by crafting legislative and constitutional safeguards for the freed blacks. Most Republicans agreed that protecting free labor, not offering free land, was an acceptable solution to black circumstances, but political considerations also hemmed in efforts at reform. The need to secure majorities, legislative and popular, moderated some proposals. Johnson's willingness to veto legislation forced Republican legislators to seek common ground in the center to override those vetoes. Such considerations rendered the confiscation and redistribution of planters' lands a moot issue; even black suffrage would not become a component of Republican policy until the passage of the Reconstruction Act in 1867. Whether these *policies* represented sufficient safeguards for achieving the "great social revolution" envisioned by Schurz was questionable. Republicans were aware that their constituents wanted an end to Reconstruction and had limited interest in a sustained federal program to protect the freed blacks.

Schurz remained active in politics over the next several years, promoting the Republican cause. He served as a newspaper editor, a delegate to the Southern Loyalist convention in 1866, and a speaker for Republican candidates. In the *Atlantic Monthly* he urged Congress to go beyond the Fourteenth Amendment to adopt black suffrage and promote public education as measures to guarantee the fruits of emancipation. In 1867 he moved to Missouri and became the coeditor and co-owner of the *Westliche Post* of St. Louis. The following year he delivered the keynote address at the Republican National Convention, unsuccessfully advocating black suffrage in both North and South and an amnesty plank, and supported that body's selection of Ulysses S. Grant for the presidential candidate.

As with Lincoln and Johnson, Schurz immediately began to offer advice to Grant. The president-elect patiently heard him out, for by the end of 1868 it was evident that Schurz might well play a role in steering administration initiatives through the Senate. In Missouri, a group of moderate Republicans, dissatisfied with the Radical politics of Senator Charles D. Drake, sought a candidate to secure the seat held by John B. Henderson, one of the seven Republicans who had voted to acquit Andrew Johnson during the president's impeachment trial. They looked to Schurz to rally German-born Republican voters to the new movement, and in exchange were willing to support Schurz for the Senate. Schurz fended off Drake's opposition and secured the Republican nomination in January 1869; his ensuing election by the state legislature was a foregone conclusion.

At the same time, Schurz began to lose interest in Reconstruction. Perhaps he thought that with the election of Grant, harmony had at last been achieved between the executive and legislative branches of the federal government; perhaps he felt that, with the Congress's passage of the Fifteenth Amendment, the securing of black suffrage nationwide awaited only that measure's ratification. As early as 1867, he pondered the possibility of party realignment. As he campaigned for Grant, he noticed that many former Confederates, aware of his stance on amnesty, had good things to say about him. In his first session as a senator, he supported the rapid restoration of Virginia and spoke against efforts to prolong the tenure of Georgia Republicans by postponing state elections.

Allied to Schurz's declining interest in Reconstruction was his assessment of his political future in Missouri. That state's Republican party had almost from its inception been divided into conservative and radical wings on the issues of slavery, Reconstruction, and black suffrage. Moreover, Drake, the leader of the Radical wing, had once been a Know-Nothing, thus making him anathema to many German-born Missouri Republicans. Schurz had capitalized on these divisions in pushing forward his candidacy for the Senate; Drake's incautious and derogatory comments about Germans and his opposition to amnesty refreshed voters' memories on these issues.

Before long, however, Schurz found himself pitted against the president over the administration's proposal to annex the Dominican Republic. Although Grant was aware of the natural resources of the Caribbean nation, he was more interested in securing it as a possible refuge for the freed blacks. The president reasoned that blacks might well exercise leverage with Southern whites if they possessed the ability to take their labor elsewhere. This, of course, was an important component of the free labor system Schurz had endorsed. Nevertheless, he joined Sumner in opposing the measure. Schurz argued that humid climates were not suitable to democratic institutions; he also implied (although he denied it) that the United States already had enough dark-skinned people. He was no doctrinaire anti-imperialist, for he made it clear that he favored the annexation of Canada. Grant grew furious with Schurz's opposition; that the senator denied German interest in the Caribbean after having helped Prussian diplomats frame a proposal in justification of a naval station there smacked of disingenuous double-dealing.

It was in these circumstances that Schurz embraced the concept of realignment in Missouri politics. It was time to move beyond Reconstruction and address the new issues on the reform agenda, notably civil service reform and free trade. Such a maneuver, if successful, would defeat Drake's efforts for reelection to the Senate. Schurz hoped that this strategy would be but a prelude to a realignment of forces within the Republican party nationwide. That black interests would suffer did not concern him. Schurz's influence over the German vote helped make the bolt from the regular Republicans meaningful. He gathered support for his new Liberal movement even as he claimed that he was reforming the party rather than destroying it. Grant did not share this opinion, and began to purge Schurz's supporters from office. Although the Liberals claimed victory on election day, electing B. Gratz Brown governor, it was the Democrats who swept to victory in the state legislature and in several congressional races.

After the election Schurz struggled to maintain an uneasy relationship with Grant. The president received Schurz at the White House as Congress convened in December 1870, and for a moment it looked as if the two men would patch up their differences. But Grant's persistence in advocating the annexation of the Dominican Republic ended all such hope. Schurz opposed a plan to send a commission of investigation to the Caribbean republic. Grant took steps to nullify the impact of Schurz's criticisms by naming Franz Sigel as the commission's secretary. The final break came when Grant and Hamilton Fish engineered the removal of the obstreperous Sumner from his chairmanship of the Senate Foreign Relations Committee. At that point Schurz turned his rhetorical guns on the president, charging Grant with conduct befitting a dictator and a party boss— a characterization that stands in remarkable contrast to later images of Grant as a weak chief executive.

In the spring of 1871 Schurz opposed legislation to protect blacks' right to vote. He claimed that the Ku Klux Klan Act, a measure empowering Grant to strike at white terrorist organizations, was an unconstitutional measure that would destroy liberty; better, he reasoned, to entrust white Southern moderates with the task of restoring order. His remarks, which stood in sharp contrast to his earlier beliefs about the need for federal protection for blacks, suggested how far he had drifted from his Radical moorings. His changing stance on Reconstruction was intertwined with his break with the Grant administration and his interest in new issues, notably civil service reform. The three themes proved mutually reinforcing. In pushing for civil service reform, for example, Schurz took aim at Grant's exercise of patronage (neglecting to add that he had had much less of a problem with the president when he had input on the selections). He also pointed to Southern Republican governments as examples of the spoils system at its worst. Such attacks presented both the administration and Reconstruction in a bad light.

The impact of Schurz's actions in Missouri meant that he had to cast about for a new political home. Whatever hopes he had entertained for fusion were dashed when Missouri Democrats secured the election of Frank Blair to the

Senate, replacing Drake. Three years before, running as the Democratic nominee for vice president, Blair had made clear his hostility to Reconstruction and his lack of interest in the fate of the freed blacks. At first, Schurz supported efforts to reform the Republican party from within and sought to rally opposition to Grant's renomination as the first step in revitalizing the party's mission of reform. Civil service reform, revenue reform, the restoration of the separation of powers disrupted by Grant—these were the themes he sounded in remarks and correspondence. Several other Republicans shared Schurz's sentiments, but Grant's skillful welding of a pro-administration coalition put an end to hopes that he would be overthrown from within Republican ranks. It was only then that Schurz accepted the idea of a new party. Speaking to an audience composed mostly of Confederate veterans in Nashville, Tennessee, on 20 September 1871, Schurz declared that it was time for an end to carpetbag regimes. Conciliation should be the watchword of national policy; Southern whites should once more hold sway. This time, however, he punctuated the traditional litany of indictments against the Grant administration by calling for a new party. Encouraged by the warm reception he received at Nashville and elsewhere in the South, Schurz deluded himself into believing that he was winning over Southern Democrats and persuading them to abandon violence as the key to regaining political power. Once more he saw the key to his future in instigating a reconciliationist realignment stressing reform; once more his political journey took him further from his original position on Reconstruction, although he never grasped what his measures meant for the future of the freed blacks.

Not all Republicans saw things Schurz's way. Cartoonist Thomas Nast's memorable renderings of Schurz in *Harpers' Weekly* represented him as a sorehead who broke with Grant over patronage matters and was out of touch with political reality. Grant supporters characterized Schurz's career as a lifelong quest for office. Schurz's behavior lent credence to these charges, for his positions on Southern policy in the 1870s stood in stark contrast to his previous stances on Reconstruction. In 1872 he supported measures to extend amnesty to all Confederates barred from holding office by the Fourteenth Amendment, explaining that the only way to end misrule in the South was to permit these white leaders to hold office once again. He attacked other amnesty proposals for not going far enough; moreover, when Charles Sumner proposed legislation calling for desegregation in public facilities, including schools, Schurz voted against his ally. Meanwhile, his efforts on behalf of a new party accelerated. In January 1872, Missouri bolters, styling themselves Liberals, gathered at Jefferson City to frame a platform for a new party founded on the principles of reconciliation and reform. They pledged their support for civil rights and the Reconstruction amendments, but this was only a token concession to conscience. More important was their call for a convention to meet at Cincinnati in May, although the exact purpose of the convention was not clear.

Throughout the winter and spring of 1872, Schurz worked hard on behalf of the Liberal movement. Sumner, well aware of Schurz's declining interest in the freed blacks, refused to join a movement he rightly suspected would oppose additional measures to protect the fruits of emancipation. Just as portentous for the movement were the people who soon flocked to its ranks. United far more by a dislike of Grant than by a common vision or agenda, these new allies did not always share Schurz's interest in reform, although the vast majority had lost interest in or become hostile to Reconstruction. These conflicts became even more apparent when Schurz entertained the notion of using the convention to nominate a presidential candidate. Without naming a candidate, it was difficult to see how the Liberals would influence the electorate; but the act of naming a candidate would erode support for the movement because those dissatisfied with the nominee would fade away and, in some cases, return to the Republican fold.

In May, Schurz presided over the Liberal assembly at Cincinnati. He urged the self-selected delegates to look beyond the defeat of Grant to a vision of reform—and then looked on in shock and dismay as newspaper editor Horace Greeley, whose credentials as a reform candidate were questionable, secured the convention's nomination on the sixth ballot. At first Schurz was so distraught that at a celebration dinner that evening, he sat down at a piano and played a funeral dirge. Then he tried to persuade Greeley to withdraw as a candidate: surely Greeley's support of a protective tariff would alienate free trade advocates, and his endorsement of temperance would drive off German voters. Eventually, Schurz resigned himself to the editor's candidacy and advocated his election, claiming that Grant's Reconstruction policy perpetuated sectional divisiveness and political corruption. The diverse members of the Liberal movement soon found common ground on the twin issues of opposition to Grant and his policy of Reconstruction. Although the Democratic party also nominated Greeley, Grant not only won reelection but did so by a decisive margin.

Greeley's defeat meant the death of the Liberal Republican movement, but some of the movement's leaders, including Schurz, did not return to the Republican ranks. Instead, these self-styled Independents tried to play off Republicans against Democrats in an effort to secure their own agenda. In this they were aided immensely by setbacks suffered by the Republican party and the Grant administration in the aftermath of the president's overwhelming triumph. Revelations of congressional corruption and greed (Credit Mobilier and the Salary Grab) dominated headlines in the winter of 1873; months later the nation's economy plunged into depression in the aftermath of the Panic of 1873. Debates about monetary policy and economic recovery, not Reconstruction, dominated the political agenda. In the South, several more states slipped from Republican control. By the beginning of 1875, only Louisiana, South Carolina, Mississippi, and Florida remained in Republican hands. The fate of these surviving regimes was rendered even more uncertain by the 1874 congressional elections, for Democrats, benefiting from the problems confronting the Republican party, secured control of the House of Representatives, effectively blocking any future Reconstruction legislative measures.

The Democratic resurgence enhanced Schurz's position, for Republicans could no longer dismiss his value to the party. Yet Schurz made it clear that he no longer supported Reconstruction. At Sumner's funeral in 1874, he used the occasion not to press for the passage of the measure closest to the departed senator's heart, civil rights, but to make the case once more for civil service reform—representing his own priorities. Months later, he spoke out against additional civil rights legislation, claiming that integration would lead to the closing of public schools. The following January, Schurz assailed Reconstruction one last time from the Senate floor. In Louisiana, Democrats had attempted to seize control of the state legislature; only the appearance of federal soldiers allowed the Republicans to retain control of the state, although the composition of the legislature remained in doubt. Overlooking the fact that it had been the Democrats who had first called on the soldiers, and that the soldiers had prevented a coup d' état, critics of Grant's policy proclaimed that the crisis of representative government was at hand as they denounced military intervention on behalf of the Republican regime.

In an impassioned address, Schurz denounced the administration, declaring that "if such things be sustained in Congress, how long before it can be done in Massachusetts and Ohio? How long before the Constitutional rights of all the States and the self-government of all the people may be trampled under foot? . . . How long before a soldier may stalk into the National House of Representatives, and, pointing to the Speaker's mace, say, 'Take away that bauble'?'' It was a speech marked by sensationalism rather than reason, and in it Schurz showed little concern for the fate of the freed blacks, although he declared that he remained "a sincere and devoted friend of the colored race." Had the nation heeded his advice in 1865, he asserted, it would have been in better shape ten years later.[13]

By this time Schurz's decision to embrace fusion in Missouri had come back to haunt him. Missouri Republicans never recovered from the 1870 campaign; whatever chance they had of winning the state legislature crumbled in the wake of economic depression. Schurz's opposition to inflation alienated money-short Missourians, and the Democrats in the state legislature wanted one of their own to take his place. In March 1875, he ended his service in the Senate. Although out of office, he remained influential, as politicians soon discovered. In Ohio, Republicans found themselves in a close contest for governor. Although party leaders had coaxed Rutherford B. Hayes out of retirement to run for a third term, they worried that Democratic nominee William Allen's appeal for currency inflation would find ready support with voters in a time of economic depression and dissatisfaction with Republican rule. Independents saw an opportunity to demonstrate the importance of their support to Republican fortunes: they, too, despised Allen's inflationist schemes. Responding to their requests, Schurz entered the canvass on behalf of Hayes. Doubtless his presence rallied German-American voters as much as his speeches punctured the inflationist cause: Hayes claimed victory by a slim margin of 5,000 votes. Even Republican party stalwarts grudgingly recognized Schurz's contributions to the result. With Grant a lame duck battling charges of corruption, perhaps it was time to extend the olive branch.

Schurz responded coyly to such courting. He persisted in maintaining his aloof attitude, and made plans to mobilize Independents to play a decisive role in the presidential election of 1876. When Hayes emerged as the compromise choice of the Republicans, however, Schurz hastily made his way to the candidate's side, much to the disgruntlement of those who preferred a third-party ticket. As he had with Lincoln, Johnson, and Grant, Schurz offered Hayes his advice and pressed his views, particularly on civil service reform and Reconstruction. The candidate proved most receptive to such notions, largely because they corresponded with his own. Hayes intended to terminate the policy of federal intervention in the South; he hoped to revitalize the two-party system in the region by wooing old Whigs and others with promises of aid for economic development. By shifting Southern politics away from questions of race, Hayes thought that both parties would seek blacks' support, promising in exchange to respect their rights.

Schurz played no role in the resolution of the electoral crisis of 1876–1877, but he was overjoyed when Hayes emerged as the president-elect. The new president wasted no time in rewarding his supporter, offering Schurz a position in his cabinet as secretary of the interior. Schurz accepted; disgruntled Republicans, recalling the nominee's earlier apostasy, could not prevent his confirmation by the Senate. Schurz supported the administration's Reconstruction policy, in large part because it accorded with his own beliefs. Intervention was fruitless, possibly counterproductive. He agreed with Hayes that attracting Southern whites to Republican ranks and realigning the region's politics promised the best future for blacks, because white politicians of both parties would court them to win votes. The strategy proved a dismal failure; Democrats retained control of the South while black political power eroded.

With the end of the Hayes administration in 1881, Schurz left public office, never to return. But he remained active in public life as a newspaper editor, columnist, and independent political organizer. In 1884 he played a prominent role in the Mugwump movement, working to deny Republican James G. Blaine a chance at the presidency. After the election he returned to the South for his first extended visit in twenty years. The degree to which his position on the region and race relations had changed over that period was evident in "The New South," which appeared in 1885, a year before Henry Grady employed the phrase. Its optimistic tone celebrated sectional reconciliation while putting as bright a face as possible on the status of African Americans in the South.[14]

It was only in the 1890s that Schurz once more reassessed his attitudes toward Reconstruction. The combined impact of lynch law and Jim Crow suggested the futility of his hope that with the end of federal intervention, Southern whites would be just in their treatment of blacks. Once more Schurz spoke out on behalf of blacks, arguing for the importance of education. Booker T. Washington asked him to speak on behalf of Tuskegee Institute. To Moorfield Storey, who had been Sumner's private secretary, Schurz remarked, "Unless the reaction now going on can be stayed, we shall have to fight the old anti-slavery battle over again." In 1904 he expressed his concern in an article in *McClure's Magazine* bearing the title "Can the South Solve the Negro Problem?" Unless Southern whites changed their ways and offered blacks opportunities to advance, most notably through education, Schurz feared that blacks would be reduced "to a permanent condition of serfdom." When President Theodore Roosevelt, overcoming his long-time aversion to Schurz, asked him for advice, however, Schurz retreated to his old belief that it would be best to let white Southerners shape their destiny.[15] He died 14 May 1906.

Carl Schurz's career illustrates the limits of Northern commitment to Reconstruction in both scope and duration. Few Republicans in 1865 pressed for more than he did, and those who did, such as Thaddeus Stevens, were never able to mobilize enough support to carry out their policies, including the confiscation and redistribution of plantation lands, an extended period of transition under federal supervision, and additional measures to secure the fruits of emancipation. By the time of the ratification of the Fifteenth Amendment, Stevens was dead, and the number of true Radicals was dwindling. Some Radicals, like Benjamin F. Wade, found themselves out of office; others, like Charles Sumner, complicated their support for civil rights when they endorsed reconciliationist measures. More puzzling were the cases of other Radicals, such as Schurz and George Washington Julian. The latter seemed to turn his back on his previous principles, declaring that the ratification of the Fifteenth Amendment "perfectly consummated the mission of the Republican party, and left its members untrammeled in dealing with new questions." Additional measures represented "military methods and the fostering of sectional hate." Such statements suggest that Julian and others were at best blind to the continued terrorist activities on behalf of white supremacy in the South, for the fruits of emancipation were not yet secured.[16]

Schurz's own course is best explained by a combination of political circumstances and considerations. His advice to Andrew Johnson in 1865 about the inadvisability of a rapid restoration of civil government tended to overshadow his desire for an eventual reconciliation between the sections. Indeed, most Republican policymakers were confounded by the challenge of securing emancipation and reunion simultaneously, especially when it seemed that one could come only at the expense of the other. Schurz's solution to the problem of emancipation embraced free labor principles and nothing more. He called for a change in white attitudes toward black labor, and for opening and sustaining of educational and employment opportunities for blacks—far short of a radical reordering of political institutions or the economic order, although it must be said that emancipation was in itself a radical change in Southern life. How even these limited changes were to be achieved without a prolonged and effective federal presence was unclear; when the changes Schurz anticipated did not come to pass, he was left without a response. Disturbed by violence in 1865, he had by 1871 decided that the federal government should not be empowered to stop it.

Partisan realities also explain Schurz's shifting position. Radical positions did not enhance his standing in Missouri; he found himself in opposition to the Grant administration by 1870. His embrace of fusion, however, accelerated his abandonment of Reconstruction and placed him squarely in the enemy camp. If political circumstances explain his shift, however, the intensity with which he denounced measures designed to achieve goals he had once feverishly endorsed suggest that his convictions about black advancement were not what they once seemed to be. Yet Schurz insisted that for the most part he had been consistent (and consistently correct) all along; he never quite came to terms with the implications of his shift during the Grant administration. His earlier proposals suggested both the possibilities and the limits of Reconstruction, for although he understood the need to secure the fruits of emancipation, he was at a loss how to secure a sustained federal presence in such a manner as to retain public support. In such dilemmas one can discover why Reconstruction turned out as it did.

NOTES

1. Hans L. Trefousse, *Carl Schurz: A Biography* (Knoxville, Tenn., 1982), 124–127.

2. Brooks D. Simpson, LeRoy P. Graf, and John Muldowny, eds., *Advice After Appomattox: Letters to Andrew Johnson, 1865–1866* (Knoxville, Tenn., 1987), 62.

3. Carl Schurz to Margarethe Schurz, 21 May 1865, in Joseph Schafer, ed., *Intimate Letters of Carl Schurz, 1841-1869* (Madison, Wis., 1928), 337.

4. Carl Schurz to Frederick Althaus, 25 June 1865, ibid., 340–341.

5. Ibid., 341–342.

6. Carl Schurz to Andrew Johnson, 28 July and 13 August 1865, in Simpson et al., *Advice After Appomattox*, 80–81, 92.

7. Carl Schurz to Andrew Johnson, 13 August 1865, ibid., 90–91; reports of J. M. Phipps and J. E. Harvey, 21 August 1865, W. A. Poillion to Wager Swayne, 29 July 1865, and J. P. Houston to Schurz, 22 August 1865, in *Senate Executive Documents*, 39th Congress, 1st sess., no. 2, 70–74.

8. Carl Schurz to Andrew Johnson, August 21 and 29, 1865, in Simpson et al., *Advice After Appomattox*, 103, 114. (Johnson pardoned Andrew in October 1865; ibid., 104–105.)

9. Trefousse, *Schurz*, 155.

10. Carl Schurz to Andrew Johnson, 29 August 1865, in Simpson et al., *Advice After Appomattox*, 112.

11. Carl Schurz to Margarethe Schurz, 2 September 1865, in Schafer, *Intimate Letters*, 349.

12. *Senate Executive Documents*, 39th Congress, 1st sess. no. 2, contains Schurz's report, supporting documents, and a letter from Grant on his Southern tour. Trefousse, *Schurz*, 158, incorrectly states that Schurz called for a redistribution of land; in fact, he anticipated such a redistribution as due to economic circumstances rather than as a result of government policy.

13. Frederick Bancroft, ed., *Speeches, Correspondence and Political Papers of Carl Schurz*, 6 vols. (New York, 1913), vol. 3, 115–152.

14. Ibid., vol. 4, 369–400.

15. Trefousse, *Schurz*, 291–292.

16. George Washington Julian, *Political Recollections, 1840 to 1872* (New York, 1970), 330–331.

BIBLIOGRAPHY

Burlingame, Michael, ed. *Report on the Condition of the South.* New York, 1969. An edition of Schurz's report presented as *Senate Executive Documents*, 39th Congress, 1st sess. no. 2.

Foner, Eric. *Reconstruction: America's Unfinished Revolution, 1863–1877.* New York, 1988.

Gillette, William. *Retreat from Reconstruction, 1869–1879.* Baton Rouge, La., 1979.

Mahaffey, Joseph H., ed. "Carl Schurz's Letters from the South." *Georgia Historical Quarterly* 35 (1951): 222–257.

Schafer, Joseph, ed. *Intimate Letters of Carl Schurz, 1841–1869.* Madison, Wis., 1928.

Schurz, Carl. *The Reminiscences of Carl Schurz.* 3 vols. New York, 1907–1908.

———. Papers. Library of Congress. (Microfilmed).

Simpson, Brooks D. "Land and the Ballot: Securing the Fruits of Emancipation?" *Pennsylvania History* 60 (1993): 176–188.

Simpson, Brooks D., LeRoy P. Graf, and John Muldowny, eds. *Advice After Appomattox: Letters to Andrew Johnson, 1865–1866.* Knoxville, Tenn., 1987.

Summers, Mark Wahlgren. *The Era of Good Stealings.* New York, 1993.

Trefousse, Hans L. "Carl Schurz, the South, and the Politics of Virtue." In Abraham S. Eisenstadt, Ari Hoogenboom, and Hans L. Trefousse, eds., *Before Watergate: Problems of Corruption in American Society.* New York, 1978.

———. *Carl Schurz: A Biography.* Knoxville, Tenn., 1982.

Joseph Smith, Mormonism, and Religious Communitarianism

NEWELL G. BRINGHURST

Joseph Smith and the Latter-day Saint movement he founded were part of the larger effort to promote social, political, and economic reform in antebellum America. Like other nineteenth-century reformers, Smith was influenced by his background, especially the economic and social situation of his family. The future Mormon leader, prior to 1830—when he formed the Latter-day Saint movement—experienced what one Latter-day Saint writer has described as "status anxiety."[1] Born on 23 December 1805 in Sharon, Vermont, Joseph Smith, Jr., the fourth child in a family of nine, was exposed to unsettled, uprooted conditions in a frontier environment. By the time he was eleven, his parents, Joseph and Lucy Mack Smith, had moved their family nine times.

In addition, the young Smith was forced to deal with the uncertainties of life within a lower-middle-class family. His father, because of continuing economic misfortune, had difficulty providing for his family—a failing that apparently drove him to excessive drinking. Young Joseph grew up with minimal formal education because of the need to work as a day laborer to supplement the family's meager income. He also hired himself out to individuals as a "money-digger" seeking buried treasure—a common practice among the poor and itinerant. The family's general poverty, combined with controversy surrounding young Joseph's money-digging activities, caused the Smiths to be snubbed by their more affluent neighbors.

There were other problems. The elder Smith apparently failed to fulfill the traditional role of male patriarchal dominance. His problems with alcohol may have been a contributing factor. Whatever the case, his wife assumed a strong role in family affairs, at least equal to that of her husband.

Exacerbating these difficulties was the Smith family's unsettled religious situation. Long before the birth of Joseph, Jr., both grandfathers had broken away from the traditional churches of New England, despite their Puritan roots. Both grandfathers, however, retained fervent religious beliefs, variously millennialistic and mystical, but could find no home within organized churches. Joseph, Sr., and Lucy also manifested religious heterodoxy; both rejected the negative view of humanity evident in the Calvinistic tenets of New England Congregationalism. They believed, instead, that free will and one's own ability could influence one's own salvation. Eschewing various established churches, they embraced "Christian primitivism," believing that various innovations within the established churches had corrupted "original" Christian teachings.

There was conflict within the Smith family over religious practice and belief when Lucy joined the Presbyterian Church following the family move to Palmyra, New York, in 1816. She was accompanied by two sons and one daughter. Other family members held back, including her husband and young Joseph. The elder Smith, holding to his deeply held mystical, universalistic beliefs, steadfastly refused to join any church, despite his wife's persistent admonitions. Such conflict distressed young Joseph.

Further complicating this situation, young Joseph was caught up in the religious fervor of the Second Great Awakening affecting Palmyra and other parts of the "burned-over" district. A number of denominations vied for his allegiance, causing him further inner turmoil. He later confessed that "my mind became somewhat partial to the Methodist sect and I felt some desire to be united with them." But he held back: "So great were the confusion and strife among the different denominations, that it was impossible for a person as young as I was and so unacquainted with man and things to come to any certain conclusion who was right and who was wrong. My mind was greatly excited, the cry and tumult were great and incessant."[2]

Deeply troubled, Smith sought divine guidance, and in the wake of a "vision" was allegedly instructed to join none of the existing denominations. Over the next several years he claimed to have experienced a number of other "visions" or divine visitations that culminated in his writing the *Book of Mormon*, completed in 1830.

The *Book of Mormon*, according to Mormon belief, was "transcribed" by Smith from a set of gold plates he found buried in a hillside near his home. It encompassed the sacred writings of three ancient American civilizations descended from a group of Israelites who had migrated from the Holy Land to the New World about 600 B.C. This work detailed their many conflicts and apostasies, culminating, about A.D. 400, with the destruction of the lighter-skinned Nephites by the darker-skinned Lamanites, the latter surviving group considered ancestors of the contemporary American Indians. The *Book of Mormon*, written in biblical prose, emphasized America's role in salvation history. Clearly millennialistic, it anticipated "the latter days" and the Second Coming as "swiftly approaching."

More important, the *Book of Mormon* served as the basis for a church founded by Smith and a small group of followers, including members of his own family,

on 6 April 1830. Smith assumed the title of "first elder," indicating "his pre-
eminence over the whole church."[3] For Smith, this new denomination, ultimately known as the Church of Jesus Christ of Latter-day Saints (or the Mormon
Church), resolved the sharp religious divisions within his own family while
allaying his deeply felt anxieties concerning the "true" source of religious authority. He apparently hoped, moreover, that revenue generated from sales of
the *Book of Mormon* would help ease his family's chronic financial problems.

The *Book of Mormon* signaled a clarion call for radical reform. It was a
critique of the "rampant exploitative individualism" evident in American society during the Jacksonian period. It rejected the "ideal" of the "self-made
man," placing community above individual self-interest. It lamented the multitude of problems—political, economic, social—plaguing American society.
Even Alexander Campbell, leader of the rival Disciples of Christ and a less-
than-sympathetic critic, noted the *Book of Mormon*'s sensitivity to "all of the
great controversies" affecting antebellum American society.[4]

As for specific remedies, the *Book of Mormon* called for a new religious-
political order based on economic equality and communal cooperation. It lamented the division of American society into distinct and separate classes. The
ideal society, Smith believed, was based on complete equality, with all individuals gainfully employed. All material things would be held in common.

The *Book of Mormon* found a ready audience, despite the radical tone of its
message—or more precisely because of it—and the fledgling Mormon Church
grew rapidly. From some 280 converts at the end of 1830, the movement more
than doubled to over 680 within a year. This came in the wake of Smith's
migration from New York to the Midwest in 1831 and the formation of a Mormon settlement at Kirtland, Ohio (near Cleveland), where Smith maintained his
principal residence with his wife, Emma Hale, whom he had married in January
1827. Smith established a second settlement in the frontier community of Independence, Missouri. By 1835 total church membership stood at 8,835, a thir-
teenfold increase in just four years. Three years later, this number had doubled
to 17,881, with over 10,000 (a majority) living in Mormonism's principal gathering area of northwestern Missouri.

The earliest converts to Mormonism were of limited means and education
and had a history of geographic mobility. Thus they mirrored the socioeconomic
characteristics of Smith himself. For example, Brigham Young, who joined the
church in 1832 and emerged as a principal Mormon leader, had been raised in
such desperate poverty that his family was broken up in 1815, when he was just
fourteen, in the wake of his mother's death. Leading a nomadic existence while
living in various communities throughout upstate New York, Young tried with
limited success to earn a living as a carpenter, a painter, and a glazer prior to
joining the Mormon movement. Other notable Mormon leaders, including John
Taylor, Wilford Woodruff, Lorenzo Snow, Heber C. Kimball, and Parley and
Orson Pratt, had been poor farmers or artisans.

Smith possessed a number of striking personal qualities that aided him in commanding the allegiance of his followers. In physical appearance he was imposing: muscular, standing six feet tall, and considered "very handsome, except for his nose, which was aquiline and prominent."[5] Moreover, he possessed a charisma particularly evident while speaking. He projected intense feeling in delivering sermons whereby "the blood drained from his face, leaving a frightening, almost luminous pallor."[6]

As Mormon leader, Smith implemented certain practices in the spirit of reform manifested in the *Book of Mormon* while maintaining control over his followers. He encouraged direct participation by church members. The church was egalitarian, with no professional clergy and virtually all adult males ordained to the priesthood. Such egalitarianism was also evident in Mormon doctrine: Smith asserted, through revelation, that virtually all humankind would be saved, including the wicked and unrighteous. Despite such universalism, the "degrees of glory" in the hereafter would vary, with the "highest degrees" reserved to practitioners of the true faith, Mormonism. Smith also established special positions of leadership for his most capable and loyal followers. These included an "assistant president"; two counselors to aid him in running the church; a Quorum of Twelve Apostles along with a Quorum of Seventies to direct the church's expanding missionary work; and two high councils to supervise affairs in the rapidly growing Mormon settlements in Kirtland and Independence.

At the same time, Smith increased his own power. In March 1835, through revelation, he proclaimed himself president of the whole church. Further enhancing the powers of this office, Smith was designated "seer, revelator, translator and prophet."[7] He used personal revelations to instruct his followers, thereby giving further divine sanction to his authority. His published revelations appeared first in the *Book of Commandments*, brought forth in 1833, and two years later in an expanded volume known as *Doctrine and Covenants*. The latter work, ultimately "canonized" as scripture in 1835, was held by the Mormons to be on a par with the *Book of Mormon* and the Old and New Testaments.

In the meantime, Smith asserted his role as a reformer in another important way. In February 1831 he called for a new economic order in his Law of Consecration and Stewardship, which was designed to transform the highly individualistic economic order of Jacksonian America into a system based on economic equality and group cooperation. Each member of the church was to "consecrate" or deed to the church all of his property. In turn, the church would grant an "inheritance" or "stewardship" to every family out of the properties thus received. Smith hoped that consecrations would exceed the stewardships, so that out of this surplus, stewardships could be granted to poorer and younger church members.

The Law of Consecration and Stewardship was designed as a leveler leading to temporal equality among all church members. Smith anticipated the "ideal" egalitarian society suggested in the *Book of Mormon*. This effort paralleled the attempts by other groups of antebellum Americans to implement their own forms of economic communitarianism, in particular the Shakers under Ann Lee and the followers of Robert Dale Owen at New Harmony. The Mormon system, however, was less all-inclusive and more akin to farm tenancy than true communal agriculture. It sought equality in consumption rather than in capital controlled or managed.

Despite its relative moderation, the Mormon Law of Consecration and Stewardship failed, and was abandoned in August 1834. Smith and other leaders could persuade only about half of the church members living in Independence, Missouri, to participate, and those involved were mainly the less well-to-do. Further upsetting Mormon plans was the Latter-day Saints' forced expulsion from Independence by hostile non-Mormons during the summer of 1833.

Much of the Missouri hostility stemmed from local reaction against Mormon antislavery views. Mormon opposition to slavery was not surprising, given that Smith and the vast majority of his followers were from nonslaveholding regions of the Northeast. The *Book of Mormon* condemned human bondage, despite concurrent and seemingly contradictory racist concepts, particularly its assertion that the Indians' dark skin reflected their degraded condition and the consequence of unrighteous behavior.

Smith, moreover, expressed deep anxieties about black slavery during the 1832–1833 South Carolina nullification crisis. Through a 25 December 1832 revelation, destined to become one of the most famous in the Mormon canon, he predicted numerous wars that would "shortly come to pass, beginning at the rebellion of South Carolina." In time "the Southern States shall be divided against the Northern States," and war would ultimately spread to "all nations." Black slaves would be involved in these apocalyptic events: "And it shall come to pass, after many days, slaves shall rise up against their masters, who shall be marshaled and disciplined for war."[8] Such cataclysmic expectations clearly fit in with basic Mormon millennialistic beliefs.

Reflecting Mormon antislavery views was a July 1833 newspaper article, "Free People of Color," published in the Mormons' official *Evening and Morning Star*; it outlined the procedures necessary for free blacks to migrate to the slaveholding state of Missouri. "So long as we [the Latter-day Saints] have no special rule in the church as to people of color, let prudence guide.... In connection with the wonderful events of this age much is doing towards abolishing slavery and colonizing the blacks in Africa."[9] Non-Mormon Missourians reacted to this article swiftly and violently, driving the Latter-day Saints out of Jackson County in 1833.

Such Mormon antislavery views helped to precipitate the expulsion of all Latter-day Saints from Missouri some five years later, in the wake of organized mob violence sanctioned by the state's governor. The so-called Mormon Missouri War of 1838–1839 resulted in Smith's near-execution and six-month confinement in the Liberty County jail. Despite their violent expulsion from Missouri, Smith and his followers continued to assert their antislavery views during the next five years. But at the same time, the Mormons remained aloof from and condemned the actions of militant abolitionists such as William Lloyd

Garrison and Theodore Weld. The Mormons also distinguished themselves from such antislavery organizations as the American Colonization Society and the American Anti-Slavery Society.

Smith showed himself to be a reformer in other ways. After 1839 the Mormon settlement at Nauvoo, Illinois, spurred further experiments in economic and political reform. By the mid-1840s, Nauvoo boasted some 12,000 residents, making it the second largest city in the state. Here Smith took charge of both economic and political affairs. In promoting the city's economy, he encouraged close economic cooperation among his followers in developing farming (the mainstay of the Mormons' economy) along with mercantile and commercial enterprises. In pursuit of this goal, Smith established the Nauvoo Agricultural and Mechanical Association in 1841.

Thanks to a liberal city charter, Nauvoo was semiautonomous. This charter also made the city's mayor a particularly powerful figure, granting him legislative, executive, and judicial authority through his concurrent position as chief justice of the municipal court. The charter, moreover, allowed the Mormons to organize their own armed force, known as the Nauvoo Legion, consisting of every able-bodied adult male resident: it numbered some 5,000 by 1844. Smith established himself as a formidable political and military figure, serving variously on the Nauvoo city council, as the city's mayor, and as commander of the Nauvoo Legion.

Smith used his political authority to promote reforms. He allowed no public drinking establishments in Nauvoo, a situation in sharp contrast with other frontier communities. His enforcement of public temperance was in the spirit of the Mormon "Word of Wisdom" put forth in Mormon scriptural writings, which called for abstinence from "wine or strong drink," proclaiming them "not good ... for the belly"[10] Smith's call for abstinence was consistent with concurrent temperance agitation in American society at large: some 5,000 temperance societies had been formed by 1834. In a similar reform spirit, Smith encouraged the Nauvoo city council to enact a strong antivagrancy ordinance and sought to prohibit prostitution.

Smith also supported reform involving women. Initially, however, such reform did not appear forthcoming because the Mormon Church had a definite male, patriarchal orientation evident from its earliest days and reflected in Mormon scripture, specifically the *Book of Mormon* and the *Doctrine and Covenants*. The *Book of Mormon* referred to only six women by name, in sharp contrast to the hundreds of men so mentioned—a natural result of this work's primary focus on relationships within male-dominated societies. Similarly, the *Doctrine and Covenants* was "generally addressed to 'men' or assumed an all-male audience." Women were mentioned only 5 times, whereas men were given over 400 references.[11]

The limited role allowed Mormon women was most evident in the prohibition on ordaining women to the priesthood. This restriction held even though women, from the earliest days of the Mormon movement, manifested special "spiritual gifts,'' including the ability to ''heal'' the sick through blessings or prayer and the gift of speaking in tongues. Also, a female member of the church by the name of Hubble ''professed to be a prophetess of the Lord . . . and had many revelations'' in affirming the truthfulness of the *Book of Mormon* during the Mormon sojourn in Kirtland.

In upholding a strong male, patriarchical role within Mormonism, Smith was apparently influenced by several factors. One of these was an apparent reaction against his childhood environment, specifically within his family, where his strong-willed mother exerted an influence at least equal to that of his father. Smith may have also been reacting against the increasingly strong role that women were asserting within various Protestant denominations during the early nineteenth century.

Despite Mormonism's strong patriarchal orientation, Smith came under pressure from women within his movement following the Mormon migration to Nauvoo. Mormon women, in particular married women, became more assertive due to increased responsibilities within their own families—a consequence of their husbands' absence. An ever larger number of Mormon males left their families as church authorities asked them to serve as missionaries, which left their wives responsible for their families. Pressure from these increasingly independent women culminated in the formation of the Relief Society in March 1842. Some 1,341 women were involved in this new organization, representing 10 to 15 percent of Nauvoo's Mormon population. These women chose as their first president Emma Smith, the wife of Joseph Smith. The major announced objectives of the Relief Society were ''to seek out and relieve the distressed'' and to ''watch over the morals . . . character and reputation of [its] members.'' In seeking ''to house the homeless and provide work for widows'' and help other dependent people, the Relief Society's role was similar to that of numerous other contemporary women's auxiliaries and benevolent and reform societies throughout the United States.[12] By the 1840s such organizations numbered in the thousands.

Relief Society activities soon expanded into the spiritual realm. Smith's mother suggested that ''the organization could provide the opportunity for women to refresh each other spiritually.'' Thus, members engaged in testimony and gospel instruction, and occasionally spoke in tongues. More important, Smith conceded the Relief Society additional powers. He characterized this organization as ''a select Society . . . a kingdom of priests as in Enoch's day'' to whom ''the keys of the kingdom are about to be given.'' He further stated that the officers of the organization were ''ordained'' to ''administer to the sick and comfort the sorrowful.''[13] These allusions to ''priests,'' ''keys'' to be given, and ''ordinations'' have led to suggestions that Smith granted Mormon women the powers, if not the actual offices, of the Mormon priesthood. Such suggestions have recently become a sharp point of debate within the Mormon community. In the short run, however, the issue of Mormon women and priesthood vis-à-vis the Relief Society became moot when church leaders disbanded the organization in 1844. This move came in reaction to attacks by certain Relief Society members on the still-secret, highly controversial Mormon practice of polygamy.

Smith's introduction of polygamy to a small, select group of followers in 1841, followed by its divine sanctification through revelation on 12 July 1843 represents his most radical effort to "reform" the role of women within both the family and the larger Mormon community. Smith's sanctioning of plural marriage was a bold departure, running counter to earlier teachings in the *Book of Mormon*, which contained five separate denunciations of polygamy, linking it with "fornication," "whoredoms," and various other forms of aberrant, immoral behavior.

Smith began moving away from his early monogamous convictions shortly after publication of the *Book of Mormon*. In July 1831 he suggested that polygamy would be implemented at some future date. It appears, moreover, that he took at least one plural wife as early as the mid-1830s, while living in Kirtland. In 1841 Smith formally unveiled plural marriage to a small group of his most trusted followers. The precise number of women taken as plural wives by each of Smith's close associates was apparently "very restricted"—generally two or three women per male. Smith took on a considerably larger number of women. The precise number of his plural wives is difficult to determine, with estimates ranging from twenty-seven to eighty-four.

Smith's precise motives for implementing plural marriage are difficult to determine. On a basic level, some historians have suggested that Mormon polygamy was the product of Smith's sexual drive or sexuality. On a higher plane, it appears that Smith looked to certain polygamous biblical figures, including Abraham, Isaac, and Jacob, as "role models" in his ongoing efforts to "restore all things."[14] On a broader doctrinal level, the introduction of plural marriage occurred during a critical stage in the evolution of Mormon theology. Through a series of revelations and important statements given between 1841 and 1844, Smith introduced a number of doctrinal innovations, including sacred, secret temple ceremonies. Smith also promoted several revolutionary concepts concerning the nature of God and humankind's relationship to the supernatural, whereby Mormons viewed God as not only anthropomorphic but also as "plural."

In promoting the latter concept, Smith asserted the existence of numerous divine beings throughout the total expanse of the universe. Moreover, he preached the even more radical concept that humans currently living on the earth had the potential to become "gods," ultimately assuming dominion over worlds of their own through a process known as "eternal progression." Ultimate godhood, however, could be secured only though strict adherence to certain Mormon ordinances and practices, including plural marriage. Indeed, plural marriage would serve as a means for faithful Mormon males to produce the largest possible number of offspring, who would be subject to his godlike authority in the hereafter.

Smith's introduction of plural marriage was also influenced by an antebellum

American society experiencing profound social change. Mormon polygamy was a means to restore the patriarchal patterns in marriage that had once been dominant in American society but were currently under attack. Smith was also influenced by the diverse forms of marital experimentation prevalent among various communitarian groups in upstate New York, where he had grown up. These ranged from the Shakers, directed by Ann Lee, who preached complete sexual abstinence, to the Oneida Community, under John Humphrey Noyes, which preached "complex marriage" that involved sexual relations with multiple partners.

In sharp contrast to the secrecy surrounding plural marriage, Smith openly promoted himself as a reform candidate for president of the United States in 1844. Rejecting the two major parties, he ran as an independent. At the same time, he adopted a broad-based reform platform clearly influenced by the two major parties, the Whigs and the Democrats, and the small but highly visible Liberty party. Echoing the Whigs, Smith called for the reestablishment of the national bank. He also expressed ardent expansionist views like those of the Democratic party and its candidate James K. Polk. Thus, Smith opposed British claims to Oregon and advocated the annexation of Texas, as well as of Canada and Mexico. Like the reformist, antislavery Liberty party, Smith called for abolition of black slavery through gradual, compensated emancipation. Three additional reforms not on the agendas of the existing political parties were prison reform, whereby virtually all imprisoned convicts would be freed; a call for a reduction in the size of the U.S. Congress by half and decrease in its pay; and, in response to earlier Mormon troubles in Missouri, a proposal giving the president of the United States authority to suppress mobs and protect the constitutional rights of all citizens, irrespective of the wishes of any state governor.

To direct his campaign, Smith utilized a newly created political organization, the Council of Fifty. This council, though separate and distinct from the Mormon Church, was made up almost entirely of church members. It dispatched more than 300 speakers to organize political rallies in major cities throughout the East and the Midwest. Expressing confidence of ultimate victory, Smith and his backers talked about building "a coalition of the oppressed" including American Catholics, who like the Mormons were a despised religious minority and victims of persistent antebellum mob violence.[15]

The extent of Smith's success in the political arena will never be known. He was killed by an armed mob on 27 June 1844 while imprisoned at Carthage, Illinois. His arrest and subsequent death came at the end of a chain of events stemming from his introduction of plural marriage, which generated increased controversy within the Mormon movement itself. By June 1844 a group of dissidents had completely broken away from Smith, denouncing him as a "fallen prophet." They formed a rival organization complete with their own newspaper, *The Nauvoo Expositor*, which openly attacked Smith and plural marriage. In response, Smith, as Nauvoo's mayor, had the *Expositor* declared a "public nuisance'' and ordered destruction of the press. But he was forced to confront the explosive situation caused by his defiance of basic First Amendment rights. To stem growing anti-Mormon violence threatening to escalate into full-scale civil war, Smith agreed to stand trial on the charges brought against him. His arrest led directly to his death at the hands of a well-organized mob that stormed the jail where he was held.

Smith and the Mormon movement left a mixed legacy relative to American reform. On an immediate level, Smith reflected many aspects of the reform impulse that characterized American society during the antebellum period— most evident in his advocacy of temperance, prison reform, and the abolition of slavery. But such proposals were minor parts of Smith's larger reform agenda anticipating an entirely new social and economic order built on the ruins of a fundamentally corrupt and decadent American society tottering on the brink of imminent collapse.

Mormonism's reform agenda, however, changed following Smith's death in 1844 and the emergence of Brigham Young as principal Mormon leader. Young, in contrast to Smith, was not an innovator or visionary reformer. He was a pragmatic, down-to-earth organizer who sought to preserve and protect his besieged Mormon followers. Accordingly, he directed Mormon migration to the isolated sanctuary of the Great Salt Lake valley. He also promoted the establishment of some 250 settlements throughout the American West. The Mormon effort to build a kingdom on the desert was an example of the self-discipline and high purpose evinced by the migration and of Mormon ties to nineteenth-century communitarianism. The migration provided the foundation for Mormon growth. Indeed, the success of the Utah experiment was itself testimony to Mormon strength and the ''truth'' of its calling.

Equally important, Young perpetuated and strengthened among the Mormon faithful a sense of group identity and purpose initially instilled by Smith. As for the specific reforms advocated by Smith, some were completely abandoned, in particular those calling for the abolition of black slavery and prison reform. Others, like communitarianism, were resurrected, albeit with mixed results. Smith's most controversial reform, plural marriage, was retained by Young and institutionalized. In 1852 Young lifted the veil of secrecy under which polygamy had been established, publicly defending it as essential to Mormon salvation. This public disclosure outraged Victorian American society and generated a crusade led by federal government officials to eradicate polygamy. Such opposition, however, had the ironic effect of generating an increased sense of Mormon group solidarity. This Latter-day Saint cohesiveness remained intact despite a formal decree issued by Mormon leaders in 1890 calling for an end to the practice of plural marriage. Indeed, Mormonism's sense of purpose and group identity has continued strong until the late 1990s, enabling the Church of Jesus Christ of Latter-day Saints to grow into a major denomination having over 9 million members worldwide.

NOTES

1. Geoffrey F. Spencer, "Anxious Saints: The Early Mormons, Social Reform, and Status Anxiety," *John Whitmer Historical Association Journal* 1 (1981): 43–53. In making this observation, Spencer builds on the arguments made by Joseph Gusfield in examining the background and motives of those involved in the temperance movement. See Gusfield, *Symbolic Crusade: Status Politics and the American Temperance Movement* (Urbana, Ill., 1963), 3.

2. Joseph Smith, Jr., *History of the Church*, edited by Brigham Roberts, 2nd ed., 7 vols. (Salt Lake City, 1978), vol. 2, 3–4.

3. Marvin S. Hill, *Quest for Refuge: The Mormon Flight from American Pluralism* (Salt Lake City, 1989), 27.

4. Alexander Campbell, "The Book of Mormon Reviewed and Its Divine Pretensions Exposed," *Painesville Telegraph*, 15 March 1831. Reprinted in Campbell's *Delusions: An Analysis of the Book of Mormon, with an Examination of Its Internal Evidences, and a Refutation of Its Pretences to Divine Authority* (Boston, 1832), 13.

5. According to Fawn M. Brodie, *No Man Knows My History: The Life of Joseph Smith*, 2nd ed. (New York, 1971), 32.

6. Ibid.

7. *Doctrine and Covenants*, vol. 88, 12–48; vol. 107, 22–40, 91–92.

8. Ibid., vol. 107, 87.

9. *Evening and Morning Star*, July 1833.

10. *Doctrine and Covenants*, vol. 89, 5, 7.

11. As noted by Melodie Moench Charles, "Precedents for Mormon Women from Scriptures," in Maureen Ursenbach Beecher and Lavinia Fielding Anderson, eds., *Sisters in Spirit: Mormon Women in Historical and Cultural Perspective* (Urbana, Ill., 1987), 45, 48–49.

12. Jill Mulvay Derr, "Making of Mormon Sisterhood," in ibid., 158.

13. Linda King Newell, "Gifts of the Spirit: Women's Share," in ibid., 115.

14. Richard S. Van Wagoner, *Mormon Polygamy: A History* (Salt Lake City, 1986), 48.

15. Kenneth Winn, *Exiles in a Land of Liberty: Mormons in America, 1830–1846* (Chapel Hill, N.C., 1989), 205–206.

BIBLIOGRAPHY

Allen, James B., and Glen M. Leonard. *The Story of the Latter-day Saints*. 2nd ed. Salt Lake City, 1992.

Arrington, Leonard J. *Brigham Young: American Moses*. New York, 1985.

Arrington, Leonard J., and Davis Bitton. *The Mormon Experience*. New York, 1979.

Bringhurst, Newell G. *Saints, Slaves, and Blacks: The Changing Place of Black People Within Mormonism*. Wesport, Conn., 1981.

———. *Brigham Young and the Expanding American Frontier*. Boston, 1986.

———. "Joseph Smith, the Mormons, and Antebellum Reform—A Closer Look." *John Whitmer Historical Association Journal* 14 (1994): 73–91. My essay is adapted from this article.

Brodie, Fawn M. *No Man Knows My History: The Life of Joseph Smith.* 2nd ed. New York, 1971.

Bushman, Richard. *Joseph Smith and the Beginnings of Mormonism.* Urbana, Ill., 1984.

Campbell, Eugene E. *Establishing Zion: The Mormon Church in the American West.* Salt Lake City, 1988.

Flanders, Robert B. *Nauvoo: Kingdom on the Mississippi.* Urbana, Ill., 1965.

Foster, Lawrence. *Religion and Sexuality: The Shakers, the Mormons and the Oneida Community.* New York, 1981.

Hansen, Klaus J. *Mormonism and the American Experience.* Chicago, 1981.

Hill, Donna. *Joseph Smith: The First Mormon.* New York, 1977.

Hill, Marvin S. *Quest for Refuge: The Mormon Flight from American Pluralism.* Salt Lake City, 1989.

LeSueur, Stephen C. *The 1838 Mormon War in Missouri.* Columbia, Mo., 1987.

Newell, Linda King, and Valeen Tippetts. *Mormon Enigma: Emma Hale Smith.* New York, 1984.

Oakes, Dallin H., and Marvin S. Hill. *Carthage Conspiracy: The Trial of the Accused Assassins of Joseph Smith.* Urbana, Ill., 1975.

Quinn, D. Michael. *Early Mormonism and the Magic World View.* Salt Lake City, 1987.

Shipps, Jan. *Mormonism: The Story of a New Religious Tradition.* Urbana, Ill., 1985.

Smith, Joseph, Jr. *History of the Church.* Edited by Brigham H. Roberts. 7 vols. Salt Lake City, 1902–1912; 2nd ed., Salt Lake City, 1978.

Smith, Lucy Mack. *Biographical Sketches of Joseph Smith the Prophet and His Progenitors for Many Generations.* Salt Lake City, 1853.

Winn, Kenneth. *Exiles in the Land of Liberty: Mormons in America, 1830–1846.* Chapel Hill, N.C., 1989.

Elizabeth Cady Stanton
and the Woman's Rights Movement

ANN D. GORDON

Advocates of woman's rights in nineteenth-century America declared no new or special rights, but claimed rights that were acknowledged for men within the family and outside it in civic life. Exact legal parallels between men and women could not be drawn. The women's realization that their relationship to men was prescribed in both spheres—in the family circle and the political arena—drove woman's rights activists to explore new and multiple meanings of equality. They attacked men's arbitrary power in familiar language derived from the colonial protest against a king and in new language aimed at the patriarchal authority preserved in common law, customs, and cultural institutions.

Elizabeth Cady Stanton was the chief writer and intellectual of the woman's rights movement during the decade before the Civil War, when the new reform found its voice and revealed its objectives. After the war, her renown spread beyond reformers. On the national lecture circuit she commanded high fees and drew good audiences year after year. Editors sought her opinion not only about women but also about street cleaning, child rearing, and fashion. Her name became synonymous internationally with the cause of women's equality. Stanton also served as an officer of national associations representing the movement's interests, beginning with the Women's Loyal National League (1863–1864), rallying support to outlaw slavery; the American Equal Rights Association (1866–1869), advocating universal suffrage; and both the National Woman Suffrage Association (1869–1890) and its successor, the National American Woman Suffrage Association (1890–1892), pressing for federal protection of woman's right to vote. She presided over the founding meeting of the International Council of Women in 1888.

Historians usually reserve the term ''woman's rights'' for the antebellum phase of the nineteenth-century movement, replacing it after the war with the term "woman suffrage movement." This shift in terminology echoes the language of the times; the National Woman's Rights Committee dissolved itself into the American Equal Rights Association, and that in turn produced woman suffrage associations. The new term underscores, without defining, an effect of the Civil War on this reform. But attention to "rights" survived the war and characterized the postwar movement through the years of Reconstruction and its demise. A case can be made that greater differences separated the early from the late stages of the woman suffrage movement than marked the transformation wrought by war.

Along with her good friend and invaluable coadjutor Susan B. Anthony, Elizabeth Cady Stanton promoted the idea that the basic tenets of American political ideology dictated women's political participation. It was an imperfect republic and an incomplete revolution that left women taxed without representation and subject to laws to which they gave no consent. She took women's fundamental equality with men for granted. Her reforms would remake law and institutions to reflect the fact. The woman suffrage movement ceased to agree on those principles sometime in the early 1880s. Suffrage attracted women who were concerned with increasing their power rather than establishing their equality and who brought late nineteenth-century political values to the cause. Many late suffragists shared the conservative mood that accompanied the end of Reconstruction, and they welcomed the drive for national unity that would replace a war over human rights. By the end of her career, Elizabeth Cady Stanton and equal rights were controversial among woman suffragists.

Born in Johnstown, New York, 12 November 1815 to Daniel and Margaret Livingston Cady, Elizabeth Cady came from an atypical background for a pioneer of woman's rights. She grew up in a well-to-do household with parents who gave her as good an education as a girl of her generation was likely to get. When she exhausted the resources of the Johnstown Academy, she attended the famous Troy Female Seminary, where Emma Willard pioneered a secular, academic education for girls. In the year of her birth, her father served in Congress; throughout her childhood, he practiced law and trained lawyers at Johnstown; after she left home, he was a member of the New York Supreme Court. From the heights of local society, Elizabeth knew no limits she was bound to respect—save her sex.

Looking for the precipitating causes of her career in her youth, the mature Stanton credited herself with early perspicacity about the injustice of being female in antebellum America. She described rebellion against the dour and fearsome theology of her family's Scotch Presbyterianism. She recounted the injustice she suffered when boys who were her intellectual inferiors at the Academy went on to college while no such opportunity was offered her; the pain of realizing, when her one surviving brother died, that sons meant more to a father than his daughters; and the woes of wives and widows consulting her father, their rights to property not protected by law.

During his courtship of the twenty-four-old Elizabeth Cady, the antislavery orator and agent Henry B. Stanton, then at the peak of his career, saw in her a woman undecided about two paths that beckoned: "the giddy whirl of fashionable follies" and the religious duty of "a person of so superior a mind & enlarged heart" to do something for "a wicked world's salvation."[1] Opting for "duty," Elizabeth Cady married Henry Stanton on 1 May 1840.

By 1848, when Elizabeth Cady Stanton called the first woman's rights convention at Seneca Falls, New York, she had blended diverse experiences into a new perspective on reform and women's part in it. Because Henry Stanton agreed to study law with his father-in-law in order to support a wife and family, marriage for Elizabeth reinforced the legal training she had begun with her father and his students who gathered around him. Yet she was attracted to reformers who spurned law for moral suasion, and to Quakers who regarded the practice of law as amoral. Marriage introduced her to the most radical women in the land: to Angelina and Sarah Grimké, who had linked antislavery activism to the liberation of women; to the Quaker preacher and abolitionist Lucretia Mott, who had joined the causes of religious individualism and equal rights; and to the Garrisonian radicals who led female antislavery societies in Rochester, Philadelphia, and Boston. But marriage also had put her at the very center of the antislavery division over the efficacy and rectitude of political action. While she learned to admire William Lloyd Garrison, Henry Stanton defied him by building the Liberty party in Massachusetts and later New York. She had a front-row seat on the future, when political abolitionism would dominate the reform and marginalize its women.

At the Seneca Falls convention, women demanded "immediate admission to all the rights and privileges which belong to them as citizens of the United States." Most notable among these were political rights. Women wanted representation and a voice in the making of law; they wanted "their sacred right to the elective franchise." Of a generation that was familiar with ceremonial readings of the Declaration of Independence each Fourth of July, and whose grandfathers fought in the American Revolution, the women at Seneca Falls turned to the Declaration to indict men's tyranny and to declare, in language hallowed in American politics, their inalienable rights. All laws that made woman the inferior of man or conflicted with her pursuit of happiness were, they declared, "contrary to the great precept of nature, and therefore of no force or authority." Laws of marriage and property were singled out for special condemnation, as were limits placed on her pursuit of education and employment. Overarching all the specifics in their "Declaration of Sentiments" and their resolutions was their claim to individuality, to being philosophically like men, similarly "endowed by their Creator," and entitled to follow their own consciences. Man had "usurped the prerogative of Jehovah himself, claiming it as his right to assign for her a sphere of action, when that belongs to her conscience and to her God."[2]

Not all of these ideas were new in 1848. Stanton's coauthors and many in attendance at the convention were veterans of women's fight to join the antislavery cause. At the Anti-Slavery Convention of American Women at New York in 1837, the language was more religious but the points were similar. Bearing equal moral responsibility with men, women needed the freedom to pursue moral causes—to lecture and preach, to educate, to petition, to join men in abolishing slavery. They resolved, in the words of Angelina Grimké, "That the time has come for women to . . . no longer remain satisfied in the circumscribed limits with which corrupt custom and a perverted application of Scripture have encircled her."[3] Although women's claims divided the antislavery forces, defense of women's right to a public role in the movement became part of the credo of the American Anti-Slavery Society.

Legal reform that would rid state codes of their most egregious examples of women's subordination to men's control of property had begun before the 1848 meeting. In Stanton's home state of New York, new law in 1848 protected the property that married women inherited from their fathers, though few women had yet seen the cause of legal reform as their own. Stanton knew that statutes were replete with exclusions aimed at women, children, idiots, and prisoners. "Think you," Stanton asked in 1848, "if woman had a vote in this government, that all those laws affecting her interests would so entirely violate every principle of right and justice?"[4]

While taking ideas from familiar reforms, the Seneca Falls convention broke with the past most decisively in its claim that woman's moral responsibility extended to herself. "The question now is," Stanton said, "how shall we get possession of what rightfully belongs to us."[5] This movement would seek women's rights because they were entitled to them, not because rights were tools in the struggle to free slaves, improve the lives of children, or purify the community.

From Seneca Falls the ideas spread, sprouting up in woman's rights conventions in New York, Ohio, Indiana, Massachusetts, and Pennsylvania within a few years. Broad principles were reiterated, the Declaration of Independence was cited, and precise objectives were spelled out. A letter from Stanton was standard fare at these meetings; her brood of young children (seven were born by 1859) kept her tied to home. Her wit as much as her wisdom won an audience. The antislavery press, the women's press, the temperance press, the health reform press—all gave space to Stanton for appeals and articles. The National Woman's Rights Convention resolved that she should write for Horace Greeley's *New York Tribune*, and she did, firing her opening shot at the midterm elections of 1854.

[R]eally, if all the women on the footstool, of every color, nation and tongue, had combined together to see what confusion they could make, they could never have equaled the men of the Empire State in this last campaign. Who ever saw such a botch, such a game at cross-questions, and silly answers. . . . Now, Greeley do you suppose the women could do worse than the lords of creation have done for the last four years?[6]

The clearest achievement of the movement in this early phase was to stimulate debate by introducing the ideas of women's subordination and resistance into political and social culture. Less obvious was the rapid schooling in political practice that activists acquired. In state after state, women petitioned their legislatures and constitutional conventions, learned to write memorials, and mastered the mysteries of legislative procedure. At the state capitals they assigned someone to oversee legislation and mobilized crowds of lobbyists as needed. Year by year their skills improved. In 1859 Clarina Nichols, an early ally, a newspaper editor from New York and Vermont, and an emigrant to Kansas, led a sophisticated and remarkably successful campaign at the Kansas constitutional convention to gain rights for women. Committee members consulted her, and the delegates asked her to address an evening session.

With Susan B. Anthony as her partner, Stanton put her ideas to the political test in New York State. Single and willing to travel ceaselessly, Anthony became the agent of the woman's rights movement who scheduled lectures, accompanied speakers into every county, distributed petitions and shepherded them back to the legislature, published pamphlets, and raised money. In 1854, assisted by their many friends in the legal community, Stanton and Anthony prepared for the legislature an itemized list of "the legal disabilities under which we labor." It included the absence of classic rights—government by consent, representation, and trial by a jury of their peers—and the imposition of disabilities by laws of marriage, widowhood, and motherhood. It defined an agenda for reform. "We ask no better laws than those you have made for yourselves," Stanton assured the legislators. "We need no other protection than that which your present laws secure to you."[7] Persistence won them rare allies and small victories before the war, especially in revised laws on women's economic rights.

Equality in the private relations of families proved early to be the most controversial part of the woman's rights agenda, though no more difficult to achieve legislatively than suffrage. When Stanton first broached her demand, in 1852, that more grounds be allowed women for obtaining a divorce, the clergy attacked her swiftly; clerical opposition would plague her for years. If marriage was a sacred institution, she asked them, then why did state law govern it so minutely? Marriage was a civil contract, and, she argued in 1860, a flawed one: the "marriage contract [is] based in the idea of the supremacy of man, as the keeper of woman's virtue, her sole protection and support," and most of the disabilities that women sought to overcome could be traced to marriage. "Out of marriage," Stanton wrote, "woman asks nothing at this hour but the elective franchise. It is only in marriage that she must demand her rights to person, children, property, wages, life, liberty, and the pursuit of happiness."[8]

Stanton continued to explore private equality through and after the Civil War. In 1869 she announced to an audience in New York City a new mission: "that as I had devoted my life heretofore to the enfranchisement of woman, my future work should be to teach woman her duties to herself in the home. . . . Thus far we have had the man idea of marriage. Now the time has come for woman to give the world the other side of this question.''[9] She overstated how she would allocate her time thereafter, but she affirmed how the personal dimension of women's lives remained central to her political agenda for woman's rights. Equality in marriage and at home supplied her with themes for many of the lectures she took to the public in the 1870s.

Before considering the contentious history of woman's rights during and immediately after the Civil War, it is useful to review the relationship between woman's rights and abolitionism. It had its troubles even before war began, but everyone seemed surprised when these problems produced serious disagreement during and after the war. Abolitionists were the best friends the woman's rights movement had. The spots in the North where agitation took root were antislavery communities, and most woman's rights leaders moved easily back and forth to meet the immediate needs of one movement or the other. The *Liberator* and the *National Anti-Slavery Standard* were the media of woman's rights as they were of abolition. However, opinions about what tied the one movement to the other varied.

Stanton, like most of her colaborers, relied on an analogy between women and slaves. Writing to the Ohio woman's rights convention at Salem in 1850, for example, she noted that a married woman ''has no more absolute rights than a slave on a Southern plantation. . . . Civilly, socially, and religiously, she is what man chooses her to be—nothing more or less—and such is the slave.''[10] A decade later she ventured to compare not only their conditions but their subjective experience as well. Men, she told the American Anti-Slavery Society, might describe ''the general features'' of the slave system, ''but a privileged class can never conceive the feelings of those who are born to contempt, to inferiority, to degradation. Herein is woman more fully identified with the slave than man can possibly be, for she can take the subjective view.''[11] She was the slave.

Antislavery feminists constructed this equation early. Celebrating her own liberation through antislavery activism, Angelina Grimké said in 1838: ''For many years I felt as if I was compelled to drag the chain and wear the collar on my struggling *spirit* as truly as the poor slave was on his body.'' A metaphor about oppression and liberation had obvious utility when explaining their oppression. It also posited a sisterhood that bound even privileged white women in the North to the antislavery cause. But did they believe it as social reality? Historian Jean Fagan Yellin observes that in time the metaphor permitted women ''to collapse the racist, sexist, and class oppression of black women into a common expression of gender.''[12] The analogy ceased to particularize the horrors of American slavery. When emancipation became a possibility and then a reality, history required that the equation be questioned. People who had implicitly accepted that women and slaves shared a common oppression did not agree about the social and political priorities for emancipation when the fate of exslaves hung in the balance.

Unanimity in the two antebellum movements about the need to redefine American rights as individual human rights obscured another problem—that woman's rights depended on abolitionists for power—and dependency undercut claims of equality. The women were, after all, lacking in the currency of politics. In theory, women's citizenship within the reform community was a prototype of long-range goals; in practice, women were dependents. In 1856, when violence broke out in Kansas over slavery and John Charles Frémont ran for president on the new Republican party's ticket, Stanton's male allies expected her to hold woman's rights demands in abeyance so as not to divert attention and resources from the national crisis or to complicate the election by raising extraneous controversies. Abolitionists needed the male electorate at this moment more than they needed their female allies, if their ideas were to gain popular support. Implicit in that judgment was a decision that slavery's abolition could occur without addressing the related question of woman's rights. During the war, the decision became explicit.

Most deeply buried of the tensions within the antebellum alliance were the implications of an independent political movement among women. Sharing the abhorrence of slavery, women had stepped easily into the opening that male antislavery leaders allowed them. Side by side they worked in an established cause with recognized leaders. Stanton venerated William Lloyd Garrison, Wendell Phillips, and their colleagues as the premier reformers of the age. Only gradually did advocates of woman's rights articulate positions that went beyond the antislavery consensus. And when they did, most often in discussions of marriage and divorce, antislavery leaders acted as if they had never heard or heeded Stanton's early proclamations that men could not represent women, that women would define issues for themselves. Instead, the men presumed not only to represent but also to lead her movement because they were leaders in their own.

In the cauldron of civil war, the demand for woman's rights was transformed, most dramatically by its becoming national in scope and federal in focus. That the cause became national during the war had less to do with the activists themselves than with national crisis. Like men, women experienced the war as an unprecedented mobilization for national ends, whether their role was to relinquish the lives of husbands and sons to battle or to serve the war machine as nurses or managers of relief efforts. They were drawn into national organizations far more centralized than anything in their previous experience, such as the U.S. Sanitary Commission. As the chief architect of the new federal focus for woman's rights, Stanton redirected women's national identities. She transformed the movement and in the process helped to fragment it.

In 1863 Stanton revived one of women's earliest political activities—petitioning Congress for an end to slavery—and created a new organization to coordinate it rather than work through the antislavery societies. Under the motto "In Emancipation Is National Unity," her Women's Loyal National League set itself the goal of gathering 1 million signatures on petitions demanding slavery's end. The names of 265,000 men and women, gathered by the League, were delivered to Congress during the winter and spring of 1864 by Massachusetts Senator Charles Sumner, as evidence that public opinion favored emancipation.

Some women were confused by the League. Drawn by its call, they expected more soldiers' relief and found its antislavery focus puzzling. Others accepted the centrality of abolition but balked when woman's rights topics surfaced. Stanton envisaged a League that would imitate, under new circumstances, the advent of women into the antislavery cause. The League would once again tie women's liberation to the emancipation of slaves. Just as Angelina Grimké had, while emancipating herself, become one of the best antislavery orators, proven women's value to the cause, and opened the way for women's equality as abolitionists, so the League, in the midst of war, would position women at the forefront of republican ideology, where their value to the nation would be appreciated. The League demanded ''for ALL the people the exercise of those rights that belong to every citizen of a republic.''[13] Congress passed the Thirteenth Amendment, ending slavery, and the League's members awaited the next step.

Reconstruction absorbed women's attention because Congress, for the first time, debated the issues that their movement had articulated since 1848. It asked what made a citizen; it examined how to create representation of an unrepresented group; it wondered how to protect new rights; it debated whether voting rights were necessary for citizenship; and it looked at how voting rights might be extended despite states' rights to regulate the franchise. Stanton seized the moment. With Anthony, Lucy Stone, and a handful of other prewar leaders, she appealed to Congress in January 1866 for universal suffrage that would enfranchise former slaves and all women. That Congress never intended to push the cause of universal liberty and rights slowly dawned on the petitioners. Woman suffrage was the demand crafted from the failure to win universal suffrage, and it was a demand now more difficult to achieve because the amended Constitution linked manhood to voting rights. Very few male abolitionists had stood with women in the fight, and none shared their bitterness at defeat. Woman's rights activists found themselves alone for the first time.

Between 1869 and the mid-1870s, the woman's rights movement struggled for a strategy that would make woman suffrage a significant national demand, take advantage of a new precedent for federal action on voting rights, and capitalize on the new use of constitutional amendments for reform. A few supporters introduced a sixteenth amendment in Congress that would match the Fifteenth and complete in tandem what could not be accomplished in a sweeping reform. Women converged for the first time on Washington, as they had on state capitals before the war, but the measure died. The constitutional amendments of Reconstruction were completed without removing what Stanton had called ''the inconsistencies of our theory and practice'' in this republic.

Suffragists divided over their response to this failure. Stanton turned against the Fifteenth Amendment for establishing the principle of man government and enshrining women's exclusion from the franchise in the Constitution. Many of her oldest friends from the woman's rights movement were appalled that she would thus attack the delicate balance that protected voting rights for the men who had been slaves. She offended them further by defining an independent political agenda for woman suffragists. Her National Woman Suffrage Association (NWSA), established in 1869, did not allow men to hold positions of leadership, refused to be guided by the Republican party, and dismissed out of hand the new Republican faith that women should go back to winning their voting rights state by state. Many of her critics found their home in the rival American Woman Suffrage Association headed by Lucy Stone.

Although Stanton and the NWSA sought a national, federal solution for obtaining woman's right to vote, they lacked a more precise strategy for several years. In fact, the initiative lay elsewhere, as women new to the cause tried to establish that their voting rights were in fact protected by the combination of the Fourteenth and Fifteenth amendments. Stanton adopted and popularized their reasoning: that by virtue of their national citizenship, women were now protected in their right to vote. By taking direct action at the polls and pursuing court cases, dozens of suffragists looked to the Supreme Court to settle the question. At the same time, others appealed to Congress for legislation that would enable their interpretation of the amendments. Congress rejected their argument, and the Supreme Court ruled that citizenship implied nothing about voting rights. In decisions that imperiled the voting rights of Southern black men as well, the Court in fact reaffirmed the right of states to regulate the franchise. By 1875 Stanton's wing of the suffrage movement faltered.

Stanton, however, revived the movement and led it through its most important campaign until the twentieth century by taking it back to the lessons of Reconstruction and reprising the demand for a sixteenth amendment. In an appeal issued in the fall of 1876, she wrote: "Having celebrated our Centennial birthday with a National jubilee, let us now dedicate the dawn of the Second Century to securing justice for Women." She acknowledged the decisions of the Supreme Court but condemned them. "If this Magna Charta of Human Rights [the Constitution] can be thus narrowed by judicial interpretations in favor of class legislation, then must we demand an amendment that in clear, unmistakable language, shall declare the equality of all citizens before the law."[14] For the next five years Stanton and the NWSA worked ceaselessly to mobilize women around this demand.

Their success with women owed a great deal to Stanton's parallel career as a popular lecturer. In the decade since the war, women of quite different experiences and values had learned to recognize her as a leader who embodied their aspirations. A call for proof that women wanted the vote elicited several thousand signatures from more than half the states, all of them gathered informally in neighborhoods and at meetings of women who came together for purposes other than gaining suffrage. Some of the writers echoed Stanton's belief in woman's rights. "I want the ballot," wrote a woman from Oshkosh, Wisconsin. "1st Because it is mine by a right, withheld by the 'powers that be'[.]" Others spoke a new language that wedded a belief in woman's moral superiority with her political ambition. "[P]eople are beginning to see," wrote a woman from Breckinridge, Missouri, "that if this hydra headed demon of Intemperance is ever subdued, *woman must have a voice in Legislation.*" Women recalled occasions when they had heard Stanton speak, and thanked her. One sent her preserves along with the list of signatures.[15]

Among men, the battle by the late 1870s was more difficult. Even to propose federal action for woman suffrage required a confrontation over states' rights, and states' rights were gaining political power. "National Protection for National Citizens" was the suffragists' theme and the title of one of Stanton's greatest speeches, delivered to senators in 1878. She combined the ideals of Radical Reconstruction with answers to the Supreme Court's denial of a federal interest in voting rights. A republic, she insisted, could not survive the separation of citizenship from voting rights that the United States attempted. Voting rights were too important to the republican idea to be left to states.

"Inasmuch as we are, first, citizens of the United States, and, second, of the State wherein we reside, the primal rights of all citizens should be regulated by national government, and complete equality in civil and political rights everywhere secured." The paralysis that kept the government from protecting the political rights of Southern freedmen she condemned as evidence of "the imperfect development of our own nationality," of the nation's historic failure to define "the limit of State rights and Federal power." On behalf of woman's rights Stanton reaffirmed the vision of universal rights. "The kind of government the people of this country expect, and intend to have, State rights or no State rights . . . is a government to protect the humblest citizen in the exercise of all his rights."[16] For nine years the Senate kept the amendment alive but locked in committee. When it finally came to a vote in January 1887, the measure failed.

Stanton retired from the lecture circuit in 1881 and spent a considerable part of the next decade abroad, where her grandchildren were growing up in England and France. Thereafter, she spoke publicly only a few times a year at special events. Although nominally the president of the NWSA until 1892, she missed many meetings and spent little time with the members. Personal pulls and political pushes alike contributed to this change in her life. Aged sixty-six, she was weary of travel. When her youngest child reached legal maturity, Stanton gave up housekeeping, and for the next twenty years relied on her children to provide her with homes, as if collecting on the debt of their childhoods, when she had paced "like a caged lioness," longing to be free of "nursing and housekeeping cares."[17]

Privacy also allowed Stanton to distance herself from the woman suffrage movement and its new demands. Success was changing the movement's membership and the leadership it required. More and more of its adherents wanted the vote to express female superiority and to empower their religious or regional views; only a faction expressed itself in the language of equal rights. Compromise with these new voices did not appeal to Stanton. With the principles in place and support growing for the idea that women deserved a political voice, agitation for woman suffrage required organizing and lobbying skills of a sort that Stanton neither enjoyed nor excelled in. It needed builders of institutions and planners of political strategy. It called for dull meetings and simplification of ideas. By removing herself from the daily demands of leadership, she could write and criticize. In the two decades that remained of her life, Stanton produced five books and hundreds of articles, published in everything from Hearst's daily newspapers to free-thought journals. She became a reformer in her own reform movement, suffragism's independent voice. She died in New York City, 26 October 1902.

Late in life Stanton had summed up the role of the reformer as she understood it. ''Let us remember,'' she wrote in the introduction to her *Woman's Bible*, ''that all reforms are interdependent . . . .Reformers who are always compromising, have not yet grasped the idea that truth is the only safe ground to stand upon. The object of an individual life is not to carry one fragmentary measure in human progress, but to utter the highest truth clearly seen in all directions, and thus to round out and perfect a well balanced character.''[18] A lofty and difficult mission, this was also a strikingly individual mission measured by personal integrity, not social effect or acceptance. In its immediate context, the passage rationalized Stanton's controversy with suffragists over her critique of clerical and biblical authority. But it clearly addressed a sense of her vocation. It recalled her admiration for William Lloyd Garrison, and it suggested tension in her own career between realizing the objectives of a reformer and those of a leader. Written when suffragists had stalled in their pursuit of winning the vote state by state and when black men were losing the right in one Southern state after another, Stanton may also have affirmed a belief that those who freed the slaves without regard for universal liberty were in error—that it was they, not she, who had compromised and overlooked the interdependence of reform.

NOTES

1. Henry B. Stanton to Gerrit Smith, 27 February 1840 Gerrit Smith Papers (Syracuse University).

2. ''Declaration of Sentiments and Resolutions, Adopted by the Woman's Rights Convention at Seneca Falls, New York, 19–20 July 1848,'' in Mari Jo Buhle and Paul Buhle, eds., *Concise History of Woman Suffrage: Selections from the Classic Work of Stanton, Anthony, Gage, and Harper* (Urbana, Ill., 1978), 94–97.

3. Dorothy Sterling, ed., *Turning the World Upside Down: The Anti-Slavery Convention of American Women, Held in New York City, May 9–12, 1837* (New York, 1987), 13.

4. Untitled address, 1848, excerpted in Ellen C. DuBois, ed., *Elizabeth Cady Stanton, Susan B. Anthony: Correspondence, Writings, Speeches*, rev. ed. (Boston, 1993), 32.

5. Ibid.

6. Letter to the Editor, *New York Semi-Weekly Tribune*, 28 November 1854.

7. "Address to the Legislature of New York on Women's Rights," 20 February 1854, excerpted in DuBois, ed., *Stanton, Anthony*, 44–52.

8. Letter to the Editor, *New York Daily Tribune*, 30 May 1860.

9. "Speech to the McFarland-Richardson Protest Meeting," May 1869, excerpted in DuBois, ed., *Stanton, Anthony*, 125–130.

10. Letter to the Ohio Women's Convention, 7 April 1850, in *Liberator*, 17 May 1850.

11. "Speech to the American Anti-Slavery Society," May 1860, excerpted in DuBois, ed., *Stanton, Anthony*, 79–85.

12. Jean Fagan Yellin, *Women & Sisters: The Antislavery Feminists in American Culture* (New Haven, 1989), 171; quotation from Grimké's speech, p. 42.

13. "To the Women of the Republic," *New York Daily Tribune*, 24 April 1863.

14. Appeal for a Sixteenth Amendment, 10 November 1876, *Ballot Box* (Toledo, Ohio), December 1876.

15. Mrs. L. M. Stephenson to Stanton, undated, and Mrs. Josephine B. Humphrey to Stanton et al., 31 May 1880, in National Woman Suffrage Association Collection (Chicago Historical Society).

16. Stanton's testimony, *Arguments Before the Committee on Privileges and Elections of the United States Senate, in Behalf of a Sixteenth Amendment to the Constitution of the United States . . . January 11 and 12, 1878 . . .* (Washington, D.C., 1878), 4–17.

17. To Susan B. Anthony, 10 June 1856, in DuBois, ed., *Stanton, Anthony*, 63.

18. Introduction, *The Woman's Bible* (1898; repr. Boston, 1993), 11.

BIBLIOGRAPHY

Aptheker, Bettina. *Woman's Legacy: Essays on Race, Sex, and Class in American History*. Amherst, Mass., 1982.

Buhle, Mari Jo, and Paul Buhle, eds. *Concise History of Woman Suffrage: Selections From the Classic Work of Stanton, Anthony, Gage, and Harper*. Urbana, Ill., 1978.

DuBois, Ellen C. *Feminism and Suffrage: The Emergence of an Independent Women's Movement in America, 1848–1869*. Ithaca, N.Y., 1978.

———. "Outgrowing the Compact of the Fathers: Equal Rights, Woman Suffrage, and the United States Constitution, 1820–1878." *Journal of American History* 74 (December 1987): 836–862.

———, ed. *Elizabeth Cady Stanton, Susan B. Anthony: Correspondence, Writings, Speeches*. Rev. ed. Boston, 1993.

Flexner, Eleanor. *Century of Struggle: The Woman's Rights Movement in the United States*. Rev. ed. Cambridge, Mass., 1975.

Griffith, Elisabeth. *In Her Own Right: The Life of Elizabeth Cady Stanton*. New York, 1984.

Hewitt, Nancy A. *Women's Activism and Social Change: Rochester, New York, 1822–1872*. Ithaca, 1984.

Holland, Patricia G., and Ann D. Gordon, eds. *Papers of Elizabeth Cady Stanton and Susan B. Anthony*. Microfilm ed. Wilmington, Del., 1991.

Stanton, Elizabeth Cady. *Eighty Years and More: Reminiscences, 1815–1897*. 1898; repr. Boston, 1993.

Stanton, Elizabeth Cady, Susan B. Anthony, and Matilda Joslyn Gage, eds. *History of Woman Suffrage*. 3 vols. 1881–1886; repr. New York, 1969.

Venet, Wendy Hamand. *Neither Ballots nor Bullets: Women Abolitionists and the Civil War*. Charlottesville, Va., 1991.

Yellin, Jean Fagan. *Women & Sisters: The Antislavery Feminists in American Culture*. New Haven, 1989.

Norman M. Thomas
and American Socialism

JAMES C. DURAM

Norman Thomas did not come to socialism as the result of any sudden conversion or of an intensive period of ideological indoctrination, but rather, as he stated, "as the disciple of events." There was little in his background, family situation, or early college experiences that suggested he would become the most prominent American Socialist in this century. There was even less to indicate that as its leader he would, ironically, witness the virtual demise of the Socialist Party of the USA during the same period that he became an object of veneration among a great many Americans.

The son of Welling E. Thomas, a Presbyterian minister, and the oldest of six children, Norman Mattoon Thomas was born in Marion, Ohio, on 20 November 1884 and spent his youth there. Because he was a sickly child, his mother, Emma, encouraged him to take up reading and intellectual pursuits. He became a voracious reader, an activity he pursued until overcome with nearly complete blindness in the closing years of his life. By the time he was a teenager, he had overcome his sickly nature and participated actively in the outdoor activities enjoyed by Midwestern youth of his day. For a time he delivered the local newspaper, which was owned and edited by Warren G. Harding, future president of the United States.

The Thomas family fit very comfortably into the Midwestern Republican conservatism that dominated small town Ohio during Norman's youth. Raised in a family where discipline was tempered with love, Thomas developed a happy, secure personality. He often spoke with fondness of his family, noting that his sharply developed sense of responsibility for his fellow human beings was the product of his Christian upbringing.

After graduating with honors from high school, Thomas spent a year at Bucknell University, which he found to be intellectually uninspiring. With the financial help of an uncle, he transferred to Princeton University, which he found to be full of intellectual ferment. There, Thomas was a tutor and held a variety of odd jobs. He excelled at debate, history, and politics. Although he had read Edward Bellamy, Henry George, and other reform authors at the urging of friends, he continued to hold conservative Republican political beliefs during his college days.

After graduating as valedictorian in 1905, Thomas became a social worker at the settlement house operated by the Spring Street Presbyterian Church in New York City. There he first confronted urban poverty and exploitation in the immigrant neighborhoods. He took a world tour in 1907, spending considerable time in Asia. His experiences there made him an opponent of colonialism.

Upon his return, very much in line with family expectations, Thomas announced his intention to study for the ministry. Although he did not realize it at the time, it was at this point that he made a choice, reflecting his broadened intellectual outlook, that kept him in an environment that permanently altered his religious, social, and political beliefs.

In 1910 Thomas became associate pastor of the fashionable Brick Presbyterian Church in New York City and enrolled in the liberal, cosmopolitan Union Theological Seminary rather than the more conservative, orthodox seminary at Auburn, New York. This decision placed him in a hotbed of the Progressive reform agitation that was transcending the traditional secular bounds of politics and greatly influencing other aspects of American life, including organized religion. At Union, Thomas came under the influence of the Social Gospel writings of Walter Rauschenbusch, who emphasized an activist application of Christian principles to social problems.

While serving at Brick Church, Thomas met and fell in love with Frances Violet Stewart, a social worker from a prominent New York family. They were married in 1910 and eventually had six children. Violet, a shy woman with chronic heart problems, created a loving, supportive home atmosphere for Thomas until her death in 1947.

After Thomas was ordained in 1911, he assumed the pastorate of the East Harlem Presbyterian Church and the directorship of the American Parish, a federation of Presbyterian churches and social agencies located in the immigrant neighborhoods of New York City. His registration as a Progressive in 1912 and his work on behalf of Theodore Roosevelt's candidacy indicate that the urban ministry had pushed him in the direction of more liberal political beliefs. A letter to his Princeton classmates in 1915 provides clear evidence of the broadening impact that experience had on Thomas:

It is a sort of school which sets hard lessons and asks some difficult questions. What is our democracy worth? How shall we apply it to our social, industrial and political problems? Are we preparing well for national safety in peace or war when so many of our workers cannot even under favorable conditions make the proper living wage?[1]

Many who read this letter must have been convinced that the Reverend Thomas had found his place in life as a Social Gospel minister to the poor. These remarks also demonstrate that Thomas was already questioning the fundamental fairness of the capitalist system.

The major turning point in Thomas's life occurred when the United States entered World War I in 1917. Unable to reconcile his strong beliefs in the gospel of Christian love and the biblical injunction against killing with the U.S. government's demand for patriotic support of a "just" war, Thomas became a vocal and active critic of American participation. In 1917 he joined the Fellowship of Reconciliation, an international organization of religious pacifists with strong social reform tendencies. He founded *The New World*, soon renamed *The World Tomorrow*, the official journal of the group, which he edited from 1918 to 1921. His editorials during this period present detailed evidence of Thomas's increasing disillusionment with the Christian church because of its uncritical justification of and support for the American war effort.

That same hatred for war caused Thomas to support the 1917 campaign of Morris Hillquit, the Socialist candidate for mayor of New York City, who ran on an antiwar platform. Fearing that his involvement with Socialists and conscientious objectors would jeopardize the financial support of the American Parish, he resigned his pastorate that same year. In October 1918, he completed his transition from Social Gospel minister to political activist by joining the Socialist party.

The Socialist party that Thomas joined had its origins in the 1901 amalgamation of the moderate, less ideologically rigid wing of the Socialist Labor party—those who favored cooperation with free trade unions, and other nonsocialist reform groups—with the even less doctrinaire, more democratically oriented, socialists who had gathered under the banner of the Social Democratic Party of America. The new party played down the immediacy of revolution in favor of a revisionist Marxism that accepted the idea of economic change through democratic gradualism. Propelled by the enthusiastic leadership of Eugene V. Debs and the reformist atmosphere of the Progressive era, the Socialist party attracted significant numbers of voters in presidential elections from 1904 through 1916, including nearly a million votes in the 1912 presidential race. Many, like Norman Thomas, were attracted to the party's pacifism and the alternative it offered to the excesses of capitalism, and shared the hope that it would become a popular political party resembling the mass-based Social Democratic parties of Western Europe.

Experience and principle thus combined to bring Thomas to socialism. As he explained:

I came to Socialism for two reasons. First because it seemed to me that only Socialist ideals implemented in a political program could deal with the tremendous problem of poverty illustrated in the East Harlem neighborhood where I then lived and worked. . . . Second, I supported Socialist opposition to American entry into World War I.[2]

The socialism Thomas accepted was democratic in its scope and content. Although he advocated the importance of public ownership of basic industries and services, he refused to accept the Marxian premise that the social order would have to be changed by force. His was the vision of a cooperative commonwealth, peaceably created.

There is considerable evidence, however, that Thomas never fully escaped the influences of his Protestant-Social Gospel background. His strong sense of conscience, his evangelical approach to politics, his frequent expressions of moral outrage, and his numerous references to biblical and historical parables in his speeches and his writings support this conclusion. As with so many other twentieth-century Americans, the departure of Norman Thomas from the religious orthodoxy of his ancestors did not mean the abandonment of his highly developed conscience.

During World War I, Thomas became greatly alarmed at the violations of civil liberties and at the brutal treatment of conscientious objectors, such as his brother Evan and other critics of the war effort, by both government and private groups. This led him to join other opponents of the war, such as Roger Baldwin, in the formation of the National Civil Liberties Bureau, which attempted to provide legal protection to those opposing the war effort. This organization eventually became the American Civil Liberties Union, and Thomas played a crucial role in its leadership throughout his life.

The decade of the 1920s, with its Republican normalcy, hyperpatriotism, economic conservatism, and intense nativism, presented Thomas with many opportunities to test his newly acquired Socialist faith. Motivated initially by both the economic needs of his growing family and his continuing preoccupation with social issues, he continued his advocacy of pacifism and Democratic Socialism in a series of editorial positions, including that of the party's daily, the *New York Leader*. The failure of the *Leader* convinced Thomas that it would be necessary for the Socialist party to carry out a long-range educational program to create a stronger sense of working-class unity.

In 1922, with his economic circumstances somewhat alleviated by his wife's inheritance (in the form of a trust fund), Thomas accepted the codirectorship of the League for Industrial Democracy, a Socialist organization dedicated to the creation of a social order based on production for use rather than for profit. Supported by a grant from the Garland Fund, Thomas and Dr. Harry W. Laidler, his codirector, worked to expand the League's activities among workers and students. The two teamed effectively to develop a varied program that included campus speaking, publication of research on industrial working conditions, fundraising to support strikers, and the defense of civil liberties. On several occasions, Thomas's active participation in meetings and picketing on behalf of workers' civil rights led to his arrest.

Thomas's keen intellect, superb oratorical skills, and leadership ability brought him to prominence in the Socialist party by the mid-1920s. He emerged as its national leader after the death of Eugene V. Debs in 1926. He soon became, by his own admission, "a chronic office seeker." Despite his singular lack of success, he was recognized as an enthusiastic, informed campaigner who discussed issues rather than spouting platitudes. He ran as the Socialist party presidential candidate in 1928 and in all subsequent presidential elections through 1948. His unsuccessful attempts to use the Socialist party as the organizational spearhead of a mass workers' party during those years absorbed much of his time and energy, and eventually taught him some bitter lessons about the realities of American politics.

Thomas's Socialist convictions, his active personal involvement in numerous reform causes, and his continuous office seeking were major influences that shaped his writing. Convinced of the need to publicize Socialist solutions for the problems facing American society, he became a frequent contributor to such reform journals as *New Republic, The Nation,* and *The World Tomorrow,* as well as the standard Socialist publications of the 1920s. These essays present evidence of the wide range of Thomas's reform interests, his firm grasp of the factual and theoretical aspects of the problems he discussed, and his belief in the superiority of Democratic Socialism over capitalism.

By the end of the 1920s, Thomas's writing formed a crucial part of his reform personality. Writing from conviction buttressed by experience, he hoped to educate and convince his readers of the worthiness of his goals. His writing was a form of secular evangelism, and its increasing volume indicated his growing faith in its potential for the propagation of Socialist ideas.

The stock market crash in the fall of 1929 ended the Coolidge-Hoover boom years of the 1920s. The ensuing Great Depression brought massive unemployment, mortgage foreclosures, and a drastically reduced standard of living to millions of Americans. Many who had rejected or ignored the Socialist critique of capitalism during the boom years became convinced of its relevance after the crash. Thomas's advocacy of public works, unemployment insurance, minimum-wage legislation, a shorter workweek, the abolition of child labor, collective bargaining, and government responsibility for the welfare of the economy struck a responsive chord among Americans. The 900,000 votes that Thomas polled in the 1932 presidential election was, to many Socialists, a sign of better things to come.

The brilliant future that they predicted failed to materialize. The emergence of the pragmatic, immediatist New Deal intensified the continuing dualism over proper tactics that had been an inherent part of American Socialist thought from its beginnings. Aligning himself with the "Militant" faction in the party (the younger, more verbally radical newer members who ignored traditional Socialist doctrine in favor of more direct action and Socialist participation in the creation of a mass farmer-labor party), Thomas rejected the insistence of the "Old Guard" Socialists that the party adhere to revisionist Marxist orthodoxy and democratic gradualism. His desire to make the party an inclusive one with room for all varieties of Socialist thought, including Trotskyite, left him alienated from Morris Hillquit and many of his former comrades.

Communist success in enticing some of the younger, more radical "Militants" into "united front" efforts in late 1935 enabled the "Old Guard" to charge that the "Militant" wing of the Socialist party was Communist-dominated. The dispute came to a head in 1936 when the "Old Guard" withdrew from the party and formed the Social Democratic Federation, taking significant amounts of the party's financial resources and publication facilities with them. Thomas must certainly bear some of the responsibility for this debacle, which left the party fragmented and weakened. His decision to make the party more inclusive and his involvement in so many outside reform activities left him too little time for its internal affairs.

Even without the intraparty strife that obviously weakened the party's electoral efforts, the Socialist party's hope of spearheading a drive for a genuine farmer-labor party based on Socialist principles was foredoomed to failure with the emergence of the New Deal. Not only did the Roosevelt administration appropriate many measures previously regarded as Socialist, but it also managed to convince many Socialists that their reform goals would be better achieved from a position of power. Consequently, many younger Socialists abandoned the party and went to work in the New Deal agencies or assumed places of leadership in the organized labor coalition that supported Roosevelt's policies.

Not surprisingly, Thomas's contemporary assessment of the New Deal was sharply critical of its shortcomings. He resented its appropriation of specific aspects of the Socialist party program, and he condemned the New Deal's lack of overall conceptualization and its neglect of basic ethical issues in the face of immediate economic problems. To him, Roosevelt's reforms represented an attempt to forestall the impending doom of the capitalist system. In later years, he reassessed the New Deal in more sympathetic terms, praising it for establishing the welfare state and strengthening democracy.

Thomas's attitude toward communism hardened during the 1930s. Earlier, he had regarded communism with some ambivalence. On the one hand, he and many other radicals had been impressed by the progress the Soviet Union had made through the use of a planned economy and the self-sacrifice of the Russian people. On the other hand, he had never accepted the Communist argument that capitalism would have to be overthrown by violent revolution. Direct exposure to the divisive, cynical tactics of the American Communists in the 1930s, coupled with careful observation of Communist behavior abroad during a 1937 trip to Spain and the Soviet Union, convinced Thomas that any cooperation between the Socialists and Communists would be disastrous.

Increasing preoccupation with foreign affairs was clearly the most dominant force shaping Thomas's reform agenda from 1935 to the outbreak of World War II. His intense hatred of fascism and his sympathy for the embattled Spanish Republic caused Thomas, with considerable anguish, to modify his belief in absolute pacifism. He did not, however, extend his support to those who urged American intervention on the side of Great Britain and France when war broke out in 1939. Disillusioned with their selfish policies and fearful that American intervention in the war would lead to the suppression of civil liberties and the rise of a fascist state in America, Thomas became an active supporter of non-intervention through his work on behalf of the Keep America Out of War Committee, rejecting the idea that collective security as propounded by those urging intervention was workable.

Thomas and his fellow Socialists paid a high price for their support of non-intervention. Because he spoke on the same platform as members of the extremely conservative, passionately isolationist America First movement, he was accused of being a member of that group and of sharing the pro-German sympathies of some of its more reactionary members. This fact and the shift of American public opinion toward support of the beleaguered Allied cause resulted in the Socialists polling even fewer votes in the presidential election of 1940 than they had in 1936.

The Japanese attack on Pearl Harbor and the subsequent American entry into the war caused Thomas to shift to a position that he defined as "critical support" of the war effort. His criticism of "totalitarian liberals" who were willing to accept restrictions on civil liberties in their haste to defeat fascism, and of those who supported the removal of the Japanese Americans from the West Coast, and his warnings against appeasement of either Soviet communism or Western imperialism, and the dangers of unrealistic peace terms drew intense critical fire from a wide range of groups in American society. The 80,518 votes in the campaign of 1944 was the lowest total in all of his presidential campaigns.

New Deal socioeconomic legislation with its overt assumption of government responsibility for the economic well-being of its citizens proved to be the prototype of the American welfare state that blossomed during the next three decades. During that time, the Socialist party saw much of its program preempted and enacted into law by the two major parties. The emergence of the American welfare state thus sealed the doom of the Socialist party as an electoral force in American politics.

Given these circumstances, the erosion of the Socialist party's power accelerated in the postwar era. Thomas, already skeptical about the wisdom of continued electoral politics, reluctantly accepted the party's presidential nomination in 1948. Although he charged that Soviet behavior constituted a threat to world peace, that Henry Wallace's Progressive party was Communist-dominated, and that the two major parties were too tied to special interests to make substantive reforms, Thomas polled only 95,908 votes. His poor showing convinced Thomas of the futility of continued Socialist party attempts to conduct national political campaigns against the two major parties.

In a move that ran sharply counter to the traditional theory and practices of the Socialist party, Thomas announced that the party should drop its electoral struggle and reconstitute itself into an educational and research unit. Such a move, he was convinced, would lead to a more effective dissemination of Socialist ideas among the American people. Unable to bring the party's leadership over to his view and convinced of the need for more youthful leadership, Thomas refused to accept renomination to the Executive Committee of the Socialist party in 1950. The Socialist presidential candidates in 1952 and 1956 fared so poorly that the party in 1960 gave up its electoral efforts and reconstituted itself as the Socialist Party-Social Democratic Federation and devoted itself to education and research.

Although Thomas never relented in his broad-spectrum advocacy of social and economic justice, the last twenty years of his life saw him increasingly drawn to the search for peace, the cause that had first attracted him to Democratic Socialism. Although he had modified his original absolutist pacifism in the face of growing fascist totalitarianism in the 1930s, he never ceased to advocate the settlement of disputes by peaceful means and the creation of a world order based on peace and disarmament. His work during and after World War II in the Post War World Council, an organization that he founded in 1942 to preach the gospel of world peace, amply testified to Thomas's deep dedication to this cause.

The advent of the nuclear age in 1945 profoundly affected Thomas's attitude toward the necessity for peace, giving it an added sense of urgency. Almost alone amid prominent Americans, he condemned the use of atomic weapons against Japan. He was influential in the founding of SANE, the National Committee for a Sane Nuclear Policy, through which he worked until his retirement from public life in 1967, to prevent the proliferation of atomic weapons through the creation of international controls.

His argument that mankind would extinguish itself unless it found peaceful means to resolve conflicts became the central thesis of his writings on peace in the postwar years. In three books, numerous articles, and hundreds of speeches, Thomas preached fervently that the development of nuclear weapons made the potential risks of armed conflict intolerable.

Convictions about the necessity to avoid armed conflict merged with Thomas's traditional Socialist approach to world affairs in such a way that they brought him into sharp conflict with American foreign and defense policies during the Cold War. Rejecting the idea that peace could be achieved by a "balance of terror," Thomas sharply criticized an American foreign policy based on the production of weapons more destructive than those of the Soviets and the Chinese. He warned that the consequence of Cold War policies would be the creation of an American "garrison state" that would be dominated by an industrial-military complex with a preference for security over civil liberties.

The stroke that finally removed Thomas from public life occurred in the midst of a speaking tour against American involvement in Vietnam, but even that did not still his pen. Shortly before his death on 19 December 1968 in a Huntington, New York, nursing home, he finished *The Choices*, a small volume that reminded Americans there were alternatives to the chaos confronting them. Not surprisingly, Thomas emphasized that the most significant choice Americans had to make was for peace. The volume is a fitting summation of Thomas's reform career, for it, like so much of what he had written throughout his life, called upon humankind to live up to its potential, to the better instincts of its nature.

It is necessary, given the American penchant to regard socialism as an alien belief, to emphasize that much of what Thomas advocated can best be understood as a twentieth-century version of the native radical tradition. His passion for social justice, his sympathy for the underdog, his civil libertarianism, his idealism, and his work on behalf of a cooperative commonwealth are all manifestations of it. Much in his background resembled those of the patrician reformers who played such an important catalytic role in the development of the American reform spirit in the nineteenth century. His family background, his superior education, and his immense appeal to intellectuals substantiate this point.

The manner and style of his activism placed Thomas in the native American reform tradition. Like most earlier American radicals, he emphasized overt, honest dissent, refusing to resort to conspiratorial techniques. Still mindful of the disruptive Communist tactics of the 1930s, he gave graphic evidence of his position with a sharply drawn contrast of Communist and traditional radical tactics:

To a very considerable degree the Communists have created a problem new in American history because they have deliberately flouted the established practices of American radicals from Colonial times on. That practice was not long-continued secret conspiracy, deceit, and concealment, but a flamboyant honesty which, for instance, led the Wobblies of old to fill the jails in towns in which one or more of their comrades had been arrested.[3]

Thomas's entire career stands as an example of open dissent.

Leon Trotsky's remark that Thomas called himself a Socialist "as a result of a misunderstanding" is significant, although not because of its accuracy. Thomas's Democratic Socialism was not rooted in the Marxian doctrine of what Thomas characterized as "salvation by catastrophe" but in the more idealistic, nonviolent, and democratic variety that had firmly established itself in America in the nineteenth century. Thomas came to socialism primarily as the disciple of events. His immersion in the political and economic developments of early twentieth-century urban America combined with his strongly developed sense of obligation to humanity to move Thomas toward the acceptance of a Democratic Socialism that permitted full freedom of such traditional American values as equality and opportunity.

Still, Thomas did not develop his socialism in isolation from his democratic counterparts in Western Europe. Thomas's correspondence, references in his writings, and later oral history interviews reflect his awareness of developments in international socialism. He often drew a clear contrast between the more nationalist American radicals of the past and the more international-minded American Socialists of the twentieth century. Perhaps too optimistically, he argued that socialism was an effective antidote to the xenophobia and hyperpatriotism that often marred the native tradition.

Much evidence exists to suggest that Thomas's contacts with Western European Socialists played an important, though not controlling role, in the shaping of his Socialist thought. The nature of his connections with the international Socialist movement worked to strengthen his well-developed belief in peaceful, nonrevolutionary change. Such contacts sharpened his perspective about the significantly different position and pattern of development that distinguished American socialism from its European counterparts.

Thomas's reform experience speaks to the failure of radicalism in America. Michael Harrington, Thomas's successor, best explained this aspect of Thomas's significance when he said:

If we are to understand Thomas as a man and much of the history of contemporary American radicalism, we must confront the fact that in part he failed. The failure lies not in the fact that Thomas never became President. Rather, it is that the impact of his leadership has been almost entirely personal, that he has not been able to build an effective, organized Socialist movement. . . . Thomas strove to work out an approach that would build a bridge between his ideas and organization and the complexities of American political life. He did not succeed.[4]

Thomas was well aware of this failure; indeed, his continuing discussion of the causes of that failure constituted one of the major themes in his later writing. He argued—in contrast to the very critical treatment of his leadership presented by Bernard K. Johnpoll in his volume *Pacifist's Progress: Norman Thomas and the Decline of American Socialism*—that the failure of American socialism resulted from forces beyond the power of Thomas and the party leadership. The differences between the American and the European situation were simply too great to overcome.

Finally, despite his advocacy of socialism, Norman Thomas can best be understood as a manifestation of the American reform tradition. Like most of the leading exponents of that tradition, he chose neither Marx nor Jesus but placed his faith in man.

NOTES

1. Norman Thomas to Princeton classmates, 6 December 1915, Norman Thomas Papers, Box 1 (Manuscripts Division, New York Public Library).

2. Norman Thomas to Alexander Trachtenberg, 18 October 1918, Norman Thomas Papers Box 4 (Manuscripts Division, New York Public Library).

3. Norman Thomas, ''The Dissenter's Role in a Totalitarian Age,'' *New York Times Magazine,* 20 November 1949, p. 78.

4. Michael Harrington, review of *Norman Thomas: Respectable Rebel*, by Murray B. Seidler, and of *Great Dissenters*, by Norman Thomas, *The Reporter,* 9 November 1961, pp. 64–65.

BIBLIOGRAPHY

Baldwin, Roger N. ''Norman Thomas: A Memoir.'' *Saturday Review* 52 (April 12, 1969): 41–42.

Duram, James C. *Norman Thomas.* New York, 1971.

———. ''Norman Thomas as Presidential Conscience.'' *Presidential Studies Quarterly* 20 (1990): 581–589.

Fleischman, Harry. *Norman Thomas: A Biography.* New York, 1964.

Harrington, Michael. ''A Socialist's Centennial.'' *New Republic* 192 (January 7 & 14, 1985): 16–18.

Johnpoll, Bernard K. *Pacifist's Progress: Norman Thomas and the Decline of American Socialism.* Chicago, 1970.

Seidler, Murray B. *Norman Thomas: Respectable Rebel.* Syracuse, N.Y., 1967.

Swanberg, W. A. *Norman Thomas, the Last Idealist.* New York, 1976.

Thomas, Norman M. ''What of the Church?'' *New World* 1 (1918): 42–46.

———. *America's Way Out: A Program for Democracy.* New York, 1931.

———. ''The Fate of a Gambler's Civilization.'' *Current History and Forum* 36 (May 1932): 155–160.

———. ''The Pacifist's Dilemma.'' *Nation* 144 (January 16, 1937): 66–68.

———. *Socialism on the Defensive.* New York, 1938.

———. *A Socialist's Faith.* New York, 1951.

———. *Socialism Reexamined.* New York, 1963.

———. ''Failure of Organized Socialism in America.'' *Progressive* 23 (January 1959): 29–32.

———. ''Pacifism in America.'' *Playboy* 12 (December 1968): 155, 278–283.

———. *The Choices.* New York, 1969.

Tyler, Gus. ''The Centennial of Norman Thomas.'' *Dissent* 20 (Spring 1985): 210–211.

Whitman, Alden. ''The Great Reformer, Unsatisfied to the End.'' *New York Times,* 22 December 1968, p. 2E.

Booker T. Washington
and Black Self-Help

LOREN SCHWENINGER

"I was asked not long ago to tell something about the sports and pastimes that I engaged in during my youth," Booker T. Washington wrote in his autobiography *Up from Slavery*. "Until that question was asked it had never occurred to me that there was no period of my life that was devoted to play."[1] Indeed, from his earliest childhood, he could remember only years of constant toil and work. It was this fact that had made him what he was, and it was a credo of hard work and self-help that would lift his race from the depths of bondage to self-sufficiency and economic independence.

Given his own struggles and remarkable accomplishments, it was not surprising that Washington would advocate self-help as a means of elevating African Americans. Born in slavery on 5 April 1856, he spent the first nine years of his life as a slave on the James Burroughs farm in Franklin County, Virginia. Even though Burroughs was not a harsh master, young Booker felt the humiliation of bondage: people were treated like "dumb animals," families could be separated on a whim, and he could not remember a single instance when his entire family sat down together for supper.

After emancipation, Washington moved with his mother, Jane Ferguson (his father was an unknown white man) to join her husband, Washington Ferguson at Malden, West Virginia. There he packed salt and worked in a coal mine. Despite these jobs, he attended night school. Later, as the houseboy for the wife of the mine owner, he received additional training and encouragement.

In 1872, at age sixteen, Washington left home and set out by train, stagecoach, and on foot across Virginia to attend Samuel Armstrong's Hampton Institute, a school emphasizing industrial training for former slaves and their children. Admitted, and finding work as a janitor to pay his way, he spent three years at Hampton. He graduated with honors. By any measure, these years had a profound influence on his life, and Washington looked upon Armstrong, a former Union general, as "the most perfect specimen of man, physically, mentally and spiritually."[2]

After teaching briefly in West Virginia, Washington spent eight months at Wayland Seminary in Washington, D.C., then returned to his alma mater to teach. In 1881 Armstrong was asked to recommend someone to head a newly established school in the Black Belt of Alabama, and he submitted Washington's name with a strong letter of endorsement. Washington was offered the position, and accepted. Upon arriving in Macon County, he discovered that the school was more a dream than a reality. Washington and his students set out to build a school from the ground up, literally brick by brick. By 1895, when he was asked to deliver a speech in Atlanta at the Cotton States and International Exposition, he could point with great satisfaction to the success of his self-help experiment. The well-kept grounds and handsome brick buildings of Tuskegee Institute seemed to have risen from the red clay soil of Macon County as if by magic.

The Atlanta address, dubbed the Atlanta Compromise by critics, catapulted Washington to national fame. "Ignorant and inexperienced, it is not strange that in the first years of our new life we began at the top instead of the bottom," he began; "that a seat in Congress or the State Legislature was more sought than real estate or industrial skill." In the "great gap from slavery to freedom," he continued, blacks should never cease to celebrate hard work and individual enterprise. "No race can prosper till it learns that there is as much dignity in tilling a field as in writing a poem." To whites in the South, he added that agitation by African Americans for "social equality" would be "the merest folly." In matters purely social, blacks could be "as separate as the fingers, yet one as the hand in all things essential to mutual progress."[3] These words were just what whites in the South wanted to hear, and the acclaim Washington received following the address launched his career as the preeminent black leader of his day.

From the outset, however, some blacks in the South and a substantial segment of the black leadership in the North felt that Washington had given up too much. Thousands of black voters still cast their ballots in various Southern states, including Alabama, and the segregation statutes were just beginning to appear. Washington, his critics said, should not have condemned black political involvement. He would "have to live a long time," one black bishop commented, "to undo the harm he has done the race."[4]

At the core of Washington's philosophy, which he continued to put forth in speeches, articles, and books, at conferences and conventions, and in personal conversations with presidents, industrialists, educators, and philanthropists, was the idea that through hard work, thrift, patience, diligence, and acquisitiveness, the children and grandchildren of slaves could make great progress in the region of their birth. Blacks should concentrate on learning skills such as carpentry, bricklaying, blacksmithing, shoemaking, plastering, coopering; they should strive to acquire farmland and raise crops for the marketplace; they should seek to establish service-type businesses; the women should learn domestic, sewing, and cooking proficiency. No race that contributed to the economic well-being of the community, he asserted, could be ignored by whites. In short, the dignity of labor and the moral value of work would lift African Americans into the middle class and lead to racial salvation.

This was not a "reform" philosophy. Quite the contrary: it fit neatly into the dominant conservative, laissez-faire business outlook of the Gilded Age. It also capitalized on the self-reliance writings and pronouncements of Washington's predecessor as a preeminent race leader, Frederick Douglass, who died a few months before the Atlanta address. Douglass had admonished his brethren to improve themselves through hard work, frugality, industry, and property accumulation. His oft-repeated speech on "Self-Made Men" articulated a heady individualism. Washington, too, espoused a rugged individualism, asserting that through strength of character and tireless efforts, blacks could raise themselves up "by their own bootstraps."[5] "The price of success means beginning at the bottom," Washington said in a typical speech. But with patience, perseverance, economy, thrift, and unrelenting toil, blacks would be rewarded; "it means struggle, it means hardship, it often means hunger." In a sense, then, as one of his earliest and harshest critics said, "Mr. Washington is leading the way backward."[6]

By using the idea of the self-made man, Washington artfully connected the long American heritage of individualism and acquisitiveness with the plight of the black masses in the South. And however pernicious such a philosophy might have seemed to the large numbers of blacks who struggled unsuccessfully to lift themselves out of debt and poverty, or to free themselves from white oppression, Washington possessed few options in choosing such a credo, even if he had been disposed to espouse a more reform-oriented philosophy. By the 1890s, the movement to exclude blacks from the political process, deny them equal access to public facilities, and keep them "in their place" had gained widespread popularity among Southern whites. Although lynching was on the decline, nearly every other day in the South a black man was lynched, and increasingly the victims were beaten, tortured, castrated, and burned. Moreover, the popular and scholarly writings of the day sanctioned Social Darwinism, with its assertions of Anglo-Saxon superiority and espousal of the view that dark-skinned peoples were inherently inferior. It was little wonder that one African American lamented in 1903 that race prejudice was then more intense and uncompromising than at any time since the Civil War.

Washington's genius was that in the midst of these stifling and oppressive conditions he could authentically articulate a philosophy of black progress and hope, one that would be accepted by the three groups whose support he sought—the "better class" of Southern whites, Northern philanthropists, and the descendants of slaves. But, as historian Louis Harlan writes in *Booker T. Washington: The Wizard of Tuskegee, 1901–1915*: "Washington had no quintessence.'' On the one hand, there were the public pronouncements that reflected ''endlessly the platitudes and dubious social science of the late nineteenth century.'' On the other hand, there was the hidden, secretive Washington who, despite his seeming acceptance of the status quo, acted in ways that contradicted his public statements. To understand the man, Harlan writes, we should focus not on ''his presumed ideology'' but on what he did. Indeed, it is by analyzing his hidden activities in behalf of black rights and his increasingly critical stance against racial discrimination that we can best comprehend his attitudes toward reform, however ambiguous and seemingly contradictory these attitudes might appear when compared with most of his public statements.

Perhaps this can best be seen in Washington's secret campaigns in behalf of black voting rights. As early as 1899, he launched an attack on the ''grandfather clause'' in the Louisiana constitution that gave the vote to men whose fathers and grandfathers had qualified to vote on 1 January 1867, a date when African Americans were not permitted to vote in the state. Although Washington favored literacy and property requirements for voting, he denounced the grandfather clause as discriminatory and initiated a test case to have it overturned, thereby bringing together various groups in the state and making clandestine contributions under the pseudonym ''X.Y.Z.'' When Alabama adopted a grandfather clause and refused to accept voter applications from African Americans solely on the basis of their race, Washington made secret contributions for the prosecution of two voting rights cases in that state. Jackson W. Giles, a Montgomery mail carrier, became the plaintiff in both cases—*Giles* v. *Harris* (1903) and *Giles* v. *Teasley* (1904)—seeking to overturn racial discrimination in voting practices. Washington not only paid Wilford H. Smith to prosecute the cases but, using code words and secret names, passed on news, advice, and money through go-betweens as the suits made their way through the lower courts to the U.S. Supreme Court.

Although none of these cases was successful, Washington was more effective in two other secret political battles. The first was halting the spread of disfranchisement statues in Maryland. In 1905 a constitutional amendment was proposed in that state to disfranchise blacks. It passed the legislature and was submitted to a popular vote. Local black leaders, including Harry Cummings, an attorney in Baltimore, appealed to Washington and others for financial assistance in attacking the proposed amendment. When the amendment was defeated by 25,000 votes, Cummings wrote to Washington: ''I cannot thank you too much for your interest in us and your practical assistance.'' Washington also provided ''practical assistance'' to fight a second battle, this one in Alabama against excluding African Americans from juries. When Dan Rogers, a black man, was convicted in a criminal case by an all-white jury, Washington secretly paid a lawyer to argue a case that a black could not receive a fair trial without blacks on the jury. In 1904 the U.S. Supreme Court concurred, overturning the conviction because qualified blacks had been excluded.[7]

Similarly, Washington worked behind the scenes to attack segregation on railroad lines. Again using lawyer Wilford Smith, he secretly assisted W.E.B. Du Bois in a case seeking to overturn a Georgia statute segregating sleeping cars. He also persuaded a Richmond black to begin a similar suit against the Virginia railroad segregation law, and contacted his longtime friend and lieutenant, James Carroll Napier of Nashville, to challenge the Tennessee sleeping car statute. Having publicly acquiesced in the "separate but equal" doctrine in transportation, by the early twentieth century Washington saw the courts as a means of taking more militant action. Even so, as Harlan notes, "There was always an element of artful dodging in Washington's actions, even as a secret militant." This was evident in 1906, when proposed amendments to the Hepburn railway rate bill guaranteed equal passenger facilities for members of both races. Washington paid a lobbyist $300 to support the amendment, but when more militant Northern blacks opposed it, he apparently realized that such a measure would give explicit congressional approval to racial segregation. Consequently, he quickly reversed himself and urged go-betweens to oppose the amendment, which was defeated.[8]

It should be emphasized that if any of these secret activities had been made public, it would have been disastrous. However ambiguous Washington's working behind the scenes and public pronouncements appeared to be, it took substantial courage to remain involved in such cases when a public disclosure would surely have raised strong opposition to Tuskegee. Revelation of support for reform would have been damaging in the eyes of some Northern philanthropists who contributed significantly to Washington's programs, and would have resulted in hostility and possibly violent retribution by Southern whites.

As if to keep his true self shrouded in mystery, Washington occasionally made public pronouncements that seemed at odds with his accommodationist philosophy. Sharing the platform with Charles W. Eliot of Harvard, steel magnate Andrew Carnegie, and future president William Howard Taft at the twenty-fifth anniversary of Tuskegee in 1906, for instance, Washington "rebuked the country for its political treachery to the Negro." According to one observer, he sounded "a warning note to the effect that free government was losing ground" by excluding blacks from the political process. Then he censured "the mob" and declared that African Americans should have "free scope" to develop themselves to their highest potential. On other occasions, Washington spoke out forcefully against racial violence, and as early as 1896 he wrote an appeal to white Americans concerning the barbarous practice of lynching: "Within the last fortnight three members of my race have been burned at the stake; one of these was a woman. Not one of the three was charged with any crime even remotely connected with the abuse of a white woman." According to Washington, the "barbarous scenes" and "shocking details" were "more disgraceful and degrading to the people who inflict the punishment than those who receive it."[9]

It appears that a personal incident of racial violence fifteen years later, in 1911, convinced Washington to speak out more openly against racial injustice.

On one of his many trips to the North, he stopped in New York City. After giving talks at two churches, he left his midtown hotel about nine in the evening and journeyed uptown to an apartment building on West Sixty-third Street, near the southern edge of Central Park. Why he went and the precise nature of his business in this somewhat disreputable neighborhood were never adequately explained. He was viciously attacked by a white man named Henry Ulrich, who beat him severely with a heavy walking stick, opening a head gash that required sixteen stitches. Ulrich and the woman he was living with accused Washington of taking indecent liberties with white women and attempted robbery. Such charges were surely fabricated, but there were also contradictions in Washington's testimony. The incident revealed the vulnerability of even the most prominent black leader in the racial atmosphere of the early twentieth century. From then until his death in 1915, Washington spoke out more openly against racial inequity.

In November 1912, Washington published an article in *Century* magazine titled ''Is the Negro Having a Fair Chance?'' In every field he discussed— education, voting rights, lynching, convict lease, jury selection, railroad accommodations—the answer was no. There was not a white man in America who would feel that he was being fairly treated if, upon being indicted for a crime, he were to face a jury of another race. Yet such was the case for African Americans. In the Southern states the amount of money spent to educate the average white boy or girl was three times the per capita expenditure for a black child. In rural areas, blacks either had no schools or schools with terms of a few months, ''taught in a wreck of a log-cabin and by a teacher who is paid about half of the price of a first-class convict.'' It was only natural that blacks should feel they were not being treated fairly by whites. In response to the article, even his arch opponent W.E.B. Du Bois admitted that Washington had ''joined the ranks.''[10]

Washington's efforts to bring pressure on officials to provide proper accommodations in restaurants, sitting rooms, streetcars, steamboats, and trains took a new twist in 1914 when he proposed that local blacks set aside two days or perhaps a week to press authorities about the difficulties of unjust treatment. He urged churches, secret societies, businesses, women's clubs, and other organizations to confront railroad officials on these days and seek redress of grievances. Washington wanted to avoid the impression that blacks were protesting against deplorable conditions—''Anxious not to use word 'protest','' he wired his longtime secretary, Emmett J. Scott, in the midst of the campaign; ''nothing to be gained by giving that impression.'' Although he was seeking to change conditions, he was not trying to overturn the ''separate but equal'' doctrine, about which, he felt, as leader of a disfranchised group, he could do nothing.

The increasing migration of blacks to cities brought another issue to the forefront during this period—urban residential segregation. Although he did not take a central role in the fight to overturn city ordinances that excluded blacks from

certain neighborhoods or districts, Washington nonetheless opposed city segregation ordinances. He also believed that African Americans should protest
openly against such restrictions. "We are sure this act is wholly unconstitutional
and cannot stand before any unprejudiced court," he wrote to Benjamin J. Davis,
of Atlanta, shortly after that city adopted an exclusionary ordinance. "What are
you going to do about it?" He advised his Atlanta friend to hire the best lawyer
he could find and fight the matter, and to let him know if he needed any outside
help. One scenario, he said, involved the loss of black-owned property, since
the moment the population shifted and a black man's house was surrounded by
whites, he would be forced to sell at a huge loss. "I should be greatly disappointed if the colored people of Atlanta do not begin to fight this unjust act and
keep up the fight until victory has been attained even if it has to go to the United
States Supreme Court."[11]

In an article in the *New Republic*, "My View of Segregation Laws," Washington spoke forthrightly about why he believed segregation was an ill-advised
policy. Not only was it unjust in and of itself, but it invited other unjust
measures, such as not providing blacks with equal public services; it appealed
to race prejudice and racial hatred; the reverse—blacks seeking to segregate
whites—would never be upheld in the courts; all black districts were a "terrible
temptation to whites" seeking illicit pleasures and illegal activities; and those
denied access to housing on reputable streets were middle-class families seeking
police protection, good city services, and vice-free neighborhoods. To the argument that whites living in close proximity to blacks suffered mental and moral
degradation, he pointed out that the president of United States, five members of
the cabinet, and a large number of U.S. senators and representatives had been
raised in the South, some of them with black mammies. And last, he appealed
for equal justice because the two races could prosper only together, since "in
the gain or loss of one race, all the rest have equal claim."

At the same time Washington was expressing his opposition to segregation,
the outbreak of war in Europe brought another issue concerning African Americans to national attention. In January 1915, Senator James Reed, a Missouri
Democrat, proposed an amendment to an immigration restriction bill that would
bar all immigrants of African descent from entering the country. Unlike previous similar measures, this one passed the Senate and went to the House of Representatives. Pressed for time, Washington quickly began a campaign to defeat
the measure. In letters to editors of many newspapers, North and South, he argued that the proposed ban put blacks under the same classification as alien
criminals, it rewarded Jamaicans for their indispensable labor on the Panama
Canal with a slap in the face, and it "bottled up" the growing populations of
African descent on the small island republics in the Caribbean.

With a sense of urgency, Washington wired his supporters throughout the
country to join him in denouncing such an "unfair slap at the colored people."
He also urged black business leagues and other black organizations and associations to write to their senators and representatives, and called on Kelly Miller,
Archibald and Francis Grimké, Whitefield McKinlay, Daniel Murray, and W.

Calvin Chase, six of the most prominent blacks in the District of Columbia, to lobby before the conference committee in Congress and ''protest against exclusion of colored people.'' In the end, the newspaper, letter, and lobbying campaign was successful. The bill was defeated, a rare instance when every faction of African Americans united behind Washington.

This was indeed a rare moment. Throughout most of his career, Washington confronted hostility and opposition from most black leaders in the North and a few in the South. Among the earliest and most vociferous critics was William Monroe Trotter, editor of the *Boston Guardian*, who excoriated Washington in editorials, public addresses, and writings. ''If Mr. Booker Washington is in any sense the leader of the Colored American people he certainly has been chosen for that position by the White American race,'' Trotter wrote in 1904, claiming that no self-respecting black man could accept Washington's doctrines of limited education, racial inferiority, and opposition to civil rights. As far as it had been in his power to do so, Trotter charged, Washington was seeking to close the door of hope and opportunity for African Americans in the South.

More balanced and more effective were the searching criticisms of W.E.B. Du Bois in his *The Souls of Black Folk* (1903), in which he called for a core of college-trained, talented black leaders who could challenge the system of racial injustice and inequality. Du Bois later founded the Niagara Movement, became a leader in the NAACP, and demanded more direct action against the denial of equal rights for blacks. There were other critics, including Ida Wells-Barnett of Chicago and J. Max Barber of Atlanta, who attacked Washington for his willingness to compromise and his ''conservative'' attitudes.

Most of Washington's critics were unaware of his multidimensional activities. They also enjoyed the luxury of living in the North, where opposition to racial injustice in the South could be expressed more openly and with less fear of physical retribution. It is true that in his public addresses and writings, Washington minimized the extent of racial discrimination, accepted the ''separate but equal doctrine,'' opposed ''social equality,'' blamed blacks for their own failures, told ''darkie stories,'' lauded materialism, and eschewed politics. But, as we have seen, his activities in behalf of black voting rights, blacks on juries, and equal rights revealed a more complex leader, one who obviously hoped for a day when blacks would be accorded equal justice, and whites and blacks would live in harmony and contentment.

Nor was Washington's educational philosophy as one-sided as his critics would contend. He did not oppose college and university training for some blacks, nor courses in academic subjects and the humanities that were part of the curriculum at Tuskegee Institute. ''We need not only the industrial school, but the college and professional school as well,'' he said in 1904, ''for a people so largely segregated, as we are, from the main body of our people must have its own professional leaders who shall be able to measure with others in all forms of intellectual life.'' It would be well to remember, he continued, that black teachers, ministers, lawyers, and doctors would prosper in proportion to the intelligence and skill of the producing class of African Americans they had in their communities. Therefore, the work of Tuskegee and most black schools should of necessity be to educate as broad a spectrum as possible, most of whom would become part of the "producing class" by learning a trade or becoming farmers.[12]

Besides his secret political campaigns, Washington might be considered a reformer, or at least someone who struggled against the status quo, in other areas. At a time when most black colleges, including Howard, Hampton, and Fisk universities, had white presidents and largely white faculties, Washington insisted on hiring blacks as administrators and teachers. For example, the architect and teacher who designed many campus buildings, Robert R. Taylor, was the first black graduate of the Massachusetts Institute of Technology, and the head of the academic department in later years, Roscoe Conkling Bruce, the son of Mississippi Senator Blanche K. Bruce, was a graduate of Harvard. The list of exceptional African-American teachers and educators who came to Tuskegee was a long one.

Another area of reform was in farming and agriculture. Among Tuskegee's most famous faculty members was George Washington Carver, the eccentric genius who not only promoted the peanut but also advocated crop diversification and other improved agricultural practices, as well as the use of acorns for hog feed and the local kaolin for whitewash. It was the discoveries of Carver and the annual meetings of farmers at the school that did much to promote new farming techniques and experimentation. Indeed, agricultural reforms emanating from Tuskegee were not inconsequential, including conferences on how to stem the tide of the boll weevil by improving "methods of cotton raising," and pamphlets such as "How to Build up Worn out Soils."

Last, despite his statements against segregation, Washington supported all-black towns, especially Mound Bayou, Mississippi, and Boley, Oklahoma.

In each of these areas Booker T. Washington was seeking to institute change. By nature cautious, circumspect, secretive, and suspicious, his public persona belied his inner attitudes and deeper feelings. It would be inaccurate to label Washington a reformer, except in a most limited sense—his growing opposition to second-class citizenship and segregation—and even this was often accommodationist in tone and style. Perhaps no clear picture emerges of Washington because he himself was ambivalent about his goals and philosophy, and because his goals and philosophy changed over time.

It is clear that during the last years of his life, Washington became increasingly dissatisfied with the course of events. Perhaps to some degree he was like the black masses he spoke for, in that it would have been impossible to live in a society based on the idea of racial inferiority without wanting to reform it and change it. If his belief that self-help would lead to the salvation of his race was simplistic and unrealistic, considering the deeply embedded racial animosities of his day, it can be said that the task of solving America's racial problems remains largely incomplete. Indeed, in some ways the situation confronting African Americans at the dawn of the twenty-first century is almost as daunting and overwhelming as the obstacles Booker T. Washington confronted when he arrived alone in Tuskegee, Alabama, in 1881, with little more than the certainty that one person could make a difference.

Although at the time of his death from arteriosclerosis on 14 November 1915, few could deny he had made a difference, it was equally true that racial hatred and racial segregation had grown steadily during his decades as America's preeminent black leader.

NOTES

1. Booker T. Washington, *Up from Slavery: An Autobiography* (New York, 1901), repr. in John Hope Franklin, ed., *Three Negro Classics* (New York, 1965), 31.

2. Louis R. Harlan, *Booker T. Washington: The Making of a Black Leader, 1856–1901* (New York, 1972), 56.

3. Emma Lou Thornbrough, ed., *Booker T. Washington* (Englewood Cliffs, N.J., 1969), 33–36.

4. Edward L. Ayers, *The Promise of the New South: Life After Reconstruction* (New York, 1992), 325–326.

5. Loren Schweninger, ''From Assertiveness to Individualism: The Difficult Path from Slavery to Freedom,'' in Richard O. Curry and Lawrence B. Goodheart, eds., *American Chameleon: Individualism in Trans-National Context* (Kent, Ohio, 1991), 131.

6. Louis R. Harlan, *Booker T. Washington: The Wizard of Tuskegee, 1901–1915* (New York, 1983), 52.

7. Ibid., 245–247.

8. Ibid., 248–249.

9. Thornbrough, *Booker T. Washington*, 72–73.

10. Ibid., 74–75; Harlan, *The Wizard*, 417.

11. Ibid., 426.

12. Ibid., 174–175.

BIBLIOGRAPHY

Denton, Virginia L. *Booker T. Washington and the Adult Education Movement.* Gainesville, Fla., 1993.

Harlan, Louis R. *Booker T. Washington: The Making of a Black Leader, 1856–1901.* New York, 1972.

———. *Booker T. Washington: The Wizard of Tuskegee, 1901–1915.* New York, 1983.

Harlan, Louis R., and Raymond W. Smock, eds. *The Booker T. Washington Papers.* 14 vols. Urbana, Ill., 1972–1989.

Hawkins, Hugh, ed. *Booker T. Washington and His Critics.* Lexington, Mass., 1974.

Meier, August. *Negro Thought in America, 1880–1915: Racial Ideologies in the Age of Booker T. Washington.* Ann Arbor, Mich., 1963.

Spencer, Samuel R., Jr. *Booker T. Washington and the Negro's Place in American Life.* Boston, 1955.

Thornbrough, Emma Lou, ed. *Booker T. Washington.* Englewood Cliffs, N.J., 1969.

Washington, Booker T. *The Story of My Life and Work.* Naperville, Ill., 1900.

———. *Up from Slavery: An Autobiography.* New York, 1901.

Tom Watson
and Populism

BARTON C. SHAW

When Tom Watson died in 1922, Eugene V. Debs wrote to Watson's widow, describing her late husband as a "great man, a heroic soul." Others were similarly moved, including the Ku Klux Klan, which sent a huge cross of roses. For a short moment, reformers and racists were united in mourning.[1]

Tom Watson's character and politics continue to perplex historians, challenging them to fathom a life filled with mystery, drama, and ambiguity. At times Watson himself seemed baffled by his career and was reduced to cryptic pronouncements upon his own work. Such was the epitaph that he wrote for himself. Although never inscribed on his tombstone, it proclaimed: "Here lies the enemy of the Bourbons, the Jesuits and the Inasmuches."[2]

Thomas Edward Watson was born on 5 September 1856 in a log cabin three miles outside the town of Thomson, Georgia. His parents were John and Ann Maddox Watson; the cabin was the home of his grandfather, Thomas Miles Watson, a planter who owned 1,300 acres and 45 slaves. In later years, Watson wrote lovingly of his early boyhood and of the plantation on which he was born. He especially remembered his grandfather, a man who strode the grounds with "the calm, dignified air of one who is used to being obeyed, and who has no anxieties; a stately, self-contained, self-reliant man."[3] The lordly air of his grandfather became an ideal that Watson sought to emulate. In this he failed. But he never forgot that through his grandfather he hailed from planter stock.

The Civil War exploded the idyll of Watson's childhood. By the end of the struggle, the slaves were gone, the barns were run-down, and the fields were choked with weeds. As if to proclaim the fall of the Watsons, their patriarch, Thomas Miles Watson, died just a few days after the death of the Confederacy. Watson's father tried to rebuild the plantation, but his impractical schemes drove his family into poverty. Afterward, he took to drink and suffered fits of anger and depression. Young Tom was sometimes the victim of his father's wrath. Many years later, Watson observed that his career might have been different "had I not been abused, ridiculed, mocked and scorned."[4]

Unlike his father, Watson's mother was sensitive and ambitious for her son. "From her . . . I got the passionate sympathy for oppressed humanity," Watson later wrote; "from her, my driving power; from her, my capacity for work." Watson's mother was indeed a remarkable woman. Although self-educated, she was a lover of books, in particular of French history. Time and again she sacrificed to provide her son with the opportunity to study. Her efforts bore fruit: Watson became a superb student and a ravenous reader.[5]

There was, however, little in the shabby town of Thomson to beckon such a boy to greatness or even distinction. But nearby there lived, at least by Southern lights, two nearly mythic figures: Alexander Stephens of Crawfordville and Robert Toombs of Washington. Stephens had served as vice president of the Confederate States of America, and Toombs had sat in the U.S. Senate and had served as a rebel general and as secretary of state of the Confederacy. Both were brilliant, charismatic, and witty; both were political mavericks who spoke for planters and yeomen. Their enemies were the so-called Bourbons, the men who promoted industrialization, railroads, and diversified farming. Watson was profoundly influenced by Stephens and Toombs and their battles. Nor was he alone. His section of Georgia—the land west of Augusta, later to become the Tenth Congressional District—was remarkable for its renegade tradition. A stronghold of Whig politics and antisecessionist thinking in the antebellum years, it possessed little love for the Democratic party. Indeed, such a sentiment helped Tom Watson bring populism to this region in the 1890s.

It was not just renegade politics that prepared the way for populism. In the 1870s and 1880s, the Georgia countryside sank into economic depression. Year after year, as the price of cotton declined, yeomen went bankrupt and became sharecroppers or tenant farmers. Among them were the once-proud Watsons. The last of their land was sold in 1873. Rather than accept the humiliation of sharecropping, they moved to Augusta, where Watson's father opened a saloon and rooming house. In time, this enterprise failed.

Despite their poverty, in 1872 the Watsons were able to scrape together a little money. That sum and a scholarship for poor boys won Tom Watson a place in the freshman class of Mercer University in Macon, Georgia. As a student, Watson especially enjoyed debate, at which he exhibited considerable skill. After two years, however, he withdrew from Mercer, unable to pay his tuition. Despite this setback, Watson's goal was clear. He would become "one of the first men of the State," he assured his father. "I have no great wish for money for myself; I only wish for fame."[6]

But until that day came, Watson was compelled to make a living. Like many poor but educated young men, he first turned to teaching. Eventually, he read law and passed the Georgia bar examination in 1875. Watson was a natural lawyer, his quick wit and clever tongue making him a formidable defense attorney. Watson soon prospered, and he became a prominent figure in his part of Georgia. In 1875 he married Georgia Durham, the adopted daughter of a local physician, and from 1882 to 1884 he served as a Democrat in the Georgia House of Representatives. Watson also turned to farming but with less success. He diversified his several thousand acres by planting fruit as well as cotton. He found, however, that at harvest time railroad shipping rates soared. His fruit, in particular, was at the mercy of the railroads, which left him with little choice but to pay the rates or let his produce rot. Such experience may partly explain his later support for government ownership of the railroads.

As the years passed, the plight of Georgia farmers grew worse. The price of cotton fell, and more and more yeomen lost their land. Out of such misery sprang the National Farmers' Alliance and Industrial Union. Founded in Texas in the late 1870s, it swept across the South in the late 1880s. By the end of the decade, it claimed 3 million members, 85,000 of whom lived in Georgia. At the local level, hundreds of suballiances offered farmers the opportunity to talk and think about their plight. Soon many of them rejected the idea that the overproduction of cotton was the root of their problems. Inspired by America's greenback tradition, they looked instead to the government's monetary policy. Since the end of the Civil War, Congress had contracted the money supply, which kept prices low. An increase in the money supply, they reasoned, would drive up prices and pull them out of debt. To this end, some Alliance members favored the coinage of more silver. But others embraced a more daring scheme. Called the subtreasury plan, it proposed that the government build warehouses in which the farmers could store their nonperishable produce at harvest, when prices were always low. In return, the government would issue them paper money worth 80 percent of their stored produce's value. The farmers would then have money and could wait until the price of cotton rose. At that point, they could withdraw their cotton from the warehouse, sell it at a higher price, pay off their debts to the government and other creditors, and realize a profit. Such a scheme possessed one additional advantage: introducing paper money into the economy on such a massive scale would cause prices to rise.

Like government ownership of the railroads, another proposal debated in Alliance halls, the subtreasury plan represented a direct challenge to the philosophy of laissez-faire; in short, the government would pass legislation that would directly aid Americans of modest means. At length the Farmers' Alliance formulated such ideas into a set of demands that became the philosophical backbone of the Alliance movement and of populism. Eventually dubbed the St. Louis Platform, it called for the subtreasury plan, free silver, government ownership of the railroads, an end to national banks of issue, the direct election of U.S. senators, and other reforms.

By 1890 the Farmers' Alliance was moving into politics. In Georgia it was especially successful, electing the governor, a majority of the state's legislators, and every member of Congress. One of the new congressmen was Tom Watson, who represented the Tenth Congressional District. As a freshman congressman, he refused to behave as a backbencher. He called for the eight-hour day for workers, demanded an investigation of the Pinkerton Detective Agency, and offered a host of bills in support of Alliance demands. All of these measures failed. Watson gained national attention, however, when he accused several congressmen of being drunk while conducting House business—a revelation that nearly brought down on him a vote of censure from his furious colleagues. Despite this, Watson was the author of one successful measure: a resolution that set up an experimental program for the rural free delivery of the mail. In later years, he was among a half-dozen men who claimed to be the father of R.F.D.

By September 1891 Watson had grown deeply frustrated by failure of Congress to enact serious reforms. For a time he remained silent about his plans, but many people predicted that he would bolt the Democratic party and join the newly formed People's party. Watson's position became clear in October 1891, when he established a Georgia newspaper called *The People's Party Paper.* Nine months later his first book appeared, *The People's Party Campaign Book. Not a Revolt; It Is a Revolution.*

In July 1892 the People's party held its first national convention, in Omaha, Nebraska. There the delegates nominated James B. Weaver for president and endorsed the St. Louis Platform. In the meantime, Watson was at work establishing the Populist party in Georgia. The party tended to attract white yeoman farmers or small planters, and it was strongest in those parts of Georgia, such as Watson's Tenth Congressional District, that had experienced a strong Alliance movement coupled with an anti-Democratic party tradition.

When the Georgia state party convention met, Watson helped write the platform, which endorsed the national party demands and called for lower state taxes and an end to the convict-lease system. At the same time, he and other party leaders realized the importance of the black vote in the coming election. Consequently, they made a daring decision: they invited a small group of black delegates to the state convention and, at Watson's urging, added a black man to the state executive committee. Shortly afterward, word swept the state that Watson had protected a black minister from a lynch mob. ''Watson has gone mad,'' a Democratic newspaper declared, and many believed that he would be assassinated. Even so, Watson had gained the affection of a host of black voters, especially in his home district. As many predicted, election day in Georgia was filled with violence. Watson lost his bid for reelection, but it was clear that the Democrats had tampered with the ballots. In 1894 he again ran for Congress, and again he was defeated. Even his opponent confessed that the results were dubious, several Democratic districts having produced more votes than there were voters. In 1895 a special election was called to determine the winner; again Watson lost.[7]

Such defeats strengthened Watson's position in the national party. The third-party press closely followed his campaigns, thundering its support for Watson and its disgust at Democratic fraud. Watson was particularly admired by the ''middle-of-the-road'' faction within his party. Middle-of-the-roaders said they stood in the middle of the Populist highway and wanted no compromising of third-party principles. Opposing them were the party's silverites. Less radical than the middle-of-the-roaders, they enthusiastically embraced the free silver issue and believed that other Populist demands should be ignored or at least deemphasized. Such a position was less radical and might make it possible to fuse with Democratic silverites.

In July 1896 the Democrats nominated William Jennings Bryan for president. Bryan eloquently defended free silver but refused to accept other third-party demands. At the Populist national convention, the schism between the fusionists and the middle-of-the-roaders threatened to wreck the party. In the end, both factions agreed to an awkward compromise: to placate the fusionists, they nominated Bryan for president; to keep the middle-of-the-roaders from walking out, they nominated Watson for vice president. The foolish hope that Bryan would substitute Watson for his Democratic running mate failed to materialize. Bryan and Watson campaigned separately, their two parties united by the weakest of links. For this and other reasons, William McKinley, the Republican presidential candidate, was elected in 1896. The defeat of the Populist ticket signaled the virtual collapse of the third party. Watson retired from politics, and in 1898 the *People's Party Paper* ceased publication.

For the next few years, Watson practiced law. By 1904 he owned 9,000 acres and had bought Hickory Hill, a mansion outside of Thomson. There he lived the life of a country squire, re-creating the world of his grandfather. He devoted his leisure hours to scholarship and journalism. Between 1899 and 1912 he wrote a novel, a history of France, and biographies of Thomas Jefferson, Andrew Jackson, and Napoleon. In 1905 he founded a national magazine, *Tom Watson's Magazine*, and a year later he established a newspaper, the *Weekly Jeffersonian*.

In 1904 Watson emerged from retirement to campaign for president as a Populist.[8] The third party was virtually dead, and he received few votes. But this token campaign gained him 22,000 votes in Georgia. With such a following apparently at his command, Watson made an astonishing proposal: he called for the disfranchisement of his former allies, the black voters. Two years later, Watson and his 22,000 followers helped elect a Democrat, Hoke Smith, as Georgia's governor. Under Smith's leadership, the voter literacy test was instituted. This, along with the poll tax, disfranchised 95 percent of black voters. Smith also led the fight to end the convict-lease system, to strengthen the state railroad commission, and to institute prohibition. With Watson's valuable support, Smith had become Georgia's most successful Progressive governor. In 1907 Watson and Smith suffered a falling out. A year later, during the state gubernatorial election, Watson shifted his support to Smith's conservative opponent. Many of Watson's flabbergasted friends deserted him. Even so, Smith was defeated.

At the same time, Watson's publications were growing increasingly bigoted. Between 1910 and 1915 Watson launched attacks upon blacks (''lynch law is a good sign''), the Roman Catholic Church (''[a] stupid, degrading faith''), and the pope (''[that] fat old dago'').[9] He wildly denounced Leo Frank, an Atlanta

Jew accused of the murder of a Christian girl in 1913. Although there existed considerable evidence to suggest Frank's innocence, Watson chose to ignore it. "Look at those bulging, satyr eyes, the protruding sensual lips, and also the animal jaw," his newspaper said of a retouched photograph of Frank. Watson's lurid invective unleashed a wave of bigotry unusual even by Georgia standards. In August 1915 his newspaper warned: "THE NEXT JEW WHO DOES WHAT FRANK DID, IS GOING TO GET EXACTLY THE SAME THING THAT WE GIVE TO NEGRO RAPISTS."[10] A few days later Frank was kidnapped from the state penitentiary and lynched in Marietta, Georgia. Watson knew in advance that an attempt would be made on Frank's life. Shortly afterward, the Ku Klux Klan was resurrected, perhaps by the very men who had murdered Frank. As one of Watson's biographers has noted, if any one person deserved credit for the revival of the Klan, it was Tom Watson.[11]

While stories about the Frank case filled the nation's newspapers, World War I erupted in Europe. Watson's thinking during this period was sometimes contradictory, but for the most part he opposed intervention, arguing that the conflict was not America's affair. When the United States at last entered the struggle in 1917, Watson sneered at President Woodrow Wilson's pronouncements about a "war to make the world safe for democracy." America was fighting, he argued, to protect Wall Street bankers and their huge loans to the allies. Similarly, Watson denounced the government's Sedition Act, which sought to silence criticism of the war. In retaliation, the Post Office Department refused to deliver Watson's newspaper and magazine to subscribers—an act that destroyed both publications. In 1918 Watson ran unsuccessfully for Congress, demanding a return of free speech and a free press in the United States. When the war ended in 1918, Watson bought a newspaper, the *Columbia Sentinel*. In its pages, he scorned the League of Nations; demanded that Eugene V. Debs, the leading Socialist and opponent of the war, be released from jail; and urged Congress to seat Victor Berger, the prominent Milwaukee Socialist. In 1920 Watson was elected to the U.S. Senate. Now old and in poor health, he nevertheless continued his assault upon the government. In particular, he criticized the standing army, which might be turned against the people.

Tom Watson died on 26 September 1922, and obituary writers set to work trying to make sense of his extraordinary life. Since that time, historians have continued the quest. Of the many questions that might be asked about Watson, three are especially important. First, to what extent did his career and personality change over time? Second, can psychological disorder or simple opportunism help explain his behavior? And, finally, what was the extent and nature of his reform zeal?[12]

Scholars have frequently used the metaphor of Dr. Jekyll and Mr. Hyde when discussing the first question. Without denying that we are dealing with the history of one man, some see distinct differences between the early and late Tom Watsons. They argue that the young Watson was surely different from the older Watson, who unleashed mobs against blacks and Jews. Other historians are less certain of this. They discern stronger connections between the two Watsons. They see, for example, a younger man who was often given to rage and violence, and who was less idealistic than is commonly thought.[13]

Whatever position one takes on the Jekyll-and-Hyde debate, there remains the question of Watson's personality. Although some scholars have passed rather quickly over the state of Watson's mental health, many think it is central to the Watson story. Psychological problems always seemed to stir beneath the surface during his early and middle years. In the last fifteen years of his life, however, they emerged in the form of depression, alcoholism, and fears of persecution.[14]

But is this the whole story? Watson was, after all, a politician. Did political opportunism ever influence his behavior? A cynic might note that when it was expedient to defend blacks, Watson defended blacks, and when it was expedient to desert them, he deserted them. As to his anti-Semitism, it should be remembered that in 1901 Watson was counsel for Sigmund Lichtenstein, an Adrian, Georgia, Jew accused of murdering a local Christian. Watson successfully defended his client, reminding the jury that Lichtenstein was a member of "that noble race of people in whose veins flow [*sic*] the godly blood of Moses, David, and the prophets." Watson ended his appeal to the jury thus: "No Jew can murder. And you know that I am not telling you anything that's not true."[15]

Perhaps the friends of Leo Frank remembered the Lichtenstein case when they searched for a defense attorney in 1913. Or perhaps they simply wanted to retain the best lawyer in the state. Whatever their motives, they approached Watson. He declined their offer, explaining that he had given up the practice of law. Did he believe in Frank's guilt—that Jews were now capable of murder? This is unknown. What is known is that Watson's newspaper and magazine remained silent about the Frank case for nearly a year. Only in March 1914 did they suddenly enter the struggle with such bloodthirsty, and lucrative, savagery. The weekly circulation of the *Jeffersonian* climbed from 25,000 to 87,000.

Finally, what of Tom Watson's politics? Whether driven by idealism, neurosis, or opportunism, where did Watson stand on the great issues of his day? Some see a career that was dangerously reactionary, bending in the direction of home-grown American fascism.[16] But others argue that Watson's loyalty to reform must not be forgotten, a loyalty that persisted, if in erratic and somewhat diluted form, into his old age. In large measure, Watson began and ended his career within the American reform camp—a camp, it should be remembered, often tainted by racism and anti-Semitism.

But where did he stand within this camp?[17] To answer such a question, one must turn to Watson's speeches and editorials. Many of his enemies believed they had revealed him as a Socialist. In 1892 Watson called for government ownership of the railroads and described populism as a "revolution"; in later years he rushed to the defense of such Socialists as Eugene V. Debs and Victor Berger; and as a senator, he called for the diplomatic recognition of the Soviet Union. "You are afraid of your own proletariat," Watson told the Senate in 1922.

That is what you are afraid of. You are afraid of the dissatisfied workman, thrown out of employment by these soulless, these heartless, these insatiable trusts and combinations of capital; you are afraid of the millions of men and women and children who do not have enough to eat in this land of bounteous harvests; not enough to wear in the very cotton fields where their hands bring forth the staple that clothes the world.[18]

Such words, however, can be misinterpreted. As a populist, Watson offered little that would have helped Georgia's rural proletariat—that is, sharecroppers and tenant farmers. He also made it clear that he loathed socialism and embraced almost all forms of private ownership. Later he championed capitalism in debates with Daniel De Leon, the editor of the *Daily People*. Watson believed, however, that the government had fallen into the hands of criminals and corporations. What followed was a patent evil: unregulated capitalism, which produced wealth for a few and poverty for many.

In the last decade of his life, Watson devoted most of his energies to foreign affairs. He scorned all forms of overseas adventurism and insisted that America stay out of the affairs of foreign states. On international questions, Watson's philosophy was closely linked to his thinking on domestic affairs. Behind the Mexican intervention, World War I, and other crises, he saw the work of mighty corporations, swelling their profits at the expense of American and foreign peoples. It made perfect sense to Watson that such interests should endeavor to silence their enemies with sedition acts and red scares.

When Watson died, editors remarked upon the bizarre, seemingly inexplicable course of his life—a life that produced much that was fine and much that was terrible. But for Watson's most devoted followers, such equivocation was unacceptable. For them a noble figure had passed from the scene. To perpetuate his memory, they erected two monuments, both of which still can be seen. One is a marble slab that rests over his grave in Thomson; the other is a statue that stands before the door of the Georgia state capitol. Both are inscribed with simple words testifying to Watson's greatness. Yet neither bears witness to the dark Tom Watson and to the strange complexity of his life. Perhaps Watson came closer to the mark with his own epitaph.

NOTES

1. C. Vann Woodward, *Tom Watson, Agrarian Rebel* (New York, 1938), 486; Harry Golden, *A Little Girl Is Dead* (New York, 1965), 296.

2. William W. Brewton, *The Life of Thomas E. Watson* (Atlanta, 1926), 401.

3. Thomas E. Watson, *Bethany: A Story of the Old South* (New York, 1904), 10.

4. Woodward, *Tom Watson*, 1–5, 12–14, 18.

5. Brewton, *Thomas E. Watson*, 15–17, 25–29, 30–44.

6. Ibid., 49–81; Woodward, *Tom Watson*, 30.

7. Barton C. Shaw, *The Wool-Hat Boys: Georgia's Populist Party* (Baton Rouge, La., 1984), 63–77, 102–123. This source indicates that the Populists were also guilty of election fraud. See also Alex Mathews Arnett, *The Populist Movement in Georgia: A*

View of the "Agrarian Crusade" in Light of Solid-South Politics, Economics, and Public Law (1922; repr. New York, 1967).

8. In 1908 Tom Watson again ran for president as a Populist. He received 28,500 votes, of which 16,600 were cast in Georgia.

9. Woodward, *Tom Watson*, 432, 420, 433.

10. Ibid., 438, 443.

11. Ibid., 450.

12. The following discussion should not be understood to mean that any historian has offered a monocausal explanation for Watson's personality or career. In fact, most scholars see a variety of influences that helped shape the man.

13. See, for example, Woodward, *Tom Watson*, passim; and Shaw, *Wool-Hat Boys*, 208–211. For Woodward's rejoinder to Shaw, see C. Vann Woodward, *Thinking Back: The Perils of Writing History* (Baton Rouge, La., 1986), 29–42. See also Charles Crowe, "Tom Watson, Populists, and Blacks Reconsidered," *Journal of Negro History* 55 (1970): 99–116; Robert Saunders, "The Transformation of Tom Watson," *Georgia Historical Quarterly* 54 (1970): 339–356; Lawrence Friedman, *The White Savage: Racial Fantasies in the Postbellum South* (Englewood Cliffs, N.J., 1970).

14. For a historian who deemphasizes the importance of Watson's mental health, see Richard Nelson, "The Cultural Contradictions of Populism: Tom Watson's Tragic Vision of Power, Politics, and History," *Georgia Historical Quarterly* 72 (1988): 4. For examples of historians who believe that Watson's mental health is an important part of the Watson story, see Woodward, *Tom Watson*, and Shaw, *Wool-Hat Boys*, 208–211.

15. Louis E. Schmier, "No Jew Can Murder: Memories of Tom Watson and the Lichtenstein Murder Case of 1901," *Georgia Historical Quarterly* 70 (1986): 453.

16. Daniel Bell, "The Face of Tomorrow: The Grass Roots of American Jew Hatred," *Jewish Frontier* 11 (6 June 1944): 47.

17. For a historian who has tried to find a republican foundation to Watson's thinking, see Nelson, "The Cultural Contradictions of Populism," 1–29.

18. Woodward, *Tom Watson*, 480.

BIBLIOGRAPHY

Arnett, Alex Mathews. *The Populist Movement in Georgia: A View of the "Agrarian Crusade" in Light of Solid-South Politics, Economics and Public Law.* 1922; repr. New York, 1967.

Ayers, Edward L. *The Promise of the New South: Life After Reconstruction.* New York, 1992.

Brewton, William W. *The Life of Thomas E. Watson.* Atlanta, 1926.

Crowe, Charles. "Tom Watson, Populists, and Blacks Reconsidered." *Journal of Negro History* 55 (1970): 99–116.

Dinnerstein, Leonard. *The Leo Frank Case.* New York, 1968.

Friedman, Lawrence. *The White Savage: Racial Fantasies in the Postbellum South.* Englewood Cliffs, N.J., 1970.

Golden, Harry. *A Little Girl Is Dead.* New York, 1965.

MacLean, Nancy. "The Leo Frank Case Reconsidered: Gender and Sexual Politics in the Making of Reactionary Populism." *Journal of American History* 78 (1991): 917–948.

McMath, Robert C., Jr. *The Populist Vanguard: A History of the Southern Farmers' Alliance*. Chapel Hill, N.C., 1975.

———. *American Populism: A Social History, 1877–1900*. Boston, 1991.

Nelson, Richard. "The Cultural Contradictions of Populism: Tom Watson's Tragic Vision of Power, Politics, and History." *Georgia Historical Quarterly* 72 (1988): 1–29.

Pollack, Norman. *The Just Polity: Populism, Law, and Human Welfare*. Urbana, Ill., 1987.

Saunders, Robert. "The Transformation of Tom Watson, 1894–1895." *Georgia Historical Quarterly* 54 (1970): 339–356.

Schmier, Louis E. "No Jew Can Murder: Memories of Tom Watson and the Lichtenstein Murder Case of 1901." *Georgia Historical Quarterly* 70 (1986): 433–455.

Shaw, Barton C. *The Wool-Hat Boys: Georgia's Populist Party*. Baton Rouge, La., 1984.

Woodward, C. Vann. *Tom Watson, Agrarian Rebel*. New York, 1938.

———. *Thinking Back: The Perils of Writing History*. Baton Rouge, La., 1986.

Ida Wells-Barnett
and the African-American Anti-Lynching Campaign

LINDA O. McMURRY

The lynchings of Thomas Moss, Calvin McDowell, and Will Stewart in March 1892 were not significant for their rarity—that year at least 158 other African Americans were killed by angry mobs for alleged offenses against white society. The location of the lynchings in Memphis, Tennessee, was also not remarkable; seventeen other black Tennesseans were lynched that year and forty-six African Americans had been killed in an 1866 race riot in Memphis. The three deaths assumed a special importance mostly because of their impact on the young journalist, Ida B. Wells. She knew all three men and was godmother to Moss's daughter. Outraged by the murder of her friends, Wells mobilized her considerable talents and energies to battle the evil of mob violence. Thus began the perfect marriage of an individual and a cause.

Born to slave parents on 16 July 1862, in Holly Springs, Mississippi, Wells was the eldest of seven children. In 1878 her parents, James Wells and Lizzie Bell, and one sibling died in a yellow fever epidemic. Wells returned from Shaw (later Rust) University and rejected plans to divide the remaining children among friends and relatives. Instead, at the age of sixteen, she assumed responsibility for her brothers and sisters and became head of the household. She began teaching and eventually moved to Memphis, where she participated in the rich cultural life of the black elite. There she might have led a conventional life but for her temperament and a series of events.

The first event occurred on 4 May 1884, when a conductor asked Wells to leave the ladies' car of a train. She refused, then bit him on the hand when he sought to remove her forcibly, and finally sued the railroad. She won the suit, lost it on appeal, and launched her career as a journalist and a firebrand. Wells became a partner and editor of the Memphis *Free Speech and Headlight* in 1889. She also taught until 1891, when she was dismissed after criticizing the conditions of the local black schools in the newspaper. Becoming a full-time journalist, she continued to write militant articles, which were frequently reprinted in other black newspapers under her pen name, "Iola." By 1892 she had become known as a forceful, energetic, and uncompromising foe of discrimination.

The lynching of her three friends that year focused Wells's anger on the plague of mob violence. Lynching, however, was not a new issue to either her or the black community. The year before, she had written an editorial of praise for African Americans in Georgetown, Kentucky, who had set fire to the town after a lynching there. She could hardly be unaware of the growing menace of racial violence—too many black Southerners were being killed in the aftermath of Reconstruction. Murder by mobs had replaced the slave master's whip as an instrument to control recalcitrant blacks. The institution of slavery had served well to keep not merely slaves but all African Americans in various states of quasi-freedom. When slavery was destroyed in the course of the Civil War, white Southerners immediately sought to find other methods of racial domination.

The white South's desire for a new form of slavery was briefly thwarted by Republican rule in the region and the Thirteenth, Fourteenth, and Fifteenth amendments. In many areas, however, violence quickly became the remedy for emancipation and black political empowerment, as in the 1866 riot in Memphis. By the 1890s, white Southerners were freed of local Republican governments and had begun to craft a caste system based upon legalized repression. That system was like a three-legged stool with disfranchisement, segregation, and the threat of violence as its supports. The lynching of almost 2,000 African Americans between 1882 and 1902 bears witness to the whites' reliance on violence to overcome black resistance to segregation and disfranchisement.

White Southerners of that era, like the slave masters before them, were equipped with consciences. They not only wanted to dominate their black neighbors; they also wanted to feel their actions were justified. They had inherited a ready-made ideological basis for discrimination: the doctrine of black inferiority. Reinforced by arguments from Social Darwinists and American imperialists, the myths of white supremacy found fertile ground and became even more deeply rooted in the North as well as the South. Segregation and the denial of suffrage needed explanation in a democracy; denial of due process and murder demanded even more compelling arguments for justification. In an ironic distortion of facts, although white men had been raping black women with impunity for more than a century, the black man was depicted as a fiendish beast who could be restrained from ravishing white women only by extreme measures. The cry of "rape" excused torture, mutilation, and murder to both Northern and Southern whites. Few whites were outspoken critics of lynching in the 1890s.

African Americans were quicker to deplore lynch law. They understood that, whatever its cause, violence was the cement of the new caste system that replaced slavery as a source of cheap labor and exploitation. Most black leaders realized that just as the slave master's whip had prevented true freedom for any African American, the ability of whites to murder blacks with impunity limited all black freedom after emancipation. Thus lynching was one issue consistently recurring in the speeches and platforms of black leaders and organizations throughout the United States. Before the Civil War the Black Convention movement had emerged in the North to fight slavery and to advance the status of free blacks. After the war, conventions were held in both the South and the North, and racial violence was included on the agendas of all. Black newspapers and such organizations as the Afro-American League denounced lynching. Every major leader publicly deplored mob violence. The chorus of cries for justice was loud and long—but still ignored. Rape was seen as far more barbaric than lynching.

So pervasive was the myth that lynching resulted from rape that even black spokesmen often did not challenge it. Many included a denunciation of rape with appeals to let the justice system do its job; they merely asked that juries and judges, rather than mobs, decide guilt and mete out punishment. Wells later wrote that before the 1892 lynchings in Memphis, "Like many another person who had read of lynching in the South, I had accepted the idea meant to be conveyed—that although lynching was irregular and contrary to law and order, unreasoning anger over the terrible crime of rape led to the lynching; that perhaps the brute deserved death anyhow."[1]

The lynchings of Moss, McDowell, and Stewart opened her eyes and made her determined to open other eyes. None of the victims were even accused of rape. All were affiliated with the People's Grocery, which opened across the street from a store owned by a white merchant, W. H. Barret. Unhappy with his new competition, Barret was hostile and provoked a number of violent encounters. He then convinced a grand jury to indict the officials of the People's Grocery for operating a public nuisance. After some outraged blacks used violent rhetoric at a public meeting, Barret persuaded a criminal court judge to issue arrest warrants for two of his competitors, on the charge of conspiring against whites. When nine deputized white men in civilian clothes approached the store after dark, they were mistaken for a mob and fired upon. Three whites were wounded, and McDowell and Stewart were immediately arrested.

Chilling stories of race riot circulated in Memphis. As panic spread, black residents were disarmed by orders of the judge, and a small army of white men helped deputies arrest thirty more "rioters," including Thomas Moss. Four days after the incident, nine whites entered the jail at 3 A.M., dragged Moss, McDowell, and Stewart about nine miles out of town, and shot them. Sorrow at the loss of "three of the best specimens of young since-the-war Afro-American manhood" mingled in Wells's mind with the horror of knowing that no one would ever stand trial for the crime.[2]

Angry and discouraged, Wells wrote a number of editorials for the *Free Speech* and suggested that black citizens migrate west to find justice. When about 2,000 did leave, a number of white businesses felt the economic impact—

especially the streetcar company, which was being boycotted. Its owners asked the newspaper to tell blacks to return to the streetcars. Wells firmly refused their requests. She also began to investigate lynchings, and discovered that only about a fourth of lynching victims were even accused of rape. In addition, many times the charges of rape were unjustified. Merely speaking to a white woman in a suggestive way could be labeled "attempted rape." Wells also ascertained that far more voluntary sexual liaisons occurred between white women and black men than white men would acknowledge. The discovery of such relationships usually prompted cries of rape.

In a *Free Speech* editorial that appeared on 21 May 1892, Wells dared to say aloud what white men did not want to hear. She wrote, "Nobody in this section of the country believes the old thread bare lie that Negro men rape white women. If Southern white men are not careful, they will over-reach themselves and public sentiment will have a reaction; a conclusion will then be reached which will be very damaging to the moral reputation of their women."[3] Whites were outraged. One editorial suggested it was the duty of whites "to tie the wretch who utters these calumnies to a stake at the intersection of Main and Madison Sts., brand him in the forehead with a hot iron and perform upon him a surgical operation with a pair of tailor's shears."[4]

Even if she had been equipped with the requisite anatomy for such surgery, Wells was beyond the reach of a mob, attending a conference of the African Methodist Episcopal Church. Wrongly suspected of authorship, coeditor J. L. Fleming fled the city before a mob descended on the *Free Speech* office and vented its anger on the furnishings and machinery. Wells heeded the warnings not to return to Memphis and accepted an offer from T. Thomas Fortune of the *New York Age* to provide him with a list of her subscribers for a fourth interest in his paper. Her first assignment was to write a series of articles on lynching.

Calling herself "Exiled," Wells wrote an extensive article in June, describing the events in Memphis and recounting similar lynchings throughout the South. Ten thousand copies of that edition of the *Age* were distributed around the nation; a thousand copies were sold in Memphis. Wells's words created a sensation within the black community but were virtually ignored by the white press. Then black women in New York provided Wells with a platform from which to reach a larger audience. On 5 October 1892, at Lyric Hall, they organized and sponsored a testimonial meeting to raise funds to restart the *Free Speech*.

Hundreds of women attended, coming from Philadelphia and Boston as well as New York. Wells cried as she told of the murder of her friend Tom Moss. Dismayed by her uncharacteristic "weakness," she was delighted to be presented with a gold brooch and $500. She used the money not to restart her paper but to expand and publish her article as a pamphlet titled *Southern Horrors*. As usual she did not mince her words. After recounting a lynching that was thwarted by armed blacks, she wrote, "The lesson this teaches and which every Afro-American should ponder well, is that a Winchester rifle should have a place of honor in every black home, and it should be used for that protection which the law refuses to give.''[5]

Wells received numerous invitations to speak throughout the Northeast. By early 1893 her words had garnered enough attention to cause the white press of Memphis to seek to discredit her by defaming her character. She considered suing the *Memphis Commercial* for libel and consulted a number of attorneys, including Ferdinand L. Barnett. She and Frederick Douglass were working with Barnett to publish a pamphlet protesting the exclusion of African Americans at the Chicago World's Columbian Exposition in 1893. Wells was diverted from both projects by an invitation from the British reformer and editor of *Anti-Caste*, Catherine Impey, to come to England to help organize an ''Emancipation League.''

With her expenses paid, Wells left for England on 5 April 1893. She sought to play a role similar to that of Douglass prior to the Civil War in motivating the English people to join the abolitionist movement. Aware that white Americans were still sensitive to British criticism, she wrote: ''The moral agencies at work in Great Britain did much for the final overthrow of chattel slavery. They can in like manner pray, write, preach, talk and act against civil and industrial slavery; against the hanging, shooting and burning alive of a powerless race.''[6] Before she returned to America in June, her hosts founded the Society for the Recognition of the Brotherhood of Man, to combat all forms of discrimination, especially lynching.

Wells returned to Chicago instead of New York, arriving in time to aid in the publication of 20,000 copies of the pamphlet *The Reason Why the Colored American Is not in the World's Columbian Exposition*. It included her article ''Lynch Law'' as well as articles describing both the repression and the achievements of African Americans. Wells joined Douglass at the Haitian Pavilion to distribute the pamphlets to foreign visitors. While in Chicago, she also helped found a women's club that was later named after her. At the same time she increased her contact with Ferdinand Barnett by joining the staff of his newspaper, the *Chicago Conservator*. He had established the paper in 1878, the same year that he received his law degree from Northwestern University. Barnett and Wells were ideologically compatible; their relationship began to blossom but did not bear fruit immediately, because Wells was once again invited to England by the Society for the Brotherhood of Man.

On her second trip abroad, Wells agreed to write a column about her experiences for the white-owned *Chicago Inter-Ocean*. Her return journey received more press attention both in the United States and Great Britain—partly because it was riddled with controversies. Wells became embroiled in a split between two leaders of the Society for the Brotherhood of Man, which placed her in a precarious financial position. Isabelle Mayo was outraged by Catherine Impey's indiscreet behavior with a black man and insisted on a public denunciation of Impey. When Wells refused, Mayo withdrew her financial support for the tour. Wells therefore had to solicit funds, thereby provoking questions about her motives. Although she would not criticize her friend, Wells was not at all reluctant to criticize Frances Willard, the leader of the Woman's Christian Temperance Movement (WCTU). Wells condemned Willard for comments in an 1890 speech in which Willard had said, ''The colored race multiplies like the locusts of Egypt. The grog-shop is its center of power. 'The safety of woman, of child-hood, of the home, is menaced in a thousand localities at this moment, so that the men dare not go beyond the sight of their own roof-tree.' ''[7]

Wells did not single out Willard for condemnation; she also attacked evan-gelist Dwight Moody, American churches that remained silent on lynching, and Southern governors who tolerated mob murder in their states. The willingness of Wells to castigate respected institutions and individuals for their ''moral cow-ardice'' provoked negative press coverage and alienated some previous or po-tential supporters. For example, Lady Henry Somerset, the president of the British Women's Temperance Union, published an interview with Willard that implied Wells had intentionally distorted Willard's position on lynching. Nev-ertheless, even when Wells's words caused resentment, they often had a positive impact. In a speech at the November 1894 national convention of the WCTU in Cleveland, Willard refuted the statements by Wells and at the same time publicly announced the WCTU's opposition to lynching.

Southern governors also responded to Wells's charges. Missouri Governor W. J. Stone wrote to the *London News* in response to its editorial about a lecture by Wells. He and Governor W. J. Northern of Georgia used novel arguments to discredit Wells. They asserted that she was an agent for a group of investors who sought to lure immigrants away from the South to the West, for personal financial gain. The charges of the Southern white press tended to be more scur-rilous. The *London Post* characterized two articles from the *Memphis Commer-cial* as ''very coarse in tone, and some of the language is such as could not possibly be reproduced in an English journal.''[8]

Undoubtedly, the favored tactic to discredit Wells was to report on black opposition to her activities. A number of African Americans did question the impact of the controversy that seemed to follow in her wake. Some moderated their support for her, for fear of alienating their white American allies, but few were willing to speak out against her publicly. Those who did were immediately proclaimed the ''legitimate'' spokespeople for their fellow African Americans by the white press in the United States. Memphis papers reported that a local black editor had proclaimed Wells's charges false and slanderous. The *New York Times* quoted a black Democratic politician who denounced Wells as a ''fraud'' and insisted, ''A reputable or respectable negro has never been lynched, and never will be.''[9] Although personal ambition likely influenced most such state-ments, Wells did alienate some black leaders by her willingness to criticize fellow African Americans for their timidity. Indeed, the list of leaders, black and white, whom Wells chastised grew over the course of her life to include U.S. presidents, Jane Addams, Susan B. Anthony, Frederick Douglass, Booker T. Washington, and W.E.B. Du Bois.

Her disdain of compromise and discreet language may have limited Wells's role as an organizational leader, but it made her written and oral rhetoric compelling. Both male colleagues and reporters were especially mesmerized by the contrast between her "feminine beauty" and her graphic descriptions of atrocities. Few reformers have provoked as many comments on their physical appearance. Reports of her English speeches indicate that audiences were often moved to tears as Wells recounted the grisly details of lynchings. In 102 lectures she constantly stressed that lynching was not about rape but about power. She also emphasized that most white American reformers were either silent on the issue or muffled their criticisms with disclaimers about the horrors of rape. Her arguments convinced numerous British leaders of the need to speak out against lynching in order to awaken and educate white Americans to its evils. During her second tour, supporters formed the Anti-Lynching Committee in London. The son-in-law of Queen Victoria headed the organization, and its membership included many distinguished persons.

Wells returned to New York in July 1894 to a mixed reception. Fellow African Americans welcomed her at a meeting in Fleet Street A.M.E. Church. The *New York Times* greeted her with a hostile editorial. It noted that the day after her arrival, a black man had assaulted a white woman in the city and declared, "The circumstances of his fiendish crime may serve to convince the mulatress missionary that the promulgation in New York just now of her theory of Negro outrages is, to say the least, inopportune."[10]

The editorial did not deter Wells from pledging to spend a year lecturing in the United States if she received financial support. Searching for funding, Wells called for the formation of a black anti-lynching organization. This was not a new idea; two previous groups had grown out of the desire to combat mob justice. T. Thomas Fortune had founded the Afro-American League in 1890, primarily as an anti-lynching vehicle; however, it lost that focus after the first convention and became increasingly inactive. In 1893 Henry McNeal Turner had issued a call for a convention that resulted in the formation of the Equal Rights Council. Both in his call and in his keynote address Turner highlighted lynching as the most critical issue facing African Americans. Nevertheless, both the Council and the League soon focused more on such issues as streetcar segregation—reflecting the priorities of the black elite that was far more likely to encounter discrimination than to be lynched. Anger over racial violence seemed to provoke conventions but not to sustain organizations.

Wells was not unusual for speaking out against lynching, but she was the only black leader to make it the focus of her efforts for an extended period of time. Perhaps lynching had touched her more personally than most middle- and upper-class African Americans. Thomas Moss had been a close friend, and his murder in Memphis brought home the fact that middle-class status did not immunize one from lynching. Probably her temperament and talents drew Wells to the issue. Her anger and fiery rhetoric were more appropriately applied to the hideous nature of lynching than to less graphic and concrete concerns.

Unable to get financial backing from any organization, Wells began to accept invitations from around the country and charge lecture fees to support her work. Her home base became Chicago, partly because that was where Ferdinand Barnett lived. As she traveled, his letters followed her. Almost a year after her return from England, they were married, on 27 June 1895. He was as militant as she was and fully supported her crusade. Four days after the wedding he gave her his newspaper, the *Chicago Conservator*, and centered his own efforts on the practice of law and politics. Even after their four children were born, Wells-Barnett returned to the lecture circuit, carrying nursing babies with her.

In addition to her newspaper work and lectures, Wells-Barnett continued her investigations of lynchings. She published her findings in periodicals and pamphlets. One such pamphlet, which appeared in 1895, was titled *A Red Record, Tabulated Statistics and Alleged Causes of Lynchings in the United States, 1892–1893–1894*. As usual, Wells-Barnett utilized the gruesome details of various lynchings to show the irrational barbarism of mob justice. She also stressed that white men continued to escape punishment for raping black women and girls. One case illustrates her tactics especially well. She described the murder of Eph. Grizzard for what she determined to be a voluntary liaison with a white woman in Tennessee. While the governor and state militia stood by, Grizzard was "dragged through the streets in broad daylight, knives plunged into him at every step, and with every fiendish cruelty that a frenzied mob could devise, he was at last swung out on a bridge with hands cut to pieces as he tried to climb up the stanchions." Wells-Barnett further noted that the mob left undisturbed in the same jail a white man who had raped an eight-year-old girl. "The outrage upon helpless childhood needed no avenging in this case; she was black."[11]

Such language in both her literature and her lectures continued to inspire white attacks on Wells-Barnett's character. In 1895 one Missouri journalist impugned not only her morality but also that of black women in general. The argument was a common one: black women did not need protecting because they had no morals to protect. Rooted in the justification for the sexual exploitation of slave women, the contention had become an integral part of the defense of the differential treatment of both black and white rape victims. The charge was particularly galling to women of the black elite, who probably valued respectability even more than their white counterparts. After the journalist mailed a copy of his letter to a black women's club journal in Boston, the club's leader decided the time had come for action. Josephine St. Pierre Ruffin, who had organized the club after she had heard Wells-Barnett speak in 1893, mailed copies of the letter to other black women's clubs and called a conference of clubwomen to meet in late July at Boston to refute his charges.

The women strongly protested the insults to Wells-Barnett and to black women in general. They also formed the National Association of Colored Women (NACW), the first permanent national organization to unite black clubwomen. Local women's groups had been instrumental in supporting Wells-Barnett from the beginning of her anti-lynching work, often sponsoring her visits to their cities. At the same time, her activities had spawned a number of those groups. Wells-Barnett hoped the NACW would become the national anti-lynching organization she had long sought. However, the women did not accept her as their leader or her cause as their issue.

Wells-Barnett was bitterly disappointed. She accused Mary Church Terrell, who had previously lectured against lynching, of purposefully ignoring the issue as NACW president, in order to reduce Wells-Barnett's influence. Actually, although the women believed in her work, Wells-Barnett was far too abrasive and controversial to be the leader of or the symbol for a group that prized respectability. Nevertheless, local women's groups continued to fight mob violence, especially the Ida B. Wells Club of Chicago. It wrote to both the president and Congress to protest lynching, and sent a delegation to visit Governor John P. Altgeld after an Illinois man was lynched.

Anger over particular lynchings and race riots continued to spark organizational efforts. The lynchings of two black postmasters in 1898 led to the revitalization and reorganization of the Afro-American League as the Afro-American Council. Wells-Barnett went with the group's delegation to ask President William McKinley for federal action on the murder of these federal officers. She also served as the Council's secretary in 1899 and later became the chair of its Anti-Lynching Bureau. Wells-Barnett used the organization as a pulpit from which she preached against the ideology of Booker T. Washington and the actions of President McKinley, until Washington and his supporters wrested control of the Council from the ''militants.''

Like most of the Southern-based opponents to lynching, Booker T. Washington made public denunciations of lynching that used relatively restrained rhetoric. The strength of his interest in lynching vacillated but later became more constant with the arrival of Monroe N. Work at Tuskegee. Work had long been compiling lynching statistics, and in 1912, he began issuing the annual Tuskegee Lynching Reports. Sent to Southern newspapers and leaders, the reports became widely accepted as accurate and provided ammunition to Southern-based, biracial anti-lynching organizations. First, however, a race riot in 1908 led to the formation of a Northern-based, biracial organization.

Every black leader was alarmed by the increasing number of race riots at the turn of the century. In riots the white mob did not murder an individual for a specific offense but instead turned its wrath on the black community as a whole, beating and killing African Americans randomly while destroying property. A serious riot in Wilmington, North Carolina, helped mobilize the newly formed Council in 1898. Over the years Wells-Barnett investigated several riots and published an account of one in *Mob Rule in New Orleans* (1900). Perhaps the most significant riot, however, occurred in 1908 in Springfield, Illinois.

The Springfield riot, like the Memphis lynchings, was not remarkable for its uniqueness. There had been many riots that were much more bloody. This type of violence, unlike lynching, had never been distinctly Southern. Indeed, black migration northward in the twentieth century increasingly made riots a national problem. The significance of the Springfield riot resides in its impact. Its location in Springfield had symbolic importance for white abolitionists and their descendants because of its ties to Abraham Lincoln. They were shocked into action.

White liberals had become somewhat complacent about race relations, perhaps in part due to the positive, conciliatory ideology of Booker T. Washington, who had become the recognized "race leader" after the death of Frederick Douglass. A number of African Americans, especially such intellectuals as W.E.B. Du Bois, had been insisting for years that things were worse than Washington painted them and that immediate militant action was needed. These beliefs were the basis for the formation in 1905 of the Niagara Movement, which emphasized lynching more than Washington had. However, the Niagara Movement attracted only a few dozen African Americans and no whites.

Other kinds of reforms had occupied most white reformers during the early years of the Progressive era. The Springfield riot, however, provided the final evidence that racial violence was becoming the same kind of blight on the nation's ideals and image that slavery had once been. The riot was the spark to action, but Wells-Barnett had supplied the kindling. The publicity her crusade received at home and abroad helped make lynching an issue that could no longer be rationalized or ignored. At the urging of fellow white Progressives, the grandson of abolitionist William Lloyd Garrison issued a call to action on Lincoln's birthday in 1909.

Oswald Garrison Villard's letter led to a conference in May and to the formation of the National Association for the Advancement of Colored People (NAACP) a year later. At the conference Wells-Barnett delivered one of the key addresses, calling for the end of "color line murder" through strong federal action. To answer the frequent assertion that the federal government did not have the power to stop lynching, she noted that it had stepped in on a number of occasions to protect foreign nationals in order to prevent international incidents. "If government has power to protect a foreigner from insult," she declared, "certainly it has power to save a citizen's life."[12]

Ironically, although lynching continued to be a major focus for the NAACP, Wells-Barnett did not remain an active participant. Once again, her uncompromising personality and militant reputation limited the organizational role she would play. At the conference a Committee of Forty was named to effect a permanent organization. Its composition was designed to attract a broadly based interracial following. Ardent "radicals" and "conservatives" were avoided, and only twelve members were black. Wells-Barnett was not among them. She was especially enraged when she learned that Du Bois had been responsible for her exclusion, over the objections of some white members. According to Wells-Barnett, Du Bois justified his action on the basis that she was already represented by the inclusion of a woman with whom she worked. His responses to other black leaders at various times suggest that he did not share the spotlight much better than Booker T. Washington. Perhaps Wells-Barnett was too bright a star for Du Bois willingly to share billing with her.

Wells-Barnett was not fully appeased by the white chairman's addition of her name and later wrote, "Of course, I did a foolish thing. My anger at having been treated in such fashion outweighed my judgment and I again left the building."[13] The incident reflects two qualities that limited her effectiveness within organizations: fierce pride and an unwillingness to compromise. She was easily hurt and angered when she did not receive the respect to which she felt entitled. Such feelings were constructive when dealing with railway conductors but sabotaged both friendships and working relationships. Even when she was due the center stage, her reluctance to yield it often hurt her more than it helped her. She frequently missed getting not only the leading role but also any role at all.

Another problem was perhaps Wells-Barnett's failure to play "appropriate" gender roles. Her assertiveness likely threatened both male and female colleagues. Her unusual status is apparent in I. Garland Penn's 1891 book *The Afro-American Press and Its Editors.* Of the eighteen women chronicled within it, Wells-Barnett is the only one to be compared with male journalists. Her designation by her male colleagues as "Princess of the Press" may mark their desire to remind her of her gender. Although Wells-Barnett attributed what she viewed as snubs by the women of NACW to jealousy, their desire for respectability probably played a major role in their rejection of her leadership. She did not reflect the image of "femininity" they wished to project. According to Susan B. Anthony, Wells-Barnett even refused to play the role of feminist properly by marrying and having children—leading to what Anthony called "divided duty." There seemed to be no niche into which Wells-Barnett could comfortably be fit.

The breach between Wells-Barnett and Du Bois never healed. They were both too proud and uncompromising to cooperate. She was further angered when Villard and Du Bois chose Jane Addams to head the Chicago chapter. The choice of Addams probably reflected the desire to recruit white moderates. At any rate, as director of publicity and research, Du Bois became the only black NAACP official, ensuring Wells-Barnett's participation would be perfunctory, given their strained relationship. In addition, as the editor of *Crisis,* the association's official organ, Du Bois gave scant attention to the activities of Wells-Barnett. Nevertheless, neither the NAACP nor Wells-Barnett deserted the crusade against lynching. From its beginning, through its transition to a predominantly black organization, the NAACP sought the key to end mob violence.

Until 1918 the NAACP relied mainly on educational projects and on pressuring local and state leaders to prevent lynchings or to punish lynchers in their communities. Lynching was one of several issues absorbing the organization's attention. In the wake of an outburst of racial violence following World War I, the NAACP dedicated the bulk of its efforts from 1919 to 1924 to finding a legal remedy for mob violence. NAACP leaders recognized that ending lynching would be difficult as long as lynchers went unpunished. By refusing to prosecute or convict lynchers, state and local law officials not only made the crime risk-free but also implicitly sanctioned it. The NAACP began lobbying for a national law that would remove lynching from local jurisdictions and try lynchers in federal courts, where there was at least a possibility of conviction.

After the Dyer Bill of 1918 encountered the roadblock of states' rights, the NAACP and its congressional allies tried various weaker formulations that punished not lynchers but local authorities who refused to prosecute them. Regardless of the wording, every federal anti-lynching bill from 1918 to 1950 stumbled somewhere along the road to enactment. Since the 1960s, however, the federal government has prosecuted acquitted lynchers for the violation of their victims' civil rights.

After the NAACP launched its anti-lynching crusade, Wells-Barnett continued her own, but at a slower pace. Her major activities were investigations of particular race riots and lynchings. These included a 1909 riot in Cairo, Illinois, and one in East Saint Louis, Illinois, in 1917. In 1919 she returned to the South for the first time since 1892, to investigate a riot in Elaine, Arkansas, during which twenty-five African Americans were killed and for which twelve more were sentenced to death. Wells-Barnett's efforts were instrumental in getting the twelve men released. She continued to denounce injustice in speeches and print.

Lynching had been Wells-Barnett's primary concern, but not her only one. Following the Springfield riot, she was able to raise funds to establish the Negro Fellowship League in 1910. It served the purposes of a settlement house for black men in Chicago. She also was active in the woman's suffrage movement and in 1913 founded the Alpha Suffrage Club in Chicago. That year she desegregated a suffrage march in Washington, D.C., by slipping into the Illinois delegation at the last moment. In addition, from 1913 to 1916 Wells-Barnett served as an adult probation officer in Chicago.

Always busy, Wells-Barnett participated in many organizations, including the Republican party. In the three years prior to her death, she began her autobiography and ran for the state senate. On 25 March 1931 death finally silenced her angry voice—a feat no other force could accomplish. That voice had forced white America to confront the myths that excused lynching. With the ugly realities of mob violence laid bare, white voices from all regions joined the black cries for justice. Less than five months before the death of Wells-Barnett, a group of white women met in Atlanta and listened to one of their own refute the link between rape and lynching. Almost four decades after Wells spoke out, Jessie Daniel Ames echoed her words and kept her message alive.

NOTES

1. Ida B. Wells, *Crusade for Justice*, edited by Alfreda M. Duster (Chicago, 1970), 64.

2. Ida B. Wells, *Southern Horrors*, repr. in Trudier Harris, ed, *Selected Works of Ida B. Wells-Barnett* (New York, 1991), 35.

3. Ibid., 17.

4. Ibid., 18.

5. Ibid., 42.

6. Wells, *Crusade*, 100.

7. Ida B. Wells, *A Red Record*, repr. in Harris, *Selected Works of Ida B. Wells-Barnett*, 231.

8. Wells, *Crusade*, 183.

9. *New York Times*, 4 September 1894.

10. *New York Times*, 27 July 1894.

11. Wells-Barnett, *A Red Record*, 213–214.

12. Ida B. Wells, "Lynching: Our National Crime," repr. in Mildred I. Thompson, ed., *Ida B. Wells-Barnett: An Exploratory Study of an American Black Woman, 1893–1930* (New York, 1990), 264.

13. Wells, *Crusade*, 325–326.

BIBLIOGRAPHY

Aptheker, Bettina, ed. *Lynching and Rape: An Exchange of Views*. Occasional Paper no. 25. American Institute for Marxist Studies, New York, 1977.

Bederman, Gail. " 'Civilization,' the Decline of Middle-Class Manliness, and Ida B. Wells's Anti-Lynching Campaign (1892–94)." *Radical History Review* 52 (1992): 5–30.

Duster, Alfreda M., ed. *Crusade for Justice, the Autobiography of Ida B. Wells*. Chicago, 1970.

Grant, Donald L. "The Development of the Anti-Lynching Reform Movement in the United States: 1883–1932." Ph.D. diss., University of Missouri-Columbia, 1972.

Harris, Trudier ed. *Selected Works of Ida B. Wells-Barnett*. New York, 1991.

Hutton, Mary Magdeline Boone. "The Rhetoric of Ida B. Wells: The Genesis of the Anti-Lynching Movement." Ph.D. diss., Indiana University, 1976.

National Association for the Advancement of Colored People. *Thirty Years of Lynching in the United States, 1889–1918*. New York, 1919.

Thompson, Mildred I. *Ida B. Wells-Barnett: An Exploratory Study of an American Black Woman, 1893–1930*. New York, 1990.

Tucker, David M. "Miss Ida B. Wells and Memphis Lynching." *Phylon* 32 (1971): 112–122.

Zangrando, Robert L. *The NAACP Crusade Against Lynching, 1909–1950*. Philadelphia, 1980.

Harvey Washington Wiley
and Pure Food Reform

JAMES HARVEY YOUNG

Harvey Washington Wiley has been accorded an accolade rare in the annals of federal legislation. Both immediately after the law's enactment in 1906, and ever since, Wiley, a civil servant rather than a member of Congress involved with the slowly evolving statute, has been termed ''father'' of the nation's first broad Pure Food and Drugs Act. This law, making the federal government responsible for the safety and truthful labeling of foods and drugs—certainly articles central to the citizens' well-being and to life itself—constituted one of the early reforms of the Progressive era.

The successful culmination of the food law campaign embodied many of the characteristics of the protean Progressive movement: a revival of earlier moral impulses linked to newer instrumental methods, the transcendence of a goal-oriented coalition over political party considerations, an effort to settle controversies within the industrial sector on a national political level, the forging of a nascent consumer movement in both cities and countryside concerned with issues of health, and the role of muckraking journalism in inciting public opinion. Wiley's role involved him with all these strands of Progressivism. A scientist who provided much of the hard data about adulteration that fueled the pure food campaign, Wiley was also a committed moralist who deemed deceiving the public as at least as dire an evil as harming their health. Wiley's career also provides evidence that the lot of the bureaucrat as reformer is not an easy one.

Harvey Wiley was born on 18 October 1844, to Preston and Lucinda Weir Maxwell Wiley, in a log cabin on a farm in southern Indiana not far from the Ohio River. In his very early years, he developed both a bent toward reform and an image of the wholesome life. His parents were ardent members of the Campbellite denomination and harbored abolition sentiments: they read Harriet Beecher Stowe's *Uncle Tom's Cabin* chapter by chapter as it appeared serially in a magazine, and the father helped conduct escaping slaves to freedom. While Wiley attended Hanover College near his home, he moved away from orthodoxy; he developed a Unitarian perspective, maintaining a deep concern for improving the lot of humankind. As a boy, Wiley enjoyed sharing in the annual labors of planting, tilling, and reaping. Throughout his life he cherished the vision of rural America as the best place for a healthy and happy life. "In the cultivation of the soil," he wrote in 1911, "is found the best of healing agencies, and Mother Nature is the wisest nurse known to Man. . . . The farm stands as Nature's sanctuary for that man who has broken down under the strain of city work, and for whom dyspepsia, neurasthenia, or kindred ills have made life no longer worth living."[1]

Wiley's college years were interrupted in 1864 by five months of military service in the Union Army in Tennessee; they ended with his discharge because of malaria and severe diarrhea. After graduating from Hanover, Wiley served a short apprenticeship with a Kentucky physician who had been one of his close army friends, then joined the first class to enroll at Indiana Medical College in Indianapolis. Simultaneously, he taught Greek and Latin at Northwestern Christian College (soon to become Butler). Wiley received his M.D. degree in 1871, then continued to teach at several institutions at once, including his medical alma mater. In 1873 he spent less than six months at Harvard, where he earned a B.S. in chemistry. Through these busy years, Wiley retained the expectation that he would eventually launch a medical practice.

In 1874, however, Wiley received an appointment as chemistry professor at the newly opened Purdue University. An imaginative teacher, he immersed his students in laboratory work. He also undertook research and began to present papers at conventions, especially at meetings of the American Association for the Advancement of Science. In 1878 he took a leave of absence to broaden his knowledge by studying with distinguished scientists in Europe. His main intention was to study chemistry in its relation to medicine. Wiley went to the University of Berlin to work with August Wilhelm von Hoffmann, but, arriving late, he could not get desk room in Hoffmann's laboratory. A fellow student introduced Wiley to Eugen Sell, chief chemist of the German Imperial Board of Health, who found a place for the American to work in his lab. There Wiley learned the essentials of detecting adulterants in foods, working especially with sugar and syrups. The "accident" by which he was thus located, Wiley later asserted, influenced the direction of his entire career.[2] Back at Purdue, he described his experiences to a member of the Indiana State Board of Health and suggested that the Board finance a survey of the adulteration of syrups for sale in the state. The cue was taken, and Wiley's first published report concerned with adulteration described how sugar syrups sold in Indiana were cheapened with unlabeled glucose. Wiley continued to present and to publish papers, expanding his reputation in the scientific community. When, in 1883, a rift developed between the federal commissioner of agriculture in Washington and his chief chemist, the former discharged the latter and put Wiley in his place.

During Wiley's first decade in Washington, his main endeavor was to seek means by which the nation could become less reliant on imports of sugar, a mission that achieved only minimal success. He did not, however, forget the problem of adulteration, a matter that had received some attention from his predecessors. Wiley's first annual report echoed his Indiana investigation: like that state's syrups, the syrups of the nation were debased by cheaper sweets. He next focused his analytical skills on dairy products. In 1887 he issued a study of butter, oleomargarine, and milk. While denying that margarine posed much danger in the diet, Wiley revealed his fundamental preference for the natural over the artificial, positing correctly that butter possessed ''many digestive advantages which science has not yet been able to demonstrate.''[3]

This document became the first part of Bulletin 13, *Foods and Food Adulterants*, that would proceed under Wiley's direction, supported by special congressional appropriations, through 9 more parts and 1,400 pages over a span of 16 years. Spices and condiments, alcoholic beverages, lard, baking powders, sugar and other sweeteners, tea, coffee, and cocoa were the food products analyzed in the early parts of Bulletin 13. The chemistry division's careful inquiry revealed that the adulteration of foods was ''generally and steadily increasing.'' Most of it posed no harm to health, although some poisonous cheapeners did cause injury and sometimes even killed. His investigations persuaded Wiley that the problem of adulteration should constitute the main business of his division, and that the only remedy for the ills he was discovering would come with the enactment by Congress of a national food and drug statute.

Adulteration had appeared early in human history when dishonest bakers and vintners began to add artificial cheapeners to bread and water to wine. Rulers down through the centuries had issued decrees forbidding such deceptions. The British American colonies imitated statutes of the mother country aimed at protecting the authenticity of foods and drugs. After the American Revolution, states continued and expanded such legislation. As food processing expanded in size and technical sophistication, and offered its wares on a national market, problems increased. The more reputable processors simultaneously found the complex of conflicting state laws a burden and the adulterated products of less scrupulous competitors an economic threat. Encouraged by recent pure food legislation enacted by Parliament in Great Britain, some American food processors thought that a federal law covering the entire nation might ease their plight.

The first broad bill to this end was introduced into the Congress four years before Wiley came to Washington, and four years after taking office Wiley gave his first testimony on adulteration before a congressional committee. He reported on lard to which cottonseed oil had been added. The pure food issue lingered on with a low priority both in the Congress and in the nation. The Granger movement and populism brought a quickening of interest, enough to get a food bill passed by the Senate. The House, however, took no action. With heavy irony Wiley bemoaned the failure of the public to press for the law's enactment. ''To be cheated, fooled, bamboozled, cajoled, deceived, pettifogged, hypnotized, manicured and chiropodized,'' he wrote, ''are privileges dear to us all. Woe be to that paternalism in government which shall attempt to deprive us of these inalienable rights.'' P. T. Barnum was right to believe that ''Americans like to be humbugged.''[4]

After 1892 the campaign for a national food and drug law languished for a time. It was revived later in the decade by the Association of Official Agricultural Chemists (AOAC), an organization of state and federal officials of which Wiley had been a founding member. When the AOAC created a committee on food legislation in 1895, the chief chemist became its chairman. The committee revamped the bill that earlier had passed the Senate; the AOAC endorsed the document; and it was conveyed to members of Congress and introduced.

Wiley also played the leading role in an inclusive assembly concerned with a federal law. In order to try to iron out disputes within the private sector between trade groups over the terms of such legislation, a National Pure Food and Drug Congress convened in Washington in 1898. Its membership was broad and diverse. Local, state, and federal agencies were represented, as were professional societies and trade associations: chemists, pharmacists, physicians, farmers, millers, brewers, fishers, beekeepers, grocers, makers of butter and of candy, even the Woman's Christian Temperance Union. Participants bargained in private and heard speeches in public, including an address by Wiley, the chairman of the advisory committee. Diplomatically playing down dangers from adulterated food, he showed his audience examples of how widespread the deception was—grape juice doctored with salicylic acid, glucose substituted for honey, aniline dyes used for coloring preserved meat, ''coffee berries'' that had never seen a coffee tree. Wiley expressed his opposition to prohibitory measures, so long as food products should be honestly labeled. ''What we want,'' he said, ''is that the farmer may get an honest market and the consumer may get what he thinks he is buying.''[5]

The compromise measure given grudging agreement moved the text away from an agricultural scientist's ideal and toward a businessman's desire. Indeed, from this point on, most trade groups rather took it for granted that eventually a law would pass. Wiley, however, deemed this private congress and two more that followed unsatisfactory as forums for making progress toward an acceptable law. ''The fewer [such gatherings] which meet hereafter,'' he wrote, ''the better.''[6] The proper site for consideration of a food and drug bill must be the two chambers of the national Congress.

It was congressional initiation, indeed, that began to bring Wiley's name and notions before a wider segment of the American public. For nearly a decade after the introduction of the first food and drug bill in 1879, several committees had reported bills or resolutions authorizing investigations of adulteration, but this power had not been acted upon. Finally, in 1899, the Senate Committee on Manufactures, chaired by William E. Mason of Illinois, undertook such an inquiry. Sitting for fifty-one days in Washington, Chicago, and New York, the committee heard testimony given by 196 witnesses. Senator Mason had gone to

Secretary of Agriculture James Wilson and asked him to assign Wiley to the committee as scientific adviser. Wiley analyzed food samples, assisted in questioning witnesses, and played the role of key summarizing witness, providing dramatic testimony that made newspaper headlines across the country. Although regarding the proportion of adulteration as small and the dangers as rare, Wiley joined other witnesses in specifying particular hazards among food additives, such as aniline dyes, chemical preservatives, and copper salts. Blatant fraud, as in the labeling of imported wines, Wiley deemed as disgraceful threats to consumer health. When the hearings ended, Wiley drafted the bill, based on earlier measures before the Congress, that Mason introduced in the Senate. "I think if there is any one man in this country," Mason said on the Senate floor, "who deserves great credit for trying to furnish the facts for the benefit of the people of this country, that man is Harvey Washington Wiley."[7]

In the years that followed, Wiley repeated with committees of both Houses the role he had played in 1899 for Senator Mason. He served as witness, helped congressmen quiz witnesses, aided with bill drafting, conferred on strategy with committee chairmen, and bargained with opponents of mainline bills in search of compromises that would let the legislative process advance. Wiley, the agrarian Hoosier, became good friends of the major proponents in Congress, most of whom came from the Midwest and Great Plains regions and desired a strong bill that would provide consumers with the greatest possible protection. These congressmen formed the crucial center of a coalition of support needed for the law's enactment. Wiley was surprised and disheartened at the lack of public interest in such a basic issue. "Measures which affect only small bodies of organized labor or insignificant manufacturing enterprises," he bemoaned, "are brought before Congress and pushed to a successful issue while the great problem of the purity and wholesomeness of human food is not able to secure a hearing."[8] Wiley determined to bind other elements to the congressional stalwarts supporting a bill and to arouse the largely indifferent public to recognize the need for pure food reform.

In his commitment to this goal, Wiley became, as a close observer later expressed it, "a one-man movement all by himself, and he carried others with him."[9] Working through individual members whom he came to know well, he sought to recruit to the cause organizations that possessed mass lobbying weight to be applied to Congress. The state chemists' society, the AOAC, was wholeheartedly with him from the start. The state food, drug, and dairy officials posed a tougher task. Some wanted an even more stringent law than Wiley thought possible to achieve; others, perhaps jealous of Wiley and beholden to business interests in their states, wanted a weaker statute. Wiley's friends within the AOAC finally secured a vote of support for the mainline bill.

Wiley had powerful allies who pledged support of the American Pharmaceutical Association to the cause, and who brought the American Medical Association's (AMA) potent lobbying force into play at crucial times. He courted the membership of the General Federation of Women's Clubs. One of its presidents

had declared: "Dante is dead. He has been dead for several centuries, and I
think it is time we dropped the study of his inferno and turned attention to our
own."[10] Purifying the food supply seemed a most legitimate crusade for women.
Women close to Wiley also converted the National Consumers' League to the
cause. In this way, the food bill Wiley favored, managed by Midwestern agrarian
members of Congress, secured support from organizations that were urban, middle-class, and national.

Wiley also gained support for his version of a law from certain segments of
business. Distillers of straight whiskey opposed to the product of so-called rectifiers and blenders came into Wiley's camp. So did a coterie of food processors
who became convinced that they could make ketchup and other food products
without the need for chemical preservatives. Wiley won over even more skeptical groups. Asked by a pea canner who eschewed preservatives to address an
assembly of canners who thought the law that Wiley favored would ruin their
business, Wiley challenged this view forthrightly. He later described the confrontation to a House of Representatives committee:

I told the canners exactly the truth . . . that they, instead of helping their business by
claiming right to put a coloring matter [or a preservative] in their goods, were driving
hundreds of thousands of American citizens away from the very stuff . . . [the canners]
wanted to sell. . . . That one man who does [use] it injures the business of every man
who does not. . . . I believe your product is one of the finest and best that can be offered
the American people. . . . You [must] take the American people into your confidence, and
. . . [tell them], "There is absolutely nothing in the goods which we present you but what
we say is in them"; and then instead of selling one can you will sell three before five
years. But if you continue to deceive the American people, and to claim the right to use
things that 95 percent of our people do not want you to use, your business is going to
suffer.[11]

One member of the audience began to clap, and then—Wiley told the congressmen—came "a tremendous outburst of applause." He had won the canners
over, he explained, "simply because when the ethical principle is presented to
the American people, the American people will respond."[12] Wiley's narration
and moral judgment evoked applause in the committee room.

Morality also was implicit in the judgments being made about evils of all
kinds afflicting American society by a new breed of journalists described by
President Theodore Roosevelt as "muckrakers." Among these writers were
some who popularized in the pages of a new wave of inexpensive magazines
the themes of food adulteration and patent medicine deceptions and dangers.
These journalists stressed the need for an effective national food and drug law.
Wiley made several efforts to get President Roosevelt to endorse such a bill,
but without initial success.

Wiley realized that the law he desired had little chance of enactment unless
the broad public became truly aware of its necessity. His indirect labors, through

journalists and women's organizations and other pressure groups, were tending toward this end. He needed, however, to enlarge his direct efforts to inform the citizenry. Wiley expanded his lecturing and made himself readily available for interviews by reporters. Still a bachelor, he had no home ties to complicate his bookings. He mingled well with people in a gregarious manner and knew how to put them at ease. As before the canners, Wiley spoke informally and with great earnestness, using wit and specific examples, in easy rapport with his audiences. Wiley was tall—6 feet, 1 inch—and weighed over two hundred pounds. His face was oval and full, his black eyes piercing, his nose prominent, his black hair receding, the lush black beard and mustache he brought to Washington shrinking in size and disappearing altogether with the new century. Wiley increasingly became a nationally recognized figure, appearing in press photographs and cartoons. His persona as well as his passion helped him persuade.

The biggest burst of publicity perhaps came unexpectedly, but Wiley took advantage of it. In 1902 Wiley, in his role as scientist and with funds allotted by Congress, mounted an experiment to test the effect of chemical preservatives upon humans. He selected a dozen robust young men who pledged themselves to eat nothing but "hygienic table"[13] food in the basement of the Bureau of Chemistry building and to provide Wiley with all their bodily excretions for analysis. The young men were their own controls. In a "fore period" they established their normal metabolism by eating food without the preservative. Then ensued the "preservative period" of just over a month, during which the chemical was consumed in steadily increasing amounts. During an "after period" the preservative was stopped while observations and analyses continued. The first preservatives tested were borax and boric acid, which in Wiley's judgment posed the least risk. At the close of the trial, Wiley published his conclusions. Borax, he asserted, retreating from his earlier more tolerant posture, should be banned from food. It had assailed his healthy young men with numerous disagreeable symptoms. Borax was only one of many preservatives in use. The total burden posed a major hazard to public health. All must be treated alike, so none should be permitted. Wiley proceeded to test other preservatives—salicylic acid, sulfurous acid, formaldehyde—with new groups of young men at his hygienic table.

Even before the first trial began, Wiley's plans found their way into the press, reported straightforwardly but with a humorous slant. A *Washington Post* reporter gave Wiley's volunteers the designation "Poison Squad," an appellation that stuck.[14] The public responded to the reporting, sometimes exaggerated, as if that name fit the case, worrying about the fate of young men deliberately dosed with chemicals that might harm their health and even put their lives at risk. Wiley regretted distorted coverage, but he kept reporters informed of developments, and they in turn called him, not without admiration, "Old Borax." Wiley knew the publicity aided his cause. When science, as represented by his experiments, affirmed that adulteration went beyond cheating to palpable hazard, then the public would become more insistent that a protective law be passed. Demands for Wiley's appearance as a lecturer increased.

Twice in the early years of the twentieth century, the mainline pure food bill passed the House but was blocked in the Senate by recalcitrant commercial interests, especially whiskey rectifiers and proprietary drug producers. In late 1905 the tide turned perceptibly. A small but diverse pro-law committee pressed the president, and Roosevelt put a paragraph of endorsement in his annual message to Congress. This time the Senate quickly passed the pure food bill, and the House lagged. Physicians and women intensified their lobbying. Public fervor increased, fueled by continuing "Poison Squad" publicity and by a series of articles in *Collier's* by Samuel Hopkins Adams blasting patent medicines as "The Great American Fraud." Finally Upton Sinclair's novel *The Jungle* described the deplorable conditions under which the nation's meat was processed for market. Sale of meat tumbled by half. Wiley and some of his congressional allies credited the impact of *The Jungle* with providing the crucial pressure for finally getting the food and drug bill through the House and conference committee. Both bills were signed by the president on the final day of the session, 30 June 1906. A recent scholar, Ilyse D. Barkan, has reversed the order of influence, arguing that it was not that the food law finally swept through Congress because of public alarm about meat, but rather that *The Jungle* upset Americans because of what they had already learned from expanding publicity about all food.

During the protracted campaign, Wiley had played the major role, a quadruple-threat leader as scientist, propagandist, organizer, and strategist in the pure food cause. As a crusader for the law, he was not an unyielding alarmist. Initially his major stress lay less on adulteration's dangers than on its immorality. "Pure" in 1906 still retained an older moral meaning as a synonym for righteous, honest. "The evils of fraud," Wiley told a House subcommittee, were "demoralizing." "No man can continuously deceive his customer and retain that high moral sense which is the very soul of trade."[15]

Wiley's "Poison Squad" experiments convinced him that unlabeled preservatives were both deceitful and more dangerous than he had earlier presumed. Such a change in his convictions, however, did not make him rigid in regard to the shaping of the law. Wiley worked with congressmen to secure the strongest terms he could get, but he did not begrudge compromises he was forced to accept to ensure enactment. Wiley's firm belief in moral values, as Robert Crunden has explained, caused him to oversimplify complex issues, blunting instrumental solutions demanded by the situation. Purity defined as honesty led Wiley to unrealistic expectations about the redeeming value of accurate labeling upon which the Pure Food and Drugs Act largely relied. Wiley had a misguided faith that the mere enactment of a law would so reform the ethics of businessmen that the task of enforcement would be simple.

To govern a complex subject, Congress produced a short statute, the Food and Drugs Act, that ran to about six pages.[16] The law's principal postulate was that adequately informed consumers could protect themselves against deception, even against danger. Some premarketing taboos might be required, aimed at especially hazardous ingredients, but even for narcotic nostrums that had killed babies and enslaved adults, only honest labeling was required, not the elimination from formulas of opiates and cocaine. Violations were not to be detected, as in the meat law, prior to marketing. Unsanitary factories were not illegal per se. Violations became detected only after foods and drugs had entered, or had been prepared to enter, interstate commerce.

Both foods and drugs were broadly defined. The act specified that the *United States Pharmacopoeia* and the *National Formulary* should be standards for drugs listed therein. For all other drugs, including proprietary medicines, a vaguer hurdle was set: they must meet their own professed standard or be deemed adulterated. A short list of narcotic and hypnotic substances, including alcohol, must be named on labels, with the quantity specified. For foods, despite a strong effort by congressional sponsors, no specific standards were prescribed; whether a product was adulterated had to be established anew in court for each alleged violation. Foods might be adulterated in six major ways, the most important being the inclusion of a "filthy, decomposed, or putrid animal or vegetable substance" or the presence of "any added poisonous or other added deleterious ingredient which may render such article injurious to health." Misbranding meant deceptive labeling. A blanket provision banned from the package or labeling of foods and drugs "any statement, design, or device regarding such article, or the ingredients or substances contained therein, which shall be false or misleading in any particular."

The law distributed enforcement responsibility with a lack of crisp precision that boded future trouble. Three cabinet members—the secretaries of agriculture, treasury, and commerce and labor—were to devise rules and regulations for enforcement. Wiley's Bureau of Chemistry received authority for surveying the marketplace, collecting and examining samples, and making a first determination that the law had been violated. The U.S. Secretary of Agriculture, given this information, should then notify the alleged violator, giving him the chance to defend himself at a hearing. If circumstances then seemed to indicate that the law had been transgressed, the secretary should certify the facts and send the evidence to the district attorney in the appropriate region to take to court. Whether the secretary, receiving from the Bureau chief an allegation of guilt, had the right of independent judgment on the evidence was not explicitly clear.

Two kinds of actions were provided for in the law. The case might be brought against an offending food or drug that had been seized. If determined violative by jury or judge, the product could be condemned and destroyed, or it might be returned to its owner for rehabilitation. Or the offending person might be prosecuted for a misdemeanor. Penalties were less severe than under the meat law. A first conviction under the Food and Drugs Act warranted a fine not to exceed $200; a second or any subsequent transgression might bring a fine not to exceed $300, or imprisonment as long as a year, or both penalties together.

As the law was in fact applied in the courts, fines were low and jail sentences extremely rare.

The new law officially took effect at the beginning of 1907, but it was nearly midyear before the Bureau of Chemistry was prepared to launch enforcement. The initial regulations had been approved by the three cabinet secretaries, and a coterie of inspectors had been chosen, minimally trained, and distributed among the laboratories across the country. In speaking to the recruits, Wiley expressed the hope that all were "Pinkertons or Sherlock Holmes's."[17] He had selected the chief inspector, Walter G. Campbell, a young lawyer from Kentucky who had been active in enforcing that state's food law. No overall regulatory strategy had yet been devised. The marketplace was in such "a state of unbridled abuse and misrepresentation," Campbell later remembered, that inspectors worked by "a sort of gum shoe method, because we could bring down game no matter where we aimed."[18] Yet the initial inspectors were handicapped, because science had still to be developed "to deal intelligently and accurately" with some of the problems they would encounter.

Wiley, designated by the law as initiator of its enforcement, was plunged into a maelstrom of activity. To judge by his correspondence, he was striving to administer his bureau; going to court; squabbling with his superiors; writing articles for popular magazines; delivering speeches; playing a role in running the Cosmos Club; keeping in touch with relatives; reading proof of a major scientific study; helping friends of friends get government appointments; keeping in touch with his allies in the food, drug, and liquor industries, on trade journals, and in state food and drug departments; counseling a Supreme Court justice on whiskey; helping Hanover College raise an endowment; serving on the AMA's Council of Pharmacy and Chemistry; and performing editorial duties for the American Chemical Society.

Despite this flurry of activity, there was a central focus to Wiley's concern: to enforce the law rigorously with respect to processed foods to which deleterious ingredients that threatened health were added. While the law had been in the course of legislative evolution, he had been willing to make compromises to move the process toward completion. Now the Congress had acted, with the president's concurrence, and the time for compromise had ended. Reform had entered a new stage. The commandments were engraved on stone and must be obeyed. Morality and science both demanded this.

"What is the great movement for purity of foods and drugs?" Wiley asked rhetorically in 1907. He then answered his own question. "Only the application of ethics to digestion and therapeutics. This is the new philosophy, namely, the morals of metabolism."[19] His ongoing "Poison Squad" continually strengthened his conviction that his science was repeatedly proving the danger of chemical preservatives in the diet. In his study of twelve young men adding benzoate of soda to their diet, Wiley concluded as to the damaging result: "If the jury . . . is polled, the verdict is eleven for conviction, and one for acquittal."[20]

As Wiley read the law, Congress had put him in charge, with final decisions to be rendered by the courts. He must act forthrightly and forcibly. When he sought to do so, the challenge to his stance and intentions, already evident before the law was passed, was renewed and expanded. The challenge came not only from industry but also from his own governmental superiors. Wiley, a reformer under siege, virtually abandoned compromise as a possible policy and fought with might and main for what he believed was his righteous cause. He finally forsook the battlefield of action, but never through the remainder of his life did he abandon his idealization of the law that in the popular mind bore his name, nor did he forsake his conviction in the correctness of his regulatory goals.

Tension developed between Wiley and Secretary of Agriculture James Wilson even before enforcement of the law got under way. Wilson had been a farmer, head of the Iowa agricultural experimental station, and a member of Congress before becoming agriculture secretary in 1897. His abiding principle in office was to help the farmer. Some of Wiley's conclusions in the ''Poison Squad'' research bothered Wilson, especially Wiley's blunt mode of making his opinions public. So Wilson, with Roosevelt's concurrence but without notifying Wiley until the action was a fait accompli, created a Board of Food and Drug Inspection to make crucial enforcement decisions under the Food and Drugs Act. The board had three members: Wiley as chairman; George McCabe, the department solicitor; and Frederick Dunlap, a young analytical chemist brought in from the University of Michigan. Wiley was upset at Wilson's creation of this body not mentioned in the law (and, hence, he thought, illegal), and his outrage grew as he was outvoted on many issues he deemed crucial. Wiley's bureau staff, likewise angered, called Dunlap a ''spy,'' ''snake,'' and ''rat.''[21]

Sometimes the three committee members did concur, as they had initially done in deciding that benzoate of soda posed a threat to health and hence should be banned from foods following the 1907 season, during which it might be used to the extent of 0.10 percent so long as its presence was indicated on the label. Pro-benzoate packers sought to get this decision countermanded. Gaining the support of Congressman James Sherman of New York, himself a canner, they took their case directly to President Roosevelt, arguing that Wiley's policies would ruin Republican business. Secretary Wilson was present, as were the three members of the Board of Food and Drug Inspection. Wiley later recalled the occasion with bitterness.[22]

''Mr. Wilson,'' the president asked, ''do you think the addition of benzoate of soda to foods is injurious?''

''Yes,'' the secretary answered.

Roosevelt put the same query to Wiley.

''I do not think, I know. I have tried it on healthy young men and it made them ill.''

McCabe and Dunlap also agreed.

''Then,'' as Wiley recalled the scene, ''turning to the Republican representatives of business, and striking the table a ringing blow with his fist, the

President said, 'Gentlemen, if this drug is injurious you shall not put it in foods.' ''

All would have been well, as Wiley viewed things in retrospect, had not the discussion turned to another product about which a debate was raging, saccharin. To the frustration of canners, Wiley opposed using this chemical sweetener as a substitute for sugar in canned corn.

''I unfortunately 'butted in' . . . ,'' Wiley remembered, and said, ''Yes, Mr. President, and everyone who eats these products is deceived, believing he is eating sugar, and moreover the health is threatened by the drug.''

''Turning upon me in sudden anger and fierce visage,'' Wiley recalled, ''the President said, 'Anybody who says saccharin is injurious is an idiot. Dr. Rixey gives it to me every day.' ''

Roosevelt's skeptical attitude about Wiley's scientific soundness rested on more than this one dramatic moment. As he explained later, ''The trouble with Dr. Wiley is, that to my personal knowledge, he has been guilty of such grave errors of judgment in matters of such great importance as to make it quite impossible to accept his say-so in the matter without a very uneasy feeling that I may be doing far-reaching harm to worse than no purpose.''[23] Distrusting Wiley's judgment, the president made a decision that had been urged upon him by Sherman and various trade groups. He authorized Secretary Wilson to appoint a board of scientific experts. Wiley had favored such a board before the act was passed, but this concept had been rejected in the conference committee. Now and ever after, Wiley believed that thwarting his bureau in a way not authorized by law represented a crass yielding to commercial pressure for political purposes.

The Referee Board of Consulting Scientific Experts consisted of five of the nation's outstanding academic scientists, chaired by President Ira Remsen of the Johns Hopkins University, the nation's most distinguished chemist, whom Wiley had admired so much that he had hung Remsen's portrait in his office. The first problem Wilson certified to the board for study was the safety of sodium benzoate, meanwhile permitting manufacturers to continue using the preservative at a low level if properly labeled. Wiley's critical ''Poison Squad'' study was ready for press, but Wilson ordered it postponed. By inadvertence, however, the bulletin was published. Wilson was angry, the pro-use packers were irate, and the public, which regarded Wiley as a popular hero, was disturbed anew about dangers in their diet. Less than a year later, the Referee Board's researches— three separate experiments done at Yale, Northwestern, and a private laboratory in New York City, using male medical students to repeat (with slight variations) Wiley's studies—came to contrary conclusions. Benzoate of soda was not deleterious, not poisonous, not injurious to health, not destructive of the quality or nutritive value of processed food. Only a single, somewhat vague precautionary sentence appeared in the report, referring to large doses: ''In some directions there were slight modifications in certain physiological processes, the exact significance of which modifications is not known.''[24] Wilson chose to accept the

Referee Board's research over that of Wiley and granted food processors the right to use benzoate of soda in any quantity so long as it was labeled.

The two contrary reports fueled a firestorm of debate that raged within the scientific community, state regulatory ranks, and the trade and lay presses. Both Wiley and Remsen were charged with proving their prejudices, devising faulty research designs, and drawing improper conclusions from their evidence. The controversy was not confined to print. At least three personal confrontations pitted members of the Remsen Board and Wiley's henchmen against each other, two of them involving Wiley himself. One took place at the convention of the Association of State and National Food and Dairy Departments in Denver in 1909. Later the two sides met in Indiana in a federal court. Finally, in 1911, the arguments were repeated before a committee of the House of Representatives.

By this time the benzoate battle had been joined by other major issues in dispute between Wiley and Wilson over how the Food and Drugs Act should be enforced, even though the Referee Board accepted some of Wiley's crucial decisions, such as those concerning copper salts and saccharin. Amid massive publicity with so many trade interests involved, it was inevitable that presidents Roosevelt and William Howard Taft become involved. Whiskey furnishes another benumbing example. Initially, Secretary Wilson accepted Wiley's ruling that mixtures of bourbon and ethyl alcohol could not be labeled "blended whisky." Rectifiers brought so much pressure on Roosevelt that he had his attorney general, Charles J. Bonaparte, render an opinion. Then the president ruled that only a mixture of straight whiskeys could be termed a "blend." Straight whiskey mixed with ethyl alcohol must be marked a "compound," and ethyl alcohol with color and flavor added must be labeled an "imitation." Rectifiers' protests mounted, causing Roosevelt to grant them a new hearing before the Internal Revenue commissioner, who would then confer with Wilson and Dunlap. Dunlap summed up in a memorandum: "imitation" was too severe a term; colored and flavored ethyl alcohol might instead pick from the words "neutral," "redistilled," or "rectified" whiskey.

Bonaparte, consulted again by the president, stuck to his guns, saying his earlier decision had survived several court tests. Roosevelt accepted his attorney general's stand. When Taft entered the White House, the rectifiers renewed their pressure, and Taft had his solicitor general meet with them and give a new judgment. This turned things to the blenders' benefit. Colored and flavored alcohol should not be called whiskey, but a mixture of straight whiskey and ethyl alcohol, if the amount of the latter was not too high to rob the product of the by-products that gave whiskey its character, deserved to bear its name. This compromise satisfied neither blenders nor distillers of straight whiskey, so Taft listened personally to their arguments. He devised another version of compromise, allowing the word "whiskey" to all participants to the fray, but requiring labeling to specify how the contents of each bottle had been prepared. Again, both rectifiers and straight whiskey distillers found reason for complaint. The three secretaries in 1910 finally, to Wiley's disgust, gave the rectifiers what they wanted: the right to label ethyl alcohol distilled from grain as "whiskey" without qualification.

As this dispute proceeded at the highest echelons, Wiley fought bitterly against Dunlap and McCabe within the Board of Food and Drug Inspection, being outvoted two-thirds of the time. Wilson, under McCabe's influence, decided in 1910 to transfer much of the board's power, especially the decision as to whether a case should be prosecuted, into McCabe's hands. To Wiley, this step seemed a direct violation of the authority Congress had given the Bureau of Chemistry in the law. This tense situation escalated when McCabe and Dunlap accused Wiley and his bureau associates of malfeasance because of the way they had illegally promised to pay an outside expert, Henry H. Rusby of the New York College of Pharmacy, to examine drugs offered for import at the Port of New York and to testify as an expert witness in court. Secretary Wilson, disgruntled by his unremitting controversy with Wiley, recommended to the cabinet that Wiley be discharged. Another protracted process of official consideration ensued, ending with President Taft's careful personal review. While this continued, the press debated the issue fiercely, and a member of the House from Indiana, Ralph W. Moss, conducted an intensive committee examination of the Rusby affair and the broader controversy about how the Food and Drugs Act should be enforced. Moss exonerated Wiley, and so did Taft. The president intimated that more sweeping action might be required.

Wiley rejoiced at his vindication and looked forward to Taft's ousting of his adversaries and strongly supporting the enforcement policies that Wiley advocated. These actions did not take place. Moreover, at the age of sixty-seven Wiley married Anna Kelton, a vigorous woman half his age, and in the spring of 1912 a baby was due. More income would be welcome. Several positions outside government had been offered at larger salaries. Wiley presented Secretary Wilson an ultimatum, consisting mainly of the demand for Dunlap's removal and the requirement that communications between the bureau and the secretary be direct, not through McCabe. Wilson refused these terms, so on 15 March 1912, Wiley left the post he had held since 1883.

All through his career, Wiley told the press that day, he had sought "to discharge . . . [his] duties according to the dictates of . . . [his] conscience, the knowledge at . . . [his] command, and the obligations of . . . [his] oath."[25] From the start of enforcement of the Food and Drugs Act, he and his superiors had regarded the nature of that task in a "fundamentally different" way. Finally, Wiley had become convinced that the gap was "irreconcilable." The law's principles had become "one by one paralyzed or discredited" as manufacturers had managed to evade decisions by the courts and had won concessions through executive branch determinations. Wiley had even had his freedom of speech circumscribed by his superiors. After he had won exoneration of false charges brought against him, he had expected the perpetrators to be removed, but this had not occurred. So he was departing government to spend the rest of his life "as a private citizen" promoting "the principles of civic righteousness and industrial integrity which underlie the food and drugs act."[26]

Wiley hewed relentlessly to this goal on the lecture circuit; in the pages of *Good Housekeeping*, to which he contributed from the time of his resignation until the year of his death; and in two volumes written during his declining years, *The History of a Crime Against the Food Law* and *An Autobiography*. Whereas his Bureau of Chemistry successors recognized weaknesses in the law and looked forward to the day when Congress might strengthen it, Wiley maintained the law was sound if only it could be enforced in the way Congress had intended. When, in 1927, Walter Campbell split off the regulatory functions under the law from the research functions of the Bureau of Chemistry, creating a new agency, the Food and Drug Administration, so as to improve enforcement, Wiley was grieved. When the reform climate of Progressivism (even though it had not fully achieved Wiley's hopes) withered, replaced in the 1920s by a more conservative Republican ascendancy that required regulators to cooperate with business in order to control abuses in the marketplace, Wiley defined the collaboration as selling out. Admiring the crusader for his achievement in securing the law, treating him courteously, Wiley's successors—many of whom he had hired—nonetheless abominated his severe criticisms, deeming him a crotchety old man whom the times had passed by. After the old warrior's death on 30 June 1930, the twenty-fourth anniversary of the law's enactment, his reputation as a reformer rebounded, especially and ironically during the five-year campaign during the New Deal to replace the Wiley law with a stronger statute, the Food, Drug, and Cosmetic Act of 1938. At an assembly celebrating the 1906 law's fortieth anniversary, a federal judge lauded Wiley's "courage and foresight . . . his determination and tenacity of purpose," and rendered thanks "for the great boon" Wiley had "conferred upon suffering humanity."[27]

"Wiley was preeminently the pioneer, the agitator, the educator," a journalist wrote some months after the chief chemist's resignation. "Obstinate, imperious, uncompromising, he won the confidence of the country in his determination to protect the people against imposition. If he cared little or nothing for the business interests affected by his autocratic decisions, he felt that the people as a whole cared no more. . . . He approached the fanatic in his zeal."[28] "If Dr. Wiley has erred," another journalist asserted, "it has been in zeal for the public welfare."[29] Wiley passed on something of his moral conviction to his successors. An agency official in 1948, after accompanying inspectors into the field, was "greatly impressed": "As one of the men said to me while riding back from a factory inspection, 'You know, this isn't just a job with us, it's a religion.' "[30]

Throughout the subsequent history of food and drug regulation in the United States, an ethical component has been constantly intertwined with the expanding laws' scientific and public health dimensions. Labeling must tell the truth. With respect to ingredients, there must be no deception. Patients recruited for clinical trials of new drugs must give their informed consent. Controversies that arise over policy often have an ethical element. Do various measures taken by the

Food and Drug Administration to speed up the drug approval process, so as to get new drugs on the market for treating life-threatening diseases like AIDS, shortcut safety considerations and thereby challenge integrity? The debate has raged fiercely. Thus the substance of Harvey Wiley's moral concerns has persisted to influence the complex calculus of food and drug policy as the twenty-first century approaches.

NOTES

1. Harvey W. Wiley, "Plow and Pitchfork Versus Pills and Powders," *Country Life in America* 20 (15 August 1911): 19–21.

2. Harvey W. Wiley, "Food Control Before 1906," *American Food Journal* 21 (1926): 559.

3. Department of Agriculture, Division of Chemistry, Bulletin 13, *Foods and Food Adulterants*, pt. 1 (Washington, D.C., 1887).

4. Harvey W. Wiley, "The Adulteration of Food," *Journal of the Franklin Institute* 137 (1894): 266.

5. *Journal of the Proceedings of the National Pure Food and Drug Congress . . . March 2, 3, 4, and 5, 1898* (Washington, D.C., 1898), 12–16.

6. Oscar E. Anderson, Jr., *The Health of a Nation: Harvey W. Wiley and the Fight for Pure Food* (Chicago, 1958), 133.

7. *Congressional Record*, 56th Cong., 1st sess., 4963.

8. Anderson, *Health of a Nation*, 128.

9. Thomas Swann Harding, *Two Blades of Grass: A History of Scientific Development in the U.S. Department of Agriculture* (Norman, Okla., 1947), 314.

10. Samuel P. Hayes, *The Response to Industrialism, 1885–1914* (Chicago, 1957), 73.

11. *Hearings Before the Committee on Interstate and Foreign Commerce of the House of Representatives on the Pure Food Bills . . .* , 59th Cong., 1st sess. (February 1906), 319.

12. Ibid.

13. Harvey W. Wiley, *Influence of Food Preservatives and Artificial Colors on Digestion and Health*, Bulletin of Chemistry 84, pt. 1 (1904).

14. Anderson, *Health of a Nation*, 151–152.

15. House *Hearings . . . on The Pure Food Bills*, 57th Cong., 1st sess., 257.

16. 34 U.S. Statutes 768.

17. Wiley's remarks to inspectors, 3 June 1907, file 12 for 1907, General Correspondence, Bureau of Chemistry, Record Group 12 (National Archives, Washington, D.C.).

18. Walter G. Campbell, "Twenty-Five Years of Food and Drug Enforcement," *Food and Drug Review* 15 (1931): 333–334. Campbell cited in unidentified clipping, Campbell file, Accession 54A477, Box 48, Food and Drug Administration Records, Record Group 88 (Washington National Records Center, Suitland, Md.).

19. Wiley 1907 speech manuscript, Box 190, Harvey W. Wiley Papers (Library of Congress).

20. Harvey W. Wiley, *Influence of Food Preservatives and Artificial Colors on Digestion and Health: Benzoic Acid and Benzoates*, Bulletin 83, pt. 4 (Washington, D.C., 1908).

21. Anderson, *Health of a Nation*, 205.

22. Harvey W. Wiley, "Why I Support Wilson and Marshall," pencil draft, Box 192, Wiley Papers.

23. Theodore Roosevelt to H. H. Rusby (copy), 7 January 1909, Box 72, Wiley Papers.

24. Food Inspection Decision 104, 3 March 1909.

25. Statement for the press, 15 March 1912, Box 105, Wiley Papers.

26. Ibid.

27. John C. Knox, "A Judge's Tribute," in *Historic Meeting to Commemorate Fortieth Anniversary of Original Food and Drugs Act* (Chicago, 1946), 163.

28. William E. Brigham in *Boston Evening Transcript*, 4 January 1913, clippings file for 1913, Bureau of Chemistry General Correspondence, RG 97 (National Archives).

29. Arthur Wallace Dunn, "Dr. Wiley and Pure Food," *World's Work* 22 (October 1911): 14958.

30. Dean Snyder to Paul B. Dunbar, 18 June 1948, Decimal file 047.3 for 1948, FDA Records, RG 88 (Washington National Records Center).

BIBLIOGRAPHY

Anderson, Oscar E., Jr. "The Pure Food Issue: A Republican Dilemma, 1906–1912." *American Historical Review* 61 (1956): 550–573.

———. *The Health of a Nation: Harvey W. Wiley and the Fight for Pure Food*. Chicago, 1958.

Barkan, Ilyse D. "Industry Invites Regulation: The Passage of the Pure Food and Drug Act of 1906." *American Journal of Public Health* 75 (1985): 18–26.

Coppin, Clayton. "James Wilson and Harvey Wiley: The Dilemma of Bureaucratic Entrepreneurship." *Agricultural History* 64 (1990): 167–181.

Crunden, Robert M. *Ministers of Reform: The Progressives' Achievement in American Civilization, 1889–1920*. New York, 1982.

Fox, William Lloyd. "Harvey W. Wiley: The Formative Years." Ph.D. diss., George Washington University, 1960.

High, Jack, and Clayton A. Coppin. "Wiley and the Whiskey Industry: Strategic Behavior in the Passage of the Pure Food Act." *Business History Review* 62 (1988): 286–309.

Janssen, Wallace F. "America's First Food and Drug Laws." *FDA Consumer* 9 (June 1975): 12–19.

Kane, R. James. "Populism, Progressivism, and Pure Food." *Agricultural History* 38 (1964): 161–166.

Okun, Mitchell. *Fair Play in the Marketplace: The First Battle for Pure Food and Drugs*. DeKalb, Ill., 1986.

Wiley, Harvey W. *The History of a Crime Against the Food Law*. Washington, D.C., 1929.

———. *An Autobiography*. Indianapolis, 1930.

Young, James Harvey. *The Toadstool Millionaires: A Social History of Patent Medicines in America Before Federal Regulation*. Princeton, N.J., 1961.

———. "The Science and Morals of Metabolism: Catsup and Benzoate of Soda." *Journal of the History of Medicine and Allied Sciences* 23 (1968): 86–104.

————. *Pure Food: Securing the Federal Food and Drugs Act of 1906.* Princeton, N.J., 1989.

————. ''Food and Drug Regulation Under the USDA, 1906–1940.'' *Agricultural History* 64 (1990): 134–142.

————. *The Medical Messiahs: A Social History of Health Quackery in Twentieth-Century America.* Enl. ed. Princeton, N.J., 1992.

————. ''Two Hoosiers and the Two Food Laws of 1906.'' *Indiana Magazine of History* 88 (1992): 303–319.

Frances Willard
and Temperance

IAN R. TYRRELL

Frances Willard was one of the towering figures of nineteenth-century American reform. For more than eighteen years after 1879 she led the National Woman's Christian Temperance Union (WCTU) to unprecedented heights of popularity and influence. Journalists hailed her as the "uncrowned Queen of America"; she was treated as a "representative woman" akin to the male business and community leaders whose portraits adorn nineteenth-century biographical compilations. Adored by middle-class American women supporters as "St. Frances," she became a figure on the world stage through the World's WCTU and her visits to England in the 1890s. After her death from pernicious anaemia at the age of fifty-nine, on 17 February 1898, the state of Illinois honored her memory in the Statuary Hall of the U.S. capitol. When Willard's marble statue was placed there in 1905, Senator Albert Beveridge described her as "the first woman of the nineteenth century, the most beloved character of her time."

Born 28 September 1839, in Churchville, New York, and raised on a Wisconsin farm by her devout Christian parents, Frances Willard developed a tomboyish streak that made her feel women could be the equal of men. Her father Josiah's discipline was harsh, and Frances gravitated emotionally toward her mother, Mary Thompson Willard, whom she venerated until the latter's death in 1892. Willard loved her father, or so she said, and nursed him until he died from tuberculosis in 1868. It was "Mother" Willard who encouraged Frances in her desire to obtain an education. Willard first attended college in Milwaukee and then in Evanston, Illinois, where she lived for the last thirty years of her life. She served after graduation from the (Methodist) Northwestern Female College in 1859 as a schoolteacher and then traveled in Europe in 1868–1869 with a wealthy former classmate, Kate Jackson. When she returned, Willard was appointed president of her alma mater; she resigned in 1874 because of a dispute with Charles Fowler, president of Northwestern University, which had taken over control of the Female College. Ironically, Fowler had been Willard's fiancé for a short time in 1861. Fowler later became a bishop of the Methodist Church, to which Willard belonged, and friction between the two persisted for many years thereafter.

The impasse with Fowler was a happy coincidence for Willard. Casting about for a new career, she turned to temperance. Although late nineteenth-century temperance reform became strongly identified with Willard, temperance did not equal women's temperance. The movement to end alcohol in America had deeper roots than the WCTU. Without the preceding decades of agitation, and the evolution of tactics before the Civil War, it is unlikely that Willard could have achieved the considerable impact that she did have.

The temperance movement began on the national stage as part of the evangelical Protestant impulse to reform antebellum society. Temperance lost its original meaning of moderation when the evangelical reformers co-opted the term to mean total abstinence from spirits. From its beginnings in the American Temperance Society in 1826, "temperance" reformers graduated to teetotalism in the 1830s through the American Temperance Union (1836), moved on to prohibition in the 1840s, achieved statewide prohibition in thirteen states and territories from 1851 to 1856, and began to concede a wider role for women in the movement. Still, most temperance organizations kept women in an inferior position; not until the 1870s did women become leaders in the temperance movement with stature equal to that of men. The Good Templars, founded in New York State in 1851, was the first to grant women a theoretical equality with men within the ranks of its organization. After the Civil War, women in the Midwest took the temperance cause into their own hands through an upsurge of social protest known as the Woman's Crusade.

The Crusade was centered in Ohio but spread throughout the Midwest, and it involved more than 56,000 women in direct protests against liquor shops. This was not the first direct action against saloons, nor would it be the last, but it was the most widespread. The impact of women engaged in marches, vigorous picketing, and court attendance in defense of the family stirred public opinion. Legend has it that the WCTU grew out of the Crusade—it was, in Willard's words, "the sober second thought of the crusade"—but recent research has indicated that the focus of the WCTU and the Crusade were different. The women of the Crusade tended to be concerned with immediate threats to the family, in particular to the sons of their own families. The rise in liquor consumption, the spread of immigrant drinking after the Civil War, and the rise of the saloon pressed them into action.

The WCTU, founded in Cincinnati in November 1874 as a response to the new temperance enthusiasm of the Crusade, had a different focus and different leadership. The WCTU sought a broader public role for women and was concerned with changing the law rather than engaging in direct action against liquor sellers. The WCTU had a cosmopolitan focus as well, rather than the local one of the crusaders. Willard fits this pattern. She had not been a participant in the Crusade; she was well educated, well traveled, and middle class. Surprisingly, she had not always practiced total abstinence; she admitted to a medicinal use of alcohol for a time after her visit to Europe. Most important, the WCTU represented a new phase in the history of women and temperance—one of consolidation and organization on a national scale of diverse women's temperance activities. In a ''search for order,'' American society embraced bureaucratic, specialized organizations in business, politics, and reform. The WCTU, part of this shift, combined bureaucracy in the form of special departments of work with a charismatic leadership and a comprehensive approach that defies easy sociological categorization in terms of specialization.

Willard's rise in the temperance movement was mercurial. Although she had been appointed corresponding secretary at the Cincinnati meeting in 1874, she did not come to full prominence in the organization until her election as Illinois state president in 1878, and national president the following year. After the short reign of the older and more conservative Annie Wittenmyer, Willard seemed a vigorous and attractive new leader. Almost immediately she began to push the WCTU toward advocacy of woman's suffrage as the foundation of what she called ''Home Protection.'' This campaign involved a massive petition signed by over 200,000 people to the Illinois state legislature, calling for women's voting rights on the liquor laws in defense of the family. Willard was the author of many such felicitous phrases as ''Home Protection,'' but this idea of using the Victorian values of ''domesticity'' to advance the public rights of women was especially important in setting the stage for the further emergence of the WCTU from its formerly narrow base of temperance into the most important organization for women's reform in late nineteenth-century America. Home Protection's organizing success became both a model for future campaigns by temperance women and a vehicle that cemented Willard's authority in the WCTU. It was in the Home Protection campaign that she first succeeded in tying the WCTU to support for woman's suffrage, and such arguments of expediency continued to be important in the WCTU suffrage campaigns even after Willard's departure.

Willard's joining the temperance movement was not sheer opportunism. Her father and mother had been abstainers, and the Methodist Church had since the 1840s been firmly in the temperance camp in the Northern states. Willard was on track in arguing that alcohol was a serious problem. Although aggregate consumption had dropped from its reputedly high levels before the 1830s, middle-class youths were increasingly faced with the temptations of drinking through the proliferation of liquor outlets and the increased availability of beer. The WCTU sought to stop this resurgence of drinking after the Civil War by closing saloons. Willard also had personal experience of the dangers of alcohol that reinforced her commitment. After the death of her brother Oliver, she had a considerable involvement in the upbringing of her nephews, Rob and Frank Willard. Frank spent time in a reform school in 1888, and Rob was an alcoholic and a gambler. In 1889 he was sent to the private Christian Home for Intemperate Men. Rob never conquered his drinking habit, and though the scandal was kept private, it intensely affected Frances, bringing home to her the fragility of the middle-class life of purity and abstinence that she valued as the basis of all reform and progress for women.

In the years after her death, historians recalled Willard, if they remembered her at all, as a leader of temperance reform. Yet she was always much more. She remains, after all these years, one of the most difficult to typecast as the representative of a single reform movement. Under her influence as national president, the Woman's Christian Temperance Union embraced an ambitious "Do Everything Policy" that included support for kindergartens, social welfare work, labor reform, woman's suffrage, peace, purity reforms such as antiprostitution and age-of-consent legislation, and campaigns for the Sabbath and against vivisection and drugs other than alcohol. Willard argued, persuasively and self-consciously, that "No one can adequately lead any movement who has not imagination enough to see that movement in its relations to others equally important."[1]

This apparent grab bag reflected the wide impact of the temperance movement, its close connection with other reforms, and the sweeping influence of alcohol as a social problem in nineteenth-century America. Drink damaged families through the propensity of males toward violence and through the loss of family income, which drinking could involve in a society where frugality and industry were pushed ahead of government social welfare or private charities as the basis of social mobility. But drink also served symbolic functions. Alcohol was closely linked to the lessening of control over sexuality. Uninhibited males could frequent prostitutes, and young women could be seduced by predatory companions. In defense of the Victorian middle-class home, temperance reform did battle against the saloon. It was a potent weapon to be able to use an articulate and well-organized lobbying group of women to accomplish this purpose after the Civil War.

While Willard moved to make the WCTU relevant to the Victorian and domesticity-oriented culture of the middle classes, she also strove to make those same classes aware of issues and rights beyond their own narrow and insular outlook. By the late 1880s, she had come to believe that wage reform and trade union development were important components of temperance reform. The Knights of Labor under Terence Powderly banned drink sellers from its membership and allowed men and women to work together as equals in the assemblies of the Knights in promoting labor reforms. Willard found this formula appealing, because she believed that women needed economic independence in order for them to engage in reform and have the economic freedom to choose suitable—that is, Christian, abstaining—husbands.

In the 1890s, Willard's radicalism went further, and she declared herself a socialist. This sprang from her commitment to the Social Gospel, a vital force for reform in urban areas in the 1890s. Willard always justified socialism in terms of "the golden rule" beloved of Social Gospelers, but she gave the cause a radical edge in her critique of great wealth and the use allegedly made of alcohol by wealthy interests. "I charge upon the drink traffic that it keeps people down," she declared in her 1893 presidential address, "and capitalists and politicians know it."[2] This was not anarchism—which she denounced, as did others of her class—nor Marxist socialism but Christian socialism of the variety championed by American reformer Edward Bellamy and some English Fabians. Willard's socialism was, because of its Christian and gradualist disposition, surprisingly influential within the WCTU. A Department of Relations Between Capital and Labor was formed in 1886, and under various names it continued to seek better working conditions for men and women into the 1920s. From its ranks the WCTU contributed a number of members of the American Socialist party, including social justice crusaders like Mary Garbutt, who headed the WCTU in southern California for many years.

Willard's broad-brush approach sometimes threatened to weaken the WCTU. Modern sociological studies confirm that the WCTU developed many ties with other reforms and that these ties reflected the prominence and respectability of the organization. To critics, this web of connections seemed ephemeral, and work done under the WCTU umbrella could be superficial at times. Certainly, much of the value of such reform work was necessarily done in so-called departments sometimes administered as independent fiefdoms by particular temperance women. For this reason, Willard cannot be assessed fairly as an individual leader but as a leader of a complex movement in which many lesser-known women contributed individually: Hannah Clark Bailey dominated peace reform, Mary Hannah Hunt spurred scientific temperance instruction in the American schools, Mary Lovell attacked the killing of animals and birds to produce furs and feathers for women's clothing, and so on. Willard "contextualized" these diverse women's activities, based on her strong friendships with other women. Departmentalization was Willard's master stroke, since it enabled women to do concrete work in their local WCTU. No local was obliged to adopt all of the causes championed at the national level, and the WCTU is best understood as a federation of these local impulses for reform coming together under Willard's galvanizing leadership.

As a symbol of woman's achievements, Willard supported the Woman's Temperance Publishing Association, run by Matilda Carse. All of the WCTU's national publications appeared under this imprint, and WCTU women contributed to the Woman's Temple, an imposing and attractive twelve-story skyscraper in downtown Chicago. Willard, with characteristic hyperbole, called it in 1891 "the noblest architectural pile ever dedicated to business purposes since the world began."[3] Under Willard's leadership, the organization grew in numerical strength from its strongest base of support, the Midwest. She worked tirelessly and made long, arduous train trips to the South, where the organization was weak, and to the West Coast in 1883. She even courted white Southern support by issuing statements that seemed to condone the high incidence of lynching in the South. At the same time, she courted "colored" support in segregated locals. Willard also sought immigrant support, and used women like the German-American Henrietta Skelton of Chicago to minister to the polyglot ethnic communities of the larger American cities. Cordial relations were developed with the Catholic Total Abstinence Union, which favored individual action to achieve temperance reform. Nevertheless, few Catholics joined, and the organization remained overwhelmingly Anglo-Saxon in origin. In this matter, the WCTU reflected the larger tendencies in the prohibition movement; most Catholics opposed the legal prohibition of all alcohol that Willard and her followers sought.

Willard's period as leader was marked by a rapid expansion in the organization both in geography and numbers. From 27,000 in just over 1,000 locals by 1879, the WCTU reached 149,000 paid-up members in over 7,000 locals in 1890. Thereafter, it was hit by the financial crisis of the early 1890s and the failure of the Woman's Temple as an economic venture. By 1897 membership had dropped to 142,000. Willard came under attack after 1895 for her connection to marginal and heretical causes. The advocacy of state-regulated prostitution by her English friend Lady Henry Somerset, and reports that she and Lady Henry had moved away from absolute prohibition toward support of high license laws and municipal management of pubs, damaged Willard's leadership. Willard denied her heterodoxy, and so great was her stature that she retained her presidency unchallenged until her death.

Equally controversial had been Willard's earlier advocacy of the Prohibition party as a third force in the presidential elections of 1884 and 1888. Subsequently, she unsuccessfully sought an alliance with the Populists. These political tactics disturbed some of her supporters in the North, many of whom tended to be Republicans. Judith Ellen Foster, formerly one of Willard's allies, led a breakaway movement in 1889–1890 to found the narrower Non-Partisan Woman's Christian Temperance Union. But the significance of this move should not be exaggerated. Willard's WCTU continued to outnumber the Non-Partisans, who, with a "limited following" in eleven states, never constituted more than a minor annoyance to the main body.

Views of Willard have changed markedly over time. From her late nineteenth-century adoration, Willard's reputation slumped after the repeal of national prohibition in 1933. Only in the 1970s was her reputation as a key woman reformer rehabilitated. The new woman's movement found in her something of a heroine. But whereas early historians had tended to see her simply as a representative of the temperance cause, feminists presented her as moving women forward into the public sphere. In their reading of her life, she emerges as a sagacious and influential woman. However, the reinterpretation can be carried too far. It is too easy to see her as a bearer, in linear progression, of the values of a future woman's movement. Even calling her "feminist" is problematic because of the shifting meanings that feminism has, and still acquires.

Not only was Willard the leader of a complex movement that cannot be reduced to temperance; she herself was a complex character. Especially infuriating is the great gap between public information on her public activities and the ambiguous and fragmentary evidence on her personal life. Like some other prominent women of the temperance cause, Willard was secretive. It is likely that we will never know the full story of the forces that drove her, for she was determined that these remain private. In fact, Willard characterized herself emotionally as "the sphinx that I have always been" on the subject of "life's most intricate equation," love. She was prepared to tantalize, but not to reveal. She wrote: "Of the real romance of my life, unguessed save by a trio of close friends, these pages may not tell." After breaking her engagement to Charles Fowler, she remained single and apparently celibate. Later in life she had a variety of female friends. From 1877 on, she was extremely close to Anna Gordon, who served as her secretary, companion, and lover. Willard also expressed love and affection for various other women. Especially influential in her impact on Willard was Lady Henry Somerset, the president of the British Women's Temperance Association, from whom she was seldom seen apart in the early 1890s.

Willard's affection for other women was not uncommon in temperance ranks. She was part of a group of single, educated, and middle-class women who dominated the reform movement's leadership from the 1870s through World War I. This was also the generation in the larger American community with the greatest number of single, educated women. Being a reform leader required much sacrifice, for the salaries were small. Willard was paid a very modest stipend, which peaked at $2,400 in the 1890s. Much of the help given to temperance, like that given by other women to reform causes, was a form of unpaid work. The women with whom Willard associated became part of what the WCTU called a "sisterhood of service," and close relations with women helped supply the domestic help, secretarial staff, part-time organizers, platform speakers, and fund-raisers the temperance movement needed. Most of the working women in the WCTU held professional and clerical occupations. Teachers and journalists were prominent, and there were also doctors, businesswomen, and lawyers in the ranks.

It would be wrong to see Willard as part of a man-hating generation, the female equivalent of a misogynist. Her study in Rest Cottage was adorned with the portraits of male reformers whom she admired: Neal Dow, Terence Powderly, John Woolley, and others. Willard praised and encouraged the roles of males in the temperance movement, recognizing that their participation was vital if the Victorian family was to be strengthened. She supported, for example, the White Cross campaign, which encouraged male sexual abstinence before marriage. Rather than spinsterhood, she encouraged what she called the "white life for two"—purity in relations between the sexes outside of marriage and an equal and sexually restrained relationship within marriage. Willard advocated women having ultimate control over the sex act; motherhood should be entered into only on terms of women's consent and equality.

Male reform groups were as important to Willard as the love and support of individual males was to the moral well-being of the American home. Since only men could vote in American state or federal elections in the late nineteenth century—with the exception of a few places in the West—it made sense to develop alliances with male-dominated groups such as Francis E. Clark's United Society of Christian Endeavor or the Anti-Saloon League (ASL), the latter group having been founded in 1895. After Willard's death and the coming of the drive for national prohibition after 1907, this alliance with the ASL proved crucial to the success of the Eighteenth Amendment. Prominent supporters of constitutional prohibition, like Representative Richmond Hobson of Alabama, courted the WCTU before and during World War I. Through this strategy of alliance with other temperance organizations, the WCTU increased its membership still further, reaching a peak of over 425,000 members in the late 1920s. But never did the movement regain the innovative leadership that Willard exerted.

Willard's character is difficult to comprehend not only because it was secretive but also because it was often so contradictory. Reared in the traditions of evangelical Protestantism—she was tempted in the 1870s by the idea of working permanently for the famous evangelist Dwight Moody—Willard nevertheless could see, by the end of her life, value in all religions. She was an enthusiastic supporter of the Parliament of Religions at the World's Fair in Chicago in 1893, calling on the Methodists to extend a hand of friendship to all peoples. Willard also differed with many Christians over their treatment of women in the churches. She supported the controversial *Woman's Bible* written by feminist Elizabeth Cady Stanton, and in 1888 she battled with her own Methodist Episcopal Church for the right of women to be delegates—a right won in 1896.

For all that, Willard never abandoned her faith. Rather, she sought to modernize it as part of the Social Gospel. She still strongly believed that Western religion alone, and evangelical Protestantism in particular, gave women hope of advancement. To the end of her life, Jesus Christ was the "Great Emancipator" of women to her, and to most of her followers.

Reform movements require charismatic and effective leaders, and Willard's success in part lies in the uncanny and multilayered appeal that she had for her class of women. This appeal was based on her impressive platform appearances and her physical presence. Willard was by no means the dour person that drab nineteenth-century photographs and the subsequent reputation of temperance might convey. She possessed a strong sense of humor and, well into her forties, a personal attractiveness that reminded followers of a beautiful young girl. She spoke to her followers in strongly rhythmic prose peppered with clever phrases and numerous allusions to the Victorian middle-class culture of polite and uplifting literature. James Clement Ambrose heaped representative praise upon her in *Potter's American Monthly* for May 1882: "As a public speaker, I think Miss Willard is without a peer among women. With much of the Edward Everett in her language, there is more of the Wendell Phillips in her manner of delivery. She is wholly at home, but not forward on the platform, with grace in bearing, ease and moderation in gesture, and in her tones there are tears when she wills."[4]

Despite her enormous appeal as a speaker, Willard preferred the medium of journalism. She especially worked through her contributions to the *Union Signal*, the WCTU's national newspaper. Founded in 1883 by an amalgamation of two earlier papers, it appeared monthly and had a readership estimated at half a million in the early 1890s. Said Willard, "The true press is a throne of power for good, a pulpit for righteousness, a telephone of heavenly magic, for while the platform speaker is reaching a few thousands, the quiet editor is reaching armies."[5]

Willard had little time for reflection, and compiled her books, *Woman and Temperance* (1884) and *Glimpses of Fifty Years* (1889) from her diary jottings, newspaper and periodical articles, and platform speeches. She was not an original thinker, but she was quick to grasp the significance of new reforms and changing social conditions for the advancement of both women and the temperance movement. For this reason, she is an excellent person through whom to study the intellectual and social influences of her time.

Willard's involvement in many aspects of health reform for women is a case in point. This included her support for John Harvey Kellogg's sanitarium in Battle Creek, Michigan, her vegetarianism, her advocacy of physical exercise for women, and her embrace of bicycle riding as a form of recreation. Willard even wrote a short book, *A Wheel Within a Wheel: How I Learned to Ride the Bicycle* (1895), to advance the latter cause. She explained there that her own early experience on the frontier had given her a physical freedom absent in the urban, middle-class woman's world, where corsets and drawing room conventions bound women down. Women's sport could become, she felt, a way to repair the physical neglect of women's moral and mental, as well as physical, health.

Willard did not confine her work to the United States. She founded the World's Woman's Christian Temperance Union in 1883 and built an alliance with British temperance women after 1886 that helped to spread American temperance reform, and the institution of the WCTU, to more than forty countries by the 1920s. Willard served as the second president of the World WCTU. She was also influential in the organizing of the International Council of Women (ICW), founded in 1888, and served as the first president of the American National Council affiliated to the ICW. The export of American reform institutions through such groups as the Student Volunteers movement and Young Men's Christian Association and the Young Women's Christian Association after about 1895, and the subsequent expansion internationally of many others, such as Alcoholics Anonymous, testifies to the contribution of American reform movements to the spread of American culture. Willard's WCTU, as one of the earliest and most successful of these organizations, provided a model for other temperance groups, like the ASL, that sought to extend prohibition to other countries after the passage of the Eighteenth Amendment in 1919.

Willard was highly regarded abroad among women's groups. She was a model for Protestant evangelical women in Australia, New Zealand, Canada, South

Africa, Great Britain, and Scandinavia. Kaji Yajima was declared "the Frances Willard of Japan"; portraits of Willard were distributed by missionaries among the mission schools of India. But like the larger temperance movement itself, her reputation never spread to any extent beyond the Anglo-American world and its missionary outposts in such places as China and Japan. Apart from her visits to Great Britain and Europe in the 1890s, to stay with Lady Henry Somerset, and several trips to eastern Canada, Willard did not tour internationally. She suffered severely from seasickness, and her health was failing. So she left the work of international organizing to such missionaries as Mary Clement Leavitt and Jessie Ackermann.

Willard's career shows in particular that American reform had impacts in other countries and at times presented a model for other countries. American reform, in turn, was influenced by events abroad and demands from admirers in those other countries. Willard's views on race, for example, were modified in a more progressive direction in 1895 as a result of British criticism of her failure to condemn lynching in the United States. Her British experience also made her aware of the complexities of alcohol production and consumption, and she was particularly interested, after her British trips in the early 1890s, in the connection of alcoholism to poverty. Her exposure to the international missionary work of the WCTU made her more sympathetic toward religions other than her own evangelical Protestantism. Finally, as part of her international vision for the expansion of the WCTU, she necessarily came to regard the improvement of relations between nations through peace and arbitration as necessary for human survival and prosperity, and pushed the idea of an international arbitration treaty with Britain.

Willard left her mark indelibly upon the WCTU. Her mother's home, Rest Cottage, where Willard lived in Evanston, became WCTU headquarters. It remains so today, and at the same time functions as a de facto mausoleum of women's temperance reform. The furniture and mementos of Willard's time dominate the surroundings and impress the memories of visitors, who are informed that nothing has changed since Willard's death. For all that, Willard's memory lives on in a world vastly changed. Her meaning today is different from that for the nineteenth-century representative woman. Frances Willard still speaks to the role of women with her concerns about the role of the family, moral values, and the tensions between family responsibilities and the search for equality for women.

NOTES

1. *Annual Report of the National Woman's Christian Temperance Union for 1893* (Chicago, 1893), 105. Hereafter these annual reports are cited as NWCTU, AR, and year.
2. Ibid., 104.
3. NWCTU, AR, 1891, 139.
4. Frances Willard, *Woman and Temperance* (Hartford, Conn., 1883), 27–28.
5. NWCTU, AR, 1891, 139.

BIBLIOGRAPHY

Blocker, Jack S., Jr. *"Give to the Winds Thy Fears": The Women's Temperance Crusade, 1873–1874*. Westport, Conn., 1985.

———. *American Temperance Movements: Cycles of Reform*. Boston, 1989.

Bordin, Ruth. *Woman and Temperance: The Quest for Power and Liberty, 1873–1900*. Philadelphia, 1981.

———. *Frances Willard: A Biography*. Chapel Hill, N.C., 1986.

Clark, Norman H. *Deliver Us from Evil: An Interpretation of American Prohibition*. New York, 1976.

Dannenbaum, Jed. *Drink and Disorder: Temperance Reform in Cincinnati from the Washingtonian Revival to the WCTU*. Urbana, Ill., 1984.

Earhart, Mary. *Frances Willard: From Prayers to Politics*. Chicago, 1944.

Epstein, Barbara Leslie. *The Politics of Domesticity: Women, Evangelism, and Temperance in Nineteenth-Century America*. Middletown, Conn., 1981.

Gordon, Anna. *The Beautiful Life of Frances Willard*. Chicago, 1898.

Gusfield, Joseph. "Social Structure and Moral Reform: A Study of the Woman's Christian Temperance Union." *American Journal of Sociology* 61 (November 1955): 221–232.

———. *Symbolic Crusade: Status Politics and the American Temperance Movement*. Urbana, Ill., 1963.

Lee, Susan Dye. "Evangelical Domesticity: The Origins of the WCTU Under Frances Willard." Ph.D. diss., Northwestern University, 1980.

Mezvinzky, Norton. "The White Ribbon Reform, 1874–1920." Ph.D. diss., University of Wisconsin, 1959.

Rorabaugh, William J. *The Alcoholic Republic: An American Tradition*. New York, 1979.

Strachey, Ray. *Frances Willard: Her Life and Work*. London, 1913.

Tyrrell, Ian. *Sobering Up: From Temperance to Prohibition in Antebellum America, 1800–1860*. Westport, Conn., 1979.

———. *Woman's World/Woman's Empire: The Woman's Christian Temperance Union in International Perspective*. Chapel Hill, N.C., 1991.

Willard, Frances. *Woman and Temperance or, The Work and Workers of the Woman's Christian Temperance Union*. 1883; repr. New York, 1972.

———. *Glimpses of Fifty Years: The Autobiography of an American Woman*. 1889; repr. New York, 1970.

Reform Chronology

PAUL A. CIMBALA

The following time line is not intended to be exhaustive in its inclusiveness. Entries generally reflect the activities of the subjects covered by or related in some way to the reforms discussed, in this volume's essays. Birth dates, death dates, and other purely personal dates relating to the reformers are not listed. Court decisions and legislation listed here are federal actions unless otherwise noted. Entries for the mid-to-late-twentieth century are arranged by month because of their immediacy. The exceptions are book publication dates; books are simply noted at the beginning of each year's list.

1775	Philadelphia Quakers organized the first antislavery society
1775	War for Independence began at Lexington and Concord, Massachusetts
1776	Thomas Paine's *Common Sense* published
1776	Declaration of Independence
1777	Vermont abolished slavery
1780	Pennsylvania adopted gradual emancipation law
1781	States ratified Articles of Confederation
1783	Court decision ended slavery in Massachusetts
1784	Benjamin Rush's *An Inquiry into the Effects of Spiritous Liquors on the Human Body and Mind* published
1784	U.S. ratified the peace treaty with England that ended the Revolutionary War
1784	Rhode Island and Connecticut adopted gradual emancipation laws
1787	Richard Allen and others established the Free African Society in Philadelphia

1787	First Shaker commune established
1787	Northwest Ordinance
1787–1788	States ratified Constitution
1789	First U.S. presidential election
1791	Bill of Rights went into effect following ratification by Virginia
1794	First of a series of American Conventions for Promoting the Abolition of Slavery and Improving the Condition of the African Race met in Philadelphia
1795–1837	Second Great Awakening
1799	New York adopted gradual emancipation law
1804	New Jersey adopted gradual emancipation law
1808	International slave trade ended in U.S.
1812–1815	War with England
1813	Robert Owen's *A New View of Society* published
1813	Massachusetts Society for the Suppression of Intemperance Founded
1813	African Methodist Episcopal Church of New York established (in 1848 it became officially known as the African Methodist Episcopal Zion Church)
1814	Noah Worcester's *Solemn Review of the Custom of War* published
1815	David Low Lodge's *War Inconsistent with the Religion of Jesus Christ* published
1815	New York Peace Society founded
1815	Massachusetts Peace Society founded
1815	American Education Society founded
1816	American Colonization Society founded
1816	American Bible Society founded
1816	Richard Allen of Philadelphia, Daniel Coker of Baltimore, and others officially organized the African Methodist Episcopal Church
1817	American Sunday School Union founded
1820	Missouri Compromise
1821	New York State built first penitentiary
1821	Charles G. Finney experienced conversion
1823	Catharine Beecher founded Hartford [Connecticut] Female Seminary
1824	First public high school for girls established in Worcester, Massachusetts
1825	American Tract Society founded

1825	New York House of Refuge established
1825	Robert Owen's New Harmony, Indiana, opened (closed in 1827)
1826	American Society for the Promotion of Temperance founded
1826	American Temperance Society founded
1826	American Home Missionary Society founded
1827	Catharine Beecher's ''Female Education'' appeared in *American Journal of Education*
1828	American Peace Society founded
1829	David Walker's *Appeal to the Colored Citizens of the World* published
1829	Pennsylvania Eastern State Penitentiary established in Philadelphia
1829	President Andrew Jackson called for removal of eastern Indians to land west of the Mississippi River
1829	Repressive black codes and violence prompted African Americans to leave Cincinnati, Ohio, to establish homes in Canada; eventually 1,100–2,200 blacks left the city
1830	Joseph Smith completed the *Book of Mormon*
1830	Richard Allen, Austin Steward, and others organized the American Society of Free Persons of Color in Philadelphia; the meeting began the National Negro Convention Movement
1830	Sylvester Graham hired as a lecturer by the Pennsylvania State Society for the Suppression of the Use of Ardent Spirits
1830	Joseph Smith and followers founded Church of Jesus Christ of Latter-day Saints (Mormons)
1830–1831	High point of Charles G. Finney's revival crusade, Rochester, New York
1831	Catharine Beecher's *The Elements of Mental and Moral Philosophy* published
1831	William Lloyd Garrison began publishing *The Liberator* in Boston
1831	Joseph Smith founded Mormon community at Independence, Missouri
1831	Nat Turner's uprising in Southampton, Virginia
1831	*Cherokee Nation* v. *Georgia*
1832	William Lloyd Garrison's *Thoughts on Colonization* published
1832	Dorothea Dix's *American Moral Tales for Young Persons* published
1832–1833	South Carolina nullification crisis
1832	*Worcester* v. *Georgia*

1832	New England Anti-Slavery Society founded
1833	Sylvester Graham's *A Lecture on Epidemic Diseases Generally, and Particularly the Spasmodic Cholera* published
1833–1849	Charles Loring Brace served as principal of the Hartford Female Seminary
1833	American Anti-Slavery Society organized
1833	United States Temperance Union founded
1833	Rev. John Jay Shipherd opened Oberlin College, which admitted women as well as men, blacks as well as whites
1834	Sylvester Graham's *A Lecture to Young Men* published
1834	Female Moral Reform Society founded
1834	Lane Seminary students debated abolitionism in Cincinnati
1834	African Americans began commemorating the British Emancipation Act with ''First of August'' celebrations
1835	Joseph Smith published *Doctrine and Covenants*, an expansion of *Book of Commandments* (1833)
1835	Charles G. Finney's ''Lectures on Revivals of Religion'' published in *The New York Evangelist*
1835	Charles G. Finney accepted appointment as professor of theology at Oberlin College
1835	American Moral Reform Society founded
1836–1844	Gag rules in effect in Congress
1836	United States Temperance Union renamed American Temperance Union
1836	New York Committee of Vigilance founded
1837	Catharine Beecher's *An Essay on Slavery and Abolition, with Reference to the Duty of American Females* published
1837	Sylvester Graham's *Treatise on Bread and Bread-Making* published
1837	*Graham Journal of Health and Longevity* founded
1837–1848	Horace Mann served as secretary of the Board of Education in Massachusetts
1837	Angelina and Sarah Grimké lectured in New England
1837	Abolitionist editor Elijah Lovejoy murdered in Alton, Illinois
1837	American Physiological Society founded
1837	Samuel E. Cornish established the *Colored American* in New York City
1838	Sarah Grimké's *Letters on the Condition of Women and the Equality of the Sexes* published
1838	Angelina Grimké's *Letters to Catherine E. Beecher* published

1838–1839	Mormon Missouri War
1838	Frederick Douglass escaped from slavery
1838	New England Non-Resistance Society founded after split in the American Peace Society
1838	Eastern Cherokees removed westward on Trail of Tears
1839	Sylvester Graham's *Lectures on the Science of Human Life* published
1839	Enslaved Africans seized the slave ship *Amistad*
1839	Mormons settle at Nauvoo, Illinois
1840	William Ladd's *Essay on a Congress of Nations* published
1840	Albert Brisbane's *The Social Destiny of Man* published
1840	Washington Temperance Society founded
1840	American and Foreign Anti-Slavery Society organized after ideological split in the American Anti-Slavery Society
1840	James G. Birney nominated for presidency on Liberty party ticket
1841	Catharine Beecher's *A Treatise on Domestic Economy* published
1841	Frederick Douglass began his association with the Massachusetts Anti-Slavery Society
1841	Joseph Smith established Nauvoo Agricultural and Mechanical Association
1841	George Ripley founded Brook Farm in West Roxbury, Massachusetts (closed by 1849)
1842	Mormon women established the Relief Society at Nauvoo, Illinois (disbanded in 1844)
1842	*Prigg* v. *Pennsylvania*
1843	Martin R. Delaney founded *The Mystery* in Pittsburgh
1843	Isabella Van Wagener took the name Sojourner Truth and began her career as a traveling preacher and abolitionist
1843	Joseph Smith announced the revelation of polygamy (previously introduced to a select group in 1841)
1843	Sons of Temperance founded
1843	North American Phalanx established at Red Bank, New Jersey (closed in 1856)
1843	Samuel Gridley Howe presented Dorothea Dix's ''Memorial to the Legislature of Massachusetts'' to that body
1844	James G. Birney nominated for presidency on Liberty party ticket
1844	Association of Medical Superintendents of American Institutions for the Insane founded

1844	Catharine Beecher founded the Central Committee for Promoting National Education (renamed the National Board of Popular Education in 1848)
1844	Joseph Smith murdered by a mob at Carthage, Illinois
1845	*Narrative of the Life of Frederick Douglass* published
1845	Frederick Douglass began a twenty-one-month tour of England, Ireland, and Scotland
1845	Margaret Fuller's *Women in the Nineteenth Century* published
1845	Dorothea Dix's *Remarks on Prisons and Prison Discipline in the United States* published
1845	New Jersey established the insane asylum at Trenton, the consequence of Dorothea Dix's lobbying efforts
1845	Annexation of Texas
1846–1848	Mexican War
1846	Wilmot Proviso
1846	Union Missionary Society, the Committee for West Indian Missions, and the Western Evangelical Missionary Society merged to become the American Missionary Association
1847	Brigham Young and other Mormons arrived at the Great Salt Lake in Utah
1847	American Medical Association founded
1847	Frederick Douglass began publishing *The North Star* in Rochester, New York
1848	Elizabeth Cady Stanton, Lucretia Mott, and other women promulgated a ''Declaration of Sentiments'' at the Seneca Falls, New York, convention
1848	Dorothea Dix proposed establishing a national land trust to fund treatment for the insane
1848	John Humphrey Noyes's Oneida Association formed in Madison County, New York
1848	Free Soil party nominated Martin Van Buren for the presidency
1849	Samuel Ringgold Ward founded *The Impartial Citizen* in Syracuse, New York
1849	American Phrenological Society founded
1850	Compromise of 1850
1850	Fugitive Slave Act prompted black migration to Canada from northern states, and Frederick Douglass to advocate armed resistence
1851–1866	Charles G. Finney served as president of Oberlin College
1851	Mary Grove Nichols and Thomas Nichols founded American Hydropathic Institute

1851	Maine prohibition law passed
1851	Mary Sharp College, Winchester, Tennessee, the first women's college with a curriculum of study comparable with a men's college founded
1851	First U.S. chapter of Young Men's Christian Association organized in Boston
1851	Frederick "Shadrach" Jenkins, arrested as a fugitive slave, was rescued in Boston
1851	Gerrit Smith, Jermaine Loguen, Samuel Ringgold Ward, and the Syracuse Vigilance Committee rescued Jerry, a fugitive slave, in Syracuse, New York
1852	Harriet Beecher Stowe's *Uncle Tom's Cabin* published
1852	Mary Ann Shadd (Cary)'s *Notes on Canada West* published
1852	Martin R. Delaney's *The Condition, Elevation, Emigration and Destiny of the Colored People of the United States, Politically Considered* published
1852	Elizabeth Cady Stanton raised the demand for expanded grounds for divorce
1852	Catharine Beecher founded the American Woman's Educational Association
1852	Brigham Young publicly defended polygamy
1853–1859	Horace Mann served as president of the coeducational Antioch College at Yellow Springs, Ohio
1853	National Council of Colored People founded in Rochester, New York
1853	Mary Ann Shadd (Cary) and Samuel Ringgold Ward began publishing the *Provincial Freedman* in Canada; Shadd became the first African-American woman newspaper editor in North America
1853	Children's Aid Society was formed in New York City with Charles Loring Brace as its director
1853–1894	Children's Aid Society transported over 85,000 children to country homes
1854	Henry David Thoreau's *Walden* published
1854	Kansas-Nebraska Act
1854	Anti-Nebraska elements began to organize themselves into the Republican party
1854	Attempt to rescue fugitive slave Anthony Burns failed in Boston
1854	Elizabeth Cady Stanton and Susan B. Anthony presented the New York State legislature with a list of the legal liabilities of women
1855	Frederick Douglass's *My Bondage and My Freedom* published

1855	Samuel Ringgold Ward's *Autobiography of a Fugitive Negro* published
1855	Elmira (New York) College, the first women's college with a curriculum of study comparable with a men's college still in existence, founded
1856	Republican party nominated John C. Frémont for the presidency
1857	Harriet Tubman rescued her enslaved parents
1857	Russell Trall incorporated the Hygeio-Therapeutic College
1857	*Dred Scott* v. *Sandford*
1858	Henry Highland Garnett founded the African Civilization Society
1859	John Brown's raid on Harper's Ferry, Virginia
1860	Harriet Tubman was severely beaten in Troy, New York, as she led the group that rescued fugitive slave Charles Nalle
1860	Secession of South Carolina
1860	Frederick Douglass began to pay increased attention to black suffrage
1861	Martin R. Delaney's *Official Report of the Niger Valley Exploring Party* published
1861–1865	American Civil War
1861–1869	American Missionary Association supported 2,638 teachers in the South
1861	Federal forces captured Port Royal, South Carolina, paving the way for a major experiment in reconstruction
1862	Homestead Act
1862	Unofficial black Union regiments organized in Kansas, Louisiana, and South Carolina
1863	Emancipation Proclamation
1863	Federal government authorized the organization of black regiments
1863	New York City draft riots
1863	Elizabeth Cady Stanton established the Women's Loyal National League
1863	Masssachusetts Board of State Charities established
1863	Seventh Day Adventists adopted Grahamism
1864	Colorado militia perpetrated the Sand Creek Massacre
1864	National Convention of Colored Men, meeting in Syracuse, New York, with Frederick Douglass as chair, issued an "Address to the People of the United States," which stressed the importance of suffrage

1865	Martin R. Delaney was commissioned a major in the Union Army, becoming the first black field officer of high rank
1865	Bureau of Refugees, Freedmen, and Abandoned Lands established with General Oliver Otis Howard as its commissioner
1865	Thirteenth Amendment ratified
1865	William Lloyd Garrison published the last issue of *The Liberator*
1865	American Missionary Association (AMA) called for a national educational system
1865–1867	Great Sioux War
1866	Elizabeth Cady Stanton, Susan B. Anthony, and others appealed to Congress for universal suffrage
1866	American Equal Rights Association established
1866	Civil Rights Act
1866	William H. Sylvis formed the National Labor Union
1866	AMA-sponsored Fisk School opened in Nashville (incorporated as Fisk University in 1867)
1867	AMA-sponsored Atlanta University chartered
1867	Howard University founded in Washington, D.C.
1867	Reconstruction Act
1868	Samuel Chapman Armstrong, with the assistance of the AMA, founded Hampton Institute in Virginia
1868	Fourteenth Amendment ratified
1869	Uriah S. Stephens and others established Knights of Labor
1869	Elizabeth Cady Stanton and others established the National Woman Suffrage Association
1869	Elizabeth Cady Stanton announced her plans to spend more time advocating equality in marriage
1869	Lucy Stone and others established the American Woman Suffrage Association
1869	Wyoming Territory enfranchised women
1870	Utah Territory enfranchised women
1870	Civil Rights Act
1870	Fifteenth Amendment ratified
1870	American Anti-Slavery Society disbanded
1870	Hiram Revels of Mississippi became the first black to serve in the U.S. Senate
1870	Joseph H. Rainey of South Carolina became the first black legislator sworn into the U.S. House of Representatives

1870	Sojourner Truth unsuccessfully petitioned President Ulysses S. Grant for assistance in settling African Americans on public lands in the West
1870	Frederick Douglass became the editor of the *New National Era*
1871	Catharine Beecher's *Woman's Suffrage and Woman's Profession* published
1871–1874	Washington Gladden edited *The Independent*
1871–1872	P.B.S. Pinchback, lieutenant governor of Louisiana, briefly served as governor of the state, becoming the nation's first African-American governor
1871	Civil Rights Act
1873	*Slaughter-House Cases*
1874	Michigan referendum for women's suffrage defeated
1874	Woman's Christian Temperance Union founded in Cincinnati
1874	Benjamin "Pap" Singleton and associates formed the Edgeville Real Estate and Homestead Association to facilitate black migration to Kansas
1875	Mary Baker Eddy's first edition of *Science and Health with Key to the Scriptures* published
1875	Civil Rights Act
1876	Washington Gladden's *Working People and Their Employers* published
1876	*United States* v. *Cruikshank*
1876	Seventh Day Adventists hired John Harvey Kellogg as superintendent of their health institute in Battle Creek, Michigan, which had opened in 1866
1877	Knights of Reliance (Farmers' Alliance) founded in Lampasas County, Texas
1877	*Munn* v. *Illinois*
1877	National railroad strikes
1878	Elizabeth Cady Stanton delivered her "National Protection for National Citizens" address
1879	Henry George's *Progress and Poverty* published
1879	Thousands of African-American "Exodusters" migrated from the South to Kansas
1879	William T. Baggett organized a Farmers' Alliance that was the beginning of the National Farmers' Alliance and Industrial Union (the "Southern" Farmers' Alliance) in Parker County, Texas
1879	Mary Baker Eddy and followers established Church of Christ, Scientist

1879	Carlisle, Pennsylvania, Indian School established
1879	Salvation Army arrived in U.S.
1880	National Farmers' Alliance (the Northwest Alliance) established in Chicago
1880	Henry George embarked on the first of five British lecture tours
1881	*Life and Times of Frederick Douglass* published
1881	Helen Hunt Jackson's *A Century of Dishonor* published
1881	Massachusetts Metaphysical College chartered with Mary Baker Eddy as president and only teacher (dissolved in 1890)
1881	Oneida became a joint stock company
1881	Federated Organization of Trades and Labor Unions established in Pittsburgh
1881	Tuskegee Institute opened with Booker T. Washington as its principal
1882–1902	Almost 2,000 African Americans were lynched
1882	Indian Rights Association established
1883	Washington Gladden's *The Christian League of Connecticut* published
1883	Henry George published *Social Problems* in response to William Graham Sumner's criticism of *Progress and Poverty*
1883	First issue of *Journal of Christian Science* published
1883	Woman's Christian Temperance Union began publishing *Union Signal*
1883	African-American laity and clergy called together by Alexander Crummell protested the absence of black bishops in the Episcopal Church
1883	U.S. Civil Service Commission established
1883	*Civil Rights Cases*
1883	Lake Mohonk (New York) Conference of Friends of the Indian
1883	Harvey Washington Wiley appointed chief chemist for federal commissioner of agriculture
1883	Frances Willard founded the World's Woman's Christian Temperance Union
1884	Frances Willard's *Woman and Temperance* published
1884	Lawrence Gronlund's *The Cooperative Commonwealth* published
1885	Knights of Labor struck Jay Gould's Wabash Railroad
1886	Washington Gladden's *Applied Christianity: Moral Aspects of Social Questions* published
1886	Colored Farmers' National Alliance established in Texas

1886	Woman's Christian Temperance Union established its Department of Relations Between Capital and Labor
1886	Henry George nominated to run for mayor of New York City on United Labor party platform
1886	American Federation of Labor established with Samuel Gompers as its first president
1886	Bombing of Haymarket Square, Chicago
1886	Stanley Coit founded Neighborhood Guild in New York City
1887	Dawes Severalty Act
1888	Edward Bellamy's *Looking Backward* published
1888	Elizabeth Cady Stanton presided over the founding meeting of the International Council of Women
1889	Frances Willard's *Glimpses of Fifty Years* published
1889	Jane Addams and Ellen Gates Starr opened Hull House in Chicago
1889	Ida B. Wells became a partner and editor of the *Memphis Free Speech and Headlight*
1890	Jacob Riis's *How the Other Half Lives* published
1890	Ignatius Donnelly's *Caesar's Column* published
1890	Mary Baker Eddy dissolved Church of Christ, Scientist
1890	T. Thomas Fortune founded the Afro-American League
1890	Jamie Porter Barrett, a Hampton Institute graduate, opened the Locust Street Social Settlement in Hampton, Virginia
1890	Cavalry troopers massacred Sioux Indians at Wounded Knee Creek, South Dakota
1890	Southern Farmers' Alliance promulgated Ocala Demands
1890	The National Woman Suffrage Association and the American Woman Suffrage Association merged to form the National American Woman Suffrage Association
1890	United Mine Workers formed
1891	Tom Watson established *The People's Party Paper* in Georgia
1892	Tom Watson's *The People's Party Campaign Book. Not a Revolt; It Is a Revolution* published
1892	Memphis, Tennessee, mob forced the closing of Ida B. Wells's *Free Speech*
1892	National Federation of Women's Clubs established
1892	Homestead, Pennsylvania, steel strike
1892	Washington Gladden chaired Congregational Church's first Committee on Capital and Labor
1892	Socialist party ran its first candidate in a national election

1892	People's Party of the United States held its first national convention, which nominated James B. Weaver as its presidential candidate
1892	Christian Science's Mother Church in Boston reorganized and reestablished
1893	Washington Gladden's *Tools and the Man* published
1893	Washington Gladden's *The Cosmopolis Club* published
1893–1922	Period of peak settlement house activity in U.S.
1893	Eugene V. Debs organized the American Railway Union
1893	Ida B. Wells embarked on her first speaking tour of England
1894	Henry Demarest Lloyd's *Wealth Against Commonwealth* published
1894	Eugene V. Debs organized strike against James J. Hill's Great Northern Railroad
1894	Pullman employees strike
1894	Eugene V. Debs's American Railway Union boycotted trains carrying Pullman cars
1894	Eugene V. Debs sentenced to six months in prison for violating strike injunction
1894	Coxey's Army marched on Washington, D.C.
1894	Bituminous coal miners' strike
1894	National Municipal League established
1894	Open and Institutional Church League organized
1894	Fairhope, Alabama, a single-tax community, founded
1895	Mary Baker Eddy's *Manual of Mother Church* published
1895	Ida Wells-Barnett's *A Red Record, Tabulated Statistics and Alleged Causes of Lynchings in the United States, 1892–1893–1894* published
1895	Anti-Saloon League founded
1895	Booker T. Washington presented his Atlanta address
1895	National Association of Colored Women founded
1896	W.E.B. Du Bois's Harvard dissertation, *The Suppression of the African Slave-Trade to the United States of America* published
1896	John Dewey established Laboratory School at the University of Chicago
1896	Populist party nominated Democratic presidential candidate William Jennings Bryan as its presidential candidate, with Tom Watson as the party's vice presidential candidate
1896	*Plessy v. Ferguson*

1897	Washington Gladden's *Social Facts and Forces* published
1897	W.E.B. Du Bois published "Strivings of the Negro People" in the *Atlantic Monthly*
1897	Charles M. Sheldon's *In His Steps* published
1897	W.E.B. Du Bois, Paul Laurence Dunbar, and other African-American intellectuals participated in the first formal session of Alexander Crummell's American Negro Academy
1897	Henry George agreed to run for New York City mayor on Bryanite splinter ticket of Democratic party
1897	National Congress of Mothers established
1898	National Pure Food and Drug Congress convened in Washington, D.C.
1898	Spanish-American War
1898	*Williams* v. *Mississippi*
1898	The Afro-American League reorganized as the Afro-American Council
1898	Charlotte Perkins Gilman's *Women and Economics* published
1899	W.E.B. Du Bois's *The Philadelphia Negro: A Social Study* published
1899	Thorstein Veblen's *The Theory of the Leisure Class* published
1899	Jane Addams published "A Function of the Social Settlement" in *Annals of the American Academy of Political and Social Science*
1899	National Consumers League established
1900	Ida Wells-Barnett's *Mob Rule in New Orleans* published
1900	National Civic Federation organized
1900	Eugene Debs ran for the presidency of the United States on the Socialist party ticket, the first of his five campaigns
1901	Frank Norris's *The Octopus* published
1901	Booker T. Washington's *Up from Slavery* published
1901	Congregational Church created Committee on Labor
1901	National Federation of Churches and Christian Workers founded, succeeding the Open and Institutional Church League
1902	Maryland passed first workers' compensation law
1903	W.E.B. Du Bois's *The Souls of Black Folk* published
1903	Frank Norris's *The Pit* published
1903	The "Boston riot" resulted in the arrest of anti-Booker T. Washington protesters, including William Monroe Trotter
1903	*Giles* v. *Harris*

1903	Northern Presbyterians appointed Charles Stelzle, a former machinist, to a special mission to workingmen
1903	Women's Trade Union League founded
1904	Lincoln Steffens's *The Shame of the Cities* published
1904	*Giles* v. *Teasley*
1905	Washington Gladden's First Congregational Church of Columbus, Ohio, established the West Side Social Center (renamed the Gladden Community House in 1920)
1905	Industrial Workers of the World (Wobblies) founded
1905	W.E.B. Du Bois and others began Niagara Movement at Fort Erie, Canada (incorporated in January 1906)
1906	Upton Sinclair's *The Jungle* published
1906	Charles Stelzle assumed leadership of the new Presbyterian Department of Church and Labor
1906	Pure Food and Drugs Act
1906	Meat Inspection Act
1906	Hepburn Railroad Regulation Act
1906	Atlanta race riot
1907	John Dewey's *Pragmatism* published
1907	Edward A. Ross's *Sin and Society* published
1907	Methodist Federation for Social Service created
1907	Northern Baptist Convention established Commission on Social Service
1908	Commission on Church and Social Service created by the newly organized Federal Council of Churches of Christ
1908	Governors' Conference called for establishment of state and national conservation commissions
1908	Springfield, Illinois, race riot
1908	Mary Baker Eddy founded *Christian Science Monitor*
1909	Herbert Croly's *The Promise of American Life* published
1909	National Negro Congress held its first meeting in New York City
1909	Rockefeller Sanitary Commission began campaign against hookworm
1909	The Niagara Movement disbanded
1910	Jane Addams's *Twenty Years at Hull-House with Autobiographical Notes* published
1910–1912	Men and Religion Forward Movement
1910	Insecticide Act

1910	National Association for the Advancement of Colored People (NAACP) officially established
1910	W.E.B. Du Bois became NAACP's director of publicity and research, and began publication of *The Crisis*
1910	Ida Wells-Barnett established the Negro Fellowship League, which served as a settlement house for black men in Chicago
1910	National Conference of Catholic Charities established
1911	Washington Gladden's *The Labor Question* published
1911	National Progressive Republican League founded
1911	National Urban League founded
1911	Triangle Shirtwaist Company fire, New York City, resulted in 146 deaths
1911	National Federation of Settlements founded
1911	Society of American Indians founded
1912	Progressive party nominated Theodore Roosevelt as its presidential candidate
1913	Congregational Church's Committee on Labor reorganized as Commission on Social Service
1913	Anti-Defamation League founded
1913	Sixteenth Amendment ratified
1914	Margaret Sanger first used the term ''birth control'' in her periodical *The Woman Rebel*, which she began publishing this year
1914	Margaret Sanger arrested for distributing *The Woman Rebel*
1915	William J. Simmons founded the new Ku Klux Klan
1916	John Dewey's *Democracy and Education* published
1916	New York City zoning law passed
1916	Margaret Sanger jailed for distributing contraceptives at a clinic in Brooklyn, New York
1917–1918	United States participated in World War I
1917	Marcus Garvey's Universal Negro Improvement Association established first U.S. branch in New York City
1917	Jeanette Rankin, a Republican from Montana, took her seat as the first woman elected to the House of Representatives
1917	Roger Baldwin and Crystal Eastman founded the National Civil Liberties Bureau of the American Union Against Militarism, the forerunner of the American Civil Liberties Union
1917	Earl Browder jailed for almost a year for refusing to register for the military draft

1917	Dorothy Day jailed for participating in a suffragist demonstration in Washington, D.C.
1918	Roger Baldwin began serving nine months in jail, having been convicted of refusing to be drafted
1918	Eugene Debs sentenced to a ten-year prison term (pardoned by Warren G. Harding on Christmas Day, 1921)
1919	W.E.B. Du Bois participated in the First Pan-African Congress in Paris
1919	Eighteenth Amendment ratified
1919	Earl Browder spent over a year in prison for antimilitary activities
1919	Volstead Act
1919	Jane Addams founded the Women's International League for Peace and Freedom, serving as its president until 1929
1919–1920	Attorney General A. Mitchell Palmer staged raids during postwar Red Scare
1920	Margaret Sanger's *Woman and the New Race* published
1920	Prohibition began as the Eighteenth Amendment went into effect
1920	Roger Baldwin established the American Civil Liberties Union
1920	Ninteenth Amendment ratified
1920	League of Nations established
1921	Earl Browder led U.S. contingent to First Congress of Red International Labor Unions
1922	Margaret Sanger's *The Pivot of Civilization* published
1922	Norman Thomas and Harry W. Lardler became codirectors of the League for Industrial Democracy
1922	Coal strike
1922	Rebecca L. Felton of Georgia became the first woman to serve as a member of the U.S. Senate
1923	Norman Thomas's *The Conscientious Objector in America* published
1923	Alice Paul and the National Woman's party instigated introduction of Equal Rights Amendment in Congress
1923	Margaret Sanger established the Birth Control Clinical Research Bureau in New York City
1923	Urban League began publishing *Opportunity*
1924	Dorothy Day's *The Eleventh Virgin* published
1924	National Origins Quota Act
1924	Conference for Progressive Political Action nominated Robert La Follette as its presidential candidate

1925	Nellie T. Ross became the first woman governor, succeeding her late husband, in Wyoming
1925	American Negro Labor Congress founded by black Communists
1925	Trade Union Committee for Organizing Negro Workers founded
1925	Brotherhood of Sleeping Car Porters founded with A. Philip Randolph as general organizer
1925	John Scopes convicted of violating Tennessee law prohibiting the teaching of evolution
1926	Earl Browder decided to champion Stalinism
1927	Roger Baldwin's *Liberty Under the Soviets* published
1927	Eugene V. Debs's *Walls and Bars* published
1927	Nicola Sacco and Bartolomeo Vanzetti executed
1927	Food and Drug Administration established
1927	*Nixon* v. *Herndon*
1927	Dorothy Day converted to Catholicism
1927	Catholic Association for International Peace founded
1928	Norman Thomas ran for the presidency on the Socialist party ticket, the first of his six campaigns
1928	Kellogg-Briand Pact outlawed war
1929	League of United Latin American Citizens founded in Corpus Christi, Texas (February)
1929	Stock market crash (October)
1929	A. J. Muste and others organized the Conference for Progressive Labor Action (May)
1930	Association of Southern Women for the Prevention of Lynching founded at meetings in Atlanta and Dallas (November) (dissolved in 1942)
1931	The Communist party became involved with the Scottsboro Boys (April)
1932	Communist Party USA nominated James W. Ford, an African American, as its vice presidential candidate, the first of two times (May)
1933	Huey Long's *Every Man a King* published
1933	Franklin D. Roosevelt's New Deal began (March)
1933	Labor Secretary Frances Perkins became the first woman cabinet member (March)
1933	Federal Emergency Relief Administration established (April)
1933	Beer legally sold for the first time since 1919 (April)

1933	John Collier became commissioner of Indian affairs (April)
1933	Dorothy Day began publishing the *Catholic Worker* (May)
1933	Agricultural Adjustment Act (May)
1933	National Recovery Administration created (June)
1933	Civil Works Administration established (November)
1933	Eighteenth Amendment repealed with the ratification of the Twenty-first Amendment (December)
1933	American Workers Party established in Pittsburgh (December)
1934	Dr. Francis E. Townsend and Robert Earl Clements established Old Age Revolving Pensions, Ltd. (January)
1934	Huey Long announced his Share Our Wealth movement (February)
1934	Earl Browder became general secretary of the Communist Party of the United States of America (April)
1934	Indian Reorganization Act (June)
1934	Southern Tenant Farmers Union, founded by Socialists Henry Clay East and H. L. Mitchell, formally organized in Searcy, Arkansas (July)
1934	NAACP formally accepted W.E.B. Du Bois's resignation as editor of *The Crisis* (July)
1934	Father Charles E. Coughlin established the National Union for Social Justice (November)
1935	Works Progress Administration established (April)
1935	National Recovery Administration declared illegal (May)
1935	Revenue Act (June)
1935	National Labor Relations Act (July)
1935	Social Security Act (August)
1935	John L. Lewis formed Committee on Industrial Organization (November) (renamed Congress of Industrial Organizations in 1937)
1936	Catholic Worker Movement established a farm commune near Easton, Pennsylvania (April)
1937	Wagner Housing Act (September)
1938	John Dewey's *Experience and Education* published
1938	Dorothy Day's *From Union Square to Rome* published
1938	Ruth De Forest's *America Chamber of Horrors* published
1938	Fair Labor Standards Act (June)
1938	Food, Drug, and Cosmetic Act (June)
1938	*Missouri ex rel. Gaines* v. *Canada* (December)
1939	Dorothy Day's *House of Hospitality* published

1940	*American Journal of Economics and Sociology* began publishing, to encourage research along lines first opened by Henry George
1941–1945	United States participated in World War II
1941	President Franklin Roosevelt delivered his Four Freedoms speech (January)
1941	A. Philip Randolph announced March on Washington Movement (January)
1941	Earl Browder began serving fourteen months at Atlanta Penitentiary for passport fraud (March)
1941	Executive order ends discrimination against African Americans in government agencies, job training programs, defense contractors (June)
1941	President's Committee on Fair Employment Practices established (July)
1942–1943	Congress and President Roosevelt began retreat from New Deal
1942	President Roosevelt authorized removal of Japanese Americans to relocation centers (February)
1942	Congress of Racial Equality founded (April) (officially named in June)
1942	Norman Thomas founded the Post War World Council (June)
1943	Detroit race riot (June)
1943	Zoot Suit Riots in Los Angeles (June)
1944	*Smith* v. *Allwright* (April)
1944	Servicemen's Readjustment Act (June)
1944	National Congress of American Indians founded (September)
1945	Delegates met in San Francisco, California, to organize the United Nations (April)
1945	Atomic weapons used on Hiroshima and Nagasaki (August)
1946	The first General Assembly of the United Nations convened in London (January)
1946	President Harry S Truman created Committee on Civil Rights (December)
1947	Erich Fromm's *Man for Himself* published
1947	Truman Doctrine announced (March)
1947	Jackie Robinson played his first game with the Brooklyn Dodgers to desegregate modern major league baseball (April)
1947	Marshall Plan proposed (May)
1947	Henry A. Wallace announced willingness to run for the presidency outside of Democratic party and went on to campaign on the Progressive party ticket (December)

1948	Water Pollution Control Act (July)
1948	President Truman began desegregation in the armed forces and the federal government (July)
1949	President Truman named his administration the Fair Deal (January)
1949	Asociación Nacional Mexico-Americana founded in Phoenix (February)
1950	David Riesman's *The Lonely Crowd* published
1950	President Truman authorized building of hydrogen bomb (January)
1950	Senator Joseph McCarthy charged Communists infiltrated government (February)
1950	President Truman authorized $10 million in aid to French in Indochina (May)
1950	*Sweatt* v. *Painter* (June)
1950	*McLaurin* v. *Oklahoma State Regents* (June)
1950–53	United States participated in Korean War (June–July)
1950	Henry Hay and others held meeting that led to the founding of the Mattachine Society in Los Angeles (November)
1952	Dorothy Day's *The Long Loneliness* published
1953	President Truman announced the successful development of a hydrogen bomb (January)
1953	*Terry* v. *Adams* (June)
1953	President Dwight D. Eisenhower prohibited employment of gay men and women by federal agencies (April)
1954	*Brown* v. *Board of Education* (May)
1954	Communist Control Act (August)
1954	Martin Luther King, Jr., moved to Montgomery, Alabama, to become the pastor of the Dexter Avenue Baptist Church (September)
1955	Emmett Till lynched in Money, Mississippi (August)
1955	Dell Martin, Phyllis Lyon, and others held meeting that led to the founding of Daughters of Bilitis in San Francisco (September)
1955	American Federation of Labor and Congress of Industrial Organizations merged (December)
1955	Rosa Parks arrested in Montgomery, Alabama (December)
1955	Montgomery, Alabama, bus boycott began (December)
1956	C. Wright Mills's *The Power Elite* published
1956	William H. Whyte's *The Organization Man* published

1956	Montgomery, Alabama, buses desegregated (December)
1957	Vance Packard's *The Hidden Persuaders* published
1957	Martin Luther King, Jr., founded Southern Christian Leadership Conference in Atlanta (January)
1957	Civil Rights Prayer Pilgrimage to Washington (May)
1957	National Committee for a Sane Nuclear Policy formed (June)
1957	Central High School, Little Rock, Arkansas, desegregated with assistance of federal troops (September)
1957	Civil Rights Act (September)
1957	AFL-CIO expelled the International Brotherhood of Teamsters (readmitted in 1987)
1958	Martin Luther King, Jr.'s, *Stride Toward Freedom* published
1958	John Kenneth Galbraith's *The Affluent Society* published
1960	Martin Luther King, Jr., assumed duties of copastor of Ebenezer Baptist Church in Atlanta (February)
1960	Greensboro, North Carolina, Woolworth's lunch counter civil rights sit-in (February)
1960	Student Nonviolent Coordinating Committee founded (April)
1960	Civil Rights Act (May)
1960	Negro American Labor Council (later the Afro-American Labor Council) held inaugural convention in Detroit (May)
1960	Food and Drug Administration approved oral contraceptive pill (May)
1960	Student League for Industrial Democracy founded Students for a Democratic Society at Ann Arbor, Michigan (June)
1960	Martin Luther King, Jr., was sentenced to four months in a state prison, prompting John F. Kennedy to intervene to have him released on bail (October)
1960–1961	San Francisco to Moscow Peace Walk (December–October)
1961	Peace Corps established (March)
1961	CORE sent freedom riders into the South (May)
1961	President Kennedy sent military advisers to Vietnam (November)
1961	Students for a Democratic Society issued Port Huron Statement (December)
1961	César Chávez resigned as executive director of the Community Service Organization to organize Mexican-American farm workers (December)
1962	Michael Harrington's *The Other America* published
1962	Rachel Carson's *Silent Spring* published

1962	President Kennedy called for new standards of consumer protection (March)
1962	*Baker* v. *Carr* (April)
1962	President Kennedy convened White House Conference on Conservation (May)
1962	Public Welfare Amendments (July)
1962	Albany [Georgia] Movement defeated (August)
1962	César Chávez's Farm Workers Association held founding convention (September)
1962	James Meredith enrolled in the University of Mississippi (September)
1962	Cuban missile crisis (October)
1963	Betty Friedan's *The Feminine Mystique* published
1963	Dorothy Day's *Loaves and Fishes* published
1963	George C. Wallace was sworn in as governor of Alabama and pledged to uphold segregation (January)
1963	*Gideon* v. *Wainwright* (March)
1963	Martin Luther King, Jr., launched civil rights demonstrations and business boycott in Birmingham, Alabama (April)
1963	Martin Luther King, Jr., wrote ''Letter from a Birmingham Jail'' (April)
1963	National television publicized violence directed against civil rights demonstrators in Birmingham (May)
1963	Equal Pay Act (June)
1963	Racial segregation ordinances repealed in Birmingham (July)
1963	Civil rights demonstrations across the U.S. (July–September)
1963	Over 200,000 people participated in the March on Washington (August)
1963	Senate approved United States, Great Britain, and Soviet Union Limited Test Ban Treaty (September)
1963	President Kennedy assassinated in Dallas (November)
1963	Clean Air Act (December)
1964	Martin Luther King., Jr.'s *Why We Can't Wait* published
1964	President Lyndon B. Johnson declared war on poverty (January)
1964	Twenty-fourth Amendment ratified (January)
1964	Senate hearings on automobile safety began (March)
1964	Mississippi Freedom Democratic party organized (April)
1964	Three civil rights workers murdered in Mississippi (June)
1964	Malcolm X founded Organization for Afro-American Unity (June)

1964	*Escobedo* v. *Illinois* (June)
1964	Harlem race riot (July)
1964	Civil Rights Act (July)
1964	Economic Opportunity Act (August)
1964	Congress passed Gulf of Tonkin resolution (August)
1964	Free Speech Movement began at the University of California at Berkeley (September)
1964	Martin Luther King, Jr., won the Nobel Peace Prize (October)
1964	University of California at Berkeley students staged a sit-in after taking over administration building (December)
1964	Police arrested about 800 students at Berkeley sit-in one day after it began (December)
1965	Daniel Patrick Moynihan's *The Negro Family* published
1965	Ralph Nader's *Unsafe at Any Speed* published
1965	U.S. began bombing North Vietnam (February)
1965	Malcolm X assassinated in New York City (February)
1965	Student teach-ins began at the University of Michigan (March)
1965	Appalachian Regional Development Act (March)
1965	Martin Luther King, Jr., led Selma and Montgomery, Alabama, marches (March)
1965	Elementary and Secondary Education Act (April)
1965	Students for a Democratic Society organized antiwar rally in Washington, D.C. (April)
1965	President Johnson convened White House Conference on Natural Beauty (May)
1965	*Griswold* v. *Connecticut* (June)
1965	President Johnson announced decision to deploy 50,000 ground troops in Vietnam (July)
1965	Social Security amendments (July)
1965	Watts (Los Angeles) race riot (August)
1965	Voting Rights Act (August)
1965	Housing and Urban Development Act (August)
1965	Farm Workers Association renamed National Farm Workers Association (September)
1965–1970	United Farm Workers struck San Joaquin Valley grape growers (September–July)
1965	Water Quality Act (October)
1965	Immigration Reform Act (October)
1966	Barry Commoner's *Science and Survival* published

1966	Washington University in St. Louis announced the establishment of Barry Commoner's Center for the Biology of Natural Systems (January)
1966	Robert C. Weaver was appointed secretary of housing and urban development by President Johnson, becoming the first African-American cabinet member (January)
1966	*Miranda* v. *Arizona* (June)
1966	Martin Luther King, Jr., took his civil rights crusade to Chicago (July)
1966	Medicare and Medicaid programs became effective (July)
1966	Demonstration (Model) Cities Act (September)
1966	Betty Friedan and others founded National Organization for Women (NOW) (October)
1966	Black Panther Party for Self Defense founded in Oakland, California (October)
1966	Edward W. Brooke of Massachusetts became the first African American elected to the U.S. Senate by popular vote (November)
1967	Martin Luther King, Jr.'s *Where Do We Go from Here* published
1967	Spring Mobilization (April)
1967	*In Re Gault* et al. (May)
1967	Martin Luther King, Jr., imprisoned for Birmingham demonstrations; began planning Poor People's Campaign (June)
1967	Race riots erupted in Newark, New Jersey, and Detroit (July)
1967	National Farm Workers Association affiliated with the AFL-CIO to become the United Farm Workers Organizing Committee (August)
1967	Demonstrators marched on the Pentagon to protest Vietnam War (October)
1968	Paul Ehrlich's *The Population Bomb* published
1968	Abbie Hoffman's *Revolution for the Hell of It* published
1968	Tet offensive began (January)
1968	César Chávez's twenty-five-day fast brought his cause national media attention (February–March)
1968	Martin Luther King, Jr., assassinated in Memphis, Tennessee (April)
1968	Chicago, Washington, D.C., Baltimore, and other cities across the United States erupted in race riots (April)

1968	Student revolts started at Columbia University, the University of California at Berkeley, and other universities (April)
1968	Civil Rights Act (April)
1968	Paris peace talks began (May)
1968	Robert F. Kennedy assassinated in Los Angeles (June)
1968	Dennis Banks, George Mitchell, and others founded the American Indian Movement in Minneapolis (July)
1968	National Housing Act (August)
1968	Protests at Democratic party national convention provoked police violence (August)
1969	Norman Thomas's *The Choices* published
1969	Theodore Roszak's *The Making of a Counter Culture* published
1969	Kate Millet's *Sexual Politics* published
1969	Stonewall Riots, Greenwich Village, New York City (June)
1969	400,000 people attended Woodstock Music and Arts Fair at Bethel, New York (August)
1969	*Alexander* v. *Holmes County Board of Education* (October)
1969	National moratoriums against the war in Vietnam (October, November)
1969	300,000 protestors participated in the March Against Death in Washington, D.C. (November)
1969–1971	"Indians of All Tribes" occupied Alcatraz Island (November–June)
1970	Charles Reich's *The Greening of America* published
1970	National Environmental Policy Act (January)
1970	Joseph A. Yablonski, an unsuccessful candidate for the presidency of the United Mine Workers, was found murdered in Clarksville, Pennsylvania (January)
1970	The first Earth Day celebration held (April)
1970	Campus protests against U.S. invasion of Cambodia (April)
1970	Four Kent State University (Ohio) students were killed by National Guardsmen (May)
1970	Two Jackson State College (Mississippi) students were killed by police (May)
1970	Protests shut down hundreds of colleges and universities (May)
1970	Voting Rights Act (June)
1970	President Richard M. Nixon created the Environmental Protection Agency (July)
1970	Mexican Americans marched in East Los Angeles to protest Vietnam War (August)

1970	NOW-sponsored Strike for Equality (August)
1970	Clean Air Amendments (December)
1971	Barry Commoner's *The Closing Circle* published
1971	Germaine Greer's *Female Eunuch* published
1971	*Griggs* v. *Duke Power Company* (March)
1971	*Swann* v. *Charlotte-Mecklenburg Board of Education* (April)
1971	*New York Times* published Pentagon Papers (June)
1971	Russell Means and other American Indian Movement demonstrators protested treaty violations at Mount Rushmore (June)
1971	National Women's Political Caucus founded (July)
1971	Russell Means and other American Indians unsuccessfully attempted to occupy Bureau of Indian Affairs offices in Washington, D.C. (September)
1972	Congress sent Equal Rights Amendment to states for ratification (March)
1972	Equal Employment Opportunity Act (March)
1972	U.S. bombing of North Vietnam prompted antiwar demonstrations (April)
1972	Dorothy Day awarded Laetare Medal by University of Notre Dame (May)
1972	U.S. and USSR signed SALT accords (May)
1972	Environmental Protection Agency banned use of DDT (June)
1972	Educational Amendments Act (Title IX) (June)
1972	First issue of *Ms.* magazine published (July)
1972	Water Pollution Act Amendments (October)
1972	Environmental Pesticide Control Act (October)
1972	Russell Means and other American Indians occupied Bureau of Indian Affairs building, Washington, D.C. (November)
1973	United States, South Vietnam, North Vietnam, and Viet Cong signed cease-fire agreement in Paris (January)
1973	*Roe* v. *Wade* (January)
1973	American Indian Movement occupied Wounded Knee on the Pine Ridge Indian Reservation (February–May)
1973	Last American troops were withdrawn from South Vietnam (7,200 civilian defense workers remained) (March)
1973	Feminists for Life organized (April)
1973	Antiabortion constitutional amendment introduced in Senate (May)

1973	National Right to Life Committee incorporated (June)
1973	Formation of National Gay Task Force announced (October)
1973	Endangered Species Act (December)
1974	Supreme Court ordered President Nixon to surrender White House tape recordings (June)
1974	Housing and Community Development Act (August)
1974	President Nixon resigned (August)
1974	Safe Drinking Water Act (December)
1975	North Vietnam invaded South Vietnam (January)
1975	Saigon fell to North Vietnamese (April)
1975	California Agricultural Labor Relations Act (May)
1976	Barry Commoner's *The Poverty of Power* published
1976	Toxic Substance Control Act (November)
1977	President Jimmy Carter pardoned most Vietnam War draft evaders (January)
1977	Clean Air Act (August)
1977	Water Pollution Control Act (December)
1978	American Indians staged ''The Longest Walk'' from Alcatraz to Washington, D.C. (February–July)
1978	*Bakke* v. *University of California, Davis* (June)
1978	President Carter attempted to facilitate Middle East peace meeting with Anwar Sadat and Menachem Begin at Camp David (September)
1978	Harvey Milk murdered in San Francisco (November)
1979	Barry Commoner's *The Politics of Energy* published
1979	The Reverend Jerry Falwell founded the Moral Majority (July)
1979	The first march on Washington for gay rights attracted nearly 100,000 demonstrators (October)
1980	The Citizen's party founded in Cleveland (April)
1980	Comprehensive Environmental Response, Compensation, and Liability Act (Superfund) (December)
1981	Betty Friedan's *The Second Stage* published
1981	President Carter awarded Roger Baldwin the Medal of Freedom (January)
1982	Gay Men's Health Crisis founded (January)
1982	Equal Rights Amendment failed to win ratification (June)
1984	Michael Harrington's *The New American Poverty* published
1984	Rachel MacNair became president of Feminists for Life (June)

1984	Walter Mondale selected Geraldine Ferraro to be his vice presidential running mate on the Democratic party ticket (July)
1987	National March on Washington for Lesbian and Gay Rights (October)
1988	President Ronald Reagan prohibited family planning clinics receiving federal funding from providing abortion-related assistance (March)
1989	*Webster* v. *Reproductive Health Care Services* (July)
1990	Barry Commoner's *Making Peace with the Planet* published
1990	L. Douglas Wilder took the oath of office as governor of Virginia, becoming the first elected African-American governor in the U.S. (January)
1990	Americans with Disabilities Act (July)
1991	Civil Rights Act (November)
1992	Russell Means, American Indian Movement, and others protest Columbus Day celebrations (October)
1992	Custer Battlefield National Monument renamed Little Bighorn Battlefield National Monument (November)
1993	Betty Friedan's *The Fountain of Age* published
1994	NATO leaders signed a document inviting former Warsaw Pact nations to join them in a ''partnership for peace'' (January)

Index

Abolitionism: African Americans and, 228, 229–33, 482; religious revivalists and, 207–9, 255, 493; William Lloyd Garrison and, 228, 230–40; women's rights and, 438–39, 441–43. *See also* Antislavery movement

Abortion: NOW and, 217–19, 222, 225, 319, 321, 323–24; opposition to, 224, 225, 316, 318–27, 397

Addams, Jane, 141, 143, 175, 386, 485, 490; concept of settlement house, 2–4, 7–8, 10–11; life, 2–3, 11; and peace movement, 11–12, 371; role in settlement house movement, 1, 7, 12–13

African Americans, reforms to benefit: birth control movement and, 404; Children's Aid Society and, 64–65; Communist party and, 71–72; educational reformers and, 341–43; Reconstruction, 411–14, 416, 417, 420, 421–22; settlement houses and, 4–5, 11. *See also* Abolitionism; Antislavery movement; Civil rights movement; NAACP; Racial justice; *and names of specific reformers*

Alternative medicine, 103, 297, 519; Mary Baker Eddy and, 189–92, 197, 199; Sylvester Graham and, 287–88, 296–98

American Civil Liberties Union, 26, 29–35, 372, 452

American Colonization Society, 206, 207–8, 230–31, 233, 234, 429

American Federation of Labor, 73, 74, 178, 264, 270–71, 375, 385; migrant farm workers and, 86; Samuel Gompers and, 277–83

American Indian Movement, 347–51, 353

American Railway Union, 130–33, 280

Ames, Jessie Daniel, 491, and anti-lynching campaign, 15, 18–25; life, 16–17, 24–25

Anthony, Susan B., 240, 322–23, 437, 440, 443, 485, 490

Antigay discrimination, 358, 362, 363–68

Anti-lynching campaign. *See* Lynching

Antinuclear activism, 123, 317–18, 378–79, 381, 456; Barry Commoner and, 98, 99–100

Antislavery movement: Beecher family and, 47–48, 207–8; early stages of, 228–30; Mormons and, 428, 432, 433. *See also* Abolitionism

Antiwar activism: during Vietnam era,

About the Editors and Contributors

EDITORS

PAUL A. CIMBALA is Associate Professor of History at Fordham University in New York City. He has published several articles on slavery and Reconstruction and was an editor of *The Black Abolitionist Papers: Canada, 1830–1865* (1986). He also is the author of the forthcoming book, *The Freedmen's Bureau and the Reconstruction of Georgia*.

RANDALL M. MILLER is Professor of History and Director of American Studies at Saint Joseph's University, Philadelphia. He has published sixteen books, including the award-winning *"Dear Master": Letters of a Slave Family* (1978; rev. and enl. 1990) and (with John David Smith) the award-winning *Dictionary of Afro-American Slavery* (Greenwood, 1988). His latest book (with Linda Patterson Miller) is *The Book of American Diaries* (1995).

CONTRIBUTORS

MARY FARRELL BEDNAROWSKI is Professor of Religious Studies at the United Theological Seminary of the Twin Cities.

KATHLEEN C. BERKELEY is Professor of History at the University of North Carolina at Wilmington.

GEOFFREY BLODGETT is Danforth Professor of History at Oberlin College.

NEWELL G. BRINGHURST teaches history and political science in the Department of Social Sciences at the College of the Sequoias.

CHARLES CHATFIELD is Professor of History at Wittenberg University.

ELLEN CHESLER is a fellow at the Twentieth Century Fund in New York City.

VINCENT J. CIRILLO is an independent researcher.

GEORGE B. COTKIN is Professor of History at California Polytechnic State University, San Luis Obispo.

WILLIAM W. CUTLER III is Associate Professor of History at Temple University.

MERTON L. DILLON is Professor Emeritus of History at Ohio State University.

JACOB H. DORN is Professor of History at Wright State University.

JAMES C. DURAM is Professor of History at Wichita State University.

R. LANE FENRICH is Lecturer in History at Northwestern University.

ANN D. GORDON is Editor of the Elizabeth Cady Stanton and Susan B. Anthony Papers project at Rutgers University.

BRIAN GREENBERG is the Jules L. Plangere, Jr., Chair in American Social History at Monmouth College.

RICHARD GRISWOLD DEL CASTILLO is Professor of Mexican American Studies at San Diego State University.

NANCY A. HARDESTY is Visiting Associate Professor of Religion at Clemson University.

ANNE KLEJMENT is Associate Professor of History at the University of St. Thomas, Minnesota.

LOUISE W. KNIGHT is an independent researcher and biographer of Jane Addams who also teaches at Spertus College.

ELISABETH LASCH-QUINN is Assistant Professor of History at Syracuse University.

RALPH E. LUKER is the editor of volumes 1 and 2 of *The Papers of Martin Luther King, Jr.*

BARBARA MCGOWAN is Professor of History at Ripon College.

LINDA O. MCMURRY is Professor of History at North Carolina State University.

ROBERT F. MARTIN is Professor of History at the University of Northern Iowa.

MARTHA MAY is Assistant Professor of History at Western Connecticut State University.

SCOTT MOLLOY is Assistant Professor of Industrial and Labor Relations at the Labor Research Center, University of Rhode Island.

JAMES G. RYAN is Assistant Professor of History at Texas A&M University at Galveston.

ERIC C. SCHNEIDER is an Associate Dean in the College of Arts & Sciences at the University of Pennsylvania.

SUZANNE SCHNITTMAN teaches in the history department at the State University of New York at Brockport.

LOREN SCHWENINGER is Professor of History at the University of North Carolina at Greensboro.

BARTON C. SHAW is Associate Professor of History at Cedar Crest College.

BROOKS D. SIMPSON is Associate Professor of History and Humanities at Arizona State University.

DOUGLAS H. STRONG is Professor Emeritus of History at San Diego State University.

IAN R. TYRRELL is Senior Lecturer in History at the University of New South Wales, Sydney, Australia.

SAMUEL WALKER is Professor of Criminal Justice at the University of Nebraska, Omaha.

RAYMOND WILSON is Professor of History at Fort Hays State University.

CARY D. WINTZ is Professor of History at Texas Southern University.

JAMES HARVEY YOUNG is Charles Howard Candler Professor Emeritus of American Social History at Emory University.

ISBN 0-313-28839-9

90000>

EAN

9 780313 288395

HARDCOVER BAR CODE